THE
GOOD
SCHOOLS
GUIDE

Amanda Atha & Sarah Drummond

THE
GOOD
SCHOOLS
GUIDE

FIFTH EDITION

MACMILLAN

Fifth Edition published 1996 by Macmillan
an imprint of Macmillan Publishers Limited
25 Eccleston Place, London SW1W 9NF
and Basingstoke

Associated companies throughout the world

ISBN 0 333 62925 5

A CIP catalogue record for this book is available from the British Library

Every care has been taken to ensure that all information was correct at the time of
going to press. The authors and publishers accept no responsibility for any error in detail,
inaccuracy or judgement whatsoever.

Typeset by Spottiswoode Ballantyne Printers Ltd, Colchester
Printed and bound in Great Britain by
Mackays of Chatham plc, Chatham, Kent

Contents

Acknowledgements

We would like to thank our co-ordinating editor, Debbie Whitfield. We would also like to thank our editor at Macmillan, Dominic Taylor and sub-editor, Caroline Curtis. Special thanks go to our agent Caroline Dawnay and assistant Annabel Hardman.

We are enormously grateful also to the countless friends, pupils, parents, staff (not to mention moles because they would rather we didn't) who have contributed valuable information and to whom we are deeply indebted.

Introduction

Ten years ago, when we first produced this book, heads were heads and appeared to be in control of the situation and enjoying themselves. Parents were silent and grateful.

Today it is a different story. The pressure on heads (not to mention staff) is enormous and comes from every direction – shrill consumer parents, the recession, greater competition between private and state schools, curriculum changes, the government demanding this and that (Children Act, Ofsted, league tables, tests, etc.), the responsibility for filling the school with the Right Stuff, the need to produce a marketable product.

We don't feel it is a coincidence that the number of scandals involving heads since we last went to press appears to have rocketed – in fact, we are surprised there have not been more. No wonder schools now take a long run at finding a new head: up to two years in some cases. The post is no longer so attractive, nor, in the private sector, so prestigious – or powerful. It is very often a lonely patch. The demands of the job require a very courageous, high-calibre candidate. There just aren't that many.

Worry over the dreaded league tables is now acute. While most of us are agreed that they are necessary, the tables are so open to abuse and misunderstanding as to be almost meaningless as an indicator of a school's overall performance. But the fact is, they *are* used blindly as indicators – almost to the exclusion of anything else, and all schools are vulnerable. 'They really make a difference', said the Head of one successful day school. 'When we were on the FT top 100, parents packed in.

When we dropped off it – and it was only by one place – inquiries tailed off.' 'Parents come in clutching newspaper league-table results and feeling they aren't getting their money's worth if their child fails to get straight As', said the Head of a highly academic girls' school.

Among the main problems are: one set of tables doesn't include schools with fewer than 40 pupils taking A-levels (for good statistical reasons, but who knows this?); most tables include General Studies, which distorts the whole picture dramatically; subjects perceived as 'hard' (e.g. further maths, history) are currently ranked equally with subjects that are considered 'easy' (sports studies, ancient history). How can you tell, from raw statistics, if the weaker candidates have been weeded out at the last minute – or indeed, weeded out of the school altogether to make way for brighter brains from outside?

It is a brave school which encourages/ allows its D stream to plough on and pull the league-table position down. It's not that the staff don't care. They usually care madly and have often done brilliantly to help little Johnny get his two Ds, but the league tables give no credit for this. 'It is not fair,' said the Head of a major state comprehensive, looking balefully at the local private schools. 'If a pupil is accepted on a course here, he or she is allowed to take the exam – elsewhere this is simply not so.'

The spotlight is now also increasingly on the governors, who are being called to shape up by the parents and the government in a way that would have been inconceivable 10 years ago. Like

Heads, good governors are thin on the ground, and when something goes wrong it is a very time-consuming business putting it right.

We wonder – is it pressure which is to blame for the apparent increase in bullying over the last year or two? We notice it affects not just the little child who isn't one of 'the pack' being bullied by his peers, but also children bullying staff, staff 'taking it out' on children, schools taking it out on parents who, for example, decide to take the child – and the fees – elsewhere. (Of course, schools are now more aware of bullying than they were when we first researched this book and the subject gets a thorough airing. Indeed there are those who would say that the pressure not to bully is producing a generation of cocky, undisciplined whippersnappers.)

Drugs – we can hardly keep up with the changing attitudes to this problem over the last decade. When we started, most Heads were unaware of their existence; then they denied it; next they admitted it and sacked indiscriminately; in the recession they did their sums and realised they couldn't afford to sack, so they invented the rotten apple syndrome and traded amongst themselves – (you take mine and I'll have yours and all's well with the bottom line); then came referendums with parents and random testings. Now it's all change again – pioneering Heads, living with the times, are offering amnesties, and pupils who confess their weaknesses will be counselled rather than kicked out.

Other general findings we note since we last went to press are:

In London, the horror of fighting for a place in a good pre-prep/primary is back again, despite the mushrooming of new schools. Some prep schools are still blatantly making up their lists of who went where (it's always Eton). Modern Languages, after a brief flurry of fashion

and despite some notable exceptions particularly at pre-prep, have sunk back into their usual inertia. English, thank God, is what the punters want (hence EFL); and in any case, as a dodgy 15-year-old candidate commented, 'I can't be bothered to go to France. Believe me, I'm getting an A whatever.' Foreigners, incidentally, do wonders for the league tables – strings of As in exotic subjects like Swahili, Norwegian, Dutch, and Mandarin (lots of those).

Back on the subject of league tables, we notice that results seem to be getting better and better every year – rather like a company report. Performance pressure is doubtless partly responsible, but could it also be that the exams are getting easier?

Economics A-level is once again out of kilter with everything else, with appalling results except in a few unlikely places. Theories as to why this should be so include tough exam boards (Oxford and Cambridge the one they're learning to avoid), poor teaching and its impossibility as a subject. Single-sex is back in fashion at the senior level (league tables again), but meanwhile the number of single-sex boys schools is still dwindling . . .

Schools are becoming ever more local and will become still more so with the increasing numbers of senior schools opening pre-prep departments (still the answer to keeping the coffers full, while also 'feeding' the senior school and using any empty space). Horizons are still shrinking on the boarding front: whereas even two or three years ago parents were apparently willing to drive two hours, now it's an hour and a half maximum. It pays for the schools to be geographically advantaged.

Schools in general are becoming, alas, more similar in their knee-jerk response to the demands of the market place. It is very noticeable that where good schools stick firmly to doing their own thing, they are often more popular and successful than ever. Ofsted we found of little help – very thorough but not brave enough to 'tell it like it is' – beware. Terrifyingly for all private schools, fashions appear more volatile than ever and based on more fragile criteria. Suddenly a perfectly good specimen which in the past has generated huge excitement is dropped for no real reason for the one across the valley.

We notice appeals for money have died away, and there is very little building. The major investment appears to be in IT (as schools are now learning to call it) – though often without the back-up knowledge among the staff. We have found excitement about 'injections of young staff' and 'better choice, better quality', but we wonder if part of the excitement is that they are cheaper?

A private moan is that schools with public relations/marketing managers are invariably twice as difficult to get information from as those with one man and a dog.

As we write, there is a feeling of impending but uncharted change in the offing. If Labour wins the election it is clear that assisted places will be phased out, but what else they have in mind is anyone's guess once you get beyond the woolly lip service to 'excellence' and 'stretching' and 'partnership'. If the Conservatives get in, we wonder if we could be seeing the first steps to privatisation of schools – save up your vouchers and go to St Paul's. Either way, it's an uncomfortable scene, and this could be why schools (unlike parents, press and government) have gone rather quiet.

Amanda Atha & Sarah Drummond
London

How to Read this Book

Read between the lines. This is a personal selection and some readers may well disagree with us. For example, 'keen' could mean just that, or it may mean enthusiastic but not actually very good. 'Lots of' may mean heaps of whatever it is, or that we are reserving judgement. The curate's egg is still with us. 'Sport not worshipped' could mean they don't play games when it's wet – and couldn't care less when they lose. 'Competitive' might imply precisely the opposite. 'Traditional' has to be seen in context. Could mean just that; or it may be time-warped.

If you are looking for the junior department of a senior school and don't find it in the prep section, look under the senior school at the bottom of the section 'Background and Atmosphere'.

If a school is not included in the book this does not necessarily mean it is not a good school – we repeat, our selection is a personal one.

Entrance

FEE-PAYING SCHOOLS

As a rule of thumb this is what you do:

1. Register the child's name in the school(s) you have chosen. Telephone the school and they will send you an application form.
2. Fill it in. This has to be done at the right moment or the 'list' may be 'full'. Embryos are acceptable at some schools. It will cost you a registration fee (usually non-returnable) ranging from £25 to £200 or more.
3. The school will then contact you and your child's current school about the next stage (it doesn't hurt to telephone and check, though, if you think they may have forgotten you – and don't forget to tell them if you change your address). They will usually get a report from the head of your child's current school and great attention is usually paid to that.
4. Next step is usually a visit to the school, a tour round it and a talk with the Head and/or Housemaster or whoever is appropriate.
5. The child is usually, though not always, put through its paces, which might mean an exam, a test or two, or 'meaningful' play, or whatever.
6. All being well, the school will then offer a firm place. You must write and confirm acceptance of this place or it may be offered to someone else. NB You will probably be asked for a large non-returnable deposit (can be hundreds of pounds).
7. Pay school fees – in advance of the term is normal practice, though the recession has thrown up variations in methods of payment.
8. Read any contract you have to sign carefully: if any doubt (e.g. what do they mean by 'a term's notice'?) a little legal advice at this stage can save you a lot of agony later.

There are a few variations on this theme. For example, schools which are ex-grammar schools will often accept entries up to the last minute, though there will be an official date for closing the 'list', from about three weeks to three terms before the exam.

TIP

All things being equal, *always* have a go at the school you think is right for your child. A combination of social trends and the recession, etc., means that even those schools you could have sworn were jam-packed may well have a place. Don't restrict yourself to trying at the 'normal' entry periods. Dare to try mid-term, and mid-academic year, or even the day before term starts. If you get a no, don't be afraid to try again.

STATE SCHOOLS

Since the 1980 Education Act, you, the parent, have been able to express a preference for the school at which you wish to have your child educated, and the local authority or school in question has a *duty* to comply with any preference expressed unless:

a) compliance with the preference would prejudice the provision of efficient education or the efficient use of resources or

b) the school is an aided or special agreement school, or has 'opted out', and compliance with the preference would be incompatible with any arrangements between the governors and the local education authority in respect of admission of pupils to the school or

c) the arrangements for admission to the preferred school are based 'wholly or partly on selection by reference to ability or partly on selection by reference to ability or aptitude and compliance with the preference would be incompatible with selection under the arrangements'.

We *think* this is talking about competitive entry . . .

If you get what appears to be a 'No' on any count you have the right of appeal, stating to an Appeal Committee why you think little Edna should go to Grunts and not St Dumps. One of the most successful reasons seems to be health: if you can get a doctor's letter stating that your ewe lamb gets asthma and will only flourish in the pure air of Grunts, you are halfway there. Like any other appeal you need to lobby like mad – the Head, the governors, the doctor, the local authority, your MP, the lollipop man – whoever seems good to you.

NB A new Labour government may change all this: at the time of going to press their intentions are not clear.

What the League Tables Don't Tell You

League tables have caused a lot of agony and misunderstanding. As we have said elsewhere, they are, as raw statistics, more or less meaningless. You will observe, for a start, that results swing wildly according to which newspaper you happen to look at. Among other things to watch out for:

1. The pupils' IQ: two Ds for some pupils is a triumph of wonderful teaching.

2. The pupils' background: how much help/support are they getting at home?

3. The school's background: is it academically selective or mixed ability? How many are on Assisted Places/scholarships? Size of class and ratio of staff to pupils – and the whole question of teaching facilities, resources, funding (books, labs, space, etc).

4. The school's policy towards A-levels: do they allow pupils to 'have a go' or to take a fourth A-level (for stretching/breadth). Do they operate a policy of dissuading borderline candidates from taking a subject?

5. What is the school's policy at Sixth Form? Are they, for example, pinching bright girls? Or are they turfing out their less able pupils? At Sixth Form intake, do they insist on very high (A grade) GCSEs in proposed A-level subjects?

6. Good years and bad years: is this a blip, a one-off? The *Financial Times* has done a five-year average, far more telling than only the present year which may be a flash in the pan. There may be exceptional circumstances, e.g. death and destruction.

7. What subjects are taken? Some are considered easier than others, e.g. ancient history. The league tables do not (at the time of writing) tell you which schools are taking General Studies at A-level: General Studies is generally agreed to push results up no end. How many AS levels were taken? AS counts for half an A-level and Heads often avoid them because they fail to push up the results (and confuse the time-tabling) – but they could be just the thing for your child.

8. The quality of education overall: depth, breadth, music, debating, etc – can he/she think for him/herself? By sheer swotting, exams can be successfully passed – but at the expense of what?

9. Watch out for Scottish schools lurking amongst the English league tables. Many Scottish schools offer two systems, i.e. Scottish Highers (usually for the weaker brethren), and A-levels. Only the A-levels show up in the league tables.

10. They don't tell you the size of the Sixth Form: are there 41 pupils or over 200?

11. Dare we say it, 'mistakes' can and do get made: particularly prevalent is muddling A–B grades with A–C grades. Beware.

INTERPRETING RESULTS
(as best you can)

This is what you need to ask the school:

1. Have they anything to declare – any special circumstances?

2. Ask for a *complete* breakdown of exam results for the last two or three years, i.e. a) The number of candidates sitting each subject; b) complete list of

subjects taken; c) number of passes and failures split into A B C, etc, all the way down to U; d) which year group took the exams – make sure that re-takes and early examinees are listed separately.

With all this in front of you (and a cold towel wrapped around your head), look to see where the weaknesses/strengths are to be found? Which are the popular and successful subjects? Is one subject pulling the overall results up? Or down? (If the latter, this gives you a chance to ask the Head what he is doing about it.) Or is a 100% A-grade pass in Norwegian translated as one pupil (with a Norwegian mother)? How many pupils are taking exams over all? A school with a Sixth Form of 40 (three children doing each subject) should find it considerably easier to come up high on the league tables than larger schools. The larger the number taking any one subject, the more commendable when the results are strong, and the wider the scope for failure. (Watch out for sudden improvements, particularly of mainstream subjects, and look warily at the numbers of candidates: if the number has halved from one year to the next, it is possible that the school policy has been to force out the weaker candidates and so manipulate the results.)

This will give you some idea of what is going on and where the weak teaching is. Now you are in a position to ask the Head to explain those appalling geography results, and to explain what he is doing about the situation? Listen carefully, because all schools have weaknesses, and the important thing is what is being done to remedy them. But at the end of the day, remember that league tables are only one, often unreliable indicator of how a school performs. And, of course, this still won't tell you which is the right school for your child.

Now turn to how to suss out a school.

Sussing out a School and Horses for Courses

Every single reference book on schools indulges in advice on this. Lists of questions tend to make Heads bristle, but going in as a parent can be daunting. The following is a list of guidelines we drew up as we went around – obviously not all are applicable to every school. Ask even half these questions and you will probably never be invited back again, but it does no harm to take them along for prompting.

ACTION

1. Send for the prospectus, a copy of the school magazine, list of governors, and ask for the last two years results and any other bumf – then read it. This saves time on crucial matters such as registration, subjects offered, exeats, etc, though NB this may be out of date.

2. Make an appointment to see the Head and to see round the school. You may find you are fobbed off with an Open Day, registrars, etc, and for big schools with large numbers of applicants this is an understandable way to start. It is, however, time-consuming for you: remember, you have to meet the Head – no amount of wonderful buildings make up for a rotten Head.

3. What to wear? Projecting the right image – not too smart (particularly if you are looking for a cut-price offer), but not dowdy either. No school wants to feel they are attracting dull people, and if you have something to offer, however humble, tell them.

4. On the day of your visit, get to the school early in order to sniff around. Approach children/staff and ask them anything (e.g. where is the main school noticeboard?). It's amazing how telling their replies can be.

WHAT TO LOOK OUT FOR

Bearing of pupils – politeness, neatness. Bearing of staff, ditto. Do they look clean, bright-eyed and bushy-tailed (or whatever you like)? Attitude of pupils to staff and vice versa. Does the Head know who they all are (you'd be surprised)? Do pupils flatten themselves against the wall as the Head passes? Do they flatten him/her against the wall as they pass? (If so, do they stop and say sorry?) Is the atmosphere happy? Fraught? Coerced or co-opted? Do you fall over pupils smoking in corners? How many are slumped in front of the television (key question when visiting around 1.30 p.m. especially)? Do the drains smell? What is the state of the paintwork, etc. – a glance at the ceiling will usually tell (not that it matters *per se*).

Grab an exercise book or three in passing and look at the standard of work and the standard of marking – this can tell you an enormous amount. Check the size of teaching groups – it's amazing how often numbers do not tally with the official version. What is the average age of the staff? All old can mean not enough dynamic new ideas or energy; all young can mean too inexperienced and also, possibly, too transitory. Ask if you can pop in to a class, or have a good long look through the peep holes, and see what is really happening: are the children dozing, is the teacher dozing, is there rapport between the teacher and the taught? Observe the state of the library: rows of dusty tomes look impressive but bright, new and dog-eared is healthier. Where is the library – is it in a useful position, do the troops use it? And, incidentally, where is the Head's study: is he in the thick of things, i.e. finger on the pulse, or is he still in his ivory tower? Look at noticeboards for signs of plenty going on, and names you know (for grilling later). Are there enough computers, and do the staff really know how to use them?

Finally, do you like the look of the parents, and would you be happy for your children to mix with theirs?

QUESTIONS TO HAVE UP YOUR SLEEVE

1. What is the size of the Sixth Form? This is a dead give-away to the overall academic strength of the school.

2. What are the results like? This is one for the Head. Watch the whites of his eyes as he gives you the answer – and see section on What the League Tables Don't Tell You.

3. How does the school monitor progress? School reports? Point systems? Incentives?

4. What is the size of the classes – biggest and smallest?

5. What is the ratio of full-time teaching staff to pupils? How many part-timers are there? How part-time are they?

6. What is the turnover of staff – do too many stay too long? NB You are unlikely to get a straight answer on this.

7. Which exam boards are taken?

(This doesn't help, but shows you are on the ball.)

8. What is the size of the library budget? What arrangements are there for getting hold of new books, papers?

9. What emphasis is there (if any) on religious teaching? Daily chapel? Daily assembly? Weekly chapel?

10. How are pupils selected? What are they looking for in pupils?

11. What special projects are currently on the go?

12. Does the school have special help on tap for special learning difficulties? If so, is it going to cost you?

13. How many pupils leave after GCSE? (They may not be honest about this.) How many are imported into the Sixth Form from outside? NB This will probably affect the school's results and needs to be looked at with a beady eye, i.e. they may be reaping the benefits of another school's hard work.

14. What is the pressure of work? Amount of work? Homework? Setting? Streaming?

15. Who are the pupils and where do they come from? (Both geographically and socially?) How many Brits and in particular how many non-Brits whose first language is not English? Too many of the latter can grind teaching to a halt – very few schools can afford to cater for them separately.

16. Where do pupils go on to?

17. What is the careers advice like?

18. What scholarships are available and won? What bursaries and funding are available when finances come adrift?

19. The cost: fees, plus real cost, i.e. size of bill? 'Extras' are usually listed on a separate sheet of paper (because they constantly rise) and tucked into the back of the prospectus.

20. Are games compulsory? CCF?

21. What subjects and extras are on offer? Can they really deliver? Beware: schools are inclined to pay lip-service. A

small school offering dozens of extras is probably doing none of them very well.

22. What languages are genuinely on offer? (Is the teacher qualified, and employed on a formal basis?)

23. How many learn a musical instrument, and for how long? Are practice sessions timetabled?

24. Who owns the school? If privately owned – though few are – are there any checks and balances, e.g. governors, PTA, etc; and to whom do you make out your cheque? Who takes over next?

25. What is the Head's attitude to discipline? Drugs? Sex? Bullying? Alcohol? Homosexuality? Stealing? Bad language? Breaking the more petty school rules? What form do punishments take? Are prefects allowed to mete it out? Ask for a copy of the school rules – this can be illuminating.

26. How many people have been expelled, asked to leave, suspended in the last two years? (This could pinpoint specific major problems.)

27. What are the present numbers in the school? What is the school's capacity?

28. What is the acreage? Or square metreage (NB there are government guidelines on the minimum amount per child)?

29. What is the structure of the school Houses, if any? What is the school hierarchy?

30. Is there any privacy for boarders?

31. Is there a shadowing system for new pupils?

32. Does the school feel responsible for pupils once they are accepted – or will it fire misfits/slow learners if they don't shape up quickly?

33. How much pocket money is suggested? A vital question, this.

34. In boarding schools how accessible are children by telephone?

35. What is the temperature at schools in the winter? (A question for Scottish and seaside schools particularly.)

36. Who would not be happy at the school?

37. What is the pastoral care like and who is responsible to whom and are problems spotted early? Is there a tutorial system (moral or academic)?

38. How good is the health care? Do they notice if the pupils skip meals? How aware is the school of the dangers and signs of anorexia? Is there a cafeteria system or a table laid and 'table talk'? How much fresh raw food is there?

39. Is there a second-hand shop?

40. Is this a *Neighbours/Home and Away* watching school, and what is the school's attitude to watching television?

41. Is there a holiday reading list, and is there holiday homework ever? Never?

42. What are the strengths of this school – and weaknesses? (Always interesting to hear the answer to this.)

43. What is the Head trying to achieve in the school? What is his/her history? What does he/she regard as most important? What does he/she really want for the pupils in the long run?

44. Until when is the Head 'contracted'? (i.e. is he/she about to leave)? Is he/she married, with children (i.e. hands-on experience)?

45. Are pupils ejected after GCSE if their results don't measure up? This is becoming increasingly common and is bad news.

QUESTIONS FOR PUPILS

1. What is the food like?

2. What subjects do you like best? (This often reveals which are the most popular members of staff.)

3. What don't you like about the school?

4. What do you like best about the school?

5. What changes would you make?

6. Where is the Head's office?

7. Are you happy here?

8. Are you allowed to get on with your own thing without teasing or bullying? (This might flush out peer group pressure to conform.)

9. Boarding school question: what do you do at weekends?

10. Have you got a brother or sister in the school, what does he/she think?

QUESTION FOR THE LOCAL SHOP/TAXI DRIVER

What is the school like? This can produce a flood of enlightening comment.

THOUGHTS FOR PARENTS

Firstly and most importantly, what is your child really like? This is your starting point for finding the school to suit him/her rather than you.

Secondly, what do you want for your child? It helps to have a game plan, even if you change it at a later date, e.g. state or fee-paying? day or boarding? single-sex or co-ed?

Thirdly, what do you want from the school? Make an honest list for yourself of everything that occurs to you, however ambitious, frivolous or peripheral it may seem. You must both do this. Your list may include, for example: happiness, safety, beauty of architecture, Daddy's old school, a stepping stone to university, very local, very convenient, exeats that fit in with your career, offers Japanese, doesn't cost too much, if anything. Are you looking for a traditional approach, or something totally different? What do you *really* feel and think about co-education?

Beware the danger of judging a school exclusively by the bottom end because your child is young – look at the end product. How and where do you want your child to end up? Is there a member of staff at the school who is on the same wavelength as yourself? There must be someone you can turn to (particularly true of boarding).

See several schools – it's a process of elimination, and comparisons are vital to make. Go by your gut reaction. Were you impressed with the Head (you don't have to like him/her, but it helps)? Did he/she appear in control of the situation? The Head really does make or break a school.

Finally, did you come out feeling good?

Money Matters

Schools in this country are mostly state-funded, i.e. paid for by the government and local authorities from taxes. A small proportion are private, funded mostly from fees paid by parents, but also indirectly by the state, given that most private schools enjoy charitable status. (Approximately 7% of children in education are at fee-paying schools.) Fees range from under £1,000 per term to around £3,000 per term for a day pupil – and £1,400 to £4,500+ per term for boarding – with wide variations depending on the age of the child, the staff/pupil ratio, and so on.

FEE-PAYING SCHOOLS: BARGAIN HUNTING

SCHOLARSHIPS: These are to attract the academically bright or specifically talented child (art, music, science, sports, and all-round) and they vary in amount. Girls' schools, alas, offer fewer and less valuable scholarships. As a rule of thumb, the old and famous foundations are the richest. (They may well disclaim this, but all is relative.) The largest scholarships awarded by HMC and GSA schools are now normally 50% of the full fees, a policy decision that was made a few years ago. However, we note that one or two schools are breaking ranks and occasionally you will get a full-fee scholarship. There are also some schools which have a statutory number of scholarships to offer (e.g. Eton, Westminster, St Paul's).

Watch out for esoteric scholarships, e.g. sons and daughters of clergy, medics,

single mothers, etc. If your name is West and you live in the parish of Twickenham there is a bursary waiting for you (at Christ's Hospital). Scholarships to Choir Schools are worth thinking about, but they may not cover full fees and the children work incredibly hard for them (and what happens when their voices break?). But NB this could well be the beginning of a music scholarship into public school.

Keep your eyes open for internal scholarships which run at various stages, Sixth Form especially. There are also increasing numbers of schools luring pupils in at Sixth Form with generous scholarships: could be worth moving schools for.

Useless scholarships – don't fall for them. It is a false economy to be flattered into going to the wrong school for £200 off the bill. By the way, it is well worth lobbying for 10% off in any case – if you have three children you should be able to negotiate a job lot. (Heads are used to this and wary of it – but take courage, this is the way the world now is. Of course, you may get a raspberry.)

BURSARIES: Usually for helping out the impoverished but deserving and those fallen on hard times – and currently stretched to the limit. We have listed them as far as possible under each school, but a more complete collection will be found in the *Public and Preparatory Schools Yearbook*, which is published annually and can be found in libraries.

ASSISTED PLACES: These are seriously good news and are fiercely fought over in most places. They are offered by the government for the children of impoverisheds who are judged to 'benefit' from private education. The scheme is means-tested, and getting into a school on an Assisted Place is at the discretion of the Head. Assisted places are now 'capped', i.e. the government will only pay up to a certain amount. This is causing difficulties for schools whose fees are above this sum – though parents are not directly affected. Not surprisingly, this scheme is controversial, politically sensitive, and will not last if a Labour government comes to power.

OTHER CHEAPOS: Certain schools are relatively cheap. The Livery Companies, e.g. Haberdasher's and also Mercers, etc, fund various schools, e.g. Haberdasher's Monmouth, St Paul's. Such schools are usually excellent value – not only cheap, but good facilities.

Also cheap, but with fewer frills, are The Girls Public Days Schools Trust (GPDST). This organization was founded in 1872 to provide schools giving girls 'a fine academic education at comparatively modest cost'. There are 25 member schools, sharing administration costs from their London HQ. Competent straight-up-and-down teaching and no frills.

It may well be worth considering sending your child as a day pupil to a big, strong boarding school. This way you will reap the benefits at a lesser price.

PAYING THE FEES

There are any number of wizard wheezes on the market. The schools offer 'composition fees', which means, in a nutshell, that you put a sum of money down one year and get a sum of money back later. The 'school fee specialists' offer endowment-backed, mortgage-backed schemes, etc, which, in effect, do the same

thing. Either way, you are stepping into difficult waters. Make sure you *totally* understand what you are doing and all the implications – how the money is being invested, what the returns are, how it compares with any other investment, what the charges are (hidden and otherwise), etc.

This does not mean you should not plan, i.e. save. The earlier you start, obviously, the better.

FINANCIAL ASSESSMENT: Given the astronomic sums involved, it is worth looking very carefully at what you are actually buying. The recession has sharpened up everybody's attitude, and a large number of schools have viable numbers again, but there are still those that are struggling, and you need to know that the school you are interested in is in good financial health. This is easier said than done. A good indicator is to compare the number of pupils this year with last year and indeed the year before that. The numbers may be similar, but NB it could be because a whole new nursery/pre-prep has been grafted on. You can find out exact statistics through the Department for Education.

Other indicators of financial problems are: not sacking troublemakers – one sacking can mean the loss of £12,000 or more a year, ('This can be the difference between profit and loss', said a Bursar); cutting corners in the curriculum, e.g. offering German one year, Spanish the next; the Head being away too much drumming up business; cheap labour – gap-year students can be wonderful, but they are inexperienced and they don't last.

If possible, pick a blue chip school with a rich foundation, e.g. with livery companies' backing: they are better positioned to ride out any storms. Look carefully at the Money Matters section on individual entries in this guide.

Scrutinize your bill carefully. We have noticed an increasing tendency to pop in items with a footnote saying that 'unless you notify the school and deduct the amounts mentioned, it will automatically be charged to you'. For example, the Old Boys/Girls society; the ISIS membership; your 'contribution' to charities? This is inertia selling: do not be shy about deducting these sums from your cheque.

Insurance needs particular care. Often policies are taken out automatically unless you say otherwise – and we know of policies on offer that only pay up once the child has been ill for at least 8 days, and don't pay up for illnesses lasting longer than a term.

GETTING IN AND OUT OF FINANCIAL DIFFICULTIES

If you do get into financial difficulties, you will not be alone, and schools are very used to this. Their attitude to bill-paying and money varies hugely. The best schools are wonderful and increasingly flexible over payment – and allow, e.g., monthly instalments. Bursars are expecting this request (no shame attached, indeed the Bursar has changed from the enemy to being the father confessor).

A lot will depend on how well funded the school is: it is worth investigating this before you go any further. Some well-funded rich schools will pick up the tab until further notice if you fall on hard times and your child is a good egg. Most of them will do their very best to see you

through exam periods, but some poor schools simply cannot afford this, however much they may wish too.

Don't assume that because they are called 'charities' that they will be charitable to you. Some may send out the debt collectors. They will hold you to the small print – i.e. one term's payment or one term's notice to quit really means it. They may well threaten to take you to court – though of course it will be an altogether different matter if your child is especially bright (see What the League Tables Don't Tell You).

ACTION

1. Speak to the Head. Mothers may burst into tears at this point.

2. The Head will immediately direct you to the Bursar.

3. Explain your position – as optimistically, positively and realistically as possible.

4. Hope for flexible arrangements, e.g. monthly payments, or deferred payment.

5. Have all the Assisted Places gone? Is there a spare bursary?

6. Assess the situation: how vital is it to keep your child in this school? Will the world fall apart if he/she leaves now?

7. If you really feel it is vital that the child stays put, try touching a relation for a loan/gift. Grandparents are still the Number One source of school fees. Investigate the possibility of an extra mortgage.

8. And if it is not vital, start looking for state alternatives. See Playing the System.

Playing the System

It helps, when planning your child's journey through the maze of state and private schools, to know the main stages of jumping from one to another. Advantages of state education are: usually close by, part of community, school bus operates in country areas (often but by no means always) avoiding need to become full-time driver, broad social mix, no school fees, probably greater understanding of the wide world at the end of it.

Advantages of the private system are: often a greater chance of doing well in public exams in many cases, often better academic (as opposed to pastoral) care, a wider range of extras and often at a higher standard, smaller classes, the opportunity to study élite subjects such as Greek and start modern languages earlier, the opportunity to board and all that that implies.

AGE 2+–4+ Kindergarten/nursery in the private sector.
AGE 4 pre-prep starts in the private sector.
AGE 5 Education is now compulsory for everyone in the UK.
AGE 7/8 prep school starts in the private sector. If you have a boy headed for the private system, you may need to take him out of the state system at this stage (NB this will make the Head shirty) in order to fit in with the changeover at 13 and to get in enough coaching to pass the entry exam (see below).
AGE 11 usually move to state school and grammar schools, both state and private. Grammar schools are by definition selective and a wheeze used by some parents is to put children into private schools until the age of 11 in order to train them up for getting into the state grammar of their choice – thus avoiding the fees thereafter. The important thing here is to be in the right geographical place at the right time to qualify for entry to good/popular ones, which are increasingly oversubscribed. However, in some areas secondary schooling starts at 12 or 13.

A few private prep schools open up a new class for very clever ten-/eleven-year-olds from state schools in order to coach them up for entry to their senior schools at 13 CE.

Girls may move from the state system to the private one at the age of 11, which can work well as there is a 'break' in both state and private systems for them. Extra tuition may be needed, usually in English and Maths – coaching after school is the answer.

AGE 13 (or thereabouts) move to most private secondary (public) schools for boys, and to private co-educational establishments, though NB some have lowered their entry age to eleven.

AGE 16 once GCSE is over, all change is possible. Boys and girls may move from state schools to private ones (almost all now have entry at 16+, sometimes with scholarships), or from private schools to e.g. state Sixth Form Colleges as petty restrictions begin to irk. You may want to leave for a school that offers International Baccalaureate.

Entry at Sixth Form level usually depends on GCSE results. Check with the school when applications need to be made. Girls applying to Sixth Form or boys' or co-ed schools may expect tough competition – though we have noticed that this is easing as the girls are now spread thinner.

NB If it looks as though A-level may be a struggle for your child and he/she has set his/her heart on university, it is possible (though the logistics may defeat you, and it will certainly mean going to school in Scotland) to change from the English exam system to the Scottish one of Highers. This is much more broadly based – more subjects at a slightly lower level – and is now accepted by many English as well as all Scottish universities.

Useful Addresses and Books

The Department for Education, Sanctuary Buildings, Great Smith Street, London SE1 7PH, Tel: 0171 925 5000. This has an information division which will give you the names of schools, pressure groups and leaflets on e.g. Assisted Places, Tel: 0171 925 5555. There is also a publications division on 0181 533 2000.

The Independent Schools Information Service (ISIS), 56 Buckingham Gate, London SW1E 6AG, Tel: 0171 630 8790; Fax: 0171 630 5013. This is the information and propaganda arm of the private sector (though NB not all private schools belong). ISIS has e.g. lists of Assisted Places in member schools.

For information on charities for parents who wish to send their children to fee-paying schools but cannot afford the fees, contact ISIS.

For lists of all schools registered in your area (state and private) telephone the County or Borough concerned (e.g. Westminster City Council, Suffolk Education Authority).

FOR HELP ON LEARNING DIFFICULTIES

For help on children with educational problems, e.g. dyslexia, misfit, behavioural problems, local authorities are usually excellent. Also worth knowing about are:

The Tavistock Clinic, 120 Belsize Lane, London NW3 5BA, Tel: 0171 435 7111; Fax (children and families): 0171 431 7057.

The British Dyslexia Association, 98 London Road, Reading, Berkshire RG1 5AU, Tel: 01734 668271; Fax: 01734 351927. This has associations for assessing and teaching dotted around the country. Contact them to find your local branch.

The Dyslexia Institute, 133 Gresham Road, Staines, Middlesex TW18 2AJ, Tel: 01784 463851; Fax: 01784 460747. This organisation also has member groups around the country. Contact this number to find your nearest.

The Dyslexia Teaching Centre, 23 Kensington Square, London W8 5HN, Tel: 0171 937 2408; No fax. Has visiting educational psychologists, and recommends others, and has a large team of specialists trained to help (adults and) children. Also offers private tuition early in the morning and after school hours (their helpers work in schools during the day).

Helen Arkell Dyslexia Centre, Frensham, Farnham, Surrey GU10 3BW, Tel: 01252 792400; Fax: 01252 795669.

The National Association for Gifted Children, Park Campus, Boughton Green Road, Northampton NN2 7AL, Tel: 01604 792300; Fax: 01604 722114. Gives advice for parents with exceptionally bright children.

USEFUL LAWYERS: Mr Peter Woodroffe, Woodroffes, 36 Ebury Street, London SW1W 0LU, Tel: 0171 730 3400; Fax: 0171 730 7900. Specialises, among other things, in advising parents about legal matters to do with fee-paying schools.

Veale Wasbrough, Orchard Court, Orchard Lane, Bristol BS1 5DS, Tel: 01179 252020; Fax: 01179 252025.

The Education Law Association, 39 Oakleigh Avenue, London N20, Tel: and Fax: 0181 445 6747. Network of solicitors who are experts in education law.

BOOKS

The private schools' 'bible' is *The Independent Schools' Yearbook* (A & C Black). This covers around 1,500 schools for children between the ages of 3–18. It is like a huge collection of prospectuses. Beware of books with entries written by the schools themselves.

Schools Catering for Dyslexia is a useful pamphlet published by ISIS which gives lists of such schools.

SCHOOLS WHICH HELP CHILDREN WITH LEARNING DIFFICULTIES

Look under individual entries in the main text of this book for dyslexic units, etc (e.g. Bloxham, Milton Abbey). Also:

Fairley House, 44 Bark Place, London W2 4AT, Tel: 0171 229 0977; Fax: 0171 727 7719. Boys and girls age 5–11.

Old Rectory, Brettenham, Ipswich, Suffolk IP7 7QR, Tel: 01449 736404; Fax: 01449 737881. Boys and girls age 7–13 come for intensive teaching for one term–two years, and then go back into the mainstream.

Stanbridge Earls School, Romsey, Hampshire SO51 9ZS, Tel: 01794 516777; Fax: 01794 511201. Boys and girls age 11–18.

Edington School, Mark Road, Burtle, Bridgwater, Somerset TA7 8NJ, Tel: 01278 722012; Fax: 01458 210111. Boys and girls age 8–13.

Shapwick School, Shapwick, Bridgwater, Somerset, TA7 9AJ, Tel: 01458 210384; Fax: 01458 210111. Senior school for Edington, founded in 1981. Boys and girls age 13–18.

THE GOOD SCHOOLS GUIDE ADVISORY SERVICE

This is a consultancy run by the authors of *The Good Schools Guide* to advise parents on choosing the best school for their child.

The authors are in a unique position to do this because they have visited hundreds of schools, and gathered an enormous reservoir of information and experience. No money is taken at any stage from the schools – all advice is impartial.

Offices at: 27a Warwick Square, London SW1V 2AD,

Tel: 0171 828 1052; Fax: 0171 932 0747;

and at 59a Cadogan Street, London SW3 2QJ.

Tel: 0171 225 2355; Fax: 0171 225 1119.

CAN YOU HELP US?

We would like to know what you think of the schools in this edition. All information will be gratefully received – no detail too slight to mention. Suggestions for schools to be included in the next edition would also be welcome. Please write to us c/o The Good Schools Advisory Service either at 27a Warwick Square, London SW1V 2AD or at 59a Cadogan Street, London SW3 2QJ.

Glossary and Abbreviations

A-level General Certificate of Education, second public exam in the UK

ALIS A-Level Information System (a statistical survey on results developed by Newcastle University)

AS Advanced supplementary level public exam equivalent to half an A-level

Assistant A young person from abroad, usually French or German, who helps teach the language (not to mention taking rugby, etc)

Assisted Places – Government-backed scheme, whereby bright children of impoverished parents can be educated in fee-paying schools. Means-tested – the government pays the short fall (up to a point)

BA Bachelor of Arts. University degree in Arts

BD Bachelor of Divinity

B Econ Bachelor of Economics

BEd Bachelor of Education. A teaching qualification

B Lit Bachelor of Literature. University qualification

Brill Slang for brilliant

BSc Bachelor of Science

BTEC A vocational qualification – alternative to A-level – awarded by the Business and Technology Education Council

Bursary Contribution to the school fees, usually given to those who are poor

Cantab Cambridge

C of E Church of England

C of S Church of Scotland

CCF Combined Cadet Force. Paramilitary training corps for the young (boys and girls)

CDT Craft, Design and Technology

CE Common Entrance Qualifying exam taken usually at 11, 12 or 13 in the private sector for entry to senior schools

Cert Ed Certificate of Education. A teaching qualification

Combined Sciences GCSE exam covering Biology, Chemistry and Physics, counts as one GCSE

CSYS Certificate of Sixth Year Studies (used occasionally in Scotland)

DfE (Government) Department for Education

DT Design Technology

Dip Ed A teaching qualification

DPhil Doctor of Philosophy

Dual Award (Science) GCSE exam in Science covering Biology, Chemistry and Physics – counts as two GCSEs.

D of E Duke of Edinburgh Award Scheme. A combination of various different activities, including demanding physical exercise, culminating in a medal

EFL English as a foreign language

Eng Lit English Literature

Eisteddfod A Welsh word for a festival of music, etc

Fab Slang for fabulous

FP Former Pupil (Scottish expression)

FRS Fellow of the Royal Society

Gap Work experience projects in year between school and university. Also name of organisation specialising in this

GCSE General Certificate of Secondary Education. First public exam in the UK

GNVQ General National Vocational Qualification. A vocational qualification

GPDST Girls' Public Day School Trust. A foundation of private schools

Grammar school A type of school which selects on academic merit and provides a rigorous academic education (and often not much else)

Grant-maintained Adjective applied to state schools which have 'opted out' of local education authority control and are directly funded by the government

GSA Girls' Schools' Association. Female equivalent of HMC. See below

Highers Higher Grades. Scottish public exam, usually taken one or two years after 'Standard Grade' (qv)

HMC Headmasters' Conference. A sort of headmasters' trade union, mostly for public schools, whose heads belong and are considered 'top' by those in it

IAPS Incorporated Association of Preparatory Schools. Organisation of prep schools. Again, generally considered the 'top' ones by those in them

IB International Baccalaureate. A public exam at secondary level, increasingly recognised for entry to university in the UK

Independent Word used by fee-paying schools to describe themselves – erroneously

Inter-denom Inter-denominational (refers to religious affiliation)

IQ Intelligence Quotient

ISCO Independent Schools Careers Organisation

ISIS Independent Schools Information Service

IT Information Technology

JMB Joint Matriculation Board

L ès L Licencié ès Lettres. French university degree

MA Master of Arts. University degree

MSc Master of Science. University qualification

NB Nota Bene

Non-denom Non-denominational (refers to religious affiliation)

OB Old Boy (i.e. former pupil of a school)

OED Oxford English Dictionary

OG Old Girl (i.e. former pupil of a school)

Opt(ed) out See Grant-maintained

OSB Order of St Benedict

OTT Over the top, as in e.g. (unacceptable) behaviour

Oxbridge Short for Oxford or Cambridge universities

Oxon Oxford

Pastoral Care Care of pupil on matters not related to their work, e.g. personal and social ones

PE Physical education

PGCE Postgraduate Certificate of Education. A teaching qualification

PSE Personal and Social Education (courses)

PTA Parent-Teacher Association

qv quod vide

RC Roman Catholic

RE Religious Education

RI Religious Instruction

RSA Royal Society of Arts

San Sanatorium, sick bay

Scotvec A Scottish vocational qualification

Set A group of children of similar ability within a form (setting is a way of sorting children by ability for more effective teaching in specific subjects)

Six-inch rule Rule applied at some co-educational schools whereby boys and girls may not come closer to each other than six inches (in case they get over-excited)

SSSI Site of Special Scientific Interest – designated as such by the government and, as such, protected

Standard Grade The Scottish equivalent of GCSE

Stream A form of children of similar ability

Suss Slang for find out, get to the bottom of, investigate, sniff out

SYS Certificate of Sixth Year Studies

TLC Tender loving care

V very

Vibes Slang for vibrations

VIP Very Important Person

VR Verbal reasoning

YE Young Enterprise. A hands-on business studies course

YMCA Young Men's Christian Association (Youth Hostel organisation)

JUNIOR AND PREPARATORY SCHOOLS

Abberley Hall

Worcester, WR6 6DD
Tel: 01299 896275, Fax: 01299 896875
PUPILS: 146 boys; 104 board, 42 day
AGES: 7–13
ALSO PRE-PREP/NURSERY with 56 boys, 25 girls
AGES: 2+–7
C OF E
FEE-PAYING

HEAD: Since 1996, Mr John Walker, BSc in psychology from Surrey (forties). Previous post was Head of Bramcote, and before that he was head of studies at Pembroke House prep school in Kenya. Went into schoolmastering straight from school and took his degree on the wing. Open personality, open-minded. Good with pupils and staff. Comments that the 'golden thing about a small school is small classes – not only can you see the problems, but you can always get on top of them'. Takes over from Mr Michael Haggard, who has been Head here since 1974 and who leaves the school in very good shape.

ENTRANCE: Informal interview, no exam. A few scholarships and awards on offer.

EXIT: The vast majority to Shrewsbury (14 in '95), some to Eton (5 in '95); also to King's Worcester and to public schools mainly in the west, including Wales (Monmouth, Christ Brecon). Steady scholarship record.

REMARKS: Extremely good teaching with high teacher/boy ratio, and, say parents, 'very good at helping the weaker brethren get up to scratch, very structured'. The outgoing Head was a keen collector of single staff 'because they don't have commitments with their own families' – a lively lot. Three/four sets. Six periods (30 mins. each) per morning, two lessons straight after lunch then out for games every day, every term. Activities: Hour each weekday allows boys to opt for a wide range of hobbies from calligraphy to climbing wall.

Keen sporting school (boys regularly put in for local and regional championships); the school has just put in a Ricochet court, and claims Abberley is the first in the world to have one. Strong DT, with Archimedes computer system. IT for all. German and Greek as options (but NB only French starts at age 8). The school did brilliantly in the 94/5 National Maths Olympiad.

The school is housed in a fascinating and remarkable Victorian country house (complete with fine crumbling stucco work, antlers on the wall, billiard tables, large gloomy Victorian paintings, huge drawing room which is home to the boys' library, etc) set in 90 glorious acres, overlooked by bizarre clock tower. Pre-prep is attached. Modern additions (including chapel, Astroturf Sports Hall, some classrooms, changing room, etc) somewhat at odds with nineteenth-century architecture. Dorms cosied up with wooden bunks.

Interesting mix of the liberal and the formal – high standards all round, and very lively extra-curricular departments, producing self-confident, articulate and really super boys. Happy and busy atmosphere. No uniform still occasionally leads to cries of 'scruffy' from parents – but discipline is firm, politeness emphasised. Boarding side somewhat hit by recession, but carries on regardless doing an excellent job. No prospectus, see the school mag instead.

3

Aberlour House

Aberlour, Banffshire, Scotland AB38 9LJ
Tel: 01340 871267, Fax: 01340 871238

PUPILS: Around 52 boys board, 36 girls
board, 12 boys day, 6 girls day
AGES: 7/8–13
NON-DENOM
FEE-PAYING

HEAD: Since January 1992, Mr John
W Caithness MA (St Andrews),
Dip Ed (fifties), previously at Merchiston
and St Andrews, and taught at Blairmore,
St Peter's Cambridge in New Zealand,
and Lathallan. Came to Aberlour having
been Headmaster of Catteral Hall (the
junior school for Giggleswick). Met his
wife, Jane, when she was Matron at
Blairmore, one son and one daughter.
Teaches Latin, German, and fills in. Well-
liked, loves teaching, and doing a 'really
good job', say parents.

ENTRANCE: By registration and interview, can take younger children in
cases of real need. Three Assisted Places
(from 11) plus four annual scholarships,
with tests in English, Maths and Verbal
Reasoning for 8- to 10-year-olds.
Additional help may be on hand from
Gordonstoun Foundation.

EXIT: No longer seen as a feeder only
for Gordonstoun. Also to Rannoch,
Strathallan, Loretto, Glenalmond, etc,
and a smattering down South – Oakham,
Haileybury and Queenswood in '95.

REMARKS: The school was founded
by Kurt Hahn in 1936 at Wester
Elchies as the prep school for Gordonstoun (qv). Aberlour House was bought
in 1947 and the whole school moved here
in 1963. The school is set in the most
fabulous countryside, well fulfilling the

founder's decree that 'our [youth should]
dwell in the land of health, amid fair sights
and sounds, and beauty . . .'. Good
classroom conversions, with passage
leading to old stable block, and fine hall.
Huge variety of (pretty vile) wallpaper
everywhere.

School run firmly along lines of Hahn's
philosophy *plus est en vous*, no class more
than 16, superb CDT, Music strong,
including the chanter (leading to bagpipes) and clarsach. There are some gifted
children and some less so – small remedial
department. Staff have gained their
qualifications from an amazing variety of
places – including an M Mus from Ohio,
an MSc from Indiana, not to mention a
Dip Ed from Callendar Park.

Masses of games, rugby, hockey,
athletics, netball, etc., but lack of other
schools nearby to play against since
Blairmore closed. Children can bring
their own ponies, however, and the
school is well-placed for skiing. No
prefects, just 'Helpers'. Serious expeditions – eight-day riding expedition,
'Hoof Prints of Queen Victoria'; back-
packing at Cape Wrath: all character-
building. Pretty up-market.

Children well behaved. Children
bussed to local Speyside Community
Centre (own pool needs a face lift), and
play games in snow. The Head believes in
positive disciplining and says 'please
walk', not 'don't run'. Lots of foreign
exchanges. School has had several
hiccups, now back on form.

Seventy-eight per cent of pupils live in
Scotland (of which 89% live within 70
miles), plus 9% from the rest of the UK
and 17% from abroad (foreign passport
holders and ex-pats) – these last two
figures dropping slightly since last edition.
The school got a shot in the arm on the
numbers front when Blairmore closed.
The prospectus information booklet has a
wonderfully helpful list of which airlines
fly into Aberdeen and Inverness airports,

and from where (e.g. Esbjerg, Business Air), as well as a list of hotels, B and Bs, restaurants, taxis, and activities for parents who might well consider combining taking a break with taking the children back to school here.

Alleyn's Junior School

Townley Road, London SE22 8SU
Tel: 0181 693 3457, Fax: 0181 299 3671
PUPILS: 208; 50/50 boys/girls
ALL DAY
AGES: 5–11
C OF E
FEE-PAYING

HEAD: Mrs Bridget Weir Cert Ed (early fifties), married to a Consultant Engineer with two children. Previously Head of St Hilary's Junior School, Sevenoaks, and educated at Tiffin, Kingston on Thames, and Homerton. Teaches handwriting to littles and RE to older ones, likes to 'hear what they are saying' and hopes to give as broad an education as possible. Grammar is perhaps not her strong point, judging by an official letter she sent to parents beginning: 'Completed in 1992, we enjoy a customed-designed light and airy building'.

Mrs Weir is the first Head of a brand new school (it opened September 1992) so 'all the mistakes are mine' (not obviously visible when we visited). Says, 'Learning must be fun'.

ENTRANCE: Name down a year in advance, already doubly over-subscribed, assessment at 5+ and 7+ (a few places possible at 9+). Most children

local, but some from further afield with brothers and sisters in Alleyn's, JAGS or Dulwich College.

EXIT: Almost all to Alleyn's (even though this is not an automatic route) and one or two to other local schools, e.g. Dulwich.

REMARKS: The latest development in the Alleyn complex: part of the South of the Thames 'Trinity Group' of schools, connected to Dulwich College and James Allen's School via the Elizabethan actor-manager Edward Alleyn under a Royal Charter of 1619. Very relaxed links between the three schools. The parents' huge enthusiasm for the birth of the school has now given way to nodding content.

This is a fabulous and exciting designer-school, with a great feeling of freedom and open space tucked somewhat unobtrusively behind Alleyn's Music School, which both schools share – but with different teachers. Junior school also shares dining hall, games complex and swimming pool, etc. Own art room, gym in hall, food technology doubles with science labs. 12 staff, all chosen by Mrs Weir. French everywhere when we visited (lessons start at 5). Some wonderfully original essays in the school mag, inspired by the number 375 (the school has recently celebrated the 375th anniversary of the Foundation).

A grown-up prep school with a cosy feel. The Head is unashamedly keen on academic excellence; classes range from 16 upwards, and there are Maths' sets for last two years. Some help can be given for dyslexia, and external tutors are on hand; children are given time off for 'extra help'.

Children respectful and very polite.

Allfarthing Primary School

St Ann's Crescent, Wandsworth,
London SW18 2LR
Tel: 0181 874 1301,
Fax: 0181 870 2128

PUPILS: 310 boys and girls, ages 4–11;
plus 45 children in the nursery class
(3 + years old)
ALL DAY
C OF E
STATE-MAINTAINED

HEAD: Since 1979, Mrs Veronica Bradbury Dip Ed (late forties); Deputy Head here five years before taking over headship. Married with two sons. Hugely admired, outgoing, very get-up-and-go, she knows all her children. Fits teaching into 20% of her timetable. 'Excellence for all,' she says, 'is the logo of the school – and I really do believe in that.' But has to remind herself sometimes that 'I'm an educationalist, not a social service officer'. Very hands-on in the school and most determined not to be swamped by admin.

ENTRANCE: At 3 to nursery, or 5; also some at 6 and 7 (often from Clapham and Putney). Preference for siblings and those near at hand.

EXIT: Wide choice of local state schools, which are varied – grant-maintained, selective, technology colleges, non-selective, as well as specialist schools. Also to fee-paying schools such as Alleyn's, Dulwich College, King's College, Wimbledon, James Allen's Girls, Godolphin and Latymer.

REMARKS: Outstanding example of a primary school. Creative but disciplined dynamic atmosphere generated by Head and her team of staff, whom she describes as 'my key resource'. They are mostly long-standing (parents love the continuity) but there is a healthy trickle of new blood too; the Head has chosen carefully for 'the chalk face'. One trained plus two assistant staff per class (about 27–30 children, divided into smaller groups by ability). The school was awarded the 'Investors in People National Standard' in '95. Commitment to high standards is visible everywhere; work is displayed throughout the school, classes make lovely books on outings/projects, etc. The school recently produced a pamphlet which is given to all parents called 'Excellence for All', setting out what amounts to a job description for parents, children and the school in the matter of educating the pupils (meant to keep everyone up to scratch).

Big emphasis on reading, with teams of parents coming in daily to hear pupils' reading; regular spelling tests, tables, etc. Individual progress monitored very carefully, slow-coaches slotted in for extra letter or number work in small groups. Way above the national and borough average in English, Reading, Writing, Maths and Science (as tested in '95). Extremely strong links with parents (four on governing body). 'It has to be a partnership,' says Mrs Bradbury, admitting also that the worst disciplinary problems are with a small minority of parents 'who need nagging to get right attitudes'.

Large playgrounds outside. Ten clubs on the go, with something on offer every day ('My children never leave school till 4.30,' said a parent), including athletics, languages (French, Italian, Spanish), choir, drama, science. Constantly take part in *Capital Woman* TV programme. Children happy and motivated. Good social mix – middle class and the socially deprived, with plenty of salt-of-the-earth in between ('this mixture has never changed in my time here,' says the Head. 'It's the geography of the area'), 30% of pupils from mixed ethnic minorities. Truancy rate is negligible, and there are no exclusions. Parents can't speak too highly of the place.

Ardvreck School

Crieff, Perthshire, Scotland PH7 4EX
Tel: 01764 653112, Fax: 01764 654920
PUPILS: 76 boys, 40 girls. Boarding: 62; day: 54. Nursery: 30
AGES: 4–13
INTERDENOM
FEE-PAYING

HEAD: Since 1995, Mr Neil Wainwright Gardner (forties), Cert Ed from the College of the Venerable Bede, Durham. Experienced primary/prep school teacher – his previous post was as Head of the wonderful King's School, Junior School, Worcester. Before that was Head of English at Aberlour, and before that in Norwich School, the Lower School. Mr Gardner is a keen fisherman and beekeeper – 'when I get the time' – so his present post should be seventh heaven. Has an optimistic turn of mind. Married to Carol, who also taught at King's School, and now 'co-ordinates learning support' at Ardvreck. They have two children, both at school in Scotland.

ENTRANCE: There is a pre-prep, but most come at 8+. All children must board for the last year. The Head comments that 'interviewing the parents is as important as interviewing the children' – you have been warned.

EXIT: Mostly to Scottish public schools, in particular Glenalmond

(it's v close), Strathallan and Gordonstoun. A handful go south, including one in '95 to Eton and one to Cranleigh. Nine scholarships in '93, 8 in '94 (almost all to Scottish schools), 7 in '95 – but spreading the net further afield, including one to Downe House, one to Canford, and the top academic scholarship to Glenalmond.

REMARKS: Purpose-built Victorian school (1883), with new(ish) swimming pool and classroom complex in the grounds, which rather lowers the tone. In 1994 celebrated its centenary as Ardvreck, with great jollifications. Two senior houses to prepare boys and girls for their public school.

Traditional teaching, and some 'terrific staff' according to parents; much fun seems to be had by all, not least the parents. Pupils mostly have oodles of self-confidence and are expected to be hardy – boys wear shorts even when the snow is thick on the ground, and there are some freezing dorms. 'Barvicks' mini-expeditions in the summer are a highlight of the year.

Extremely strong on games, particularly in rugby – usually gets through to quarter- or semi-finals of Rosslyn Park; also at netball (recent tour to Malta); is pre-eminent at shooting throughout the UK and has had national shots. Music is also strong, particularly in singing, and the school won, for example, several firsts in the Perthshire Musical Festival, including the City of Perth Rose Bowl: Senior Choir. Nor is the piping to be sneezed at.

Edinburgh and Borders 'smarties' tend not to send their children here; the school has a reputation as the backwoods Scots' Scottish prep school. Pupils are, by and large, happy and keep up friendships and links long after they have left.

It's too early to comment on the new regime, except to say that the signs are good.

Arnold House

3 Loudoun Road, St John's Wood,
London NW8 0LH
Tel: 0171 286 1100 Fax: 0171 266 0655

PUPILS: 230 boys
ALL DAY
AGES: 5–13
C OF E in theory, but all are welcome
FEE-PAYING

HEAD: Since 1994, Mr Nicholas Allen, BA, PGCE (forties). Formerly head of Ipswich Prep School. Wife teaches at Queensgate School. Has three school-age children – including one in the school, which gives him an instant window on to what is going on. A thinker – dry, with a quiet charm and a slow delivery which is a bit disconcerting at first. Read History and Archaeology at Exeter, and this is where his interests lie. Teaches religious instruction to the top of the school. Comments on his progress so far that he has tried to introduce more (formalised) communication, e.g. a very useful newsletter which goes out to parents.

ENTRANCE: Formerly on a first-come, first-served basis, which made the school so popular. Now, alas, this is on the way out in favour of interviews with the child, followed by 'assessment . . . not a test'. Pupils come from all round, also Islington, which the head describes as 'a black hole' (in prep school terms).

EXIT: Most to Westminster (take a look at the ancient honours boards in the basement, which includes nice little never-say-die touches such as Blogg (Prox Acc) got a music exhibition Here. OBs – John Tavener the composer, C. Tickell.

REMARKS: A school which feels as though it is changing from the cosy and popular, not-too-pressured prep school it used to be under the previous Head, Jonathan Clegg (who is now in the throes of building up Phoenix House). It is difficult to comment on the new regime at the moment, however, as it is so new, and obviously changes are afoot.

School lunches are reported by one and all to be outstanding – old boys write back fondly to their younger school mates, saying 'enjoy them while you can'. Some good evidence suggests the boys are being taught drawing, though we have seen more originality elsewhere.

Class sizes are still about 16, the biggest being 17. The top two classes are now streamed – 'cosiness is not all' says the Head. There is a 'part-time' special needs teacher. Greek for some in 'year 7'; spoken French from the beginning – 'because it becomes more academic in years four to six'. Mr Allen has made a point of breaking the eight years the children spend at the school into 'three distinct experiences . . . remembering that year 7 is the beginning of secondary education'.

The school's playing fields are at Canon's Park (at the end of the Jubilee Line tube), and boys are bussed out there for games twice a week (soccer, rugby, cricket, athletics, etc); there's an all-weather pitch – though the school does not seem mad keen on games. Big sports hall. Lots of distinctive stripey red and green ties for e.g. industry, sport, responsibility.

The school is opposite the American School (which looks like a prisoners' pound), and housed in three large houses – away from the busy through road to the A1, and with what is by London standards a large tarmac playground, and a pretty garden.

Founded in 1905 by Miss Hanson. It currently sports three ex-heads on the staff – a sort of knacker's yard for Headmasters. Parents (some pretty demanding) include some distinguished media names; the professions are 'pretty well represented'; and there are lots of second-generation OBs' sons. The school is being watched a bit nervously by parents. All change.

Ashdell Preparatory School

266 Fulwood Road, Sheffield S10 3BL
Tel: 01142 663835 (no fax)

PUPILS: Approx 130 girls
ALL DAY
AGES: 4–11
C OF E
FEE-PAYING

HEAD: Since 1984, Mrs Jane Upton (fifties), brought up in Cumbria, further education in France, teacher training in Sheffield. Married; husband is Deputy Head of Silverdale School in Sheffield – a powerful couple in Sheffield educational circles. Gentle, inspiring, tireless, with a sense of humour. Ambitious that the school should be 'excellent in what it does best', and for this reason has policy not to increase numbers radically. Runs the school by the seat of her pants – at her post all hours, has no Deputy. Comments that when she took on the job she had 'no idea how all-consuming and thrilling it would be'.

ENTRANCE: Parents are interviewed 'to see how much they are doing and what they want'; if their aim for their child is the local comprehensive the Head advises them it would be unfair to send the child here. Next the child is interviewed and tested for ability. Register any time.

EXIT: A number to Sheffield High and schools in Yorkshire and the north of England, e.g. Casterton, Queen Margaret's York.

REMARKS: Excellent as ever, and presided over by one of the best heads in the business. Rare commodity in this area – a 'proper' girls' prep school with the feel of a boarding school: doors open at 7.30 a.m. and clubs still going strong at 5 p.m. Standard of handwriting excellent – five-year-olds turning in performances which would not discredit people twice that age, and school regularly wins competitions. Mrs Upton reckons to achieve 'very high standards', academically speaking.

The acquisition of a new mid-Victorian building behind the current site on Fulwood Road (nice views over Sheffield and the near 'brother' school of Westbourne Prep) has eased feeling of crowding, and planning permission has recently been granted to expand the gym and build a large new music room.

Coaching given not only to those falling behind in the race, but also to the extra bright ('it is unfair not to'). Parents are doctors (local hospitals very handy), lawyers, landed, and builders, etc.

Children are well-behaved but perhaps a bit lacking in zip, laden with briefcases and musical instruments. All children get the chance to experience a week's boarding while in the school – ostensibly to give them an opportunity to abseil or whatever, but the 'hidden curriculum' being to introduce them gently to life away from home.

School founded in 1949 as a dame school by the coal-and-steel Baronet Roberts; now a charitable trust. Cheery, cherry-red jackets and boaters with snowdrop crest – 'a humble flower, and the first sign of spring'.

9

Ashdown House

Forest Row, East Sussex RH18 5JY
Tel: 01342 822 574, Fax: 01342 824 380

PUPILS: 133 boys, 54 girls
ALL BOARD EXCEPT FOR AROUND 5
AGES: 8–13
C OF E
FEE-PAYING

HEAD: Since 1979, Mr Clive Williams MA (early fifties), educated at Eton and Cambridge. An old boy of Ashdown, he taught at Elstree. Contracted until 2004. Affable, and modest, he teaches Classics, English and Scripture (about 16 periods a week). His wife Rowena also teaches (Scripture), as well as managing the school's premises both in England and in France. Three teenage girls, one boy.

ENTRANCE: Put names down three years in advance 'though one's lists are more volatile now'. Interview one year ahead. 50% from London, 20% from overseas (a handful of foreigners), 20% local, 10% other.

EXIT: Mostly to smart boarding schools – Eton topping the list. NB the school is only interested in girls leaving at 13, 'Because we like girls in the top slots at school'. Hmmm.

REMARKS: A fashionable/sought-after school which bucked the boarding trend in the recession and goes from strength to strength. (Pupils include children of the Head's friends.) Traditional English prep school with family feel (though not without a certain formality), humming with activity (4 plays a year, a choral work, etc), especially over lunch time. Very handsome Georgian house (listed Grade 2), soft grey stone, overlooking the Downs, with much tactful building-on behind. New indoor swimming pool, classroom block, and more dorms (the 'East Wing') opened in '94 – 'But we won't go beyond 200').

Lovely setting in rolling acres, 'jungle' area for camps, etc. Strong on the games front. Good food eaten in huge dining hall, cafeteria style ('A pity,' comment parents of young children). Keenly musical – around 150 play an instrument and portable instruments are often practised in dorms. Reading rest period in theatre for all ages after lunch – 'Very difficult to get children to read nowadays,' moans the Head. He reads to the youngest forms nightly, sitting in his study, his voice broadcast to their dorms. Children awaken at 7.15 a.m. to Radio 4.

Classes of 15, streaming after two years, scholarship class varies in size from year to year. French getting a higher profile since the acquisition of a Château in Normandy (the Château de Livet, near Falaise) which they let out to other schools. Pupils initially go to the château for two weeks, then for half a term, and fax French diaries back every day. Master in charge of French at Falaise is a young (English) Oxford College lecturer. 'Still very few girls,' comment parents – Ashdown continues to feel like a boys' school with some girls in it.

Aysgarth School

Newton-Le-Willows, Bedale, North Yorkshire DL8 1TF
Tel: 01677 450240, Fax: 01677 450736

PUPILS: Around 136
ALMOST ALL BOARDING IN THE MAIN SCHOOL
AGES: 3–13
C OF E
FEE-PAYING

HEAD: Since 1988, Mr John Hodgkinson MA Cantab (early fifties). Previously Housemaster at Uppingham. Married (wife, Hilary, helps in the school doing 'all the usual things'); three daughters.

ENTRANCE: By interview – 'we never, ever write a child off'. No scholarships into school, but occasional bursary, including one from the Charles Leveson-Gower Memorial Fund.

EXIT: Mostly to smart English public schools.

REMARKS: Once the automatic choice for Yorkshire toffs, but no longer; intake, though, is from the same (smart) Yorkshire families. Lovely grounds, purpose-built school with tower and romantic (but dour) old classrooms with uplifting Latin mottoes around the walls, e.g. *Pereunt et imputantur*. Latin for all at nine and ten – though 'one or two drop off'. NB, apropos of the dour classrooms, the head comments that they have a running programme of redecoration throughout the school.

IT – one timetabled lesson a week, but boys 'popping in and out the whole time'. Very successful petite extra-tuition teacher. Good Carpentry, lively Art, and the Head points out that in the last edition we failed to mention how good the Music was – lots of distinctions, not to mention 6 boys being taught the organ, to the degree that they can play for Sunday-morning chapel.

Traditional, old-fashioned school. Friendly boys. The first eleven were unbeaten for a (record?) 100 matches, but, alas, lost a game in Summer '95. Exeats every three-and-a-half weeks; also Sunday exeats if 'special family occasion'. Chapel every morning. Buildings freezing when we visited (but, says Head, 'you happened to visit on a very cold day'). Rest on beds after lunch for the youngest boys.

Numbers were seriously down, but now, with the opening of the pre-prep and nursery departments (both bubbling), look much perkier – indeed, have grown by about 40 per cent since we last visited. Some happy reports from pupils; one or two, less so.

Beaudesert Park School

Minchinhampton, Stroud, Gloucestershire GL6 9AF
Tel: 01453 832072, Fax: 01453 836040

PUPILS: 94 boys, 63 girls. 66 board, 91 day; Pre-prep: 62 boys, 63 girls.
AGES: 4–13
MOSTLY C OF E
FEE-PAYING

HEAD: Since 1995, Mr and Mrs John R W Beasley MAs Cantab and St Andrews respectively (thirties). They took over from Mr Keyte, who was here for 25 years and was the third generation to teach at the school, which was founded by his grandfather and became an educational trust in 1968. Mr Beasley's previous post was as assistant master teaching history at Eton. Lists his interests as reading, playing cricket and golf, refereeing rugby, writing children's poetry, black and white photography and people. Golf blue (3 times). His wife, Ann, was previously assistant teacher of history at St Helen and St Katharine, Abingdon. One young son, Tom.

Continuity is being provided by the school dog, Nina, who has been living in the Garden Cottage on the estate chez the long-serving Deputy Head, Mr Stevens.

ENTRANCE: Popular. Visit and register.

EXIT: Lots to Malvern, Marlborough, Cheltenham, Clifton and a wide variety of other schools. Usually a trickle to Radley and Eton. Girls go to Cheltenham Ladies' College, Stroud High, Stonar, etc. Won a record 16 awards to senior schools in '95, including seven for music/art.

REMARKS: Too early to comment on new regime. School is perched at the top of a hideously wiggly drive up a hill on the edge of Minchinhampton Common (with fabulous views over the golf course). Splendid Victorian Gothic with many additions (sympathetic Cotswold stone at the front), surrounded by 12 acres of stepped playing fields.

CDT strong, lots of computers, mega-gym with fabulous adjoining swimming pool tiled like a Roman bath (much-envied). Good art, lots of options, fabulous drama. Friendly.

Lots of weekly boarders – the Gloucestershire set. Most board for the last two years. Can deal with dyslexia. Vegetarian meals available and salad on every table, every day.

Beeston Hall School

West Runton, Cromer,
Norfolk NR27 9NQ
Tel: 01263 837324, Fax: 01263 838177

PUPILS: 100 boys and 70 girls. 105 board, 65 day
AGES: 7–13
MAINLY C OF E
FEE-PAYING

HEAD: Since 1986 Mr John Elder MA (forties), educated at St Andrews and Edinburgh. Historian (teaches the top

five forms Maths, and the scholars English). Dutch wife, three young children. Leads from the front, talkative, a prep-school boy at heart. One-man band: 'It's very much the headmaster's school – which has its advantages and disadvantages,' commented a parent. Indefatigable visitor of senior schools – visits 15 a year, 'seen 100 in the last decade and some at least five times'.

ENTRANCE: Entry tests in English and 'numbers' (very rare to be found unsuitable), but all children are seen about six months before entry. Subsequently they come (in groups of 12) to try out a day's timetable (and may 'try out' boarding).

EXIT: Widespread (with most girls staying till 12+ or 13+). Gresham's has had by far the largest numbers in the past 3 years, followed by Oundle and Oakham; after that it's all over, mostly in ones and twos – Harrow, Milton Abbey, Rugby, Tudor Hall, Downe House, Sedbergh, Gordonstoun, etc, including RC contingent to Ampleforth.

REMARKS: Gloriously happy school run as a big family. Very much a country school, and mostly catering for proper country children (only 20 from London). Half a mile from the sea, this pleasant Regency white house with additions is set in 700 acres and surrounded by National Trust estates. Good facilities for everything and bright classrooms. Art work, which is outstandingly good, is framed and hung throughout the school, a joy to see. Very thorough teaching, with subject teaching from the start (regular French lunch table with real Madame), and extremely flexible class system (groups of 14), whereby fast movers can go up one at the end of a term (this could mean two years in the Sixth Form and a scholarship chance), or it may mean one year and more in the same class. 'Good for the bright and the non-bright' according to a parent with both kinds; remedial help given at no extra cost.

No prep at all: the Head firmly believes that 'children would rather be taught' – but groups (half a class) are often sent off to work on a project, solve Maths problems, etc, while a formal class is in progress. Good work goes straight to the Head (sees and signs 1,800 per term), also bad (50 per term), and poor work (50 per term). Astonishing number of cups (120), and prize-giving every single term.

Fantastically strong emphasis on drama (main stage is in the indoor sports hall), at all times and all levels; wildly popular. Mothers press-ganged into sewing costumes with Mrs Elder. Good music; loads of computers (Archimedes, BBCs, Amigas and Amstrads), taken seriously.

Huge amount of sport (and unusually varied for a prep school) with House matches as well as many with other schools, some as far afield as Scotland. Geographical position something of a disadvantage, with lack of local competition and long journeys for matches. The school is very successful, however: in 1994–5 they played 281 matches in all, won 213, drew 16, lost 52, and over 150 children took part. The first fifteen won 18 out of 19 matches in '94/95; county champions in cross-country and cricket and Under-13 girls' hockey, second in national prep schools golf in '94, second in prep schools riding in '95 – and more, there isn't room to list it all. No specialist for gym or PE; taught by the devoted and committed staff.

Books everywhere (poetry learned by heart), also magazines – public school mags, *Newsweek*, *Focus*, etc. Interesting general knowledge system: common-room notice board (for 10+) posted weekly with aspects of news, e.g. on the United Nations, geography, also art and music, which children look at, 'absorb by osmosis' and are later quizzed on.

The youngest children sleep in the main house (cosy rooms); newish boarding house for the rest (boys and girls share this); biggest dorm has eight beds, all rooms well provided for with Monopoly, Scrabble, etc. Super common rooms (French bar football, mini billiards, etc). All children provided with a school cheque book for Church money, tuck, etc.

Children allowed out in groups of three (to the beach, to the tiny town $1\frac{1}{2}$ miles away. 'It's an area you know they are safe in', says a parent). Long (50-minute) morning breaks, for music practice, climbing trees, play, etc. Many clubs/activities for evenings and action-packed weekends. Children given duties – postman, sweeping up after lunch, etc. Long exeats (but fairly far between).

Delightful and outstanding little school, currently slightly over-full; deservedly popular, it has confident, happy children.

Belhaven Hill

Dunbar, East Lothian EH42 1NN
Tel: 01368 862785, Fax: 01368 865225

PUPILS: 70 boys, 5 girls; 65 board, 10 day
AGES: $7\frac{1}{2}$–$13\frac{1}{2}$
NON-DENOM
FEE-PAYING

HEAD: Since 1987, Mr Michael Osborne MA, educated at Radley and Cambridge, read Economics (qualified as an accountant), and considered by some to be 'the best teacher in Scotland'. Separated from wife and lives with his two sons (one in school) and four-year-old daughter. Popular Head –

the boys love him (he knows his 32 times table and 57 times table – 'well actually any times table'). An enthusiast, good at advising on senior schools, boys keep up with him after they leave (and he writes back).

ENTRANCE: No test, but register as early as possible. Boys spend a day at Belhaven the term before they come.

EXIT: In the last two years, 10 to Eton, 5 to Oundle, 4 to Glenalmond, 3 to Loretto, 2 each to Harrow, Stowe and Winchester etc.

REMARKS: The Scottish prep which focuses on sending children to public school in the south. It has had one or two upheavals since we last went to press.

School based in late eighteenth-century sandstone house, with imaginative new addition and tower (library, classroom and huge mega-windowed dorm above – Osborne's folly), flanked by familiar hotch-potch of extra classrooms.

Streamed at top end, staff increased to ten (stay on average ten years plus). Remedial help on hand. Computers scattered throughout. Greek, German and Spanish options. Pianos everywhere, and a good Music Centre. Piping lessons by Mr McCreadie and Housemaster David Conran-Smith.

Boys' dormitories under one roof, teddy bears, bunks, duvets and old tartan rugs. Magnificent Sports Hall which adapts for school plays and air rifles. One or two reports of bullying recently.

Night store heating throughout. Well-kept grounds with two cricket pitches (successful '94/'95 season), artificial slips, a putting course and an eighteen-hole golf course 'over the wall'. Regular trips to Hillend ski slope. Archery and carpentry both popular; boys encouraged

to have their own bit of garden. Outward Bound, Mastermind Competitions; hot on chess.

Parents are encouraged to play a large part. Upper-middle to upper class; most local or with Scottish connections if not local, though an increasing trickle from south of the border. Day girls 're-introduced' in September 1995 and new girls' house for boarders scheduled for '96.

Bousfield Primary School

South Bolton Gardens,
London SW5 0DJ
Tel: 0171 373 6544, Fax: 0171 373 8894

PUPILS: 200 boys, 200 girls
ALL DAY
AGES: 5–11
NON-DENOM
STATE

HEAD: Since 1990, Mrs Vicky Plotkin B Sc (forties), previously Head of a north London infants' school. Delightful, both gentle and firm.

ENTRANCE: Priority given to brothers and sisters and to children who live nearest the school. 20 per term: 2 reception classes.

EXIT: One-third go on to independent schools – heading the list are Latymer, Putney High, Godolphin and Latymer, Queen's College, Queen's Gate and Westminster Under. State favourites are Holland Park, Shene and Elliott.

REMARKS: Continuously and deservedly popular, much sought-after primary school in a v useful central

London location. English is not the first language of about half of the pupils – 39 different mother tongues (Arabic and French chief among them). Well run, fun, strong on parental involvement. Bousfield busily fosters the creative arts – Music especially good, also Art. The school now tends to attract teachers with musical skills who teach recorder, guitar, etc.

The Head is dead keen on good manners, minds about discipline (not a problem), and there is a homework policy obligatory for all junior classes – children throughout the school take work home regularly. Mrs Plotkin is currently working to improve the Maths. Well-used and well-stocked libraries. Children heading for private schools typically get extra boosting (for a year or more) from outside on both Maths and English. Classrooms all bursting with colourful and creative project work.

The school is on the site of Beatrix Potter's childhood home, built in 1956 (and now a listed building), with light airy classrooms ('too small,' sighs the Head) and grass play area, plus very large playground, the envy of local private central London schools. Central body of the building consists of two large halls mirroring each other for infants and juniors, used for dance, productions, gym, assemblies, etc. Governors have control of a fully delegated budget; the Head, School Admin. Officer and School Services Manager work out all payments, 'from staff to loo paper – so there's not much time for me to teach!' However, Mrs Plotkin oversees everybody and often 'goes walkabout'. A nursery department opened in April 1996.

Brambletye School

East Grinstead, West Sussex RH19 3PD
Tel: 01342 321004, Fax: 01342 317562

PUPILS: Around 160 boarders, 55 day. All boys
AGES: 7–13. Plus pre-prep, 45 boys and girls, ages 4–8
C OF E
FEE-PAYING

HEAD: Since 1969, Mr Donald Fowler-Watt MA (fifties). Educated at Harrow and Cambridge. Once a stockbroker. Three grown-up children (sons both teachers, daughter works for the BBC). Runs the school with his wife Sheila, a wonderful person who inspires confidence most especially and importantly in mothers, who know that their sons are in excellent care. She is also the inspiration for the wives of new young heads (speaks at conferences, etc). Retiring in '97.

ENTRANCE: Book early, this is a sought-after school. No entry test, but previous school fills in a telling form for pupils. Entry at 7/8; sometimes places available later. Large number of children from London, 30–35 Brits from abroad.

EXIT: To at least 17 different boarding schools each year – regularly to Harrow, Radley, Charterhouse, Eton, Wellington, King's Canterbury, etc. Also one or two to e.g. Epsom, Eastbourne College and Milton Abbey. Awards to Harrow, Sherborne, Winchester, Wellington, etc in '95.

REMARKS: Could be one of the happiest boarding preps in the land; has a strong family atmosphere, hence its continued popularity as a boarding establishment. Not a hothouse but thinks of itself as 'quite academic' (and senior schools note Brambletye boys are well grounded in most subjects). Seven- and eight-year-old entry classes separately taught. Classes of 18 or 12; scholarship group is formed at 11.

Set in lovely countryside (though just on the edge of East Grinstead), it was once the Abergavenny family house and looks baronial, though the atmosphere is cosy in a grand kind of way: lots of polished wood and panelling and fires. Top-quality staff of long standing. Much on offer, including shooting, golf, fishing. Good music, and outstanding art. Terrific theatre produces fine drama. Very full sports programme; 'fearfully competitive' said a pupil in a neighbouring school.

New library opened in '94 with full-time librarian on site. The money – as usual at this school – comes from the school's own resources (including a donation from a grateful parent, 'The most expensive present we have ever had'). But no appeals to parents – other bursars/heads please note.

Accessibility to London means strong parental involvement, with parents calling by with cake, etc, on a child's birthday. Manners are important, boys very sparky and self-confident.

Bramcote School

Filey Road, Scarborough,
North Yorkshire YO11 2TT
Tel: 01723 373086, Fax: 01723 364186

PUPILS: Approx 90 boys (plus girls from '96)
ALL BOARDING
AGES: 8–13
C OF E FOUNDATION
FEE-PAYING

HEAD: From September 1996, Mr Peter Keith, who was previously Housemaster at Glenalmond. Married with two daughters. Takes over from Mr John Walker, who was here three years before moving to Abberley. In the past few years, there has been too much changing of Heads for the good of the school.

ENTRANCE: No entrance exam – all comers taken, and about two of these a year need 'Extra English' 'for whatever reason', says the Head. Pupils from all over Yorkshire, and a few from 'outside' (by which he means outside Yorkshire).

EXIT: A typical year would be 2/3 to Winchester (long tradition of links with Winchester, and current Head of Winchester is an OB), 2/3 to Eton, 3/4 (or more) to Shrewsbury, 2/3 to Uppingham (or whichever school takes parents' fancy in a two-hour radius); plus one or two to Sedbergh, Oundle, Repton etc. On average 25% of boys get scholarships, which, given comprehensive intake, is not nothing ('very good', comments school).

REMARKS: Founded just over a hundred years ago by Sir Samuel Servington Savery, whose brother George opened Harrogate Ladies' College. Traditionally more for sons of professionals than landed compared with rival school Aysgarth, but this has altered in recent years with marked swing in popularity towards Bramcote. That said, school had a tough time weathering recession owing to geographical position – out on limb with sea on three sides (not much catchment area) – and for being (hitherto) boys only.

Basically a good traditional all-boys' boarding school – full boarding only, with exeats every three weeks. Straight-forward, no-nonsense preparation for

Common Entrance. Standards geared to high demands of Winchester entrance exam – Latin for all (except those doing 'Extra English'), lots of basic grammar, Greek for scholarship boys, solid grounding in traditional subjects. The National Curriculum is shadowed and school has opted to be tested for this, which will be interesting. Excellent history, under John Horton, with charts on wall when we visited listing e.g. important dates in 1909: 'Edward VII died; Bramcote played first match against Aysgarth'.

Academic class sizes a 'variable feast' – occasionally split forms, average 11–12. First years called 'Toads' (as it is kindly and at great length explained in the prospectus) though the school admits that parents don't always like to think of their children being called 'toads'. Music: 90% play an instrument and practice takes place every day after breakfast – 'there is plinking and plonking and scratching in every corner of the school,' says the outgoing Head. A new Director of Music was appointed in '94.

School housed in what looks like a large red-brick seaside hotel up above the seafront. Do not be daunted – behind the façade everything is in good working order, with super playing fields, all on same site, and wonderful views of the sea from one or two of the dormitories. In one corner of the playing fields is a pavilion which used to belong to the North of England Tennis Club (a museum piece). Steamy, hot indoor pool; good indoor ball-bashing-about room; new sports hall with cricket nets, etc opened in 1995. One of the houses has been refurbished in preparation for the GIRLS.

NB A senior master who has seen these comments says he doesn't recognise the school at all – it's much more fun than this.

Broomwood Hall

74 Nightingale Lane,
London SW12 8NR
Tel: 0181 673 1616, Fax: 0181 675 7805

PUPILS: 308 children, Co-ed
AGES: 4–8 boys, 4–12 girls
C OF E
FEE-PAYING

JOINT HEADS: Since 1984, Mrs Colquhoun B Ed (thirties, pronounced cahoon), and her husband Malcolm, a Scotsman. They have two young children plus older step-children (his). Home in Scotland. Mrs C is considered by many to be imposing, but she is tremendously confident and enthusiastic. Having opened Broomwood's 'brother' school, the Colquhouns are now planning a secondary school for 500 girls.

ENTRANCE: At 4, also at 7 and 8. Get on the list early. One-to-one interview for young children, tests for the older ones. Mixed ability. NB Catchment area rules for children no longer applies – you don't have to be local, though most live in fashionable Wandsworth.

EXIT: Boys (at 8) to London day schools Northcote Lodge, Dulwich College Prep, and to boarding schools including Cothill, Sandroyd, Caldicott. Girls to boarding schools St Mary's Wantage, Downe House (scholarship here in '95), Heathfield, and the St Mary's Calne, Ascot and Shaftesbury; also to day schools e.g. Streatham Hill and Clapham High, Francis Holland and More House.

REMARKS: A charming school, set up by Mrs Colquhoun in 1984, which has grown successfully from a dozen

... s and is now hotly sought-after by south London parents. Girls' ages extended to 11/12 in 1991. 'Babies' are round the corner in the Vicarage. Very traditional and structured in every respect (lots of emphasis on manners), friendly competition (cups galore, many donated by leavers' satisfied parents). Box for 'slips' of good behaviour marks, and (rare) poor marks. Extremely cheerful and friendly children, from Sloaney backgrounds.

The school is a large plain Edwardian house, once the HQ of SOGAT, with a splendid garden and playground, and enviable space. Homework rule: parents must set the conditions, leave the child alone to work, and knock when time is up (no extra time allowed). Strict party rule: no parties during the week, 'It ruins two days, the day of the party and the day after.'

Good system of swaps with Paris school for girls in the top year ('It took me years to find the right school'). Girls correspond for a year before, and exchanges sometimes continue for years ahead. 'I wish I had worked harder at French before I went to the Paris school,' commented one pupil. Latin (very popular) begins at 8.

Throughout the school, children are taught in ability groups within the same class. Mrs Colquhoun considers her main thrust is preparing children for boarding. 'It's important that they have a liking for themselves, and feel comfortable with themselves,' she says, adding that the academic side of school life is far easier to get right. 'I see my job as helping them to feel in control of their lives.'

NB Broomwood has a 'brother' school in Northcote Lodge (under the same ownership). Head: Mr Desmond Bain, Tel 0171 924 7170. Opened in '93 and looks promising – parents nod that they are satisfied with it.

Bute House Preparatory School for Girls

(formerly St Paul's Girls' Prep)

Bute House, Luxemburg Gardens, London W6 7EA
Tel: 0171 603 7381, Fax: 0171 371 3446

PUPILS: 254 girls
ALL DAY
AGES: 4–11
NON-DENOM, PREDOMINANTLY
  CHRISTIAN
FEE-PAYING

HEAD: Since 1993 Mrs S C Salvidant B Ed (forties). Formerly Head of Rupert House School, Henley-on-Thames. Has worked in the state sector; commutes (by train, with her husband) to London; grown-up daughter going into teaching. Firm, matter of fact, straight down the line manner, and the children adore her. Believes 'all children have gifts and strengths, we value everyone'. Teaches RE to the eldest, and to the rest on a roving basis.

ENTRANCE: Non-selective ballot entry at 4+; children's names must be registered two years in advance, by September 30. Selective entry at 7+: 25 places, school chooses from over 100 girls (seen by three members of staff in groups of ten, testing and teaching – the school is very secretive about what is actually involved in these tests, but the emphasis is on initiative; they are looking for girls who have inquiring minds and a 'spark' that can be fired). Sisters get priority for places.

EXIT: Large numbers to St Paul's (15 in '95); also to Godolphin and Latymer, and one or two elsewhere. Less often to boarding schools, but three apiece to Wycombe Abbey and Downe House in '95. Awards won regularly – including art and music.

R EMARKS: Currently the reigning London academic girls' prep school, a position which is well deserved. Lots of happy comments from parents: 'The best possible start,' said one. 'Children skip into school like Enid Blyteenies . . .' Senior school headmistresses also comment that the girls come up 'well prepared'. The system appears informal, but this is deceptive. Work comes back with remarks not marks, no streaming, no positioning, no weekly or termly tests – which can make parents twitchy at the top end of the school; but 'don't believe all the stuff about no competition, no streaming', commented a parent. 'The standard is very high indeed. My daughter is doing things at 8 I didn't do at an exceptionally academic school until 11 or 12'. Timed tests are reserved for the last year.

Classes changed and mixed every year: from '94 entry children have been in the correct academic year groups, so there is now no need for girls with autumn birthdays to repeat a year.

Interesting mix of all abilities ('though you probably wouldn't choose to send a child here unless you had high expectations,' says the Head) plus selected entry.

Specialist teachers for 8 and 9+ (unusual in a girls' prep). Much time is devoted to extra help if a child doesn't grasp spelling, etc. Some 'absolutely marvellous' teachers, say parents, including the adored reception class teacher, Mrs Harris, and the glamorous Miss Barnes – 'she only has to raise an elegant eyebrow and [she] has 25 five-year-olds gasping with attention'.

Impressive science labs (and lots of hands-on); lovely Art, on show at every turn. Chess and debating societies, as well as the usual crafts, sports etc.

Strongly musical, with all instruments (including trombone and all the strings) taught in school hours (why can't all prep schools do this?); two general music lessons per week. Two choirs – senior and junior, and two orchestras – the main school one, and a 'training' one.

The school is set in glorious grounds, lots of space, and sunny rooms overlooking a beech tree. There are picnics in summer, and a bright Wendy house for play. Also wonderful hot food (meatballs and sunshine tart a 'special favourite').The large assembly hall acts as gym, dining and drama hall and looks out over senior St Paul's playing fields, which Bute House may use at allotted times.

The school has an unusually large library and each class has its own library as well. CDT in the art room. Fortnightly meetings for community discussions – children are involved at all levels (table-setting, litter-picking, etc). Recently introduced drama, games and swimming clubs after school.

Parents are: political, arty, media, performers, not rich.

The school is firing strongly on all its many cylinders, and much deserves its continuing success. It is well worth bustling about to get into this school.

NB: The school is not – and never was – the prep school for St Paul's, despite its erstwhile name and proximity, and notwithstanding the numbers of girls going on there – often doing well in the academic scholarship stakes.

Butterstone School

Arthurstone House, Meigle,
Perthshire PH12 8QY
Tel: 01828 640528, Fax: 01828 640640

PUPILS: Around 52 girls: 40 board, the rest day. 11 in pre-prep. 30+ in nursery
AGES: 3–13
INTER-DENOM
FEE-PAYING

HEAD: Since 1986, Mr Christopher Syers-Gibson MA (Cantab) (sixties) via Wellesley House, St Michael's Choir School and Horris Hill. Teaches Latin and Scripture. There 'till retirement', ably assisted by his wife, Anita (Cert Ed), who teaches English and speech. Aims to produce 'well-rounded children' capable of tackling their next school with confidence and ability.

ENTRANCE: By interview. Two full assisted places and one part assisted place (age 10). Some bursaries and scholarships on offer.

EXIT: Got the top scholarship to Downe House in '95; other pupils went to North Foreland Lodge, Wycombe Abbey, Kilgraston, etc. In '94 got one music and one all-round scholarship to Gordonstoun.

REMARKS: The only all-girls' boarding prep school in Scotland, a haven of horses, rabbits, music and happiness. Tiny toffs' school with tiny classes to encourage academic excellence. All girls learn at least one instrument. Dancing, Art and English speaking board exams popular compulsory subjects. Three girls won awards in the NatWest UK schools junior Maths' challenge in '95. Good remedial support. Run as an extended family, the school is very popular and the staff friendly and helpful.

Financially secure since 21 parents joined with bank to buy fabric of school, which is leased back to Butterstone School Trust for a peppercorn rent. Numbers are rising again, with strong local demand for the nursery (Little Butterstone) – in '95 the school recorded the largest intake since '47. A part of the stables was converted to create extra space for – amazing to relate – an increased number of boarders.

NB: The school is not to be confused with Veronica Linklater's The New School, which is in Butterstone House, Tel: 01350 724 216, Fax 01350 724 283 (Head: Dr Bill Marshall) and is for the 'educationally fragile' – v useful place to know about if you have a child in need of special attention. Some children funded by local authorities.

Caldicott

Farnham Royal,
Buckinghamshire SL2 3SL
Tel: 01753 646214, Fax: 01753 647336

PUPILS: Approx 250 boys, 140 board (including all pupils in the last two years), the rest day
AGES: 7/8–13
C OF E
FEE-PAYING

HEAD: Since 1993, Mr M C B Spens MA (early forties). Educated Marlborough and Cambridge, where he read Natural Sciences. Previously Housemaster at Radley for 10 years, and taught geology at Radley for ten years before that. Made this increasingly common, if unusual, career move in order to retain a sense of being among the pupils while running his own show. Married to Debbie, who is a part-time dyslexia coach. They have one young son (featured in PR photos), a daughter and three dogs. Has many interests, including climbing and sport. We commented in the last edition that he seemed quiet and perhaps a bit over-serious, but Mr Spens reports that his friends find this the 'most inaccurate description' they have ever read.

Heads and ex-heads Mavor, Silk and Morgan are governors.

ENTRANCE: Test and interview. Majority of boys live within an hour of the school.

EXIT: To M4 corridor schools – Radley in particular, Harrow and Wellington; also to St Edward's, Oxford in largish numbers. Number of scholarships fluctuates considerably. Two scholarships to Oundle in '95 and one to Eton.

REMARKS: Highly structured, traditional boys' prep school (perhaps slightly buttoned-up, though 'not true' says Head). Emphasis on boarding, but, in common with national trend, increasing number of day boys. Founded 1904, moved in '38 to present site – now 40 acres of choice Home Counties surrounded by seas of computer commuters. The previous Head, Mr Wright, instigated a dynamic building programme and presided over a huge increase in numbers during his long reign. The result is large numbers of carefully thought-out, purpose-built blocks – the new block, the 'new new block', the 'academic block', etc – all light and spacious and with noticeboards everywhere (more than at any other prep school we have visited and boys walk past them mesmerized – 'not true', says Head).

Very complicated streaming – 'I might die if you asked me to explain it,' said a boy. The object of the streaming, comments the Head, is 'nothing to do with "pushing scholars" and everything to do with looking after weaker candidates'. Early Ofsted report commented that the quality of learning was one of the major strengths of the school – 'satisfactory or better in more

than nine out of ten lessons observed; it was good or very good in six out of every ten'.

Dorms in long corridors and wings off corridors, numbered from 23 to 1 – very much in keeping with the logical structure of the rest of the school. Large common rooms for boarders (slight feeling of 'them and us' between boarders and day). Noisy dining room. Some accommodation for staff in yet another block of houses. Headmaster's study, masters' common room and admin slightly cut off from rest of the school.

Keen rugby school – long tradition; the wall is plastered with trophies. Hot competition from the Dragon and Papplewick. Art teaching still very good – job shared by two Art teachers (mothers!) with real hands-on technique. Good music facilities, including a pianola. Drama traditionally strong – the school is patronized by a clutch of actors' and media sons.

A nice feature of the school is the handful of Thai children, who can be seen learning English in corners. Also Japanese, Chinese, Colombians etc. Says Head: 'we like a "smallish" number of foreign nationals'.

The structured and disciplined atmosphere has rubbed off on the boys, who are kind and thoughtful but perhaps lacking in zip and in need of opportunities to let off steam. Ofsted report comments on the 'exemplary' behaviour of the children – we think it is possibly *too* good. Burnham Beeches – 700 acres of wild, wild woods – are on the doorstep, but not a place you would want to go on your own (panic!).

Cameron House

4 The Vale, London SW3 4AH
Tel: 0171 352 4040,
Fax: 0171 352 2349

PUPILS: 100 (40 boys, 60 girls)
ALL DAY
AGES: 4–12
C OF E
FEE-PAYING

PRINCIPAL: Since 1980 Mrs Josie Ashcroft BSc (thirties). Founder and owner of the school. Mother of two tiny children, married to a lawyer. Charming and competent, a classicist and educational psychologist by training. Taught at Thomas' and coached children privately before setting up her own school here, initially called the Learning Tree and specializing in helping dyslexic children.

HEAD: Since 1994, Miss Finola Stack BA PGCE (early forties). Previously co-founder and co-principal of Finton House (qv). Two children in the school. Swimming instructor and 'keen student' of karate. Sensible and thoughtful and parents report her 'ok'.

ENTRANCE: Put child's name down asap; visit the school 10 months in advance of child's entry. All pupils given an informal assessment.

EXIT: Some boys (decreasingly) leave for traditional boys' boarding preps at 8; others transfer at 11 (to Thomas', etc) or go to junior houses of boarding schools. Girls to Francis Holland, Queen's Gate, Heathfield.

REMARKS: Small and caring school. An excellent place for children to learn self-confidence (at least six pupils have gone on to become Heads of their subsequent schools). Bright colours everywhere, walls well-decorated with work and projects. 'The environment helps children think and become curious,' comment parents. Teeny playground (indeed, the whole outfit is dinky); use of nearby Paulton Square for reading and drawing.

At the time of our visit, there was a debate in progress in top class, on the Inuit and modern man – six-a-side, plus four children judges, under the auspices of a charismatic young American, one of two floating teachers in the school. French at 5, Latin at 9. Science extremely popular, worms and pigs' hearts dissected.

Good singing, ambitious drama. Clubs keenly attended after schools hours; outstanding karate taught by Mrs Lavender Ralston-Saul, one of Britain's few full-time female Black Belt 2nd Dans. 'Academically well prepared,' commented another Head. A charity-minded place, with strong parental involvement.

Cargilfield School

37 Barnton Avenue West,
Edinburgh EH4 6HU
Tel: 0131 336 2207, Fax: 0131 336 3179

PUPILS: 84 boys, 41 girls, 82 board, 43 day
AGES: 3–13+. Junior School (Benbow House) 22 boys, 14 girls. Nursery 25
NON-DENOM
FEE-PAYING

HEAD: Since 1991, Mr Alan Bateman MA (fifties), educated at Trinity College, Dublin. Taught at Colet Court and Canadian secondary boarding schools, and joined Cargilfield in 1986. Assisted by his wife Suzanne, MA, who oscillates between a housekeeping role and teaching English.

Bow-tied Mr Bateman, who teaches History and RE, hopes children will leave Cargilfield with 'enough confidence to start to get to know themselves' and to have a 'shot at all sorts of things'.

ENTRANCE: Bulging waiting lists. No longer guaranteed through nursery and pre-prep. Interview and assessment. Tests if learning difficulties are present.

EXIT: All the Scottish public schools: Gordonstoun, Loretto, St Leonards, Merchiston, less now to Strathallan. Small trickle South: Downe House, Framlingham and Oundle in '94 and '95. Won 13 academic and two Music awards in the last two years.

REMARKS: Edinburgh prep full of 'pushy Edinburgh parents' commented one, increasing in popularity once again: 'droves of people queuing up to come'. Boarding numbers now on the increase again, against every trend, but note that this still feels over-full of day pupils for what is (or was) essentially a boarding school.

The drastic staff reorganisation which we reported in last edition is now reported to have stabilised. Pupils move round amongst the staff; at ten, they are setted and streamed; scholarship class. Learning support available. Computer studies (new computer room with 8 networked Archimedes computers); enviable CDT unit about to be computer-linked.

Latin is strong, as well as Art and Music. There are daily games for all pupils, with a huge choice – new excitements include judo, karate and fencing. Won all but one of its first-eleven hockey matches in '94/'95. Clubs for everything. Much used mini-buses for Edinburgh facilities.

Twenty weekly boarders, and expanded girls' boarding in the pipeline (school quite rich following land sale some years ago). NB Day children can stay when parents are away if space allows.

Boys' dorms huge and airy, girls' much cosier above the Head's flat.

Founded in 1873 and moved to present site in 1899, with magnificent (and very chilly) War Memorial chapel/theatre. Dynamic board of Governors who have just had a think tank on 'Where should we be in 2010?'. Tough on bad payers. There are 23 Service bursaries. Fair quantity of first-time buyers; otherwise mixture of traditional parents (boarders predominantly from the West of Scotland), professional East-coasters and Edinburgh yuppies.

Chafyn Grove School

Bourne Avenue, Salisbury, Wiltshire SP1 1LR
Tel: 01722 333423, Fax: 01722 323114

PUPILS: Around 75 girls, 134 boys (82 board, 122 day)
AGES: 7–13; plus pre-prep with 60 boys and girls, ages 4–7
C OF E
FEE-PAYING

HEAD: Since 1993, Mr David Duff-Mitchell BA, Cert Ed (forties), educated at Canford and did his Cert Ed at Southampton University, took a degree through the Open University. Previously Head of Northcliffe, and has also worked in state sector – thinks all those teaching in private sector should do a spell in a state school. Has open-door policy, lives above the shop with his wife Heather, daughter (at Godolphin), four cats and one dog. Energetic and positive. Keen sportsman, cricket especially.

ENTRANCE: At 7 or 8, assessment 'to make sure they will fit in'.

EXIT: Boys and girls to Bryanston, Sherborne, Canford, Dean Close and Marlborough – and to long list of other schools, day and boarding.

REMARKS: Purpose built (in 1876, co-ed since 1980), on the northern edge of Salisbury, with somewhat gloomy, Virginia creeper-clad face, but at the back the school looks out over its own grounds to fine view of Salisbury plain.

Splendid Creative Arts Centre, with huge high-ceilinged hall, good keen Art (including pottery and workshops), also Drama and Music. All children play recorders at age six, and the violin at 9 – varying numbers stick with it. Big library (with large display area). Sports hall, glass-backed squash courts.

Day pupils come in from fairly far afield. Flexi boarding is also available. There is a good week-end programme, and boarders are well catered for; a notice-board advertises competitions, lost and found, anagram, etc. Pupils come from a broad cross-section, with first-time buyers, service parents, professionals.

Friendly unassuming atmosphere. Unobtrusive but firm discipline – 'We give them a nudge when they need it' says the Head, who is keen to get parents' co-operation over manners especially. Family school, well spoken of by locals (though one or two local parents are not so keen).

Cheam Hawtreys

Headley, Newbury,
Berkshire RG15 8LD
Tel: 01635 268242, Fax: 01635 269345

PUPILS: About 160 boys. About 128 board, the rest day
AGES: 7–13
C OF E
FEE-PAYING

HEAD: Since 1994, Mr Chris Evers BA (Oxon) (fifties), previously head of Cheam *tout court*. The day we visited he had a bad cold and was not a bundle of fire, but he did comment that his aim was 'to continue the boarding tradition in whatever guise boarding evolves . . . we still think boarding in the country is the best education you can give them'. By 'we', he means him and his wife, Penny, who works constantly at his side and is a very considerable presence in the school. Mr Evers teaches current affairs to the top form and to the babies. He was the IAPS Chairman for 1995–6 – which kept him very busy.

ENTRANCE: By 'assessment' – which means that would-be pupils visit the school to get to know it and it to know them. Mr Evers has a horror of London-type high-pressure entrance exams. 30% of pupils are from London, 60% from within a 100-mile radius, and 10% ex-pats/foreigners (including a Russian, a couple of Thais and a brace of Spaniards when we visited).

EXIT: List not given, but all the usual public schools in the area. The advent of Hawtreys boys, among other things, has meant a higher proportion now go to Marlborough. Famous OB (of Cheam): the Prince of Wales, who hated it, of course, and has not been back.

REMARKS: Cheam Hawtreys is a new hybrid cultivated during the recession, a cross between two famous prep schools (Cheam and Hawtreys) who needed, when times were hard, someone to get into bed with – financially speaking. The *official* result is an amalgamation of two similar schools. The *actual* result is that Hawtreys bit the dust, their buildings reverted to the freeholder, while Cheam has emerged (temporarily at least) fatter and financially fitter with 47 boys from Hawtreys and 6 of Hawtreys' brightest and best staff, and plans to build a more permanent structure than the current Portakabin to help house the extra numbers. The new school (the merger was in 1994) has, by the way, just celebrated its 350th anniversary . . .

There is a star teacher of tinies, Colyn Moore (ex-Hawtreys), who is ably helped by her spaniel, Bumble. The enthusiastic Head of Music, Mr Dowbekin (also ex-Hawtreys), is packing in the punters (125 of them are doing an instrument – or two) both because he is good, and because he has a brilliant boy-friendly music processing programme for the computer – Cubase, with which the school has even been known to sing-a-long in chapel.

By and large, though, the atmosphere and the teaching are still very traditional in outlook – small classes (sixteen pupils maximum, but the most we saw were seven or eight), which are streamed from age 9, with sets for French and Maths. There is lots of talk and chalk and an overall sense of being subdued by the awesome task of Common Entrance – never far from the thoughts of the older classes and their teachers. NB Parents (with boys at Cheam) have complained to us that too much of the school's efforts are thrown into the scholarship class.

The pupils we met were poppets, with excellent manners – almost *too* good, perhaps, and too silent to be healthy (though this could just have been their reaction to us).

Points worthy of notice: there are rows of computers, and the Science Master organises a science competition between CH and the local prep schools. Tea is at 4.15 p.m., followed by 40 minutes of play, prep, supper, free time, then hot drinks – by which the boys set great store – and a 'winding down' time, so that the boys don't hit their beds at the run, but are suitably calmed. There is a very nice light library – with bright well-chosen books,

all set at boy height. On the subject of bullying, the Head comments that 'the important thing is communication . . . getting the bullied and bullying together' to discuss things.

The school is housed in a beautiful Edwardian country house (designed by Detmar Blow), with formal gardens leading down to an outdoor swimming pool (now heated for summer swimming), and games fields stretching out to the back. New buildings have been grafted on to blend in and the whole is pleasing. The tinies' boarding house – Denham – is separate, one side of a quadrangle, and the rest are tucked up at the top of the main building, in myriad dormitories (carpets, some bunks) with matrons placed at strategic intervals, and jolly jungle pictures painted on the walls by the boys.

Cheltenham College Junior School

Thirlestaine Road, Cheltenham, Gloucestershire GL53 7AB
Tel: 01242 522697, Fax: 01242 526553

PUPILS: 238 boys, 12 girls, 60 board, rest day.

AGES: 3–13. Plus Kingfishers Junior School, 35 boys and girls 3–7. NB from '96, girls will go up to 11.

HEAD: Since 1991, Mr Nigel Archdale BEd, MEd (forties). Educated John Lyons School, Bristol University and Edinburgh University. Previously Headmaster of Wolverhampton School and before that at the Edinburgh Academy junior school. Keen sportsman (swims or runs every morning); a linguist.

Three young children, his wife is a teacher (career on hold). Since he came he has turned the school around. Writes plays and librettos for children in spare time. He 'adores teaching and young children'. Keen on going for the individual's 'ceiling'. 'Smashing head,' commented a parent.

ENTRANCE: At 3, 4, 7, also 11. Boarders by and large from ex-pat families living abroad.

EXIT: 90% over the road to Cheltenham College.

REMARKS: Dynamic school, previously all boys, now co-ed, with fine teaching. There are high standards in many departments – especially good is Music (the choir tours regularly), and French under an excellent Madame (the 'martins pecheurs' start at 3, with daily lessons). Lovely Art, strong Drama, and a keen technological department with power boats being built. The school, in splendid grounds and setting (across the A40 from the public school), uses some of the senior school facilities.

The first lesson is at 8.15 a.m., and children can stay till 5 p.m. Full weekend programme for the boarders (Technology department open; dry ski-slopes not far away; 'brilliant' 100-foot-long model railway, super (shallow) lake with exciting rope bridge, etc). All boys housed in the main Victorian block, where the dorms have been refurbished.

There is a careful balance for all children of organised extra-curricular activities (including a popular Scout troop) as well as free time for children to organise as they will.

Kingfishers opened September '93 (to a chorus of delight from locals). It is very attractive and bright, in a cosy well-defined area within the main junior school block. Co-education was being phased in, ostensibly to form a pattern of 'family' education below 11, single-sex through the growing years and Sixth Form co-education. However, the senior school is now going co-ed throughout. See also entry on senior school.

Christ Church Primary School

1 Robinson Street, Chelsea,
London SW3 4AA
Tel: 0171 352 5708, Fax: 0171 823 3004
PUPILS: 210 boys and girls
ALL DAY
AGES: 5–11
C OF E voluntary aided
STATE

HEAD: Since January 1993, Miss Anna Kendall, BEd Hons (early forties). Specialises in Religious Education, and Special Educational Needs. Formerly an Advisory Teacher for the Royal Borough of Kensington and Chelsea, Camden and Westminster. Interested in the theatre.

ENTRANCE: Application by February for the following September as the child is rising 5. All other ages on an ad hoc basis. Priority given to: i) children having siblings in the school; ii) children of families who are regular worshippers in St Luke's or Christ Church, Chelsea; iii) children living in the Parish; iv) children of families who are regular worshippers in a neighbouring parish church.

EXIT: Elliot School, Pimlico School, Lady Margaret's, Fulham, Greycoats, Westminster City, Salesian College, etc; about 30% to private London day schools – JAGS, City of London, St Paul's Girls', etc.

REMARKS: Excellent primary school in super location tucked away in a quiet corner of Chelsea, with – by London standards – lots of space, including a good-sized playground and an extra area of courts and grass. Founded 1840, affiliated with local churches (the Rev Gerald Beauchamp of Christ Church is Chair of Governors). Cherry-coloured uniform.

Bright classrooms – but note that the older classes are top-heavy with girls as boys peel off to go to prep school. Class size 30 maximum. Approximately 40% of pupils from Chelsea, 24% from Wandsworth, the rest from Westminster and beyond – a mixed intake. Popular with media folk.

The school is funded by the government local education authority, the church and parents. There are good Science and Technology departments (new hardware/software, CD-Rom, sound card, etc). All children have experience with computers. Maths and English are also good. French for everyone in years 5 and 6, swimming to year 3. PE in the much-used all-purpose school hall. Keen games, with the school participating in inter-school competitions. Keen Music, and the opportunity to sing in the Christ Church choir – the choir master liaises between the church and school.

Colet Court

Lonsdale Road, London SW13 9JT
Tel: 0181 748 3461, Fax: 0181 563 7361

PUPILS: Approx 440 boys, day (plus one small boarding house)
AGES: 7–13
C OF E
FEE-PAYING

HEAD: Since 1992, Mr Geoffrey Thompson (forties), who has more qualifications than you ever dreamed of: BA from Newcastle in Biology, M Ed, Cert Ed, M I Biol, C Biol, Fellow of the College of Preceptors, Fellow of the Linnaean Society. In other words, the man's a hotshot biologist. Also Fellow of the Royal Society of Arts. Educated (in the first place) at Hemsworth Grammar, West Yorkshire. Taught at Colet Court years ago. Appointed here following posts in senior schools – previously Head of Licensed Victuallers' School in Ilkley.

Bluff Yorkshireman, old-fashioned schoolmaster – 'might fit in better in a senior school?' query parents. Is responsible to the High Master of the senior school – ties have been strengthened beween the two establishments as a matter of policy. Married to a teacher. No children. House in the middle of the school site, overlooking the Thames.

ENTRANCE: At 7+, 8+, 10+ and 11+, these last two ages mainly for assisted places. Name down asap – the list closes at 500 names, though the Headmaster has a 'supplementary list' for those who have been living outside the area and for those who do not understand the system. Intake of 2 forms of 18 at 7+, plus two at 8+, making 4 forms in all. Test usually in January – Maths, English and verbal reasoning (non-verbal for 6/7-year-olds), followed by interview for those weeded out by the exam. (The school was a feather-ruffling pioneer in bringing the entry age down from 8 to 7.) Children come mainly from pre-preps in Battersea/Clapham. Internal academic scholarships; music and a choral scholarship offered to outsiders.

NB Parents must sign that St Paul's is their first choice of school on being offered a place at Colet Court.

EXIT: Around 98% to St Paul's (qv); otherwise, scholarships to Eton, etc.

REMARKS: The school is sited in truly horrendous '60s buildings (the architect should be shot) on a fabulous site on the banks of the River Thames. Newly redecorated classrooms, (but with mean little windows): 'institutional', volunteers the Headmaster. The music block is in an ex-Thames Water building with new furniture and new double-glazed windows.

The school remains one of the two most sought-after academic preps in London – the other being Westminster Under – with parents rightly viewing it as an entry point to St Paul's. Common room of high-powered academics, old and new; not an easy place to be. Around 11 women. Boys are bespectacled and bulging with brains, mainly from professional families; keep the staff on their toes – withering scorn when one of them makes a floater.

Class sizes 18 at bottom, 22 at top (max 24). Talk and chalk everywhere (mostly chalk). French and Latin from second year (which, with new 7+ intake, is now the third year). French *assistant*. 'Some' Greek for scholars. Sets from third year in some subjects; in fourth and fifth year one scholarship class and three equal ability classes – setted in most subjects. IT offered all through the school. The school has a specialist on the staff who will assess pupils with learning difficulties, and once a week someone comes in to tutor where necessary – NB this is absolutely not the place for dyslexics.

Games 'as strong as always'. The school uses all the facilities of the senior school, which is on the same site. (NB Colet Court has far more outdoor space than any other central London prep). Every sport is on offer except rowing – according to experts the Thames' current is too strong for the littles – though they can use the rowing tank. The school plays all the usual games, twice a week, with matches against Dulwich, Whitgift, Haileybury, etc.

There is one boarding house with a handful of boarders, but if e.g. parents are away from home, boys can clock in for short periods on a pro rata basis. Some pretty meaty poetry in the '95 school magazine – on dead dogs, punishment ('Hate! Pain! They're mindless, I'm different . . .'), the bully ('. . . He looked such a wimp I could've chopped him in half . . .'), the victim. Some boys adore the heavy academic atmosphere of the place, others hate it. Don't be tempted by the designer label unless your son is both bright and keen.

Cothill House

Nr. Abingdon, Oxon OX13 6JL
Tel: 01865 390800, Fax: 01865 390205

PUPILS: 260 boys. All board
AGES: 8–14, plus day 'arm' for boys and girls ages 5–11
C OF E
FEE-PAYING

HEAD: Since 1976, Mr Adrian Richardson Cert Ed, Oxon (forties). Popular with parents and boys, respected by other Heads; (too?) self-assured. Lovely wife Rachel (strong mother appeal), who still refers to 'our ghastly mad system of sending children away to board – so it must be as much like home as possible'. Three young children. School is brimful, and all-boarding (a great rarity) – 'But we're probably living on borrowed time.'

ENTRANCE: Early registration advised. Interview plus assessment, 'to encourage and reassure, not to eliminate'.

EXIT: Some to Radley, also Eton and Harrow, Stowe ('for support'). Occasionally Oundle.

REMARKS: Still flourishing. Very strong family feel pervades – the main building is large, white and uninstitutional, and the way in is through the Richardsons' living quarters, where new little boys are allowed to play Lego, help cook, befriend the family's au pair, etc. Cosy (huge teddy count) at all levels, but also deeply traditional. Vast numbers of clubs. Emphasis on reading (a book by each boy's bed), two libraries (4,500 volumes in the reference library), plus classroom libraries.

Well-designed modern teaching blocks; lots of female staff (grannies and young). Three streams with Maths workshops to 'sort problems'. Good CDT, Art and choir. Rifle range and golf course.

Boys divided into Greeks, Romans, etc, and are competitive over obtaining good markings generously given (good work, being tidy, etc). Remedial help 'not brilliant' – 'The school doesn't really want to know about children with learning difficulties,' moaned a mother.

Each boy must write a 'personal report' at the end of each term answering a questionnaire on books he's read, his opinions on staff, food, etc. Manners are considered very important. Exeats are kept to a minimum, but boys are kept busy at weekends; parents much encouraged to visit for matches (which suits Londoners), though complaints that 'only parents of match children' are allowed to attend.

Château de Sauveterre (near Toulouse) was bought by the school in '89, 'the best thing we ever did'. This produces sour grapes comments from some other schools – e.g. 'But of course the children speak English almost all the time.' All boys spend at least one term out there,

and some of them two. Great for boosting their confidence on many fronts, 'first and foremost they lose the fear of speaking French,' comments Mr Richardson. Children (boys and girls) from other schools often come too. Teaching starts in English and moves into French (French staff are on hand).

This is a lovely happy school (for most), doing a fine job (and viewed with envy by others): against the trend of the national drop in boarding numbers, here is a boarding-only school which is fuller than ever. However, it could be in danger of becoming a bit swollen headed, though the Head denies this, commenting '. . . We are only too well aware of our good fortune and daily marvel at it . . .'.

NB Cothill's latest addition is Chandlings Manor, Tel 01865 730771, 3 miles away, it is the school's day-pupil 'arm'. This was officially opened in September '94 and the idea is that by about the year 2000 it will be a co-ed day school for 200–250 boys and girls aged 5–11. Boys could then transfer to Cothill. Cothill Sixth Formers now sleep at Chandlings (and feel very grown-up to be a five-minute bus ride away from their juniors). Chandlings belonged to an Arab who built, spread-eagle style, on to the original manor house, an indoor swimming pool, squash court, fine grounds, etc.

Cottesmore School

Buchan Hill, Pease Pottage, West Sussex RH11 9AU
Tel: 01293 520648, Fax: 01293 614784

PUPILS: Around 100 boys, 45 girls. All board
AGES: 7–13
C OF E
FEE-PAYING (private limited company)

HEAD: Since 1971, Mr Mark Rogerson MA (fifties). Educated at Eton, read History at Churchill College, Cambridge. Taught at Wellesely House, Summer Field and Windlesham (where he met his wife). Wife Cathryn plays vital supportive role in this family business. Grown-up children.

ENTRANCE: One-third of parents live abroad (but there are only around 10 foreign children). Many from London and the Home Counties, a few Services' children. April and September entry (a rarity nowadays).

EXIT: Girls to Woldingham, Tudor Hall, Burgess Hill, Benenden, plus co-ed public schools, e.g. Bryanston. Boys to all manner of schools, including Charterhouse (by far the largest number have gone here over the past five years), Sevenoaks, Tonbridge, Reigate Grammar, Mill Hill etc.

REMARKS: Family-run prep school (the present Head took over from his father, after two years of joint headship), now a limited company. Extremely happy, vibrant co-ed, full of siblings, sited in a splendidly grand house (the architect was Lutyens' teacher) built in the 19th century for a French gentleman, whose fortune was based on ostrich feathers, which are painted on ceilings. Splendid views and fine grounds, with lots of (modern) cottages on site for staff.

All children do Latin and French; plus 'tasters' of Greek, Spanish and German after CE. Keenly competitive children ('girls more so than boys'). Small enough to be cosy, yet with a sense of space and tradition – oak-panelled corridors with rows and rows of school photographs. Not overly tidy. Boys and girls do everything, 'they're busy, busy, busy'. The Gatwick Express is used for London outings.

The school wins a great many games matches (the First Eleven, Second Eleven and Colts cricket were all unbeaten in '94/'95); also keen and exceptionally good swimming (won the team swimming in the IAPS team swimming competition in '94/'95); the first fifteen won eight out of their nine matches. Riding, judo, very nice music (e.g. *The Mikado*, piano only). Mini-billiard tables everywhere. The school exchanges with Ecole St Martin, Portoise. Help is given for the dyslexic.

There is streaming in the third year. Chits (for good work, etc) get signed and seen and praise is liberal. Exeats are every two weeks, when the entire school empties out: ex-pats must have handy relations/guardians. Long 'catching up' period daily at breakfast time, when pupils can catch teachers, practise games, musical instrument, do prep.

Numbers are apparently unaffected by the recession (though lists are more volatile); it is one of the eight boarding-only prep schools left in England. This is a super place; there are dynamic photos both in the prospectus and the school magazine. Very low profile.

The Dragon School

Bardwell Road, Oxford OX2 6SS
Tel: 01865 315400, Fax: 01865 311664

PUPILS: 610 boys, 150 girls. 230 boys board, 380 day boys. 20 girls board, 130 day girls. Plus 180 boys and girls in Lynams pre-prep (3–7-year-olds) on separate site

AGES: 3–13
C OF E
FEE-PAYING

HEAD: Since April 1993, Mr Roger Trafford MA (Oxon) (fifties), married to Cheryl, with two grown-up sons. Educated at Forest School, London, then Hertford College Oxford; a historian. Previously Head of Clifton Prep, via Head of King's College Taunton Prep, and Colet Court (Head of English and Housemaster). Known as 'Traff' to the children. 'Substitute teaches' when there's a gap in English or History. Accessible, moving his office to the middle of the Campus (keeps door open); a beady-eyed wandering Head, he turns up everywhere, in the classroom, on the games field. 'Never know when Trafford is going to come round the corner.' Knows school, little boarders have tea chez Traffords, and leavers' dinner in groups of 15. A super, helpful Head.

Aims to give the children 'two feet to face the world', ('the world's getting tougher'), and to develop their interests 'to the best of their abilities'.

ENTRANCE: By early registration – embryos OK – though immediate places available in exceptional circumstances (and in the middle of term for visiting profs to Oxford). Non-competitive academic assessment year before entry; Head sees parents. Waiting lists. Easier to get in as a boarder than a day pupil. Lots of pupils from abroad, particularly Hong Kong and ex-pats. One of the schools which fields state school pupils bound for Eton. Chic little prospectus with Oxford-blue cover.

EXIT: To 95 different schools over the past few years, but most to Eton (has over 100 here at any one time) and St Edward's Oxford. Largish numbers to Magdalen College School, Marlborough, Winchester, Abingdon, Headington, even one or two to Westminster. Regularly wins squillions of scholarships for everything.

REMARKS: One of the best, most exciting academic prep schools in the country. This is a genuine co-ed, with boarding houses cleverly broken down to give a sense of belonging and a feeling of cosiness in what is, in fact, a very large prep school.

The school projects an image of informality – scruffy cords, the scruffier the better (bomber jackets worn only by day pupils), and even scruffier casuals after school. This *laissez faire* attitude to outward appearances charms the children who feel that somebody somewhere is on their side. Underneath, however, the school is very disciplined with a rigorous academic timetable and absolutely no messing-about allowed in class. Horizontal tutorial systems throughout. Terrific staff loyalty, all computer-literate or trained in special needs teaching in the classroom. Remedial help available. There are 6/7 streamed forms in each year after the junior school, but the school will fast-stream a child up three forms if necessary (or drop). In each of the top two years, 40/50 pupils do Greek, a little German and Spanish. Masses of computers everywhere (produces own CD-Roms), and more are scheduled.

Very good Music, with choirs, orchestras, boys' jazz bands, etc. State-of-the-Art theatre with grown-up sound box and lighting (operated by the boys). Lots of options.

Boarders have extra TLC in tiny houses (up to 20 pupils live with house parents, matron, etc). All meals are moving to central feeding (new hygiene regulations, alas), but tinies will still have bun break and tea in houses. Day houses opened in '95.

Masses of sports, traditional rugby, hockey, tennis, cricket, but also sculling (good at that), canoeing, shooting. Enthusiastic rather than outstanding at mainstream sports – words such as 'slow start', 'promising' and 'frustration' feature in the school magazine write-ups. Terrific parental support, however.

Days are long, 'teaching preps' till 6/6.30 p.m. for day boys. Punishments for class disobedience, with the five-minute rule which can end in detention or copying out. Occasional sacking for theft or OTT behaviour.

Conglomerate of purpose-built blocks mingling with Victorian North Oxford; girls' boarding house (Strads) opened September '94 by parental request. School has recently bought another site about a mile away (for pre-prep).

Children can play by the river when they have passed their 'clothes test' (two lengths of the swimming pool in clothes). Many Dragon traditions, including Draconian (school mag), Christmas fair, Stooge's dinner; the list goes on forever. Favoured staff have nicknames, (Jumbo, Tuckshop Tim),while house parents are known as Ma and Pa (though some are called Sue, Jane, Henrietta). There is fierce old-boy loyalty. A very exciting school to be at.

Dulwich College Preparatory School

42 Alleyn Park, London SE21 7AA
Tel: 0181 670 3217, Fax: 0181 766 7586

PUPILS: Approx 742 boys, 707 day, 35 boarders
AGES: 3–13
C OF E
FEE-PAYING

HEAD: Since 1991, Mr George Marsh MA (early fifties), previously Head of Millfield Junior School and before that taught for eight years at the Dragon School. Tactful, beady-eyed and – rarer than you might think in this world – genuinely loves children and enjoys their company. Has 'softened' the approach to children and introduced a system of 'good show ups' in which children come to see him and get a star and a chat when they have done well – so they don't associate the Headmaster solely with bad show ups.

ENTRANCE: Through own excellent nursery school, otherwise normally at five or seven, into cosy, lively infants' school. All children who are registered are assessed – numbers registered are restricted.

EXIT: Around one-third to Dulwich College, fair numbers to Westminster, Winchester, Harrow, Marlborough, Tonbridge and other academic schools. Regularly gets lots of academic and music scholarships (21 at senior level and 7 at 11+ in '95).

REMARKS: Absolutely wonderful academic prep school doing everything and doing it very well (and by the way, no relation to Dulwich College). Very large and much prized in South London, with a five-star Head.

Five streamed forms in each year from the age of ten; average class size 20. Set on the edge of leafy Dulwich, with an asphalt playground behind. Land bought from next-door state school now boasts a multi-purpose building which would not disgrace a university.

Music under the outstanding Michael Spencer is top class – all children can read music by the age of nine, there are several choirs (including one for parents), and the school puts on ambitious and wonderful performances including e.g. a Beethoven symphony and chopsticks. The art department is also super – imaginative work, tireless staff and good teaching. There is a good school bookshop – manned mostly by older boys. The

Maths, French and English teaching is excellent. The school is also a Centre of Excellence for DT and IT. Lots of clubs and activities; parents are deeply involved (so this is not a school to patronise if you haven't got lots of time). The new super Deputy Head is working wonders on the pastoral system.

School has its own little boarding house, Brightlands, just down the road – 13 acres in woodlands with capacity for about 35 boys. Run by Mr and Mrs Symmes, it is weekly and flexible.

Dunhurst (Bedales Junior School)

Petersfield, Hampshire GU32 2DP
Tel: 01730 262984; Fax: 01730 267443

PUPILS: Approx 170 in Dunhurst; 80 in pre-prep Dunannie; boys and girls. Approx 70 board
AGES: 3–8; 8–13
NON-DENOM
FEE-PAYING

JOINT HEADS: Since 1983, Mr and Mrs Michael Heslop. Michael Heslop MA PGCE (fifties) went to St Edward's School and Trinity College, Dublin, read History. Previous post – Deputy Head of Ditcham Park.

Harriet Heslop BA PGCE (fifties), also went to Trinity College and read History. Her previous post was Deputy Head of Bedales. They have four children, and both Heads comment that their spare moments are spent looking after them. Great charm and natural warmth, as well as enthusiasm; excellent rapport with staff and children.

HEAD OF DUNANNIE: Since 1987, Miss Sarah Webster (forties),

trained at the Froebel Institute, did MA in psychology, has taught in America, travelled in Africa and worked in France for two years. Came here from the Unicorn School in Kew. Top-class professional, dedicated and thoughtful.

ENTRANCE: No testing of littles, who move on automatically from Dunannie. Older children are tested for everything, and come for 48 hours ('like a junior civil service exam') to spend two nights boarding and getting to know the school. Entry at 8, 9, 10 and 11 and occasionally at 12.

EXIT: Bedales, apart from one or two.

REMARKS: As an old boy remarked, 'Until I went to Dunhurst I did not know what happiness was.' No praise is too high for the way in which the staff of this school relate to the children: they treat them as people (still a fairly novel idea among prep schools) and the result is children who are friendly, confident, and look you in the eye. More five-star staff here than any other school we have visited – there is a mix of ages and experience, but all staff have the requisite energy, enthusiasm and personality to teach and to make learning fun.

As the majority of pupils go on to Bedales, the school is not stuck in the straitjacket of Common Entrance (for those who want to go elsewhere, 99.9% of schools will make adjustments for the difference in curriculum, says Head). No streaming, but sets for French and Maths; at 11+ start secondary curriculum. Good maths staffing – two staff in room at a time – allows for more flexible help for the one who's stuck without holding up the rest. The biggest class has 24; Art not more than 12; lower down the school the class average is 15. Follows national curriculum in some subjects, shadows in others to keep curriculum as broad as possible, e.g. a class might spend a fortnight studying the Bayeux Tapestry.

Art, Music, and Design and Technology (all excellent) are timetabled – and form an integral part of school life. Pupils have three supervised music practice sessions a week (148 out of 170 now learn an instrument) and 'we like them to perform publicly, even if they are beginners'. The 11-year-olds do prep in study periods which are timetabled, and keep their prep recorded. At 11/12 each child has a tutor and individual sessions each week to go through their whole work file – so that, by the time they get to Bedales, they should be able to work on their own. There is no formal competition, and no public marks. Good PE facilities (use of Bedales where necessary). Other preps pour scorn on Dunhurst's (lack of) prowess on the games field – but without reason. Comments the Head, pupils 'can be keen as mustard and you've got to cater for it'; at various sports in '94/'95 they did brilliantly.

One boys' boarding house and one girls'. The Heads live in a flat in the middle of the school and are available at all hours. No formal splitting of their work, but Harriet tends to oversee girls' boarding and Michael the boys'. All children involved in local charity work. Lots of trips, particularly to Edale.

Meanwhile at Dunannie – 4 teaching staff plus 4 assistants, 2 members of staff to each class. Class size 14–18. Carefully structured timetable from 8.30–12, then 'more free-flowing afternoon'. Takes part in the Nuffield Design and Technology project, and this is excellent in both schools. Good library, and the classrooms have no doors; wellington boots are kept at eye level (so they don't get kicked around). The school has its own garden (and gardens for the children to cultivate), a large sand pit, and an adventure playground (designed by the children).

Edgarley Hall (Millfield Junior School)

Glastonbury, Somerset BA6 8LD
Tel: 01458 832446, Fax: 01458 833679

PUPILS: Around 445, boys and girls. Around 235 board, the rest day (more boys than girls)
AGES: 8–13 (junior school); (also pre-prep in the middle of Glastonbury, ages 4–8)
INTER-DENOM
FEE-PAYING

HEAD: Since September 1996, Mr Simon Cummins MA (early thirties – yes, it's young blood). Previously Head of St Michael's Prep in Otford, Kent. Married with two children. Rumoured to be sporty.

ENTRANCE: Generous scholarships – exam held February for entry in September. Otherwise interview and report from previous Head.

EXIT: Majority to Millfield.

REMARKS: Pleasant houses, good facilities (including use of senior school facilities at times). The generous staff:pupil ratio means there is effective streaming and setting. The school is used by the National Association for Gifted Children – this means a layer of genius in the top stream. It also has an outstandingly good remedial department.

Genuine comprehensive intake – though with the increase in the number of day pupils, the school has the feel of a local school and boarders from further afield tend to feel a bit bleak at school

34

functions. Girls' boarding houses half a mile or so down the road (which means constant ferrying by school minibus); boys' houses on the campus.

Smart Music School. Still very strong on sport (thanks to the Millfield ethos) though it has been known to be beaten by preps that are ostensibly much weaker. Lots on offer, as well as mainstream sports – hockey, netball, rounders, tennis and athletics (for girls), rugby, football, hockey, cricket, athletics and tennis (for boys). There is a smart new indoor swimming pool.

Much too early to comment on the new regime.

Edge Grove

Aldenham, Hertfordshire WD2 8BL
Tel: 01923 855724/857456,
Fax: 01923 859920

PUPILS: Around 140 boys, 70 board, 70 day
AGES: 8–13 (Also 130 mixed from 2½–7 in St Christopher's Edge Grove)
C OF E
FEE-PAYING

HEAD: Since 1985, Mr Jolyon Waterfield Cert Ed (fifties). In the Navy for 27 years (as a submarine commander), before coming to teach at Edge Grove, which was started by his father and by the father of the previous Head, Mr Jimmy Pratt. Avuncular and sensible. Nice wife, who works in school looking after the boys and the domestic side of the school.

ENTRANCE: Registration and non-competitive test two terms before the pupil is due to come into school. Many pupils from within a one-hour radius of the school. Over 10% of parents live abroad.

EXIT: A rich mix, including lots to Harrow, to nearby Aldenham, and to Haileybury, as well as one or two to Eton and other schools.

REMARKS: Low-key prep boarding school with an increasing day element, set in a fine seventeenth-century building with grounds in apple-pie order. (Formerly the property of J P Morgan.) The atmosphere is more like a country house party than a prep school. The largest dormitory is an elegance of wood panelling – hence no posters. Wooden floors, highly polished, and flowers. The Head and his family live 'over the shop'; the five-star gardener has a cottage in the grounds. The back of the buildings, though, is less prepossessing than the front.

Good modern Science block, as well as a new computer centre. Horizontal and vertical streaming – 10 forms, As and Bs; children are moved in the middle of the year, or earlier if up to it.

An open family school, which, said a parent, 'unlike some of them, gives some awareness of the real world'. Firm on discipline. Some extremely long-serving and loyal staff. Good support team – parents bustle about. School privately owned until 1969; now a charitable trust.

Enthusiastic Music – three-quarters of pupils play what Mr Waterfield calls a 'proper' instrument. Games played with enthusiasm but 'should not be taken too seriously', said Head, 'and the less able ones should be catered for as well'. Keen ski club.

Pupils have exquisite manners and apropos these, the Head comments that although they have some very good academic successes, the important thing is 'being part of a team and getting on with other people' – an approach which is less common in prep schools than you might think.

Elstree School

Woolhampton, Reading,
Berkshire RG7 5TD
Tel: 01734 713302, Fax: 01734 714280

PUPILS: Around 160 boys. 100 board, 60 day
AGES: 3–13
C OF E
FEE-PAYING

HEAD: Since 1995, Mr S M Hill MA (Cantab) – read Geography and Education – (forties), previously a Housemaster at Malvern College. A big man with a sporty background – soccer and tennis blue – and a sense of humour (we think). His wife, Jane, is 'much involved in the school'. Takes over from Mr McMullen, who has retired.

ENTRANCE: No test. 25% from London, a few from abroad, rest from the Thames Valley.

EXIT: 80% to Bradfield, Eton, Harrow and Radley; also Winchester, Marlborough, Wellington, Stowe, Pangbourne.

REMARKS: Traditional prep school in a fine Queen Anne country house with extremely stylish additions (designed by Basil Spence) – including lots of play space, and marvellous classrooms, dorms, dining room.

Streaming, setting for senior classes, good teaching for dyslexics. Reasonable scholarship record. French continues to be a special strength; DT is also good and there are computers all over the place. Marks given first for effort.

God is very important – the Sports Hall doubles as Assembly for morning prayers, and there is a quiet period observed nightly for reading, particularly Bible reading (more than one-third of the boys ask for Scripture Union notes).

Lots of games – rugby, football and hockey throughout the two winter terms as well as squash, shooting and golf on the school's own course. Strong tennis. Good Art and Music (boys design the stage sets themselves for the annual musical). Strong on extra-curricular activities, including astronomy (the school has a 12-inch reflecting telescope).

NB Pre-prep, Home Farm School, opened in 1991, in a lovely eighteenth-century farmhouse in the grounds. It proved popular at once; staff here headed by Mrs Watson, described by parents as 'magic'. 39 children, including girls.

Too early to comment on new regime.

Falkner House

19 Brechin Place, London SW7 4QB
Tel: 0171 373 4501, Fax: 0171 259 2493

PUPILS: Approx 140 girls
ALL DAY
AGES: 4–11
CHRISTIAN NON-DENOM
FEE-PAYING

PRINCIPAL: Mrs Flavia Nunes, a star, who founded the school in 1954 and was/is the driving force behind it; she is now a partner in it with her two daughters and son-in-law. Keen sailor. Famously talkative. Catholic family.

HEAD: Since September 1988, Mrs Jacina Bird BA Hons (forties) – Mrs Nunes' daughter. Educated More House in London and Trinity College, Dublin. Mother of three. Tireless energy; good administrator. Married to Derek ('Dickie') Bird, ex-army, who now has a facsimile portrait business (photos of ancestors) – the fruits of which are hung wonderfully around the walls of the school. Mrs Bird comments – sincerely – that the school is 'one big family', and that it runs in her blood (she was brought up in the school). Also talkative. Not everyone's cup of tea.

ENTRANCE: Girls tested by educational psychologist at age three, and 'only the bright ones' are picked. Mrs Nunes firmly believes it is possible to winkle out brains at this stage, though she also comments that she has the national average of children with learning difficulties. Worth trying for a place later.

EXIT: To London day schools (e.g. Godolphin and Latymer, More House), also a fair number to boarding single-sex schools, e.g. Benenden.

REMARKS: Housed in two large, light, prettily decorated red-brick buildings behind Old Brompton Road, with a playground in front. Solid phalanx of very experienced staff, plus one or two younger.

Inspired Music – children learn violin in groups, playing two parts at the age of six. French from the age of four. Latin from age of nine (grammatical approach). German club. Other languages could be arranged if requested. No science lab, but, says science mistress, 'so much can be done without one'. Growing collection of computers. Excellent grounding in the three Rs.

Head very keen on homework (tells the children to 'use their homework notebooks like Filofaxes') and talks about pupils learning to complete a task in their own free time before 'doing something they really want to do' – all good old-fashioned nannying stuff (which foreigners may not always appreciate). Also, on the same tack, almost neurotically careful about children's

safety. Mrs Nunes' tenet is that private schools must be flexible if they are to survive into the 21st century and, with this in mind, she has started the 'early' and 'late' Bird system (please note the pun) – children can be dropped by e.g. fathers driving in from the suburbs at seven in the morning, and left after school till seven at night. Bliss for overburdened mothers.

Maximum class size 'usually' 20. No streaming or setting. Despite its posh image, the school accepts from all backgrounds and all are welcome. Mrs Bird teaches tapestry on Friday afternoons. Her study is at the top of the house, away from the hurly burly, but, she says, the door is always open.

Lunch is served in a tiny basement room (a miracle), and all children take home a cooked treat at teatime. Lots of nice little touches: much thought goes into the school day and many opportunities are grasped, courtesy of Mrs Bird's extensive networking. The school has recently bought Bina Gardens – a secret garden square 120 yards away. There was a slight rumpus among parents last year over an unpopular reshuffle of staff, following the leaving of a much-favoured member of staff. School now uses a PR company.

Farleigh School

Red Rice, Andover,
Hampshire SP11 7PW
Tel: 01264 710766, Fax: 01264 710070

PUPILS: Around 163 boys and 57 girls ages 7–13; around 88 boarders (boys and girls), rest day. Kindergarten and pre-prep with around 116 boys and girls ages 3–7
AGES: 3–13
RC but other faiths welcome
FEE-PAYING

HEAD: Since 1993, Mr John Murphy BSc Hons, PGCE (late forties), read Geography at Durham University. Previously Head of St Joseph's, Cornwall, and before that Deputy Head at All Hallows Prep, Somerset. Apparent diffidence masks humour and competence. Supported by his wife Hilary, whose duties he describes as 'without portfolio'. Three children. Sports enthusiast. Very keen on fostering courtesy and kindness.

ENTRANCE: At 7/8. Children need to be well grounded in the basics; letter from previous school. Also to the kindergarten.

EXIT: Mostly to non-Catholic schools – including in particular Cheltenham at the moment, Marlborough, one to Winchester. Two to Ampleforth in '95. Girls to St Mary's Calne, St Swithuns, etc. Good scholarship record – six in '95.

REMARKS: Lovely school – happy, busy, involved children with loads to do, using very good facilities in an attractive setting. Clever children encouraged, less clever not harried (remedial help on hand). Some excellent teaching, and the staff (ten resident) are popular with parents and pupils; eight dogs also on the staff.

Children are divided into three sets (used to be two). Encouragement and praise generously given; with stars allotted for effort. French at 8, Latin at 9. Super Art. There are loads of Archimedes computers, with lesser computers 'cascaded down' to other departments. Splendid new Sports Hall with lots of natural light (unlike most); also good new Music Centre.

Not a rich school but there is a brilliant financial adviser on the governing board. The Head has revamped and moved the library – re-organizing books and methods, and above all 'getting children to know how to use the resources'. Library tables set up with chess boards, at the time of our visit, ready for play by club members.

The school is set in a fine Georgian country house with many later additions (mostly inherited from the former incumbent, Red Rice College – Farleigh, founded in 1953, moved here only in the eighties). Handsome stucco work, fireplaces, fine proportions, polished wooden floors; the whole building is light and airy, charmingly painted in shades of yellow and blue (school colours), including the Chapel (once the ballroom). Ratio of 60:40 RC and non-Catholics: no proselytizing, but Christian values very much underpin the ethos. Entire school attends Mass on Wednesday; voluntary attendance on daily basis.

The dorms (named after Saints) are alive with teddies and jolly duvets. Girl boarders admitted for the first time in '94 (16 as we write), making this slightly more of a co-ed enterprise than a boys' school with some girls. Lovely grounds with 40+ acres of grounds and outstanding specimen trees.

Strong sports, major and minor. Loads of activities and clubs – the speciality of Deputy Head Philip Watts (prep school born and bred, son of co-founder of Moor Park). Many day pupils stay till 5.30 p.m. every day. Unusually full weekend programme for boarders.

Boarding numbers holding up, while the day intake increases (some convert later, 'convenience boarding' on offer), helped by improvements to the A303 – pupils come from as far as Winchester, Warminster, Romsey. Hummingly good reports.

Finton House School

171 Trinity Road, London SW17 7HL
Tel: 0181 682 0921, Fax: 0181 767 5017
PUPILS: 71 boys, 118 girls
ALL DAY
AGES: 4–11
NON-DENOM
FEE-PAYING

HEAD: and Founder, in 1987, Miss Terry O'Neill (forties), previously Head of the Vale School, London, and before that taught at Eaton House. (Co-founder has since left the school and is now head of Cameron House, qv.) Miss Terry (as she is known) is firm, forceful, and widely respected (especially by parents) as a 'brilliant teacher'. Totally confident in her belief in what her school is about: 'working with parents and staff to give the children a sound and good basic grounding, both academically and socially'. Has a thorough working knowledge of the London schools systems and the pressure problems.

ENTRANCE: Much sought-after. First come, first served – but this means entering child's name at birth. Tests abhorred. 36 children at age 4; majority in the autumn term (half or full day), rest (full day) January.

EXIT: Some boys leave at 8 for other prep schools, i.e. boys heading for CE at 13+; others stay for 11+ entry to, e.g. Dulwich, City of London, Alleyn's, King's Wimbledon, etc. Girls go to Roedean, Benenden, Woldingham, the Ascot schools, JAGS, Wimbledon High.

REMARKS: Handsome and well-proportioned Victorian house sensitively adapted/transformed for school use, with light rooms, good library, and a big playground; delicious food. Smallish school with family feeling – and parents (unusually) heavily involved. Deeply traditional (Latin motto – *apertis cordibus manibusque ductis* – as well as a uniform, termly exams, homework notebooks, etc). Two parallel classes per age group, all of mixed ability, within which there is a great deal of individual teaching so that children develop at their own pace. All staff know all children extremely well. French now throughout the school. All children swim once a week and play games twice. Music department notably strong with music tuition for all pupils plus individual lessons. Very active after-school clubs: sports, soccer, rugby, art, swimming, drama, chess, computer, Scottish dancing, cookery. Useful, no-nonsense magazine, which, for once, feels as if it is for the children and parents rather than for PR purposes.

One of the few schools to integrate special needs pupils (as per the Warnock report); offers 10% of places (for which there is fierce demand) to special needs children (epilepsy, partially sighted, etc). The school's own team of therapists means specific learning difficulties can be helped on site.

School charging on despite the plethora of new fee-paying schools that opened south of the river in September '93; emphasis on individuality and family values, and results without pressure are its forte. Children are bright-eyed and bushy-tailed.

Francis Holland Junior School

Graham Terrace, London SW1 8JF
Tel: 0171 730 2290, Fax: 0171 823 4066

PUPILS: 160 girls
AGES: 4–11
ALL DAY
C OF E
FEE-PAYING

HEAD: Since 1984, Mrs Molly Bown Dip Ed (late forties), elegant, sparky, and on the ball. Came to teaching late, her first career was as a ward sister. Grown-up son and daughter (husband works in the medical world). Turned the school around. 'I'd seen really good schools and knew what I wanted.' Has chosen some outstanding staff to work with her. Encourages girls to 'say what they think – I tell them they don't have to agree with me, I want to know their views,' and also emphasizes manners.

ENTRANCE: At 4. Children are 'tested' in January for the September term: Mrs Bown and staff see 100 for 17 places (potential is sought). More come at age 5.

EXIT: About one-third go into the senior school (via CE). The rest regularly choose St Paul's, Godolphin and Latymer, JAGS; Wycombe, Calne, Benenden, etc.

REMARKS: Strong girls' pre-prep and prep school with happy children, in the centre of London, with the senior school on site across the playground. Modern block with large, light and bright classrooms; computers, PE, pottery and some Art, also Music done in the senior school. Pictures on the wall everywhere, and slogans such as 'Jolly Jennifer eats juicy jellies'. All girls are reading by the age of 6; very regular spelling homework (help for learning difficulties, but they rarely crop up). Really sound basic 3 Rs. French from 8.

Exceptionally strong project work, involving research encouraged from the age of 8 onwards. Girls choose a composer to write about, or choose from a range of inventors, scientists, pioneers, and are guided towards source material. This is a regular weekend homework, and the projects are madly popular, e.g. for a World War II project locals are invited to speak from experience and girls go and grill Chelsea Pensioners. Pupils also learn to talk about their subject to the rest of the class for five minutes. Not surprisingly, these children are extraordinarily articulate and fearlessly tell adults of their interests and work. The Science club is very popular.

Good mixing with senior school: Sixth Formers come over to hear reading, etc. Mrs Bown reckons the children don't need remedial teaching, but as there are two staff to each class, she can whip them out and train up at odd moments as necessary. Girls in Houses, as per main school, so children of all ages mix. Plays, music and charity fund-raising galore. No PTA and some complaints that parents don't feel they have direct access to the staff; parents also find, to their surprise, that the prep school 'is not autonomous'.

Garden House School

53 Sloane Gardens, London SW1W 8ED
Tel: 0171 730 1652, Fax: 0171 730 0470

PUPILS: Approx 270 girls, 65 boys
(number of boys growing)
ALL DAY
AGES: girls 3–11; boys 3–8
NON-DENOM
FEE-PAYING

PRINCIPAL: Since 1973, Mrs Jill Oddy BA Hons, the owner/administrator. A five-star mover and shaker, with a keen eye for the main chance.

HEAD (OF GIRLS): Since 1993, Mrs Rosemary Whaley BSc, from the City of London ex-poly, PGCE (mid-thirties). Mother of two. Studied at Guildhall for 2 years, trained at National Opera Studio and came to Garden House as Head of Music in '84, then became Deputy Head. Appointed to Headship on departure of previous Head, whose appointment did not work out, to general consternation and staff changes. Strong presence and probably no nonsense – though one or two parents have complained that she is too elusive. Comments that she 'likes to "stretch" the children as much as possible, and to give confidence'.

HEAD (OF BOYS): Since 1995, Miss Rachel Macintosh, BEd in religious studies from the Froebel Institute (early thirties). Appointed from within the school. Particularly keen on music and is choir mistress of the boys' choir.

ENTRANCE: At 3 and 4, later if/when places arise (always worth a try). Entry test one year before entry. Put down name asap. NB In common with other inner-London preps, charges an astronomic fee on firm offer of place – £750 at time of writing. This concentrates parents' minds wonderfully.

EXIT: Boys mainly to Sussex House, three to Ludgrove in '95, also to other London schools e.g. Northcote Lodge. Girls to London day schools, including Francis Holland, Godolphin and Latymer, also to posh boarding schools.

REMARKS: Until recently, a dear little girls' prep school in central London, a stone's throw from Sloane Square. The school is now mushrooming out into new ventures, with a separate site in Pont Street for the boys (see below).

Girls: Charming main house – carpeted, flowery, and light with nooks and crannies for individual tuition, pretty pictures on the walls, and a friendly and gentle atmosphere. The big drawback is no outside space, and the communal gardens are a no-go most of the time – it's off to Battersea Park or Burton Court for games (by minibus). Meals are in the basement – cramped but perfectly OK. There is also a little science lab in the basement with a top-class science teacher. Hot news: the school now has a 'scholarship class' (unusual) and a PTA – sighs of relief. Parallel classes for girls all the way up the school. Size of classes 15–20. Ambitious parents have been known to take out their children half-way up the school for less charming more 'stretching' establishments. Investigative maths – puzzles, learning to think for themselves. 'Serious' work from the word go. French at 4, French nationals on tap.

Parents are doctors, architects, solicitors/American bankers (lots of Sophies and Charlottes); the school has lots of siblings. Charming children, charming staff. Clubs after school. Lots of music and poetry. Homework 'club' till 5 p.m. every day.

Boys' school: 26/28 Pont Street, SW1, but use main switchboard above. Lots of space when we visited – nice big rooms, albeit a fair amount of it in the basement. Lots of sport including fencing and judo. New computer/media room is based here and is for both sexes. Size of classes 10–15. Could be a very good solution for central London parents.

Kindergarten: four rooms in a church in Seddon Street.

George Watson's Primary School

Colinton Road, Edinburgh EH10 5EG
Tel: 0131 447 7931, Fax: 0131 452 8594

PUPILS: Around 431 boys, 360 girls
ALL DAY
AGES: 5–12
ALSO NURSERY: 100 children
AGES: 3–5
NON-DENOM
FEE-PAYING

HEAD: Since 1989, Mr Donald McGougan Dip Ed (forties), educated at Campbeltown Grammar School, then Moray House. Unmarried. An internal appointment: was a form teacher in 1970 and graduated to Deputy Head before achieving this post. No thought of 'trying to produce a typical Watsonian: not all in the same mould'. Wants children to be happy and clamps down on bullying. Aims to produce 'well-educated children who excel in every possible area'. Chuckles.

A wandering Head, 'pops into the odd classroom': assisted by a 'timetabled wandering gang of three Assistant Heads (one of whom doubles as form teacher) and two Deputy Heads'. Nothing escapes their notice. Head teaches each of the six Primary Seven forms.

ENTRANCE: At 5 and every term thereafter if space available – can take next day if ditto. Assessment and test at five; 8-year-old tests tied to the National Curriculum – look for an indication of potential. Serious waiting lists at 5 and 11 (from State schools). No automatic transfer from nursery: no special bias in favour of FPs' children.

EXIT: Very occasional leakage at eight to traditional prep or public schools

(they usually go at 13 anyway), most go on to senior school unless outside circumstances dictate otherwise.

REMARKS: Cosily encampused on George Watson's mega site, surrounded by, and with use of, all senior school facilities. Shares labs, Science and Technology, Home Economics, but has own Music staff and Modern Language staff.

Clubs for everything: orchestra from 8, pipers, Brownies, Guides, Computer Club, art and drama, etc. Games include hockey, jogging, cross-country; there is also a sports hall.

Classes vary in size from 22 in Primary One, to 25/6 in Primary Seven: Famous with the senior school for teaching dyslexics; 'the Cabin' is without rival in Scotland. Full- and part-time teachers; pupils either receive support teaching in the class or go for individual lessons at the Cabin. Support staff are constant throughout.

Glendower Preparatory School

87 Queen's Gate, London SW7 5JX
Tel: 0171 370 1927, Fax: 0171 244 8308

PUPILS: Around 185 girls
ALL DAY
AGES: 4–12
INTER-DENOM
FEE-PAYING

HEAD: Since 1986, Mrs Barbara Humber BSc (forties). Previously at Colet Court, where she was Head of Science for nine years. Very keen that girls should be taught science and provided with the same facilities as boys.

ENTRANCE: At 4½; also ten places for 8-year-olds. All potential pupils are interviewed (though not IQ tested). Put names down early, and be prepared for vociferous disapproval if you change your mind.

EXIT: Mostly at 11, some stay for 12+. To day and boarding schools – St Paul's, Godolphin and Latymer, Grey Coats, also to boarding, e.g. Woldingham, St Mary's Calne (though this list changes yearly). Note large Catholic contingent.

REMARKS: Strong girls' prep school with unusual (for this sort of school) emphasis on Science.

Good sound teaching and starts things at an early age (French at 4). Computers used from age 4 onwards; combined Science for all at 8. Setting at 9; Latin at 10 for all. Girls do electronics and soldering (in spare time as well as class). Tuition room for slower children to catch up (included in fees). Parents still report that they are keen on the school because it 'stretches' children, though there have been one or two murmurs of dissatisfaction recently.

Somewhat cramped space, but well used. Class sizes: up to 22 in lower school (each class has one qualified teacher and one assistant); upper school 14–16 pupils. Strong on projects, very good Music. Delightful Art – fresh, and without the dead hand of the teacher in it. Lots of visits and lectures; clubs after school four days a week. Teams win most netball matches; school uses Imperial College swimming pool. Active Parents' Association.

Startling purple uniform. Glendower progressed from a dame school (founded in 1899) to a well-established jumping-off place to high-powered senior education.

All school lunches are vegetarian – and formally served in classrooms, which leaves 'a lingering smell of cauliflower' reports a parent.

Godstowe Preparatory School

Shrubbery Road, High Wycombe, Bucks HP13 6PR
Tel: 01494 529273, Fax: 01494 429001
PUPILS: 130 boarders, 140 day girls
AGES: 7–13, also pre-prep of around 132 boys and girls ages 3–7
C OF E
FEE-PAYING

HEAD: Since 1991, Mrs Frances Henson BA (early forties), previously Deputy Head of Thornton College. Quietly spoken, and firmly efficient. She has a house in the grounds with her husband (who is an accountant), and two children.

ENTRANCE: No tests (for either pre-prep or main school). 'Healthy waiting lists' for both day and boarding. Academic scholarships available at 8 and 11 years.

EXIT: Mainly to boarding schools, and with a distinguished scholarship record – Wycombe, Cheltenham Ladies, Downe House, Benenden, St Mary's Wantage. Also local strong day schools. Popular co-eds: Rugby, Bryanston, Oundle.

REMARKS: The first girls' boarding prep school in England, founded 1900 and purpose-built. On the edge of High Wycombe, but quietly set with agreeable grounds. Faintly formal feel despite 'family' claim (especially when compared to some boys' prep schools).

43

Oldest girls recently given 'flat' in the garden (to foster their teenage independence) where they can make tea, etc.

Pretty pale colours in newer dorms, sick-bay in bright primaries; some school decor done by the girls.

Good computing. French from 5, Latin for all at 10. One of the few all-girl schools aiming girls at the 13+ entry (only a few leave earlier). 'They can preserve their innocence here,' says the Head. Strong on all fronts – academic, games, swimming, extra-curricular, Brownies, outings, ballet, etc. Outstanding sewing and textiles.

Eight teaching staff always on duty at weekends for clubs/options, etc. Very popular with ex-pats (40% of the boarders), including services' children and a few diplomats'. Streaming from the start, one-to-one help given where needed. New boarding house recently opened – boarding numbers up, against all the odds.

Successful school with unspoilt children getting good results; has recovered from a difficult period. Good reports.

The Hall School

Crossfield Road, Hampstead,
London NW3 4NU
Tel: 0171 722 1700, Fax: 0171 483 0181

PUPILS: Around 400 boys
ALL DAY
AGES: 5–13
C OF E
FEE-PAYING

HEAD: Since 1993, Mr P F Ramage MA Hons (fifties). Educated at Warwick School and Cambridge – Historian and cricket blue (he describes himself as 'quite gamesy'), keen on the theatre, and on antiques. Previous post was as Head of St John's Northwood; before that he was at Bedford Prep ('for six happy years'); started his teaching career in the senior school of UCS so, in geographical terms, he says, he has 'come full circle'. Mrs Ramage, who is a splendid soul, teaches craft in the junior school and is involved in admin and social matters in the school – a very present help ('she is everything', comments Mr Ramage). They have three grown-up boys.

Deputy Heads are Julia Allen and Paul Ilott (the latter in the senior school).

At last, after landing the school with three Heads in three years, the governors seem finally to have got it right – going for the safe and steady choice, who has a good track record, and is unlikely to move before retirement if all continues to go well. The new Head is a twinkly soul, calming, with a great sense of humour, and warmth for all under his care – including the littles. He says modestly that really all he has had to do so far is 'bring some stability to the place'. Mr Ramage is enthusiastic but also laid-back – perfect for this particular school. He also projects an air of confidence, which is much appreciated by one and all.

ENTRANCE: You must register early to stand a chance – at birth if possible, but certainly by the time the child is two, though it is always worth approaching the school for gaps at odd moments. The school registers the first 125 names which come in – to avoid taking registration fees under false pretences (there is, however, a registration fee – a modest £50 at time of going to press). Children come from all the local pre-preps – Stepping Stones, Broadhurst Gardens, Phoenix House, the Children's House in Islington, etc. Fees are just under £2000 a term time at time of writing.

EXIT: More to Westminster than anywhere else – and, according to Mr Ramage, there are apparently more boys from the Hall at Westminster than from any other prep school. Otherwise it's Highgate, St Paul's (a bit of a way to travel), UCS. Got four top scholarships to major schools in '95, plus two music scholarships – one to Marlborough, and one to Aldenham.

Plenty of famous OBs, including Stephen Spender, who bequeathed a bijou gem to the school including the lines,

'It would be such a hackneyed thing;
I must not write about the spring.'

Among distinguished former Heads (of the junior school) was E H Montauban, who was one of the founders of Stowe (parents of Hall boys subscribed for the first library there).

REMARKS: A highly academic prep school which has, in the two years of Mr Ramage's reign, climbed painfully back into its position as the *numero uno assoluto* boys' prep school in north London. It is now once again a privilege to be in the school, and for parents, well worth bustling about to get in. But it is by no means perfect.

The school is on two sites – littles aged 5–8 are in a nice light house surrounded by its playground in Buckland Crescent. The Head's house is above the shop here, so he gets to know the children particularly well, treading among the trail of scarves and pink blazers which litter the junior school (but not the senior school – older boys think they are 'cissy').

The 'senior' school (and note there is a very firm line drawn between the two schools) is in Crossfield Road and has a very school-boyish, bubbling atmosphere. There are no carpets, a strong smell of science stinks as you walk through the front door, and very little is in the best of decorative order – (well-scuffed surfaces everywhere) – not exactly a pretty sight. There is, however, some excellent art on the walls and good IT in the basement where the boys get to grips with basic principles and obviously find it very refreshing after the academic grind (and it is a bit grindy).

There is a constant state of unpeaceful co-existence in the road, (thoughtless double-parking), but recent purchase should help relieve pressure on space.

Class sizes show 'a little flexibility': 15 in the class but 'it could be 18'. Nothing in the way of setting until 10, then setting for Maths and English. At 11 and for the first time 'we identify a "quicker form" – two parallel forms'.

There is a wonderful and very keen computer man – Mike Fitzmaurice, who has survived the successive Heads. And another enthusiast, in the shape of Mr Gilbey-Mckenzie, who is in charge of the scholarship form, is particularly keen on drama. Every form puts on a play and Drama is on the timetable even at the top of the school – where it is set against current affairs (a sound idea). Latin for all at 9, but Greek for none, surprisingly. Science for all – investigative work goes ahead of the course.

Endless patience is taken with those who fall by the wayside, and the school is very astute at spotting those with problems at home – both these virtues are great and unexpected strengths of the place.

The school uses Hampstead Cricket Club for games twice a week (soccer, cricket, etc.), and reports that it has become very good at fencing – it is number one among prep schools at the time of writing, beating even Sussex House.

Parents are north London high-powered barristers, media professionals, etc, with a surprising number of fathers at the top of their professions with much younger wives. Traditionally a very demanding difficult lot. However, Mr Ramage appears to be totally in control of the situation.

The school was started in the 1880s by Francis John Wrottesley, who as a 'father of a growing family of boys' decided that the best way to educate them was to start his own school. From this time it has grown in strength and distinction – get a copy of *One Hundred Years in Hampstead* for a fascinating read; it even includes some of the school songs (*Carmina aulariensia*).

Hanford School

Childe Okeford, Blandford,
Dorset DT11 8HL
Tel: 01258 860219, Fax: 01258 861255

PUPILS: Approx 100 girls
AGES: 7–13
C OF E
FEE-PAYING

JOINT HEADS: Since 1995, Mr and Mrs McKenzie-Johnston (Mr and Mrs 'M-J') (early forties). Mr (Lt Col, though he's dropped that) M-J read Economics at Cambridge, and ended up teaching at Shrivenham before coming here, where, (he says) he can hardly believe it's work. Mrs M-J is an occupational therapist – and so doesn't teach.

The M-Js take over from the Sharps, who owned the school, and from Miss Sarah Canning MA (early sixties). Sarah (never Miss Canning) is the daughter of Clifford Canning, the distinguished Head of Canford, who, with his wife Enid, founded the school. She is still very much present in the school, running things, looking after the ponies and being generally splendid.

The school is still privately owned, with Mr and Mrs M-J now part of it and easing their way gently in to the driving seat with what appears to be an immense amount of give, take and tact. The Sharps are at the telephone if needed, but never interfere and are not on the doorstep. Sarah at the moment still lives in the school, while the M-Js are in 'Fan's House' (a not too special building in the grounds), but the idea is that eventually they will move into the school, with its lovely drawing room. They appear to be the perfect couple for the job – he is fun, and enthusiastic while she is an exceptionally warm and friendly soul, totally 'unheadmistressy', brilliant at being with the children and at treating them as human beings. Mrs M-J is an OG of the school. They have 3 daughters, one in the school.

ENTRANCE: All are welcome. Pupils are very English, some locals, girls from the south and west, Londoners in need of real country life, and numerous families posted abroad. One small music bursary – the Helen Smith award.

EXIT: Over half the girls go to Sherborne Girls'; others mainly to girls' boarding schools in the south. Regularly gets scholarships to Division One girls' schools. Got an art scholarship to Heathfield in '95.

REMARKS: One of the nicest, if not *the* nicest, girls' prep boarding schools in the country, with a gentle, friendly, enthusiastic and genuinely family atmosphere. A place you can feel absolutely confident leaving your daughter in, with the knowledge that the school will probably do a better job of looking after her than you would, and will, almost as a side issue, give her a thorough grounding in CE subjects, and a fun time with it. Some outstanding staff, all very experienced (if anything there is too little turnover) and indeed one of the cooks has been in the school for *fifty* years.

Excellent French under Mrs Bolton who champions the French series *Il était une Grenouille* – the pupils are usually way past the standard of their senior school by the time they leave, and all articulate with good pronunciation. There are three streams, and setting within those streams can split right down to one pupil if necessary – 'we're desperately flexible' says Mrs M-J. Maximum class size is 15 at the moment. Note that computers come nowhere in the general scheme of things. No EFL but the school has a full-time remedial teacher, who helps with any difficulties.

The Art is outstanding under Ann Babbington: girls produce work which would not disgrace an art foundation course in a wide variety of disciplines – in particular, wonderful sculptures. Good grounding in technique, but this does not dampen the pupils' creative excitement.

Sport is also top class, under the jolly Ann Ford, who was trained at Bedford. The school regularly wins everything (in particular, short tennis) and again, although they do not train teams ('you train the school'), very thorough teaching is given, though when we visited the whole school had actually been tobogganing. The gym club is still v popular, and is outside in summer; visitors arrive to find girls standing on their heads.

Excellent pastoral care – 'it's all done by trust'. Kindness and common sense rule. There are 'no punishments' says Mrs M-J, but they get SYRs – (Serve You Rights) – if they do something silly, and these could involve writing down some truly boring, long poem while everyone else is having fun. Pupils are labelled (and re-labelled every week with great excitement amongst their peers) according to their good manners – starting with 'Piglets' (the bottom) and scaling the heights to 'Royal guest'. There

are no fixed exeats 'so parents can choose', no uniform (except for games) and basically 'no changes,' says Mrs M-J, from the previous regime.

A terrific feature of the school is the large number of furry Thelwellian ponies they own (28 at last count) – all can ride and there is a covered riding school. The ponies have walk-on parts in the school plays which are memorable, and every girl takes part. There is a wonderful wardrobe room.

The school takes the look of shabby gentility to an art form. The main building is a glorious 1623 manor house (instantly seductive to parents and children) in an antique landscape (Iron Age barrows, Roman fort remains, rolling Dorset countryside). Inside, lots of polish, wonderful old rugs, slightly peeling paint, well-worn wood, and dorms which are quite Spartan – one ('Oak') has a carpet, otherwise you're lucky if there's a rug. Old iron bedsteads groan with teddies – 'as many as they can fit in' says Mrs M-J. In the garden, there is an enchanting chapel in beautiful grounds, and the vegetable garden supports the school, except for potatoes. Teaching is done in a series of what feel like rabbit hutches – a bit sad and squashed looking, though no one seems to care (but NB one classroom has a bas-relief in it rather on the lines of the one that Canford sold for such huge sums recently . . .).

The High School of Glasgow Junior School

27 Ledcameroch Road,
Bearsden, Glasgow G61 4AE
Tel: 0141 942 0158, Fax: 0141 959 0191

PUPILS: Around 167 boys, 190 girls.
Nursery 50 boys and girls
ALL DAY
AGES: 4–10
NON-DENOM
FEE-PAYING

HEAD: Since 1974, Miss Eileen Robertson MA, Cert Ed, (fifties), educated at Perth Academy, Edinburgh University and Moray House. Has total autonomy with staff appointments. 'In the classrooms all the time.' Aims to 'educate the whole child'.

ENTRANCE: At 3½ or 4. Waiting lists, though vacancies may become available throughout the school. Priorities to siblings, FPs' children, then the rest of the field.

EXIT: Automatic transfer to senior school. Slight leakage to traditional prep schools. Some go on to other private schools, and to state schools.

REMARKS: The Glasgow prep they all fight to get into. It is set in an elegant Victorian house almost totally surrounded by a cunning collection of additions. Classrooms are off the buttercup-yellow main passage with a cosy area for tinies, and a room upstairs for learning support.

Group teaching, aggressively academic: tinies start to learn at four. Good learning support which carries through to senior school (with the same staff). Computers in classrooms, IT strong, French throughout – but no Latin.

The junior school shares senior school facilities, and is bussed to Anniesland for rugby, hockey and swimming at the Allander Centre. It has a lot of (good) Music and plays.

There is very strong local support; Lord MacFarlane of Bearsden (FP) is Honorary President of the school and much in evidence. Parents include many of first-time buyers; middle-class bias, doctors, lawyers, and high work ethos.

Highfield School

Liphook, Hampshire GU30 7LQ
Tel: 01428 722228, Fax: 01482 727164

PUPILS: 120 boys, 55 girls
BOARDERS: 140, 35 day pupils (all pupils must board by 10)
AGES: 7–13
C OF E
FEE-PAYING
ALSO: Brookham pre-prep on site, 80 boys and girls.
AGES: 3–7.

HEAD: Since 1993, Mr Nigel Ramage MA (fifties), educated at Winchester and Trinity College, Dublin; PGCE. Brief period Oxford Playhouse, then Media, followed by Director of Studies at Hampstead School of Language. Head of English and Drama at Highfield since 1984. Now teaches English and RE. His wife Katy works in the school Treasurer's office. Two sons, both at Highfield.

ENTRANCE: By registration and interview; must be up to scratch on their reading and writing; visit school for informal test. Most from within A3 corridor from London. Two or three foreigners, many ex-pats. Good naval links. Waiting list for day pupils to 1999.

EXIT: Recently to Charterhouse, Marlborough, Winchester, otherwise one here and one there to all manner of schools from Bedales to Wycombe Abbey and Bryanston.

REMARKS: A purpose-built red-brick conglomerate with masses of wooden additions in 170-acre grounds. Large woods, cows, pets, and a school donkey. The school has a traditional chapel, good games hall, and a theatre (with hideous hard benches), Drama in Chapel and Assembly as well as a school play each term. Music is thriving; the Head of Music is a composer in his own right. Superb art, with a new Art Centre opened by Penelope Keith in '95. Greek only as a hobby. Children can play games on computers in their free time. The tennis courts are good and the children play hockey by floodlight in winter. There is an outdoor swimming pool.

New library and Junior house recently revamped. The girls' dorms are jollier than the boys', but there are posters and own duvets everywhere. New central heating and hot water system throughout school.

There are daily reports for slacking. Serious naughtiness equals no sweets on Wednesday. Parents include 'quite a few' first-time buyers. The school is full to bursting and refuses to take weekly boarders. It has a relaxed family atmosphere, and works well.

Highgate Junior School

Cholmeley House, 3 Bishopswood Road, London N6 4PL
Tel: 0181 340 9193, Fax: 0181 340 7674

PUPILS: Approx 360; 120 in pre-prep.
All boys in prep; co-ed in pre-prep
ALL DAY
AGES: 3–7 pre-prep; 7–13 prep
C OF E FOUNDATION
FEE-PAYING

HEAD: The Master since 1992, Mr Simon Evers BA in English, Cert Ed (forties). Previously Head of Worksop College prep, before that wide-ranging experience from VSO to trainee booking clerk in Cooks. Comes from a teaching dynasty – one brother is Head of Cheam/Hawtrey's, one teaches Classics at Farleigh, grandfather was Housemaster at Rugby, father was head of Sutton Valence. Laid-back. Married with two sons – his wife helps in school.

One of the Head's first changes on being appointed was to move his office from the top to the main body of the school where all rush past. Members of staff have commented that perhaps he could be tougher on discipline – but the Head says that no one has ever said that to him.

ENTRANCE: Main points of entry are 7+, 8, 10 and 11 (though try any time). Entrance exam in January and February for September. Some from local primary school, St Luke's.

EXIT: To Highgate Senior School – see separate entry. Boys sign a form on entry to junior school saying they intend to go on to the senior school.

REMARKS: Junior school for Highgate (qv) in the grounds of the senior school; it is increasingly popular owing not just to geography but also to the increasing success of the senior school. Very popular pre-prep run by Mrs Barbara Rock, who has had children at Highgate. Good sports facilities (uses the senior school facilities), e.g. 18 fives courts, (is this a record?) Housing for a proportion of the staff – an enormous draw in this expensive area of north London (though it can foster unrest in those who don't have it).

Set in super green country-like site between Highgate Village and Kenwood – a cluster of buildings grouped round the playing fields of the main school, with lots of room. Shares dining hall – modern light block with a good choice of food, the youngest eat in a separate room. Uniform reverses colours of senior school.

Streaming and setting from 11, but no year places and no form places – assessment only twice a term for attainment and effort. School has the relaxed feel of an establishment which exists for education rather than for passing CE. Form tutors are the first contact with parents, parents collect littles from the classroom.

Pre-prep in a separate bizarre-looking building tucked away; it was formerly a boarding house. The 7–9-year-olds also have their own quarters – Field House. Super form rooms of 20 or so – three forms at 7+, four at 11+. Largish numbers of ethnic minorities. The school has an anti-bullying code, and the Head has introduced 'circle time' – a time of self-assessment when pupils can express their feelings and thoughts honestly.

Pupils are the sons of local professionals, some actors. (John Betjeman was taught here by T S Eliot.) The school has an inspired Art master. The science labs use Westminster-type modules. Computers are easily accessible, lining the walls in classrooms. Thoughtful touches – e.g. younger boys change in classroom, leaving pile of clothes on each desk to avoid the chaos of changing rooms.

Hill House International Junior School

17 Hans Place, London SW1X OEP
Tel: 0171 584 1331, Fax: none

PUPILS: Currently around 1067: around 700 boys, 400 girls

ALL DAY
AGES: 3–13
NON-DENOM
FEE-PAYING

HEAD: Owner and founder in 1951, Colonel H S Townend OBE MA (Oxon) (eighty-seven in 1996 and still going strong). Educated at St Edmund's, Canterbury, read Mathematics and Science at Oxford, followed by a diploma in French, German and Italian. He has become an educational institution. When he does retire, his son Mr Richard Townend (forties) (Westminster School and Royal School of Music) will take over, assisted by his wife, Janet (Saffron Walden Teachers College, Cambridge). It would be a miracle if the Colonel's son were as good as his famous founding father.

Enormously charming and fun, the Colonel wears his years well, claims 'never to sleep in England, only on an aeroplane or in Switzerland' where he spends half of every week running the Swiss side of Hill House.

He runs the school without secretarial or bursarial help, and takes a dim view of Schools Inspectors – he considers their reports to be not worth reading.

ENTRANCE: The school is open to parents on Wednesdays, between 8 and 8.30 a.m. when prospective parents may tour the main school. After Assembly in Pont Street Church Hall they are introduced (or not, as the case may be) to the Colonel to whom they hand a green slip of paper with their child's name, date of birth and required date of entry. Two weeks later they are sent an official confirmation, which is followed nearer the proposed entry date by an information pack. The school has four terms or quarters, starting in January, April, August and October; but the Colonel will admit any child at any time, as the need arises.

EXIT: As you would expect, some to traditional prep schools at 8. Otherwise boys to Westminster, St Paul's School, Dulwich College, Harrow, Eton, Stowe, etc. Girls to More House, Francis Holland, St Paul's Girls, JAGS, Benenden, Cheltenham Ladies, Downe House, etc.

REMARKS: A unique school: people love it or loathe it. Colonel Townend *is* Hill House, and he places a terrific emphasis on challenge and sport. Almost 50% of pupils are foreign. The school is scattered around Knightsbridge and Chelsea, with different ages in different locations, and crocodiles of orange and brown knickerbockered children (girls can opt for culottes or skirts) moving in orderly (or not) file to swim at Chelsea Baths, or play sport (lots of it) at The Duke of York's Barracks, in Hyde Park, or the local church hall. Buses for almost everywhere else, though the Bentley shooting brake is also labelled as the 'school bus'.

Many young staff, many from South Africa, New Zealand and Australia, all called Tutor; regular (some parents comment 'too high') turnover. Staff paid small sum for attending evening meetings. Each department has its own Head.

Very cosy small school in Flood Street, through Milner Street, Pont Street, Cadogan Gardens (380 children) and Hans Place. School fondly nicknamed 'Hell House'. All buildings are self-contained, with own dining room, etc. Tiny classes at bottom rising to no more than 16 at top – pressure now descends heavily upon the children during the last two years. All children learn the recorder; pianos and music rooms everywhere, as are computers. Good Science, Languages, Art, etc. Special help for those with learning difficulties or needing extra English. HRH Prince Charles was here briefly, and all parents are known as

'Charles' Daddy' (or Charles' Mummy). Huge eclectic mix.

The school opens daily at 8 a.m. and closes by 1 p.m. on Friday. Usual punishment is detention before lunch on Fridays (their only free time), otherwise children sit cross-legged on the floor outside the Head of Department's door. The junior department is super, girls are hived off for entrance exams at 11 or 12 and, in the main, are taught separately from the boys.

Twenty 'Middles' (8/12 – girls or boys separately) spend four-week periods at the Swiss base of the school, La Coline at Glion above Montreux, with lessons as normal during the week and skiing or water-skiing at weekends

---

Holmewood House

Langton Green, Tunbridge Wells, Kent TN3 0EB
Tel: 01892 862088, Fax: 01892 863970

PUPILS: 449 boys and girls (two-thirds boys, one-third girls) 51 boarders, 398 day
AGES: 3–13.
INTER-DENOM
FEE-PAYING

HEAD: Since 1980 Mr David Ives MA (Oxon) (late fifties, contracted until he is 65). Avuncular. Charming and enthusiastic with his finger absolutely on the pulse: very hands-on Head. Cosy wife. Two grandchildren in the school.

NB School was put on road to fame and fortune by the famous Mr Bairamian.

ENTRANCE: At 3 and 4 for nursery and pre-preps (no tests, but the 'unsuitable' would be weeded out). Also at 7 and 8 (and some at 11), with school's own tests.

EXIT: Boys most frequently to Tonbridge, Sevenoaks, King's Canterbury. Also the Judd, Eastbourne, and many other schools. Girls to St Leonard's Mayfield, Benenden, Roedean, King's Canterbury, Marlborough. Long list of scholarships and awards: '93–'95 fifty-one awards, including the top scholarship to Winchester, King's Canterbury and Tonbridge.

REMARKS: Strong prep. Boarding numbers fell heavily during the recession, but the school still runs very much as a boarding school (and the Head, determined to continue this, is busy courting boarders). Saturday-morning school (almost always followed by matches), day pupils stay until 6 or 6.30 p.m. in main school.

Every department is ticking away, and the staff (numerous, all ages, vociferous) are fantastically committed, well paid and energetic. Also, an unusually interesting bunch – the Head has been busy collecting from all over, e.g. Natalie Clarkson ex-Olympic gymnast; Chris McGovern ex-Lewes secondary school History Head who lost his job for allowing some pupils to do the Scottish History exam, as well as the English History exam, and who is now part of the team re-writing the History curriculum for our schools. Good New Zealanders, Zimbabwean teacher, etc., who add an extra dimension – as do a handful of foreign students (TEFL lessons given) including Russians/Ukrainians.

There is an excellent remedial department (run by an ex-parent, fully trained) helping children via a special gym as well as by more conventional methods, e.g. eye testing.

Streaming all the way. Homework is, in principle, done at school. Pupils bright and bouncy, well aware of high expectations but outgoing and playful. Wonderful CDT (jars stuffed with pipe cleaners, screws); also much IT. Good science labs with tiered seating for lectures/demonstrations. Lovely Art. There is a well-used and well-stocked library with a full-time librarian – rare in a prep school. Food 'not that healthy' report parents, correcting our previous impressions.

The school was founded after the war, and was privately owned until the current Head took over. Went co-ed in 1989; there is also a new purpose-built pre-prep.

In Decimus Burton house, the boys' dorms have recently been modernised (not before time). There are live-in houseparents in flats adjacent to the boarding houses. The other buildings tagged on at the sides and back are a mishmash, but produce outstanding results nonetheless. A new Music block is being built. Good views at the back and all the playing fields are here, in an unlikely setting on the edge of an executive homes' estate.

Expensive – £2,340 per term for day pupils; £3,485 per term for boarders. Notwithstanding, parents move into the area to send children here.

Honeywell Junior School and Infants' School

Honeywell Road, Battersea,
London SW11 6EF
Tel: 0171 223 5185 Fax: NONE

PUPILS: Around 360 boys and girls in junior school; 325 in infants' school
ALL DAY
AGES: 3–7 (infants); 7–11 (junior)
NON-DENOM
STATE

HEAD: Since 1992, Mr Dick Cooper BA Hons, PGCE (forties). The only Head who has commented that 'MAs from Oxford are spurious'. Educated Royal Grammar School, Guildford, and Christ Church, Oxford, where he read Philosophy and Psychology – useful for teaching. (Head of Infants' School is also a philosophy graduate.) Previously Head of Fircroft School, Tooting Bec. Keen on music, gardening and classic cars.

ENTRANCE: Via infants' school – entry here guarantees a place in Junior school. Harder to get into than some of the private schools round here – oversubscribed, with waiting lists. It helps to live in the right catchment area. 'Occasional' vacancies for other children.

EXIT: To Wandsworth grant-maintained schools, and a third to private schools in South London, in particular Alleyn's, also Dulwich, JAGS, Emmanuel and 'the GPDST schools' – Streatham, Wimbledon, etc.

REMARKS: Described by the Head of a public school in London as 'the best prep school in South London'. Huge old purpose-built building, with its own tarmac playground. Disciplined and well-structured, the school follows the National Curriculum. Lots of attention is given to less able (though NB large class sizes – 30 maximum never more – make this difficult). Computer studies are timetabled. There is a jolly art department, producing some good work. Also good Music – this is one of the very few schools to offer free tuition, and to loan instruments (recorder, violin, 'cello). Lots of clubs. The nursery class caters for half-day and all-day attendance. There are happy reports from parents; a large contingent of middle-class impoverished parents who comment 'if you can get into

Honeywell we see no point in going anywhere else'.

Horris Hill

Newtown, Newbury,
Berkshire RG15 9DJ
Tel: 01635 40594, Fax: ex-directory

PUPILS: Around 160 boys; 150 boarders, 10 day boys
AGES: 8–13
C OF E
FEE-PAYING

HEAD: From September 1996, Mr Nigel Chapman BA (early fifties), who takes over from Mr M J Innes MA, who – to the great good luck of the school – has been teaching here for a record thirty-five years, eighteen of them as headmaster. Valete.

Mr Chapman was previously co-head at Lockers Park, educated at Felsted and London University. Married to Sue, with two children; a keen family man.

The school 'dame' is now Miss Susan Young, who comes from eight years' experience in the girls' house at Loretto.

ENTRANCE: By registration. No entrance examination but there is a 'little placing test' and it is sometimes gently suggested, but not insisted, that a boy might do better at a school more geared to remedial teaching.

EXIT: A seventeen-year breakdown of where boys go on to shows Winchester at the top of the list with 126, and Eton second (125) – some record. Radley third (49 – numbers to this school up again) and Marlborough fourth (38). Good scholarship record. OB: Richard Adams.

REMARKS: A famous country prep school which has managed to hang on to its traditional feel while softening the edges of discipline, environment, etc. One of the few academically successful boys' prep schools at which boys have time to play with model aeroplanes, etc, have regular pit stops for 'cocoa', and generally behave like little boys rather than potential Derby winners.

That said, the school works and plays hard. No horizontal streaming but the school adopts the 'filtering' approach and boys are constantly on the move upwards (which, says the Head, 'keeps teachers on their toes'). The average rate of movement is once every two terms. Good remedial help.

Outstanding Art department under Ian Keen (and keen is the word). Over 100 boys learn one musical instrument; 23 learn two and 1 learns three. The Head of Music adopts a hands-on approach. There is an entire room dedicated to a wonderful model train set – the school's pride and joy. Floodlit fives courts, squash courts. Very keen football and cricket: both first and second football elevens were undefeated in '94/'95; cricket first and second eleven also undefeated – and the team toured Barbados. Sports hall doubles as theatre – keen thespians here. Classrooms are a bit bleak and the desks battered – but currently being spruced up, and carpets added. The average class size is 12.

There are no prefects – masters fulfil this role – no speech day, and no motto – 'no humbug', to quote the founder, who was an (ex-) master of Winchester aiming to train up boys for entry to that school (date of foundation, 1888). Both boys' and masters' houses are dotted around the grounds, which are pleasant and spacious, though the main school building is of such hideous Victorian red brick that the prospectus features it heavily camouflaged with snow. Other schools may change in response to market forces, but 'Horrid Hell' (as some of the children call it) is, as we write, still good and popular withal.

Ibstock Place

Clarence Lane, Roehampton,
London SW15 5PY
Tel: 0181 876 9991, Fax: 0181 878 4897
PUPILS: About 114 boys, 142 girls; plus senior school, with around 78 boys, 113 girls, ages 11–16
AGES: 3–11
ALL DAY
NON-DENOM
FEE-PAYING

HEAD: Since 1984, Mrs Franciska Bayliss (forties), Froebel Dip Ed. Attractive, sensible and well respected. Married to a lawyer, two grown-up children. Very energetic, encouraging and persuasive. Taught at the Unicorn (a Froebel school), and was briefly Head of junior school at Surbiton High. Proud of the 'high level of accountability and communication at all levels' in the school. She is Headmistress of both junior and senior school.

NB Mrs Bayliss and the marketing director/registrar strongly disapprove of the style of this book.

Head of 3–7 department: Mrs J Webbern, Froebel Cert Ed.

Head of 7–11 department: Mrs A-L de Buriane, BEd, Froebel Cert Ed.

ENTRANCE: At 3 and 7 – book early, there are waiting lists. Selective at 7+. Oversubscribed kindergarten set to expand, doubling its numbers (morning and afternoon sessions) from 1997 to meet demands.

EXIT: At 8 or 11 for prep or public mainstream schools. Popular choices are Hampton, King's College School, Wimbledon, Latymer, and Godolphin and Latymer for girls; pupils also go on to the senior school.

R EMARKS: Both kindergarten and primary classes are bursting with energy and excitement. Children are kept busy, the walls are full of their work; colour is everywhere – a very rich environment. Strong sense of the inter-relatedness of subjects. Work in the early years is topic-based, with emphasis on projects. This is a place where you know your child will get an excellent educational start, in an unstressed environment. The pupils are articulate.

Set in six green acres, on the edge of Richmond Park. From the age of 9, children are taught in the main building, a large Queen Anne-style house (designed by Chesterton, founder of the estate agency). School founded in 1894, and based on the educational principles of Friedrich Froebel, the German educationist (d. 1852), who pioneered kindergartens and women teachers. Good facilities.

The senior school (with fewer pupils) stops after GCSE. Previously in the alternative education category, but the liberal progressive image has faded considerably, and indeed the school considers itself to 'have a straight bat'. High staff:pupil ratios, with the emphasis on 'social skills' – open dialogue, getting on with people, communication. Pupils go on to Sixth Form Colleges, Hurtwood, Godolphin and Latymer, Lancing, Bedales – scooping up a good array of scholarships at this stage.

In our view, the real strength is the junior school; however, the senior school works well and may be a solution, if transport is not a problem.

James Allen's Preparatory School (JAPS)

East Dulwich Grove, London SE22 8TE
Tel: 0181 693 0374, Fax: 0181 693 8031

PUPILS: Approx 177 in middle school; 108 in lower school; boys and girls (from 1996, boys 4–7, girls 4–11).
ALL DAY
AGES: 4+–11
C OF E
FEE-PAYING

H EAD: Since 1992, Mr Piers Heyworth MA, PGCE (forties). Educated at Marlborough and Christ Church, Oxford, where he read English and founded the Oxford Survival Society (keen on the environment).

Previously the celebrated Head of English at JAGS, and his appointment here was an unusual but inspired choice – there's even more scope for his enthusiasm. Comments that the school takes 'a hundred and ten per cent of my time'. 'A good front man' commented his previous headmistress at JAGS. Unmarried. As school recently expanded to double the size, more than half the staff are his own appointments.

E NTRANCE: From 'a hundred different nurseries', mainly in Clapham. Entry test in January for September, child psychologist on tap to watch out for what he calls 'adventurousness of spirit'. Followed by interviews.

E XIT: In all, 20 scholarships in '94, including ten to JAGS (qv). Boys will go on to Dulwich, etc.

R EMARKS: God's gift to the people of Dulwich. Part of the same foundation as JAGS, etc, and consequently very well funded. Formerly the prep department of JAGS, now spreading its wings, with IAPS membership, co-education and an identity all of its own. On two sites – the littles in a Gothic mansion down the road, the 'middle school' tucked beside JAGS, with a large extension opened in '93 to include a large sports hall, and super library with its own librarian – light and much used.

Separate IT room, timetabled computing for all (National Curriculum), large sunny Science room, specialist staff. 'Immersion' French from age 4, with Mlle Pascale Bizet, who speaks entirely in French; so far children have not cottoned on to the fact that she speaks English as well – children play lots of fun games, have impeccable accents, and by the time they leave the school will need special fast streaming to keep up the good work. In the middle school French is taught in half classes by another French specialist, who also teaches some other subjects (e.g. Drama, Music, Geography) *in French*.

Eighteen per class in lower school, rising to 24 above that, though most classes have two members of staff and can be split. The brilliant Art teacher, ex-Jackanory producer Mrs Pauline Carter, earns her salary several times over in art prizes won by the school. Drama strong (Head keen and experienced). There are 55 clubs after school, and about 125 pupils turn up for 'Saturday School' – the brain child of staff member Miss Beverly Sizer – Music, Drama, Dance from 8.30 a.m. till 1.30 p.m. – a wonderful way for pupils to work off excess energy, and parents to get to Tesco's in peace.

School absolutely full of fizz, with top-class staff; strong all round. Has to be a contender for the best London prep south of the Thames.

Kensington Preparatory School

17 Upper Phillimore Gardens,
London W8 7HF
Tel: 0171 937 0108/9,
Fax: 0171 937 0797

PUPILS: 200 girls
ALL DAY
AGES: 4–11
NON-DENOM
FEE-PAYING

HEAD: Since 1993, Mrs Gillian Lumsdon MEd (early fifties), previously Head of Whitford Hall Prep school in Bromsgrove. Married (husband is a lawyer) with three grown-up children. Educated at Oxford High School, read Pharmacy at Nottingham University and more recently for an MEd at Warwick University. A charming woman, lively, open-minded, enthusiastic, with a keen sense of humour. Teaches Technology, one of many departments she is expanding. 'It's a very good place to watch girls' thinking skills develop.'

ENTRANCE: Register child's name up to the time of testing (4 and 7). NB No advantages given to early registration, and no charge for registration (unusual). Testing on a one-to-one basis, followed by group assessment for those who have cleared the first hurdle. Places for 16 girls at the age of 7, occasionally at other stages as and when vacancies occur, always via testing.

Some parents complain about over-bearing behaviour by the school on the whole question of entry.

EXIT: The majority to day schools: Godolphin and Latymer, St Paul's, Francis Holland, South Hampstead High,

Putney High in large numbers; also batches to Wycombe Abbey, Downe House, St Mary's Calne, etc.

REMARKS: No longer the Holy Grail for academically ambitious parents of London girls – though it acts as though it were, judging by comments from parents. It is now one among several strong preps. Parents' tendency to hype and neurosis at exam time is still fairly pronounced, and the school continues to attract pushy, ambitious parents who double-park and await collection volubly, while the children carry on in their normal bright and happy fashion, under a team of (mostly) extremely contented and steady staff. The Head 'treats the children as people, not just as "little girls",' commented a mother.

Atmosphere decorous in large Kensington house with a super, big garden at the back – much larger than most London preps, but still slightly cramped (less so than some of its competitors), and children may not play on the grass except in the summer; otherwise they use the tarmac playground where staff park their cars, 'and endlessly come home with sticking plasters,' complained a mother. Inside some rooms have now been amalgamated to make them fewer and bigger.

The standard of work is very high, and teaching is rigorous. There is a firm emphasis on spelling and handwriting, also reading. Classes of 20 children at the bottom of the school, then two parallel classes of 18. Mrs Lumsdon has 'opened the school up', with more visits, more matches, and more after-school activities, including ballet, chess, computers. Discipline and order are important aspects of school life.

This is the odd one out of the GPDST group, being junior only. The Trust is firmly committed to keeping the school, though most definitely looking for larger premises within the same catchment area i.e. somewhere between Holland Park, Kensington and Fulham. This is still one of the strongest London girls' prep. schools, despite having considerable competition nowadays.

King's College School

West Road, Cambridge CB3 9DN
Tel: 01223 365814, Fax: 01223 461388

PUPILS: 184 boys, 95 girls. 39 boarders (including 16 choristers and 6 probationers); 240 day (including all the girls)
AGES: 4–13.
C OF E
FEE-PAYING

HEAD: Since 1993, Mr Andrew Corbett MA (early forties), took over from the renowned Mr Gerald Peacocke. Educated at Marlborough, read History of Art at Edinburgh. Approachable, a man of action, not a musician ('I never thought they'd take me for that reason'). His wife is a teacher, two young daughters both in the pre-prep. Previously Director of Studies, Head of History and Housemaster of a girls' house at Port Regis, and before that Head of History at The Hall.

ENTRANCE: At 4, 7, 11. Fairly broad intake, from the average to the very bright. Provision for three dyslexics per year ('but they must be bright'). Annual choir auditions. Assessments at 7+ and above. Around 30% children of academics, offspring of farmers and business people. Both the pre-prep (which opened in '92) and the dyslexia unit are over-subscribed, so register early.

EXIT: Mainly to the Perse (boys and girls), The Leys, Oundle, Uppingham, St Mary's Cambridge, Westminster. Also Oakham, Eton, Downe and elsewhere. Girls leave at 11 and 13.

REMARKS: One of *the* two prep schools in Cambridge (the other is St John's). The two fluctuate in the popularity stakes. Exceptional music – of course: the school provides choristers for King's College (a splendid sight in their gowns, top hats and stiff collars). King's choristers are of world renown, and still best known for the Nine Lessons Carol Service. They are well used to being in the public eye, and are sophisticated (as well as unspoilt) over making recordings, travelling, etc. They are also well integrated with the rest of the school – it is not unusual for a chorister to be also an academic scholar. Music plays a major role in school life, with 147 children learning one instrument, and 79 learning two. Also, there are no less than 29 visiting music teachers, and a Deputy Head of the Music department.

Many staff are long-standing, and there are stimulating high standards of teaching in all areas – somewhat taken for granted by one and all. Head of History particularly popular; Latin and Science masters are also well liked. Staff somewhat other-worldly and not clamouring for change. Director of Studies is a new appointment. Pupils help decision-making within the school via a committee. There are regular visiting speakers, 'Here we are in Cambridge, let's make use of the brilliance,' says the Head. Saturday-morning school still goes on and is still (as per the last edition) 'under review', with children wanting it to continue. Girls' numbers are gradually increasing. The fascinating list of Old Boys include Orlando Gibbons, Michael Ramsey, Christopher Tugendhat, John Pardoe.

(Some) boarding facilities recently renovated – 'And frankly they needed it,' from a parent. The whole place has been freshly painted since we last went to press. Five-minute walk over to King's; founding of this school dates back to 15th century, though premises are undistinguished red-brick 19th century (plus huts, additions, etc). The atmosphere is definitely friendly, liberal, informal: 'They seem to *encourage* the boys to let their shirts hang out,' commented one dismayed mother. Notwithstanding the rigorous academic and music standards which underpin everything, this is a happy place. But we hear a few less satisfied reports.

King's College Junior School

Wimbledon Common, Southside, London SW19 4TT
Tel: 0181 255 5335, Fax: 0181 255 5339
PUPILS: 461 boys
ALL DAY
AGES: 7–13.
ANGLICAN (other faiths welcome)
FEE-PAYING

HEAD: Since 1976, Mr Colin Holloway MA (mid-fifties), educated at University College School and Christ's College, Cambridge (Classics followed by Theology). Taught at University College Junior School and UCS (third master). Teaches Latin to the bottom sets – 'Their minds go at the same speed as mine' (i.e. 'not very speedy'). He spends a huge amount of time on admin. and showing prospective parents around.

Wife is Head of English (elsewhere), two grown-up children. A charming, modest man whose gentle manner belies enormous energy and efficiency. Due to retire in '97. Recently Chairman ('94–'95) of IAPS (the prep schools' association).

ENTRANCE: Most at 7 and 8; some at 9, 10 and 11. Mr Holloway interviews every single boy himself, 'It's fascinating, always different, completely unscripted, but a spark will show through'. (Last year, for instance, he interviewed 257 boys for 107 places, – at least 2 boys per place; boys advised to re-apply the following year are not re-interviewed). Chooses boys with intense care, looking from the start 'for that real love of learning'. (Do not despair, it is worth applying later since occasionally boys leave to board due to changes in parental circumstances).

NB A most illuminating booklet tucked into the prospectus gives details of admissions procedure and examinations and also gives a useful children's reading list. There are 5 Assisted Places at 11. Bursaries (considerably increased these to help those hard-hit in the recession). Early registration advisable.

EXIT: Boys go on to the senior school (qv) (gaining most of the scholarships, academic and musical), although two or three per year go elsewhere e.g. Emanuel, Stowe, Epsom.

REMARKS: As we have said before, this is an outstanding prep school, with excellent standards in absolutely everything. On the same site as the senior school, neatly tucked at one side. Heart of its main building was once Tudory-Victorian, but was brutally destroyed and built over in the '60s ('the very worst period,' groans Mr Holloway). Softened, face-lifted and altogether improved in the '80s, and the grey and beige impersonal corridors have now been enlivened by pupils' work/paintings/maps, and pos-

ters. Good library wih a terrific on reading (lists galore).

Most subjects taught in subjec (rare in prep schools). Art, Mus.. and Technology departments (all close by the junior school) are shared with the senior school. Science labs are also shared (Science is taught as three subjects from the very start). Juniors share the dining hall, Sports Hall, swimming pool as well as the very fine on-site games facilities (including more acres a 10-minute drive away and a Boathouse) with their elders. Indeed some staff teach most ages (i.e. 7–18) – unusual? 'Certainly very challenging,' says the Head of Art. 'The idea sometimes alarms new staff.' All this, says the Head, 'requires extremely careful time-tabling'.

Latest acquisition is Rushmere, the large handsome Georgian house which backs on to the main junior school building (divided by a garden and now a jolly playground). Bought from the sculptor David Wynne, it is the home base for the new 7-year-olds (first entry in September '93), sheltered and self-contained with cosy classrooms (the children also have their own dining room here, which doubles as the hall).

At 8+, after a quiet start, boys bustle busily. Broad social mix. Bright red blazers, Dad's cast-off briefcase a popular alternative to the satchel. Touch-typing in the IT room for 7- and 8-year-olds. From 10 onwards, the children are setted in French, Maths, Latin and (extremely unusually) Music: Music immensely strong, many choirs including the Chamber Choir, with the senior school (more complex timetabling). Lots of clubs; chess and debating keen. Drama hall (shared with senior school) has tiered seats that fold and run to the wall at the press of a button so that six table-tennis tables come into their own every lunch time. Table-tennis coach – boys were national champions at under-11 in

1995. Also champions in tennis and cricket.

Despite the numbers, this feels like a small school, cosy and caring. Mr Holloway remarkably persuasive about the wisdom of boys staying in the same environment from 7–18: he talks of 'the rhythm of study' and supportive surroundings, and about boys 'settling in to breadth and depth'. From his point of view, there is the joy of seeing the fruition at 18 of the love of learning, first spotted at 7 or 8.

Knighton House

Durweston, Blandford,
Dorset DT11 0PY
Tel: 01258 452065, Fax: 01258 450744

PUPILS: 140 girls. 100 board, 40 day
AGES: 7–13. Pre-prep with 40 children, including 20 boys, ages 4–7
C OF E
FEE-PAYING

HEAD: Since 1986, Mr Roger Weatherly BA, PGCE, FRGS, (forties) previously Head of Geography at Bryanston. Madly supportive wife, four children. Much liked, with a strong sense of purpose for the school – emphasis on the individual and the community. An energetic visitor to senior schools.

ENTRANCE: Via pre-prep, or at 7 or 8 (informal interview plus report from previous school).

EXIT: At 12 or 13 mainly to Sherborne, Bryanston, St Antony's Leweston, St Mary's Shaftesbury, Godolphin, Royal School Bath. Reasonable record (and building) of awards and scholarships. Pre-prep boys go on mainly to Sandroyd, and the Old Malthouse.

REMARKS: Charming, happy, and unassuming, country school for girls, with a family atmosphere. A village school, set in marvellous Dorset country (founded by Christopher Booker's parents). Many later additions (the building programme is all managed out of fees), includes the music school, the all-purpose gym/assembly/performance hall, and the splendid dining room (small tables, emphasis on manners). Healthy and good food with loads of home-grown vegetables and fruit.

Good teaching in all areas (but bear in mind that this is not an academic hothouse). Occasional use of nearby Bryanston's facilities (the swimming pool, riding in their grounds). Girls greatly encouraged to read; breadth considered important. Regular internal curriculum reviews at the instigation of the Head: 'He's always tinkering with it,' said an approving father, 'Complacency is not allowed'. Music a special strength, with 15 peripatetic music staff, and high standards chorally and instrumentally (115 out of 140 in main school learn one instrument, 20 learn two). Girls fundraise seriously. Enthusiastic sport, and lots of outdoor life, including keen riding (ponies can be kept here).

An increasing number of girls stay on until 13, and a housemistress for senior girls has just been appointed. Red dungarees (which fade to pink) are the uniform, – 'We love them.' Girls are friendly, mutually supportive, natural and unspoilt, many from country homes. As we said before, this is a school where girls can stay relatively unsophisticated until they are 12 or 13.

Breeds contented parents and pupils. Numbers are healthy, with parents recommending the school to their friends.

Lady Eden's School

39/41 Victoria Road, London W8 5RJ
Tel: 0171 937 0583, Fax: 0171 376 0515

PUPILS: 160 girls
ALL DAY
AGES: 3–11
NON-DENOM
FEE-PAYING

HEAD: Since 1988 to July 1996, Mrs G A Wayne (forties). Retiring July '96. Stop Press: New Head: Mrs J A Davies BA, previously Deputy Head of Bromley High School.

ENTRANCE: Book in young for main entry to kindergarten at three years. No formal test. Some vacancies thereafter, subject to informal assessment. Lots of siblings, and daughters of former pupils, and consideration given to those 'who live in the road'.

EXIT: London day and boarding schools: traditionally and currently to Godolphin and Latymer, St Paul's Girls' School, and Francis Holland, Wycombe Abbey, the St Marys, (Calne, Ascot and Wantage), Tudor Hall, Heathfield and Downe House, etc.

REMARKS: Undoubtedly smart and upmarket. School founded in 1947 by the late Patricia, Lady Eden, and still privately owned by Lord and Lady Eden, who live above the shop and take a very active interest in the running of the school: Parents' Council Meetings are held in their drawing room.

Light airy classrooms in a double-fronted house near Kensington Gardens. Academic matters tightly structured with computers in every classroom, from the tinies upwards, and two new computer area recently created with CD-Roms. Sixth-formers do a touch-typing course before they leave. Solid groundings in the basics, high standards in everything. Serious Science, Latin at 9, and French from 6: leavers put on a French play each year. Lovely Art.

Remedial teaching (from external specialists) available as an extra. Parents are closely involved and help with reading, clubs, outings and plays. There are many visits to museums, theatres, and the schools is good on extra-curricular activities and clubs, e.g. fencing, gym, games, dance, bridge, cookery, etc. Plenty of sport and gym are laid on.

Good fresh food is prepared in the school's own kitchens. The uniform is smart, and includes a boater in the summer (no longer blue).

A dear little school which achieves a lot in an atmosphere conducive to serious learning, and produces happy and confident children.

Lambrook School

Winkfield Row, near Bracknell,
Berkshire RG42 6LU
Tel: 01344 882717, Fax: 01344 891114

PUPILS: Around 90 boys, 60 board, 28 day, plus 2 girls (Masters' daughters)
AGES: 8–13
C OF E
FEE-PAYING
Also own pre-prep started September 1993, 13 boys and girls (new intake of 4/5-year-olds September 1994)

HEAD: Since April 1993, Robin F Badham-Thornhill BA (Hons), PGCE, (forties), married to Angela with two young daughters. Educated at Cheam and Cheltenham, read History, Economics and History at Exeter, and previously taught at King's School, Bruton.

Teaches, keen on PR, and is currently spending time on raising the image of the school. 'Gradually' stamping his own imprint on school, changing Heads of Departments and 'kicking school into 21st century, while retaining old traditions'. Believes in expecting a lot, also in giving praise and encouragement 'which leads to greater confidence'.

Preparing to go fully co-ed from September '97.

ENTRANCE: By registration. No exam, but a reading and writing test a year before entry. Boys accepted any term at any age.

EXIT: Most popular currently are Wellington, and Bradfield, but boys also go on to Eton, Sherborne, Harrow; otherwise widespread, e.g. Durham, Gordonstoun, St Edward's, Pangbourne, Stowe, etc.

REMARKS: Fair quantity of first-time buyers among parents 'who like the idea of a traditional prep school but also want to keep their darling at home' (i.e. day pupils).

Small classes in a collection of small modern classrooms. Scholarship Greek, some dyslexic and EFL help available. Boys say 'sir', stand up and open the door, and are friendly and interested. One-way French exchange during summer term (they visit Lambrook), but plans afoot to make it two-way.

Good Music, with a choir, and woodwind band. There is an enormous new Sports Hall with short tennis only, and an indoor swimming pool. A keenly gamesy school.

Lots of weekend options, including a thriving Magic Circle and good CDT facilities in old gym. Golf and rifle-shooting are popular.

Two bursaries and two scholarships offered (up to 50% of fees); 'might help with financial difficulties'.

The school has been one of the top traditional preps, and after a bumpy ride is now well spoken of by current parents: 'There's so much emphasis on education of the child inside and outside the classroom' said a father, and the pre-prep is generating much local enthusiasm.

Lathallan School

Johnshaven, by Montrose,
Angus DD10 0HN
Tel: 01561 362220, Fax: 01561 361695

PUPILS: 145 boys and girls (92 boys, 53 girls); 88 day, 57 board (plus Kindergarten with 60 children ages 3–5)
AGES: 5–13
INTER-DENOM
FEE-PAYING

HEAD: Since January 1993, Mr Philip Fawkes MBA, Cert Ed (forties), educated and taught at Embley Park, Hampshire. Did his Cert Ed at Southampton University, and MBA in Education at Keele – a rare commodity, 'and it shows,' commented a parent. Teaches Scripture and some History, and is applying 'man management' and 'marketing skills' to making Lathallan (previously a somewhat sleepy establishment) into a force to be reckoned with in Scottish education. Assisted by his wife Jane, plus Gigi the golden retriever and Daisy the Yorkshire terrier. One daughter (at the school).

ENTRANCE: From local primaries, and own kindergarten.

EXIT: Boys mostly to Scottish public schools, Glenalmond, Strathallan, Fettes, Merchiston, plus tiny dribble south: Eton, Wellington, Bradfield. Girls to St Leonards, St George's Ascot; also to Dundee High and Robert Gordon's.

REMARKS: The school has vastly increased in numbers since the introduction of day children, with regular buses from Aberdeen and Montrose (both full) doing a morning and evening run. Boarding numbers are increasing, and weekly boarding is now a popular option especially among local Scottish land-owning and farming families (there is no Saturday-morning school). Day pupils offered B & B after late-evening activities. Some first-time buyers, occasionally from Shell and Conoco families.

Structured day; good teaching staff, with small classes; scholarship stream. Provision for dyslexia on one-to-one basis if necessary, with child withdrawn from class. CDT currently in Old Hall and being moved, marvellous computers (children can bring their own). Great feeling of family; table napkins.

Set in own 60 acres, with 13 acres of playing field overlooking the North Sea (bracing). Excellent games (and thrashing all-comers). Rugby tour to Ireland in '95. Top-notch Drama and Music, own pipe band.

Children sleep in a Victorian castle (the girls in the servants' quarters); dorms have recently been carpeted, but are still rather chilly. Much store is set by lighting a fire in the hall and leaving dorm doors open. Classrooms are in the converted stable block which also houses the kindergarten. There are lots of trips and links abroad at this increasingly popular and good local prep and pre-prep school, which goes from strength to strength.

Lockers Park

Hemel Hempstead, Herts HP1 1TL
Tel: 01442 251712, Fax: 01442 234150

PUPILS: 110 boys. 40 day, 70 board
AGES: 7–13

C OF E
FEE-PAYING

JOINT HEADS: Since 1983 Mr Roger Stephens BA (early fifties), educated at Repton and Durham. Small jovial bachelor, every inch a schoolmaster. Organises the day-to-day running of the school as well as the pastoral side; also teaches the top end.

New Co-Head not announced at time of writing, previous Co-Head has left to become Head of Horris Hill.

ENTRANCE: No problem. At 7 or 8, with a one-to-one test, fairly wide ability range. All boys are encouraged to board at 11 (until recently they were required to do so – the decision is now made by the parents).

EXIT: Harrow, Stowe, Shrewsbury, Radley, Eton, Aldenham, Berkhamsted. Reasonable scholarship record.

REMARKS: Popular local choice. A small, traditional, slightly old-fashioned prep school purpose-built in 1874, in a pleasantly rural setting despite the nearby city and suburbs. Links with founding family (Draper), but the school is now a charitable trust and for historical reasons has joint Heads.

Noticeably friendly boys, very much listened to by staff, who are friends with them. CE always in sight. Maximum class size 16, but usually 13. Remedial help is on hand. The school has a very well-thumbed library; technology and computing are integrated. Boys move up by ability allowing two years at the top for the scholarship stream. Notably strong Music. All boys play the violin for a short time at least (regular Music scholarships, including to Eton, no mean feat); extremely good singing.

Keenly sporting, with French windows

looking out onto slightly sloping playing fields – 'annoying for visiting teams' admit the boys gleefully. Good drama. Chapel plays a central role. Firm discipline ('Stand up, you're making a nuisance of yourself'), but also a free-range outlook: boys are good at expressing themselves in all manner of ways.

Pleasantly scruffy school, neither rich nor smart – though it has been fashionable. The impressive list of Old Boys includes Lord Mountbatten, (excellent classroom blocks are named after him), also Keith Joseph, Paul Channon and the Nawab of Pataudi.

Ludgrove

Wokingham, Berkshire RG40 3AB
Tel: 01734 789881

PUPILS: 195 boys
ALL BOARD
AGES: 8–13
C OF E
FEE-PAYING

JOINT HEADS: Since 1972, Mr Gerald Barber MA (fifties), and Mr Nichol Marston MA (fifties). Both educated at Eton and Oxford, both from prep school backgrounds: Mr Barber is the third generation to run the school (now a charitable trust), Mr Marston's father was Headmaster of Summer Fields. Mr Barber previously taught at Mowden in Sussex, where he met his wife Janet whose family still run that school; they have three grown-up children. All three are charming, friendly and popular with parents and pupils. Parents and Heads are immediately on Christian name terms.

ENTRANCE: No exam, but reasonable standards are essential. Numbers are up since our last edition, despite the waning boarding-prep trends elsewhere. School is booked up till 2001 (i.e. lists are full, but bear in mind that they are also volatile). (Entrants from Scotland have decreased, probably as a result of the recession.) Names need to be registered at birth. One or two signs of post-Royal blight, with parents switching choices to other Eton feeds.

EXIT: As always, almost two-thirds to Eton; also Harrow, Radley, Wellington.

REMARKS: Has always been among the top ten toff prep schools in the country. Breeds tremendous loyalty and has large numbers of old boys' sons (who find the place unchanged in essence). It is very much a choice for Eton families, aristocrats and now Royals. As we said before, it says much for the school that despite the young princes (Harry is still a pupil) the school has not changed one jot. Press observed and were shocked by the homeliness, scruffiness and battered old desks. Also, that despite the unselected intake, the school continues to get large numbers of boys over the Eton hurdle (top marks for this).

Cosy, friendly, understated, unpressurized and in some respects laid-back, with a strong family feel. Large country house (only one hour from central London) with masses of later additions and conversions, in fabulous 130 acres. Large woods for camps and free-range games, with most pitches out of sight. Very strong games, lengthy fixture list. The Victorian-Tudor house contains all the main school rooms and dorms (bathrooms with 16 baths surprised the Children Act Inspectors, 'though they came to see the sense of it'), overlapping with the Barbers' quarters (sick children use the Barber children's bedrooms in isolation if needs be).

Traditional in every respect, with sensible care, minimum fuss (and uniform) and much emphasis on manners: 'We're always banging on about table manners, and the importance of considering others.' Good food, lists of all boys' names on boards in the dining room (which spills out into the old camellia house). Excellent pastoral care; the school has stood firm in not allowing boys instant access to telephones, and all problems are channelled through staff, mainly Mrs Barber (called Ma'am by the boys, as are all the female staff). Regular exeats from Friday midday till Sunday evening.

Much building and re-vamping since we last went to press, including new specialist classroom blocks, with a second lab. Teaching throughout is very traditional. Maths teaching is 'brilliant' say parents. Two remedial teachers are now employed – 'a big help' say parents.

There is a huge Sports Hall/theatre, clapboard chapel, computer room, squash and fives courts, a tiny indoor swimming pool as well as new Art, CDT and pottery rooms in converted cowsheds. Most parents (like boys) are happy as larks, but occasional criticism reaches us from those who think the school is not 'moving with the times' – a comment firmly refuted as 'nonsense' by the school.

The Mall School

185 Hampton Road, Twickenham, Middlesex TW2 5NQ

Tel: 0181 977 2523, Fax: 0181 977 8771

PUPILS: 285 boys
ALL DAY
AGES: 4–13
C OF E
FEE-PAYING

HEAD: Since 1989, Mr T P A MacDonogh MA (fifties) (pro-nounced MacDonow). Educated at Winchester and Cambridge, previously Deputy Head of Berkhamsted Junior School. Keen musician, teaches IT and Maths, emphasizes school as a community.

ENTRANCE: First come, first served with the main unselective entry in the September nearest the fifth birthday – there is a waiting list, so book early. Also at 7+ and 8+ subject to test.

EXIT: Wide selection, mainly day. King's College, Wimbledon, Hampton and St Paul's are the most popular. Recent boarding includes Wellington, Charterhouse, Harrow, Canford. Gets an average of six academic awards per year.

REMARKS: Traditional prep school with unusually informal and friendly atmosphere. Classes of 20–24, but in the final year boys are in three or four sets (smallest grouping for those who need most attention), and the scholarship class (where they spend two years). Little ones are 'mothered' for three years, the 6-year-olds' computer is programmed for them, and there is a CD-ROM in Form 1, where 5-year-olds know how to use it quicker than their teacher. This class bakes, sews and learns joined-up writing. Cosy and traditional in a nice balance all through the school. Remedial help is available for minor cases.

Strong sport and Music (two choirs, two orchestras). Lots of plays. Good on clubs and projects – with boys queuing up before 8 a.m. (Daddy drops them off) to get stuck into their activities (table tennis is popular). Judo, fencing, chess, computing, and carpentry are all on offer.

A considerable amount of new building in the last three years has greatly improved the facilities, classrooms and space. The fourth side of the quad is now under attack – planning permission was granted but the school has gone back to the planners with a more ambitious scheme.

As we have said before, there is a notably strong rapport between parents and staff, intimacy and warmth being the keynote of the school. 'Nothing else like it around,' comment parents clamouring to get boys in. Very hard-working.

Malsis School

Cross Hills, North Yorkshire BD20 8DT
Tel: 01535 633027, Fax: 01535 630571

PUPILS: Around 150 boys, 125 board, 25 day

AGES: 7–13. Plus pre-prep, for boys ages 3–7

C OF E

FEE-PAYING

HEAD: Since 1994, Mr Norman Rowbotham, Cert Ed (fifties). Previously Assistant Headmaster here, and has been in the school since 1978.

Enthusiastic sportsman, madly keen on walking and sailing. Teaches French and runs the Outdoor Pursuits. His wife Jane helps run the school (some would say she does run it) and teaches younger boys. They are both very hands-on, and live on site.

ENTRANCE: Interview and informal tests. No longer Yorkshire only. 'We're attracting families we didn't use to attract.' Boys come to the Scottish borders from West Cheshire, Lancashire, and a handful from abroad.

EXIT: Strong stream to Uppingham, Oundle, Shrewsbury, Giggleswick, Sedburgh, but also to Eton, Harrow, Winchester, Ampleforth, Stoneyhurst, Loretto, etc. In the last five years, 36 scholarships, including Art and Music.

REMARKS: Lots of specialist teachers. Day boys called 'Home Boarders' and have to be in school for breakfast at 7.45 a.m. and stay till 7 p.m. most nights.

School founded in 1920, as the prep for Giggleswick, and since then much expanded. Marvellous John Piper War Memorial Windows in Chapel, plus the flags which used to hang on the Cenotaph in London. Chapel converts to hall/theatre. School housed in flamboyant Victoriana, with many additions. Light airy classrooms, but overall impression is fairly scruffy.

The school is keen on DIY to smarten the place up, and has its own team of craftsmen who finish tradesmen-built shells (of rooms, furniture, etc). Massive improvements recently, and outstanding 'Victorian' ceilings and cartoons all over by Cedric (who used to be the carpenter). Curtains and carpets, and cunning home-made permanent beds nailed to the floor.

Boys learn French from 9, small classes and dedicated staff. Labs with pet shed off biology lab (recently extended). Good and active special needs unit, with visiting staff from Harrogate Dyslexia Institute. Superb facilities, Music Dept, huge Art hall (and ceramics), DT plus craft (i.e. computer-aided design, models and the like) in converted stables. (The previous Head and parents co-owned in syndicate two race horses, now a thing of the past in school life not to mention school publicity, and a loss to the race-crazy Yorkshire crowd.)

Good drama. Absolutely masses of outdoor activity, including caving and long-distance hikes, as well as soccer, rugger, cricket and golf. There is a large sports hall, plus a proper gym and swimming pool, and communal showers beside the changing area. Staff live within ten minutes, so there are lots of busy weekends.

Bad boys 'go on the card' which is

signed by staff at inconvenient (for the boys) moments, and 'generally have their wings clipped'. Pre-prep opened in January '96, in redesigned surplus building next door to the main school.

The school breeds pheasants and peacocks, and also turns out splendid well-rounded chaps, though some of them seem a little large for shorts.

NB There was a recent court case involving the choir master, Mars Bars, computers, sexual fantasies.

Maltman's Green

Gerrards Cross,
Buckinghamshire SL9 8RR
Tel: 01753 883022, Fax: 01753 891237

PUPILS: 340 girls
ALL DAY
AGE: 3–13
NON-DENOM
FEE-PAYING

HEAD: Since 1988, Mrs M Evans BA (fifties), read History at Royal Holloway College, formerly Head of Roedean's junior house. Sensible, competent. Teaches current affairs; 'also I do drugs and interview technique and all that sort of thing' to the top two years. Very realistic about the social and financial changes affecting boarding and is entering the school's new phase with competence and confidence. Has three Cavalier King Charles 'who earn their keep as comforters and aids to PSE lessons.'

ENTRANCE: At age 3; also at 4 (selective), 7 (tests). Prospective pupils spend a day in the school prior to entry 'to see how they are'.

EXIT: Increasingly now to day schools – a good area for grammar schools

with Beaconsfield High and Dr Challoner's; Wycombe Abbey is within day-girl distance. Also to Queenswood, Cheltenham Ladies, St Swithun's, Downe House, Roedean amongst many others. Most girls leave at 12+, but some stay for 13+ entry. Good on getting scholarships.

REMARKS: Boarding is now a thing of the past (due to Lloyd's, service cuts, recession, social attitudes). The boarding house was immediately put into action for new kindergarten intake – which is already booked up for three years ahead. Children will automatically move up the school, but if it transpires that they are 'not the right material' they will gently be hived off to more suitable establishments.

The school is housed in what looks like just another grand stockbroker's pile in a ritzy suburban belt of Gerrards Cross, tile floors gleaming with polish. Strong on all fronts, with subject teachers for everything at 8+ (including a native French Madame). Particularly good Design Technology (girls were making small battery-operated vehicles at the time of our visit), and computing (20 networked Nimbuses) – the English, Geography, Maths, etc, staff bring girls up here to use computers as and when. There is a good Music department, and the Art department is an Aladdin's cave. Fine Science labs. Exceptional gymnastics, with girls winning all manner of medals. PE every day; the gym is used for plays too. The school is set in eleven beautifully kept acres, with an outdoor heated pool, adventure playground, etc.

Some help for children with learning difficulties, though the school is down-playing this a bit.

This is a busy, happy and bright place – ditto the children who are confident and outgoing, zooming about in their purple uniform. Good food. Good on trips and outings. The school made a smooth conversion to all-day, with a slow run-down, and all staff staying put, erstwhile matrons becoming nursery helpers, a housemistress being in charge of the new extended day programme, i.e. activities/hobbies galore between the end of school (4 p.m.) and the end of the day at 6 p.m.

Girls can come in at 7.30 a.m. for breakfast if it suits their families: 'It's like boarding school, but they sleep at home,' commented a parent. 'Practice boarding' weeks and fortnights offered during the summer term for girls who are going on to senior boarding schools.

Milbourne Lodge

Arbrook Lane, Esher, Surrey KT10 9EG
Tel: 01372 462737 (constantly engaged), Fax: 01372 471164

PUPILS: about 200 (too many, in the Head's view); mostly boys, but about 20 girls as well
ALL DAY
AGES: 7/8–13
C OF E
FEE-PAYING

HEAD: Since 1949, Mr Norman Hale MA (seventies), who is still on line for an entry in the *Guinness Book of Records*, and looking fitter, more active than ever; a National Living Treasure. Says he occupies his spare moments with expensive holidays and trips to Annabel's, where he has been known to bump into parents. Has a seriously glamorous wife, who in a weak moment last time said she was in charge of 'buns, bursar and bogs' – an excellent description.

Both Mr and Mrs Hale have a phenomenal amount of energy (in our view) and work with giant enthusiasm for the school which, incidentally, is owned by them. They are an inspiration to us all, and have a good sense of humour and proportion with it. The only Head we have seen going round clutching *Kennedy* as though his life depended on it. Mr Hales was educated at Shrewsbury and Lincoln College, Oxford, where he read History.

The Hales live on the site, through a little wooden gate from the playground.

ENTRANCE: Register asap – lists are permanently full. But this part of the world has a shifting population, so always give it a try. Stiff test, but, says the Head, if you are at all worried, the thing to do is to come and visit the school informally with your infant and the school will give him/her an OK to go ahead (or not). Some children come from Squirrels in Wimbledon, some from Milbourne Junior School (which has *no* connection with this school) and from 20 other pre-preps roundabout. Some 'transplants' also from other schools in the area.

EXIT: Has consistently got probably more scholarships per head than any other prep school in the country – over an enormous number of years, and year in, year out. Not just any old scholarships either, but Winchester, Eton, Harrow, and King's College, Wimbledon. Girls at the moment are sent to Roedean and Wycombe Abbey (though this could be because the Head has heard of them . . .)

REMARKS: In terms of scholarships, this is probably the most successful little prep school in the country. It is a day school, but feels very like a traditional boys' boarding school, with a few girls thrown in for good measure (mostly the sisters of boys in the school). The success appears to be due to rigorous and unrelenting attention to the academic subjects set in CE, by staff who manage to make the hard work (slightly) fun: 'I say,

"I want to be *entertained*," ' says the Head, ' "Let's have *fun* in the classroom." ' Staff roll their sleeves up and have strong minds.

The day starts early, and for the older children, doesn't finish till 6 p.m. or later – 'whenever I've finished with them,' says the Head. There are A and B streams – two classes of 24 for the tinies (thus proving that small classes are not everything), going down to about 18 or 16 in the higher classes – the head is quite flexible about this. Latin for all from the start, and Greek for the A stream from the third year (11-year-olds, *Greek for Beginners*) – the school is one of the last outposts of Classics, and this in itself finds favour with the academic public schools, who recognise the need for some demonstrable mental discipline. Physics comes as a light relief to this under the brilliant teaching of Miss Carroll, who was formerly in the state sector. Computers are hardly to be seen. Miss Carroll looks sternly at one which looks as though it has been made to stand in the corner for bad behaviour: 'We run *it*,' she says, 'not *vice versa*'.

Lest you get the impression that it's all swot and no sport, let it be said that the whole school does games *every afternoon* (football, rugby, cricket, some tennis). There is also a 5-minute run-round between lessons, and the place hums with the energy of 200 children letting off steam at all available moments. The school has the most wonderful games fields – rolling acres stretching out towards the wild, wild wood of Ardbrook Common (mature broad-leaved trees, excellent for dens). This comes as a surprise after the rather unprepossessing approach to the school – up a rather suburban-looking, stockbroker cul-de-sac, set about with modern houses.

Extra-curricular activities are what go to the wall in the quest for academic excellence – not that the school doesn't get the odd Music scholarship, but you feel that this is more thanks to pressure from home rather than from in-built Music timetabling. Not much sign of caring for art, good or bad. Some good poetry in the school magazine, however, e.g.:

The alarm rings – morning –
My last few moments.
Curled up like a croissant.

There is no gym or swimming pool and no plans for them either. CDT is done as a concentrated course once CE is out of the way. There is also an absolute minimum of Nissen-hut extra buildings – and again, no plans for any building expansion as we write.

The school is housed in a cramped but quite pleasant-looking suburban Gothic building – desks practically touching each other and the surrounding walls in the Upper VIth (the last year) 'but that's because that form room is lucky for us,' says the Head. The pupils don't mind, but some of the staff looked rather uncomfortable.

The original school was founded by the father of Woodrow Wyatt in a house up the road. The prospectus (all one page of it) is laconic in the extreme. Pupils are solidly from the professional classes (with an actor or two) and go on to Oxbridge and thence to be upstanding citizens, particularly fat-salaried ones – doctors, surgeons, lawyers, etc. Parents are ambitious (from the sushi/BMW belt), and are quite likely to have moved into the area to be near the school, though some children commute huge distances from London. Both parents and staff (and there are some very long-serving of the latter) comment that this is a one-off place, inspiring, charismatic, and managing to get results without over-punishing little spirits. For what it sets out to do, it is hard to fault (though, by the way, the school lunches Could Do Better).

Moor Park

Ludlow, Shropshire SY8 4EA
Tel: 01584 876061, Fax: 01584 877311

PUPILS: 251 boys and girls. 130 boys, 89 girls

AGES: 3–13. (158 in prep school, 7–13. 70 board, 88 day).

RC (but only one-third are Catholics)

FEE-PAYING

HEAD: Since 1988, Mr J R Badham BEd Oxon, BA, OU (forties), educated White Friars Grammar School, Cheltenham, previously Head of a north London prep school. Lives with his wife and four young children 'above the shop'.

ENTRANCE: Tests for children 'if necessary' entering at 7+ and 8+.

EXIT: Boys to Downside, Ampleforth, Worth, Eton, Shrewsbury and a wide variety elsewhere. Girls to the leading Catholic schools, Moreton Hall.

REMARKS: Founded in 1964 in a large country house and enjoyed rapid growth, followed by a slide in the popularity stakes. Like other prep boarding schools in rural areas, this one has suffered in the last two/three years from declining boarding trends, though demand appears to be 'picking up again', and it remains a popular local choice. Boarders largely from a 30-mile radius (Londoners and children from abroad a rarity nowadays), and the Catholic proportion of the school has diminished.

Lovely chapel (in the old ballroom); Christian values underpin everything but religion is not forced down anyone's throat. The school is very much run as a boarding school with a recently elongated day – there is an activity/hobby session for children between 5.30 and 6.30 p.m., and there are games sessions every weekday. Good Drama, Music ('on the up' report parents, 'especially the choir'), and strong on games (with the best teas for miles around). School has been first nationally in the St David's Shield Shooting Competition.

Pastoral care is good and all House-parents are married. Boys' dorms are cosy, girls' quarters are comfy. Extended-family atmosphere, where children are given plenty of encouragement under the Head's aim to stretch but not drive them.

Mount House School

Mount Tavy, Tavistock,
Devon PL19 9LJ
Tel: 01822 612244, Fax: 01822 610042

PUPILS: Approx 150 boys, 110 full boarders, 40 day; and from September 1996, girls.

AGES: 7–13; plus own pre-prep for boys and girls ages 3–7

C OF E

FEE-PAYING

HEAD: Since 1984, Mr C D Price BA (early fifties). Educated Clayesmore and Open University – read English. Was previously Assistant Headmaster at Cheam. Teaches Geography and English. Hobbies – sailing, model railways, sport and the 'latest boys' crazes'. An enthusiast who carries all before him. Boys appear to regard him as a human being – a rare state of affairs, in our observation, which speaks volumes for his talent as a teacher. Tireless in promoting the school to the outside world, and regularly plays host to Heads of public schools. Steady back-up from his wife Sue – who does everything from running the clothing shop to serving match teas and 'loves it'. Their son teaches at a prep school; their daughter, an ex prep school matron, is married to a prep school master.

Some useful governors, including headmasters, accountants, a surveyor, and the editor of the *Dragon Book of Verse* (who teaches at Eton).

ENTRANCE: From local and far-flung corners of the West Country. Also some service children (though fewer of these) and others 'from Elgin to Penzance', not to mention those now from Hong Kong, Dubai, Singapore (the children of diplomats, bankers, etc). Interview, assessment and test.

EXIT: 13 scholarships in '95, 10 in '94, 11 in '93, including to Radley, St Edward's Oxford, Stowe, Clifton, Sherborne, King's Bruton, King's Taunton, Blundell's, Plymouth College, Kelly, Milton Abbey and Stonyhurst – this reflects where pupils go on to, though some also to Eton, Winchester, Wellington College, etc. Thirty-one leavers to 15 public schools in '95. OBs: include Ed Bye (producer of Jasper Carrott, etc), Philip de Glanville, David Owen and the Cashier of the Bank of England.

REMARKS: Huge changes afoot, i.e. *girls* will be admitted from September '96: the build-up is likely to be fairly slow. Also, moving with the times and making financial sense, is the purpose-built pre-prep for boys and girls from the age of 3 – with little competition in this area.

School still billed as the best in the West by senior school Headmasters – 'nothing to touch it for miles' said one, though how girls will affect this remains to be seen. Particular strengths are those intangible unquantifiable qualities – politeness, friendliness, children who look you in the eye, hold their heads up, and are confident without being cocky.

The main building is a glorious old manor house overlooking Tavistock with a view – on a good day – to Cornwall. Super site, surrounded by Dartmoor (tendency to mists and gloom), and with a river running through the bottom of the playing fields (the school has riparian rights).

Enthusiastic Music (tour to Poland in '95); much diligent practice, which wins Music scholarships from time to time. The Head is good at fostering talent in this area, however slight. Good Art department. Keen games; the school will travel miles for a match with traditional preps such as Caldicott. Smart sports hall, with a full-size tennis court and two squash courts in it, also a CDT centre.

Strong on natural history – not surprising, with so much scope for study on the doorstep. Pupils streamed and setted in English and Maths, and are turned out well-prepared for their public school. New head of Classics – otherwise no staff changes for eight years.

Sunday chapel a bit of a feature here – much attended by parents still, and regularly persuades public school Headmasters to preach the sermon. Parents by and large professional – lawyers, accountants, services, medics (one or two who work in London but have weekend cottages in the area), etc.

Two exeats each term plus three Sundays out – 'we never have a child left behind at an exeat' says the Head. Average class size 13, maximum 16.

Mowden Hall School

Newton, Stocksfield,
Northumberland NE43 7TP
Tel: 01661 842147, Fax: 01661 842529

PUPILS: 83 boys, 38 girls. 93 board, 28 day
AGES: 8–13. Plus pre-prep: 72 boys and
girls, ages 4–8
C OF E
FEE-PAYING

HEAD: Since September 1991, Mr
Andrew Lewis MA (early fifties),
educated Marlborough and Cambridge;
previously Housemaster at Repton.
Charming and polite, a keen cricketer.
Wife is wonderful and energetically
supportive, four children.

ENTRANCE: No exam or test, aims to
take a wide spectrum of abilities.
Children from North Northumberland,
the Scottish Borders, Cumbria, Yorkshire. Three-term entry.

EXIT: A wide spectrum including day
schools, also Sedbergh, Loretto, St
Leonards, Casterton, Eton, Shrewsbury,
Oundle.

REMARKS: Traditional country prep
school, with a family feel, set in a
pleasant house with lovely parkland.
Efficiently run and much loved. Not a
rich school, but with good facilities on a
modest scale, all well used. Lots of
enthusiasm, with a good atmosphere that
balances discipline (children are on a rota
system for clearing plates, etc) with
freedom; the emphasis is on work and
play. Two streams from 9 onwards,
scholars in the top year only. Keenly
sporty (girls' hockey especially
successful), with matches on weekdays to
leave weekends free for activities. Lots of
fun expeditions (Roman Wall, the
beach), camp-fire cooking, and playing in
the woods.

The school has a very good library,
with a much-used suggestions book.
Quiet time after lunch, ostensibly for
reading. The stable yard has now been
brilliantly converted into a magnificent
Science, Art and Technology Centre –
which is also bustling with activity during
club time in evenings and at weekends:
'It's made a *huge* difference,' say
approving parents, as has the newly
appointed Head of Art and Technology.
Stop Press – recently acquired a half share
in the Château de Sauveterre (see
Cothill).

The super pre-prep (which opened in
September '93) is bursting and successful,
with waiting lists for all age groups (and it
is rare for a child not to go on to the main
school).Three-weekly exeats for prep
boarders recently introduced (Friday 11
a.m. until Monday morning), to suit far-
flung parents.

A happy place, with nothing similar for
miles around.

Newcastle Preparatory School

6 Eslington Road,
Newcastle-upon-Tyne NE2 4RH
Tel: 0191 281 1769, Fax: 0191 281 5668

PUPILS: 270 boys and girls
AGES: 4–13
ALL DAY. Plus approximately 30
children in the kindergarten
C OF E
FEE-PAYING

HEAD: Since 1988, Mr G Clayton
MA, Cert Ed (forties).

REMARKS: Very popular prep and
pre-prep school which prepares
children extremely well for the next stage.
The school has grown since our last
addition, and will continue to increase
its numbers as the newly acquired
neighbouring property is converted.

Bright, busy and happy, with good reports from parents. Has been going for over one hundred years; Cardinal Basil Hume is an Old Boy. Lots of individual attention and jolly music, playlets, art.

Alternatives for Newcastle parents would be Ascham House School and Newlands Preparatory School, both boys only, both in Gosforth. NPS is in the thick of Newcastle's highest-flying senior schools, right opposite the Royal Grammar School and Central Newcastle High School to which most pupils move on. Other exit lines are Dame Allan's, Church High or Westfield.

New College School

Savile Road, Oxford OX1 3UA
Tel: 01865 243657

PUPILS: Approx 135 boys
ALL DAY
AGES: 7–13
C OF E
FEE-PAYING

HEAD: Since 1990, Mr J Edmunds BA (forties), degree in History from Warwick University. Was choral scholar at Forest School in North London. Ran junior school at West Buckland School in Devon before coming here, and has taught in a state comprehensive. Says he was 'surprised' to be offered this post, though to us he seems a perfect Wykehamist choice – dry humour, quiet, polite, intelligent, interested in music, particularly early music, etc. Has written local history books, and is currently writing a history of the school. Comments as though he means it: 'The individual child is the most important

thing here.' Divorced, with one grown-up son, who lives with him – in flat above the school.

ENTRANCE: School runs a week of testing in February for 7-year-olds. They come to the school in groups of six with their friends, have a 'little test' (IQ – NFER) in Maths and English, play Lego, etc – i.e. the school is selective, especially given its geographical position. Choristers have a voice trial at 8; parents pay one-third of fees – Head chooses choristers 'by their eyes – if there's a spark there'.

EXIT: To the musical schools, with lots of music scholarships – Uppingham, Eton, Winchester (though NB only one or two here – despite the foundation link). Also mainly to schools within an hour-and-a-half's radius – Magdalen College School and Abingdon are popular choices; one or two to Cokethorpe, St Edward's. OBs include Richard Seal, Ian Partridge, Andrew Lumsden, Howard Goodall (composer – *Black Adder, Red Dwarf*, etc), Ian Fountain (pianist).

REMARKS: Feels like an elderly, indigent relation, clinging to the coat tails of the big brother – the mighty foundation of New College, in whose shadow the school squats. Do not, however, be put off by the unritzy surroundings, the standard asphalt playing ground and the functional classrooms. Energy has been breathed into the place by Mr Edmunds, and by the Head of Music Roger Allen, who, according to a delighted parent, is 'fabulous, has opened up the Music so that whereas before it all revolved round the choristers and college, now there are all sorts of events for the rest of the school' – including a regular St Matthew Passion and St John Passion – with help from parents.

Meanwhile, choristers sing all manner

73

of wonderful things, particularly early music, under the direction of New College's choir master, Dr Edward Higginbottom, who came in '76, has seven children (some in the school), wears a Rupert Bear scarf and treats the children as adults (too adult?). 'I see it as an enabling job,' comments Dr Higginbottom, 'to get out of them what they can do.'

Teaching is traditional – the three Rs. One class in each year group all taught together – i.e. no streaming or setting. Saturday morning is all devoted to culture – the Head has taken this out of the weekday curriculum, so children can now do four out of seven or eight options, e.g. creative writing, music. Soccer can be dropped at the age of 9 – 'we're very civilized here'. The school uses New College playing fields just across the road; has a small gym. Grey shorts are changed for long (rather naff) trousers in the pupils' third year. The boarding element – mostly for choristers – has now closed. Parents mainly lawyers, doctors, dons.

A good low-key Oxford prep which could do with more funding? NB No prospectus, ask to see the termly newsletters.

Norland Place School

162–166 Holland Park Avenue, London W11 4UH

Tel: 0171 603 9103, Fax: 0171 603 0648

PUPILS: 158 girls, 90 boys (to age 8 only)

AGES: 4–11

NON-DENOM

FEE-PAYING

HEAD: From March 1996, Mr David Alexander (thirties) BA, educated at Grosvenor High School, Belfast and University College, Wales. Married, a musician and keen glider. Previously Deputy Head and Head of Music at St Paul's Cathedral Choir School. He takes over from Mrs S J Garnsey, who still owns the school and has run it since 1966, latterly with the aid of live-in Bursar Patrick Richardson.

ENTRANCE: Babies names put down at birth. Special cases for children of Old Girls, including grannies (NB school founded in 1876), and siblings. First come, first served basis – and very popular as such. OBs: TRHs Prince William and Prince Harry.

EXIT: London day schools, e.g. St Paul's, and boarding schools – no pattern. All girls sit three day schools 'as a safety net'. Boys leave at 7 or 8 for Colet Court, Westminster Under School, Westminster Cathedral Choir and Sussex House, or to board, usually at Summer Fields, Ludgrove or Cothill.

REMARKS: Once the fashionable London choice (and one of the rare co-eds). Now one of many popular prep and pre-preps, and being watched with interest under the new Head.

Three houses joined together, which means rabbit warrens of twisty stairs and half-landings, with every inch of space in use. Two much-used playgrounds, a long narrow gym/dining hall, with a splendid Head of Gym, Stephanie Price (who swam for England). High teaching standards, and everything going full-blast. After-school-hours clubs are popular – Science, Art, swimming, French, Drama, Music and Netball. Newly equipped Science, IT and Art rooms. Boys and girls split at 8, and are bright as buttons.

Assessments are carried out at the end

of Spring Term after the child's entry to the school, usually at the age of 4. They are not overly popular with parents, who must pay for these assessments: block testing is carried out by two female Educational Psychologists. The assessments are not absolutely compulsory, but are 'much encouraged', because it throws up the very bright, and also any learning difficulties. Remedial help is on hand.

Difficult to comment at the time of writing, as the new Head follows the lengthy and successful reign of the owner and Head, Mrs Garnsey.

The Old Malthouse

Langton Matravers, Swanage,
Dorset BH19 3HB
Tel: 01929 422302, Fax: 01929 422154

PUPILS: Around 90 boys. 65 board, 25 day. Pre-prep 25 (including 8 girls)
AGES: boys 4–13, girls 4–8
C OF E
FEE-PAYING

HEAD: Since September 1988, Mr Jonathan (Jon) Phillips BEd (forties), previously Deputy Head at The Downs, Wraxall. Educated at Canford School and St Luke's College, Exeter. Teaches Junior French and PSE to boys in their final year. Very proud of the school, enthusiastic and fun. Married with two children, James and Georgina.

ENTRANCE: At 7 or 8, register early, own entrance test. Best route is through pre-prep. Pupils 'mainly Dorset', eight via London train and eight 'from abroad'.

EXIT: Blundell's, King's Bruton, Millfield, Bryanston, Sherborne,

Bournemouth School, Poole Grammar, Monkton Combe, etc.

REMARKS: Slightly surprising entrance off main street, but delightful converted Old Malthouse (one dorm still called 'The Granary'). There is a splendid new multi-purpose hall with music rooms below and adjacent. A classroom and dormitory block was completed in 1990, and six new classrooms built in 1995.

The school has a solid tradition of a scholarship stream, but also caters well for the less able. The school has a well-run exchange system (parents and boys are enthusiastic) with a French school in Normandy – boys spend ten days on their own in French families and attend French lessons. Teachers exchange too.

Very structured; discipline includes cleaning silver, mucking out mini-buses and extra work. Boys say 'Sir', stand up, have table napkins. The dining Hall (with lovely old benches) doubles for assembly and chapel on Sundays, when the dining hatch to the kitchen converts to an altar.

No longer the Spartan place it used to be. An outdoor swimming pool has replaced 'Dancing Ledge', but lots of boyish activities abound – target shooting in the old gym at break, clay shooting, judo, cookery and lots of outdoor pursuits. There are good games pitches in the school's 15-acre grounds, including one all-weather area for tennis and hockey.

Senior boys and Captains have their own room with 'toyes' (curtained off private work areas), where they do their assignments as preparations for public school. A good strong school, with a very friendly atmosphere. It works well.

Orwell Park

Ipswich, Suffolk IP10 OER
Tel: 01473 659225, Fax: 01473 659822

PUPILS: 151 boys, 46 girls. 149 board, 48 day
AGES: 3–13
INTER-DENOM
FEE-PAYING

HEAD: Since September 1994, Mr Andrew Auster BA (forties), previously Head of The Downs School, Colwell, and before that Director of Music at Shrewsbury. Keen rugger player (played for Durham and Cambridge Universities), accomplished musician. Gentle voice and manner belie the inner steel. Caring with a strong social conscience and ambitious plans to help poor children from Russia and Brazil. Married with three children.

ENTRANCE: By registration, thence by careful screening. Not difficult.

EXIT: Not a feed for anywhere, but a feeder for public schools; last year boys went to Harrow, Eton, Oundle, Uppingham, Oakham, Rugby, Gresham's, Framlingham, Epsom, etc. Girls to Benenden, St Swithun's and elsewhere.

REMARKS: A famous East Anglian prep school which has changed/adapted – and is still in the process of so doing. Co-ed (since '93), with girls' numbers gently swelling, and a new popular pre-prep. Overall softening at the edges (it had been robustly traditional, and terrific with it, with boys helping to clean the school, embarking on Outward Bound-ish activities, etc). The Head has innovated some clever changes in the use of space. Quite a change in staffing too.

Academically, the ethos remains: not a swot shop, but teaching goes well beyond the confines of CE, with an initial extremely strong emphasis on spelling, tables, reading (the first activity of the day). Children kept busy at all hours and given many opportunities – they build all kinds of things, sail well, play games four times a week (there are now enough girls to make up teams and beat some all-girl schools), and use the army-built confidence (i.e. assault) course. The school has its own observatory (manned by the local astronomy club) with a 10-inch refractor telescope and radio station. Lovely Art studios; good Music, with pianos all over the place and dozens of music practice rooms in the cellars. Busy clubs (including radio club); many options (free time is one, 'But you can't always choose that'). Library with bean bags (an excellent idea, why don't more prep schools do this?); IT room open at all times.

The school has a glorious setting, in 95 acres of parkland and overlooking the River Orwell. An attractive and dignified large Georgian-style house in mellow red brick with turn-of-the-century additions including brick skin; beautifully proportioned rooms. Boarding numbers have held up (though, as elsewhere, are less in demand), and flexi-boarding is available on demand, but overall numbers are down from our last edition, despite the wider age range and the girls. Dormitories are user-friendly. Mr Auster has re-introduced 'formal family' meals (previously a free-for-all) in the large dining room. The immense, ritzy facilities may mean some children are in for a shock when they get to their secondary school and find it cannot compete.

Children fizz with enthusiasm. Traditionally the sons of landed gents and farmers, but the intake has now very considerably broadened; several from abroad (including a regular intake of Spanish).

Some parents of older children have found it hard to adapt to changes.

Packwood Haugh

Ruyton-XI-Towns, Shrewsbury,
Shropshire SY4 1HX
Tel: 01939 260217, Fax: 01939 260051

PUPILS: 145 boys, 75 girls. 130
boarders, 90 day
AGES: 8–13. Plus small pre-prep
department (opened '93) ages 4–7
C OF E
FEE-PAYING

HEAD: Since 1988, Mr P J F Jordan MA Cantab (fifties), previously Head of the Old Malthouse. Considerate, thoughtful, a keen games player and musician, but some parental criticism that he is not a good communicator. Has successfully 'softened the edges' here. Wife busy on all fronts, two children.

ENTRANCE: Short informal assessment on Maths and English; academic scholarships sometimes awarded. Help for the needy. Children from Shropshire, Cheshire, Wales, London and also abroad.

EXIT: Boys mainly to Shrewsbury and Oundle, also Ellesmere, Eton, Harrow, Rugby, King's Chester and elsewhere. Girls often opt for Moreton Hall and Cheltenham Ladies, also Malvern Girls, Oundle, Wrekin and elsewhere. Very good track record of gaining awards – academic, Music and Art.

REMARKS: Academic and traditional country prep school surviving

successfully after a tricky patch (at the tail end of the previous Head's incredibly long reign), though boarding numbers are affected by the national trend against boarding (boarders down by 60 since the last edition, day numbers almost double). Boys and girls work hard, and play hard too. There is a good remedial department, and careful streaming. High academic standards apply and on average *fourteen* children each year gain awards to their senior school though there is no sense of pressure-cooking. The outlook is broad – there is something for everyone to shine at, and a good choice of options and activities. Sensible use of free time. The school is keenly sporting – boys and girls do well in a wide variety of sports; Astroturf pitch floodlit for after-dark games. Music, Art, CDT, and Drama all play major roles.

Spacious and handsome purpose-built boarding house for the girls, run by the charming Head of Science and his wife. Boys' dorms are in the main building. Fine grounds, including a famous topiary of the Apostles in the garden, and lots of space. Flourishing pre-prep.

Papplewick

Ascot, Berkshire SL5 7IH
Tel: 01344 21488, Fax: 01344 874639

PUPILS: Around 200 boys. 150 board,
50 day. All must board by 11
AGES: 7–13
C OF E
FEE-PAYING

HEAD: Since January 1992, Mr Rhidian Llewellyn BA (Hons), Dip Ed (late thirties). Educated at Pangbourne College, followed by University of London and Dip Ed at Oxford, previously taught at Arnold House, and The Dragon, where he was a Housemaster. Friendly, confident and fun. His wife, Sue, an interior designer, is in charge of housekeeping, and teaches stencilling to the boys. Head teaches English and General Paper to scholarship boys, but would probably rather be playing, coaching or watching cricket (despite his horsey background – his uncle is Harry of Foxhunter fame). He also edits the seriously challenging school STAG mag. Ably helped by his black Labrador, Orlando.

ENTRANCE: Non-competitive entrance exam: apply early. 60% from Berkshire, 20% from overseas ('mostly ex-pats, perhaps 10 real foreigners'), 16% from London and 4% 'from wherever'.

EXIT: Very good record of scholarships/awards (thirty in the last three years), academic, art and music. Sends more boys to Wellington than elsewhere, also Eton, Harrow, Marlborough, Bradfield, Stowe, St Edward's, Cheltenham, Sherborne, Milton Abbey and many other schools besides. One or two leave at 11.

REMARKS: Strong academic school, with inspired teaching (and teachers), small classes, and brill computing and CDT facilities (and output). There is a well-used dyslexia unit. Latin for all. Staff must stay late twice a week, most live on campus (and those that don't are housed by the school locally) and boys only exeat three times a term (including half-term). Parents may visit until lunch time on Sundays, afternoons are devoted to mega-activity time, with all staff on duty – they have a day off in lieu during the week.

Mr Llewellyn says his cleverest appointment was that of Father Eddie Phillips-Smith as Chaplain (previously at Edgarley Hall, where the children commented that he took 'wicked' [pupil-speak – meaning top-class] assemblies, e.g. turning scrambled eggs purple).

Campus currently tiny and twee, 'tiresomely well-manicured' said a (rival) Head. Cars and games pitches are all squashed into a 13-acre site opposite Ascot No 7 car park, with lots of activities on the Heath and in nearby Windsor Great Park. But (complex and lengthy) negotiations are under way to buy adjacent land/property, and the plan is to move tiny boarders here, tack on a pre-prep (for 5–7-year-olds, opening in September '97) and expand the staff accommodation.

Papplewick Cricket tour of Zimbabwe in March/April '95. Swimming pool, local riding. Latest developments since our last edition include a brand new Science laboratory and the new Studio Theatre, with the superb newly enlarged Media Centre which has a full-blown recording studio, pre-set camera markings on the floor and regular Sunday a.m. broadcasts on Radio STAG. Good with tricky children.

Boys wear short trousers till their tenth birthday and board by their eleventh. Classrooms and dorms are higgledy-piggledy throughout in best Ascot-Georgian style, with a cunning extending chapel. Twenty-four-bed dorms tucked under the eaves are much the most sought-after (i.e. 24 good bounces). Worn carpets, some bedrooms cramped, shabby furniture, ditto bathrooms.

Local parents can and do use squash courts, tennis courts, etc. Good parent/teacher contact but no Association; friendly camaraderie. 20% first-time buyers and recession no problem – 'dropped one or two by the wayside'. The growth area is now London parents who currently account for 23%.

Two 50% scholarships annually. Strong sense of cheerful Christianity and well-organised and happy children. Breeding ground for Headmasters.

Pembridge Hall Preparatory School for Girls

18 Pembridge Square, London W2 4EH
Tel: 0171 229 0121, Fax: 0171 792 1086
PUPILS: 250 girls
ALL DAY
AGES: 4+–11
C OF E
FEE-PAYING

HEAD: Since April 1995, Mrs Laura Marani, Cert Ed, (prefers not to disclose her age) following the two-term Headship of her predecessor. Has been Deputy Head here since 1986, and is widely respected by staff and parents. Now she carries on the work of the redoubtable Mrs Elizabeth Collison, who took Pembridge Hall from 80 to over 250 pupils during her reign. Married with two grown-up daughters, who have been 'through the London system, and that's a great help,' says Mrs Marani.

ENTRANCE: Complicated. Two entry dates per annum (now a rarity): September (for those born between September and February) and April (for those born between March and August). Definite places are offered to the first five children born in each month (applications should be in before the child is six weeks old), and thereafter up to five girls per month are put on the waiting list (which usually closes 6/8 months after birth). Girls may then be added to a supplementary waiting list (the father of a 2½-year-old was being given the bad news

when we visited!). Twenty-four girls join the school at each intake, few are taken later, though occasional spaces do arise.

EXIT: To all the top London Day Schools: Godolphin and Latymer, Francis Holland, St Paul's, Queen's College and Queen's Gate. Between a quarter and a fifth go to boarding schools: Downe House, Wycombe Abbey, Benenden, North Foreland Lodge, etc.

REMARKS: School founded 1979. Tinies are taught by Teacher and Assistant for the first three years, and classes seem 'to fall away' down to about 18/20 by Upper School (7-year-olds). Staff:pupil ratio 1:11. Classes are mixed, not streamed (and totally integrated by Upper School). French from 8, daily. Computers throughout.

Special needs are catered for in a rather jolly room at top of house; girls often want to have reading difficulties to go there.

Whole school is in a cunning conversion of a former police house, with music rooms under the pavement, a science lab on the roof, and a super great hall in the basement for Gym and Drama, which Pembridge Association also uses. Science combines with CDT – put an electric circuit in your doll's house.

Much use of local facilities: Queen's Club for skating, Allendale Park, West London Stadium and Perks Field for rounders. Girls use the Square gardens after lunch. No catering on site; girls bring packed lunches and there was a competition running when we visited for the most imaginative.

Lots of clubs and societies; all but the tiniest can stay after school for 5 p.m. collection. Ethnic backgrounds mixed, but most children are British.

Very successful, very popular and deservedly so. It has a low profile, and has survived unscathed the recent wobble at the top, now under steady leadership.

The Pilgrims' School

The Close, Winchester,
Hampshire SO23 9LT
Tel: 01962 854189, Fax: 01962 843610

PUPILS: Around 180 boys. About 75 board, the rest day. 38 choral scholars (at half fees)
AGES: 7/8–13+
C OF E
FEE-PAYING

HEAD: Since 1983, Mr Michael Kefford MA, Dip Ed (fifties). Educated Lancing and St John's Cambridge. Previous post Head of Colston's Preparatory School, Bristol. Married with two teenage children. Of the *mens sana in corpore sano* persuasion. He is a lay preacher in C of E; runs five miles a day in school holidays.
Stop Press: Retirement in July '97. New Head: Dr B A Rees BA, BD, Dip Min, PhD. See Bedford Preparatory School.

ENTRANCE: Voice trials for choristers and quiristers in November or by individual appointment at other times. Half fees for these. Test at 7+ for ordinary mortals. Day places over-subscribed.

EXIT: About half to Winchester (but NB as able children are placed in the school by Winchester College, this does not give a true reflection of the home-grown product). Otherwise hither and yon (Eton, Lancing, Sherborne, Charterhouse are popular choices); in particular to schools offering Music scholarships.

REMARKS: Traditional, buttoned-up little prep school in the most glorious site in the shadow of Winchester Cathedral (with tourists milling round). School was originally for the 16 quiristers (pronounced kwiristers) who sing in Winchester College Chapel, and for the 16 choristers who sing in the Cathedral. The present incarnation of school was founded in 1931 to add 'commoners' and turn what had been a choir school into a 'proper' prep.

Music is understandably strong – 140 boys learn one instrument, 80 learn two and Music scholarships are regularly won. 'They emerge', said a mother, 'as little professionals.' And sometimes exhausted with it. Choristers at a recent concert appeared to be half asleep and not watching the conductor. School has a 'split' feeling as choristers go in one direction, quiristers to Dr Christopher Tolley in another, and the rest e.g. to assembly.

School day for day pupils = 8.30 a.m. – 4.45 p.m., then, after first two years, hobbies (known as 'Commoners Hour' – as the singers are singing at this point) till 6 p.m., supper 6.10 p.m., then prep. NB When we wrote the last edition of the book the school was two-thirds boarders, now it's one-third – the balance has tipped but the school still operates as though still all-boarding. Maximum class size 18. Loyal parents.

'Gentle' streaming. Timetable computing, satellite French – French from 8, German in last year. Large numbers of Oxbridge graduates teach in the school, which the Head considers a Good Thing. Uniform is Lovat green sweaters, grey trousers and a bashful look.

Buildings are an interesting hodge-podge from the wonderful medieval Pilgrims' Hall, in which it is thought that pilgrims rested from their exertions at St Swithun's shrine (it is now the school hall), to a new wooden chalet in the school grounds put up at cost of £50,000 to provide an extra classroom. Dormitories in the middle of school are spick, span, and Spartan – though this is strongly denied by the Head, who points out that there are duvets, wall-to-wall carpeting and teddy bears. 'They learn good habits right from the start here', says the Head, 'it's a long tradition'. (He can say that again.) Twenty-three also sleep in the 'quiristers' house' which is just down the road. Music rooms and practice cells are in what was probably the stables – incredible old oak. There is a huge model railway (another of the Head's enthusiasms) in the same block.

However, conflicting reports reach us: e.g. 'We are thrilled,' said one parent. And another: 'We much prefer Twyford.'

Port Regis

Motcombe Park, Shaftesbury,
Dorset SP7 9QA
Tel: 01747 852566, Fax: 01747 854684

PUPILS: 316 boys and girls; 195 boys, 121 girls, (most board, 83 day)
AGES: 7–13. Plus new pre-prep (currently 36 pupils, places for 66), ages 4–7
C OF E
FEE-PAYING

HEAD: Since January 1994, Mr Peter Dix MA (Cantab in Classics) and BA Hons (Natal University) (forties). Short spell in the City. Previous post: sixteen years at King's Canterbury, the last five as a Housemaster. Wife Liz, elegant and dynamic (BA Hons in Fashion and Textiles and has been teaching the same at King's Canterbury). Two children. Keen on gardening, team games, cooking, computing, chess. 'Preparatory school should be preparing children, not forcing,' comments Head. He also believes in working as a team: 'There's too much talk about the individual, forgetting we all must work

together.' Lively couple – some parents are fans, some are not.

ENTRANCE: Still overbooked (for girls especially) – book a year or two in advance. Annual academic, music, gymnastic and all-rounder scholarships. Head and/or his wife show parents/ children around: looks for potential.

EXIT: Bryanston, Marlborough (more girls than boys), and also to single-sex schools and other co-eds absolutely all over the place. 21 awards won in '95 (and this is fairly typical) – 5 academic, 5 Music, 1 Art and 10 all-rounders. Girls almost all stay to 13.

REMARKS: Still an astonishingly strong and vibrant school, certainly one of the most go-ahead in Britain (also among the most expensive prep schools). Exceptional facilities (far better than some public schools) – purpose-built specialist classrooms, each with its own teaching office (a luxury and rarity among prep schools), county-standard Sports Hall, and a national centre for junior gymnastics with incredible French equipment (by Gymnova), opened by HM the Queen (when wearing both crown and granny hat – the Princess Royal chose this for her children). All this may be bewildering to some.

Staff are fantastically committed, hard-worked (and very well paid), and the new Head, like his predecessor, is encouraging them to do their own thing. Many young staff (some with state school experience). 'The facilities are quite outstanding,' muses the Head, 'but one could scoop up the staff and children, take them to a farm down the road, and still have an absolutely first-class school.'

For all the sophisticated facilities, this is definitely a country prep school, set in rolling Dorset parkland: the main house was originally built for the Duke of

Westminster, and the atmosphere is fun, friendly and informal.

Outstanding facilities include Cunningham Hall of Technology, consisting of art and pottery studios, a technical drawing and design studio, computer-aided design, woodwork, a magnificently equipped technology centre, an IT room, specialist Science laboratories and Maths classrooms, plus a lecture theatre – phew! New boys' boarding house (opened January '95) with en-suite wash-basin, clothing storage and desk, to complement the girls' house. Also new since we last went to press is the Astroturf all-weather hockey pitch plus nine tennis courts. The pre-prep (it opened in September '93) is useful for siblings; the tinies can stay until 6.30 p.m.

Children are immensely self-confident, happy, motivated (very), and used to a fairly free-range existence; they are liberally praised and encouraged by staff and kept 'wildly busy.' Loads of staff are on duty at weekends. There is a strong tutor system, with children choosing their own. At least 20% of the timetable is not geared towards exams. Seventy different hobbies on offer (is this a record?), and 15 sports – they win almost everything. Big theatre, much used.

Parents repeat 'It's like an upmarket holiday camp,' and admit that the holidays can be a bit of a let-down, with children in need of a rest. The next stage of schooling often comes as a shock to children who have been given nothing but the best and whose expectations are immensely high. Other establishments may appear somewhat dozy in comparison. Flexi-boarding is, of course, increasingly popular. Morale is sky high and the school charges on with confidence and élan.

Queen's Gate Junior School

133 Queen's Gate, London SW7 5LF
Tel: 0171 589 3587

PUPILS: Around 135 girls
ALL DAY
AGES: 4–11
NON-DENOM
FEE-PAYING

HEAD: Since 1987 Mrs Ann Karol Cert Ed (age not given). Works closely with the Principal, Mrs Holyoak (see entry for Queen's Gate School).

ENTRANCE: Put names down early (preference given to grand-daughters/daughters of old girls, and sisters). Children spend a morning in the school a year in advance of their entry to make sure they will 'fit in'.

EXIT: At least a dozen per year move on up into the senior school (qv); others choose other London day schools or board. Horses for courses – and the school puts no pressure on pupils to stay put at the senior school.

REMARKS: Still a delightful and busy school, the walls bulging with pupils' work. Loads of clubs and extra-curricular activities to be enjoyed – including cooking, sewing, music. Clever grouping of children and use of staff enables children to work at their own pace. Remedial help for those in need, but every single child takes a turn with the specialist teacher so 'no-one feels odd'. French from the age of 6, Latin for all at 10, computing from 8. Very good use of space (e.g. the entrance hall lobby turns into a quiet corner for reading when needed). The junior school has its own front door and takes up a comfortable chunk of the ground floor; also uses some of the senior school facilities, e.g. Science laboratories, music rooms, etc.

School flowers brought in by class rota. No garden or playground, but daily walks and lots of games. Strong PTA and parental links (loads of old girls' whose own mothers were here). Minimal uniform (Harris navy-blue coat, knitted wool hat; blazer and boater; plus games clothes). Lively and cosy. Collection time (double-parking) a cracking bore for passing traffic.

Riddlesworth Hall

Diss, Norfolk IP22 2TA
Tel: 01953 681246, Fax: 01953 688124

PUPILS: 150 girls; 80 board, the rest day. (90 in the prep school; 30 in the pre-prep, ages 4–7; 30 in the nursery, ages 2½–4)
AGES: 2½–13
C OF E
FEE-PAYING

HEAD: Since 1991, Miss Susan Smith BA (forties), read Music at Bristol University; previously Director of Music at a Malvern senior girls' school. Energetic, with bags of enthusiasm; also lots of hobbies, including theatre, opera, cookery and entertaining, walking, archaeology, reading, travel.

ENTRANCE: Registration and interview.

EXIT: All over the place, mainly to single-sex boarding schools. Tudor Hall, Benenden and Wycombe Abbey are all popular choices. Also Gordonstoun and Oundle.

REMARKS: A charming posh country school in a beautiful listed stately home with fine plaster mouldings and chimney pieces, and glorious grounds with lovely trees in one of the most unspoilt areas of the country. Bright classrooms in the converted stable block. Startling dome-design pre-prep department (which has its own adventure playground) opened by the Princess of Wales, who was a pupil. The latest addition, from September '96, is the dear little nursery school department, opening in response to popular demand.

A traditional family-feel school (where table manners and being nice to each other matter) with the emphasis on spelling, tables, etc. French from 4+ and Latin from 9 (this is early by many girls' schools' standards), German from 12. There is some setting; remedial help is given where necessary, including EFL for the foreign children (there is a regular flow from Spain). A big emphasis on creative arts – 'The girls adore all that,' enthused one mother.

Strong on extra-curricular activities – flourishing Brownies, masses of pets (belonging to the girls), riding available, also archery, clay-pigeon shooting, plus a terrific indoor swimming pool (huge windows and potted palms), and a super adventure playground – with the declared aim of helping girls develop leadership and team skills plus confidence. Happy and busy in rural isolation.

Rokeby School

George Road, Kingston-upon-Thames, Surrey KT2 7PB
Tel: 0181 942 2247, Fax: 0181 942 5707
PUPILS: 365 boys 949 2366
AGES: 4–13
ALL DAY
C OF E
FEE-PAYING

HEAD: Since 1985, Mr Roy Moody (fifties), MA, educated at Felsted and Clare College, Cambridge. A Classicist, and a keen games player, particularly of real tennis. Quietly humorous, unassuming, charming. Married (his wife is an occupational therapist) with three grown-up children, one in the teaching profession.

ENTRANCE: At 4 (first come, first served) and also at 7, 8 or 9 via tests. Put names down early.

EXIT: King's College Wimbledon in large batches (often with scholarships, also exhibitions); also Radley, Charterhouse, Eton, Epsom, St Paul's, and many other schools besides. A very distinguished record of scholarships.

REMARKS: A super prep school, traditional but also forward-looking. Enviable setting, almost like a country prep, in a very leafy part of Kingston, with golf courses more or less all round. Founded in 1877 and has been going strong ever since. Became an educational trust in the 1960s, and the school belongs to the parents, who, elect the governors – some of them parents and ex-parents. The main building was the childhood home of John Galsworthy – built in the collegiate style in red brick with steeply pointed eaves, and added to and adapted often; a large number of newer buildings. Good facilities throughout, including two new Science labs with good space and light; strong Design and Technology.

Loads of specialist teachers, and specialist teaching rooms for the top two years. 23 per class maximum. Scholarship class for the last two years. High expectations all round and boys work hard, with formal teaching and regular testing – 'The boys thrive on it,' said a father. Heavy emphasis on Maths and English through all stages. Latin for all from 8/9, and there is always a clutch of clever boys doing Greek too. The Head keeps a Red Book where pupils' names are recorded for exceptionally good work. Cups and prizes for just about everything. 'The school is best for the brightest boys,' commented the mother of a middle-of-the-road child, wistfully. But remedial help is on hand and – unusually – speech therapy, 'particularly useful at the junior stage' says the Head.

Good food provided by a catering family. Parents are busy running bookshops, second-hand clothes and lost property, etc.

Unusually lively debating society, the Athenaeum, is organised and run by the boys. There is a good range of well-attended after-school activities – Judo, music groups, etc. Sports hall and Astroturf on site, and two large split-level playgrounds at the back of the school where the boys roar about – occasional reports of 'too much and a bit rough' from parents of (delicate?) boys reach us. Super sports grounds nearby, and the school is keenly sporting – with lots of Saturday matches. Ambitious theatre and good Music: regular singing competitions, three choirs, and small groups playing to the rest of the school. A record for gaining Music scholarships to senior schools is building up nicely. A new music room is one of the most recent additions.

The pre-prep is self-contained and purpose built, with its own playground plus adventure playground. It appears to produce cheerful and fearless chaps. Junior Rokeby has its own Principal, but Mr Moody is the Head of the whole enterprise – and he is one of the breed that knows all his boys, no mean feat with 350 of them.

St Anselm's

Bakewell, Derbyshire DE4 1DP
Tel: 01629 812734, Fax: 01629 814742
PUPILS: Around 100 boys, 50 girls. About two-thirds board.
AGES: 7–13. Also pre-prep of about 30 boys and girls, ages 4–8
C OF E
FEE-PAYING

HEAD: Since September 1994, Mr Richard Foster BEd, from St Luke's, Exeter (early forties). Previously Deputy Head of the school and before that Head of Pembroke House, Kenya (a school which has produced two heads for English preps in the last three years). Married to Rachel, who helps run the school with him, they are in charge of all the boy boarders. Three young children.

NB All but one of the governors have (had) children in the school.

ENTRANCE: By registration.

EXIT: Impressive scholarship and exhibition list – to Repton, Oundle, etc. Children also go to Wrekin, Cheltenham Ladies', Radley, Uppingham – and all elsewhere.

REMARKS: The site is tucked up behind Bakewell church, with well-designed purpose-built blocks overlooking fields of sheep and cows. The school is only on to its fifth Head since it started in 1888 – this gives the place a totally family feel and the Head's house is practically in the middle of the school, with toys and treasured possessions scattered about. There are three girls' boarding houses, all run by married couples, with small groups of children in them. The general appearance of the school has been considerably upgraded since we last wrote.

The school has a record of academic success that is outstanding (given the mixed intake) – partly attributed to the staff-pupil ratio, with classes of a maximum of 10, and partly to that precious commodity which boarding schools have in abundance: time. The heavy schedule is, the Head admits, much harder on the day children. Busy schedules with well-designed trips to France, a super school newspaper *The St Anselm's Advertiser*, very jolly plays, serious Music (Music scholarships to Uppingham, Repton and St Mary's Ascot in '95). Pupils are the children of doctors, lawyers, and farmers and also some ex-pats.

Dedicated and gentle staff, including Classicists and linguists, not to mention the Head of Maths, who is an English rugby cap (which he got while at the school).

The school has a computer room and is terrifically keen. Pottery outstanding, with the wife of one of the masters coming in to inspire and direct.

The school is streamed after the first shake-down, but St Anselm's definitely does not force feed. Philosophy pervades to learn what trying is – 'when you are 40 down in a match . . .' Sport on 'only' four afternoons a week; options otherwise. Main games are rugby, football, hockey and 'mad keen' cricket.

The school deserves to be better known. 'Good at getting the less academic up and running,' said a neighbouring Headmaster.

St Anthony's School

1 Arkwright Road, Hampstead, London NW3 6NP
Tel: 0171 435 0316 Fax: NONE

PUPILS: 270 boys
ALL DAY
AGES: 5 (from September 1996) –13.
RC BUT OTHERS WELCOME
FEE-PAYING

HEAD: Since 1994, Mr Nigel Pitel BA (Oxon), PGCE (thirties), a Historian, educated at Ampleforth and Oxford, married with two daughters and a son. Takes over from his uncle, Tim Patton, who reigned for 32 years. Nigel joined St Anthony's in 1986 and has been Joint Head since 1992. Earnest, committed and caring. Pledges to continue his Great Grandfather's ethos 'that learning must be fun'. Being watched with interest.

The school is privately owned, and Nigel is the fourth-generation Headmaster. Tim (jeans and tie, balding, bearded and pony-tailed) has transferred his shares into the Trust, and is taking off to 'blow fire and run Street Theatre in Ireland'.

ENTRANCE: Currently interviews take place two terms before arrival, but entry age has been dropped to five. Boys admitted at any time if place available, and come from as far away as Islington, though most are fairly local.

EXIT: Primarily to London Day Schools – University College School, Highgate, Haberdasher's Aske's, St Paul's – and only occasionally to boarding schools (Harrow and King's Canterbury in 1994; almost never to 'proper' prep schools).

REMARKS: The school is split between the junior school (to 9) in Fitzjohn's Avenue, and senior school in Arkwright Road, nearby. Marvellous facilities for a London school: a heated and covered swimming pool, good CDT, fish pond, and lots of play area.

Plans were underway at the time of writing, and are due to be completed by the time we go to press, which will expand the Junior Dept, remove the Portakabins, extend the dining area (smelling rather strongly of cauliflower when we visited), and turn Tim's flat into classrooms.

The school is very firmly a jeans (with tie) place – though Nigel is introducing grey trousers in junior school – 'but in no way will we become a grey school'. Special coaching for dyslexics can be arranged and is done at school.

Academically, children are stretched. Teaching is imaginative and streamed at the top. Staff are known by their first name, and classes are called e.g. '6G' = Six Gerald. No bells ring. 'Guys' get a huge choice of extra-curricular activities (chess, stained-glass making, producing their own 'playettes'); hobbies, with 24 different activities, are after school and are on offer on different evenings of the week. Boys have their horizons broadened and their 'minds blown with the excitement of it all': currently masses of mime and theatre, with art in all directions intermingled with a serious 'strong moral and spiritual dimension'. Senior boys compose their own prayers; mass is celebrated at school three times a term.

The school has a strong anti-bullying policy, and there is a great emphasis on self-motivation. Both sex education and the 'major survey on Pot, Speed, the Barbiturates, Cocaine, Acid and Heroin' are detailed in the Prospectus.

The curriculum is currently being revamped but Nigel has no thoughts of drastically changing this most unusual school. The staff, many of whom are Irish Catholics, have a Rock Band, and musical happenings are known as GAWs or Groove Awhiles.

Sisters can only be green with envy.

St Aubyns

Rottingdean, Brighton, Sussex BN2 7JN
Tel: 01273 302170, Fax: 01273 304004

PUPILS: Around 110 boys, approx 75
board, 35 day
AGES: 7–14. Plus own pre-prep with
about 25 children.
C OF E, NON-DENOM
FEE-PAYING

HEAD: Since 1974, Mr Julian James,
IAPS Diploma, Cert Ed (fifties),
educated at Charterhouse. Three sons;
wife Hilary works in school. Lives in
Tiggywinkle-type house in the grounds
of the school. Dedicated professional,
with a particular understanding of what
makes children tick. At school as both
man and boy: was a pupil here and came
back to teach when he left school.
Follows up news of Old Boys with keen
interest, and comments: 'We have been
particularly thrilled to have received such
good reports of our leavers at the end of
their first term at public school.'

ENTRANCE: By assessment, interview
and report from previous school.

EXIT: Eastbourne and St Edward's
Oxford have been popular choices
recently, otherwise spread about, with a
handful to Eton, Winchester, Radley,
Stowe etc. Reasonable record of scholarships.

REMARKS: Sad to report, changes are
afoot: all set to go co-ed from
September 1996, and the pre-prep (which
opened in September '95) is now set on
course, building up from the bottom,
having started by taking 4-year-olds only.
Initially a dormitory was taken over for
the tinies' classroom, but as we write the
school is putting up its own pre-prep
building.

Boys are streamed but not set as the
school is too small – basically, there is one
scholarship class and one CE class all the
way up the school, with 'vertical'
streaming for pushing on the bright ones.
Good links with France and have French
boys, also Spaniards, in the school. Super
Art, with a good record of gaining Art
scholarships to senior schools.

Children are notably cheerful, outgoing, articulate and enthusiastic. They
call the Head 'Sir', but have a very good
rapport with him. Both Mr and Mrs James
have a great understanding of the lurking
terrors of being sent away to prep school
at an early age – and do everything to
lessen the shock, meeting new boys at
Victoria Station at the beginning of the
school year and making sure that there is a
video, general fun and time to settle in. In
January boys come back at lunchtime (to
avoid the depressing dark) in time for a
pantomime visit.

The school on the edge of the sea
(which is a geographical disadvantage as
far as the catchment area is concerned), in
the village with playing fields rising up the
hillside behind. Super matrons – the
dormitories are a bit Spartan, but immaculate and gleaming, with wonderful
iron bedsteads. Cheerful, seaside wooden
architecture. A slightly grim chapel (the
entire school disagrees with this description), small and full of memorials to
the war dead – but, says Head, 'we are
very proud of our chapel.'

Perkins the dog (a very experienced
operator by this time) is still on hand to
tuck children up in bed at night. Bible and
prayers before bed and a good routine of
winding down and kind thoughts at the
end of the day.

Flexible arrangements on boarding to
suit parents and individual boys. Saturday
morning school and Saturday afternoon
games for one and all; the school is proud
of the sports record. Do not be put off by
humble surroundings and a slightly old-

fashioned feel. If pastoral care and an understanding of young children is what you are looking for, it is well worth considering.

St John's College School

Grange Road, Cambridge CB3 9AB
Tel: 01223 353532, Fax: 01223 315535

PUPILS: Around 260 boys, 180 girls. 50 boy and girl boarders, 390 day
AGES: 4–13
C OF E
FEE-PAYING

HEAD: Since 1990, Mr Kevin Jones (late thirties) MA, plus an unfinished thesis on how best to acquire knowledge and preserve creativity. Educated Woolverstone Hall (state boarding) and Caius Cambridge. Previously Deputy Head in the school and before that Head of Drama and English at the Yehudi Menuhin School. Married with one son – in the school – and one wild toddler. A thinker, good with children. Worthy successor to the great previous Head, Mr Mould.

ENTRANCE: The Cambridge prep. Name down from embryo on. No testing at 3+ ('ridiculous') – but test at 7. Yearly scholarships for up to five boy choristers a year. Means-tested scholarships and bursaries at 11+ for outstanding academic, musical, artistic or all-round ability.

EXIT: Every year gets a clutch of scholarships to strong Music schools – Eton, Uppingham, Winchester. Also gets academic scholarships and awards. Feeds The Perse School in Cambridge,

also sends pupils to Oakham, Westminster, Harrow, Radley, Tonbridge, King's Canterbury, Oundle, and one or two East Anglian schools. About half the girls leave at 11+, usually for The Perse Girls' and St Mary's Cambridge; the rest generally opt for co-ed boarding at King's Canterbury, Oundle, Oakham.

REMARKS: Wonderful prep school – well worth bustling about to get in. It feels like a honeycomb of schools – the kindergarten department is in a separate house, 'so it feels like home'; 5–8-year-olds are in a wing of the smart, tailor-made Byron House which was refurbished and reopened in 1990 (to replace a multitude of Portakabins) and provides not only classrooms, but a smart hall/gym, Drama Studio, DT, and a Music department for the tinies. A bit of a squash. Older pupils are in a house next door; boarders live above the shop with their own private, recently refurbished and upgraded quarters – part of the £1.5 million building development (you name it, they've now got it, from an indoor swimming pool, to a junior library and a new Music School, the latter not completed at the time of writing).

Claims to have (and we would not dispute it) the best computer facilities of any prep school: a network of 25 PCs housed in a new building on the senior site, and a network of BBCs for the 4–9-year-olds. More importantly, the school has the staff to go with them. Recognised as a National Expert Centre for all prep schools for Design Technology and Information Technology.

The present Head's aim is to 'meet the individual needs of each child, so the most (and least) able children get what they need'. With that in mind he has come up with a number of developments: study skills (teaching children the skills of individual learning) are now an integral part of the curriculum; an advanced tutorial system, with one member of staff responsible for 'knowing all there is to know' about no more than ten children and their families; a reporting system that allows parents to be 'fully involved' in their children's education. There is also an 'individual needs department' – qualified specialists backed by an educational psychologist on staff. Approximately 20% of pupils at any one time receive help with a 'learning difficulty', but, having said that, the academically weak would struggle with the hotshot children of dons, government ministers, etc. 'It really is pressured,' observed a parent.

Classes are never more than 20 and these are subdivided in senior years to make classes of 12–18. High calibre of teachers who draw all that is best and most original from pupils. School has super, steady, rock-like houseparents – Liz and Simon Hickes (he is a recently published author of children's picture books). Jolly red uniform.

Choristers are under the tutelage of organist Christopher Robinson. Terms now fit in with other schools and not university terms as hitherto. Most helpful, flexible school day and week includes weekly boarding, 'day' boarding (i.e. until 8.15 p.m.) and 'staying on' (until 6.00 p.m.) – a miracle for working parents. No longer Saturday morning school, but sports coaching and optional activities.

Not a professional games school, but has lots of sporting options including real tennis and rowing (has produced national real tennis champions). Also the usual sports – rugby, hockey (for the girls).

St Peter's Eaton Square Primary School

Lower Belgrave Street,
London SW1W 0NL
Tel: 0171 730 8855, Fax: 0171 259 9174

PUPILS: Intake 30 each year to the Nursery and 38 per year to the Reception Class
ALL DAY
AGES: 3–11
C OF E
STATE

HEAD: Since 1992, Mr J Wright BEd in Education with Geography and Mathematics (forties). Previous career in state system in London Borough of Merton and in Beaconsfield. Keen on music, especially opera, also on theatre and travel. Fantastically efficient and makes a real point of knowing his pupils, his staff and the parents well. Keen on 'the corporate ethos' and has a real talent, said one teacher, for getting us 'to work as a team', not to mention encouraging parents to help.

ENTRANCE: Register name after first birthday for the nursery, and after the second for the reception class. Visit school. Priority given to children whose parents attend St Peter's (very high) Church; children with siblings in the school; children whose parents attended the school; children baptized as Anglicans. Always oversubscribed at the early levels, and there is no automatic transfer from nursery to reception classes. Offers are made eleven months before a pupil is due to take up a place.

EXIT: To local state schools, particularly Greycoat Hospital, St

Marylebone School, Lady Margaret's, Westminster City, Pimlico, London Nautical. 30% to private schools – JAGS, Alleyn's, City of London, St Paul's Girls, etc.

REMARKS: Super central London primary school. Good social mix – everything from duchesses to dustmen and politicians, who make loyal parents and have a good PTA (good fund-raisers, these). Exceptionally committed and dedicated professional staff. Terrific swimming school (uses nearby Queen Mum's Sports Centre pool) – continues to hold all the Westminster trophies and children regularly compete at county level. Good Music, and getting better all the time, with the recent appointment of Kevin Minns, the Head of Art, also now in charge of Music. Keen on computers.

Maintenance of school is supported by London Diocesan Board. Every inch of the school is used, and though the space is tight-ish, by cunning timetabling and doubling-up of rooms for various purposes it doesn't feel too cramped. Maximum class size 30.

Jolly shouts from the playground (playtimes are staggered – a clever move), with a regular supply of mothers overseeing fair play, etc. The newly housed library is again under the management of a rota of mums. Food reported to have improved.

Strong links with St Peter's Church, and the clergy pop in and out. Super nursery opened in 1992 in the crypt of St Peter's church (now tarted up totally following an attack by an arsonist). NB Previous nursery in the crypt was privately run. Morning or afternoon sessions, with groups of 25, with a gem head teacher, a nursery nurse and two helpers – not nothing. Alas, this is (of course) a windowless crypt, but it has lovely 'areas' for different activities.

Drawbacks of the main school are that it is very cramped for space (though NB, many local private schools are even more cramped) while the playground can be horrifically noisy and bursting at the seams at break time. No French or Latin.

Children are not 'pushed' academically – you may consider this a bad or a good thing: ambitious parents may prefer a more hothouse atmosphere.

St Philip's

6 Wetherby Place, London SW7 4NE
Tel: 0171 373 3944, Fax: NONE

PUPILS: Approx 95 boys
ALL DAY
AGES: 7/8–13
RC
FEE-PAYING

HEAD: Since January 1990, Mr H Biggs-Davison MA (early forties), educated St Philip's Downside, Fitzwilliam College, Cambridge, where he read Geography – and came straight back to St Philip's to teach in 1978. Aims to run an 'even more excellent little prep school and develop it, not in terms of expansion but as a place'. Good at recruiting and good with children; open. His wife is the one with ideas.

ENTRANCE: Several tests, but priority is given to Catholics, so intake is more comprehensive than the majority of London preps.

EXIT: A variety of private schools, both day and boarding, including St Benedict's, Ealing, Westminster and St Paul's; Downside, Worth, Haileybury, etc.

REMARKS: One of central London's few Catholic private prep schools and has powerful Catholic patrons (Hume and assorted abbots). Housed in a large red-brick Kensington building which has been ruined by having to comply with fire regulations. Cramped classrooms – even by London schools standards – but the saving grace is a wonderful leafy and muddy playground which runs the whole length of the block, with room for everyone to let off steam.

The top two forms are streamed. Pupils (including the children of restaurateurs, diplomats, MPs) are a riot of different nationalities – Italians, Portuguese, a Kuwaiti, a Japanese – some of whom do not speak English as a first language. Mr B-D is confident, however, that the school has the resources to train these up into the main stream of teaching – 'we have small classes at the bottom of the school and can give them a lot of individual attention – and they catch up very fast'.

Excellent Art – the Art teacher does picture-framing in spare time. Not the smartest school in London, but most parents report it's 'absolutely super, kind and friendly staff' – though there are one or two dissenters to this view.

St Ronan's School

Hawkhurst, Kent TN18 5DJ
Tel: 01580 752271, Fax: NONE

PUPILS: Approx 90 boys and girls. 50% boarders, 50% day
AGES: Main School boys 7–13, girls 7–11
PRE-PREP: 36 boys and girls, ages 3–7
C OF E
FEE-PAYING

HEAD: Since 1970, Sir John Vassar-Smith (sixties), educated at Eton. Charming. Johnny, as he is known, took over from his father, 'Sir Rich' (Bart), and runs the school with his wife, Bobby. Two sons. Voluble, and fantastically experienced, having taught here now for forty years. This has been a family-owned school, but now the Head is poised to retire, first selling off some property to endow the school and changing it into a charitable trust. He tells parents: 'You choose the school, and we'll get him there.'

Headmaster designate is Edward Yeats-Brown (thirties) BA, who was a boy here, and after a spell in the City, taught at Yardley Court where he met his wife Joanna. They have two young children.

ENTRANCE: By interview. No exam, but boys have to be of fairly good standard (if only because of that rash promise); school nonetheless covers a wide ability range. Pre-prep, 'the puppies', now come in at age 3, and there is even a teeny nursery class for 2½-year-olds. Girls can stay up till 11, and this is on girl/parent-driven demand: their numbers in the main school are still token, but will be feeding up from 'puppies'. Pre-prep still under the wing of the highly competent Linda Smith.

EXIT: Pupils go on to a wide range of public schools. In '95 got the second scholarship to Eton, the third at Tonbridge, half-fees scholarship at Sevenoaks (a particularly good year). Lancing is a popular choice, also Bradfield, Sherborne, King's Canterbury and Cranbrook.

REMARKS: A happy and relaxed school, 'It's school in a home,' explained one cheerful new boy. The Head's door is always open and boys pour in and out to use the computers. Nightly games sessions on these – 'We have the best and most expensive,' says the Head shamelessly, 'I know some mothers don't approve, but I think after a hard day's work, boys need to relax . . .' Day boys are included in everything (prep ends at 7.30 p.m. every day) and most demand to board sooner or later. Saturday morning school, and lots of afternoon matches.

Maximum class size 18, average 10–12. Latin is taught as a major subject from early on, with traditional methods of teaching – grammar, syntax, the lot – and exceedingly popular, under Henry Husey who has been teaching here for 25 years. Very flexible classes means mixed ages, with boys moving up at their own pace, and being taught in mixed-ability groups. 'We like it that way, it helps the slower ones, and stretches the staff.' Scholarship class for a possible three years, but may be only one; again mixed ages from 10–13. Children sleep and eat with their own age group.

Impressive red-brick pile, acres of parquet flooring, pleasantly battered and much loved. The splendid one-time ballroom (with sprung floor and painted ceilings) doubles up as theatre, reading room, billiard room, indoor football room, etc. Walls everywhere groaning with photographs of teams down the years, and every leaver's name is enrolled on boards in the chapel. The chapel is used every morning and every evening for ten minutes, and Bible reading is encouraged in bed. Each dorms has a theme, e.g. the nautical dorm has info on morse code, flags and a knot-tying corner.

Strong sports – First and Colts elevens were unbeaten at last check, and the First Seven won the Battle Abbey Shield again. Shooting and golf – school has its own course – also popular.

OBs include Piers de Laszlo and cartoonist Sir Osbert Lancaster, whose Latin master used to tear up his sketches and demand prep instead. Popular with the Services and other professions – 'Volvos, not Rolls-Royces'. The school combines a wonderful family atmosphere with good results and yet is not above

sending for Mum if child is ill and Mum handy.

Currently feels like a boys' school with a few girls in it (which is indeed the case), but this will gradually change as feeder pre-prep grows up.

St Vincent de Paul Primary School

Morpeth Terrace, London SW1
Tel: 0171 828 8834, Fax: 0171 931 7413

PUPILS: Around 280–300
DAY
AGES: 3–11
RC
STATE

HEAD: Since 1986, Mrs Eileen Weller BEd (age not given). Previously Acting Head, before that, Head of St Patrick's Kentish Town. Comments 'The vision of our school is to create a warm, loving, learning environment, to live by the Gospel. And to enable each individual to realise his or her full potential.'

Chairman of Governors – Mrs Garel-Jones – excellent choice; rich Spanish, with five children.

ENTRANCE: Must be practising Roman Catholics.

EXIT: Cardinal Vaughan, The Oratory, St Thomas More, Sacred Heart Hammersmith, etc.

REMARKS: Super primary school in the shadow of Westminster Cathedral, with a large (for Inner London) playground much coveted and occasionally used by other local schools.

Main building designed by Street. Full of local Spanish and Portuguese waiters'/cleaners' children. A large basement means plenty of room for Brownies, etc. Good library. Shot to brief fame when the ex education minister John Patten revealed that his child was here and that he had put her where his job was.

Sandroyd

Rushmore, Tollard Royal, Salisbury, Wiltshire SP5 5QD
Tel: 01725 516264, Fax: 01725 516441

PUPILS: 134 boys; 125 board, 9 day
AGES: 8–13
C OF E
FEE-PAYING

HEAD: Since 1994, Mr M J (Mike) Hatch, MA, AFIMA (fifties). Educated at Wells Cathedral School, and Trinity College, Oxford. Mathematician; keen cricketer. Previously Housemaster at Sherborne, before that was at King's Canterbury. Married to Christine, who has pursued her own teaching career, and now teaches here; two grown-up children, one a teacher.

ENTRANCE: Requires fluency in reading, writing and arithmetic, assessment nine months before entry.

EXIT: Radley, Sherborne, Bryanston, Marlbrough regularly, also Harrow, Eton, Stowe, Winchester, Charterhouse, etc.

REMARKS: Has survived its trauma remarkably well (the previous Head left following a sex scandal). According to one and all, the situation was handled with speed and skill by the governors and helped by the loyalty of parents.

A traditional prep school run on family lines in the Pitt-Rivers family house, with open fires (well-guarded) and the marvellous long hall which is the focus of school. Benches for all and super oak furniture everywhere, while the grounds (70 acres in the middle of the Rushmore estate) are *beautifully* kept. The boys are terribly polite, say 'Sir', and stand up as soon as you appear; table napkins and firm discipline – punishments include 'sweeping out boot room', emptying bins or being deprived of free time. Several boys keep their ponies here (the stables have been rebuilt), have pets, bikes and gardens. Day boys introduced in '95 (all at the lower end of the school), maximum of 10 – a sign of the times, previously there was an over-my-dead-body attitude on this.

The whole school is under the same – somewhat sprawling – roof, with a super swimming pool built to celebrate the school's centenary in 1988. Computers all over, CD-Roms, strong Art, very good Music (three choirs, orchestra) and Drama booming. Vibrant CDT department. God important; boys attend chapel (recently revamped) five days a week. Delicious food. Busy on the sports fields (boys often play seven days a week), and regularly successful.

Remedial teaching (for about 20%), two teachers, but otherwise classes streamed after two years. Some new staff in key positions. Maximum of 15 per class (staff pupil ratio of 1:7). Senior boys spend their final year in a separate wing, in study bedrooms ('It's great!' they agree), with their own common room area, computer, telephone etc.

Good social mix. Strong army links; most children from Wessex, 10% OBs' sons. OBs include the Lords Avon, Carrington, Snowdon, also Sir Ralph Fiennes and Sir Terence Rattigan.

Sarum Hall

15 Eton Avenue, London NW3 3EL
Tel: 0171 7942261, Fax: 0171 4317501

PUPILS: 162 girls (including pre-prep)
ALL DAY
AGES: 3–11
C OF E
FEE-PAYING

HEAD: Since 1984 Lady Smith-Gordon BEd (fifties), former Head of Garden House. Smart, jolly and firm.

ENTRANCE: No tests. First come, first served.

EXIT: Mainly to day schools – all the north London ones, e.g. North London Collegiate, South Hampstead High, Queen's College Harley Street, Francis Holland, Channing; also Haberdasher's Aske's, St Margaret's Bushey; smaller numbers to boarding schools such as Wycombe Abbey, Downe House, Cheltenham Ladies' College.

REMARKS: Solid small school which grounds the girls well in all the basics. There is a strong emphasis on reading and also the learning of poetry. Senior schools remark on the fact that girls arrive well-taught and keen, which speaks volumes. 'We are ambitious for them,' says the Head, but pressure appears minimal.

Physical education (gym, games or dancing) every day. The garden play area covered with sensible rubber flooring, contains a netball court doubling as four short tennis courts.

The school moved in September '95 (further down the road) to what is currently London's only new purpose-built private preparatory school for girls. It also opened its own pre-prep for boys and girls in this new building.

Summer Fields

Oxford OX2 7EN
Tel: 01865 54433, Fax: 01865 510133

PUPILS: 251 boys; 238 boarders, 13 day
AGES: 8–13
C OF E
FEE-PAYING

HEAD: Since 1975, Mr Nigel Talbot-Rice, MA (fifties), contracted until he is 60. Nicknamed Small but Nice, also Talby. A five-star head and a real pro – particularly on the Eton feeding front. Educated at Charterhouse and Oxford (read History). Wife Joanna runs a Sunday school (for the staff's little children) amongst other things; five children, mostly grown-up, two in the teaching profession. The school's first married head since 1939 (had the Head's house built as well as many other buildings, extensions, improvements). 'The school is my life' – taught here for ten years before becoming Head. Immensely efficient, keeps his eye on absolutely everyone and everything, pursues excellence in all aspects of work and play, and minds like mad about manners. Widely considered to be one of the most able Heads in the business, he knows all the boys well, and most of their families, too. Firmly refutes criticism that the school is an academic hothouse.

ENTRANCE: Put names down early: this is one of the very few boarding prep schools that remains full and with a waiting list despite the national anti-boarding trend. Parents seen when boys are six 'Parents get weeded out if they won't fit in'. Once a very upper-class establishment, now a mixed bag with a lot of 'Fulham Aga parents – do you know what I mean?' said a parent. Entry assessment two terms before the boys are due to join the school.

EXIT: Eton feed – 60% here (excellent tradition of scholarships, 5 or 6 per year, annually celebrated with feasts on the lawn); also to Radley; occasionally to Winchester; some regularly to Harrow and Stowe.

REMARKS: Hugely successful and happy school that hums with energy and enthusiasm. Founded in 1864, and set in 60 acres (feels less) in the suburbs of north Oxford, the main building is a large bow-windowed house with many additions, almost all of them attached. Facilities are exceptionally good, including the newest, the Wavell building, large and light, for Art (which is outstanding), Science, and Technology, and an IT room – the school now has 32 computers, including 16 with CD-Rom. Brilliant equipment everywhere and the just completed sports hall is splendid, with a rifle range, three squash courts, two fives courts, and a climbing wall. There is an outdoor theatre and the former gym has now been converted into a theatre and concert hall.

Elsewhere classrooms are bright and light (16 per class), and teaching is evidently a pleasure both to the teachers and the taught – curiosity, interest and a desire to learn is the norm, as witness the sparklingly lively boys. Not all are geniuses by any means; there are plenty of the average as well as the very clever, and all of them are fully stretched. The school is particularly good at gearing up the less academic and getting them in to Eton. Boys are competitive, but not un-pleasantly so; work and play is very carefully monitored with lots of tests, lots of homework. Scholarship classes are set apart for the last two years, and there is almost invisible streaming from the start. There is a strong emphasis on reading (the main library is very grown-up, more like a public school) with two reading periods per day, one after lunch, overseen by hovering masters, the second before lights out. There are very few female teaching staff, but handfuls of very pretty very young matrons – wowing fathers and staff alike. A good-looking housemaster wows the mothers.

Chapel plays a major role (keen organists nip in to practise whenever they can); the altar cloth is embroidered with what could be taken as the school's motto: 'A good seed brings forth good fruit.' Staff are of a notably high calibre: Mr Talbot-Rice is a good picker (and stands no nonsense), very much a team effort.

Recent addition is the use of a château (near Cherbourg) – boys' visits build up from short to longer stays as they go up the school. Summer Fields staff accompany them over, and a former senior master and the Head of French and his wife remain with the boys during their stay.

Sport is extremely strong. 'We don't mind if we don't win, but we usually do.' Almost undefeated cricket, rugby, soccer. An indoor and outdoor swimming pool allows the boys to swim every single day, and there is a 9-hole golf course and a splendid adventure playground – 'You name it, it's there and the boys do it full throttle,' said one parent who knows his son finds holidays and home offer rather less. Music and drama are also remarkably strong.

Cosy homely dorms have individual bedside lights and wallpaper. The fine dining hall (where the food is good – sausage and mash highly recommended) has portraits of the great and good, mostly old boys, including Macmillan and Lord Wavell. The news (recorded at 6 a.m.) is broadcast daily at breakfast time. Day boys ('whose numbers will not increase,' says the Head) are often dons' sons. Exeats have recently been slightly increased, to general cries of delight.

This is, without doubt, one of the strongest prep schools in the country. For the boys, this is where networking begins.

Sussex House

68 Cadogan Square, London SW1X 0EA
Tel: 0171 584 1741, Fax: 0171 589 2300

PUPILS: Around 175 boys
ALL DAY
AGES: 8–13
C OF E
FEE-PAYING

HEAD: Since 1994, Mr Nicholas Kaye MA (early forties). Read English at Cambridge. Previous post Deputy Head of the school – has been here for yonks. Has also taught in Ethiopia and runs a Trust there. Unmarried. Bags of mother appeal. Rides a bicycle. Ambitious for the school.

A shrewd operator. Keen on Victoriana – and has undertaken tremendous restoration work and renovations to the school's superb red-brick Betjemanesque building, including the magnificent original ballroom. Even keener on music (a serious amateur), and regularly conducts concerts, and directs the St Mary Magdalene Church Music Society (of which Mme Duruflé is President). Lives above the shop, as do one or two other members of staff – a great perk.

NB The school is once again a charitable trust, having been the object of a management buyout, with a parent or two acting as guarantors for part of the loan. The trustees are Mr Kaye plus two ex-parents.

ENTRANCE: Own paper taken at Sussex House, plus interview. NB There has been a major increase in numbers of boys applying since the new developments. Punishing £500 deposit required on entry.

EXIT: Not a feed for anywhere in particular. Boys go on to very wide range of fee-paying schools, e.g., at time of writing, City of London (6), Westminster (3) St Paul's (2), Dulwich (2), Harrow (2) and also Rugby, Eton, Stowe, Latymer, Cheltenham.

REMARKS: A mellow prep school in the wonderful elegant surroundings of Cadogan Square – the lease from Cadogan Estates has been renewed until into the next century; the school also owns an annexe round the corner (usually in need of Jeyes' fluid). Huge upheavals over the last few years: the new Trust is now well established, and major developments have occurred on all fronts.

Since we last went to press, there is a new Science lab and a new computer lab. Recent appointments include the Deputy Head previously at Shiplake (a keen sportsman) and the Head of Mathematics, Mr Donald Duncan from Hawtreys, who now takes – among other things – regular Maths' 'Clinics' for 'those experiencing difficulties' (i.e., you can go and confess you don't understand without fear of holding up the rest of the class). The new Director of Music is excellent. One or two 'retirements' made way for the newcomers.

Teaching is very structured, straight up and down, with 'endless dry tests and repetitions' to quote a dissatisfied parent, though another, satisfied one, commented on the 'endless trouble the school takes to get its weaker candidates up to scratch'. Whatever, all are agreed that CE is never out of sight for long. Maximum class size is 20 – though 16/17 is nearer the average. School has 'modified' streaming in the last year (depending which school the child is trying to get into). French and Latin for all from the start. Pupils are winkled out for extra help 'where really necessary' – given by staff in the school.

The school day ends at 3.45 p.m. (do not go near Cadogan Square at this time – mothers are double-parked and gossiping away). Children mostly local, however, among them diplomats' sons and dual nationalities.

Pupils wear tweedy jackets and carry lunch boxes. Staff also carry lunch boxes. The school is best known for prowess in the fencing world – has the controversial Welsh International Mark Nelson-Griffiths and was invariably National Prep Schools' Champion (beaten in '95); has been London Schools Champion as well. There is a new games programme using nearby Royal Hospital pitches, and FA coaches for the seniors. Games are 'taught', and not just 'taken'. Voluntary football on Saturdays. NB There is no playground, but occasional limited use of Cadogan Square (though absolutely no ball games). Weekly assemblies in St Simon Zelotes round the corner (whose vicar is the school chaplain).

Thomas's

28–40 Battersea High Street,
London SW11 3JB
Battersea branch: Tel: 0171 978 4224;
Fax: 0171 585 0463.
Kensington branch: Tel: 0171 938 1931;
Fax: 0171 937 6782.
Clapham branch: Tel: 0171 924 5006;
Fax: 0171 924 1114

PUPILS: 432 boys and girls in Battersea;
205 boys and girls in Kensington;
approx 350 boys and girls in Clapham
AGES: 4–13 (Battersea); 4–11
(Kensington); 4–11 (Clapham)
ALL DAY

C OF E
FEE-PAYING

PRINCIPALS/OWNERS: Mr and Mrs David Thomas. Whizzo entrepreneurs both, enthusiastic, tireless and courageous; they much deserve their great success. Vice Principal (from September 1996) is Miss Jill Kelham, BEd, previously Headmistress of Thomas' Battersea. The Thomases' son Ben is now Headmaster of the Kensington branch (see below) and son Tobyn is director of administration for all the schools – sorting out transport, maintenance, etc.

Mr Thomas, an ex-Gurkha, is hot on property – the family has acquired three top-class sites. Mrs Thomas is alive with ideas, has an eye for detail and design, and is the one who started it all – in a church hall in Pimlico. NB Involvement of the Thomases means that – unusually in these tricky times – the school Heads can get on with the business of running the school, less troubled by PR and marketing matters.

HEAD: of Battersea site from September 1996, Mr Andrew Sangster, MA, BD, M Phil AKC (early fifties) educated at Dover Grammar School and King's College, London. Has taught in the state sector, also in New Zealand, at Eton, and most recently was Head of St Edmund's, Hindhead. Energetic, enthusiastic, keen on chess and debating. His wife Carol also has long experience of teaching. Two grown-up sons.

HEAD: of Kensington branch since September 1995, Mr Benjamin Thomas BA (late twenties) appointed amid much brouhaha and cries of nepotism. Educated at Eton and Durham University, taught at a school in Lesotho, worked for Barings (but left before it collapsed).

HEAD: of Clapham branch, which opened in 1993, Mrs Carol Evelegh, (thirties), Dip CE (Hamilton), who has been with the Thomases for years, in all their ventures. Fizzy and with a Scottish upbringing, she says she would rather not be described as a Miss Jean Brodie (it's tempting). This school is busy expanding: the top age at the time of writing is 11, and will go up to 13 in two years.

ENTRANCE: Treat the three schools as one school on three separate sites, advise the Thomases (not to mention two kindergartens – one in Pimlico, and one in a wonderful site on the river in a Battersea church crypt). Name down asap (at birth no bad idea) – registration fee of £36; test at 4, exam at 8. Hefty deposit required on accepting a place (£950 at time of writing – not returnable till the child leaves the school and no interest is paid on it). Automatic transfer from Kensington to Battersea at age 11. School 'keen to take siblings – very few turned away'.

EXIT: Some boys leave at 7 and 8 to go to all-boys' prep schools. Otherwise girls go to London day schools or smart boarding, boys mostly to day schools – Dulwich is a popular choice.

REMARKS: The school was founded in 1977 by the empire-building Thomases (see above), and went from strength to strength through the '80s. The main school is now housed in an ex-grammar school on the rat run in Battersea – dignified old red brick, with softening touches of carpets, curtains and flowers provided by Mrs Thomas. The building is large by London prep standards (unlike the Kensington branch, which is two large formerly private houses and has a cosy, more nursery feel to it).

Thomas's was the people's choice for London prep education for many years, not least because, unlike most rival establishments, it was co-ed. Expansion has somewhat dampened this pressure, and other schools have moved in to view.

The energy spent on the latest venture (i.e. Clapham, now going strong) produced a few tart comments about the need to consolidate the existing schools. Since the last edition Thomas's Battersea has been re-organised, and has a new art room, new Physics, Chemistry and Biology laboratories and a large purpose-built Design Technology room. At Kensington, one building was internally gutted and rebuilt. New minibuses with seatbelts. All the libraries have been computerised on the Saint system – 'they're far better now' say parents.

The new Clapham branch is housed in an old girls' grammar school – a magnificent red-brick building which must appear daunting to 5-year-olds coming from cosy nurseries. However, it is made user-friendly inside by elbow grease and inspiration – budding interior designers should take a good look, particularly at the magnificent school hall. Children were initially rattling about here, but numbers have shot up. The grand plan is to build from the base and only those children are accepted who will, according to Mrs Evelegh, benefit from the particular Thomas 'mix' of work and play.

There is an unusually strong PTA. Children get a fairly gentle start to teaching, which is imaginative, with high expectations but more emphasis on non-exam work than usual in London preps, though the day is still highly structured. Projects from 8, French from 5, Latin for all at 9, streaming from 8 onwards. By 8 the only subject-taught classes are French and Science. Around 20 per class. Remedial help is arranged where necessary – both in the school, and out of it.

Lots of extra-curricular activity is fitted into the long school day – ice-skating, computing, ballet, swimming, lots of clubs and far more exercise and sport than at some London schools. Battersea has three-quarters of an acre of playground, with pitches marked out everywhere, a gym, an assembly hall/theatre and many labs (the legacy of the grammar school). Good food.

Lots of enthusiasm and bright, cheerful children. Children are bussed everywhere – the Kensington lot have Science lessons in their last year in the Battersea building – it has better facilities and 'it gets them used to the place for when they move,' say the staff (and children say they are chuffed to be in with the seniors).

Trevor-Roberts

55–57 Eton Avenue, London NW3 3ET
Tel: 0171 586 1444, Fax: 0171 722 0114

PUPILS: 175; 95 boys, 80 girls
AGES: 5–13
ALL DAY
NON-DENOM
FEE-PAYING

HEAD: Principal and founder, since 1981, Mr Christopher Trevor-Roberts LVO (early sixties), educated Bromsgrove, taught at various prep schools and set up (in the '50s) his own tutorial establishment preparing boys for CE. A really keen educationalist, who is convinced that 'self-esteem and confidence are what make for happy children ... Confidence is 80% of learning – perhaps more, it's easily destroyed.' Extremely enthusiastic musician (photographs of well-known musician friends/parents all round his study); he originally trained as a singer. Lives above the shop. His son Simon (thirties, BA,

married with two children) is Headmaster of the junior school and poised to take over when his father retires.

ENTRANCE: Main entry is now at 5 but some places are available at other ages, by interview (children and subsequently parents).

EXIT: Hugely wide range of schools, day and boarding. Most girls stay till 13; co-ed schools are popular for girls.

REMARKS: This has grown since our last edition: the starting age is now 5 (previously it was 8). Despite shedding its original tutorial tag and now officially a prep school with its own pre-prep, it has overtones of a 'tutorial' establishment at the top end. The staff, an unusually close-knit team, are all in the business of getting children excited about their work – and getting them to work. 'In fact, we get them more interested in studying, not just working.' Non-competitive, no orders, no public marks – but half-term reports and all progress exceedingly carefully monitored. Some children arrive here as refugees from other schools where they were wobbled, lost concentration, turned work shy – 'And they get made whole,' commented a mother. Very careful streaming. No form teachers, but subject teachers all the way. All six main subjects are taught every day. The Head is very insistent on children becoming self-reliant, thus for homework there is no notebook, no parental monitoring, no telephoning around.

Computers are housed elegantly against a background of William Morris wallpaper ('We try to make it home-like'), 'but we're very traditional, I expect we should be using computers more,' says Mr Trevor-Roberts.

The school is in a large Victorian house with rooms of a good size (some folding doors open to double the space for plays, assembly, etc); well-designed black folding furniture. Bright dining room and good food.

The paved playground is used for outdoor teaching, and as a theatre, also for games, i.e. basketball and soft hockey (this is not the place for a football-mad boy, though there is now a weekly football club using a local pitch, and it is popular with pupils). No matches against other schools, however. PT every day; swimming (at Swiss Cottage) twice a week.

The most recent acquisition (bought from Eton College, which is at last selling freeholds in this area) is the neighbouring house (previously a school for the blind), used by the junior department – ages 5 to 8. As well as housing their classrooms, Science laboratory, and dining room/gym there is also an Art room and Music room used by the whole school. Music plays an important role throughout the school, and children arrive to piped classical music (the programme is written up in the hall). Also features every morning at assembly with mini playlets, poetry readings, etc.

Twyford School

Winchester SO21 1NW
Tel: 01962 712269, Fax: 01962 712100

PUPILS: Approx 180 in prep school, of which 40 girls; 80 in pre-prep, of which 32 girls
DAY AND BOARDING for boys; boarding house opened for girls September 1994
AGES: pre-prep 3–8; prep 8–13
C OF E
FEE-PAYING

HEAD: Since 1983, Mr Richard Gould (early fifties). Educated Sherborne, Cert Ed. Inspired choice of head by governors; before this post he was stipendiary steward for Hong Kong Jockey Club and before that in the English Jockey Club (though before that was at Summer Fields teaching French).

Comments people 'must come and see us and feel the atmosphere'. Bags of bonhomie, hail-fellow-well-met and nervous energy; five-star sense of humour, which can leave potential parents gaping if they are off guard. Very experienced, very professional. A bit of a showman. Wife Jane helps in school with 'matron, kitchens, that sort of thing'.

ENTRANCE: Children come for a day's informal assessment a year before they are due to come into the prep school. Priority given to boarders, then girls, day boys last (but lots of these).

EXIT: About 10/11 to Winchester, the rest in ones and twos to Radley, Charterhouse, Sherborne, Harrow, Eton, Wellington, St Swithun's, Godolphin, etc.

REMARKS: Currently regarded by locals as probably the strongest prep school in this area and in our opinion it deserves its reputation. An interesting place – dates back to the middle of the seventeenth century, and its current C of E foundation for the 'sons of Middle Class Persons' to 1809 – the school lays claim to being the oldest 'proper' prep school in the country. Riveting history (see *Shades of the Prison House* by the Rev R G Wickham) which the current Headmaster pays scant attention to (though he is strongly supportive of the archives department). Impressive list of OBs, including Hubert Parry, Douglas Hurd. Current pupils predominantly upper and upper-middle class. The school motto *Vince Patientia* has been lovingly translated and engraved above fireplace as 'Dogged as does it', and there is a picture depicting the hare and tortoise (the Headmaster's tie sports a tortoise, the Second Head's a hare . . .).

Streaming into two sets at 10, and into three (scholarship class, middle and the rest) in final year. No class more than 18, smallest 10. Science is taken seriously. French from age 8, Latin for all, Greek an option, other languages may be available, but there again, they may not. One or two old sticks among the staff.

There is a top-class Art department and evidence of pupils' work are displayed on walls cheerfully all over the school. Music is traditionally strong, with three choirs (which sing from time to time in Winchester Cathedral), a jazz band and three orchestras – not bad for a small school. Large, light music room with a soundproof studio, overlooking the playing fields; below it there squats an open-air amphitheatre.

Pleasant 20-acre country site close to Winchester, which includes the original old school hall (wood panelling and the vibes of centuries of schoolboys). Fairly scruffy. Charming chapel. Excellent swimming pool and sports hall; good coaching. Very strong on games for the boys – currently winning too much to begin to list it and all must play something. The Head is very keen that all should have a go; those who aren't much good at rugby, for example, will do 'shinty' – a form of hockey. Cricket in summer (the cricket team toured Barbados in 1994).

Each pupil has a 'tutor' responsible for overall welfare, and keeps the same one throughout. There are weekly sessions with the tutor to record the state of play. The Head is very keen on recording everything – has book in which all matters, great and small, are written up. Eternal vigilance on teasing so that it is not allowed to develop into bullying. Children in houses – Wasps, Mos-

quitoes, etc. All dormitories have been redesigned, refurbished and repainted since we last went to press, and dayrooms (upstairs) include computers, music centres, football games, etc. Pupils on the whole are cheerful, bouncy, casual and the school appears to achieve the delicate balance between learning and allowing boys to be boys with shirts hanging out, etc. The dining hall has long tables and benches – anyone can sit anywhere, but pupils must ask to leave table. Fax machine for pupils to keep in touch with parents (as well as the statutory telephone, of course).

This is a traditional, friendly school which still feels like a boys' boarding school, though it is in fact predominantly day. Girls are still at a rudimentary stage (they were let in around '87 – the Head is a bit hazy about exact dates) – treated as honorary boys and play football, etc.

Walhampton School

Lymington, Hampshire SO41 5ZG
Tel: 01590 672013, Fax: 01590 678498

PUPILS: Around 98 boys, 72 girls (currently 52 boys board, 46 day; 36 girls board, 36 day)

AGES: 7–13, plus pre-prep of about 50 boys and girls aged 4–6+ and nursery of 12 boys and girls

C OF E

FEE-PAYING

HEAD: Since 1983, Mr Andrew Robinson MA (fifties), educated at Repton and read History at Oriel College, Oxford. Previously Head of a co-ed prep in Derbyshire, he has successfully 'weathered the recession'. Introduced – with his wife, Rachel – a nursery in '95. Not a showman, but has flashy eyebrows. Retires in 1997.

ENTRANCE: Either via pre-prep or between ages 8–10. Assessment during year before entry. Children typically come from within one hour's drive from school, plus M3 corridor, south-west London and, increasingly, from the Esso installation at Farleigh (often first-time buyers).

EXIT: To 'Wessex' private schools, especially Bryanston, Clayesmore, Canford, Dauntsey's. A trickle to Winchester (there is a special board in the hall). Girls to Downe House, etc, and, progressively as day numbers mount, to King Edward's Southampton.

REMARKS: A school which still feels like a boarding school, but is now changing its character with a large drop in boarding numbers and a consequent influx of day pupils.

Based in a superb Norman Shaw adaptation of an earlier Queen Anne building; original cornices are still in evidence on a classroom floor. The fabulous 95-acre grounds have climbing frames and two ornamental lakes – Walhampton is regularly the prep school windsurfing champion – plus topper sailing, etc. Pupils can and do bring their own ponies (usually cared for by the owner but ridden by all). Masses of options, IT, lots of sport.

Flexi-boarding is on offer, so that day pupils' parents can park their children in the surplus boarding space; there are also 'boarding in' weeks, when day children are 'invited' to sleep over. Very successful. Excellent pastoral care, with little boys at the Lodge, seniors in the main house and girls in the Clockhouse. Girls' dorms vary from 2 to 13 – not necessarily a happy compromise. Oodles of responsibilities devolve on more senior

pupils via a system of dorm leaders, 'patrols' and 'patrol leaders'.

Maths is streamed at entry to the main school, with scholarship class for 11-year-olds, plus optional Greek. Good remedial help is on offer – children are given support in class or withdrawn – but serious cases are not accepted anyway. Not enough computers in evidence throughout the school; pupils with a new machine in library were totally at sea: 'we're not very good at computers'. Brilliant Music with everyone learning the violin and recorder at 8, and Music scholarships won.

This is a nice, cosy school in beautiful surroundings which needs kicking into the '90s. Three of the current staff are doing MBAs; perhaps could do with some fresh blood.

Wellesley House

Broadstairs, Kent CT10 2DG
Tel: 01843 862991, Fax: 01843 602068

PUPILS: 106 boys, 43 girls. 136 board (including 22 weekly boarders), 13 day
AGES: 7–14
C OF E
FEE-PAYING

HEAD: Since 1990, Mr Richard Steel, BSc (forties), previously Head of York House School. Has young children, and wife (a trained teacher) is 'everybody's mummy'.

ENTRANCE: Interview, occasionally assessment as well.

EXIT: Widespread, and regularly the most popular choices are Eton, Harrow, King's Canterbury, Benenden, Roedean.

REMARKS: Classy and traditional tiny prep school, suffering (as very many others) from the trend away from boarding and from its geography. But it continues to get good results without pushing the children (fairly rare).

Sunny red-brick buildings set in 15 acres of manicured games pitches surrounded by the suburban sprawl of Broadstairs, and one mile from the sea. An adjacent property recently purchased for IT purposes and the subject is now included on the timetable. German is now an option. Good facilities include a heated indoor pool, also an impressive Music, Art and Pottery complex. Lots of hobbies/activities: wonderful carpentry, keen sewing, extra music, current affairs. The library has been refurbished and re-equipped since the last edition.

Excellent games/sports, with especially strong cricket: for the third time in four years Wellesley won the National Prep School Under 13 knockout championships in 1995. Also keen golf (a pro from Sandwich comes weekly).

Girls have their own house across the games field, cramped, cheerful, and very feminine. Dorms throughout have been refurbished and beds painted in bright colours. There is also an animal complex. Children are friendly and chatty; the school is popular with City and establishment parents. Small school atmosphere with lots of charm. Good reports reach us from parents. The chapel is used every morning.

Westbourne (Preparatory) School

50–54 Westbourne Road,
Sheffield s10 2QQ
Tel: 01142 660374, Fax: 01142 670862

PUPILS: Around 165 boys
ALL DAY
AGES: 4–13
NON-DENOM
FEE-PAYING

HEAD: Since 1984, Mr Colin Wilmshurst BA from Open University (fifties), promoted from assistant, formerly at Crawfordton House (his father-in-law started Crawfordton and Mr Wilmshurst was a pupil there). Studied educational psychology and the arts. Qualifies for all the adjectives used to describe a good Head – friendly, approachable, experienced, with understanding, full of good ideas and much liked by the boys and the locals.

Hobbies: archaeology, model cars and ancient postcards. Mrs Wilmshurst used to help in the school but is now a psychotherapist outside the school. Mr Wilmhurst's study is a caricature of a prep school Head's study – lots of trains and toys within easy reach, a big untidy desk, pictures of his holiday cottage, etc.

Some loyal staff – 6 people represent 110 years of service at the time of writing.

ENTRANCE: First come, first served. Interview with Head and form teacher.

EXIT: Six scholarships in '95 (about par for the course) – to Repton, Gresham's, two to Trent, Birkdale, St David's. Most boys used to go on to public school, now increasingly they are headed for local schools as well.

REMARKS: The best 'proper' boys' prep in Sheffield and indeed for miles around. The atmosphere is a good mix of friendliness, fun and hard work. Outstanding French language teaching – formerly from age 8, but French *assistants* come into the lower school, and start informally, speaking nothing but French in class most of the time (immaculate accents). Latin from age 10, 'even if dyslexic'. Mixed ability intake, with no streaming until 11 – one class intake before that and 'we're too small to set'. Excellent support staff coach pupils up to standard – used by 'even the brightest', says the Head – for any specific problems. The school has had the National Under 15s Dyslexic Arts Champion for two years running.

There is a pleasant light wing of classes for tinies, with books thoughtfully arranged in tiers at a height which allows a pupil to help himself. The large asphalt playground can get a bit overheated – however, the staff room (with nice cosy old chairs) overlooks it, and a watchful eye is kept. The site is in Sheffield Hallam, on the hill in what has been described as the 'greatest academic concentration in any mile in Europe' – there are two universities within easy reach and countless schools. The nucleus of the school is a large private house, which has sprouted additions. The sign at the school gate now reads 'Westbourne School', which now projects (even if subconsciously) the image of a non-privileged, non-elite establishment (no bad thing in Sheffield, which is David Blunkett's stronghold).

Nice touches – breakfast is now offered to all (including parents) from 8 a.m., which has been a big hit with families where both parents work. Parents are professionals – medics in particular – even the occasional football manager. There are clubs after school and a crèche till 5.30 p.m. The Head has a 'headmaster's surgery' twice a term so people can get at him without having to make an appointment. Every Friday there is a 'good work assembly'. Games is a serious business – with specialist games teacher – on site until the age of 8, then the school uses Sheffield's prestigious Abbeydale Sports Club – every child is an associate member of it.

Westminster Cathedral Choir School

Ambrosden Avenue,
London SW1P 1QH
Tel: 0171 798 9081, Fax: 0171 798 9090

PUPILS: About 95. Choristers (between 20 and 30) board, the rest day
AGES: 8–13
RC
FEE-PAYING

HEAD: Since September 1995, Mr Charles Foulds, BA (early forties). Previously at Stonyhurst in various posts, his last one as Assistant Headmaster with special responsibility for discipline (no mean task). Easy to get on with, outspoken and sensible.

Has three young children, all of them currently at St Vincent's just over the wall. Read Modern Languages at Swansea and Durham; wife, Elizabeth, was at the Royal Academy of Music. When we visited him early on in his Headship here he was holding all his cards clutched to his bosom, commenting 'I am watching . . . if that doesn't sound too . . .' Mr Foulds can communicate with the boys on their own level, and there is every sign that they judge him to be just the ticket.

ENTRANCE: Too many ramifications to explain, but basically by exam and interview at 7+ around Jan/Feb. Choristers have separate entry procedure, with voice trials normally in Feb, and academic assessment at the same time.

Children come from e.g. Eaton House, the Vale, Wetherbys, Falcons, etc. You do not have to be RC to join the school – a third of the school now is not (but NB all choristers are RC).

EXIT: A pretty catholic (joke) mix, mostly of middle-ranking public schools, both RC and not. In '95 didn't do so spectacularly in scholarships, but in previous years there has been an outstanding collection of music scholarships, mainly to RC schools, but also to Eton, Harrow, occasionally to Highgate.

REMARKS: In our previous entry we reported that reports from disgruntled parents made it difficult to comment. This produced a snowstorm of letters from very gruntled parents protesting that the place was tiptop in all respects, and socially smart to boot. We stand corrected.

The cramped school buildings with a tarmac playground are umbilically linked to Westminster Cathedral (you can get through to the school via a little door behind the high altar). The library – which was criticised in the Ofsted report – belongs to the Cathedral, and as we write it does feel very dusty, full of old tomes and not in the least boy-friendly. The other criticism from Ofsted concerned the IT provision – compared with switched-right-on prep schools it is almost non-existent.

Apart from these matters of fine tuning, it's all go. Enthusiastic, confident boys get endless practice standing up and performing (musically) in front of adults. The school has a super chaplain. Excellent French; the most terrifyingly imaginative pictures line the walls on the way to the Art department, depicting in black chalk monks with ecstatic obsessed faces, but when you get to the art department it's jolly, light and has the requisite model aeroplanes swinging from the ceiling. Teaching is traditional in nature (indeed, some have said it is over-traditional). The biggest class is 22, the smallest 17. As boys move up the school there is 'some streaming'. There are games twice a week (three times a week for the tinies) and the school has some use of Vincent Square.

The choristers have the usual horrendously long day, which they appeared to cope with amazingly well. All choristers are boarded in one big light dormitory with bunks – and posters squashed on the walls (not much wall space for each boy). From Tuesdays to Fridays they sing at evensong in the Cathedral, (also twice on Sundays), and this is the most important part of their activities, says the Head. The Master of Music, James O'Donnell, is a genius with the boys, who produce a wonderful, clear, robust and merry noise, though it is difficult to tell the quality of the voices, as the amplification in the Cathedral would flatter a bullfrog.

The choristers obviously overshadow the rest of the school's musical activities – it is, after all, why the place is there – but in the way of many choir schools, most of the rest of the school are dragged up (musically speaking) to a level way above the average and practice sessions go on all day in every cupboard and corner.

The Head has a flat in Ambrosden Avenue (cheek by jowl with MPs) which makes it handy for him to have supper with the boarders and matrons. We agree with him that what strikes you first here is a sense of community. Added to that, a minuscule chapel for the boys and staff right in the middle of the school makes a very definite statement about the priorities of the place. This is still definitely an old-fashioned, traditional prep school on which the Roman Catholic church leans heavily, but the result is a place of strength, warmth, and, particularly in matters of music, excellence.

Westminster Under School

Adrian House, 27 Vincent Square,
London SW1P 2NN
Tel: 0171 821 5788, Fax: 0171 821 0458

PUPILS: 260 boys
ALL DAY
AGES: 8–13
C OF E
FEE-PAYING

HEAD: Since 1992, the Master, Mr G Ashton MA (forties), who came here from seventeen years at Westminster School – where he headed the Spanish department, was subsequently House-master of a day house, then of a boarding house and latterly the Registrar. Married with three school-age children (was a parent at the Under School). Teaches French and Latin to some, reads with the youngest. Busy encouraging more dialogue between parents and school, mingling parents, staff and boys in fêtes, fairs, leavers' celebrations, etc. This hands-on approach is welcomed by parents.

ENTRANCE: Probing and competitive entrance exam (taken at the school), with 150 boys chasing 40 places. (Lists left open until near the exam; no need to sign on a dotted line that you wish your son to proceed to Westminster School, 'the Great School'.) At 10+, 20 boys (via exam) from state primaries (occasionally from private schools). NB No plans to lower entry age to 7, 'Unless we were to move to larger premises and start a pre-prep.' Some boys travel for miles, as the map in the school hall shows.

Eight assisted places at 10+ (which pupils may carry through to Westminster School – but nowhere else). Music bursaries of up to half fees to incoming boys at 10+ or boys of that age already in the school.

EXIT: 48 out of 60 typically go on to Westminster School – and the percentage is creeping up. The others go to Eton, Winchester, Radley, Wellington, City of London, Dulwich. Approximately 8 boys sit the Challenge and 3 or 4 usually gain Westminster scholarships.

REMARKS: Marches strongly on. One of the two top London boys' academic prep schools. Exceptionally high standards of teaching throughout, including outstanding English under Mrs Gillian Howarth (ex-wife of MP Alan). There is a terrific emphasis on reading, with inter-house competitions, boys declaiming poetry and prose ('Rather old-fashioned,' said the Head half apologetically).

Sciences and Classics are also immensely strong: the boys' developing intellectual curiosity is satisfied and fed. Acorns everywhere (and squirrelled away, of course, in the computer room), with older boys, totally computer literate, belting out sophisticated projects. The 10-year-old entry is kept apart in order to catch up with French (this is the beginning for many), though the whole school starts Latin at this stage.

Two scholarship classes (15 in each) are chosen and set aside in the last two years only; up till then classes work on parallel lines, with a minimum of streaming (relatively gentle start). Many more than will actually get scholarships (but will sit the exams nonetheless) are part of the scholarship classes, 'because many boys can profit from advanced teaching', and CE would seem humdrum. (Also Westminster and Eton like this arrangement as it gives them a better insight into boys' potential.)

Music is of a high quality, with lots of it: it occupies the entire basement, there is a Head of department plus an Assistant Head, and 20 peripatetic teachers. Free violin or cello for first-year boys. There are junior and senior choirs and orchestra, a jazz ensemble, chamber group, etc, and the school provides choristers for St Margaret's Church. Boys regularly win music scholarships to Westminster. Lovely Art and pottery, and incredibly enthusiastic Drama performed in an eyesore of a hall.

Over the road is Vincent Square (shared with Westminster School), the envy of all central London preps and used daily for breaks. (The Head is desperate to build an adventure playground, because boys must keep off the playing fields or it would be a mud bath.) Twice-weekly games sessions – 'Not enough sport' is a regular complaint. Weekly swimming and PE.

The school building (previously a hospital) is well loved, well worn, well used. Dingy basement hall for dining, plays, etc. During lessons you could hear the proverbial pin drop; out of lessons, the place shakes with noise, rush and high spirits. Occasional grouse from parents, who are liberal with praise on the academic front, that the boys don't 'absorb much social polish at school'. Parents are a complete mixture of well-off and badly off, public school and first-time in the fee-paying sector.

Extra-curricular activities are a big strength – the school is very strong on outings and trips (exchange with a school in Marseilles, annual trip to Pompeii, camping in the Lake District, one-offs, e.g. bicycling in Holland, safari in Zimbabwe – all the results of staff enthusiasms and receiving strong support from parents and boys). Sophisticated debating at the top of the school. Being

bright is not enough: robustness is an essential ingredient for boys here. Some reports of bullying reach us. And: 'The school does not care what happens outside the school gates,' said a parent, though many would disagree.

Winchester House School

Brackley, Northamptonshire NN13 7AZ
Tel: 01280 702483, Fax: 01280 706400

PUPILS: 75 boys, 59 girls; 93 boarders, 44 day pupils.
AGES: 8–13. Plus pre-prep with 95 boys and girls, ages 3–7
C OF E
FEE-PAYING

HEAD: Since 1975, Mr D R Speight (pronounced Spate), MA Oxon (late fifties), contracted until 2002. Educated at Stowe then Christ Church. Came to this school (where he was a pupil) from Oxford; previously Assistant Headmaster, i.e. has been here as man and boy. Teaches History (eight lessons a week to the top end). Fun, not married, sitting room filled with comics and tapestries (done by his mother), reckons 'to know all the children well'. Flat-coated retriever Satchmo accompanies him everywhere and tucks pupils up at night.

ENTRANCE: All three terms. Day pupils move up via pre-prep, others come for an informal test ('we walk round the school and do a spot of reading and 'rithmetic'). Most boarders come from within 100-mile radius (including Lincolnshire and London); a few from abroad.

EXIT: To schools within 100-mile radius, especially Rugby, St

Edward's, Oundle, Uppingham, Rugby, Stowe, Bloxham, also Malvern, Winchester and Eton. A good collection of awards over the years.

REMARKS: Traditional co-ed prep school with its own thriving pre-prep, comfortably set in a converted Victorian hunting lodge with a chapel and (mini) billiard room/library in an earlier Tudor building. The school was founded in 1876 and moved to its present site in the town of Brackley in 1923. God is very important: prayers each morning are followed by 15 minutes' religious instruction in the classrooms. Sound teaching on all fronts, with strong Classics (including Greek for the brightest) and good French and Maths. Some setting. There are two remedial helpers for children with (mild) learning difficulties.

Keen games; athletics meetings here are still a great favourite. A sports hall is under construction. Playing fields over the road include tennis courts, and also the very-well-run pre-prep plus nursery. The new library block (attached to the main building) also houses the IT centre. Art, Music and CDT all popular.

Weekend activities are 'building up nicely,' said a mother – scouting is popular, also boating, orienteering, camping trips to the Peak District, etc. The school appears to have weathered the chill winds of the recession, and has recently had an injection of younger staff, a new Head of Maths and a new bursar. Also, it has had an injection of money – by selling off some property in the high street. Weekly boarding has just been introduced – by popular demand of day pupils. Breeds happy and self-confident boys and girls.

Windlesham House School

Washington, Pulborough, West Sussex RH20 4AY
Tel: 01903 873207, Fax: 01903 873017

PUPILS: 220 boys, 130 girls
ALL BOARD
AGES: 7–13
C OF E
FEE-PAYING

HEAD: From September 1996, Mr Philip Lough (forties) MA, PGCE educated at Sherborne and Trinity College, Oxford. Modern linguist and a keen sportsman, previously a Housemaster at Marlborough. Married to Christine, who is also a linguist, teacher and keenly sporting; they have three children. Succeeds Mr and Mrs Ian Angus who took over from the much-loved Maldens (and were the first ever non-Malden Heads), and lasted but briefly.

ENTRANCE: 25% from London, lots from Sussex and Hampshire, brothers and sisters galore, over 100 children of ex-pats and diplomats – more diplomats' children than any other school in the UK. Entry via interview.

EXIT: To seventy different schools in the last three years, both co-ed and single-sex, with substantial numbers going to Bryanston, Marlborough and King's Canterbury (good scholarship/awards at all these schools), also Eton, Harrow, Roedean, Benenden. Girls occasionally leave at 12.

REMARKS: Has been in limbo, following the sudden departure of the previous husband-and-wife team of Heads, who took over from the long reigning owners, Mr and Mrs Malden. Windlesham was once the flavour of the month and the envy of all other co-ed preps; it has been an outstandingly strong prep school, flourishing in all departments. Much of the teaching is geared to non-examinable subjects, and is co-ed in everything; pupils are set for almost all subjects. IT is extremely strong: this is not taught as a subject ('That way everything gets locked away'), but everyone uses IT where and when appropriate, and staff move round with portables. Children are busy producing the school newspaper ('Boys love doing the layout'), designing it and preparing camera-ready copy. There are two Nimbus network rooms and more computers dotted around.

Strong links with Europe (all 10-year-olds spend some time in France) and one or two foreign children (here for a term or three, and come by word-of-mouth recommendation) get EFL lessons. There is help for learning difficulties ('We don't call it dyslexia, it sounds like a disease'), and staff note more children need this now 'probably because they are less well taught at an early stage'. All do French and Spanish (added at 9), brighter ones Latin at 11/12. Loads of games, lovely Art (strong on textile printing especially), Design Technology. Everyone cooks and sews. 'Sometimes it's a let-down going on to the senior school.'

Super drama – on Open Day all twenty forms put on a play (some outdoors); once a year a production includes every single child in the school. The new Malden Family Theatre is a brilliant piece of design that acts as a Sports Hall most of the time, with fold-away seats (10 mins. to put up), and a floor that opens for a pit orchestra; they can even bring in flying machines for some productions. All manner of activities include yoga (very popular) and dance (boys and girls). Children have a full day – many go home

(exhausted) after Saturday morning school returning on Sundays, but 'if we stay at school we have a very jolly time – sometimes it's more fun than being at home,' say pupils. The parent profile has changed over the years from upper crusty to a mixed bag.

There are large numbers of husband-and-wife teaching staff (9 pairs currently, including the marvellously competent deputies). Despite the large size of the school, it is definitely cosy (bedtime stories are broadcast to tinies nightly, cuddles from matron) and manages a nice balancing act between the informal and highly structured. No uniform. School (and some children) is slightly scruffy to the dismay of some but 'like a well-lived-in much-loved home,' commented one parent. Good follow-up on pupils, right to university level.

The school was founded in 1837 by the Malden family and still run as a family trust; cheques for fees made out to the Malden Family Trust. It is a splendid house set in 60 acres of well-used grounds (lots of staff houses), with games pitches, tennis courts, etc.

Currently being watched with interest, not to mention bated breath – can it recover from its recent upheavals?

Woodcote House

Windlesham, Surrey GU20 6PF
Tel: 01276 472115, Fax: 01276 472890

PUPILS: Approx 100. About 81 boarders, 19 day boys, who 'usually board after a year or so'
AGES: 8–13
NON-DENOM
FEE-PAYING

HEAD: Since 1990, Mr Nick Paterson BA (early forties), educated at Westminster and Exeter University.

Called 'Mr Nick' by one and all. Runs the school with the help of Mrs Nick and his parents, Mr and Mrs Mark, who themselves ran the school for 30 years before him. Mr Nick's grandfather bought the school in 1931 when it was going 'but only just'. It is now a private limited company. Super wife, with older children; one son currently at school here.

ENTRANCE: Send for what is still one of the smallest prospectuses in the country (though Ludgrove and Sunningdale come close), small 'because it is vital they (the parents) come and see us with the boy, and really we must get on pretty well'. School also sends 'little test'. Always prepared to talk to parents right up to the last moment. Takes new boys in at the beginning of all three terms.

EXIT: Widespread – to Wellington as it is close by, also Lancing, Eton, Sherborne, Radley, Milton Abbey, Harrow, Cranbrook, Pangbourne, etc.

REMARKS: Super little school where each boy is carefully cocooned so that the shock of leaving a 'nursery environment' will not be too much. The main problem might be the shock of leaving Woodcote for public school. Exeats every third week, though an ex-pupil commented it was more fun staying at school during an exeat than going home because they did all sorts of nice things like playing golf with the Paterson family. Monthly magazine, keen chess, bridge, fishing, calligraphy.

Set in its own thirty acres, which includes some attractive woods, the main building is Regency and elegant but is delightfully worn at the edges, with additional, modestly built classroom blocks round the back and a charming little chapel across the lawn, made of corrugated iron (painted black) and wooden inside. Uniform duvets in the dorms. A Barbour and/or Husky is part of the uniform, with corduroy trousers and a rather dreary brown sweater.

Lots of golf played (on site), as well as cricket, squash (which uses courts up the road), rugger and shooting. The Head concentrates on placing boys in the school of their parents' choice rather than on getting scholarships. There is a small and very competent remedial unit. One or two gems among the staff include the dynamic Head of Science, and the archetypal schoolmaster, Colin Holman, who is the Assistant Headmaster, has been here for yonks, lives in the lodge and, amongst other things, looks after the grounds lovingly.

A development programme means the school now has a new Science lab, computer centre, new Art and Music block, even new changing rooms (not before time, some might say), as well as new Astroturf hockey pitch/tennis courts.

About one-third of pupils are sons of soldiers or ex-pats (Foreign Office, Gulf, etc), one-third London or local, and one-third from 'far afield', by which they mean Dover. Also one or two Thais (long-standing tie with Thailand, no pun intended) and a few Europeans (by which they mean not British).

One of a dying breed – the family-owned school – and, unlike some, by and large it works. Good reports.

SENIOR
SCHOOLS

Abingdon School

Abingdon, Oxfordshire OX14 1DE
Tel: 01235 521563, Fax 01235 559851

PUPILS: 783 boys, 658 day, 125 board
(including 70 weekly boarding)
AGES: 11–18
SIZE OF SIXTH FORM: 260
C OF E
FEE-PAYING

HEAD: Since 1975, Mr Michael St John Parker MA (fifties), read History at King's College, Cambridge, formerly Head of History at Winchester, and also taught at King's Canterbury and Sevenoaks. Married, with four children. Something of a stickler for discipline, a traditionalist; fondly referred to as 'our eccentric headmaster' by some of his staff. Very fast-talking, humorous but stands no nonsense. Liked by the boys; occasional mutterings about 'high-handed' style of management from parents and staff. Highbrow. Comments that he hopes boys leave here 'Knowing *how* to think' and 'happy with themselves.'

ACADEMIC MATTERS: Strong across the board, with best results in Chemistry, Maths, Art and Music in '95 (67% A–B grades). Classics are small and impressive; also Modern Languages (including Russian – on offer even for 11-year-olds – also Japanese). The Head of Modern Languages is Adam Pettitt, who inaugurated teaching Germanic languages first, Romance languages later. Sciences do well; outstanding performers in the national Physics Olympiad. Economic Business type subjects are hotly pursued. Large classes (around 27), decreasing to 20–21 in GCSE years, but staff are adept at drawing boys in. There is a good general studies programme (non-examinable) for Sixth Form.

A fine new teaching block, (opened September '94) has 15 classrooms and departmental suites (generous help was given by the Mercers Company). The school has stunning hi-tech – a huge IT centre, with all departments making use of it, networking, 6 CD-Roms, plus computers increasingly dotted about classrooms. Teaching is interfaced with research, masterminded by David Haynes, considered to be a 'bit of a whizz'.

There have been several staff changes and additions: a lively bunch, some long-serving (25 years), leavened by interesting new young recruits, among them an ex-City broker already itching to be a Housemaster.

GAMES, OPTIONS, THE ARTS: Rowing is especially strong, and has regular successes. The Boat Club generates huge enthusiasm. Plenty of sport is available (compulsory twice a week right through to Sixth Form) though pupils don't live or die by it. There is a not brilliant (heated) outdoor pool, and a Sports Hall shared with the local community. The school has a strong music tradition with 30 peripatetic teachers, numerous orchestras and chamber groups (National Youth Orchestra, National Jazz Youth Orchestra players), and good choral work. Very successful Young Enterprise teams. Concerts and plays are sometimes put on in conjunction with Headington Girls (qv) and other girls' schools. There is a super theatre. Energetic charity fund-raisers.

BACKGROUND AND ATMOSPHERE: This is an ancient foundation; an ex-Direct Grant school which has grown to become one of the largest schools in the region, and numbers have risen since our last edition. 'We're cheaper than a lot of other schools,' says the Head. Sprawling, red-brick Victorian Gothic, with steep roofs and turrets and new complex built in the vernacular. The latest addition, in executive homes style, Mercers' Court, was built at a cost of £2.5 million, to which the Mercers contributed substantially. This now houses the Head's offices – posho, but are they isolated from the heart of the school, being at the far end? The whole school is psychologically and geographically separated from the centre of Abingdon by parkland.

Morale is high, and there is a terrific sense of purpose. Feels – and operates – like a boarding school (though boarders are a small minority), with Saturday morning school, matches on Saturday afternoons, etc.

Houserooms (some still battered, a refurbishment programme is in hand) are the centres of social life, featuring lockers, toasters, pool tables. Separate houses for day boys and boarders, whose accommodation has much improved with the creation of study bedrooms (singles for Upper Sixth).

PASTORAL CARE AND DISCIPLINE: 'Far more sensitive to bullying issues nowadays,' commented a parent. Thorough pastoral care system, with regular reporting between tutors/housemasters and pupils. Poor work means detention. The Head is keen on pastoral care going far beyond the school gates – advises on Saturday parties, etc and describes parents as 'responsive'.

PUPILS AND PARENTS: Popular with business, Oxford gown, professional and service families, and plenty of first-time buyers. Some computer-sophisticated parents are attracted by the computing facilities. Boys are unpretentious, lively, relatively well-groomed and industrious. There are 40–50 ex-pats and foreigners, including Hong Kong and Malaysian scholars. Boys living over 45

minutes' bus ride away must board. Scores of buses to fetch and carry.

ENTRANCE: An increasingly popular choice for day pupils, particularly at 13. Complicated: at 11 via own competitive exam, at 13 via CE (but boys must also take the 11-year-old exam at the appropriate time). Lots from the Dragon, (a few from Chandlings). 15–20 enter at Sixth Form (including some refugees from more expensive schools, a recessionary plus for Abingdon).

EXIT: 97–100% go on to degree courses, some after a 'gap' year. 20 is the norm to Oxbridge. Engineering is popular, also Geography. There is a slight bias to science subjects.

MONEY MATTERS: Good value; 15 assisted places per year, plus 5 at Sixth Form. Several major and minor scholarships at 13, plus one for Art and Design, one for Music; bursaries.

REMARKS: Jolly good boys' school, benefiting from the national swing towards day schools, and currently riding high, with good facilities, some fizzing staff, producing boys with polish and qualifications.

Alleyn's School

Townley Road, London SE22 8SU
Tel: 0181 693 3422, Fax: 0181 299 2671

PUPILS: 464 boys, 465 girls
ALL DAY
AGES: 11–18
SIZE OF SIXTH FORM: 264
C OF E
FEE-PAYING

HEAD: Since 1992, Dr Colin Niven MA (Cantab), Dip Ed (Oxon), L es L from Lille (fifties). At Dulwich as man and boy. Educated at Dulwich College (he was School Captain) followed by Cambridge, and Nancy University. Then taught in France, at Sedbergh, Housemaster at Fettes and Head of Modern Languages at Sherborne. Also Principal at Island School, Hong Kong, and St George's English School, Rome. Chairman of the European Division HMC, etc. Single, he still teaches Modern Languages.

ACADEMIC MATTERS: The school believes in supporting and stimulating pupils – 'we are pupil centred'. Perceived as Arts-orientated. There are two sets of theatre studies. All three science departments boast published authors amongst their teachers. Dual Award for the majority, three separate sciences for high fliers at GCSE. Classics in the Trinity Group. Everyone does one year Latin, and Greek A-level is available; very successful results for the one or three who do it. French in first year and German and Spanish introduced in second year; bilingual pupils are encouraged to take GCSEs in their own languages (Urdu, Swedish, Japanese, etc).

League table talk: this school has jumped up since '92, from a low starting place. Results are now very good (63.6% A–B grades at A-level in '95); English, Maths, French are all strong, also Theatre Studies, History, Physics. NB Potential parents should ask to see a detailed breakdown of exam results, which lists separately girls' results and boys' results. The Head claims 'We've become more academic without losing the ethos.'

Reports reach us from some disgruntled parents that slack work is not picked up early enough, and that slackness is not immediately reported back to parents.

GAMES, OPTIONS, THE ARTS: One afternoon a week is devoted to sport (in the first and second years, girls and boys have combined games) all in the 20 acres of grounds surrounding the school – including netball round the parked staff cars. There is a Sports Hall and a girls' gym, and sports on offer are badminton, serious hockey, cricket, basketball (very popular), strong netball and fencing coached by Professor Moldovanyi, said to be the last person alive to have seen a duel to the death. The school has a strong swimming tradition, and girls take on JAGS and St Paul's GS and beat them regularly. Voluntary CCF is popular.

Pupils can also engage in conservation work, gardening, or helping with handicapped children. Workshop with Primary Schools, and work shadowing in Fifth and Sixth forms.

Fantastic Drama everywhere, particularly popular in the 'bear pit' in the old gym. The Art Department has got all A grades at A-level and GCSE (13 leavers in one year recently went on to art college); terrific pottery. Photography at GCSE. Fabulous Music in a spectacular converted brewery which links with junior school. Recently produced choirboy of the year; some children play in the National Youth Orchestra.

Lots of lunchtime and after-school options, – Railways Society, music, table tennis. The school has a Field Centre at Buxton in Derbyshire. Staff attend regular Institute of Education refresher courses in their subjects (the school keeps a special fund for such training).

BACKGROUND AND ATMOSPHERE: Part of the South of the Thames Trinity group of schools, connected to Dulwich College and James Allen's School via the Elizabethan actor-manager Edward Alleyn under a Royal Charter of 1619. It became fully independent of the other two schools in 1995, (the 375th anniversary of the Alleyn Foundation) and now has its own board of governors, etc. It was a bit in the shadow of nearby Dulwich College until it went fully co-ed in September 1979.

Set in a large Victorian building in South London red-brick surrounded by a higgledy-piggledy collection of purpose-built blocks. Still retains the atmosphere of a direct grant school: committed staff, and intelligent children from a wide variety of backgrounds and nationalities but strictly unsmart.

Fairly laid-back atmosphere but underneath some tight lines; it is an extremely friendly place – and this may be the first thing you observe.

PASTORAL CARE AND DISCIPLINE: There are tutors for all, a strong house system, and good links with the Head, Deputy Head and Head of Lower School (first two years). Staff are deeply caring and committed to pastoral care, attending counselling courses, etc. Drugs on campus means instant dismissal – the school has been known to sack in the run-up to exams on this front – otherwise suspension for fags and booze. Pupils may drive to school with parents' and house master's permission.

PUPILS AND PARENTS: A wide cross-section: 'Loyal following.' 'More Dulwich than Dulwich.' There is an enormously strong Alleyn's Association with a sports club. Some parents really struggle to keep their children here; there are lots of first-time buyers. A huge ethnic mix. Several hundred primary schools have submitted pupils for entrance and pupils have been known to come from as far away as Sevenoaks and Knockholt. The school shares buses with Dulwich College and JAGS. Former pupils include CS Forester, VS Pritchett, Julian Glover and Simon Ward.

MONEY MATTERS: Twelve Saddlers' and Foundation scholarships at 11, one at 13 and another for the Sixth Form. There are 35 Assisted Places in total. Extra bursaries can often be found for genuine cases of hardship.

ENTRANCE: From Alleyn's Junior school (qv), on site. Some from Dulwich Hamlet, and from Wandsworth schools. Approx 550 candidates sit for 130 places at 11. Each child is asked to read a passage and questioned on it; later there are tests in Maths, English and Verbal Reasoning. ('What we are looking for is an enquiring mind and potential. We see all parents too, and there we need support.') Around 10 children are accepted at 13, and 20 or so at Sixth Form Entry.

EXIT: 90% to universities. 9–14 to Oxbridge annually.

REMARKS: This is a good all-round South London school with improving academic results and plenty on offer – still the only major private school in London offering co-education throughout.

Ampleforth College

York YO6 4ER
Tel: 01439 788224, Fax: 01439 788330

PUPILS: 563 boys (all board, except for 3)
AGES: 13–18
SIZE OF SIXTH FORM: 222
RC
FEE-PAYING

HEAD: Since '92, Father Leo Chamberlain MA (mid-fifties). Clear-sighted Father Leo cuts a generous figure 'not unlike Friar Tuck' comments a parent, not unkindly. He has been man and boy at the college since the age of nine (his great-grandfather started here in 1835) with a brief interlude as scholar of University College, Oxford, where he read Modern History (he teaches an A-level set). Comments on the defection of RCs elsewhere, 'We must respond to the needs of the present day. Catholic boys should go to Catholic schools and our job is to be so good that they would want to come to us.'

ACADEMIC MATTERS: Top of the Catholic league but it makes no bones about a non-élitist intake – from A stream scholars to fifth stream pupils with IQs of around 105 who get extra help with English and Maths. NB 90% of this bottom stream achieve three A-levels: 'That the strong should be given something to strive for and the weak should not be over-burdened,' is Father Leo's statement of purpose. 'They never discard,' says a parent, 'the boys gain self-respect, the monks have an ability to home in on potential, to unlock talent to achieve.' There is a core curriculum plus compulsory Religious Studies throughout; most take three separate sciences at GCSE although the lower stream take the combined award. Liberal Arts have traditionally had the edge here but Science and Maths have picked up significantly in the last two years. English Literature and History are the most popular subjects at A-level; Greek and Politics are among the options. NB Boys are allowed to have a go at an A-level subject even if they obtained only a pretty modest grade at GCSE. Two-thirds of the staff are lay (a number are women), 25 are monks.

GAMES, OPTIONS, THE ARTS: A powerful games school (games are compulsory, including rugby); virtually unbeaten First Fifteen. 'We have a depth of expertise' says the Head. Also cricket, cross-country, hockey, athletics, squash, golf, fly-fishing, renowned beagling. Twelve Rugby fifteens, seven cricket elevens, four tennis teams, a 25-metre swimming pool, and a Sports Hall.

Strong CDT in a newish centre (which includes photography and electronics). Excellent Drama, with a main and studio theatres. CCF is now voluntary. D of E; Scouts have now been taken over by an Outdoor Activities Group. Clubs for everything from debating to bee-keeping. An annual pilgrimage to Lourdes for senior boys.

The monks of Ampleforth singing plain chant are now known to millions via *Classic FM* – a nice little earner.

BACKGROUND AND ATMOSPHERE: The school was founded in 1902, in a fine setting in a lovely Yorkshire valley – very isolated, but, as Father Leo points out in his drive to attract day boys 'the half hour it takes to get boys here daily from York is as long as many London day-school runs'. NB The fast train from London to York takes less than two hours. There is a rather austere 1861 Victorian Gothic main wing plus Giles Gilbert Scott's huge abbey church and school buildings (1930s) with late '80s additions: 'the Benedictines have joined forces with Holiday Inn,' commented an architect, though the school points out indignantly 'There are other views!'

There is a huge central hall 'rather like a liner' according to a pupil, and a study hall with carrels (individual study desks). Houses are autonomous and vary considerably in character with a deliberate spread of ability throughout, and are run by ten housemasters, 'deeply thoughtful men, they've seen it all before' – 8 out of 10 are monks, 2 are married laymen. There is no choice here, boys are allotted to houses.

Though remote and very much a country school, Ampleforth has links with the outside world via excellent and regular lecturers (Kate Adie, Norman Lamont, William Dalrymple recently), and far-away projects e.g. Chile and Eastern Europe (about these Father Leo has been described as 'mustard keen'). 'It's perfect for parents abroad,' says one such, 'so much going on at weekends there and too far away for exeats.' There are no exeats except for the winter term, otherwise half-terms. A handy list of local hotels, restaurants and B & Bs is sent out to parents in the comprehensive book *'Confirmation of Entry – Your Questions Answered'*. The warmth of the welcome to parents and visitors is legendary: 'It's part of the Rule of St Benedict to welcome guests in Christ,' comments Father Leo.

Plans for central feeding are going ahead (at a cost of £2 million), and will be in operation by Spring '97, with pupils seated by house for supper in sub-divided areas within the main dining hall.

PASTORAL CARE AND DISCIPLINE: Father Leo is continuing to clamp down on discipline. Consciences are still worked on rather than harsh restrictions imposed; several boys were expelled for drugs in '94, others suspended. There is a fine for smoking (£7.50 for first offence). Lower Sixth upwards can have two pints of beer with a meal in local market towns e.g. Helmsley – but suspension for spirits. Bad language is censored: 'they see tennis stars disputing, footballers spitting, we ask for standards to be different.' Pastoral care, say parents, is 'unique' – but see below. 'The housemaster is a priest and a friend as well, there is a tremendous loyalty from boys in return who come back to the Abbey to be married, and to have their children christened.'

Stop Press: the suicide of a monk in the grounds in '96 is still causing shock waves.

PUPILS AND PARENTS: The scions of top and middle Catholic families from all over the place. Also lots of Forces children. The notoriously untidy-looking boys chased up by a sharper regime into sticking somewhat closer to the no-uniform 'dress code' of jacket and trousers with black or sports 'colours' ties. Old Boys include Frank Muir, Rupert Everett, Piers Paul Read, Hugo Young, Christopher Tugendhat, Lord Nolan, James Gilbey.

ENTRANCE: Common Entrance (60% pass required) with exceptions always allowed especially 'for reasons of faith or family,' or simply because boys have come up through the junior school.

EXIT: 90% to university, on average 15–18 to Oxbridge (with fewer scientists among them), otherwise mostly to old universities, a few new. Subjects include History, Classics, Theology, Music, Medicine, Estate and Business Management.

MONEY MATTERS: A generous 17 major and minor scholarships available, and others internally awarded. Also 7 Music scholarships of varying value.

REMARKS: Going well: the major school of the liberal Catholic tradition emerging a little leaner and fitter after the recession and the fall-out to other schools, with more than a nod to the market expectations of its highly supportive parents, among whom a detractor is scarcely to be found. 'The philosophy is absolutely right,' says a parent, 'it is no good succeeding in life if you fail yourself.'

Aylesbury Grammar School

Aylesbury, Buckinghamshire HP21 7RP
Tel: 01296 84545, Fax: ditto

PUPILS: Around 1,057 boys
ALL DAY
AGES: 12–18
SIZE OF SIXTH FORM: 350
NON-DENOM
STATE

HEAD: Since 1992, Mr Ian Roe, BA, Dip Ed (fifties), educated at the Royal Grammar School, High Wycombe and Leicester University. Came to the school in 1961 to teach French and worked his way up: 'Every time I thought about leaving, they offered me something else. I couldn't have enjoyed myself more.'

Rewrote the school's Policy Document in consultation with staff and discussion with children, emphasising that children should challenge themselves to do their personal best and have confidence in themselves as people.

ACADEMIC MATTERS: Gets formidably good results year after year. Excellent Maths; also Business Studies (no failures at A-levels for 5 years, out of 300 students). Strong Science A-level results in '95, with over 50% at grade A in Physics. Latin and Greek on offer. There is a powerful Computer Science centre, and Computer Studies popular, with over 100 pupils studying this for A-level; the school markets its own programmes, and computers are used with everything, even Latin. Sixth Form learn IT with basic desk-top publishing.

Has the occasional real high-flier (e.g. in '95 three boys achieved 6 A grades at A-level, and not long ago a 13-year-old recently got into Oxford, and assimilated well into the school having previously been taught at home). Extra learning support, including for dyslexia, is available where required and comes out of the school budget.

GAMES, OPTIONS, THE ARTS: Particularly strong rugby side. Currently also has some outstandingly strong tennis players, including the current national champion for division 7; the under-15 team are South of England champions and have won the Buckinghamshire Cup every year since 1985. Strong cricket. Streams of teams for most sports. Swimming if wanted before school in the morning. Also keen on sports abroad – skiing in Canada, cricket tour to Trinidad, rugby tours to Wales and France.

The school timetable is linked with the Girls' High School next door, so there are lots of joint clubs and activities, and increasing numbers of these. The schools combine for drama, and the choir. There is also an orchestra. Masses of visits, trips and exchanges, with extra help available for those who might not otherwise be able to afford them.

Remarkably successful at Public Speaking events – the school has produced 3 individual world champions in the last 6 years.

BACKGROUND AND ATMOSPHERE: The school was founded in 1598, and moved to its present site in 1907; an oasis of green in the town. The original school building is now surrounded by a mass of specialist buildings (some rather ugly).

Boys are tidy and uniformed; the occasional ponytail. There are photographs of achievements everywhere. The school was recently revamped – a special environmental team (flowers) was created, and a wizard ceramic tile composite by Juniors depicts life at the school in main hall.

PASTORAL CARE AND DISCIPLINE: Boys relate to the Head of Year and Head of House, who report serious misdemeanours to the Head. Expectations are high on this front.

PUPILS AND PARENTS: Half from Aylesbury, half from surrounding areas. Middle-class parents without capital behind them still move here in droves. They mix well, are helpful and supportive.

ENTRANCE: Highly competitive. Via school reports and examination. Around 95% from state schools, rest from prep. There are 20–30 boys in Sixth Form from public school and roughly the same from the state sector. Top 30% of ability range. Pupils can come in at other times, but there is a stringent entrance test. Waiting lists.

EXIT: Around 24 to Oxbridge, and the rest to other Universities. Boys join the professions, become engineers, business managers, etc. Serious University counselling and careers advice is given.

MONEY MATTERS: Extra help is available for extra-curricular activities. Sixth Form oversubscribed because of recession.

REMARKS: As we have said before, this is one of the few, old-fashioned 'free' grammar schools – possibly too old-fashioned. Run on the lines of a traditional public school; an occasional criticism is that it is 'more like a public school than a public school'. Still outstanding, however.

Badminton School

Westbury-on-Trym, Bristol BS9 3BA
Tel: 0117 962 3141, Fax: 0117 962 8963
Junior School Tel: 0117 962 4733

PUPILS: Around 300 girls, 200 board, 100 day
AGES: 11–18
SIZE OF SIXTH FORM: 86. Plus junior school on site, ages 4–11 (20 board, 60 day)
C OF E
FEE-PAYING

HEAD: Since 1981, Mr Clifford Gould, MA (fifties), educated at Haileybury and Trinity College, Dublin. Teaches English to Oxbridge students, 'and I stand in for pregnant English teachers.' Wife was previously Head of Mathematics, now involved at national level on model UN and European youth parliament; two sons. Previously Deputy Head of Frensham Heights (and with his wife jointly ran the girls' boarding house), before that taught at Latymer Upper. Knows all the girls, and is respected ('I look fierce when I'm not frowning'); hot on the subject of boundaries and freedom/identity. Quietly impressive. Unusually clear about the school's identity and aims. Hopes girls are allowed to keep their femininity and compete with men. At co-ed schools learnt the secret: 'You don't push girls, you pull them: come and try this; whereas boys respond to go and do that.'
Stop Press: Head retiring '97.

ACADEMIC MATTERS: Good and rising steadily – over 5 years, the school rates 50th nationally according to the *Financial Times* ('I'm [still] surprised', says Head), but bear in mind this is a small school. One of the few Heads who is openly glad about league tables 'because it's done us a lot of good and attracted good people here – the critical mass'. Good Maths A-level results, also Biology. Sciences are taught to younger pupils according to sets, as three subjects or the Dual Award. The school got 28 out of 58 starred A grades at GCSE in Dual Award Science in '95. Humanities are slightly squeezed. Most staff are female (35 women, 8 men), not many are young. NB For girls in cosy boarding schools wanting to expand their horizons at Sixth Form, this is well worth considering – ask to see the Sixth Form prospectus.

Teaching staff go home by 7 p.m. 'That way they're far more willing to come in over the weekend and do Duke of Edinburgh or whatever.' Seriously good advice on universities and careers.

GAMES, OPTIONS, THE ARTS: Music continues to be a real strength: 90% of pupils learn an instrument, choir practice (twice a week) at 8.15 p.m., all manner of concerts and strong quartets, with four orchestras, four choirs, numerous ensembles – quite something for a school this size. Good drama. Excellent batik and textile department, enthusiastic jewellery making and keen art, with a super new Art Centre (completed '95). There is an arts circus for junior girls, whereby they move round art and technology departments. Sports matches are kept to day schools ('to avoid two-hour drives'). Lots of options and activities, often purposefully clashed with prep times during the day – 'It's a subtle way of getting girls to join activities and find time later to do prep.' Very successful European youth parliament speakers, also model UN (unusual in a small girls' school). Good on trips and outings at all levels.

BACKGROUND AND ATMOSPHERE: Founded in 1858, as a place where girls would learn to compete with men in a man's world, and has been through ups and downs.

It used to be fashionable among Fabians. After a blip, it is once more going up the fashion stakes, though has sadly been hit by dwindling numbers of boarders even since the last edition. Its present site, a 19th-century Renaissance-style country house, set in 20 acres on the smart edge of Bristol, is encircled by stone walls, with curiously bent yew hedges. There are many new buildings including an excellent indoor pool, a pleasantly painted yellow Sixth Form house and a fine light library (with classrooms below) designed by Sir Hugh Casson (an ex-parent). The junior school and playgrounds are also on site; there is an overall sense of muddle in the layout with not much space in a small campus.

A strong work ethic is firmly in place, and a fairly full weekend programme too. Prevalent no-nonsense attitude. Team of three head girls (voted by pupils). The jolly, bright, busy junior school has its own pre-prep (girls now come at 4).

PASTORAL CARE AND DISCIPLINE: There are fairly tight rules (the Sixth Form booklet mentions the school's emphasis on 'moral, intellectual and social welfare' in that order). Pupils are friendly and everyone knows everyone else. 'We're not wild on parties here,' says the Head. Boarding staff (practically all graduates) are not teachers, by and large; also 19-year-old Australians, plus French, German and Spanish *assistants*. Discipline is not much of a problem (only occasional drinking misdemeanours). Access to Bristol centre is not very easy – 'luckily' say parents.

PUPILS AND PARENTS: Mixed: 7% foreigners (Malaysians, Kenyans, Hong Kong Chinese), as well as families from Devon, Cornwall, Hereford and Worcester and also the London M4 corridor. Professional parents who don't want 'prissy girls' boarding schools, but who don't want co-education either,' said one.

Girls are distinctly articulate, very busy and stretched; well-motivated and career-minded. Uniform of naff baby blue jerseys. Some complaints from boarding parents over inflexibility of exeat rules, 'at variance with weekly boarders and day girls' freedom'. But day and boarding pupils are well-integrated.

ENTRANCE: At 11 (many from junior school), 18–20 places; also at 12 and 13 (one of the first girls' boarding schools to offer places at 12 and 13 in order to cater for girls from co-ed prep schools). Also at 16 (regularly from the traditional girls' boarding schools where less is offered/expected). Old girls include Iris Murdoch, Indira Gandhi, Claire Bloom.

EXIT: Leakage to co-ed (usually) schools post-GCSE, 80%–90% stay on to Sixth Form. Rare for a pupil not to go on to get a degree; 4–10 a year (7 in '95) to Oxbridge. Medicine is a particularly popular destination, also engineering, and an unusually wide variety of subjects and careers followed.

MONEY MATTERS: Careful with money, 10% of fees are spent on the buildings, so the school is well maintained with constant improvements. No Assisted Places, but 'help is available'. Variable scholarships – 24 were awarded last year (academic, music and art, and general all-round) worth between 10 and 50% of fees.

REMARKS: A strong all-round small girls' school, more aggressive than the 'nice' little all-girls' schools, with a lot to offer, but suffering from the anti-boarding fashion, plus the large numbers of private schools in Bristol.

Bath High School

Hope House, Lansdown, Bath BA1 5ES
Tel: 01225 422931, Fax: 01225 484378

PUPILS: Around 670 girls, including separate junior school at 3–5 Grosvenor Place, Bath BA1 6ES
ALL DAY
AGES: 4–18
SIZE OF SIXTH FORM: 100
NON-DENOM
FEE-PAYING

HEAD: Since 1985, Miss Margaret Anne Winfield, BA (forties). Ex-grammar school girl; read History at Leicester University. Previously Head of Hulme Grammar School, Oldham. Prime of Miss Jean Brodie figure in yellow Moygashel. Goes around with a permanent smile on her face 'as if her one idea of heaven is to look after a whole lot of grumpy adolescents,' says a parent. She is a 'legend in her own lifetime,' says a local taxi driver. Great inner strength; happy and on top of the job. Firm disciplinarian: 'benevolent dictatorship is one way of looking at it.'

Stop Press: retiring; successor is Mrs Emma McKendrick.

ACADEMIC MATTERS: A consistently good performer in exams. Gets excellent results, including a high A-level pass rate with 68% A–B grades in '95. Hot on Sciences – both Dual Award and 'triple science' at GCSE, available through options scheme. The usual one or five take Greek and Latin. All Sixth Formers take a General Studies course. Philosophy and Physical Education are both on offer at A-level. There are six male members on the staff in the senior school, plus peripatetic music staff. Heavy on prep.

GAMES, OPTIONS, THE ARTS: Sport plays a minor but 'significant' role says the Head. A wide range of activities are on offer and Bath High girls have been the county netball champions. Keenest matches (called 'rallies') are the ones against other GPDST schools. Girls are very enthusiastic about the Ten Tors walk. On-site sports facilities are 'soon to be improved'. Music department is thriving; Art department is enthusiastic and productive. Technology now covers IT, Design and Realisation, Food and Textiles. Some parents comment they would like to see more after-school life/hobbies, etc, 'though of course it's impossible because of the vast radius from which children come'. An after-school supervision scheme operates in the Junior Department to suit working mothers and big sisters.

BACKGROUND AND ATMOSPHERE: Georgian houses knocked together in a lovely crescent with views over the City of Bath, and beautiful grounds. Elegant hotel across the road in what the school likes to refer to as 'gracious surroundings' was bought in August '95.

Businesslike and efficient, no-nonsense atmosphere, but is slightly Spartan-looking inside. It is very much a city school – no space is wasted. Girls appear neat, tidy and cheerful. A Sixth Form Centre also houses Art/Music facilities. A GPDST school. Junior school now housed in Georgian houses at Grosvenor Place, about 1 mile away.

PASTORAL CARE AND DISCIPLINE: PSE programme. Girls have heads down, and discipline is by and large not a problem, though NB Bath is one of the West Country's drug centres with New Age travellers, social outsiders, etc, all over the place; the school authorities would like it pointed out that they put much emphasis on pastoral care.

PUPILS AND PARENTS: Approximately half from Bath, half from the surrounding counties, many arriving by coach or train. Predominantly middle class – nice girls with ponies, etc – wholesome, good manners, ordinary.

ENTRANCE: At 11+ and 14+ by test and interview, also at 16+ (dependent on GCSE results plus interview). Head considers cramming for entrance 'most unwise'.

EXIT: Considerable fall-out after GCSE (for Sixth Form Colleges or co-ed schools), but intake at Sixth Form more than makes up for its size. Practically all go on to higher education, and later take up professions.

MONEY MATTERS: GPDST scholarship awarded on entrance for excellence; Sixth Form scholarships on examination and interview (open to girls within and without the school). There are 18 Assisted Places at 11+, and 2 at Sixth Form.

REMARKS: Good steady middle-of-the-road academic girls' day school which gets successful exam results – parents are thrilled, though they may need to educate and extend their daughters in the non-academic areas of life.

NB Amalgamating with the Royal School, Bath over two years. This means a major reorganisation, including a new name – Royal High School, qv.

Bedales School

Petersfield, Hampshire GU32 2DG
Tel: 01730 263286,
Fax: 01730 263286 day;
    01730 267411 night

PUPILS: Around 400 boys and girls, in approximately equal numbers (around 75% board)
AGES: 13–18 (but see entry under Dunhurst for Bedales Junior School)
SIZE OF SIXTH FORM: Around 160
NON-DENOM
FEE-PAYING

HEAD: Since 1995, Mrs Alison Willcocks MA (forties). Educated at Cambridge and Birmingham (B Mus). Previously taught at Portsmouth High School, and was Housemistress, then Deputy Head at Bedales – an inspired appointment from within the school. A very capable lady, whose interests include literature, music, history and child psychology. Commands wide respect. Two teenage children, and her husband Jonathan is director of the junior academy at the Royal Academy of Music. Mrs Willcocks has recently been made a member of the HMC. Takes over from Mr Ian Newton whose appointment was not a success.

ACADEMIC MATTERS: Operates very much on university lines – broad curriculum, with pupils learning to organise themselves and work on their own – working habits that are taught in the junior school. This can be tricky for pupils coming in from schools taught by more straight up-and-down methods, but they are well supported here.

There are some outstanding staff, some of very long standing. One parent commented the school had 'given my daughter a love of English and theatre which will last her for the rest of her life'.

Surprisingly, A-level Theatre Studies in '95 resulted in 3 Ds, 3 Es, 3 Ns and 2 Us. Voluntary extensions in several subjects are available for pupils who want to be stretched beyond exam courses. The school gets excellent results, considering the mixed intake. 9–11 GCSEs are the norm. Dual Award Science at GCSE. Setting in Maths, Science and French.

Subjects are balanced between boys and girls – including Science. Pupils are encouraged to do arts with science. There is an exceptionally strong, stable Common Room – it's a way of life school. Participates in 'swap' training scheme.

GAMES, OPTIONS, THE ARTS: The school has had a reputation of having a strong Art department – several leavers go on to art foundation courses – but currently Music is stronger, under Nick Gleed, and has produced some outstanding work; and NB there are good opportunities for the less skilled, too. Drama is also lively – a good place for budding thespians, particularly with the building of the new Olivier Theatre.

Sport is something else. There is no rugby and the school mag, the *Bedales News*, was recently over the moon at what it described as its 'thrashing' of Winchester at football, but the very excitement tells its story: team games are not worshipped here; indeed, it was pointed out to us by the junior school that the politically correct (and more accurate) name was 'PE'. Pupils oblige by tipping up to push a ball about on fine days, but there is a strong feeling they are doing everyone a favour by their presence (we exaggerate, but you get the picture). NB The Head disagrees with this part of our entry and would like it known that though 'sport had a less enthusiastic reception at one time,' there are now 'significant teams' and 'excellent facilities'. That said, there is an alternative to games, Outdoor Work – hands-on farm and conservation work on the school's estate – and this is taken up by many. A strongly imaginative and green environmental policy affects all aspects of school life.

BACKGROUND AND ATMOSPHERE: The school was started in 1893 by J H Badley in an attempt to retain the best features of traditional public schools, while reforming the narrow bias towards Classics, muscular Christianity and rugby. One of the oldest co-educational boarding schools – a true mix, in which boys and girls relate to each other on equal terms. Much more unusual, pupils are on equal terms with the staff; they call all staff by their Christian names (including the Head), and this, says a pupil who has also been in a school where more conventional modes of address are used, 'has the immediate effect of putting them on the same footing as you. They cannot be stuffy, and you cannot be in awe of them.' The present Head considers communication 'a vital aspect of school'.

The school has the reputation of being liberal and letting it all hang out, but this is a surface impression, more or less confined to the dress code (or lack of it), which give pupils an illusion of freedom, while allowing staff to run the place with a firm structure. There is no uniform – the school is a contender for the scruffiest in the country; all clothes go in the washing machine and come out grunge-coloured. Pupils go round like walking ragbags, – 'it's the fashion now,' said one. Hair is also freedom city – dye it sky blue or pink if you wish.

The school is a mishmash of old and new buildings, from a fine example of Arts and Crafts to 1960s utilitarian structures. The glorious mellow library is well stocked (with 40,000 books). Barns have been restored by students for an ODW (Outdoor Work) centre.

Girls, excepting Upper Sixth, are all housed in one giant rambling building with corridors, and annexes – quite ghastly for newcomers; it gives the school a feeling of being very large and soulless. However, a smart new boys' boarding house, the school's pride and joy, looks like a ski chalet. There are three main boarding houses, with the Upper Sixth now in the newly refurbished house which aims to provide a 'good pre-university atmosphere of controlled co-ed boarding.' Until Upper Sixth, boys and girls are in mixed-age dorms (which causes mixed reactions). Food is not brilliant but the few complaints of hunger appear a thing of the past.

PASTORAL CARE AND DISCIPLINE: The school is justly famous for the strength of its pastoral care – staff are highly experienced at watching for and sorting out problems, and handling rebels with the lightest of touches. Excellent house staff. The school has various customs which bring the unruly into line, such as everyone shaking everyone's hand at end of term, and at 'Jaw' on Sunday evenings (the nearest the school appears to get to the high moral ground). Punishments can be based on labouring for the community.

A large number of pupils go home at weekends. They have an excellent relationship with the village of Steep, in which the school is sited – a good test of how a school is functioning. Discipline on 'issues that really matter' can be tough but fair. Students (NB they are *not* referred to as pupils here) know where they stand. There is a firm emphasis on self-discipline, with scope for making mistakes and – hopefully – 'growing through them'.

PUPILS AND PARENTS: Famous for its arty media parents (large numbers of sons and daughters of luvvies), but also lots of Foreign Office. Two members of Pink Floyd were parents here, also Peter Hall, Princess Margaret, and Sylvia Plath's children were also here. The most pinned-up famous OB currently is Daniel Day-Lewis.

ENTRANCE: Half from Bedales' own junior school, Dunhurst (see separate entry), the rest from co-ed preps such as Windlesham, from London and the south-west. Entry at 11 and 13, and into Sixth Form. Potential pupils come down for Civil Service-type two-day residential tests over a wide range of subjects and performance – also excellent for pupils to get to know and judge the school. 16+ entry via interviews.

EXIT: A few to Oxbridge in recent years, including three choral scholarships in '95/'96. Also other universities, art colleges, etc. Lots take a gap year; travel scholarships are available.

MONEY MATTERS: During a previous Head's reign, school built up excellent reserves, and so has developed its facilities; while not among the ritzier of establishments, it isn't missing anything important. The school bends over backwards to help parents in financial distress and on this score alone earns its charitable status. There are 5 assisted places in each year of Sixth Form. Scholarships are available for general excellence at 13+, music throughout, and for art and design and academic at 16+.

REMARKS: A one-off. You either like it or loathe it. It is now back on course as a top-class, co-education boarding school – strong, thriving and full, in the steady hands of its new Head.

Bedford School

Burnaby Road, Bedford MK40 2TU
Tel: 01234 340444, Fax: 01234 340050

PUPILS: 720 boys (over one-third board). Plus Prep School, with 400 boys (ages 7–13).
AGES: 13–18
SIZE OF SIXTH FORM: Approx 300
C OF E
FEE-PAYING

HEAD: Since 1990, Dr I P Evans, MA (Cantab), PhD, MRSC. Former Scholar, Churchill College Cambridge. Educated at 'a maintained Grammar School' in North Wales, then got a First in Natural Sciences at Cambridge, followed by PhD at Imperial College, London. Came here via St Paul's where he was Head of Chemistry and Chief examiner for A-levels at the University of London Examining Board. A keen committee man.

An enthusiast, keen on cricket, the organ (which he plays), and poetry; also a Welsh-speaking Celt whose non-conformist views ('muscular Christianity at work') are reflected in his passion for Pastoral Care. 'Good civilised values are supported by the power of working together.' Teaches chemistry. His wife is also a PhD in chemistry. A fast talker; his eyes twinkle only slightly more than his watch chain. Bubbly, caring and urbane.

ACADEMIC MATTERS: Impressive – computers throughout, as well as a myriad of labs, and language labs, and separate buildings for science, IT. The most marvellous facilities: a full-blown weather station is incorporated into the Geography department. Much use of visual aids. Latin is on offer and a little Greek. Classes of 18–20 throughout the GCSE programme, 10–12 at A-level. 'High degree of scholarship among the staff.'

Uses five different exam boards (one of the many schools which have opted for this). 1995 results up on 1994, with Chemistry, Physics and Maths tops followed by Geography, English, History. Over 64% A-level passes grades A–B '95; 28 pupils achieved A grades in all their subjects. Good grief!

GAMES, OPTIONS, THE ARTS: The superb Design Technology building is still a little under-used; has marvellous wood-working facilities, etc. The Art room is burgeoning with ideas, with its own library and slide dept. The Music department is well equipped, with children working quite late on their own compositions. Impressive standards, with an unusually large batch of grade 8 players of various instruments. Gave a spectacular performance with three other schools of Benjamin Britten's *War Requiem* in the Birmingham Symphony Hall.

The Recreation Centre combines a purpose-built Theatre (huge depth of stage) attached to a Games Hall the size of 7 Badminton Courts, and a vast Swimming Pool (with space to paddle canoes). Also a keep-fit room. Games are taken very seriously; recent under-16 National Indoor Hockey Champions, rugby still strong, also basketball. CCF is very popular. Leadership values strongly emphasised. School makes full use of river and usually thrashes all-comers in local regattas.

BACKGROUND AND ATMOSPHERE: Letters Patent 1552; endowed by Sir William Harpur 1556; moved to present site 1891. The main school burnt down in March 1979 and the internal structure was subsequently radically reshaped, with a mega hall on the first floor. There is a good feeling of space, with fifty acres of playing field-filled campus, dominated by the school chapel designed by G F Bodley (a restoration programme is under way) – God is strong at Bedford.

A hotchpotch of ancillary buildings culminates in the most current construction: the building of a 500-seater hall, attached to a new building for DT.

A 1960s boarding house was recently closed, and there has been much revamping, with a newly purchased Victorian boarding house nearer campus opening in its stead. There is now a Sixth Form international boarding house. Boys move from dormitories to study bedrooms: all very cosy with carpets and duvets and the occasional poster. Day boys are allotted to the same six houses: there is no apparent rivalry between the two.

Bedford Preparatory School, (Tel: 01234 352007, Fax: 01234 345048). Head since 1991, Dr B A Rees BA, BD, Dip Min, PhD (forties), Canadian and a rare bear of enormous charm and tact. A super prep school, self-contained but able to use the facilities of the senior school. Strong on games and music. French from 7; German, Spanish, and Latin from 11. Five-star hotel-esque boarding house. All boys go on to the senior school with rare exceptions (logistical, financial, or when they don't make the grade).

PASTORAL CARE AND DISCIPLINE: Relies on houseparents, and tutors – pupils have the same tutor throughout. 'Discipline not a problem' – based on co-operation. 'No problems in school' with drugs but would sack if discovered; cigarettes totally banned anywhere in school – staff as well as pupils. Has a very strong anti-bullying programme. Children helped write the Policy Document.

PUPILS AND PARENTS: Much loyalty to school and most UK boarders have strong Bedford connections or live within a 50/60-mile radius. Buses from all over Bedfordshire and as far as Milton Keynes: a wide net. Around 25 boarders have service connections (mostly RAF). There are substantial numbers of overseas pupils, mainly in the Sixth Form, including boys from Hong Kong, Japan, Thailand, Malaysia and Brunei (government scholars and private pupils), also Germans, Spaniards and other Europeans. OBs include Paddy Ashdown and HH Munro (Saki).

ENTRANCE: From own Prep School, and elsewhere by CE at 13. Special arrangements for boys entering from state schools.

EXIT: 100+ pupils to Universities, around 7–11 Oxbridge places annually. The '95 breakdown of subjects reveals that Social Sciences tops the list, followed by Engineering, then Business Administration. A few leavers go straight into business, occasionally the Services.

MONEY MATTERS: The Harpur Trust helps out Bedfordshire families generously. Up to 4 Assisted Places at 13+ (some bring them at 11+ from the junior school), and 3 Assisted Places at 16+.

REMARKS: Gritty and purposeful traditional boys' school that has a good following, good social mix, and outstanding facilities.

Benenden School

Cranbrook, Kent TN17 4AA
Tel: 01580 240592, Fax: 01580 240280

PUPILS: Approx 442 girls
ALL BOARD
AGES: 11–18
SIZE OF SIXTH FORM: Approx 140

C OF E
FEE-PAYING

HEAD: Since 1985, Mrs Gillian duCharme (pronounced Dewsharm), MA Cantab (fifties), formerly Head of private co-ed day school in Manhattan. Divorced. Read Modern Languages at Girton, (tennis blue), worked for British Council. Tall and chic, she jogs around the grounds by way of relaxation. Sees her job as 'training adults, as well as educating children'. Wants girls to 'make something of themselves, whatever they're good at: if they can achieve home and work, I think that's lovely – but it's really hard: we're not pushing anyone out to do careers'. Hot on the subject of self-confidence (Head clearly has oodles) – 'Girls must feel good about themselves'. Some complaints (strongly denied by the school) from parents and would-be parents that Mrs duCharme has not enough time for them.

ACADEMIC MATTERS: Used to be stronger on Arts subjects; now more evenly balanced. English, Maths and Economics are especially good (it is rare to find any school achieving good results in this last subject). Setting in Maths, Latin, French, and GCSEs are now taken early in these subjects (the Head has seen the light on this). The inspiring English master, the Dutch Welshman Nicholas van der Fliet, is still doing his stuff. All 11–13-year-olds now do two modern languages on entering the school. Design Technology and Theatre Studies are also on offer.

The '95 results are impressive – their best for several years, with 12 out of 17 pupils getting A grades for Economics, and half the Eng Lit girls achieving A grades at A-level.

GAMES, OPTIONS, THE ARTS: Traditionally keenly sporting:

lacrosse, 15 tennis courts (including all-weather), squash, etc. There is a strong tradition of riding at the excellent nearby stables (see Old Girls). Judo also on offer and dance (there is a studio); the indoor swimming pool is 25 metres long. The school has an area well-thought-out for seminars. A Technology Centre opened in 1991. Lots of Music and Drama; the school holds an annual arts festival, for which they manage to get top writers, designers, etc, to come and participate. The whole campus is now networked with e-mail for staff and students.

BACKGROUND AND ATMOSPHERE: Founded in 1923 by three mistresses from Wycombe Abbey. The huge, elegant and slightly gloomy Victorian mansion was built by Gathorne Hardy, first Earl of Cranbrook, and set in 244 acres, with lots of rhododendrons. Generally mixed-age dorms in six 11–16-year-old houses, plus Sixth Form Centre. Girls may wear trousers or skirts; the uniform is not oversmart despite a tie and the darkest of navy blues. There is a rogues' gallery close to the staff room with a named photograph of every pupil, ditto staff.

Its isolated position makes the school self-contained, and life is boyless – not good news for Sixth Formers, though NB the Sixth Form is currently full. In the traditional all-girls' boarding school manner, crushes and passions still run high ... Shades of Angela Brazil. General atmosphere on the steamy side.

PASTORAL CARE AND DISCIPLINE: There is a new policy on television watching, following parental angst. No 'set' night for television: the thinking behind this is that they will watch less, and 'must learn to budget their time'. Houses are now smaller, with more married Housemistresses and also Housemasters ('I wouldn't want to be a single parent

with 50 or 60 kids, would you?' asks the Head) and the atmosphere is less institutional and more like family life, a fact that was amply demonstrated in the rosy-tinted television programme on the school, which showed happy matrons cheerily coming in and drawing back the curtains. But 'It's not like that at all,' say pupils.

Academic tutors are now attached to each house – caring for 6–8 students each. Smoking is not allowed (there are fixed penalties). Sixth Formers may drink a limited amount of alcohol with 'specific permission'.

One girl was recently and summarily 'asked to leave' following a fight with another. Some mutterings from parents and pupils that this matter was 'Not well handled.'

PUPILS AND PARENTS: Interesting and rich geographical and social mix – upper crust, new money, first-time buyers, overseas pupils (approximately 10%). The most famous Old Girl is HRH Princess Royal; also Charlotte Brew (the first lady to ride in the National); Liz Forgan; Joanna Foster (Chairman of the Equal Opportunities' Commission); the Reverend Angela Berners-Wilson (a pioneer woman priest); and – wait for it – Lady Moon (founder of the worldwide Old Bags' Society for rejected wives, following a wonderful headline case in which she cut off the sleeves of her erring husband's suits, and distributed his wine cellar about the village).

ENTRANCE: By CE and interview – from 50 different preps at 11+, 12+ and 13+. A few at Sixth Form – and keen to have fresh blood at this stage. £50 registration fee; also 10% of a term's fees on acceptance of a place (i.e. just under £400 at time of writing).

EXIT: 98% go on to degree courses, including 6 to Oxbridge in '95.

MONEY MATTERS: Sixth Form (academic, music and art) and lower school (academic and music) scholarships are held at the school in January. Both major (up to 80% of fees) and minor awards. Don't hold your breath, though – the school is not well-endowed. Some bursaries available for hard times, with priority normally given to students about to sit public examinations.

REMARKS: A famous and traditional girls' country boarding school which appears to have slipped in the popularity stakes. But why?

Birkdale School

Oakholme Road, Sheffield S10 3DH
Tel: 01142 668408 Fax: 01142 671947

PUPILS: Around 780 boys, including the prep and pre-prep school; around 20 girls in the Sixth Form
ALL DAY
AGES: 4–18
SIZE OF SIXTH FORM: around 221
C OF E
FEE-PAYING

HEAD: The Rev M D A Hepworth MA (fifties). Educated at Birkdale. Read Theology at Emanuel College, Cambridge. Ordained in '67, not to be a vicar, but so he could be chaplain in a school, because he was interested in 'being involved with the whole person' – an idea which, he confesses, does have a tendency to sound pi. Comments also that he is 'much more interested in what pupils do at university and beyond' [than at school] – a good point.

ACADEMIC MATTERS: The school has built up a good Design Technology department which was working on a project to replant the centre of Sheffield when we visited, as part of an A-level course and Art Department. There are good staff here, but the school is woefully short of space. Everyone does General Studies at A-level (and the Head has gone into print on the subject of the misleading league tables that are the result of this subject).

Only the most mainstream subjects are currently being studied, though one or two slightly more exotic ones are offered – e.g. Politics and Music. No one is currently doing Further Maths or Latin, and few do languages though the school has wonderful *assistants* to help. Currently 34% of the staff are female – unusual in a boys' secondary school, but, of course, standard in a prep school. Separate sciences and Dual Award sciences on offer at GCSE. Class sizes are a maximum 24, but average 15 in the senior school, and staff:pupil ratio is a respectable $11\frac{1}{2}$:1.

GAMES, OPTIONS, THE ARTS: The school buses the pupils to sports fields. There are too few girls for team games but they can go into town and play badminton, do ice skating, etc. – that is, said one or two of the boys darkly, 'when they are not shopping'. Not a place which sets a lot of store by games success. Rugby is compulsory for the first two years of the senior school, after that the pupils can play e.g. basketball. Some joint activities with Sheffield High.

Everyone in the Lower Sixth does a week's work experience (the school has good contacts with industry, not least among the current parents). Everyone also does 'leadership training', also in the Lower Sixth. Strong Outward Bounding.

BACKGROUND AND ATMOSPHERE: The school was founded at the turn of the century as a private prep school, and remained that way until 1978 when the school moved upwards to 16-years-old; then in 1988 it started a Sixth Form, sharing teaching with the very nearby Girls' Public Day School Trust School, Sheffield High. For various boring reasons this did not work out in the long term, and Birkdale now runs its own Sixth Form, grafting on new subjects as and when it can.

The school started on the site which is now the senior school, and this explains the generally cramped feel and the impression of bursting at the seams, with extra buildings being tacked on as and when. The Sports Hall, for example, was built on what had been the swimming pool (there now isn't a swimming pool). There is a nice octagonal gazebo for concerts. The main School Hall is shrill and much too small for current numbers. There is a separate Sixth Form block – the Grayson Building (named after a governor), which has lots of little boxes opening off narrow corridors, and spills into an old house which used to be offices. It was cold when we visited, and the pupils acknowledged this was a problem. The atmosphere is lively, scruffy and quite fun, however, and the actual site of the school is in one of the nicest parts of Sheffield – Education Corner, up by the university, and near the other schools.

PASTORAL CARE AND DISCIPLINE: The school prides itself on its pastoral care, though we saw no evidence of it being better than anywhere else. The school is structured into five age 'layers', with a head for each layer, there are also form tutors. School uniform (black and grey with vying red striped ties) is worn right the way through. Girls wear neat jackets and skirts with white blouses.

PUPILS AND PARENTS: Local lads, many first generation in private education. Large catchment area – one at

time of writing even comes from York. OBs: Michael Palin, Martin Stephen (High Master of MGS), a brace of judges, lawyers etc.

Junior School: On a separate rather nice site, overlooking the Botanical Gardens, in what was once the family home of the Osborn family. Compared with the senior school, the prep school feels vast – good big corridors, rooms with space, music rooms in the basement (which feels a bit damp and sweaty), and its own noisy gym. Not a cosy place, even the pre-prep forms, which are in their own wing. The (new) Head had 'flu when we visited – but there is a very nice, experienced Deputy Head.

ENTRANCE: The school is not selective at the age of 4 – but boys coming straight to the senior school are tested – so it's semi-selective.

EXIT: Formerly to Northern and Midland public schools and grammar schools. Now to first division universities, to ex-polys with good specialist courses, a sprinkling to Oxbridge (mainly to bridge), one or two to art colleges. Most of the pupils we talked to currently in the Sixth Form wanted to become lawyers . . .

MONEY MATTERS: Coining in money from fees (which are reasonable). Has applied for assisted places. Academic scholarships of 25% of school fees are on offer – which can be topped up in case of need.

REMARKS: Still feels like a junior school, albeit one which has hit the jackpot in terms of providing private schooling in Sheffield for boys up to the age of 18 for the first(?) time, fulfilling what was obviously a great need. The school has now outgrown its strength. It could be that numbers have grown too fast – concentrating on quality, rather than stopping to build up and consolidate departments and smooth the rough edges. Nevertheless, even greater numbers are projected and the school looks set to become the much needed grammar school that Sheffield has not had since the local schools went comprehensive.

Blackheath High School

Vanbrugh Park, London SE3 7AG
Tel: 0181 853 2929, Fax: 0181 853 1537

PUPILS: 350 girls
ALL DAY
AGES: 11–18
NON-DENOM
FEE-PAYING

HEAD: Since 1989 Miss Rosanne Musgrave MA (forties). Educated at Cheltenham Ladies' College and Oxford (read English) before second MA at Reading (Linguistic Studies) and PGCE London. Approachable, direct, energetic woman with steel-rimmed glasses. Has taught in both state comprehensive and mixed grammar schools ('all teachers should do their turn in the maintained sector – we shadow the National Curriculum here, so they keep their freedom to manoeuvre'); previous posts at Channing and as Head of English at Haberdashers' Aske's. A hands-on, clear-headed administrator, she is unusual in going herself to visit potential entrants in state sector schools. Accessible to staff and parents: 'I see four or five sets every week' – and not afraid to act as a trouble-shooter in child–parent clashes at home: 'I want girls to leave here confident, flexible, able to run their own lives.'

ACADEMIC MATTERS: Strong, traditional grammar-school teaching with innovative 'cross-curricular' approach for the first two senior years 'to bridge the gap between project-based and subject-biased teaching,' e.g. the building of a town for which girls went to study life in Boulogne, visited London museums, made scale drawings in Maths and Geography, printed their reports on Miss Musgrave's own press, and even made and fired their own bricks for building models in Technology.

The three separate sciences are taught to two-thirds at GCSE, with recent option of Combined Science for the rest. Around 25 to a class, 1:3 male:female teacher ratio; 9 GCSEs the norm – 'There's no point in doing too many, I want them to go on playing the tuba and swimming.' Good advice is given over A-levels; Maths and English are the most popular choices, with Economics on offer. Girls add an extra GCSE with their A-levels: choices include Spanish, drama, photography. Good careers advice is also given.

The school's league table placing does not look too hot; however, since exam results have not been shown to us in any form, it is impossible to comment.

GAMES, OPTIONS, THE ARTS: Girls go by bus to 5-acre site at Kidbrooke Park for hockey and netball. Popular rowing for Sixth Form at Royal Victoria Docks. The bizarre listed '50s 'gull-wing' chapel is under conversion to a Music Centre. A strong husband-and-wife team heads the flourishing Music department; two-thirds learn an instrument and there are three choirs, an orchestra and recorder groups. Also plays, takes part in GPDST poetry competition and has keen Art (life class offered) with a trip to Amsterdam.

BACKGROUND AND ATMOSPHERE: The school moved at the end of the summer term '94 to an imposing Victorian brick pile across the Heath in Vanbrugh Park, formerly a Church Army training college with renovated rear annexes. 'But it's not all roses,' muttered a member of staff of the school move. A hall is badly needed.

Bustling, friendly, unsnobbish girls wear navy-pinstriped blouses; no uniforms in Sixth Form – lots of trousers and DMs on show as they sit chatting over coffee in Sixth Form common room. Morning assembly 'generally uplifting monotheistic, so as not to offend.' Cafeteria food is ordered hospital-style the day before.

Junior school: Wemyss Road **SE3 0TF** (0181 852 1537) Head: Mrs Patricia Norton BEd, MIL. Moved into the refurbished premises which recently housed the senior school: 1880s fine purpose-built premises with a Palladian-style hall with balustraded double staircase. A good move for the juniors, now expanding from 250 to 300 4–11 years-olds. Most go on to the senior school.

PASTORAL CARE AND DISCIPLINE: The school has a strong policy centering on form tutors, joined by older girls who help in junior classes – 'they love it', comments Head. Homework books are sent home for parents to sign or comment on, and there is lots of space on report brochures (designed by Miss Musgrave) for pupils' and parents' comments, target attainment ratings. A 'tame' educational psychologist is on call; PSE classes. Immediate expulsion for drugs, suspension for drinking – 'the nearest I've got is sending a girl home for the day who came in with a can of lager,' says Head.

PUPILS AND PARENTS: An ethnic and social melange drawn from gentrified Blackheath, also from Rotherhithe, Deptford and Catford. One-third black and Asian, but 'race is not an issue here,' says a Sixth Former. There is an active Social Services programme: the school has links with a handicapped children's centre, and girls 'adopt' and visit local OAPs, funding an annual old people's party by means of discos and socials. The very friendly parent body ranges from top professional classes to blue-collar; it raises £10,000 a year for the school.

ENTRANCE: From state primary and local preps at 11. Exams in Maths and English, plus Miss Musgrave's Blackheath Paper III surprise – 'might be a design problem – build a paper platform – or questions on a video. It's to see how they reason. Prep schools hate it,' enthuses the Head. Interview to suss out 'a good sense of humour and enthusiasm for life – we don't want little silent gnomes'. School is part of the South London Consortium (pioneered by Miss Musgrave).

EXIT: 95% to higher education, nearly all into first-choice university, 2–5 to Oxbridge. Old girls include Margaret Jay, Katie Stewart, Mary Quant.

MONEY MATTERS: Very reasonable fees (about £4,000 p.a.), paid mostly by monthly direct debit. There are 14 assisted places; the Head is a great supporter, 'They're always filled, often by very needy one-parent families.' Some entrance and Sixth Form scholarships, plus the Minerva fund for hard times.

REMARKS: A strong, unpretentious, multi-ethnic, expanding city school turning out confident, educated, realistic girls for bargain outlay, under a powerfully efficient Head.

Bloxham School

Banbury, Oxfordshire OX25 4PE
Tel: 01295 720206, Fax: 01295 721897
PUPILS: 315 boys, 41 girls in Sixth Form
(252 board, 104 day)
AGES: 11–18
SIZE OF SIXTH FORM: 173
C OF E
ANGLO-CATHOLIC
FEE-PAYING

HEAD: Since 1991, Mr David Exham MA (Cantab) (early fifties), unmarried, educated at Radley, read Maths at Christ's College, Cambridge, then PGCE at Nottingham and came via St Peter's York, King's Taunton (Head of Maths), Second Master at Repton. Fun and giggly.

Still teaches Maths ('not a lot') and looks to produce 'friendly children, who come out as themselves, not clones, contributors, who have achieved their academic potential'.

ACADEMIC MATTERS: GCSE and A-level results improve annually. Very strong French, English, Maths, Art, with German, Spanish and Chinese at GCSE, as well as Hungarian, History, Geography, and three Sciences. Economics and Business Studies are increasingly popular. IT has expanded.

There are superb remedial facilities for dyslexia under Hugh Alexander but the school is not keen to be known as a school for dyslexics and says it is 'not interested in [dyslexic] children with less than an IQ in the high 120s'. Computers are everywhere, networked and in most classrooms. Strangely, though, no key-boarding taught as such, and notepads are not much used in classrooms and not at all in exams.

GAMES, OPTIONS, THE ARTS: Rugby is excellent and teams have toured Australia, the Pacific Basin and Canada; also cricket and hockey. Masses of Oxfordshire squads, and representative on England hockey team at 16 and player in England rugger squad. The school has a mega Sports Hall, swimming pool, and all-weather hockey pitch, and is applying for planning for international standard lights. Won the Millfield Schools' Polo Trophy at the National Schools' Championships in 1995.

A fantastic Music department is centred round an old converted gym (great fun), with myriad orchestras, saxophone and swing blocks inspired. Lots of groups and bands. Also superb Art, with all sorts of fabric: concrete and fibreglass sculptures. Lots of Drama, with an active small theatre.

Young Enterprise, D of E; the Art school is open at weekends, workshops ditto, and computers are totally accessible. Staff contracts stipulate that they must live in the Parish of Bloxham and be available for weekends.

BACKGROUND AND ATMOSPHERE: Founded 1860 and given to Woodard Foundation in 1896. Set in 80 acres of playing-field-filled grounds, this is a handsome building of Horton stone (dug from foundations), surrounded by modern ramifications. A splendid new kitchen/dining area released the basement area for an IT department, and a new technology centre is underway. The school bought the nearby Methodist chapel to convert into an extra theatre. They also bought the local pub, the White Lion, for junior (11–13) day boys, and lowered the entry age to 11 – a popular move with local parents, but not necessarily with other schools.

Boys graduate from dorms to study bedrooms. There are six houses, and girls join one of the boys' houses, as do day boys. Girls' houses are out of bounds to boys, but they may visit boys' houses. The school has a strong Christian tradition, a good working Woodard relationship, and a magnificent first-floor chapel.

PASTORAL CARE AND DISCIPLINE: Strong tutorial system via houses – pupils stay with same tutor throughout. Discipline 'not as big a problem here, on the whole a very reasonable and sensible collection', 'a small school where you feel you might be letting someone down'.

The Head sacked a pupil for drugs on his second day, but there have been no recent incidents. Booze not a problem, cigarettes mean a gating; will suspend for serious offences, 'a short cooling-off period', and talk about it with parents.

PUPILS AND PARENTS: Lots of first-time buyers. Typically within an hour of Bloxham, up and down the M40, and dyslexics from wherever. Masses of parental participation. Lots of farmers, businessmen, the Services: a considerable mix. 'Not perceived as socially upmarket.'

ENTRANCE: From traditional prep schools (Swanbourne, Winchester House, New College, etc, at 13), CE pass of 50% required. Test and assessment for state entrants. Sixth-form interview and report from previous school. But entry at any time if space available. Lower school (11–13) by entrance exam.

EXIT: A small leakage after GCSE; 85% to Universities – huge mix, with 8 to Oxbridge in a good year.

MONEY MATTERS: In the past there were some problems with bad payers, but the school will help real need via the 'dreaded blue form'; Woodard Foundation could give help in an emergency. Bursar is a 'brilliant entrepreneur' and the school is let for Language School and summer activity

school in summer holidays which provides extra cash for bursaries, etc. Assisted Places at 13+ keenly taken up.

REMARKS: The school has come up dramatically in the academic field over the last twenty years: no longer seen purely as 'Bloxham for Blockheads'. A very decent place, with strong Christian values.

Blundell's School

Tiverton, Devon EX16 4DN
Tel: 01884 252543, Fax: 01884 243232

PUPILS: 385; 286 boys, 82 girls (two-thirds board, one-third day)
AGES: 13–18, 11–18 from September 1996
SIZE OF SIXTH FORM: 182
C OF E
FEE-PAYING

HEAD: Since 1992, Mr Jonathan Leigh, MA (early forties), educated at Eton and a Cambridge Choral Scholar; historian – teaches the first-year Sixth Form. Married with two young children. Previously Second Master at Cranleigh. A housemasterly Head – holds the reins but delegates; often to be seen with his equally approachable black Labrador. Hot on pastoral care, and still remembered with admiration by those in his house at his previous school.

ACADEMIC MATTERS: Middle-of-the road in most subjects, with some classy results in Modern Languages. Theatre Studies and Sports Science are new additions at A-level and proving very popular; also successful A-level Photography. Broad intake, maximum class size 20, with four ability bands and some setted subjects. There is a smart new computer room. Science teaching is rock solid. Staff are mainly male (the Head is redressing the balance gradually, also introducing zippy young staff), some staff are long-timers, some of whom have tremendous enthusiasm outside their official realms, e.g. the English teacher on astronomy and astrology. There is a good scheme of supplementary studies for the Sixth Form. Head is busy stretching the scholars well beyond the curriculum, convinced that 'if the award holders fly the middle, the rump will rise in their wake', to which end award holders now play an active role in school life at various levels, e.g. leading debates, etc.

GAMES, OPTIONS, THE ARTS: Plenty of sport: there is a new Astroturf pitch, and the Ten Tors walk is taken seriously. Lively Music department, with a good and full programme of concerts, currently stronger on choral work than orchestral, and one brilliant piano teacher, ex-Royal College of Music. Good workshops (textiles, silversmithing, cabinet-making, engine repairs). CCF is compulsory for one year; fairly strong community involvement.

BACKGROUND AND ATMOSPHERE: On the edge of Tiverton, on a 100-acre site, calmly set in the most beautiful country. Dignified collegiate main blocks, cloister and chapel; over the road is the newer music block, a huge dining hall, and the excellently designed Ondaatje Hall housing the theatre plus facilities for photography, art, pottery, named after its Old Blundellian benefactor, brother of the Booker Prize winner. Typical public school red-brick boarding houses have spacious, carpeted study beds for groups of six working down to singles for top-year pupils. There is a new Sixth Form centre. Un-pressurised atmosphere, but with a character-building ethos. Uniform still

gingery brown tweedy jackets, with patched elbows.

The school was founded in 1604 through the will of a local clothier, Peter Blundell. It has a long association with the Amory family, whose endowments have been generous. Went fully co-ed in 1993, and girls' numbers are slowly increasing, but has had girls in the Sixth Form for some time; numbers overall are gently rising after taking a severe dip, and NB from September '96, the entry age is 11.

The school is mentioned in *Lorna Doone*.

PASTORAL CARE AND DISCIPLINE: Good supportive care; work and motivation are well monitored. Occasional misdemeanours over drink, but nothing serious.

PUPILS AND PARENTS: Parents working in the professions (probably also looking at King's Taunton); radius is closing in, but a few far-flung pupils, including Londoners with West Country connections; gentle middle class plus a healthy sprinkling of landed families (who have often sent boys for many generations). A fair number of Forces. 12% foreign nationals including Germans, pupils from the Eastern bloc, Japanese, Canadians. Strongly loyal and supportive Old Boys, including Donald Stokes; Michael Mates, MP; Anthony Smith. Pupils are pleasant, unpushy and unspoilt.

ENTRANCE: CE, from traditional prep schools (e.g. Mount House) – one of the few schools in the area to take pupils at 13. Also at Sixth Form.

EXIT: 90% go on to further education; in '95, 5 to Oxbridge – more than usual. Bristol, Edinburgh, Exeter in substantial numbers. NB School has traditional links through Peter Blundell with Sidney Sussex College, Cambridge and Balliol College, Oxford. Sport Science is a popular subject.

MONEY MATTERS: There are a generous number of scholarships, academic and also for Music, Art, Technology and Drama, at 13+, Fifth Form and Sixth Form: well worth enquiring about. Approximately one-third of entrants hold awards of some sort, up to 50% fees. Foundation places for some day boys.

REMARKS: As we have said before, this is a small, truly rural public school with charm. It combines discipline with a sense of values, and pupils won't sink without trace. Gradually becoming fully co-ed.

Bolton School (Boys' Division)

Chorley New Road, Bolton BL1 4PA
Tel: 01204 840201, Fax: 01204 849477

PUPILS: 1,026 boys; plus own junior school, with 150 boys ages 8–11.
ALL DAY
AGES: 11–18
SIZE OF SIXTH FORM: 240
NON-DENOM
FEE-PAYING

HEAD: Since 1983, Mr Alan W Wright BSc (fifties), educated at Manchester Grammar School, and Birmingham University. Arrived via King Edward's Birmingham, and Head of Chemistry and Sixth Form Supervisor at Newcastle upon Tyne Royal Grammar School. Married, three grown-up children. Approachable and under-standing, Mr Wright has transformed the school (he would say allowed it to evolve) during his time in office. He comments that there has been an 'enormous amount of adapting to modern needs'. Beady-eyed. Deals with problems with great sensitivity.

ACADEMIC MATTERS: No streaming or setting – not necessary as pupils are all bright. A huge range of subjects is offered. School's best ever A-level results in '95 with 71.7% A–B grades (but NB this includes General Studies). Chemistry continues to reign supreme but the school is also strong in Maths, Biology, Physics, Geography. Three separate sciences for all boys at GCSE. Excellent Careers Dept. Early retirement scheme for staff (high-powered, lots of PhDs, etc).

Superb Russian teaching (from First Form): teachers wrote their own textbook which is sold to other schools, and there are regular trips to Russia. It is popular up until GCSE, with good results, but very few take it at A-level.

Inspired Computer/Technology department, with designs being patented and sold: everything to a truly profes-sional industrial standard. IT has been transformed from within the school, lots of serious machinery. There was a complete refurbishment of the Technology department in '94 under the innovative Mr Whitmarsh. New and second-hand computers (lots, every-where); the Geography department sports a satellite weather station. Technology-Design courses at A-level linked with the Girls' Division (qv); also Classics and other Sixth Form minority courses.

GAMES, OPTIONS, THE ARTS: Surrounded by pitches: this is a soccer school. Matches to as far away as possible. Rugby gaining in popularity; also hockey, cross-country, tennis. Games Hall the size of four badminton courts; multi-gym and fitness training centre. Water polo is popular.

There are regular timetabled residential holidays at a hostel in Ullswater operated by the school in a former Victorian lakeland mansion, Patterdale Hall. Parents contribute £20 towards food. Boys go sailing, abseiling, rock-climbing, etc. Very strong Scout and Cub Scout troops.

Music and music technology. Good Art, and Arts and Language Bureau attached to 25-metre swimming pool – shared with the Girls' Division (qv). The Language Bureau is open and much used by local businesses – from 8 a.m. each morning; a good source of cash.

Clubs for everything during the lunch hour, and joint with the girls' school. Also shares the theatre.

BACKGROUND AND ATMOSPHERE: Independent since 1524, with links tracing to before 1516, the school was re-endowed in 1913 as a single Foundation by the first Viscount Leverhulme in equal partnership with the Girls' Division (founded in 1877). Set in 32 acres on the western edge of Bolton, with excellent motorway links and 22 school buses (for girls too) criss-crossing the local countryside.

A collegiate Edwardian sandstone structure, with oodles of passages and modern buildings, surrounded by playing fields. There is an impressive 'chained library', as well as an operational one.

Junior School: Bolton School (Boys' Division) Junior School. Master in Charge: Since 1990, Michael Percik, BA PGCE (forties). Entrance via test, with no automatic entrance from the school's own pre-prep, Beech House (with 200 boys and girls 4–8, on junior school site). Super and strong feeder prep, just across the road from the senior school, to which virtually all boys progress.

PASTORAL CARE AND DISCIPLINE: Yearly form tutors, who report to block tutor. Form tutors meet with class twice a day and do mega termly interviews with each boy – and also deal with any crisis. The Head and Deputy Head deal with serious offences.

There is one official counsellor, the Art mistress, plus several other staff specially trained in a small team led by the second master, Henry Jackson. Discipline is a co-ordinated exercise/campaign. Sackings for involvement off-campus with drugs (a drugs counsellor is on staff); also immediate expulsion for drugs within school or trading. Drink less of a problem than in previous years. 'No vast smoking problem.' Expulsion for bringing name of school into disrepute.

PUPILS AND PARENTS: From far and wide, including lots of merchants' and local businessmen's sons. Enormous parental support. 95% regularly turn up for year meetings. Not many 'non-professional, non-white pupils': 15% – very few, if you think of the catchment area. Unsophisticated by London standards.

ENTRANCE: Oversubscribed. 400 interview for 140 places. Fourth- or fifth-form entry, depending on applicants, and no automatic entry from junior school. Each child is tested on own merits: no preference is given to siblings.

Sixth-form entry to balance the books (around 20 each year). All candidates (including those already in school) must normally get As or Bs at GCSE in subjects they want to study at A-level, and not less than C in Maths and English.

EXIT: Some 10–15 post-GCSE. Otherwise 90+% to Universities, and between 7 and 10 to Oxbridge. The majority widespread, old and civic universities favoured. *Lots* of engineers.

MONEY MATTERS: Can and will help if real need arises; the recession increased bad debtors, 'but not catastrophic'. Bursaries available, plus music scholarship i.e. free Music Tuition. There are 38 Assisted Places, plus five at Sixth Form. Student, travelling and 'initiative' grants available.

REMARKS: Strong boys' day school. Huge variety of choice, lots of options. Good work ethos.

Bolton School (Girls' Division)

Chorley New Road, Bolton BL I 4PA
Tel: 01204 840201, Fax: 01204 849477

PUPILS: 940 girls
ALL DAY
AGES: 11–18, plus own junior school, with 150 girls ages 8–11
SIZE OF SIXTH FORM: 240
NON-DENOM
FEE-PAYING

HEAD: Since September 1994, Miss Jean Panton, formerly of The Merchant Taylors' School, Liverpool, who says she 'would prefer the school did not appear in this book.'

ACADEMIC MATTERS: Strongly academic. 'All year groups are unstreamed', but Maths is set from the second year. The curriculum is elastic enough to allow a huge option at GCSE. Most take (and get) 4 A-levels, including compulsory General Studies, with a predominance of Assisted Place pupils getting the As; pie charts to prove it. Detailed breakdown of results were not forthcoming, but in the past Sciences were the strongest suit; Dual Award at

GCSE. Some Classics. English is popular. All pupils must do one Modern Language (French, German or Spanish) at GCSE. There is an enormous range of optional subjects in Sixth Form studies. GCSE Drama, and PE, A-level Art, Textiles (the school writes its own curriculum), Home Economics, Religious Studies and Classical Civilisation. Girls and boys join up for specialist courses.

Computers are everywhere; they are not networked, girls and staff can take them home for weekends and holidays.

GAMES, OPTIONS, THE ARTS: Lacrosse, netball, swimming, all strong. Large sports hall, 18 tennis courts, and swimming pool – all shared with the Boys' Division (qv). Lots of minor sports: golf, squash. Fabulous Fabric and Art departments. Good Music. Regular toing and fro-ing with boys, lots of joint clubs (at lunch time – little activity after school). Newish Arts and Language Bureau attached to the 25-metre swimming pool – shared with the boys.

Senior girls help with Juniors, and Beech House (coat duties), and do occasional reading practice.

BACKGROUND AND ATMOSPHERE: Founded in 1877, under the auspices of the first Viscount Leverhulme (the soap sud king), who endowed the school in 1913 as a single Foundation in equal partnership with the Boys' Division, and moved it to its present site of 32 acres on the western edge of Bolton. Cloned with the Boys' Division (qv).

Junior School: Around 150 girls, ages 8–11, plus 200 boys and girls in Beech House, the pre-prep. Mistress in Charge: Mrs K M Critchley. Entrance via test at 8; also for children who have been in the pre-prep. Shares the campus with the senior school and uses some of its facilities. Thriving on all fronts: French starts early, lots of computers, good library, superb cooking and fabric facilities. Most girls transfer to the senior school via tests.

PASTORAL CARE AND DISCIPLINE: Yearly form tutors, who report to 'block' tutor. Form tutors meet with class twice a day and do mega termly interviews with each pupil – and also deal with any crisis. Staff 'pop in' to the girls' Sixth Form room and boys slip out of the other door – persistent offenders are reported across the quad. Sixth Formers allowed considerable latitude, clocking in each morning, but can then 'go shopping' if no classes are timetabled. Five hours' homework per subject per week, which may be done either at school or at home.

Detention, letters home for repeated minor offences, and sackings for the usual – drugs, pregnancy. Drugs educational specialists are on call.

PUPILS AND PARENTS: As per Boys' Division. Old Girls include Ann Taylor MP; Harriet Steele MP; and Dame Janet Smith QC.

ENTRANCE: Highly competitive. Own exam at 11+ (pupils from 57 different state schools currently applying), no automatic entry from junior school. Test and interview. Enormously oversubscribed with about four girls trying for each place. Entry at Sixth Form, test again, plus As at GCSE in A-level subjects.

EXIT: Trickle after GCSE. Almost all to University, with around 10 to Oxbridge.

MONEY MATTERS: There are 38 Assisted Places at 11+, five at 16+, with topping up from the school's Open Door Appeal Fund in keeping with the 'principal objectives of the first Lord

Leverhulme – that no boy or girl of potential who qualified on academic grounds but whose family were able to offer limited support would be debarred from entry to the school'. Can and will pick up unexpected financial crisis.

REMARKS: Still a worthy, progressive, well-endowed and sought-after academic city day school, with a strong work ethos and high aspirations.

Bradfield College

Bradfield, Reading, Berkshire RG7 6AR
Tel: 01734 744203, Fax: 01734 744195

PUPILS: Around 500 boys; 80 girls in Sixth Form (mostly boarding, about 30 day pupils)
AGES: 13–18
SIZE OF SIXTH FORM: About 280
C OF E
FEE-PAYING

HEAD: Since 1985, Mr Peter Smith, MA (forties), educated at Magdalen College School and Lincoln College, Oxford. Previously Housemaster at Rugby. Married with two teenage daughters. Known in the Thames Valley, says a parent, as 'the Chief Executive'. Former Oxfordshire cricket captain.

Affable but laid-back, or possibly shy. Plays cards close to his chest. Headmaster's office feels slightly isolated, given the sprawl of the school, but the Head assures us this is not so. Has an efficient secretary, Mrs Coutts.

ACADEMIC MATTERS: Some unusual and some excellent teaching. Japanese is a genuine option, taught by a native Japanese speaker (though the take-up is minimal). Eng Lit, Maths, Chemistry, Geography, are strong and

Biology results are much improved. Rather heavy amounts of Es (Economics in particular), also Ns dotted about A-level results. First-class honours graduates teach Maths, Biology, History, Religious Studies, Physics, English and Classics (for what that is worth in teaching terms). Severe streaming. Girls no longer bump up the results, according to the Head; League Table results are creditable, given intake. NB ALIS (see glossary) shows that the majority of Bradfield's academic departments do better than the norm as compared to other schools in the project, with English, Chemistry, Politics and Art candidates performing especially well.

GAMES, OPTIONS, THE ARTS: Seriously sporty – turns in solid wins in cricket and soccer and, says the school mag, in major block football fixtures. The First Eleven had their most successful ever post-war season in 1995, scoring 58 goals, winning more matches than any previous first eleven, and the Colts were undefeated – Phew! 'Games and games players are worshipped at Bradfield,' sighed a Sixth Form girl. A terrific new Sports Complex, built at a cost of £3 million and officially opened by OB Lord Owen, is huge and impressive. Girls also play a mean game of cricket, not to mention lacrosse, hockey, tennis, sailing, and riding (there is a riding school nearby). All manner of extras are also on offer such as fly-fishing, clay-pigeon shooting. Has one of the most beautiful cricket pitches in the country, The Pit. Keen CCF.

The school is famous for its open-air classical Greek theatre, in which is performed every three years a Greek play, in (classical) Greek; this draws enthusiasts from all over the world. The play is performed by the best thespians (rather than the classicists – there aren't a lot), – with a drama coach, and input from Classics masters. In 1994 it was Euripides'

Trojan Women. The theatre has an amazing atmosphere, stone seats surrounded by bosky glades, and it is also used for speech-day picnics, etc, as it can hold the whole school – definitely worth a detour.

Excellent Art department, with an atmosphere conducive to inspiration, and showing good work. Excellent school mag – the *Bradfield College Chronicle* – worth a browse to give some idea of the strength of extras.

BACKGROUND AND ATMOSPHERE: The school, founded in 1850, occupies a whole village just off the M4 and pupils are constantly walking up and down the road from one building to another. There are three purpose-built girls' houses – the ritziest we have seen, with en suite bathrooms which, according to a housemaster, only cost an extra £30K or so to do – well worth it. Most of the houses – particularly the girls' houses – are in sunny positions with views, and French windows opening out onto sunny lawns. The boys' houses are altogether tougher in aspect – choose house with care. Compulsory chapel three times a week, pupils still wear gowns. Beer is available in Blundell's, the school bar. Numbers have grown by 100 over the last eight years – more boys as well as the addition of girls, and NB with the opening of the third girls' boarding house (September '96) there is provision for 40 more girls.

PASTORAL CARE AND DISCIPLINE: The school freely offered us a copy of the local authority report. Head says he welcomes the inspection, to alert him to possible problems. (NB Given the geographical layout of the school, it is difficult for the Head, or indeed anybody, to keep tabs on everything at the same time.) Every family is regularly handed a large questionnaire to be filled in by parents after consultation with boys, giving, e.g., rating of communication with Housemaster from 1–5 – a very good chance to spot problems. Machismo still alive and well in one or two houses. 16 female members of staff (i.e. *gradually* increasing).

Not always an easy school for boys to settle in at 13+: 'It's tough,' said one.

PUPILS AND PARENTS: Jolly good chaps. Families mostly from business and high-tech industries in the M4 corridor. Around 15% from overseas, 10% sons of OBs. Famous OBs include David Owen, Richard Adams, Nobel prize-winner Martin Ryle, Leslie Glass and Stephen Milligan.

Girl talk: the school is the second choice for some – who then love it. Girls given pep talk early, encouraging them to join in everything – 'then you'll meet everybody'.

ENTRANCE: By CE or scholarship exam. Sixth Form entry for girls and boys (10–20 of latter at Sixth Form) on interview, IQ test, assessment and school report (and expectation of 'good grades' in 5 GCSEs). Draws pupils from 40 different prep schools (Elstree, Brockenhurst, St Andrew's Pangbourne, Papplewick, Hall Grove, King's House Richmond, Pilgrim's, St Neot's, Twyford, etc regularly; in '95, 40 boys came from 6 prep schools), but keeps in touch with 80 preps.

EXIT: Virtually everyone to higher education, most to degree courses, a few to drama and Royal Academy of Music, art. A handful to Oxford, lots to Edinburgh and other places north. Produces engineers and businessmen and a small percentage to the Services.

MONEY MATTERS: Up to 15 scholarships on offer of 10–15% of fees, with provision for upping this to 90%

in case of need. Up to 4 music scholarships of 20–50% of fees plus free tuition. Assisted places at Sixth Form. Parents who fall on hard times are asked to fill in a financial circumstances form, then the school does what it can to see pupil through to a sensible moment. Endowment is a freehold of 200 acres in Bradfield.

REMARKS: Strongly traditional public school which for some reason fails to catch the fashionable selector's eye despite all its advantages. Still retains its male atmosphere despite the softening influence of girls in the Sixth Form. Boys who survive to top are on the whole charming, however. Head comments the school is 'not for non-doers'.

Bradford Grammar School

Bradford BD9 4JP
Tel: 01274 545461, Fax: 01274 548129

PUPILS: 887 boys, plus 31 girls in the Sixth Form. (Also 179 boys in the Clock House, the junior school)
AGES: 11–18
SIZE OF SIXTH FORM: 292
NON-DENOM
FEE-PAYING

HEAD: From September 1996, Mr Stephen Davidson BSc, PGCE, (forties) educated at Tynemouth Grammar School, and read Metallurgical Engineering at Manchester University. Previously Head of the middle school at Manchester Grammar School. Married, with one young son. Takes over from the ebullient Mr David Smith: a hard act to follow.

ACADEMIC MATTERS: A really powerfully academic school, strong right across the board – Sciences especially so, particularly Chemistry, and 7 out of 10 pupils got A grade at A-level Electronic Systems in '95; History, Maths (29 out of 30 at A grades – gosh), and French also all doing extremely well, though overall fewer A grades in '95 than in some previous years – which said, 66% A–B at A-level. All five Latinists got A grade. Business Studies continues to be a highly popular subject. School keen on AS – 'good for stretching'. Super GCSE results. Expectations are incredibly high, and pupils work hard. Pupils are highly competitive, 'But not necessarily when we arrive here' confided one – and they thrive on it. Staff are 'amazingly devoted and committed' – and teach Sixth Formers 'as if they are university students,' said a parent. Low turnover of staff.

GAMES, OPTIONS, THE ARTS: Strong rugby – all credit to Mr Wappett, who continues to preside in a scruffy office at the back of the school. Recently coached the England Under-18 team. 'Really, Mr Wappett,' said a pupil, 'you know, he could train anybody.' (alas, leaving for Sedbergh). Both the First Fifteen and the Under-15 sides were semi-finalists in the *Daily Mail* National School's Cup, the first time the school had got as far as this. Cricket is good too; some outstanding results for the Under-16 tennis team. Keen Drama. Three full-time teachers for Design and Technology (and increasing numbers choosing it as an exam option). Art in somewhat cramped rooms. Visiting speaker every Friday. Half day each week is given over to sport, drama, music.

BACKGROUND AND ATMOSPHERE: The school dates back to the 16th century. Formerly a Free Grammar, became Direct Grant, then private (following abolition of Direct Grant). Pleasant setting on the outer edge of Bradford, in twenty acres of grounds, and all classrooms, games, etc, are on site – the present sandstone buildings were planned with 'incredible foresight'. There is a pleasing feel of space to corridors and quads between buildings. Subjects grouped together in Classics 'row', Geography 'row'. There is a large modern library and well-equipped IT rooms. Huge indoor swimming pool in the midst of the class blocks. No pre-fabs, though the new science block is extraordinarily badly designed. Pupils and staff are all purposeful and fully stretched – faint sense of production line.

Daily morning assembly. Very traditional, and quite hierarchical.

PASTORAL CARE AND DISCIPLINE: A lack of self-discipline is heavily frowned upon – and relatively rare. The Northern hard-working ethos is very much in place – but there is plenty of space to let off excess steam.

PUPILS AND PARENTS: Sons – and some daughters – of local businessmen, professionals, 15% Asians (usually bright and hard working – 'It suits us well here,' said one Sixth Former Asian girl). Old Boys include David Hockney (who comes back to the school), Denis Healey, Adrian Moorehouse. Pupils are courteous and self-confident, and neatly dressed. Recession has meant a continuing drop in numbers.

ENTRANCE: 50% from state school, via selective exam, average IQ is 120. Half the 11+ entry come in (also via exam) from the Clock House (for 8, 9, 10-year-olds), which has expanded since we last wrote and is going strong, tucked away at the side. Sixth Form girls get in on interview plus GCSEs.

EXIT: 23–33 to Oxbridge, it used to be between 40 and 50, but now 'the competition [from other universities] is greater'. *Bradfordian*, the school's magazine, is full of interesting charts on, amongst other things, university choices and subject choices and swings in these. Durham, Newcastle, Bristol, Nottingham, Edinburgh, Liverpool, Manchester, Birmingham are all popular choices, with streams reading History, Engineering, Modern Languages and Business Studies (often in combination with another subject); also Medicine.

MONEY MATTERS: Fees are kept purposely low – a bargain. 'I can look mothers in the face,' said the previous Head, 'and say, yes, it is worth going out to work.' 25% of pupils are on Assisted Places, plus various scholarships.

REMARKS: Steams successfully on. Still a first-class outward-looking grammar school, now in the hands of a new Head.

Bristol Grammar School

University Road, Bristol BS8 1SR
Tel: 0117 973 6006, Fax: 0117 946 7485

PUPILS: Around 1,040 boys and girls in the main school, plus another 270 7–10-year-olds
ALL DAY
AGES: 11–18
SIZE OF SIXTH FORM: Just under 300 in total – one of the biggest academic sixth forms in the south west.
C OF E
FEE-PAYING

HEAD: Since 1986, Mr Charles Martin MA (fifties). Historian (Cam-

bridge), not to mention ornithologist and sometime bee-keeper. An efficient, likeable chap, who has presided over a significant rise in numbers right through the recession, and in the teeth of large competition. On the National Assisted Places Committee. Came here via Leighton Park, Sevenoaks, Pocklington; then King Edward VI, Camp Hill, of which he was Head. Teaches the youngest class; his Deputy, the wonderfully steady Roger Perry, who has been here since the 1960s, teaches them Latin.

ACADEMIC MATTERS: The Head is anxious to disperse the perceived view of the school as a home from home for geniuses – 'your good average will do well here' he says, and points to the good academic results, in the light of this comment. The grammar school has some outstanding staff in all departments, putting in good rigorous teaching while at the same time – so it seemed to us – putting life into things.

Regularly produces a clutch of students studying Russian (the Head of Modern Languages is married to a Russian and writes Russian textbooks), and the school does an exchange with St Petersburg. Also Classics is alive and well here (indeed, 'year eight' – the youngest – nominated Latin as one of their two favourite subjects.

Class sizes are a maximum of 30 at the bottom of the school, 15 at the top (but often far fewer). GCSE results are outstanding – just to pick one from an embarrassment of good choice – Maths '95 got 37 starred As, 53 As, 51 Bs and 7 Cs – nothing less. Among the top fifty GCSE results in the country. General Studies not taken at A-level.

No streaming or setting when pupils first enter the main school; first setting is in Maths in 'year 8'. The school does not reckon to have to cater much for learning difficulties, but that said, there are 'little groups' all over the school doing extra lessons in e.g. the lunch hour.

GAMES, OPTIONS, THE ARTS: Strong, no-nonsense DT department. Boys do rugby, hockey, cricket; girls hockey, netball, tennis and athletics. PE is mixed – the girls seem to hold their own, though the boys are noticeably more enthusiastic. The school owns large acres of playing fields at Failand (as do other Bristol schools) and pupils are bussed out – it's part of Clifton school life. There is a gym on the site, much used (a large fencing class was in progress when we visited, both girls and boys). Interform competitions are held at lunchtime ('we eat quickly', commented a pupil).

Over 140 pupils are 'going through to gold' in the Duke of Edinburgh's award scheme – an amazing number for a school without an Outward Bound tradition. Public speaking is a popular option (the school was recently regional winner of the *Observer* mace competition).

Stunningly good library – county standard, and with a £15,000-a-year budget, beautifully catalogued and laid out; a joy to use.

BACKGROUND AND ATMOSPHERE: Founded in 1532 as a boys' grammar school, with the usual worthy objectives, by the Thorne brothers – hence the school's motto, – *ex spinis uvas.*

The school is dominated by the huge, hangar-like Gothic, old School Hall, which has wooden seats carved into the walls where masters sat, warming their feet on the (only) hot pipe, with assorted pupils ranged in front of them. Today the old hall is used for concerts, for lunch etc, and provides a distinguished focal point. All around this, the school has mushroomed out, perched up on the hill, just beside the university (Sixth Formers

sometimes use university labs). The school has even gone into 'layers' with IT underneath, and a grassy walkway on top.

The atmosphere is unbelievably bouncy, almost rough, with girls being swept aside as the boys play ball games in the slightly confined playgrounds. There is also an impression of excitement, fun and hard work, and the senior mistress commented she would like to think that the school was 'a place where the eccentric can be safe in' – a wonderful thought.

PASTORAL CARE AND DISCIPLINE: The first two years are housed in the Princess Anne Building (so called because she opened it), under the care of Mr Huckle, who, said a parent, is 'tremendous . . . he treats each child as if his own'. Before the new children come to the school, the staff go out to the children's previous school to introduce themselves, and generally go out of their way to make new pupils feel at home. Each pupil is given a booklet, which seems to be modelled on many state sector booklets we have seen, and is full of simple, useful reassuring information, such as what to do if you're feeling unwell.

Thereafter, each year has its tutor groups, and an overall Head of Year. Bullying is reacted to fast, and although some drugs must be expected in an inner site not far from a notoriously druggy area, our impression is that the school is too open (every corner being used for legitimate purposes) and too busy for the drug culture to get much hold.

Going co-ed (over the past 15 years), with all the changes that this entails, has been accomplished under the calm and thoughtful eye of Mrs Pemberton, who comments that girls 'learn the same things differently'. Sixth Formers confess themselves so at ease that they literally have to think twice before working out how many of each sex is in any particular set.

PUPILS AND PARENTS: Sons and daughters of Bristol businessmen, lots of first-time buyers, and a fair amount of *vin* pretty *ordinaire*. Surprisingly few famous old boys, given the long-standing strength of the school: Tom Graveney the cricketer is one, also Allen of Penguin fame, otherwise it's clergymen, doctors, solicitors, etc.

ENTRANCE: Entry exam at 11+ (earlier, if 'mature') held in January for September – held in conjunction with several other Bristol private schools. One-third of pupils come up from the Grammar School's own junior school (on the same site, but separated by a high wire fence), the rest from schools not just all over Bristol, but all over Avon as well – as far flung as Weston super Mare. Typical feeds are Henleaze, Elmleigh and Stoke Bishop primaries, Colston's Primary in Cotham, Westbury Park, Westbury C of E, plus Clifton, Redmaids, Redlands, Clifton High etc.

EXIT: Mostly to the strong, popular red-brick universities – everywhere but Bristol, really. Few to Oxbridge, for a Sixth Form of this size. They go on to be teachers, doctors, solid citizens.

MONEY MATTERS: Fees just under £4,000 a year as we write – a bargain. There is an unspecified number of assisted places, but 'it is rare for assistance not to be available for all able pupils whose parents' income qualifies them for fee assistance'. A few academic and music scholarships (the latter paying for music tuition only). One-third of the pupils are on 'assistance of some sort'. The school is part of the Bristol Municipal Charities.

This is not a rich school, but selling land in the city has produced some endowment, and, given the large growth in numbers, the school does not have a problem laying hands on the money it needs out of fee income.

REMARKS: Once the state grammar school catering for the academic cream of Bristol's male youth. Now a private sector grammar school producing top class academic results with a less selective intake. In most areas comes top of the 10 private schools in Bristol, though it is not the place for social climbers.

Bryanston School

Blandford Forum, Dorset DT11 0PX
Tel: 01258 452411, Fax: 01258 484661
PUPILS: Around 400 boys, 260 girls. Around 600 board, the rest day
AGES: 13–18
SIZE OF SIXTH FORM: 260
C OF E
FEE-PAYING

HEAD: Since 1983 (and says he's staying till 2005) Mr Tom Wheare, MA (early fifties), educated Magdalen College School and Cambridge, where he read History. Married with two daughters, one at Bryanston. A good front man for the school, very professional, and easy to talk to. Hobbies are music and drama – he sings in school, and occasionally directs plays. Wife, Ros, is one of the school's 'independent listeners' – someone to talk to in confidence – set up in response to the Children Act, Esther Rantzen and all that. Mrs Wheare also runs the fortnightly OAP community visits. A zealous PR head – some would say too zealous.

ACADEMIC MATTERS: School has reputation for being arty, but in fact Sciences have a substantial following at A-level, Physics especially, with 18 out of 37 candidates gaining A grade in '95. Separate sciences and Dual Award science both on offer. Economics is also popular and the Economics master, Peter Hardy, has written a very readable book on Mrs Thatcher's Britain. English is far and away the most popular subject at A-level at the last count, and does very well; also a strong History department and good French. The school has an active exchange programme with both Europe and with the States. A wide range of subjects is offered and taken up at both GCSE and A-level, including Sports Studies, and the school will let you do a subject even if you are the only one (Spanish, surprisingly, had only one pupil recently) or even Turkish – an unusual and refreshing/expensive attitude, not often to be found, sadly. The school is continuing to 'explore' the possibility of offering vocational courses.

Pupils are assigned an academic tutor on entering school and keep the same tutor all the way up the school. Much is made of the school's use of the American Dalton system of timetabling – lots of chart filling, and free periods in which weekly projects 'must be done', with tutors on tap at specific times. This is meant to give a little preparation for the tutorial-based system at university. Some parents are slightly nervous about the temptation for pupils to pull the wool over staff's eyes. All academic subjects are setted. The number of As at A-level is creeping up. Brilliant CDT Centre designed by Piers Gough (observe the column on entrance – large left-handed screws). Size of classes 12 – 20. Staff:pupil ratio 1:10. This is the first choice school for dyslexics, with good backup.

GAMES, OPTIONS, THE ARTS: All staff take three afternoons of games or pioneering work a week, and are supposed to be available to pupils three evenings a week. Pupils must do something sporty twice a week, but this is not a school which worships the team game. Rowing school, with the glorious River Stour flowing at the bottom of the games fields.

'Pioneering' (= community work) is, however, compulsory and a big feature of the school – chopping logs, visiting old people, maintaining the school grounds. Art is *still* desperately uninspiring – despite years of complaint (but a new art building is planned for 1997). Drama is good and enthusiastic – '60s Coade Hall and Greek theatre. Music is strong.

BACKGROUND AND ATMOSPHERE: The Norman Shaw house for Viscount Portman is 'more like a town hall than a private house,' to quote John Betjeman. Grand buildings make it a great favourite with staff and parents to visit for a summer ball, etc. Stunning grounds, with approach by a long drive which, says the Bursar (Mr Goucher, a five-star fellow), always wows the parents – 'by the time they get to the front door they are sold on the place'.

The House system is rudimentary – school is centrally run from a huge notice board in the 100-yard front hall (parquet flooring everywhere), and much lingering about goes on in and around there. Some boys and all girls live in purpose-built blocks (girls' houses all have hair-dryers). New boarding accommodation for boys, and some live in the main building.

Excellent food from a self-service in the basement, with an omelette bar capable of flipping out omelettes at a rate of 150 in 40 minutes.

Recent changes to dress guidelines (to make pupils neater). Atmosphere of *je . . . m'en fiche* and let-it-all-hang-out vis-à-vis appearance appears to be still in evidence. This laid-back image is at odds with the formality of the surroundings.

The Sixth Form common room can provoke strong parental reaction: 'Cosy atmosphere would be putting it mildly – it's like a fairly sleazy night club,' said a father, adding, 'But they love it.'

PASTORAL CARE AND DISCIPLINE: Heavily into pastoral care; not so heavily into discipline. There is a slightly obsessive, American-style preoccupation with relationships, feelings, etc. Given the liveliness of the place and the trickiness of some of the inmates, it's a difficult place to manage. Head comments that the Children Act has given them the 'opportunity to be positive' – and has set up an intricate system for complaints, problems, etc, which, he said, was well patronised to start with, but has now dwindled as the novelty wears off (pity).

Expulsion is automatic for drugs or for pupils being caught in bed together. There is a tiered system of punishment for smoking (many parents are in despair over this), drinking, etc – gatings, warnings, etc. 'Night wandering' – climbing on to the roof and racing round the parapet – is still the occasional excitement. The Head must consult the chairman of governors for a pupil to be 'withdrawn out of time', and if they have to let a pupil go, he does his utmost to find another school. There is a chapel in the grounds, but there is not much evidence of organised religion.

PUPILS AND PARENTS: Middle-class trendies' children, and media. About 100 ex-pats, including lots of Service families, and a wide selection of foreigners. Articulate, but a tendency to self-obsession can result in slight gracelessness. OBs include Quinlan Terry, Lucien Freud, John Eliot Gardiner, Frederick Sanger, Mark Elder, and some Conrans.

ENTRANCE: Via scholarship exam, CE, or school's own entrance exam. The recession has wiped out the large waiting list, and it is now worth applying at the last minute. Pupils come from prep schools all over the country, particularly co-eds. Useful entry at Sixth Form – qualification is 'they need to be capable of taking A-levels'.

EXIT: Some leakage post-GCSE. Solid chunks go to Oxford, Bristol, Cambridge and London universities. Otherwise scattered around the south, mostly to higher education. 20 to new ex-polytechnic universities.

MONEY MATTERS: Fees are 'always in the top ten'. Around 7% of fee income goes on bursaries. If parents are in genuine financial difficulties, the school tries to work out something – 5% reduction, 10% – 'if I can help, I will,' says Head. Also, 8 academic scholarships, 4 music, 4 sport and 1 art at 13, 2 academic and 2 music at Sixth Form.

REMARKS: All round co-ed liberal education. In its heyday, it had a long run as one of the two top co-ed boarding schools in the country and now faces far greater competition, but it has fallen in popularity and feels, dare we say it, a bit tired. ... Which said, this is a home from home for wild live wires, and is well suited to the socially buoyant.

Burford School and Community College

Cheltenham Road, Burford, Oxfordshire OX18 4PL
Tel: 01993 823303, Fax: 01993 823101

PUPILS: Approx 1,200, boys and girls (approx 85 board, the rest day)
AGES: 11–18
SIZE OF SIXTH FORM: About 220

INTER-DENOM
STATE (boarding fees approx £1,650 a term)

HEAD: Since 1995, Mr Patrick Sanders BA, FRSA, (forties), with a degree in English and American Studies from Hull, (PGCE from Bristol). Teaches English in the Lower School. Previously Head of the Cotswold School, Gloucestershire, and before that Deputy Head of Wallingford School. Married, with two children; a keen family man, and an enthusiastic sportsman. Comments that 'My main job is to consolidate.'

ENTRANCE: Comprehensive intake. Siblings get priority, then locals, and of those from further afield, boarders will get priority – for obvious financial reasons.

EXIT: Wide and interesting next steps. Large numbers to ex-polys, also to long-established red-brick universities (Newcastle, Bristol, etc); some straight into employment; and a handful do a 'gap' year. One or two to university abroad.

REMARKS: Large state comprehensive with a boarding element which is useful to know about, and useful to have on your doorstep. Exam results are not brilliant. Keen on extra-curricular activities.

A good range of subjects is offered at Sixth Form level – not just the usual subjects, but Theatre Studies, Sports Studies, Photography, Environmental Science, IT, etc – much stronger than the average private school. National Curriculum followed. Some setting after the first year. Senior students are expected to do two hours' homework a night. Maximum class size: 'we're always stretching it, but the average in the first three years is 26 or less' (this is good for a

state school). The A-level results are still significantly above the national average. A special needs department gives help both in and out of class. The school's spelling policy brings tears of joy to middle-class parents. Staff are enthusiastic and helpful; teaching exchanges are encouraged. GNVQs now in place.

Mainly middle class, including 40+ RAF children, and around 60% of boarding children have parents in the Forces.

The school farm (approximately 40 acres) has just been re-introduced and put into working operation by the new Head (it had been closed for a couple of years). A great plus for giving students hands-on agricultural experience and preparation for GCSE subjects, e.g. Rural Science.

Founded by Charter in 1571, it has been through different stages. Beautiful surroundings; reasonably attractive front buildings. There are some grammar school hangovers – including house systems, prefects, ushers, uniform. The boarding house is in the old grammar school site in picturesque Burford (Lenthall House, for both sexes), and is cheerful and friendly – which is true of the whole school.

Suffers on occasion from low expectations. 'You have to teach them at home,' commented a parent with two children in the school.

Camden School for Girls

Sandall Road, London NW5 2DB
Tel: 0171 485 3414, Fax: 071 284 3361

PUPILS: 840, including 60 boys in the Sixth Form
AGES: 11–19

ALL DAY
SIZE OF SIXTH FORM: 275
NON-DENOMINATIONAL
STATE

HEAD: Since 1989, Mr Geoffrey Fallows MA, FRSA (early fifties). Educated at Shrewsbury, read Classics at Oxford. Previously Deputy Head here, and has taught at College in the USA, a boys' grammar school and the largest London comprehensive. Married with two grown-up daughters. Traditionalist.

ACADEMIC MATTERS: National curriculum plus; classical studies of some sort for all, some do Latin and Greek – both are available. Setting for Maths, Sciences and Languages mainly in Key Stage 4, and pupils of widely differing abilities stretch the immensely dedicated staff, who start here early in the morning and often give girls extra tuition. The school has high expectations and proudly continues the founder's tradition of 'promoting opportunities for girls'. Over 60% have achieved A–C grades for GCSE in '94, 70% in '95. A-levels also do well – large numbers transfer from other schools including the private sector, with English far and away the most popular subject, followed by Art, then History. AS-level and GNVQ courses are also on offer, the latter fairly recently introduced.

Sixth Form numbers have now stabilised (they were previously too large, but are still very large), and the school works as partners in a Camden consortium at Sixth Form.

GAMES, OPTIONS, THE ARTS: Particularly strong in the arts, and Music is ambitious with several choirs (Mozart Requiem, Haydn Mass, etc) and orchestras, with several pupils in the London Schools Symphony Orchestra. Big range of Drama events.

BACKGROUND AND ATMOSPHERE: Founded in 1871 by that great pioneer in women's education, Frances Mary Buss (who also founded North London Collegiate (qv). The hotchpotch of buildings, old and new, are all prefabricated; there are three workshops for Design and Technology and one for Sixth Form classes. The Sixth Form is bursting at the seams of its now too small building. Facilities are good despite some overcrowding. The school has a relaxed atmosphere with a buzz of excitement in some areas, e.g. art. No uniform (which means eye-catching dressers at the top end).

PASTORAL CARE AND DISCIPLINE: The truancy rate is low; staff are 'fairly strict' about courtesy ('but not always successfully so,' notes a parent). A supportive and fairly tight system is particularly good with children in difficult circumstances.

PUPILS AND PARENTS: Very broad mix. Mixed race, with 40% black or Asian; substantial numbers of well-off middle-class girls and also the socially deprived. Well-heeled middle-class parents continue to opt to live in the area in order to benefit from the school. Always a bunch of talkative, expressive, independent-minded girls. Old Girls include Emma Thompson, Sara Kestelman, Kate Saunders.

ENTRANCE: Heavily oversubscribed for year 7 entry. 107 places are available. Preference for sisters, and for up to 5 Music places (new since '95), then for a small number of girls granted social or medical priority; remaining places allocated on the basis of distance from the school – in practice a mile is usually too far. At 16+ by interview (distance not a factor at this stage). Boys admitted since 1989.

EXIT: 70% continue into the Sixth Form; 70% continue into higher education (5–8 a year to Oxbridge), art college a popular choice.

MONEY MATTERS: Parents and girls are expected to help with – and are good at – fund-raising to help building programme/maintenance. All parents are asked to give £10 per term to supplement school funds.

REMARKS: An exciting and lively London comprehensive state school which encourages self-motivation and also feminism, led by staff with high expectations.

Canford School

Wimborne, Dorset BH21 3AD
Tel: 01202 841254, Fax: 01202 881009

PUPILS: 411 boys, 94 girls. (283 boys board, 128 day boys; 65 girls board, 29 day girls)
AGES: 13–18
SIZE OF SIXTH FORM: 242
C OF E
FEE-PAYING

HEAD: Since 1992, Mr John Lever, MA (Hons) (Cantab), PGCE, (forties), educated at Winchester; read Geography at Trinity, Cambridge, and a Rowing Blue. Taught briefly at St Edward's School before returning to Winchester for sixteen years where he became Head of Geography and was Housemaster for eight years. Married to Alisoun, with three young children.

Teaches PSE and thinks that a 'positive attitude to their own talents and other people's values is absolutely critical.' Keen on 'encouraging a greater sense of intellectual curiosity.'

Thoughtful, humorous, and an enthusiast, he is passionate about boarding – 'develops unselfishness', and 'extends sense of community'. Has involved Canford much more with the locals: pupils help with local charities, Riding for the Disabled, give swimming lessons to local handicapped children in the Canford pool and help tinies at local primary schools with reading.

ACADEMIC MATTERS: The Biology department hums with excitement, a 'terrific place', under Head of Department, Andrew Powell, who 'leads from the front'; very popular trips to almost everywhere – deep-sea diving in Israel, visits to Costa Rica, charting flora off Old Harry (rock), plus trips to Wales and overseeing the local SSSI. They also write and design their own software (and sell it: *Arachne*), and write and sell their own Geography software too.

John James, Head of English, was organising 'A Conflict Week' when we visited, with tanks in the grounds, exhibitions in the Library, food rations, and streams of lectures: Kate Adie, Vernon Scannell; General Sir Brian Kenny, GCB, CBE; G B Jameson MC.

The Physics and Design Technology departments organised 'Engineering Week' in '95 including visits and demonstrations by Rover (with Go-Karts) and Lotus (with cycle); university lecturers came in to talk about bridges, bio-engineering, vibrations etc. This all generated much excitement and similar operations are in the pipeline.

Pupils are setted for Maths, French, Latin; max 22 per class, top movers streamed. Computers throughout, plus a busy Computer Room (which staff also use). IT is linked to Business Studies A-level.

Results are good and steady, particularly considering the relatively wide ability range. Sciences, including Chemistry, particularly strong, also Geography and Art. Remedial help and individual lessons are organised.

GAMES, OPTIONS, THE ARTS: Strong on games, with Astroturf hockey pitches also used by locals – i.e. Bournemouth Clubs, who also pay to use Royal tennis court, squash and golf course (v popular). Has a new Sports Hall with a full-sized indoor hockey pitch. The 300 acres of superbly sculpted grounds with a pool, hard tennis courts and games fields are enjoyed by pupils and staff alike.

Sailing on the flooded quarry at Ringwood, racing at Poole Harbour, and sculling on the River Stour which runs through the estate. Girls are keen and good coxes. Rowing going well. CCF is popular; shooting an option.

Prominent Music, also theatre (outdoor theatre). Art is fun and thriving, with good ceramics. The CDT department has doubled in size.

BACKGROUND AND ATMOSPHERE: Founded in 1923 in a marvellous gothic Barry design, built for the Guest family according to a (not much visible) Norman design; ponderous 19th-century interiors, but a splendid dining hall (with 21st-century facilities – vegetarian meals are popular). Building in progress includes an Art School extension, and, coming next, a theatre.

Girls have a state-of-the-art new house – Marriotts – with single and double bedrooms (and sewing machines and kitchens). A second girls' house is currently in the final stages of being built, and will be open by the time this book appears. Day houses are mixed, and single-sex boarding houses have rooms for socialising with the opposite sex. The school went fully co-ed in September '95 (though girls have been in the Sixth Form since the early '70s), with 21 girls in the first intake, who will work their way up.

The Norman chapel in the grounds is used for services in rotation (too small for the whole school) and by Canford Magna for weddings, etc. The school is ringed with a security trench, and only one entrance is in use. The library has been revamped. Popular student newspaper, Young Enterprise and D of E Award. Juke box in Tuck Shop. Bar for older pupils at weekends.

PASTORAL CARE AND DISCIPLINE: Housemaster/mistress plus three tutors and matron in each house. Each pupil has a tutorial (either individual or by group) with a tutor each week. Local ex-parents act as independent listeners. Some super matrons, and 'good mature pastoral care,' commented the Head of a neighbouring prep school.

One drugs incident since we last went to press. The anti-drugs policy is 'to keep pupils busy', and teach them 'how to say no'. 'No hesitation in throwing child out for bullying', but the prefectorial system works well. Eternal vigilance is the watchword here.

PUPILS AND PARENTS: Most from within a one-and-a-half-hour drive; huge car park for older day pupils. Few foreign nationals – eight to ten. Large number of Forces children. Growing numbers of first-time buyers. Fairly laid-back.

ENTRANCE: CE (50% pass required); interview. Prep school recommendation matters: 15 regular feeders, Castle Court and Dumpton the largest.

Girls and some boys arrive after GCSE at A–C. Sixth Formers come from local state schools, and from other fee-paying schools.

EXIT: 91% to Universities: 18 to Oxbridge in 1994 – an unusually good year, 12–15 the norm. Strong on engineers, professions. Southampton popular for scientists.

MONEY MATTERS: Assisted Places at 13+ and 16+. Total capacity of 35 in school is not all taken up. Scholarships at 13+ for Academic, Art, Music, and 'Allrounder'. Will keep child in exam year if real financial need, 'work with parents'. No bad debtors, but extended payments. Numbers increasing.

Coffers given a terrific boost in July '94 by sale at auction for £7.7m, of a 3,000-year-old Assyrian bas-relief, which had previously hung unrecognised in the school tuck shop.

REMARKS: Confident, decent, unpressurised boarding and day public school with a dash of pizzazz and good vibes, which does well for the middle-of-the-road; co-ed now taking off. Could be just what you are looking for and hadn't thought of.

Cardinal Vaughan Memorial School

89 Addison Road, London W14 8BZ
Tel: 0171 603 8478, Fax: 0171 602 3124

PUPILS: 580 boys, plus 40 girls in Sixth
  Form
ALL DAY
AGES: 11–18
SIZE OF SIXTH FORM: 160
RC
STATE

HEAD: Since 1976, Mr A S J Pelligrini BA, FRSA (early fifties). Formerly Deputy Head. First lay head appointed. Likeable, hands-on Head, who teaches liberal studies and religious education in

the school. Read History at LSE (Italian Renaissance). Unmarried.

ACADEMIC MATTERS: Religious Education considerable – at least as many take religious studies at GCSE as take English and Maths. Sciences – 'we cream off our ablest scientists after the second year and they jolly well do Physics, Chemistry and Biology as specialist subjects.' All other children are required to do 'balanced' sciences' (i.e. Dual Award). Small but competent Classics Department. In '92 increased the working week by one hour to fit everything in – 8.30 a.m. to 3.40 p.m. Over 25% female staff at last count. Five recently refurbished labs; brand new Arts and Technology Centre.

Hallelujah – a school which breaks down A-level results by sex. It shows that here at any rate the girls are strongly biased towards arts, and overall do not do quite as well as the boys – which is against the national trend.

According to league tables, the school consistently does well by Inner London state school standards – not that that is saying much, alas, and Deputy Head Michael Gormally points out that in the 1995 results, the school was 'placed among the 200 top-performing state schools in country', a position it has maintained for a few years.

GAMES, OPTIONS, THE ARTS: Extremely active sports – soccer the main game, but also bussed to river for rowing (strong), and fencing. Pupils go to Kensington Sports Centre for swimming. Excellent playing fields next to Rugby Football Ground at Twickenham. Pupils do one whole afternoon of games a week, plus PE in school. There is a new IT Centre. Lots of school trips to e.g. Lourdes. Really strong choral music – choirs taking part in events all over London, e.g. the English National

Opera's production of *Carmen*, and also performing abroad.

BACKGROUND AND ATMOSPHERE: Built at the turn of century as a memorial to Herbert Vaughan, third Archbishop of Westminster, whose chief claim to fame was the building of Westminster Cathedral. Originally a private grammar school, it changed tack in 1945 following the 1944 Education Act. Super site (leafy) behind Holland Park. Upper and Lower school split, however, by a busy one-way road – parts of the school are warm and mellow, parts '60s functional. Black and grey uniform (school hot on that). Busy, friendly atmosphere, and a feeling of safety, unlike many Inner London state schools which are jungles.

PASTORAL CARE AND DISCIPLINE: Good: taken seriously. Sex education is entrusted to the Religious Education Department. All members of Upper Sixth are appointed prefects – to set a good example to younger boys. A 'homework centre' is available each evening – good news for working parents. There is a daunting list of thou-shalt-nots – including 'The use of corrective fluids and thinners is strictly forbidden'.

PUPILS AND PARENTS: School is fed by 'strategically placed' RC primaries, including Our Lady of Victories Primary School, St Joseph's Maida Vale, St Francis, Notting Hill.

ENTRANCE: By test on application for 'balanced intake'. Primary criterion for admission – 'evidence of baptism or reception into the Roman Catholic Church'. Head points out that it is untrue to say the school creams off talent from less RC establishments. Always oversubscribed – Head points to heart-breaking piles of letters going out rejecting hopeful candidates. Entry at Sixth Form for both sexes.

EXIT: Large numbers leave post-GCSE. Of those that stay on to do A-level – lots to London University, also to nearby ex-polys, some scattered further afield (Leicester, Exeter, Bristol, etc), and a handful to Oxbridge. Also Chelsea College of Art.

MONEY MATTERS: Grant-maintained.

REMARKS: A kind, religious state school with dedicated staff, and a comprehensive intake which appears to be doing better academically.

Casterton School

Kirkby Lonsdale, Cumbria LA6 2SG
Tel: 01524 271202, Fax: 01520 271146
PUPILS: 348 girls (of whom over 80% board)
AGES: 8–18 (40 aged 8–11) plus 30 boys and girls in pre-prep
C OF E
FEE-PAYING

HEAD: Since 1990, Mr Tony Thomas, MA (Cantab) (fifties), educated at William Hulme's Grammar School in Manchester. Previously Housemaster and Head of Maths at Sedbergh. Lacrosse international (he coaches lacrosse), keen on drama. Described by one parent as a 'surprising appointment, he wouldn't set the world alight'. Another one comments he is a 'sound, commonsense man'. Very keen on single-sex schooling, 'girls work jolly hard'. Norwegian wife, Kirsti, and two sons, at Sedbergh and Shrewsbury. The third headmaster at Casterton.

ACADEMIC MATTERS: Steady results, with over 51% A–B grades at A-level. Has been top in GCSE league tables in the past. Strongest in English, History, and Modern Languages good, also good A-level Economics results. Maximum class size is 20, new Science/-Maths building opened in 1995, and two new computer rooms opened in 1993. Can deal with 'mild dyslexia'. Mixture of male and female staff.

GAMES, OPTIONS, THE ARTS: Lacrosse (obviously) as well as hockey and netball. Strong parental demand for all-weather pitches. A Creative Arts Centre opened in 1990, and much used for lots of jolly productions (musicals a favourite), sometimes with Sedbergh boys. Indoor swimming pool. Good Music and Drama. Successful Young Enterprise groups.

BACKGROUND AND ATMOSPHERE: The Brontës' school, founded in 1823, as the Clergy Daughters' School; the central house includes a dining room and library. Sensible through and through: 'They long for glamour,' says a parent. Lots of good limestone conversions, and houses are dotted around the tiny, friendly village (18-year-olds can go to the local pub). Own riding stables.

Sixth Formers have study bedrooms. Most do D of E. Strong links with local boys' schools – particularly Sedbergh, but also Stonyhurst and Barnard Castle. Regular trips to Manchester, Leeds, Liverpool and London, plus work experience.

PASTORAL CARE AND DISCIPLINE: 'Haven't sacked for many years now.' Will expel for 'usual reasons' – automatically for drugs.

PUPILS AND PARENTS: Mostly local: though 'a dozen' or so real foreigners. 'Not a snobby school', with lots of first-time buyers and 'new money' said a parent. Also lots of Forces children.

ENTRANCE: Own entrance exam: most pupils come via Brontë (the Junior House), but entry at any time. New pre-prep started in September 1993, and is going well.

EXIT: Tiny leakage post-GCSE: around 95% go on to higher education, and NB this percentage is considerably increased since we last wrote, even taking into account national trends; previous parental grumbles (hotly denied by the school) 'that they have to do all the work' (finding the courses available), appear to be fading and career guidance is 'getting better'.

MONEY MATTERS: Numbers on the up (and consequently so is the school's income). Around 50 Assisted Places, not all taken up – particularly at Sixth Form level. Regular bursaries and scholarships (out of income) at 11+, 12+, 13+; but basically support is provided for real emergencies, rather than on ability basis. Not a rich school.

REMARKS: Friendly girls' boarding school – cosy, happy, but lacking muscle. Popular with locals, and numbers gradually increasing.

Central Newcastle High School

Eskdale Terrace,
Newcastle upon Tyne NE2 4DS
Tel: 0191 281 1768, Fax: 0191 281 3267
PUPILS: 596 girls
ALL DAY

AGES: 11–18
SIZE OF SIXTH FORM: 180
NON-DENOM
FEE-PAYING

HEAD: Since 1984, Mrs A Chapman, MA (early fifties), educated Teesside High School, Bristol University and the Sorbonne. Previously taught at neighbouring Church High. Very charming and articulate, keen tennis player, actively interested in careers. Teaches French to Sixth Formers in small groups. Tells youngest girls, 'Always ask, why?' Hot on confidence, far from being a feminist, but informs the Sixth Formers, 'If you know your value, then you will get ambition from that.' Urges them to stay calm: 'If you want something and are really determined – so few are – and remain quietly determined, you will get it.'

ACADEMIC MATTERS: Far and away the most academic girls' day school for miles around, and gets consistently good results. Sciences are particularly strong, and a remarkable number of girls go in for medical careers. Over half the girls take all three separate Sciences at GCSE, the rest two, occasionally one. An eighth laboratory is currently being built in a neighbouring building, which will also house more teaching rooms and an enlarged IT department. Languages are especially strong (Japanese, Arabic, Italian on offer for Sixth Formers; also Japanese pen friends). Choice of French and Spanish, or French and German in alternate years. French exchanges at 11 ('targeted academically rather than socially') are very successful. Philosophy recently introduced for 11-year-olds – and proving highly popular. AS Psychology is also a successful addition to the menu.

A General English course is offered to non-English A-levellers, and broadening 'general interest' programmes for all Sixth Formers, some subjects for a full year, others in 10-week blocks. Girls often notch up yet another GCSE in the Lower Sixth, or AS French; Maths refreshers also available. 28 per class, but fewer in teaching groups. The Northern work ethic is in place, though the Head points out that such is the atmosphere that girls apply pressure to themselves: 'I tell them they must have a good holiday during Christmas.' Work and progress is carefully monitored at all stages. The Careers department received a boost from the Tyneside TEC 'matched funding' initiative and now boasts sophisticated information systems in a newly constructed careers office.

GAMES, OPTIONS, THE ARTS: Outstandingly strong tennis, boosted by a new indoor tennis court – under-11 national tennis champions two years running, and under-14s doing well. (Mrs Chapman is convinced that playing tennis well has a good effect on concentration). Parents still think there is not much for the also-rans on the sports side, but team opportunities are not always taken up by girls. The school does consider itself gamesy (golf is now on offer) and it is notably more 'rounded' than some sister GPDST schools. The very enthusiastic Art department is housed in part of a former synagogue. Music was recently given a 'much needed boost', commented one mother. New Music School houses a keyboard laboratory and recording studio.

BACKGROUND AND ATMOSPHERE: The school, founded in 1895, is in a quiet area of Jesmond (convenient for the underground), just along the road from the Royal Grammar School (qv). The Sixth Form have their own house round the corner; the gym is round another corner; the erstwhile synagogue now serves as a coffee shop used by Sixth Formers from both Central High and RGS (manned by parents). Parents and staff are extremely committed.

PASTORAL CARE AND DISCIPLINE: A caring school, with a firm emphasis on 'basic values'.

PUPILS AND PARENTS: Solidly middle-class. Brothers are often up the road at the Royal Grammar School. Miriam Stoppard is an Old Girl.

ENTRANCE: Hard to get in (many come up via the school's own junior department, not far away); fairly tough competition at 11+ (though some choose the gentler Church High and Westfields, both are much less academic).

EXIT: Rare for girls not to go on to university, 9–10 a year to Oxbridge, 'though it's often not the first choice.' Medicine is especially popular.

MONEY MATTERS: There are 18 Assisted Places at 11+, and 5 at Sixth Form; 3 academic scholarships (of varying worth), 1 bursary.

REMARKS: Strong and consistent, this is a flourishing and sought-after academic girls' day school, with no local rivals, under firm leadership. Super all round.

Channing School

Highgate, London N6 5HF
Tel: 0181 340 2328, Fax: 0181 341 5698

PUPILS: 325 girls
ALL DAY
AGES: 11–18

SIZE OF SIXTH FORM: 68
NON-DENOM (Unitarian)
FEE-PAYING

HEAD: Since 1984, Mrs Isabel Raphael MA Cantab (fifties). Educated at Cheltenham Ladies' ('large and impersonal, a tremendous contrast with Channing'), read English and Classics. Came here from City of London Girls' (she had previously taught at Channing). Two grown-up sons; formerly married to a journalist and has lived in (amongst other places) Paris, Vietnam, New York. Extremely clear-headed, both gentle and steely, with a reputation for fighting hard to keep the brightest girls on through Sixth Form. Knows all her pupils well.

ACADEMIC MATTERS: Doing well and coming up the academic ladder: ranked 48th nationally in A-level league tables (but NB 40 girls sat A-levels in '95, compared with double/treble this at larger schools) and 97th in the *Financial Times* five-year results. Strong English (distinctly well taught, with 14 out of 17 getting A grade), and good results in Biology with far more girls taking this at A-level. Several Heads of Department are men. Dual Award Science for GCSE. All girls study IT to certificate level, and get it over and done with before the GCSE run-up. Classes of 25–26, shrink for GCSEs. The Head of RE, a Unitarian Minister, teaches comparative religion.
  Library newly enlarged, formally opened by Booker prizewinner Penelope Lively.

GAMES, OPTIONS, THE ARTS: Not really a sporty school, though there are tennis courts on the site (doubling up for hockey) and over the road at the junior school (used by parents during the holidays), as well as playing fields near by. Which said, Channing won almost all its matches in '94/5 against larger schools and does very well at athletics. Big sports hall (refurbished in '94). No Saturday matches ('perish the thought').

Good and enthusiastic art. Main orchestra with Highgate boys. Sixth Formers go over (5 minutes' walk) for lunchtime talks, and are hand-picked for drama. 'But we don't invite them back – they'd have all the best parts.'

Very successful Young Enterprise – girls win all manner of prizes in this.

BACKGROUND AND ATMOSPHERE: Looks and feels uninstitutional, a mixture of 18th-century and 1980s buildings, founded in 1885 for the daughters of Unitarian Ministers and others, set in 3½ acres (swings, playground and garden) at the very top of Highgate Hill: stunning views. Main buildings are linked by a curious warren of staircases; cooking smells chase all along corridors. Recent improvements now include a huge new top-floor studio, and a complete refit of the computer lab (Apple Macs); also a hugely popular Sixth Form Centre, which appears to be alluring enough to keep the troops here post GCSE.

Morning assembly starts with singing (more likely to be a bracing or spiritual song rather than a Christian hymn) 'Because it's good for everyone to sing once a day,' says Mrs Rafael.

Junior School, Fairseat. Head: since 1994, Miss Elaine Krispinussen. The school is over the road with 144 girls, ages 5–11. Set in lovely grounds, the handsome old buildings are about to undergo another round of conversion to develop facilities.

PASTORAL CARE AND DISCIPLINE: Firm and fair. Summary justice meted out.

PUPILS AND PARENTS: Quite a racial and religious mix, but predominantly nice girls from professional families. Head firmly calls on parents 'To come in and talk and help,' hence Highgate media parent Robert Fox of the *Daily Telegraph* roped in to talk about Croatia, plus the *Archers'* Shula and Brian Aldridge to do voiceovers. Old Girls include Baroness Cox. Girls appear slightly protected but there is no prototype. Beastly brown uniform.

ENTRANCE: Half from the school's own prep, Fairseat; the rest from state and private schools in equal numbers.

EXIT: Most to university (approximately 50% opt for a gap year first) to read a vast variety of subjects.

MONEY MATTERS: No assisted places; some scholarships and bursaries. Weathering recessionary storms, but relatively expensive – like so many small schools.

REMARKS: Traditional and small day school doing a sound job and feeling good about itself, successfully building up its academic muscle in recent years. Still best, however, for girls not suited to the bustle of big, competitive schools – and does well by them.

Charterhouse

Godalming, Surrey GU7 2DJ
Tel: 01483 291600, Fax: 01483 291647

PUPILS: 640 boys, 80 girls (in Sixth Form all board except for 25 day)
AGES: 13–18
SIZE OF SIXTH FORM: 330
C OF E
FEE-PAYING

HEAD: From September 1996, Revd. John S Witheridge MA (forties).

Educated at St Alban's School, University of Kent and Christ's College, Cambridge, also Ridley Hall Theological College Cambridge. Married with four children. Previously the Conduct at Eton.

Appointed in the wake of the resignation of his predecessor whose sex scandal with an eighteen-year-old call girl hit the headlines.

A CADEMIC MATTERS: Does very well indeed, especially considering the (relatively) broad range of IQ at intake. Sciences are particularly strong – the Head of Science likes taking boys on trips, e.g. to Frankfurt, 'so they really see the subject applied to industry, and it's not just theoretical'. Science labs are all finely updated and modernised with their own excellent resource library – the same is true of several departments, including Politics, which continues to have a strong following at A-level (52 candidates in '95). Modern languages are another strength (including Italian), with 19 A grades out of 29 at French A-level in '95. Very strong GCSE results. Glorious main library.

G AMES, OPTIONS, THE ARTS: Keen cricket, good soccer, also shooting. Many sports on offer – karate, canoeing, fencing, water polo, archery – you name it. There is a splendid new Sports Centre. Well-supported CCF, also Scouts (Baden-Powell was here). Has one of the best public schools' theatres in the country – named after OB Ben Travers. Music is very good and on the up, and had the Young Composer of the Year ('93) among its pupils. Nearly 50% of pupils learn an instrument. (NB Vaughan Williams was here.) Numerous societies: 'A good place to discover and develop interests for life,' commented a parent. Girls coming here from all girls' schools are enthusiastic about all this: 'I can't believe how much there is on offer,' said

one. There is an excellent post-GCSE period when pupils organise (under supervision and with staff blessing) all manner of trips (groups of three, 'vaguely educational', boys must report on experience to school) which relies much on trust (that is 'not often broken', said a master).

B ACKGROUND AND ATMOSPHERE: A suburban place, with idyllic cricket pitches surrounding the turreted and Gothic brickwork of the main building. The towering chapel (by Sir Giles Scott) has name upon name of OBs who fell in the World Wars, and an awe-inspiring organ. There is a strong feeling of fellowship, and the school breeds tremendous loyalty (though a few, like Max Hastings, loathed their schooldays here). New houses look like ocean liners rising out of the grounds in '60s-university-campus style. Buildings are spread far apart over much ground – 'I walk MILES every day just getting places,' said a boy.

Founded in 1611 in London by Thomas Sutton, and moved to its present site in 1872. Boarding houses are all very different (so choose carefully); the oldest have cubicles and rooms for Sixth Formers of shabby luxury. Girls are in their own house for one year, then farmed out (in twos and threes) to staff families. This is generally considered a good system, 'because it's not so school-y.'

P ASTORAL CARE AND DISCIPLINE: There was a well-publicised case (early '94) of a couple being found together in bed and expelled instantly. Rules are clearly defined. Occasional drugs problems; smoking an irritant. There are good staff/pupil relationships, and parents feel their young are well looked after. Pupils may go home over night every three weeks. The appointment of Andrew Morrison as Second

Head and overseer of all the years below Sixth Form has helped the pastoral care.

PUPILS AND PARENTS: Surrey stock-brokers, Londoners. Also contingents from far corners of the UK; 100 from overseas (mainly British families but there are several Thais, Germans, etc). Some charming chaps, thoughtful as well as full of bounce. Girls, often from day schools, (including state), are fun and outgoing. OBs cover all walks of life – e.g. Joseph Addison, Max Beerbohm, Don Cupitt, John Alliot, the Lords Wakeham, Prior and Griffiths. Judges, statesmen, soldiers, scholars galore. The school has strong yuppie appeal – 'There's a brash smell of money,' commented one parent.

ENTRANCE: CE results must be good across the board (i.e. average will do nicely). Also entry at Sixth Form.

EXIT: In '94 28 to Oxbridge. 98% go to university (and half take a year out). They go on to a wide variety of subjects, more sciences than humanities. A small number always go on into the Creative Arts.

MONEY MATTERS: There are generous scholarships at 13+ and 16+. 12 academic, 3 exhibitions, 5 Music, 2 Art at 13+. Various academic, art, music scholarships plus 5 assisted places at Sixth Form (bargain of a lifetime, given what is on offer). The school continues to maintain its position as one of the most expensive in the country – pots of money about, and the school is most definitely well run. New Sixth Form scholarships have been introduced for those with special leadership potential and no family funds.

REMARKS: Undaunted by the recent unwelcome publicity, this charges on fashionably, much helped by its geographical position. Some reports describe the school as 'offhand'.

Chelmsford County High School

Broomfield Road,
Chelmsford, Essex CM1 1RW
Tel: 01245 352592, Fax: 01245 345746

PUPILS: 680 girls
ALL DAY
AGES: 11–18
SIZE OF SIXTH FORM: 200
NON-DENOM
GRANT-MAINTAINED STATE
    GRAMMAR

HEAD: Since 1990, Mrs Bernice McCabe, BA, MA, FRSA (forties): 'It's all about expectations, the word 'weak' is not in our vocabulary here.' Appointed Head at thirty-seven and still raring to go on 'indefinitely, I want to open up horizons, inspire, maximise potential. Giving up on someone in any area is the worst thing you can do.' 'Yes,' she admits, 'I am probably a bit of a slave driver.' Neat, vital, power-dressed, she won't talk about her personal circumstances but reveals a private education (Clifton High School before University of Bristol, English degree and PGCE). She teaches the new intake and Sixth Form and Oxbridge candidates: 'I love it.' Directs operations from her flower-filled study lined with framed press-cuttings (of pupils' extra-curricular activities). She burns with an almost American-style fervour and tireless enthusiasm, 'Yes, I do have some spare time at weekends, so I'm doing an MBA.'

ACADEMIC MATTERS: Highly selective, producing chart-busting results, e.g. 26 Sixth Formers got three or more grade-A A-levels at the last count (down on '94, when it was 33 girls), 4 of those with five grade As apiece. Also 38 girls got eight or more grade-A GCSEs (starred or plain), 14 of those with ten A-grades. The committed long-serving staff (largely female and on expensive top-of-scale salary grades) are hard driven by Head; endless appraisals 'for academic success, our top priority'.

Class sizes around 20 with setting in French and Maths. Teaching styles vary from traditional to National Curriculum requirements for girls to take responsibility for their own learning through project and investigation – in the Biology lab we found girls hatching out chicks.

Compulsory three separate Sciences up to GCSE, taught in the new 8-laboratory Science block (funded by a government grant of £850,000, the second highest single grant to a GM school that year) as part of a 10-subject GCSE package, including French, German, Spanish, Russian, Latin (one-third take Latin, 80% grade A – no Classical Civilisation on offer). There are 19 subjects on offer at A-level plus FLAW (French Language at Work business qualification for those not doing a language). Three weeks' post-GCSE work experience for all (part of the Trident Project) with placings including the Cabinet Office, local accountants, a Brunei hospital. Good careers advice is given, with professional parents asked to come in to give talks and interviews.

Results always make this one of the best, if not *the* best state school for GCSE and A-level (64% A–B passes at A-level, excluding General Studies, in '95). Mrs McCabe is a rare league table supporter: 'I'm keen on accountability and openness; parents aren't stupid and can compare like with like.' Hmmm.

GAMES, OPTIONS, THE ARTS: A team of games captains cover hockey (Eastern Counties Champions), netball, tennis, fencing, athletics, dance, swimming. Regular Saturday matches – four hockey pitches, five tennis courts, and a Sports Hall for PE, weight-training, fencing.

Eleven musical groups include choirs taught by keen Sixth Formers, likewise Drama groups (in a dance/drama studio). Compulsory community service involves each class in serious fund-raising.

Home Economics, Textiles, Electronics, computing (Nimbus); D of E Debates with boys' grammar school. Stunning Art and Ceramics – teeming art studio; art and history trips; in-house Royal Academy 'outreach' workshops, life-drawing.

BACKGROUND AND ATMOSPHERE: This is a solid Edwardian red-brick, ivy-clad, two-storey, purpose-built (1906) school with a dismal refurbished '50s extension and the odd Portakabin. Neighbouring detached villas for Sixth Formers provide them with own common room, kitchens. A development appeal is now successfully underway for a Performing Arts Suite, artificial turf pitch, etc. Buildings stand off the main Cambridge road near the soulless Chelmsford centre but 'buzz with life' as the Head says – spotless corridors, gleaming lino, landings with trestles of immaculately finished ceramics – 'No, we have no vandalism here.'

PASTORAL CARE AND DISCIPLINE: The Head's male Deputy is in charge of pastoral care but 'we don't expect problems'. A homework 'log-book' is sent home for parents to sign/comment; questionnaire for home views on school's 'strengths and weaknesses'.

PUPILS AND PARENTS: The majority from white professional middle classes, 40% from Chelmsford, otherwise Essex, Suffolk, Herts. Up to one-third transfer from the private sector after 'feeling the pinch'. Tidy, biddable, navyblazered girls (Latin motto, *'We carry the lamps of life'*) in pleated grey skirts ('dress-code' only for Sixth Formers – but no extremists) smile helpfully above neatly knotted ties.

Parents and Governors (including a Provost, a judge, a bank chairman) are drawn from the professions and 'committed to education'.

ENTRANCE: Annual intake of the 112 highest scorers on 11+ examination (verbal reasoning, Maths and English) – no interview, but IQ range 115–140 – 'I get lots of calls from parents asking how to make sure their daughters get in,' comments the Head. Appeals system for despairing near-misses. Head is careful to point out that not every able child opts for selective education. About an extra 20 taken on in the Sixth Form with a minimum of five or more GCSE passes at grades A–B.

EXIT: 98% to higher education including a regular troupe to Oxbridge. Lots of medics, lawyers, international bankers, engineers; also the Forces, business studies, teaching, arts foundation.

MONEY MATTERS: State-funded, grant-maintained. £2,000 per annum opt-out budget per hand-picked pupil.

REMARKS: Highly selective, old-fashioned grammar school delivering top-quality exam results, which they care about desperately. The tough, image-conscious Head drives a high-calibre staff hard to prise the potential from the elect of Essex women-in-the-making: 'It's not a rest-cure here.' Truly impressive nonetheless.

Cheltenham College

Bath Road, Cheltenham, Gloucestershire GL53 7LD
Tel: 01242 513540, Fax: 01242 577746

PUPILS: 485 boys, 85 girls in Sixth Form. (Two-thirds of the pupils board, one-third day) NB girls from 13 as from September '98.
AGES: 13–18
SIZE OF SIXTH FORM: 290
C OF E
FEE-PAYING

HEAD: Since 1990, Mr Peter Wilkes MA (fifties), educated at Radley and Trinity College, Classicist. Third generation in education – his father was Warden of Radley, grandfather was Head of Shrewsbury and Eton. Taught in Zimbabwe and Iran, also Rugby (House-master); previously Head of Ryde School on the Isle of Wight. Wife has her own teaching career. They have three grown-up children and a house in the South of France. Sensitive beneath a somewhat bluff manner.

ACADEMIC MATTERS: Results are variable, and the intake is very broad (IQs from 100 to 130+). Good English department, with much liked Head of Drama. French now doing well; good Maths record. Sciences are strong. Some interesting staff (NB only six in the common room are over 50, the average age is 34) – the Head of Biology is an opera enthusiast ('actually, I'm a fanatic') who regularly encourages a coach load of boys up to Covent Garden and brings them back singing. 5 or 6 sets for most subjects. IB is no longer an option (due to lack of take-up).

An outstanding Electronics department places huge emphasis on the subject from the start, though even girls coming in at Sixth Form and new to the subject have been known to win national competitions. The school regularly wins all the top electronics prizes (two or three each year, with all manner of inventions, under the watchful eye of an inspiring Head of Department, who arrives in a Porsche). Also a big emphasis on IT throughout the school, with computers all over the place. Career department has good industrial links.

GAMES, OPTIONS, THE ARTS: A sporty school – everyone partakes of some sport on Saturday afternoon. Rugby and cricket are the main games ('It's annoying,' said a hockey-playing girl), with huge numbers of teams and matches. NB The Head groundsman was a former England fast bowler. Keen polo school, which plays at Cirencester; pupils box own pony or make arrangements locally – particularly popular with Gloucestershire day boys. The school has a boat house at Tewkesbury. Very strong CCF. Good Art, also Drama (small studio theatre plus proscenium arch theatre hall); also good Music, some with the Ladies' College. Good numbers of activities/clubs on offer at all stages.

BACKGROUND AND ATMOSPHERE: Proud of being the oldest of the Victorian public schools (founded for 'the sons of gentlemen'), with strong army links. On the edge of the city, fine views of Cotswold hills. But it has sold much land over the years and now the A40, roaring with traffic, slices the school buildings in two, dividing the main campus from subsidiary blocks. Fine Gothic collegiate architecture in honey-coloured stone; the dining hall (with hopeless acoustics) used to be the chapel; extremely fine library (looks like a chapel). Chapel service starts with school notices (good acoustics and rousing singing) every morning at 9.15 a.m., i.e. after the first lesson.

PASTORAL CARE AND DISCIPLINE: Two were sacked for drugs in '94. A list of pubs/cafés/restaurants pupils may visit, plus the forbidden places, is on public display. Parents are 'urged' to get to know their offspring's tutor, but note with 'dismay', said one father, 'that remarkably few tutors live in the Houses'.

PUPILS AND PARENTS: Army links have decreased but are lingering. Increasingly pupils come from within a one-hour radius. Day pupils from the far side of Swindon, Gloucester, Broadway. 8% non-Brits. Boys' hair, appearance and manners get 8 out of 10. Girls wear uniform even in Upper Sixth – and don't complain. Old Boys include Scott of the Antarctic's companion Edward Wilson; many distinguished soldiers, e.g. Field Marshal Sir John Dill, Lt General Sir John Bagot, 14 VCs (the largest per capita number of any school apart from Wellington). Not to mention more Old Boys rumoured to have been eaten by tigers than any other school.

ENTRANCE: CE not a high hurdle. Many via own extremely good prep school (see separate entry). Competitive entry for girls at Sixth Form.

EXIT: Fewer dropping out post-GCSE (though clever locals opt for Pate's Grammar School). 17–20+ per year to Oxbridge. Most to university, occasionally into the army or art college.

MONEY MATTERS: Was badly hit by the recession. There are 6 scholarships of 50% fees; others between 10% and 40% on academic merit; help for the needy.

REMARKS: Solid, if somewhat un-inspiring, second-division public school (once one of the greats) with a marked technological emphasis, fighting its corner – now poised to go co-ed throughout from 1998.

The Cheltenham Ladies' College

Cheltenham, Gloucestershire GL50 3EP
Tel: 01242 520691, Fax: 01242 227882

PUPILS: 843 girls (641 board, 202 day)
AGES: 11–18
SIZE OF SIXTH FORM: 272
C OF E
FEE-PAYING

HEAD: From September 1996, Mrs Anne Tuck, MA, PGCE, MIL, (forties), who comes here from City of London School for Girls where she was Deputy Head. Takes over from the redoubtable Miss Enid Castle, an iron fist in a velvet glove, and being watched with interest.

ACADEMIC MATTERS: Continues to be seriously strong, particularly in Maths, French and Latin (classes up to 20). Streams of As at A-level (e.g., in '95, 42 out of 52 pupils got A grade in Maths; Physics also strong results). Good take up of Sciences at A-level, especially Chemistry and Biology. Greek for those that want it, also Spanish (poor results in '95), German, Russian, Mandarin Chinese, also Japanese classes available: Italian at Sixth Form. Well-supported History of Art and well taught. Overall, 71% of the A-level passes at grades A–B in 1995 – phew!

Modern languages labs contrast with the old-fashioned (and much loved) desks. Science labs were quite recently renovated, all 15 of them, with a shower in lab area. IT is strong, (the college is fully networked) and CDT is much encouraged. Computers throughout. (A new Art, Design and Technology block is planned for '97).

Huge staff, 95 full-time plus part-timers, with a low turnover, not many come here for their first post. Can cope with 'mild dyslexia'. Superb careers department, work shadowing in holidays and work experience in term.

GAMES, OPTIONS, THE ARTS: There is a huge gym in the main building, a new games hall, a fitness room, indoor tennis, a new competition-sized indoor swimming pool which generates great enthusiasm and spectacular results. Slight grouch from pupils that 'we are not allowed enough time for Field' (i.e. games). The school has its own riding school nearby, and girls are allowed to bring ponies (popular among younger children especially); polo is now an option – quite a rarity at girls' schools. Teams for everything.

Strong music – 600 music lessons weekly, masses of choirs, and an orchestra – all under John Sanders, organist at Gloucester Cathedral and, by tradition, Director of Music. John Rutter gave a master class in '95. Drama is strong with the theatre studio recently revamped, and a new editing suite for filming, etc fitted out. Cooking; excellent fabric design; the pottery and art studios are now open at weekends.

Debates, concerts and occasional drama with Cheltenham College (now co-ed, 'Which doesn't help,' said one pupil) half a mile away and also plenty of 'unofficial contact'. Strong on charity work. D of E.

BACKGROUND AND ATMOSPHERE: Founded in 1853, and granted a

Royal Charter in 1935, the main school revolves round a huge purpose-built Victorian campus – with magnificent stained glass, a marble corridor, Princess Hall, vast library, etc – in the middle of Cheltenham.

Based on the model of boys' public schools: pupils go back to their house for lunch, tea and at night (where they have pets, table napkins, pianos, and sewing machines). Most houses are about 10 mins' walk away, and each girl has a 'walking partner' who must go with her at all times (you have a late music lesson, she does prep in the old hall).

Junior boarders live either in rooms converted into 'cubs' (cubicles), or in open-plan dormitories (much preferred); 'Friendlier, you get to know each other better,' say the girls. Sixth Formers have their own houses (1 day, 4 boarding), boarders sleep and work in charming individual rooms, each with its own panic button ('with 222 girls in the middle of town, what else can we do?' said one Housemistress), but retain strong links with their junior house.

Housemistresses in junior houses are non-teaching, whilst Sixth Form housemistresses also have academic responsibility. TVs, videos, computers and sewing machines (again) for Sixth Formers who can 'have dinner in town' (taxi there and back) and invite their boyfriends back – 'the boys often become house friends'.

Called 'greenflies' by townfolk, the girls wear magnificent loden coats and staff have been known to accost total strangers wearing the school coat 'on the lawn' at the National Hunt Festival.

There are food committees in all houses; letter from parents required for vegetarian meals; few anorexics. Girls carry their books in 'sacks'; send internal messages via 'slab' and have names for almost everything: Slodge (Sidney Lodge), St Mags (St Margaret's), the bunny run. No bells, just clocks.

PASTORAL CARE AND DISCIPLINE: Class teachers liaise with housemistresses for junior girls, Sixth Formers have tutors. Two day houses and a Sixth Form house are based at the Day Girl Centre with their own housemistresses.

A confidential conselling service is available to all girls run by professionally trained counsellors (2 teaching staff, 2 independent external counsellors, employed part-time). 'No shame attached,' said a girl.

Drugs – 'not that I am aware of'. Worst offence 'getting out at night and risking the security'; house doors are locked at dark. Otherwise, punishment depends on the offence: smoking, fine £10 for first offence, then one week's suspension. Girls are asked to leave for going OTT. Some girls complain about feeling 'locked in' and 'locked up' – even Sixth Formers. Each House organises its own weekend activities, 'but you can't make them join in,' said a housemistress.

PUPILS AND PARENTS: Ambitious parents of academic offspring queue up in droves. Middle class, 20% from abroad, ex-pats, (the Services rather than foreigners, though some from Hong Kong). Very caring of one another, outspoken and charming. Perhaps a trifle jolly hockey sticks. OGs: Rosie Boycott; Mary Archer; Cheryl Gillan; Rachel Lomax, Vice Chairman of the World Bank.

ENTRANCE: Stiff competition, at 11+, 12+, 13+ CE and own exam post-GCSE.

EXIT: Well over 90% to universities (with a slight bias towards Sciences), around 20 to Oxbridge (25 in 1995). 'All girls are destined to have careers.'

MONEY MATTERS: There are 5 Assisted Places at 11, plus discounts for siblings, plus 2 major and 2 minor academic and music scholarships, and 4% of fee-income available for bursaries. Maximum award 50%, but can 'top up according to means'. Currently huge queues for Assisted Places.

Currently less demand for boarding at 11+; girls wait till 12+ or 13+, and waiting lists at Fourth Year.

'No problems' with the recession, always above budget anyway.

REMARKS: One of the best girls' boarding schools in the country, now with increasing numbers of day girls. Wonderful facilities, impressive all round and very traditional. Increasing numbers of good reports from parents reach us. But as we have said before, this is not the place for the timid girl, however clever she may be.

The Cherwell School (Cherwell Upper)

Marston Ferry Road, Oxford OX2 7EE
Tel: 01865 58719, Fax: 01865 311165

PUPILS: Approx 940 in all, boys and girls
ALL DAY
AGES: 13–18
SIZE OF SIXTH FORM: Approx 300
NON-DENOM
STATE

HEAD: Since 1981, Mr M H Roberts, MA (Oxon) (fifties), educated at Christ's Hospital and Merton College, Oxford (Historian). Previously taught at Leeds Grammar School, then went into state comprehensive system and has stayed in it. Married to Diana, who is a social worker; son and daughter. Lists his hobbies as squash, dog-walking and writing history books for schools.

ACADEMIC MATTERS: Good, though not considered anything out of the way by locals, who live in the academic hothouse of Oxford. Some reports of sloppy teaching, though HMI report very complimentary. Sets for Maths and Modern Languages. Block subjects now on timetable, so departments can organise groups as they wish. History of Art is well taught.

Growth at Sixth Form level in recent years, with two-thirds of the pupils now staying on, and up to 30 or 40 new pupils coming in. To cater for a wider range at this stage, GNVQs are being introduced alongside A-levels from September 1996.

Two successive years of financial cuts ('95/6 and '96/7) in Oxfordshire mean that class sizes are larger, learning support has been cut and there are five fewer staff.

GAMES, OPTIONS, THE ARTS: Under-19 county champions at football in 1993; netball and basketball have a good local reputation. Strong and enthusiastic Music department – lots of extra-curricular bands and concerts – and superb A-level results. Drama and Theatre Studies are particularly strong. DT on course.

BACKGROUND AND ATMOSPHERE: Modern brick and prefab buildings off Banbury Road. The cramped and ugly school assembly hall is seriously overused. The whole school bursts with energy, with some staff radiating interest in and concern for the wellbeing of their charges, like kindly shepherds – there is a feeling of safety and spiritual warmth. Interestingly, the school started life as a secondary modern. A £1 million building programme is due to start in September 1996, to include 3 Science labs, 2 Technology labs, 12 Workshops.

PASTORAL CARE AND DISCIPLINE: Each class has the same Form Tutor who relates to the same Head of Year for first three years: the Sixth Form have their own Form Tutors and Heads of Year. Senior Head of Year is pastoral co-ordinator. Pupils go 'on record' and parents are informed for slacking or truancy; disrupting lessons and fighting can 'lead to suspension'; drugs and threatening or violent behaviour leads to 'permanent exclusion'.

PUPILS AND PARENTS: Some middle class, some connected with the University, but also large numbers from nearby housing estates. Seriously popular locally, buses from all over. Ability range is a fair spread.

Maureen O'Connor, ex-education correspondent of the *Guardian*, is Chair of the Governors. Six staff have their own children in the school. Good parental links and consultations.

ENTRANCE: Majority from the Middle School. (NB Oxford has middle and first schools.) Oversubscribed for all years. A staggering 20+ come at Sixth Form level from local private schools.

EXIT: Very few at 16; most do two years in Sixth and on to university.

MONEY MATTERS: A local 'winner' – the Head and governors have more to spend and much more discretion in that spending than formerly.

REMARKS: State comprehensive which should be better, with an enlarged Sixth Form, now offering GNVQs as well as A-levels, and doing its best in the face of financial cutbacks.

Christ's Hospital

Horsham, Sussex RH13 7LS
Tel: 01403 211293, Fax: 01403 211580

PUPILS: Approx 481 boys, 328 girls (all board)
AGES: 11–18
SIZE OF SIXTH FORM: Approx 220
C OF E
FEE-PAYING – but see paragraph on Money Matters

HEAD: From September 1996, Dr Peter Southern MA, PhD (late forties), previously Head of Bancroft's School and before that Head of History at Westminster.

ACADEMIC MATTERS: Strong academic tradition, particularly Sciences and Maths. Maths has had a wobble, but appears to be firming up. Satellites sprouting up on Physics labs (weather signals feeding in) and Language Departments. Science at GCSE is compulsory (Dual Award). Offers Classics, Russian, Italian, as well as French and German. Girls tend to do more Arts subjects here, with better results. Unusual subjects on offer include British Government and Politics, and Archaeology. Very strong Art and Design, and all pupils have scored A or A* for the past three years in Art and Design at A-level and GCSE. In '95, 5 grade A, one B (out of six candidates) at A-level Music – quite a feat.

GAMES, OPTIONS, THE ARTS: The school now claims to have the 'best' sporting facility of any school in the country opened by their President, HRH the Duke of Gloucester, at a cost of £3 million, which includes a social centre and even disabled facilities – as ritzy as any we have come across.

Very strong musical tradition. The school band leads the Lord Mayor's procession in London each year and hundreds of people turn up to hear the school beating the retreat – an old tradition. The band also plays while the school marches in to lunch and it is considered a status symbol to be in it (though it makes you late for a rather good lunch). The school has five organs – a record? A good Arts centre with a super theatre seating 500 that is said to be the inspiration for the Swan Theatre, Stratford. Lots of good productions, both school and professional – much appreciated by all.

BACKGROUND AND ATMOSPHERE: Founded in 1552 by the boy king Edward VI for the education of London's sick and poor, and still sticks by and large to the spirit of this aim. In 1902, the school moved from its 5-acre site in the City (good grief!) to 1,200 Sussex acres (is this a school record?). The large complex with avenues and quads designed by Victorian architect Sir Aston Webb, looks like a huge, smart, red-brick barracks with gracious cloisters. Vast dormitories – think of Florence Nightingale and you've got the picture – have now been converted into units of study/bedroom accommodation. Still feels a bit institutional. Dorms are spartan, but 'cosy psychologically' commented a mother.

In September 1985 joined forces with the sister school which moved down from Hertford.

Boys wear wonderful ancient uniform (and bring it home at half-term to be washed, stiff with dirt) of floor-length blue wool coat, black breeches and saffron-coloured stockings, and tab and 'broadie' buckle on leather belt. Girls wear the same blue coats in winter, and picturesque navy suits with old-fashioned cuffs and buttons. Pupils could all step straight into a Tudor play, without changing a thing. Parents love the flapping cassocks on November evenings.

The uniform is provided free, and is worn seven days a week – and often smelly by half-term – but the children love wearing it.

PASTORAL CARE AND DISCIPLINE: A swift turnover of Heads entailed period of disruption and disaffection, but the school has now settled down. Things were tightened up considerably under the outgoing Head, whose message to the children on sex was 'If possible, wait'. There are still occasional outbursts of trouble (drink in particular).

PUPILS AND PARENTS: Anybody poor and deserving from miners' sons to those of bankrupt bankers and 'we even have prostitutes' children here,' said a member of staff. NB Largish proportion of single-parent families. Mostly from south-east, though school is trying to rectify this. Both working class and a few distressed gentle toffs. OBs: lots of distinguished ones, as you might expect, including bouncing-bomb man Barnes Wallis, William Glock, Bernard Levin, Colin Davis, cricketer John Snow, Coleridge, Leigh Hunt.

ENTRANCE: Very complicated, owing to the ancient charitable foundation and Counting House which oversees the procedure. For the majority of places, the school will only consider children whose parents cannot afford boarding school fees and who have a definite 'need'. It helps to be in the Church, the RAF, or to be a single parent or down on your luck. .

The school sets its own exam. Places are gained either by competition or by 'presentation' – governors and certain Livery Companies have the right to sponsor a child. (This means that the 'presentees' have to reach a minimum standard, while the competitive candidates have to be brighter, and to compete.) Get the up-to-date governors' list from the school to see who may help.

Caveat: the whole process is humiliating but persevere.

EXIT: Most to university, and very widespread, though the school gets some fall-out from children whose family circumstances make it impossible for them to continue.

MONEY MATTERS: The school's revenues are largely derived from property – and are recession hit. Fees assessed according to income, from nil, if the family income is less than £10,650 at time of writing, to £10,688 for incomes above £41,857 gross at time of writing. You will need a good accountant.

REMARKS: This is an ancient foundation which, unlike most, still operates as a genuine charity, and is without the snobby aspects of the usual public school. A parent comments that the 'traditions knit the troubled backgrounds.'

City of London School

Queen Victoria Street,
London EC4V 3AL
Tel: 0171 489 0291, Fax: 0171 329 6887
PUPILS: Around 865 boys
ALL DAY
AGES: 10–18
SIZE OF SIXTH FORM: Approx 240
NON-DENOM
FEE-PAYING

HEAD: Since 1995, Mr Roger Dancey MA (early fifties), educated Lancing, Exeter University (read

Economics and Government), previously Headmaster of King Edward VI Camp Hill, Birmingham, and before that Senior Master at RGS Worcester. Married with two children, both teachers (and as such the family were the subject of a Radio 4 programme, *Peoples' Peace – A Dynasty of Teachers*). Outgoing and charming, extremely keen on the theatre (the play *Les Liaisons Dangereuses* was dedicated to him by the playwright), also cinema, cricket and golf.

ACADEMIC MATTERS: Grammar school ethos. Some setting. No specialisation below Sixth Form level. Strongest in Mathematics (distinguish themselves in the Mathematics Olympiad), and Sciences doing very well. History, Politics and English are all notably thriving departments, with a remarkable English master, Jonathan Keates, the distinguished author of biographies on Stendhal and Purcell, and 'a brilliant teacher' say the boys. Staff are considered supportive and friendly – 'they'll invite us round to their houses'. Results are distinctly good – the school has been in league table top thirty for the last three years.

GAMES, OPTIONS, THE ARTS: Certainly more sporty than Westminster, with lots of staff involved on games side. Seventeen acres of playing fields at their disposal 35 minutes away, whence the under-14s are bussed one afternoon a week plus keen over-14s. Judo, fencing, squash (three courts), shooting (run by their Cadet Force) are amongst a number of options, with the competitive edge going to swimming (there is a super 25-metre swimming pool) and water polo. The sports facilities on site are superb and well used, and even include a sauna; most sports have to be travelled to, but can be done (e.g. real tennis at Queen's).

A flash Design/Technology Centre opened in 1991. The Music Department is extremely good. There are 30–40 clubs operating at lunch break, and pockets of energetic after-school activity; rehearsals (boys as young as 14 take up directing), a jazz group. Very lively political debates.

BACKGROUND AND ATMOSPHERE: The present school started in 1837 on a medieval foundation. In 1986, the school moved to a new purpose-built high-tech building right on the Thames just east of Blackfriars Bridge. The school is cut in half by the main road, producing rabbit-warreny levels linked by windowless corridors. There are stunning views of St Paul's, attractive terraces for the boys, and a constant hum of boats from the river. The new school boasts an attractive small theatre and drama studio for use only by the English Department (drama is part of the curriculum up to Third Form), and a Great Hall with a splendid Walker organ. The good library has an annual £10,000 book allowance. It is a high-pressured day – but there is a feeling of shut-down mid-afternoon.

PASTORAL CARE AND DISCIPLINE: Well-developed tutor system, all boys report to tutor first thing each morning and afternoon. The new Head is very keen 'to promote links with parents' and goes out of his way to make himself accessible for parents and pupils – 'Much appreciated,' said one father. Interviews all Senior Sixth about their UCAS applications.

PUPILS AND PARENTS: The location makes it extremely handy for sons of yuppies (Daddy drops son at school en route for the City). Also popular with bright East End dwellers. No defined catchment area – to some extent the school is 'pig in the middle' – but most come from North London (75–80%), in a great arc that reaches from north-west London down to Essex – lesser numbers from South London. All are hardened commuters (lots of homework done that way), and very mixed socially, economically and ethnically – no readily identifiable CLS type. Unsmart, gritty, efficient, no cachet. Very conscious of how the world outside works. OBs include H H Asquith, Mike Brearley, Kingsley Amis, Julian Barnes, Denis Norden.

ENTRANCE: The school's own exam is set at three different standards according to age group (entry at 10, 11, 13 and 16), 'all a bit of a bear garden, as almost all candidates are trying for at least two and sometimes as many as five schools'. Interviews last 20 minutes. At 11 65% come from state sector; at 13 almost all come from private preps, and occasionally report that 'it can be difficult to integrate.' Not the pressure on places that there is for elsewhere, (will this change?) but not everyone makes it. Entry into Sixth Form requires six A–C GCSEs, with A or B grades in subjects to be studied at A-level.

EXIT: 98% to university or medical school, including nearly 20% to Oxbridge.

MONEY MATTERS: Financially in the thrall of the Corporation of London – not short of a bob or two, but a Byzantine system for organising it. There are 20 Assisted Places at 11+ stage, 5 for entry to Sixth. Academic Corporation scholarships at all ages, and for music (amount offered is a movable feast). Several Livery Company scholarships. Choristers of Temple Church and Chapel Royal, St James's, are bursaried pupils. Some bursaries are available for hard-pressed parents.

REMARKS: Good busy cosmopolitan London day school on the up, possibly on the impersonal side, (its Brave-New-World high-tech appearance frightens off one or two traditionalist parents), gets strong exam results. Dynamic new Head.

City of London School for Girls

Barbican, London EC2Y 8BB
Tel: 0171 628 0841, Fax: 0171 638 3212

PUPILS: 656 girls
ALL DAY
AGES: 11–18
SIZE OF SIXTH FORM: About 150
NON-DENOM
FEE-PAYING

HEAD: Since 1995, Dr Yvonne Burne BA, PhD, FRSA (forties), educated at Redland High School in Bristol, read Modern Foreign Languages at Westfield College, and first taught at Harrow County School for girls. Moved to Washington with her diplomat husband, and embarked on a career in educational publishing. Latterly Head of St Helen's Northwood. Two teenage children.

ACADEMIC MATTERS: Gets impressive results. Thorough teaching, and girls are expected to work hard (they do). Some staff have been here for many years ('too long' commented one father, 'they are real old pros, mind you'). Good Science teaching, with all doing Dual Award at GCSE. Emphasis on aural skills at Modern Language GCSE level annoys some parents ('Shouldn't they be writing more?'). German or French (chosen by 75%) as a first choice, then girls take up a second modern language or Latin one year later. Russian, Spanish and Greek are

offered from fourth year. A-level results strong in Maths, Biology, History, English and Biology, though Ds, Es, Ns and Us are still showing up; nonetheless school ranks well in the league tables. Latin A-level group the usual handful but always does extremely well; Theatre Studies are very successful, with three-quarters of pupils gaining A grades. About half the pupils do Maths for A-level, and a quarter do Chemistry. Work and progress is well monitored at all stages, including Sixth Form.

GAMES, OPTIONS, THE ARTS: Keen and fairly gamesy especially given the concrete-jungle location. Splendid indoor pool, large gymnasium and all the usual girls' school games. Music is strong – as you would expect from a school whose neighbour is the Guildhall School of Music and Drama – with good orchestras, singing and instrumental tuition. Girls performed in a new opera, Anna, written especially for the school's centenary year, by David Bedford, and premiered as part of the City of London Festival of the Arts in 1995. Girls occasionally take part, via audition, in Guildhall productions.

Extremely good Art, and much in evidence, with stunning textiles. CDT up and running. Very active D of E, including some participation with boys from the brother school.

BACKGROUND AND ATMOSPHERE: Purpose-built in the 1960s in the midst of the concrete, faceless Barbican blocks, also ancient historical monuments – a truly urban environment bang in the City centre. The school was founded in 1894 on Victoria Embankment by coal merchant William Ward, with the express intention that girls receive a broad and liberal education with the emphasis on scholarship. The centenary year has seen much building and revamping – facilities are greatly improved (paid for by the Corporation of London), with, among other things, an extended music block, extended Sixth Form libraries, a dark room, studies, tiered seating in the main hall.

Part of the Corporation of City of London, has connections with Livery Halls, and City Corporation appoints the governing body – all this seen as a mixed blessing by some. In principle, these links make the girls aware of the great world outside – though parents have doubts. Which said, lively noticeboards show Third World awareness.

There is a general air of get-on-with-it: opinions vary from finding the place challenging and exciting, to monotonous and downright ugly. Foyer with gladioli and reception kiosk, 'You could be entering a hospital,' said a visitor.

City of London School for Girls Preparatory Department Tel: 0171 628 0841, Fax: 0171 638 3212 104 girls, ages 7–11. Head: Since 1991, Mrs G M Thomas Cert Ed. Umbilically attached to the senior school and a sure way in (with rare exceptions). Entry via whole day assessment. Shares some of the facilities (Design Technology department, gym, pool, etc.) with the senior school.

PASTORAL CARE AND DISCIPLINE: Not a problem, with a work ethic firmly in place. All Sixth Formers act as prefects. Democratic use of school council and suggestions book.

PARENTS AND PUPILS: A similar intake to City of London Boys with heavy loads from Islington, and commuting in from Buckinghamshire and Essex. Broad ethnic, also social mix – offspring of Lords and Commons, children of shipbrokers and shop-keepers. Talkative girls, not at all afraid of holding their own in an argument with anyone.

'But they don't always aim high enough,' commented an ambitious mother.

ENTRANCE: Enormously over-subscribed at 11+ (400 for 50 places), many via junior school. Exam, and interview – this part is important, with staff seeking 'flair, open minds and children who can respond'. Variable numbers of Sixth Form entry to fill up leavers' places.

EXIT: University for one and all, 10–15 per year to Oxbridge. Some leave post-GCSE, usually for boys' schools, though dwindling numbers nowadays.

MONEY MATTERS: There are 20 Assisted Places at 11, plus 5 at Sixth Form. Also 3 full scholarships a year (which may be spread thinner and wider, depending on the intake).

REMARKS: Strong and highly sought-after city girls' school which somehow lacks cutting edge, despite (because of?) its location/Corporation ties, and which should be making more of a noise. Now being watched with interest under the new Head.

Clifton College

32 College Road, Bristol BS8 3JF
Tel: 01179 739187, Fax: 01179 466826

PUPILS: 440 boys, 190 girls (378 board, 252 day)
SIZE OF SIXTH FORM: 262
AGES: 13–18
C OF E and one Jewish House
FEE-PAYING

HEAD: Since 1990, Mr Hugh Munro, MA (forties), educated at Rugby and Pembroke College, Cambridge.

Married, with two teenage children. Historian, Rugby Blue. Previously Head of Worksop, has also taught in America and worked in industry. A very popular fellow (and widely admired by other Heads), open, forward-looking, humorous. A good ambassador for the school. Still keen to get everyone here – staff and pupils – 'talking more'. Considers his main job 'to develop the width of talents'.

ACADEMIC MATTERS: Good English department, ditto Science, with research emphasis, enabling challenging investigations at all levels, including purposeful trips, e.g. to the rain forests of Nepal. Science schools in large Victorian block, ultra-modern computer system in the science library. Some subjects (e.g. History) are taught away from the main campus. Overall academic results in '95 the school's best ever since league tables started with 64% of A–B grades at A-level; best results in Maths, Physics, English and Economics. Good GCSE results too, particularly given that the intake is of a very mixed ability. The Director of Studies meets every pupil at the end of their first year to discuss options (he also trains the British Mathematicians for the Olympiad teams). The Head has reduced the average age of staff, and limited the tenure of Heads of Departments. There is a smattering of interesting/eccentric staff. Effort grades for each subject are publicly displayed in each House bi-weekly.

GAMES, OPTIONS, THE ARTS: Famous for its sporty poem, 'Play up and play the game', written by Old Boy Sir Henry Newbolt. Girls (whose numbers are *gradually* increasing) do well at rowing and fencing. The main games field (86 acres) is on the other side of Clifton Suspension Bridge; pupils are ferried back and forth. Sports Studies an A-level possibility.

Fine Drama, and lots of it, with a splendid theatre (used by Bristol Old Vic and visiting companies). Good Art and outstanding pottery, enthusiastic Textile department.

Keen CCF (girls are very enthusiastic), strong D of E. A really really good activities programme was recently introduced, with a master in charge, whereby 'pupils must take part in some options'.

BACKGROUND AND ATMOSPHERE: Huge mass of high Victorian Gothic buildings, with the main campus overlooking the Close ('*There's a breathless hush in the Close tonight*' runs the poem). School buildings spread over the road, next door to the zoo (10p entry for pupils provided they are in uniform) in Bristol's smartest residential area. The school, founded in 1862, by Bristol merchants, went fully co-ed in 1987. Dining hall has been redecorated, and has unusually small tables (for 6 or 4). Regular compulsory chapel, and compulsory (day pupils included) chapel every second Sunday. There are 11 houses (3 for girls, 5-star of course), including Polack's, for Jews (currently 40) – the Head made enquiries and found Yes, this is still a need, despite dwindling numbers. It breeds a very pleasant tolerance among pupils, 'And it makes us more orthodox, more observant of the rules than we would be at home,' volunteered a Jewish pupil (fresh from a 24-hour Yom Kippur fast). Own synagogue in house. Jewish girls, on the other hand, are integrated into girls' houses.

There is a firm emphasis on inter-house competitions in every sphere. Some flexi-boarding (the Head sees this as important for the future). There is a slightly split-personality feel with day/boarding elements. Saturday morning school (a recent re-introduction, this) for everyone except the Jewish students.

Quite a cosy atmosphere prevails, despite the spread of the lay-out.

Clifton College Preparatory School, The Avenue, Bristol Tel: 01272 737264, Fax: 01272 467565. 450 boys and girls ages 3–13. Head since 1993, Dr R J Acheson MA (fifties). Not far from the main school, with plenty of space, kindergarten for 3–8-year-olds down the road, numbers and girls building up under tireless Head. Boarding now down to one-third of total prep children, many from overseas (Far East and expats). Fine school, not simply a feeder for Clifton.

PASTORAL CARE AND DISCIPLINE: Pastorally good. No drugs incidents since '93. Pubs are the temptation – the Marshal makes regular raids round the likely ones on a Saturday night. Homework notebooks are considered 'effective' particularly for the shambolic.

PUPILS AND PARENTS: Professional parents, hordes of 'businessmen'. From Wales, Hereford and Worcester, West Country. A fair number of Forces children; also of foreign nationals. Pupils are pleasant, friendly, streetwise. OBs include Sir Michael Redgrave, Trevor Howard, John Cleese, Earl Haig, Sir David Willcocks, Roger Cooper (quoted soon after his release from prison in Iran as saying 'prison experience is not unlike public school', which resulted in a large number of enquiries from potential parents).

ENTRANCE: Not a high hurdle – 50% at CE (negotiable) and NB there are always some high fliers. Some from own prep. At 13 and 16 (an average of 15 leave post-GCSE). Could do with more pupils, but not alone in this.

EXIT: 95% to university, 20 to Oxbridge each year in '92, '93, '94 and '95. University subjects, like careers, are widely varied. The Head is pushing the gap year.

MONEY MATTERS: Several scholarships (depending on the calibre of pupils) of varying worth, also a Music scholarship and Art scholarship all at 13. Some academic scholarships (internal and external) for Sixth Formers. Some bursaries available, and Assisted Places (usually brought by pupils awarded them at age 11). The recession has increased the day element, decreased boarding: two boys' boarding houses amalgamated (September '93).

REMARKS: A co-ed public school beginning to hold its own in a city loaded with day schools, and gently rising from the ashes.

Clifton High School

College Road, Clifton, Bristol BS8 3JD
Tel: 0117 9730201, Fax: 0117 9238962

PUPILS: 414 senior girls, (about 24 board, rest day)
AGES: 11–18
SIZE OF SIXTH FORM: About 131. Plus own nursery/pre-prep and prep and junior school school with 341 boys and girls ages 3–11
C OF E
FEE-PAYING

HEAD: Since January 1996, Mrs Yvonne Graham, previously Head of Lavant House, Chichester. Took over from the admirable Mrs Walters, and being watched nervously.

ENTRANCE: Exam at 11+, with many girls coming up through the excellent on-site junior school. Some at Sixth Form.

EXIT: University (5 a year to Oxbridge) – Edinburgh, Birmingham, Nottingham are current favourites, and usually some to art college.

REMARKS: A traditional girls' day school, with a small boarding element (Sixth Form only) in the poshest part of Clifton, much sought-after by locals. Founded in 1877, main school building (once a private house, and seen on TV in *The House of Eliot*) has fine entrance and staircase.

Gets super – and sometimes outstanding – academic results, e.g. '95 produced the best ever GCSEs with almost half the entries A or A★. At A level 62% A–B grades, and in the Sciences, the figure was 90%. Sciences are outstandingly strong year after year – in '95 one girl was named the best A-level Chemistry candidate nationally by the Cambridge board, another's STEP papers in Chemistry and Maths for entrance to Cambridge University were classified 'outstanding', a rare accolade. (GCSE option of Dual Award or separate Sciences; all the ablest girls directed towards the latter), History, Maths. 'Thorough teaching and high expectations seem to be what makes the place tick,' commented a mother, 'And a lot of encouragement for the girls to get on and *do* something with their lives.'

Large numbers stay on for Sixth Form Studies here, and new girls come in. New additions and improvements include attractive and functional Sixth Form facilities and a new technology department, including powerful computers for design. There is a good careers department, and girls are encouraged to think boldly.

The school is well equipped with computers, good library. Excellent Textiles, and Home Economics department, also nice Art. Drama and Music are both strong (choral works with nearby Clifton College). This is a traditionally sporty school, though the main sports grounds are a bus ride away: Jo Durie is an OG; also Sarah Keays and Mary Renault.

Boarders (including ex-pats and foreigners) have a comfortable house (two to a room, or singles) and sensible doses of freedom. 'And there's very good social life with so many other schools round about,' say the girls. Pupils are articulate, streetwise and unspoilt. The uniform has recently changed from an unbecoming grey and green to heathery blue sweaters plus kilts.

The school has been going from strength to strength on the academic front, and is well spoken of by local parents.

Cranleigh School

Cranleigh, Surrey GU6 8QQ
Tel: 01483 273997, Fax: 01483 267398

PUPILS: Around 440 boys, 73 girls in Sixth Form (422 board, 91 day)
AGES: 13–18, plus own junior school
SIZE OF SIXTH FORM: 260
C OF E
FEE-PAYING

HEAD: Since 1984, Mr Anthony Hart, MA (Oxon), (fifties), educated at City of Bath and read PPE at New College. Ex-Treasury, and devoted to graphs and pie charts. Teaches British Constitution to new boys and some A-level Economics to Sixth Formers. Knows the boys, and is sympathetic and good-humoured. Aims to produce 'well-balanced, sane adults for this fast changing world.'

Stop Press: retiring in '97.

ACADEMIC MATTERS: A middle-of-the road school: '95 A-level results were disappointing compared with the previous year. Strong Maths; Eng Lit also does well; History and Geography both popular. Small and successful Theatre Studies, as a fourth A-level only. Some very sound teaching 'But I wish they could get pupils to work harder,' muttered a parent. Classics is 'virtually dead' in the Sixth Form, no Greek. Dual Award Sciences from '94 for 'weaker brethren' at GCSE (around half). Individual learning support via the Helen Arkell Institute. Extra courses to keep scholars from getting bored.

Many other things going on – including RSA computer qualifications, the computer facilities were upgraded in '95, and computers are classroom-based and networked. Regular progress reports via Profiles. The superb library is linked to the British Library by CD-Rom. Enterprise Week gives masses of careers experience.

GAMES, OPTIONS, THE ARTS: Games-y: rugby is strong; also hockey (also for girls), helped by the new floodlit Astroturf pitch; cricket (also for girls); tennis; clay-pigeon shooting; and riding, including polo as well as show-jumping and showing (with school and private horses). Serious swimming pool – indoor, heated (and used by Cranleigh Prep School), and water polo does well. Cranleigh village can use the facilities via Cranleigh Sports Club.

Outstanding Drama – and lots of it, *far* more than most schools, with professional theatre under Andrew Fowler-Watt. The addition of the Vivian Cox studio at the back of the stage extends the scope enormously (total stage depth is now 50 ft), as well as being used for concerts, ensembles, etc. Sir Michael Redgrave was Director of Drama in the 1930s and would not be embarrassed to play here.

Three theatres and an outdoor theatre. Superb changing rooms and green room.

Music is also important: musicians performed at the Albert Hall in '95. Good organ, and lots of foreign tours. Lots of Art: 15–20 A-levels annually.

BACKGROUND AND ATMOSPHERE: The school, founded in 1865, is an imposing red-brick building with central quad, plus neo-Queen Anne block, 1928, and newer additions. Originally established to educate the sons of local gentlemen farmers. The elegant and much-used chapel only just holds the entire school. A handsome new house, Loveday, has been built like the main school block around a central courtyard. East House just revamped and now boasts university-style accommodation. (Good for letting to conferences/summer schools?) All set in over 250 acres overlooking the Surrey Downs.

Houses are divided into 'Inner' and 'Outer ' – lots of friendly rivalry, and girls (introduced in 1971) live in flats next to the warden of each house. Pupils graduate from dorms to cubicles (also known as areas or complexes) to study bedrooms.

A magnificent staff Common Room cost £500,000. Staff contracts stipulate that they must live not more than 'ten minutes from school on a bike', so there are lots of them around at weekends. NB A lot of staff go on to be Heads of Departments elsewhere, also Heads of schools.

Fortnightly exeats, lots of parent/staff/school contact; and newly introduced is the Flexeat – allowing weekly exeats, which are easier to obtain as you go up the school.

Cranleigh Preparatory School Tel: 01483 273666, Fax: 01483 277136. Has 185 boys, ages 7–13. Just over the road and uses some of the main school's sporting facilities, but by and large is self-contained. A super school. Sends boys to all the major public schools (Charterhouse, Tonbridge, Wellington popular), but many go on to the big brother school.

PASTORAL CARE AND DISCIPLINE: There is an increasing emphasis on the need to 'work closely with parents' in the wake of some 'concerns about discipline.' The Head says, 'We do think we know our people very well indeed.' Pupils have a yearly tutor, and can choose their tutor in the Sixth Form: 'there is always someone here you could talk to'.

Very anti-drugs, and has sacked four in the last 10 years ('they went immediately'). Hot on theft, smoking and bullying, though 'the things they do are daft rather than bad'. Gating, lots of reporting and getting a card signed, cleaning up and mucking out the stables.

Out for sex (two incidents in 11 years), but we 'don't go looking for trouble immediately'.

PUPILS AND PARENTS: A local school. 60% from Surrey and Sussex, 20% further afield (particularly the girls), 20% from abroad (mainly ex-pats, though 8% foreign). School has strong links (still) with multi-nationals, oil companies – Shell and BP – and airlines (it is midway between Heathrow and Gatwick).

It is likely to become more local with much courting of day pupils, whose school day ends at 5.45 p.m., strings of buses to ferry to and fro Guildford, Horsham, Godalming, Haslemere.

ENTRANCE: Pass of 55% CE, 'sometimes a bit below, but not below 50%'; not oversubscribed. 30 or so from Cranleigh Prep, otherwise from local prep feeders: Brambletye, Aldro, Penthorpe, St Aubyns. 'They come in penny packets.' At Sixth Form, com-petitive entry exam, mainly girls, about ten boys. 3 Bs and 3Cs in GCSE, girls chosen almost more for 'their suitability, than their academic ability'.

EXIT: Faces stiff competition at Sixth Form level from surrounding schools (e.g. Hurtwood House). Vast majority to university (95%), with 75% going to traditional universities, and 1 in 10 to Oxbridge. Lots of traditional professions.

MONEY MATTERS: Fees have been held back until other schools catch up – this used to be top of the expensive tree. Bursaries for financial problems – well worth investigating about these. There are 35 Assisted Places throughout, and streams of scholarships for Academia, Art and Music – all of which are subject to continued good performance and good behaviour.

REMARKS: A well-heeled traditional public school, with good opportunities on offer, but puzzlingly low results.

Dr Challoner's Grammar School

Chesham Road, Amersham,
Buckinghamshire HP6 5HA
Tel: 01494 721685, Fax: 01494 721862

PUPILS: 1,090 boys
ALL DAY
AGES: (11) 12–18
NON-DENOM
STATE

HEAD: Since January 1993, Mr Graham Hill, MA (Hons) (Cantab) (fifties), educated at Bacup and

Rawtenstall Grammar School, Lancashire, read Natural Sciences at Trinity College, Cambridge, followed by PGCE. Previously Deputy Head, having started as Assistant Science teacher at Marlborough and Head of Science at Bristol Grammar.

Came to school in 1978, and is the author of several successful textbooks. Chairman of the Association for Science Education for two years, followed by a year as Fellow at York University – during which time he had secondment from the school.

A no-nonsense, caring Head, with clear-cut ideals and great vision. Looks to produce boys of serious academic standing, who are involved in their community and have enjoyed the range of extra-curricular opportunities and activities of the school.

ACADEMIC MATTERS: Very strong exam results (NB selective intake), rated by *The Times* league table as the 12th most successful state school in 1995, their best ever results. English, Sciences, Maths and Foreign languages (French and German: Spanish on the way up) all equally powerful. Language laboratories are very well used. There is a computer-linked satellite weather station in the Geography department. Computers throughout. CDT and IT linked to Business Studies. A BP Link school, given a bursary for advice on how to build an assault course for D of E and expeditions, etc., (which will then be designed and built in school).

Maximum class size 30, down to 28 in GCSE years, 18 in Sixth Form. No streaming for first two years, then 'banded' rather than set: top two bands take Maths and French a year early. Almost all boys take Dual Award or three sciences to GCSE. No Greek, not much Latin. Streams of boys getting As in GCSE and A-level. Thirty (out of 57)

achieved A grade Physics at A-level in '95 – wow! Remedial help is on hand.

GAMES, OPTIONS, THE ARTS: Strings of National and County representatives in football, basketball, athletics, gymnastics, cricket (tour to Caribbean '94), cross-country, athletics and long and triple jumpers; plus cycling and swimming. Desperately cramped site, with a small sports hall, but superb achievements: in '94/95 the school was Buckingham County Champions in 4 different sports at junior level, and 5 different sports at senior level.

Music is brilliant, and boys sing in Central Hall Westminster and Albert Hall. Plus two orchestras, three choirs, barber's shop group, jazz, Dixieland band, swing band – in other words, a 'tremendous amount of music going on', often in conjunction with sister school, Dr Challoner's High (qv). They also combine for drama. Art rooms are always open; strong ceramics and traditional pottery; popular photography.

There are strong exchange and work experience links with schools in France and Germany. Regular expeditions to North Africa (Egypt, Morocco), occasionally to Southern Africa, South America, North America. Work experience is arranged pre-Sixth Form: linguists do it abroad.

BACKGROUND AND ATMOSPHERE: Founded in 1624, and moved to present site in 1903, co-ed till 1962. Rather cramped (the Head would rather we said 'compact') site encompassing the main Edwardian old school building, overshadowed by a '50s tower block, and enhanced by a charming cloistered brick-built library and classroom extension, which also contains the Sixth Form Common Room. Both senior and junior libraries well stocked.

New extensions to include a Drama

Studio, departmental offices and suites for History and Geography are due to be completed by the time we go to press.

Boys wear uniform below Sixth Form, when dress is 'relaxed but smart and conventional': overall impression is neat and tidy. 'Fair number' of female staff. 12 Head Boys, 50 prefects; all share responsibilities. 200 metres from the Metropolitan Line station.

PASTORAL CARE AND DISCIPLINE: Chain of command via Form tutors (Division tutors in Sixth Form), Heads of Year, and Deputy Head; all have a weekly meeting with Head. All are very available to parents: if Head is not around, Deputy Head, Matron (SRN) or one of four trained counsellors can be contacted immediately.

There is a strong anti-bullying policy, including a bully box where boys can leave notes, not necessarily signed, without feeling they are telling tales. Rather, it shows a concern for each other.

Serious wickedness equals either temporary or fixed-term exclusion, or expulsion (i.e. for supplying drugs or for other major misdemeanours) but boys almost always get a second chance. The Head reckons he is firm, but fair.

PUPILS AND PARENTS: 'Very much commuter country', droves of middle-class parents with perhaps 7% ethnic. Hard-working, conscientious and very supportive. Parents join The Friends of Dr Challoner's Grammar School, with heavy fund-raising events plus links with the school – wine tasting as well as careers advice.

ENTRANCE: At 12 (very occasionally at 11); 40/50 feeder schools (fee-paying e.g. The Beacon, Gayhurst, Chesham Prep) as well as local middle schools. By county-administered VR

test, preference given to siblings and Head Teachers' reports, but the school has 'no say whatsoever'. The Head believes that boys who arrive might be one-quarter of those who put Dr Challoner's first on their list, but no accurate information is given to the school.

Entry to Sixth Form is by interview: 30–40 annually; 70–80 usually apply.

EXIT: A small number leave post-GCSE, either relocation, or to take up employment (two or three annually) or go to Art Foundation Courses or co-ed Grammar Schools. Otherwise 90% to universities (40% to ex-polys), including regular 18–25 to Oxbridge.

MONEY MATTERS: Funds are available for the financially hard-up for extra-curricular activities (but these are currently on a growing curve); 2 travelling scholarships in Sixth Form.

REMARKS: A highly successful traditional old-style grammar school, going from strength to strength.

Dr Challoner's High School

Cokes Lane, Little Chalfont, Buckinghamshire HP7 9QB
Tel: 01494 763296, Fax: 01494 766023

PUPILS: 875 girls
ALL DAY
AGES: 12–16
SIZE OF SIXTH FORM: 283
NON-DENOM
STATE

HEAD: Since 1993, Mrs Sue Lawson BA (forties), educated at Queen

Mary's College, London, followed by Northern Counties Teacher's Training at Newcastle University. Married to civil engineer, one daughter. Came to teaching via Coal Board and personnel. Previously taught peripatetically (thanks to husband's job), and came to Dr Challoner's from George Abbot's School in Guildford.

ACADEMIC MATTERS: Maximum class size 30, unstreamed except in Maths, a strong department. Early language diversification with French, Spanish, German and Latin on offer at 12/13; girls can choose two languages for GCSE. Dual or single sciences are available; large take-up in all three Sciences at A-level. Classical Civilisation is on offer. Computers are used throughout, and Maths Dept uses palm-top Hewlett Packard computers (with Derive Software); keyboarding teaching in lower school. Super new library, still 'about to be enlarged'.

GAMES, OPTIONS, THE ARTS: Sport popular, national and county level athletics, hockey and swimming (but does not have own pool), and county level netball. Strong on extra-curricular sports clubs, and ballroom dancing is an option with the boys of Dr Challoner's Grammar School (qv).

There is a superb new arts and technology faculty, with Art and Design, Technology, Electronics, Multi-media workshops. The school produces good Art, which festoons the building; also masses of Drama, mostly via the English Dept, and lots of competitions. Music is strong, with lots of peripatetic teachers; string, wind, brass ensembles, hugely adaptable. Choirs and good links with Dr Challoner's Grammar School for orchestras, societies, drama etc. There is an Arts Week in the summer term, with master classes, and artists and a dancer in residence.

Work Experience, D of E, and clubs for everything. Good charity involvement. Also lots of foreign visits.

BACKGROUND AND ATMOSPHERE: Founded in 1624 by Dr Robert Challoner, becoming co-ed in 1906. The girls were hived off to Little Chalfont in 1962, concentrating, in the words of the then Headmistress, 'not on looking backwards, but upon a forward vision'.

On a splendid suburban site, with mature trees and acres of playing fields, the school is a combination of ghastly flat-roofed '60s and marvellous curving brick-built recent extensions, (two-thirds already open, one-third to go), encompassing an outdoor amphitheatre. Very close to the Metropolitan Line.

PASTORAL CARE AND DISCIPLINE: Girls have the same form tutor from the time they arrive until Sixth Form level. There is a girl-orientated School Council, and parents are involved in the pastoral curriculum – 'an awareness-raising programme'. Personal, Social and Health education in place; little bullying; will 'probably' exclude for involvement with drugs – mutual support with all schools in area i.e. you exclude, they take in and vice versa.

PUPILS AND PARENTS: From all over Buckinghamshire and down the Metropolitan Line, predominantly middle class, with a fair share of ethnic-minority backgrounds. Parents are very supportive financially, they underwrote the original computer lab.

Parents can visit any time, with the Head's clinic on the first Monday of every month for parents with queries.

ENTRANCE: 150 pupils each year at 12+; administered by LEA. School has no say in intake, though preference is given to siblings and girls within the catchment (Grammar schools in Bucks take approx. top 30% of ability range).

Sixth Form entrants apply direct to school and need a minimum of five GCSEs at C or above, and a minimum of B in the subjects they want to do at A-level.

EXIT: Dribble leave after GCSE, usually to do different A-levels elsewhere, otherwise 95% to university. 8–12 annually to Oxbridge.

MONEY MATTERS: Parents' Association is involved in fund-raising events.

REMARKS: Strong and worthy academic traditional state school with a dynamic Head, and definitely perceived as an excellent solution for the impoverished middle class.

Dollar Academy

Dollar, Clackmannanshire FK14 7DU
Tel: 01259 742511, Fax: 01259 742867

PUPILS: Around 550 boys, 550 girls (150 board, 950 day)
AGES: 5–18
SIZE OF SIXTH FORM: 250
FEE-PAYING

HEAD: Rector since 1994, Mr John Robertson MA (forties). Formerly Assistant Head at Stewart Melville, and Deputy at Dollar for several years. English specialist.

ACADEMIC MATTERS: Scottish system – using A-levels occasionally. There is a wide range of subjects and a flexible timetable to fit pupils' options, rather than the other way round. French or German in junior school. Japanese studies possible at Sixth Form – the school has close ties with the Japanese faculty at Stirling University. Classes of 21–25 in junior school and in senior school 17–22. Mixed ability classes; no setting.

GAMES, OPTIONS, THE ARTS: The school has successful teams – rugby for boys, hockey for girls. Lots of extra-currricular games on offer. Lots of games fields, plus a large hall and indoor pool. Strong choral tradition in the school and there are two orchestras. The enthusiastic Pipe Band wears McNabb tartan. CCF, Drama, D of E, work experience in local hospitals, etc. The school has good facilities, and plenty of clubs.

BACKGROUND AND ATMOSPHERE: Founded as a co-ed boarding school in 1818 by Andrew Mylne, the local minister, with a legacy from John McNabb. Formerly Direct Grant but in 1974 became private. Elegant Playfair façade, but following fire in the '60s, the main building was rebuilt entirely. New building in 1995 for Computing, Business studies and Maths. Boarding houses are 'OK', say the pupils. Geographically useful, given the school's position vis-à-vis the Forth Bridge.

PASTORAL CARE AND DISCIPLINE: Firm discipline often involves cleaning up the school. The family atmosphere in houses was praised in HMI report in '95. Boarders complain of not wearing their own clothes enough – school uniform has be worn to all meals at weekends.

PUPILS AND PARENTS: Pupils from all over Scotland and children of ex-pat Scots, but the vast majority from a 20-mile radius; plus large numbers of Forces children. Some fourth-generation pupils.

Rector says pupils are perhaps 'too conservative' and an English master said 'they would have difficulty discussing the concept of rebellion'. An OB is Sir James Dewar (inventor of the vacuum flask).

ENTRANCE: At 5, 10 or 11, the latter two by examination, which is very selective. Well oversubscribed.

EXIT: The majority to university and some each year to Oxbridge.

MONEY MATTERS: There are 55 Assisted Places; 4 academic scholarships of 50% at 11, 2 at 15/16. Very reasonable and excellent value.

REMARKS: A solid, traditional school which is not setting the world alight, but is very popular locally.

Downe House

Cold Ash, Newbury,
Berkshire RG16 9JJ
Tel: 01635 200286, Fax: 01635 202026

PUPILS: 612 girls (580 board, 32 day)
AGES: 11–18
SIZE OF SIXTH FORM: 164
C OF E
FEE-PAYING

HEAD: Since 1989, Miss S R Cameron, BA (fifties), educated at Wycombe Abbey, and read History at London University. Previously Head of Cobham Hall (briefly), and before that a Housemistress at Sherborne. Has had, regretfully, to give up teaching because of the weight of administration. Comments that the school does not produce a 'type', and sees part of her role as ensuring that girls leave 'knowing their strengths and their weaknesses and that they are able to get on with people even if they don't like them'. A great believer in broad and balanced education, in preparing not protecting, and thinks it very important that girls also enjoy life (surprisingly rare to hear a Head stress this). Hopes she teaches girls to 'use their feminine wiles positively'. Positive is her watchword. Has charming spaniels.

On the current success of the school, she comments, 'We're doing something right, but I can't quite think what. Geography and fashion must both have something to do with it . . .' Full to bursting point at the time of writing.

Stop Press: Miss Cameron leaves the school at the end of the summer term '96 to go to – of all unlikely places – North Foreland Lodge. Two deputies appointed as Acting Heads.

ACADEMIC MATTERS: A *very* good performer and rising – results get better each year, and are a joy to look at (77.7% A–B grades at A-level – phew! – with remarkably little below a C grade). Sciences are doing distinctly well (NB the school has a splendid and inspiring Science block). Successful Modern Languages, with a 'taster' term for all 11-year-olds of Spanish, German and Russian. Ecole Hampshire (in the Dordogne) has been acquired on a long lease ('Lucky, because we had an overflow of pupils'): 11-year-olds go out for an entire term (in batches of 25), and *love* it. 'Magic for the French, of course,' says a mother. Projects, art, music, etc, also benefit from the French experience. Class subject rooms are rationalised, cutting down on endless movement hither and thither. Good IT. Technology was fairly recently introduced ('We're starting gently') and is proving popular. Can cope with mild dyslexia.

GAMES, OPTIONS, THE ARTS: Round-the-year tennis coaching

(oodles of courts); strong on lacrosse, also very strong swimmers – there is a splendid pool. Music everywhere (90% of girls play one instrument), and there are practice rooms in nuns' former cells; also a particularly good choir. Cookery and needlework for everyone. Exciting Art (several girls go on to foundation courses/ art degrees), with textiles and screen painting and ceramics. Very enthusiastic Drama – 'and', said one girl, 'quite a lot of it'. Good Young Enterprise, D of E, also CCF.

BACKGROUND AND ATMOSPHERE: Whitewashed building in Hispano-Surrey style, disjointed and scattered (lots of to-ing and fro-ing, with the library well down the hill), set in 110 acres. Definitely a house-orientated school. The first two years lead a cosy life apart, under strict management. A second Sixth Form house is now open (Lower and Upper mingled, large single rooms for upper, doubles for Lower), with huge TV-viewing/common rooms. A cafeteria system has now been introduced ('We know our manners have gone downhill'), and good food.

The former Convent Chapel is too small for the whole school, but is much used, with some complaints of 'too much'. This is a highly structured set-up, but subtly so, with uninstitutional buildings and atmosphere (which comes as a disappointment to potential parents who imagine it might be a really traditional girls' public school). The weekend programme has considerably increased options (Saturdays and Sundays), 'but some girls still choose to mooch around'. Strong work ethic.

PASTORAL CARE AND DISCIPLINE: Smoking is a persistent irritant, 'no matter how disagreeable the evidence against it,' sighs the Head. Girls very much on trust. Ages mix freely, also plenty of staff to turn to. There was a drugs incident in '95.

PUPILS AND PARENTS: Upper-class parents with cohesive backgrounds and values, with a fair number of Forces children. Geographically fairly wide-spread (Scotland, Cornwall and of course London and the Thames Valley). De-lightful and open girls, a good advertise-ment for their school who comment on themselves, 'We're very untrendy – lessons finish at 6.30 p.m., and no one bothers to change into mufti afterwards.' OGs include Baroness Ewart-Biggs, Dame Rebecca Murray, Geraldine James.

ENTRANCE: By exam at 11+ (the bulk), also 12+, 13+ and some at Sixth Form. 'Full up to the end of the century' according to a spokesperson. Currently represents the Holy Grail for some.

EXIT: A few leave post-GCSE, but far more come in. Almost all to university, 17 to Oxbridge in '95 (extra coaching for Oxford and Cambridge applicants); increasing numbers take a 'gap' year.

MONEY MATTERS: Major and minor scholarships at 11+, 12+, 13+ also at Sixth Form; 2 open Music scholarships and 5 Assisted Places.

REMARKS: Currently the flavour of the month, strong and nice with it: successful, flourishing, all-girls' boarding school with breadth and depth that keeps girls busy and makes them thoughtful too.

Caveat – has grown substantially since we last went into print. Too fast?

Downside School

Stratton-on-the-Fosse, Bath BA3 4RJ
Tel: 01761 232206, Fax: 01761 233575

PUPILS: 291 boys, 2 girls (in Sixth Form);
all board except for 9. Plus own Junior
House, with 35 boys ages 10–13.
AGES: 13–18
SIZE OF SIXTH FORM: 113
RC
FEE-PAYING

HEAD: Since July 1995, Dom Antony
Sutch MA (forties), aka the Monk
of Mayfair, the Monk of Manhattan, also
Tone. 'My motto, as it were, for the
school is that we have been given life in
abundance and should live it accordingly.'
Totally in agreement with his predecessor
that 'The timescale for a Downside boy
should be eternity and not the passing
moments.' Educated at Downside, read
History at Exeter. Became a chartered
accountant before becoming a monk,
then went to Oxford and took a degree in
Theology. Taught Theology and History
at Downside, was a Housemaster, and
responsible for bringing down 'some of
the more exciting members of our world'
to speak – the great and the good, with
whom he naturally mixes. Writes for *The
Spectator,* occasionally for newspapers.
Lives with his four predecessor headmasters.

ACADEMIC MATTERS: Mixed for-
tunes for a very broad entry criteria.
The new Head bears down fiercely on
'idle boys suffering from their own
idleness', and within his first six weeks
asked four boys to leave. Supervision of
work has been tightened up; boys are
now chased up over slack work. Bright
boys are given a 'good crack' to quote a
parent of one.
    Modern Languages have a good
following and do well (Russian, Chinese,

Arabic, Spanish, German, Italian,
Portuguese, French – and tutors for other
languages can be brought in). Sciences are
distinctly well taught (separately or
combined at GCSE). There are around
15 teaching monks, the rest are lay,
including a handful of women. Business
Studies A-level has been introduced.
Dyslexic help and EFL on offer. Lots of
trips, e.g. geographers to French Alps,
language exchanges all over the place,
historians to Rome with insider access to
the Vatican museums.

GAMES, OPTIONS, THE ARTS: Keen
sport, especially rugby (coached by
Jonathan Callard, Assistant Housemaster,
capped for England as star penalty-kicker
in an historic victory over the All-Blacks);
also soccer, hockey, cricket, golf,
orienteering, fencing. The school has an
indoor pool, and space-age Sports Hall.
Flourishing CCF (Army and Royal Air
Force scholarships clocked up recently)
includes Ten Tors walk and a summer
camp in Cyprus. D of E being 'given a
boost'. There is an annual pilgrimage to
Lourdes, where boys remain on helper
duty throughout the night.
    The 'Twenty Club' invites high-
profile speakers to talk to Seniors e.g.
Lord Hailsham, Charles Moore.
    Fine Music under David Lawson: EMI
have asked for a recording. Boys have
sung at Westminster Cathedral as well as
at Sting's birthday party – which led to a
lot of engagements. Slaughterhouse
Seven jazz band is constantly on tour, and
duly renowned, raising money for
charity, often abroad. Boys play in
concerts in Abbey Church with professional soloists. Half the boys learn an
instrument and all try one out free for the
first year.

BACKGROUND AND ATMOSPHERE:
Part of the Benedictine Monastery
(which still owns the 300-acre farm)

transferred to rural Somerset from Flanders in 1814. True to Benedictine tradition as a seat of learning, *Downside Review*, a slim theological quarterly, is internationally known. The hexagonal monastery library with 500,000 books – 'We have some that aren't in the British Museum' – is used by scholars from all over the world. The Abbey Tower dominates the lush landscape for miles around. Neo-Gothic architecture by Giles Gilbert Scott, plus many additions.

The vast roof encompasses virtually all the Downside buildings. Two boarding houses have closed (due to falling numbers), giving GCSE boys individual study bedrooms – much welcomed. House kitchens and leisure areas are now in place. 'Boys mix easily and there is a spirit of camaraderie,' approves a parent who chose Downside 'campus' over the more disparate Ampleforth. Requirements of the Children Act has split larger dormitories into cubicles. Monastic and scholastic bells jointly divide the day, and even during a cricket match play stops for prayer when Big Bede is rung.

Boys 'on own request' are back in the old pre-war uniform of black jackets and pinstripes – murmurings of 'media hostility to the men in grey suits'.

PASTORAL CARE AND DISCIPLINE: Tightening up under the new management. There have been massive changes in the management team, with three lay masters put in as Deputies: one in charge of pastoral side (this includes discipline of both boys and staff), one in charge of studies, one in charge of admissions. Rustication for drinking; expulsion if, on suspicion of drug-taking, a urine test is refused. Otherwise 'early parade' for misdemeanours – 'more of a pain for the adults supervising than for the children.' Foul language is being targeted by the new Head.

'Wonderful humanitarian approach' to foreign boys, e.g. Italians and Spanish, in helping them cope and settle, though some are reported to have bolted initially – one was recaptured at Heathrow.

PUPILS AND PARENTS: More sons of old boys than most other public schools (30–35%), often three or four generations. 20% are from overseas – widespread, and a fair number of Forces children. Lots of Spanish with English links (Sherry), Maltese, Italian and newly forged links with Russia, Poland and sister Benedictine schools in Hungary. A handful from Hong Kong; also South and North America. Most of Catholic Western Europe is represented – St Benedict is the patron saint of Europe.

OBs (Gregorians) make an aesthetic line-up, including Sir John Pope-Hennessy, Michael Noakes, David Mlinaric, Rocco Forte, Rupert Allason MP, sportsmen Simon Halliday and Richard Cohen. Auberon Waugh is the most prominent *enfant terrible*.

ENTRANCE: No problem. At 10 to Junior House (Plunkett), or at 13 to main school at CE. Family links can clinch a place: 'We do admit boys who haven't done so well if we know who they are.' There is a huge range of ability.

EXIT: Around 94% to universities; 8 to Oxbridge. Otherwise arts foundation, Cirencester Agricultural College, business courses, study abroad.

MONEY MATTERS: There are 3 major scholarships plus a number of minor ones. Maths scholarship, Art scholarship, several Music scholarships from half fees to instrumental cover; Choral scholarships for Junior House. Some Sixth Form scholarships. 'Kind' to those in financial difficulties.

REMARKS: A traditional monastic school, being given a thorough shake-up by its new high-profile Head, who is hoping to bump up numbers.

Dulwich College

London SE21 7LD
Tel: 0181 693 3601, Fax: 0181 693 6319

PUPILS: Around 1,385 boys (around 85 board)

AGES: 7–18. (Divided into Lower School: 7–13; Middle School: 13–16; Upper School: 16–18)

SIZE OF SIXTH FORM: 380

C OF E

FEE-PAYING

HEAD: From January 1997, Mr Graham Able MA (early fifties), educated at Worksop College, read Chemistry at Trinity College, Cambridge. Wife has her own teaching career, two children. Direct, highly competent, widely admired. Keen hockey player, puts a big emphasis on tolerance, and dismissive of league table 'games'.

Takes over from an interrugnum of the Deputy Master, Mr Christopher Field JP, MA (Cantab), ARAM (mid-fifties).

Follows in the footsteps of the enforced resignation of the much liked Mr Anthony (Tony) Verity, following the accusation by his secretary of sexual harrassment, of which he was cleared. This matter rocked the school, and was considered by many to have been badly handled by the governors and to have brought into question the whole role of governors at schools. Which said, the running of this school is so efficient that during the protracted problem period, life went on as normal. The senior management team has terrific muscle.

ACADEMIC MATTERS: The school has a strong work ethic, and is distinguished academically; considering the school has a much wider ability range than Westminster or St Paul's, it has excellent A-level results. There is an increasing number of mixed Arts/ Sciences courses (separate sciences at GCSE); very strong staff in English, History, Modern Languages, Sciences. Disappointing results in Economics in '95, also Maths with Statistics. A very large number of A-levels is offered.

There are 125 staff in all, with a very low turnover, and extraordinarily committed, full of Value Added. The school has excellent careers provision – the department even drums up paid jobs for pupils. The National Curriculum is followed with 7+, 11+ tests. Help for dyslexics and for those 'who slip through the net'.

GAMES, OPTIONS THE ARTS: Famously brilliant under-15 rugby side in recent years – trounces everybody. The school has an enormous gym, used for international baseball matches (baseball is very popular), and used daily for martial arts, weightlifting, fencing, etc. Also huge numbers of playing fields and floodlit Astroturf. Friends of Dulwich College can use the school's sports facilities, including the swimming pool and magnificent new Fitness Centre (deep envy). Strong Army, Navy, Air Force with three oversubscribed troops of Scouts, plus a Venture Scout unit.

Many clubs, computing, biology (rocketry – i.e. making rockets and firing them off – still popular in Middle School). Super Music: all children learn a stringed instrument at eight ('sometimes it sticks'); the choir tours internationally. Drama everywhere: 'Difficult to drag Dulwich boys off the stage.' In the purpose-built theatre, over 30 plays are produced annually – girls come from JAGS. Good

Art. A Field Centre in Wales is also used for Sixth Form Studies.

BACKGROUND AND ATMOSPHERE: Founded by the Elizabethan actor-manager Edward Alleyn (1619). (The school has a first folio edition of Alleyn's Shakespeare and diaries of the Globe and Rose theatres). The 1870s stately pile is not totally at odds with late 20th-century buildings. Spectacular frontage, and set in handsome grounds with trees, parks, woods, the sheer size automatically confers a sense of considerable privilege in the otherwise mundane red-brick South London. A stone's throw from Railton Road, Brixton (where the riots were).

Inside, corridors are wide and spacious, with no noise or suggestion of over-crowding. The school has exceptional facilities, with two fabulous libraries (one for staff only) and the Wodehouse library has replica of his study. The paperback book shop is open daily. The amazing school 'magazine' is in the form of a hardback book. The huge dining hall offers a vegetarian option; staff eat there too.

The Lower School is self-contained and set apart but is still on the generously large green campus. From the age of 10 boys start using specialist facilities at the main school (e.g. labs, Art, Design and Technology rooms).

It has the general atmosphere of a proper country public school, and looks like one too.

PASTORAL CARE AND DISCIPLINE: The school recently introduced a formal contract on a code of conduct to be signed on admission by parents, pupil and school – will other private schools follow?

Tutorial system introduced after fourth form. Drugs are an 'occasional problem' and mean instant dismissal. But for day boys 'they usually know where to draw the line; there is little overlap between parties and school'. Sackings for persistent theft, perhaps one or two a year in total, otherwise detention *and* it's on Saturday mornings. A visiting Imam comes once or twice a term. Resident school counsellor. There are occasional complaints from boys that staff 'don't even know our names'.

PUPILS AND PARENTS: A very *very* wide but not conspicuous social and ethnic mix, including Hong Kong Chinese and other Asians, not to mention new trickles from Eastern Europe. Over 25 mother tongues are spoken in the school. Lots of Bank/City children. There are three boarding houses (though numbers are dwindling), including weekly boarders and overseas boys; the majority at the top end of the school, but some younger.

Boys are fairly street-wise as you would expect but very 'anti-attitude'. Buses with Alleyn's and JAGS from all points out, including Wimbledon. Lots of locals (the richest and the poorest). Children can and do drive to school. OBs include P G Wodehouse; Shackleton, whose Antarctic expedition boat is on display.

ENTRANCE: At 7, 9, 11, 13 and some into Sixth Form. By exam and interview. The school has its own entrance exam – though NB not when you'd expect it (January for 11+, February for 13+, 60 places, also 20 more places via CE): get details from the school, it's complicated and not like other public schools. Foreign children can sometimes be admitted throughout the term if that is when their parents hit this country. Automatic entry via Lower School.

EXIT: Conservative. More than 90% to universities – a wide spread, including northern. In '95, 32 to Oxbridge, reading traditional subjects, English, History, the Classics, Sciences, Languages. Imperial College London is popular.

MONEY MATTERS: A very wealthy foundation. There are substantial numbers of academic scholarships, also for Music and Art; bursaries; Sixth Form scholarships and bursaries. 50 Assisted Places in all (mostly at 11+, some at 13, plus 5 at Sixth Form). There is an ongoing Bursary appeal (set up in the recession to help the hard hit), with £500,000 from an Old Boys' endowment.

REMARKS: A distinguished school suffering slight post-trauma nerves but marching onward. Broad, strong and tolerant.

The Edinburgh Academy

42 Henderson Row,
Edinburgh EH3 5BL
Tel: 0131 556 4603, Fax: 0131 556 9353

PUPILS: 540 boys (490 day, 50 board)
Plus own prep school (311 boys, ages 5–11), and nursery (53 boys and girls ages 3–5).
AGES: 11–18
NON-DENOM
FEE-PAYING

HEAD: Rector since 1995, Mr John Light MA (forties), educated at Sedbergh, read Modern Languages at Clare College Cambridge. Did a diploma in Business Administration, and worked in industry before teaching: taught at Glenalmond, Uppingham, Haileybury, then Sedbergh as a Housemaster. Keen

sportsman, and singer. Married with four children, two at university, two at school. Very straightforward and a good communicator. Busy strengthening the continuity between prep and senior school. Works closely with a strong management team (Deputy, Bursar, prep Head). Keen on pupils emerging as 'flexible people who can take initiative where necessary, but be part of a team when appropriate.' And currently laying particular emphasis on 'ambition within and without the classroom.'

ACADEMIC MATTERS: Broad academic range of pupils in mixed-ability classes, considered to be beneficial to all, 'more normal, more balanced'. The emphasis (as so often in Scottish schools) is on breadth of education – choices are left late. Most Sixth Formers do Highers in their first year, and take A-levels the following year; a minority spend two years on Highers. GCSEs before that for everyone. A-level boys start with four subjects, then drop one after a year.

Strong Sciences, (12 out of 18 pupils clocked up an A grade at A-level Physics in '95); good Modern Languages department, with taster German, Russian now a Sixth Form option; traditionally good English. Overall results could do with sharpening up. General sense of could-do-better ...

The tradition of 'dux', the brightest boy in the school (Magnus Magnusson was dux in his day), has now been enlarged to include a clever group of dux-worthy boys.

GAMES, OPTIONS, THE ARTS: A gamesy school – famous on the rugby field, most matches, still on Saturday mornings, involving a large numbers of boys. Main games fields 2 miles away. CCF, keen D of E.

Outstandingly fine Art department, headed by John Brown, a real star in the

Art education world: pupils notch up A grades galore at A-level, and also GCSE, and growing numbers take Art at both levels. Life class (of course). DT going well. Strong music, especially on the choral side; also a string group, pipe band and orchestras. Academy Action recently launched – involving Accies in the local community, e.g. with charity-raising sleep-outs. Also forging links outside with luminaries of Edinburgh, 'making use of the place – it's no good just sitting on our backsides,' to quote a member of staff.

BACKGROUND AND ATMOSPHERE: The school was founded in 1824, in a dignified classical building with a Greek inscription on the portico ('*Education is the mother of both wisdom and virtue*'). Wings and additions, traditional classroom blocks all around a huge tarmac yard, some cumbersome layout, e.g. Biology behind Art, well away from Physics and Chemistry. Famous oval assembly hall. Boarders live 15 minutes' walk away by the junior department, near the Botanical Gardens and Inverleith Park (the green lung of Edinburgh North). The school owns a Field Centre in Angus. Girls are very much a minority – this feels like a boys' school with a few girls. At the bottom end, much work continues behind the scenes to strengthen continuity between Prep and Upper.

Unpretentious, quietly civilised atmosphere.

The Preparatory School, 10 Arboretum Road. Tel: 0131 552 3690, Fax: 0131 551 2660. Head, since 1995, Mr CRF Paterson MA, Cert Ed. Children come in at 3, 5, and 7; boys and girls in the nursery, then boys only. A good place, buzzing with energy and enthusiasm. Work is displayed everywhere; lovely art; ambitious music and plays; lots of games. Set in a large building (opposite the Rector's house), daunting outside, but cosy inside. Increasingly strong links between senior and prep school. Some boys go on elsewhere.

PASTORAL CARE AND DISCIPLINE: Head ephor (Prefect) is a key link with Head and school. 'Far more care now,' said a parent, glad that the new Head emphasises the necessity for courtesy – as well as encouraging ambition. City temptations are close.

PUPILS AND PARENTS: All sorts, with large numbers of professionals from Edinburgh and Lothian. Farmers' sons and foreigners board. Boys wear tweedy jackets in winter, blazers in summer, Sixth Form girls neat in navy blue blazers. Pupils are pleasantly self-confident and polite. Sir Walter Scott was one of the school's founders, and FPs include Robert Louis Stevenson and J M Ballantyne.

ENTRANCE: Up from the junior school (no exam is necessary), also entry via English and Maths assessment at 11+, 12+, 13+ and some (boys and girls) at Sixth Form.

EXIT: Most to universities, mostly Scottish. About 7 per year to Oxbridge. Business Studies, Art, Biochemistry and Engineering are equally popular subjects at university. The gap year is a popular option. A few re-takers in recent years.

MONEY MATTERS: Some scholarships, including several for Art; Assisted Places throughout.

REMARKS: A traditional and distinguished academic day school which has had a rough ride, and is trying to re-establish itself under (yet another) new Head. We are getting mixed reports.

Emanuel School

Battersea Rise, London SW11 1HS
Tel: 0181 870 4171, Fax: 0181 875 0267

PUPILS: 720 boys, 4 girls, and going fully
co-ed from 1996
ALL DAY
AGES: 10–18
SIZE OF SIXTH FORM: 160
C OF E
FEE-PAYING

HEAD: Since 1994 Mr Tristram Jones Parry MA (forties), educated at Westminster and Christ Church, Oxford (Maths and computers). Taught at Dulwich, then Westminster – where he was Under Master for seven years. Very tall, appears lugubrious. Widely acclaimed as a 'brilliant Maths teacher'. Bachelor, who lists his interests as reading, travel, walking, cycling and watching sport. A stickler for discipline ('Not someone to get the wrong side of, was a typical comment.)

ENTRANCE: At 10+, 11+. CE at 13 (automatic entry from the lower school), when 300 chase 80 places. Also at Sixth Form. (Entry now fully co-ed at all ages).

EXIT: Post GCSE leakage appears to have ceased. 90% go on to further education after A-levels. Old Boys include Michael Aspel; Dr J B Phillips, the Bible scholar; Stuart Surridge, cricketer and founder of sports outfitters.

REMARKS: Sound, low-profile, traditional South London day school, poised to go fully co-ed (though NB the take up of girls in the Sixth Form when doors were opened to them in '95 was minimal), and as such is a rare animal. It takes in a fairly broad range of abilities and does well for the average. Good Maths, Chemistry and Physics. Has a traditional approach to teaching. Second Master, Mr Jeremy Edwards, is a gifted English teacher (also an international oarsman).

Distinguished rowing (boathouse by Putney Bridge), successful rugby, and enthusiastic parental support for sports. Keen drama, music, CCF, community service and CDT. There are a good range of lunch-time clubs for younger boys.

The school was founded in 1594 by Lady Dacre (whose descendants are still on the governing board) and moved to its present ivy-clad Victorian Gothic block (originally an orphanage) in 1883, a 12-acre oasis with fine trees, in the middle of busy Battersea. There is a newly built Sixth Form centre (basic, 'But it gives us independence' commented pupils warmly). The school is committedly Christian 'Godliness and good learning' are stressed by the statutes, and there are two full-time chaplains. Pupils are decent and polite (both facts regularly remarked upon by locals), with 39.89% on Assisted Places. Boys carry yellow cards (identity, timetable, plus conduct marks). The broad social and ethnic mix, a jolly jumble, from a wide catchment area, includes first-time buyers and refugees from boarding schools. Not upmarket.

Epsom College

College Road, Surrey KT17 4JQ
Tel: 01372 723621, Fax: 01372 726277

PUPILS: 660, including 65 girls in Sixth
Form. (360 board – of whom 236
weekly boarders, 130 full boarders,
300 day). Going fully co-ed from
September 1996, taking girls at 13
AGES: 13–18
C OF E
FEE-PAYING

HEAD: Since January '92, Mr Anthony Beadles, MA (fifties), educated at Epsom College, read History at Christ Church, Oxford. Three children; collects 19th-century glass and watercolours, plays golf, and is a voracious reader. Previously Headmaster of King's Bruton, and before that a Housemaster at Harrow. Quiet, unassuming, widely respected as a good manager on all fronts. Tightening up pastorally – 'Stricter, but we see less of him than we did of his predecessor,' commented a pupil. Introduced prefect training scheme, a mini-managerial course which pupils like.

ENTRANCE: Via CE at 13, also at Sixth Form (mostly girls). The Royal Medical Foundation helps 'medical practitioners and their dependants in distressed circumstances and has generous scholarships and bursaries'.

EXIT: University for most, 15 per year to Oxbridge; substantial numbers study medicine. Art college for some.

REMARKS: Founded for the sons of doctors in 1855, and claims to produce more doctors than any other school, though now largely a local school (57 come from abroad, including Malaysians and Hong Kong Chinese). 'In the good old days medical families automatically sent sons here.' – 17% sons of medics currently. Set in 80+ acres, a green oasis in a sea of suburbia, the red-brick Gothic gives a homogeneous feel, even including the latest addition (1993) of staff flats, nicknamed 'Eldorado'.

A-level results are consistently impressive and the school rates highly in national league tables. Extremely good science teaching (of course), with the subjects taught and examined separately throughout; the strongest A-level results in Mathematics (32 A grades out of 65 candidates), and in Chemistry (37 out of 77 candidates getting A grades). There is a nice (unique?) little biology/natural history museum on site (all manner of pickled objects).

Art is exceptional: here is one of the country's outstanding art departments, under Mr G Poupart, with Jeremy Broadway in charge of brilliant pottery. Several pupils doing three sciences take Art as their fourth A-level (and get an A or a B). Both Graham Sutherland and John Piper are old boys (also a large number of medical bigwigs).

Finely equipped in all departments (far better than some more famous schools), contradicting the College claims not to be well off. A new Library (in the quadrangle) will be open by the time we go to press. IT has been revamped, fitted above the now outmoded swimming pool. The Design Technology department has shining equipment.

Strong sports, with two Sports Halls, any number of squash courts, a huge fencing salle (fencing is currently on a winning streak), Astroturf, hockey/cricket/soccer grounds galore. There are regular sports tours abroad, and an excellent army assault course (the army make use of it).

The Sixth Form girls' houses (built for medical pensioners) are cosy and comfy, and at the time of writing preparations are in hand for the 13-year-old girls. Boys' accommodation is sparse, at odds with the school's teaching facilities. The pub-like Sixth Form common room has leather banquettes, fruit machine. Pupils are polite, neat, friendly, middle class, and kept very busy. Some reports of bullying reach us.

Saturday night is 'peaceful' say staff, 'dull' say boarders, with the loss of day and weekly boarding pupils. But life hums into action again on Sunday evening (concerts, prep), and the school lives well up to its claims of operating as a boarding school (and is good value, especially for day boarders) with a six-day week in which the various categories of pupils integrate well. Well mentioned now by prep school heads.

Eton College

Windsor, Berkshire SL4 6DW
Tel: 01753 671000, Fax: 01753 830167

PUPILS: 1,275 boys (all boarding)
AGES: 13–18
SIZE OF SIXTH FORM: about 504
C OF E (other faiths 'excused' chapel);
160 RCs, who have resident chaplain
FEE-PAYING

HEAD: Since September 1994, Mr John Lewis BA (fifties), quiet, scholarly New Zealander still being watched with interest. Dapper; not the gentle soul he first seems, but possibly without the iron strength needed to head this establishment: appears, noted a disenchanted parent, 'like a startled rabbit.' Nicknamed Peter Jones. Classicist. Teaches scripture to junior boys. A very private man, who loathes personal publicity, plays his cards close to his chest and incidentally does not care for the style of this book.

Antipodean drawl, 'Which you may find charming,' commented a father, 'or you may wonder if it's hiding something.' (His Kiwi accent is mercilessly imitated by the boys.) Mr Lewis was Master in College before becoming Headmaster of Geelong GS in Australia. Danish wife, no children. Comments that any changes he makes are just in the direction of 'extremely fine tuning'. He has handled the arrival of the heir to the throne in the school ('there were very lengthy preparations') and the press with tact.

NB Eton is ruled by triumvirate: Head, Provost, Vice Provost. Mr Lewis takes over from the widely admired Dr Eric Anderson, and was appointed after much song and dance. Previous Provost was Lord Charteris – another hard act to follow; current Provost is Sir Antony Acland. Sarah Hogg has been made a fellow.

ACADEMIC MATTERS: First-class all round. Outstandingly good teaching – Eton can pick and choose. 'It's what we're paying for,' said a first-time buyer parent. Boys are setted by ability from the first year, and all take GCSE Latin and French one year early, then seven or eight more the following year. Plenty of to-ing and fro-ing among sets, so boys are constantly changing beaks (pluses and minuses) and peer groups. Very highly structured: lots of sticks and carrots, monthly order cards, show-ups and all that.

The greatly admired Head of English, Nicholas Welsh, is 'a reminder of what good teaching can be like,' said a master from another school. Outstanding languages – one of the most successful departments in the country in terms of results – packs in the results with talk and chalk. In '95, 49 out of 76 pupils got A grade at A-level French, and 18 out of 23 in German, also 12 out of 20 in Portuguese. Japanese is an option. (NB If Eton offers a subject it really happens – unlike many other schools which often have an element of window-dressing.) Geography is another strong department, so is History.

A choice of thirty A-levels is genuinely on offer, and results are a joy to behold. Classics are waving the flag: at the last count ('95) 10 boys took Greek, 7 got As; 14 boys took Latin, 10 got As. Fewer boys take science subjects than arts at A-level, and get super results. There were huge numbers of A* and A grades at GCSE as well.

Twice-yearly internal exams ('trials'), and very detailed reports to parents; work is thoroughly monitored at all stages. Boys need considerable stamina and self-discipline to cope with it all and with the structured academic day, and occasionally fall by the wayside. NB No quarter is given if this is the case.

Some complaints that parents 'find it hard to get at' information on A-level choice implications, university subjects and careers.

GAMES, OPTIONS, THE ARTS: Excellent all round: every conceivable extra-curricular activity is on offer to amazing standards, but no concessions are made to not fitting in your work. Music, under Mr Ralph Allwood, is generally acknowledged to be one of the best departments in the country – and attracts the brightest and best in music scholarships. Very polished concerts. Wonderful chapel choir. Good Art department producing some remarkable work. Very fine Drama, and a lot of it, with a mixture of 'traditional' and boys plus masters writing their own plays.

Main games are soccer, rugby, fives, hockey, cricket (21 cricket 'squares'), boats (40% row, and a rowing lake is now under way), plus Eton's own Wall Game and the Field Game. Good fencing, swimming, water polo, sailing, also judo, polo, beagling. But the school does not appear to be winning everything the way it once did, and sport is no longer worshipped the way it once was: academic matters reign nowadays. CCF, social services.

Considerable numbers of outings, visits, field trips, with regular exchanges with schools in France, Germany, Spain and Russia. Part of the Casa Guidi in Florence was recently acquired to provide study opportunities for boys. There are vast numbers of societies (mainly run by boys, often held in the evenings).

BACKGROUND AND ATMOSPHERE: Founded in 1440 by Henry VI (and is the sister college of King's, Cambridge, which was founded a year later); 70 King's Scholars still live in the original buildings (most elegant dining hall). The buildings are of mellow old red brick, and the grounds run down to the Thames. The magnificent chapel was built by Henry VI and there is a second chapel for Lower boys. RCs are looked after by Father Forrester, the ex RC chaplain to the University of Oxford, and hear Mass in the beautiful Upper School hall. 24 boarding houses (single-study bed-sits for all from the start) are strung out along the streets. Wildly differing housemasters, from the traditionally eccentric bachelor to those more in keeping with the school's newly acquired profile as a meritocracy. Major extensions to Art and Music schools are now in train.

Sartorial note: boys still wear traditional tailcoats and stiff white collars (an expensive uniform, this); however, much changing and half-changing goes on throughout the day and full-fig is no longer worn out of school hours. Incidents of antagonism between Etonians and the town have been reported again since we last went to press.

Atmosphere very much alive, not easy; every day is highly structured and active. Everyone – boys, beaks – are on the go. School, under the previous Head, has unfurled itself to the world a little. Still rich in its own language, which can exasperate outsiders.

Royal note: HRH Prince William's house is Manor, headed by the excellent Dr Steven Gailin. Boys 'feel sorry' for the security officers, who are on watch 24 hours a day (though often invisible). Security everywhere has been tightened up, with coded locks all over the place – expensive. Boys have been forbidden, on pain of expulsion, to talk about Prince William to the press – considered well OTT by some who point to the Prince's parents' record in this respect.

PASTORAL CARE AND DISCIPLINE: Broad-minded and liberal in principle though in fact exercises a tight day-to-day structure and is quite capable of firing a pupil at a moment's notice, often to the consternation of parents. Drink is a perennial problem, drugs from time to time (including an Old Etonian pusher, and several other inside cannabis cases in '96). Random drug-testing was recently introduced. The Housemaster, Dame (Matron), Division Master and Academic Tutor oversee each boy – 'which means,' said a mother, 'that problems should be spotted early'. However, minimal tradition of parental involvement can and does cause Mummy angst.

There have been reports of bullying – isolated cases, but some fairly serious, including 'initiation' rites (which are supposed to be outlawed).

Popular American padre.

PUPILS AND PARENTS: Most certainly confident and privileged, more socially mixed than it once was. Currently 35% are sons of Old Etonians, an increasing numbers of first-time Eton buyers, plus yuppies. A slight tendency to self-obsession lingers on. Among numerous Old Etonians: Hubert Parry, 19 Prime Ministers, Captain Oates, the poets Gray and Shelley, Keynes, Fielding; Humphrey Lyttleton, Harold Macmillan. Fewer real stars among living Old Etonians but: Mark Fisher, Tim Dalzyell, Grey Gowrie, William Waldegrave, Nicholas Soames, Douglas Hurd, David Nickson, Charles Moore, Darius Guppy, Ranulph Fiennes.

ENTRANCE: Registration is essential by 10½; NB boys are called up for inspection ('interview') and exam (VR) at 11 (one out of three fall at this hurdle). CE at 12+ or 13+ (minimum of 65%, and there is a 6–7% failure at this stage): boys should be able to cope socially, physically and intellectually in order to survive.

Entries for King's Scholarships (14 per annum) are accepted until the beginning of May for exam in May at 12+ or 13+. Up to 4 junior scholarships a year for boys from state schools at 10, at which point Eton pays for three years' prep school education in traditional Eton feeders for the successful candidates. Also 4 scholarships for state school pupils at Sixth Form.

EXIT: With a network second to none in the land. Average of 70 boys to Oxbridge, with an exceptional 102 in 1994 (though NB this did include some reapplications). Also successful on organ scholarships to Oxbridge. All boys go on to university – to Edinburgh in droves, plus over 70 different institutions in the UK, 10–15 abroad. Lots of gap year pupils shaking the dust of Eton from their heels. Thereafter, the City, journalism, family estates, politics, the army, the police – and jail.

MONEY MATTERS: Probably the best endowed school in the country. It can afford to, and does, pay its staff properly. At the top end of the public school fees range, but with all it has on offer it is most definitely good value. The Foundation income goes mainly on the upkeep of historic buildings, as well as on providing new facilities or scholarships. Large numbers of bursaries, etc, for parents on hard times (and this has been put to much use by Lloyd's-hit and recession-hit parents). However, pots of money still in evidence among parents.

In addition to scholarships detailed under Entrance, there are also 8 Music scholarships each year, plus Exhibitions.

REMARKS: Terrifically strong, still the Number One toffs' school in the country, and rising above the invasion by royalty and media. It provides an excellent all-round education and, in our view, has been turning out a more balanced and less arrogant product under the outgoing Head. Perhaps sliding very gently in the fashion stakes?

Felsted School

Dunmow, Essex CM5 3LL
Tel: 01371 820258, Fax: 01371 821232

PUPILS: Around 360 pupils, including 90 girls. (310 boarders, 50 day pupils).
AGES: 13–18 (Also prep school of 165 pupils, and pre-prep of 105)
SIZE OF SIXTH FORM: 170 (including 45 girls)
C OF E FOUNDATION
FEE-PAYING

HEAD: Since 1993, Mr Stephen Roberts, MA (thirties), nicknamed 'Loopie'. Not one of your outgoing heads, according to pupils, but friendly withal. Educated at Mill Hill and Oxford, where he read Physics. Previous post – Housemaster at Oundle, where the troops had little to say about him, one way or another. Started life as a merchant banker. Married – wife Joanna helps with the pastoral side of the school. Two young sons. Hockey player.

ACADEMIC MATTERS: Middling, and rising. The statistical average number of A-level 'passes' per candidate is 3.2 with 58% at grades A–B (good-o). Girls in particular tend to 'over-achieve', according to a master – though all is relative. Maths, CDT and Science are traditionally strong here – solid results. English popular (with girls?); also, as you would expect in Essex, CDT and Economics (though results in this last are, as elsewhere, not in line with results in

other subjects). English or Maths can be done with anything at A-level, and any other combination is organised, provided there is a viable set (i.e. 5–6 pupils). Dual Award sciences at GCSE. Modern Languages are reasonably good. Some excellent teaching staff. There is a new system of screening for dyslexia, and remedial help is in operation.

GAMES, OPTIONS, THE ARTS: A school well known for prowess on the games field and the competitive attitude of the 'professional' games players. The cricket captain of '95 played for the English Schools XI, and an under-14 boy won a national bowling award. It is an immensely strong hockey school (only Bedford competes) – and the girls shape up well, espcially considering that the school only went co-ed in 1994, with teams touring South Africa. The shooting teams are, as usual, distinguishing themselves. Pupils unkeen on games now have a 'rolling programme of health-related fitness'.

The school is still in the grip of the official computer buff (Head of Computing) Chris Dawkins, who has more or less succeeded in his ambition to wire up the whole school into one huge network – one of the first and few to have done this – into which anyone can plug at any time and check on e.g. whether Smith is currently on a bicycle ride/ill/doing exams. 'Even the unkeenest pupil will sooner or later want to use it,' says Mr Dawkins, 'if only to look up the latest Test score on Prestel.'

The school also has a wonderful old farmhouse next door (The Bury), left to the school by an OB in the '30s in which all manner of societies take place. The school has some distinctly good Art, and the school has a noted Director of Music, Jasper Thorogood, from the Royal Academy of Music, who has galvanised the place in this direction, with lots of super and ambitious things on offer in the Felsted Arts Festival.

Impressive community service.

BACKGROUND AND ATMOSPHERE: Set in the heart of the yuppie East Anglian commuter belt, surrounded by fat Ferraris, BMWs and flitches. The school is on good terms with the local village in which pupils flit to and fro, and a local commented that it was a 'lovely school' (it is unusual to get a compliment like this).

Founded in 1564 by Richard, Lord Riche, Lord Chancellor of England, who came and 'buried his conscience here' after his successful part in the decapitation of Thomas More. For 300 years thereafter, the Riche heirs were patrons of the school, which still solemnly celebrates the existence of this arch-baddie on Founder's Day.

Peaceful, pleasing and quietly purposeful, the school is almost civilised to look at, though some Dickensian horrors are tucked away out of sight. Modern buildings in the grounds (diligent groundsmen) are well planned and unobtrusive. The main buildings are now Grade I and II listed, which has necessitated reorganisation and refurbishment. There is a large modern dining hall and the school is mostly now central feeding (alas). One Sixth Form house; two new houses for girls lower down the school. The smallish numbers of girls below Sixth Form look a bit lost.

PASTORAL CARE AND DISCIPLINE: All members of staff are attached to a boarding house and every pupil has a tutor. Good San (also wired up to the computer). The school makes use of the Writtle Foundation for counselling expertise. Occasionally it makes local headlines for live wire behaviour.

PUPILS AND PARENTS: 'Lack get up and go – motivation,' according to a visiting educationalist. 'Broad' spectrum of backgrounds, from around Felsted, Hertfordshire, Southend, also London and south of London. Local accents predominate. The most famous Old Felstedian is Richard Cromwell, son of Oliver (a letter from him hangs in the rather static-looking library). The most famous present OB is probably Kenneth Kendall. Lots of engineers among OBs.

ENTRANCE: By CE or exam. Special provision for pupils from state schools. School has own prep school over the road; pupils also come from local prep schools.

EXIT: Keen on gap year, then higher education and yuppie careers, also Services, farmers and the occasional vicar.

MONEY MATTERS: An unspecified percentage of fee income goes towards bursaries and a variety of academic, music and art scholarships worth up to 50% of the fees at 13 and 16. Scholarships also for 11+. There are 3 Assisted Places for 13-year-olds; 5 day places for Sixth Form. School does not have heavy endowments. Numbers of pupils are down – recession problems and too much local competition.

REMARKS: Formerly a macho boys' public school with dwindling numbers, now co-ed, though girls are a tiny minority. Low profile, and still formidable on the sporting front.

Fettes College

Carrington Road, Edinburgh EH4 1QX
Tel: 0131 332 2281, Fax: 0131 332 3081

PUPILS: Approx 236 boys plus 215 girls (365 boarding, the rest day)

AGES: 10–18
SIZE OF SIXTH FORM: 170
NON-DENOM
FEE-PAYING

HEAD: Since 1988, Mr Malcolm Thyne (to rhyme with pine), MA (fifties), educated at the Leys and Clare College, Cambridge, where he read Natural Sciences. Married with two children. Has had a rough ride – which he sees as 'taking a firm stance which has been supported strongly by parents,' over the past few years, concentrating on discipline, appearance and manners, which he believes slid somewhat during the eighties. Comments, 'I would like any pupil who comes here to get recognition.' Formerly Headmaster of St Bees, Cumbria.

ACADEMIC MATTERS: A large part of the Head's brief has been to improve academic standards, and this has been done as the school's graphs show: '92 was the peak year, since when there has been a gentle downslide, but still the school appears to have done much better than when the Head took over. The school plays the system – A-levels for some, Scottish Highers for others (spread over two years). Very difficult to comment, given the two-tier system, and English league tables are absolutely meaningless in this context. Clear advice is given; one or two complaints that dodgy candidates are steered away from A-level, 'but parents' wishes at the end of the day are followed.' Sciences are taught and examined as three separate subjects.

French, German and Spanish are on offer as mainstream languages all through the school, Russian is a Sixth Form option; otherwise exotics can be 'arranged on an ad-hoc basis'.

English department is traditionally strong. Foreign pupils with minimal English are accepted. Good ratio of staff to pupils.

GAMES, OPTIONS, THE ARTS: Enthusiastic games, and results have been perking up – though OBs point to the presence of *girls* reducing the pool of talent for teams. Good cricket; also some noted rugby successes in '95, 'returning to its former glory,' hoped the son of a former pupil. The school has an all-weather pitch which, says a pupil, is used non-stop. Blood matches with Loretto still. Girls play lacrosse – the Sixth Form are not forced to play team games – swimming will do.

The Head of Music is from King's Canterbury; keen Drama with imaginative productions, and the school always perform at the Edinburgh Festival (have won awards). Art is on the up.

BACKGROUND AND ATMOSPHERE: A vast Grimm's fairy-tale of a building, turreted and with acres of dark wood panelling, purpose-built in 1870 by Bryce. Various Victorian edifices are scattered about the school's wonderful 90-acre grounds plonk in the middle of Edinburgh. Acres resold off to raise £3 million for major refurbishing of boys' houses (now five star, by boys' school standards). The sold land developed into 'Fettes Village' – little boxes all on one side. Food includes good Scottish fare. NB to Mums: choose a low-lying house if you can – the wind whips straight in from the North Sea on the more exposed parts of the school (though 'modernisation' helps keep it at bay nowadays). The atmosphere has gradually metamorphosed from a traditional boys' public school to co-ed, (girls have been Head of School for the last five years) with quite an international flavour.

PASTORAL CARE AND DISCIPLINE: 'One puff is enough,' says the Head of his policy on smoking pot (NB Edinburgh is the drugs capital of the North, and running a school in the middle of it is a challenge, to put it politely). The Head describes himself as 'unyielding on standards of discipline'. Tough school, with an operating anti-bullying policy. The girls' houses we visited are well and sensibly run.

PUPILS AND PARENTS: Now unashamedly cosmopolitan – pupils from Europe, ex-Iron Curtain countries, China (several taking Chinese). Some Forces children, some diplomats' children. Also large phalanx of Edinburgh lawyers' offspring, also from remote corners of Scotland and the Isles. Parents can and have been vociferous in complaint. Old Fettesians = Iain Macleod, Selwyn Lloyd, James Bond, Tilda Swinton, and Tony Blair. Former Headmaster, Chevenix-Trench.

ENTRANCE: CE, or the school's own exam for foreigners. Approximately 30 places at Sixth Form level – the school can 'pick and choose' girls, but boys are at a premium.

EXIT: 95+% to higher education. Five places a year to Oxbridge for '95 (four girls, 1 boy); otherwise to universities hither and thither.

MONEY MATTERS: Well endowed with academic scholarships. There are around 38 Assisted Places. Also foundation awards for children whose parents cannot afford the fees.

REMARKS: A famous Scottish public school which has had a rough ride and now appears to be holding its own again, enjoying its burst of publicity as the Labour leader's old school and busy tapping the new overseas market. However, some criticisms still roll in.

Framlingham College

Near Woodbridge, Suffolk IP13 9EY
Tel: 01728 723789, Fax: 01728 724546
PUPILS: 283 boys, 169 girls (310 board, 136 day)
SIZE OF SIXTH FORM: 195
AGES: 13–18
C OF E INTER-DENOM
FEE-PAYING

HEAD: Since September 1994, Mrs Gwen Randall, BA (forties), who studied French at Bristol University and comes here from Dauntsey's (Deputy Head); before that she was Head of Modern Languages and Drama at St Mary's Calne; she has also taught in Germany. A very live wire (and the first woman to join the HMC). Married to a helicopter instructor, with a teenage daughter.

ENTRANCE: No problem.

EXIT: Degree courses, agriculture, the Services, medicine, teacher training, business.

REMARKS: Numbers are up again, particularly the girl count, with an enlarged number at Sixth Form. Both the GCSE and A-level results are reasonable, especially considering the mixed intake. This is not a hotshot, but it does well for the middle-of-the-road. Science and Technology do well, and Modern Languages have had a boost, with large numbers of Sixth Formers following courses at various levels.

The school has good facilities, with well-equipped labs, a geography school and a drama studio. On the social side, there is a much-used Sixth Form Centre, also a Fifth Form Centre (unusual), and a covered courtyard which acts as a central meeting place for all pupils.

Pupils are regarded as students and individuals 'which change of ethos ... requires greater self-discipline and self-reliance', commented a member of staff. Strong D of E, lots of games, a golf course, and floodlit Astroturf.

The College was founded in 1864 as 'Albert Memorial College for Sons of the Middle Class' to commemorate the Prince Consort. It is in a beautiful setting with well-tended grounds (50 acres of playing fields) perched on one of Suffolk's few hillocks. Outgoing, bouncy, relatively unsophisticated boys and girls from middle-class backgrounds; increasingly popular locally with parents seeking more opportunities for daughters than is offered by sheltered single-sex schools.

Increasingly well spoken of by locals as a place with a lot to offer and good value. Popular with the Forces.

Francis Holland School

Ivor Place, Clarence Gate,
Regent's Park, London NW1 6XR
Tel: 0171 723 0176, Fax: 0171 706 1522

PUPILS: 370 girls
ALL DAY
AGES: 11–18
SIZE OF SIXTH FORM: Around 90
C OF E
FEE-PAYING

HEAD: Since 1988, Mrs P H Parsonson MA (fifties), educated at Casterton and St Hilda's College, Oxford (read Maths). Mother of four, and her husband used to run a house at Harrow School.

Previously Head of Maths, and subsequently Director of Studies, at North London Collegiate. Also has experience of teaching in state schools. She is an impressive Head – brisk, intelligent but with warmth. She gives the impression that all things are possible, and really not that difficult either. Plays golf, gardens, and plays the violin in her spare moments. 'Once prospective parents talk to her, they are always won over,' commented a member of staff at another London girls' school.

ACADEMIC MATTERS: Biology, English, History and Maths were the subjects best patronised at A-level in '94 and '95. An excellent range of languages are on offer at this level also, including Italian and Greek and it is possible to do more exotic languages (e.g. Japanese) on a one-off basis. Physics is still almost non-existent, but otherwise the school continues to have good steady results across the board. Excellent GCSE results as you would expect, including 15 A★s in French and 14 in Science (Dual Award). The school doesn't do General Studies as an examined subject.

Maximum class size is 28 at the bottom of the school (taught in half classes for some subjects), 16 at the top (though most classes we went in to were much smaller). There is a good collection of options at Sixth Form, e.g. Spanish from scratch, Drama (one-year course). Useful careers department.

A school where, by and large, you can currently count on pupils getting the results you would expect of them – if not better – in an atmosphere which feels conducive to learning. There is a pleasant, not very large, library, light and airy, and well supplied.

GAMES, OPTIONS, THE ARTS: No room for games – Regent's Park is about two stones' throws away (for hockey, netball, rounders and tennis), but as usual in inner London girls' schools, there is no great feeling of enthusiasm here and pupils appear nonchalant to find themselves Middlesex under-14 netball champions in '94. Music, though, is another matter – the school were finalists in the National Choral competition recently and did a concert (along with other finalist schools – and very good they all were) in the Queen Elizabeth Hall on the South Bank; as we visited this time they were in the throes of rehearsing *My Fair Lady*. Some excellent three-dimensional Art – showing real imagination here, in a good light area. Clubs in the lunch break, with keen Drama and debating.

BACKGROUND AND ATMOSPHERE: The school was founded as a church school in 1878 by Canon Francis Holland, whose portrait hangs in the front hall (this was the first of the schools he founded). It has no endowment, however, but the school appears to be managing its funds extremely well, and was just hitting the £400,000 mark on its building appeal when we visited. This unlikely talent for making money spills over into the monies raised for various charities by the school – the noticeboards are alive with statements saying the school has raised e.g. £450 for the Terence Higgins Trust, and is organising to supply desks to children in Kimilili, and many more.

Although the school is known as 'Francis Holland, Clarence Gate' to distinguish it from the Graham Terrace school of the same name, it actually lurks on the edge of Park Road (where the traffic whistles down into Baker Street), next door to the Rudolph Steiner establishment, and it is quite easy to miss. The building – once you find it – is a very distinctive wedge shape, like a large thin slice of cheese, and it is the thin end of the wedge that has the main door in it. There

is no feeling of ceremony about the place, but the minute you walk in, it really does feel friendly, with broad smiles and a welcome, and it is this, says the Head, which over and over again parents give as the reason for choosing the school.

The wedge is in the process of being turned into a bigger ritzier wedge, with a whole new range of classrooms etc at the wide end of it, and an imaginative plan for what amounts to an atrium at the top, making lots more room, with a Sixth Form centre, swimming pool and new labs (the old ones are, as is so often the case in London, buried in the basement of the school). When we visited, the school had a rabbit-warreny feel to it, and it is difficult to see how this will change much, given the lack of space overall.

PASTORAL CARE AND DISCIPLINE: Parents do query whether the bright lights of Oxford Street, etc are a temptation, but the Head reassures us, as do the girls – 'it's a long walk,' they say realistically. No particular problems at time of writing.

PUPILS AND PARENTS: Gentle folk, and polite – 15% Jewish (around eight a year), 10% Muslim, daughters of diplomats, and inner London parents looking for something a bit less shrill, more laid-back, than some of the local day schools. Famous old girls: Joan Collins, Jackie Collins, Margaret Budy, editor of *World Tonight*, Amanda Donohue, Saskia Wickham.

ENTRANCE: Own exam at 11; one of the 'North London Consortium' of schools who – praise be – co-ordinate their entry for January (names down by end of November). Some spaces at Sixth Form to make up the numbers.

EXIT: Lots to London University, a handful to Oxbridge, another handful to vocational courses, e.g. hotel and catering at Westminster College. A broad, strong offering of subjects, showing however a bias to the Arts. The usual slight exodus post-GCSE – the largest numbers to Sixth Form colleges.

MONEY MATTERS: There are 2 scholarships at Sixth Form (half fees) internal and external; two exhibitions (one-twelfth fees) at 14+; 1 music scholarship at 11+. Generous bursaries for those already in the school. Also 5 assisted places at 11+ (and has applied for more). Fees a bit less than some comparable schools.

REMARKS: A pearl of a girls' day school, tucked back from the swirling traffic. Lively and friendly, academic but without the feeling that nothing else counts in life. Much to be recommended, certainly while the current Head is in place.

Francis Holland School

39 Graham Terrace, London SW1W 8JF
Tel: 0171 730 2971, Fax: 0171 823 4066

PUPILS: Around 180 in the senior
  school; (plus 160 in the junior school,
  see separate entry)
ALL GIRLS
ALL DAY
AGES: 11–18
SIZE OF SIXTH FORM: About 45
C OF E
FEE-PAYING

HEAD: Since 1982, Mrs Jennifer Anderson, MA Cantab and MA London (fifties). Educated at St Paul's Girls' School and read French and Italian

at Cambridge. Previous post teaching languages at school's sister school at Clarence Gate. Has three children and two step-children. Divorced, and remarried, to poet William Anderson. Teaches French literature to the Sixth Form.

ENTRANCE: Half from school's own junior school (qv), otherwise from local preps. One of the North London Consortium Group 1 (with St Alban's, Heathfield, Notting Hill and South Hampstead). There is a written exam in English and Maths; most who take the exam are interviewed, and must participate in a lesson to see how they react. Sixth Form entrants must have minimum four Cs at GCSE.

EXIT: Interesting spread in ones (including Cambridge, Durham, Oxford Brookes, Bristol, Newcastle, Manchester, Camberwell College of Art, Imperial College), which reflects what the school is good at – finding the right course for the pupil.

REMARKS: A small Church of England girls' school founded 1881. On a useful site at the edge of Belgravia – surprisingly roomy behind a terraced façade, with good playground and hall (stained glass windows of famous biblical women). Pupils are daughters of diplomats, bankers, one or two politicians' children. Neat uniform.

There is a strong English department, with good Languages (German, French and Spanish, plus Italian in the Sixth Form). Very good Computer Studies under Chris Chisnall, with timetabled lessons through much of the lower school, and pupils taking the RSA exam. Good careers advice.

The library is expanding under the aegis of a new librarian. Lots of visits to galleries, etc. Has links with St Mary's Church round the corner and the vicar,

Bill Scott, comes in on Thursdays to take prayers. The Bishop of Fulham is a governor. That said, there is no particular feeling of religious propaganda – all are welcome and the school has 'lots' of Catholics and Muslims.

One or two small bursaries and scholarships, also help for clergy daughters. Class size – 25–30 in first three years, but subdivided for 'almost everything' (two teachers per form); after third year, almost all are in groups of 15. Combined sciences and Dual Award offered (in the latter 10 A*s, 16 As and 4Bs at GCSE). Detailed breakdown of results not given out by and large, but overall A-level results were better in '94 than '95.

A massive appeal is in progress to build a new wing (planned to be ready for September 1997) on an adjacent site for Science, Technology, Computing, Art and a new gym and a new library plus a Sixth Form Centre. After this, the senior school will expand and, rumour has it, take on a new Head.

At the time of writing, this is a *very* small school (though the Sixth Form numbers have been creeping up from 13 in '93 to 20 in '95), and rather limited with it – just not in the same category as the sister school.

Frensham Heights

Rowledge, Nr Farnham,
Surrey GU10 4EA
Tel: 01252 792561, Fax: 01252 794335

PUPILS: 147 boys, 153 girls (134 board, 166 day). Plus own junior school with 23 boys, 19 girls, ages 4–10 (all day)
AGES: 11–18

NON-DENOM
FEE-PAYING

HEAD: Since 1993, Mr Peter de Voil, MA (late forties), educated at Northampton Grammar School, read Classics and English at King's College, Cambridge. Married, no children. Previously a Housemaster at Uppingham. Sensitive, sensible and humorous, clearly happy to be out of the straitjacket of traditional public school life. 'What I most like about Frensham is that it teaches values in a subtle way: people really do treat each other as part of a community, with the emphasis on the individual.'

ENTRANCE: At 11, 13 via exam and some post-GCSE with variable scholarships/awards offered. By interview from junior school (St George's).

EXIT: All children go on to further education, universities, art colleges, and drama schools perennially popular.

REMARKS: This is an unusual very small co-ed school (founded in 1925, with links to St Christopher's Letchworth, qv), which opened its own junior school in '95. Liberal progressive, but has tightened up very considerably over the last decade and most notably under the present excellent Head ('quite a tough egg' commented a parent). Five years ago academic results began to be taken seriously, sciences in particular upgraded. Now 17 A-levels are offered, three pupils went to Oxbridge in '95 (the norm), and the school is sprouting with talent. Staff are kept on their toes teaching an extremely wide ability range, with some dyslexic children (given remedial help).

There is a huge emphasis on the creative and performing arts: at GCSE every student takes two Art subjects, out of art, ceramics, CDT, drama, dance or music. Music is remarkable (especially choral work and piano), both among staff and students (several go to Royal College of Music Junior on Saturdays); one current pupil has reached the semi-final of Young Musician of the Year competition. Loads of drama for all (there are several children of film and theatre parents in the school); the National Youth Music Theatre rehearses here during the holidays, sometimes providing nice openings for young hopefuls.

A magnificent Edwardian pile (built by a brewery magnate) set in very beautiful grounds with stupendous views, where a former stable block is used for classrooms and there are many later buildings for the arts. The boys' houses have been refurbished, girls have bright rooms at the top of the main house. Children are unpretentious, friendly and a broad mix, including currently two Bosnian refugees (given EFL lessons), paid for out of fee income – part of the school's philosophy of helping the less privileged. Sir Claus Moser is an old boy (and was here as a refugee from Nazi Germany). Social consciences are alive and well. There is no uniform, no competition, and all Sixth Formers are counsellors and help younger pupils.

Sport plays a minor role, but is gradually building up; the school has a brilliant outdoor Adventure Centre (mini-Outward Bound). Weekend expeditions are also building up, though there is 'a bit of an exodus' with boarders going home at weekends.

A one-off. Alternative education with a strong ethos and emphasis on relationships and individuality; worth considering after a period of being wildly off track. On the up again.

George Watson's College

Colinton Road, Edinburgh EH10 5EG
Tel: 0131 447 7931, Fax: 0131 452 8594

PUPILS: 1,260, boy:girl ratio 55%:45% (1,230 day, 30 board). Plus own junior school (qv)
AGES: 12–18
SIZE OF SIXTH FORM: 400
NON-DENOM
FEE-PAYING

HEAD: Principal, since 1985, Mr Frank Gerstenberg, MA (Cantab), PGCE London (fifties). At school at Glenalmond, and previously Head of Oswestry School. 'Not a Committee man', he describes himself as 'fairly shy' (outgoing would be nearer the mark), and reckons to have the 'most challenging job in Scotland' – 'there's an awful lot happening'. He should know: since his appointment he has transformed the place.

Very hot on industrial liaison and work-shadowing, now also in Europe. Aims to produce the 'best parts of a comprehensive without the worst parts'. Mr Gerstenberg teaches History 'a little', during the first and last year.

ACADEMIC MATTERS: An enormous range of subjects on offer, though it is easier to get good grades in Sciences than the Arts ('you can't go wrong with practical stuff'). Pupils do the Scottish system, Standard Grades followed by Highers and CSYS: academic results are high, and the brightest (usually around 50% for English and History and 25% for Maths and French) skip Standard Grades and go straight to Highers. Very strong on Science, Maths, Economics, English and French. Modern Languages are also strong, and Sixth Formers can take German, Italian, Spanish and Russian as modules; also, Mandarin Chinese and Gaelic.

There is a marvellous Technology building. Rows of computers everywhere; enormous library.

The school gives the best dyslexia help in Scotland, under Dr Charles Weedon, who was previously at Perth Grammar. Dr Collins (the expert in dyslexia) is staying on as a consultant. Six children with specific learning difficulties are taken each year for special help in the Cabin.

GAMES, OPTIONS, THE ARTS: Strong games traditions: rugger is good (lists of internationals). Games fields on campus, plus a refurbished swimming pool, and outdoor gym adjacent to sports hall.

Art and pottery are strong. Music dominates, with orchestras throughout and regular trips to Assisi. There is also a wind band, Baroque orchestra, jazz band and full-blown pipe band; Clarsach (Scottish harp) also popular, D of E award, and masses of exchanges with Europe. Lots of ancillary sports, Scouts, Guides, community service ('granny bashing') and there are clubs for everything.

BACKGROUND AND ATMOSPHERE: The school was founded in 1741, and moved to its present site in 1932, a magnificent sandstone building, purpose-built, long-corridored totally symmetric, and sporting the Merchant Company boat. There is a superb hall much in demand for dances, political rallies and the like. Also many modern conversions and additions.

Co-ed throughout since 1974, class sizes are max 25, smaller for practical sessions. Timetabled on a seven-day cycle. Pupils are positive, doing a lot, particularly extra-curricular. The school is no longer fettered to the Merchant Company, but loosely linked, needs permission to buy and sell land, and have budgets and accounts approved, it now appoints its own (very dynamic) Board of Governors, and has more freedom of action within the Company.

PASTORAL CARE AND DISCIPLINE: Each year has a Head of Year who stays with pupils until they leave, and is responsible for pastoral care. This works well. Houses are purely for competition. The Deputy Head is in charge of discipline, 'firm but fair'. There was an incident of drugs last year (sacked). 'Sackings are relatively rare.' Otherwise detentions, occasional suspensions for second offence smoking, extra work or litter-picking.

PUPILS AND PARENTS: The offspring of Edinburgh professionals and from outlying suburbs as far as Kirkaldy and Peebles. Some boarders are ex-pats. Border farmers' children, a fair quantity of first-time buyers and FPs' children. There is a strong Watsonian tradition (new parents conform quite quickly). FPs include Malcolm Rifkind.

ENTRANCE: At 12 and 16 by interview, assessment and test. Straight through from the junior school. Suitable candidates can be fitted in at any time if space is available.

EXIT: Very occasionally to traditional public school at 13 – both Scottish and English; a little leakage after Standard Grade. Otherwise 180 per annum to university (either after Highers or CSYS), about 10 to Oxbridge.

MONEY MATTERS: Bursaries and scholarships for hardship, both Music and Academic. Regular winners of national Arkwright Technology scholarships. Lots of Assisted Places – all taken up.

REMARKS: No change: a huge co-ed day school, stronger than ever, with a remarkable Principal. The school produces friendly children, who come out as themselves, not clones.

Giggleswick School

Settle, North Yorkshire BD24 0DE
Tel: 01729 823545, Fax: 01729 824187

PUPILS: Around 320 boys and girls (290 board, 30 day). Plus own junior school, with 121 boys and girls, ages 8–13 (73 board, 48 day)
AGES: 13–18
SIZE OF SIXTH FORM: 120
C OF E
FEE-PAYING

HEAD: Since 1993, Mr Anthony Millard, BSc (forties). Economist with experience in industry and the European Commission. Previous post, Head of Wycliffe College. Married to tennis coach, four children.

REMARKS: A co-ed boarding school doing a good job for a broad intake in this relatively isolated area. Good solid staff. Three streams for separate and combined sciences offered at GCSE. Setted for GCSE in English, French, Maths, Science. The best A-level results in '95 were in Geography and Chemistry. Class sizes 24 maximum, 10–14 for A-level. There is a support system for dyslexia.

The school runs a Sixth Form course with 'international module' (a wide-ranging vocational course, with hands-on across Europe with language, business studies, culture, etc – v useful for the pupil who does not know what he/she wants to do next). There is a super Sixth Form centre.

Beefy games, with strong girls' tennis and successful junior netball. The swimming pool has been revamped. Keen Drama started by the late Russell Harty. Ballroom dancing is now on the menu. One-third of pupils learn an instrument. Outward Bound, CCF (including girls). Exchanges with schools in France and Germany.

Set in the Yorkshire Dales – sheep country – 60 minutes' drive north of Manchester, Giggleswick was founded in 1512 and moved to its present site in 1869. The cluster of grey houses are spread throughout the tiny village beneath an incongruous mini-St Paul's (copper dome and all), the gift of another benefactor. A much needed revamp of some living quarters has been completed. Happy atmosphere.

The school has many local children, in a large catchment area, with more boys than girls. Stalwart lads and lassies (the school has been fully co-ed since '83 – one of the early ones). Also 5% foreign, ditto ex-pats, as well as Forces children – and popular with all these. Parents in professions. Entrance at 8 via own test and reports; CE at 13. Entrance into Sixth Form is by five GCSEs at C grade (about 20 a year). About 80% of pupils go on to further education. Some leave after GCSEs to go into business or another school/Sixth Form college. There are 5 Assisted Places a year, of which two go to 11-year-olds in the school's junior department, Catteral Hall, which is on the same site. Several scholarships are also available, including General Distinction, Art and Music.

Traditional and steady with it, and good at character building.

Glenalmond College

Perthshire, Scotland PH1 3RY
Tel: 01738 880205, Fax: 01738 880410

PUPILS: 294 pupils (238 boys, 56 girls; all board except for 32 day pupils)
AGES: 12–18
SIZE OF SIXTH FORM: 117
EPISCOPALIAN
FEE-PAYING

HEAD: Warden, since 1992, Mr Ian Templeton, MA, BA (fifties), previously Head of Oswestry, taught at Daniel Stewart's, Melville and Robert Gordon's. Educated at Gordonstoun and read Maths and Logic at St Andrews, then took a degree in Philosophy in London. His jolly wife, Aline, writes thrillers; two grown-up children. He was appointed following a disastrous period for the school, and was initially cautious. Appears dour and slightly hands-off, but this could be deceptive – 'It takes me six seconds to get from my bed to my desk.' His study overlooks the courtyard, and pupils are well aware that he is watching. Keen singer. Teaches Maths to the third years. Basking in the '95 Inspector's Report, which described 'strong effective leadership.'

ACADEMIC MATTERS: Some very good staff at all levels – including the English department, and a young Wykhamist Biology teacher (who runs the jazz band). The Head has injected new young staff to counter-balance long-servers ('It's a community and a way of life,' said one who has been here well over

20 years). Highers and A-levels available (the majority go for A-levels, about one-quarter go for Highers and do them over two years). A-level results have much improved, with 46 A grades in '95 (it claims more than any other school in Scotland), 62% A–B grades; Highers results are also rising, and ditto GCSE, with one-third at A grade. English, History, Modern Languages are all strong at A-level (but NB the ablest students are likely to take A-levels, and in '95 the largest number of pupils taking any one subject was 21 – i.e. it is hard to compare with big schools with large Sixth Forms). Sciences do less well overall.

Setting in the third year. Scotvec is available. General Studies broadened out for Sixth Form. Economics, Geology and Theatre Studies now on the menu. But 'Is my son being made to think for himself?' queried a father, conceding improved league table results.

GAMES, OPTIONS, THE ARTS: Strong rugby (distinguished tradition); also skiing (with its own artificial ski slope and regular trips to Glenshee). The school has a 9-hole golf course and private fishing (on the River Almond). However, games are sometimes interrupted by weather conditions, though the school is rich in all-weather courts (for tennis/netball). Also a Sports Hall and indoor heated pool. 'The facilities,' commented a pupil, 'are fantastic.' There are enough girls now to muster full strength sports teams.

Distinctly good Music is headed by the inspiring Christopher Tambling (who has a wonderfully busy office covered with papers and books and musical instruments); he is a talented composer (musicals, hymns). Fine Design and Technology department – sophisticated equipment and know-how, loads of space. CCF and pipe band. Glenalmond Enterprise (own version of YE) popular and successful.

BACKGROUND AND ATMOSPHERE: A spectacular and elegant self-contained quadrangle of cloisters, with a chapel at the centre, set in just under 300 acres of fine parkland against a backdrop of wild Perthshire hills and grouse moors. Founded in 1841 (as a theological college) by the Prime Minister, William Gladstone. Formerly known as the Eton of the north. The Head's wife is busy cosying up the boys' quarters, with carpets and colour. The furthest away boys' house is now closed (proximity is 'better for discipline'), and pupils move up from tie-dye draped dormitories via horse-boxes to double/single bedrooms. The brown panelling, brown corridors, etc, are still much as Daddy knew it. Girls live in modern comfort. Several modern additions, including the Basil Spence music block, are clustered at the back.

All staff live on the estate and most on the premises (part of the conditions). Girls and boys 'kept pretty occupied most of the time,' commented a parent. A busy weekend programme introduced by the Head, (in contrast with previous regime), has pupils doing their own Blind Date, etc. Sunday evening is now the only 'free' evening.

PASTORAL CARE AND DISCIPLINE: Tightening up 'and not before time,' say parents. The civilising effects of girls is seeping through. Chapel daily (no-one complains), God-loving not God-fearing (NB several Bishops on the Council). Drink and smoking are perennial problems. Reputation for drugs and past bullying is hard to shake off entirely: it is gentler than it once was, but children report that it is 'still tough' and that there is still bullying.

PUPILS AND PARENTS: Produces extraordinary loyalty among FPs, who will do/have done anything for the College: vast donations, harpsichord, etc.

FPs include Sandy Gall, Miles Kington, Allan Massie, David Sole, Robbie Coltrane. Went co-ed in 1990. First took day pupils (home at 6.30 p.m.) in '91 (from Crieff and Perth). The friendly, open, polished pupils get on well with all ages. Traditionally Scottish upper-middle and middle class, army, Highland families; very small number of foreigners. Some complaints from parents that they themselves are not involved or informed enough on their children's education.

ENTRANCE: Numbers are up since we last went to press, and registration lists 'looking healthier' now following a fallow period with huge leakage and the troops staying clear. Own entrance exam at 12, most at 13+ CE. Some at Sixth Form. Selective up to a point (claims to be).

EXIT: 85%+ to university, with several taking a gap year; a few to art college, to HND courses, the odd top-up resit. Between 3 and 10 per year to Oxbridge. Edinburgh and St Andrew's are popular, otherwise widespread.

MONEY MATTERS: There are 5 Assisted Places. Approximately 6 academic scholarships at 13+, 3 or 4 at Sixth Form, plus 2 or 3 Music, 1 or 2 Art scholarships. No endowments, but some bequests which school manages.

REMARKS: Shaping up and gaining confidence now with numbers, girls, results all on the up – having been the object of a huge PR exercise which appears to be paying off, and still hoping to regain its former glory. Saved by the belles?

Godolphin School

Milford Hill, Salisbury,
Wiltshire SP1 2RA
Tel: 01722 333059, Fax: 01722 411700

PUPILS: 402 girls (209 board, 193 day)
(plus preparatory department with 45
girls ages 7–11)
AGES: 11–18
SIZE OF SIXTH FORM: 103
C OF E
FEE-PAYING

HEAD: From September 1996, Miss
Jill Horsburgh MA Oxon (forties).
Previously Assistant Head at Benenden,
where she was a Housemistress, and
before that taught at Downe House.
Modern History is her subject, she also
went to Sheffield Business School. Keen
musician, photographer and horse-
woman. Arrives to find the school in
extremely good shape. Outgoing Head,
Mrs Fender, will be a hard act to follow.

ACADEMIC MATTERS: A broad intake
and certainly not a hothouse,
(though there are usually a few exceptionally clever girls here). There are 22
subjects on offer at A-level, and the
school claims that any sensible
combination is possible, and subjects are
never precluded through timetable
conflicts. Science teaching 'gives us lots of
practicals and hands-on explanations –
most of us need that'. The Sixth Form has
grown dramatically over the past few
years (comings and goings). All take 8 or 9
GCSEs; steadily rising results. A-level
results are commendable, with Business
Studies far and away the most popular
subject, with equal numbers of A and C
grades, followed by English, Maths and
History. Higher education is taken
seriously, a long process that starts in the
Lower Sixth. Half the teaching staff are
male (most unusual in a girls' school).

GAMES, OPTIONS, THE ARTS:
Exceptionally strong on extra-
curricular activities, 'the best thing about
the school,' say many pupils. An unusual
after-school course is offered in baby-
sitting (childcare/first aid) – 'so many of
our girls babysit for extra pocket money';
car maintenance for Sixth Formers;
jewellery making, sailing, fashion design,
enthusiastic D of E. Strong Music (75% of
pupils learning one or more instruments,
and 20 pupils at the time of writing
holding places in national, county and
regional orchestras and choirs; one pupil
is currently studying instruments at the
Royal College of Music Junior School in
London – thanks to a good train service).

Large five-studio multi-media Art
department – open at all hours. Com-
missions from the local railway station, etc
for art work puts girls in 'real life'
situations, considering suitability,
practicality, etc. In September '94 a
Technology and 3D Art workshop
opened. Work is in progress on a 350-seat
Performing Arts Centre. Lots of sport
(strings of girls represent county teams in
lacrosse, tennis, etc).

BACKGROUND AND ATMOSPHERE:
A distinctly uninstitutional cluster of
purpose-built houses and classrooms atop
chilly Milford Hill (with a fabulous view
of Salisbury Plain). The school is divided
by unpavemented road (footbridge
mandatory for juniors). The school
moved here in 1890, founded under the
terms of Elizabeth Godolphin's Will of
1726. All girls to the Sixth wear blue
sleeveless cotton pinnies (popular); cloaks
and boaters. Day/boarding girls are well
integrated (despite a fairly strict exeat
programme for boarders). Day girls must
stay till 4.45 p.m., many stay much later
(casual boarding as and when).

In need of a Sixth Form Centre,
especially with increasing numbers at this
stage.

PASTORAL CARE AND DISCIPLINE: A caring school, with the emphasis on the individual. Pupils communicate often and easily with staff, and trust is paramount, very carefully nurtured, especially among seniors. All House staff are married (lots of young families about the place, lots of men, 'It's normal'.) Smoking is the main irritant (not drink) – a punishable offence that could end in expulsion.

PUPILS AND PARENTS: All sorts, from the landed to modest first-time buyers; lots of Forces children. Parents are not wealthy. Friendly, chatty girls, who enjoy life and 'have their priorities in the right place,' commented a parent. Famous OGs: Dorothy L Sayers, Jilly Cooper.

ENTRANCE: 11+. Also for boarders only at 12 and 13, and at Sixth Form. As popularity has increased, so has the pressure on places – 5 or 6 applicants per day girl place (register names at 7). Also from the school's own dear little preparatory department (just down the road but still on site).

EXIT: Degrees, at universities old and new, (1, possibly 2, high-fliers per year to Oxford or Cambridge), art colleges – and thereafter all manner of careers.

MONEY MATTERS: There are 6 foundation scholarships (originally destined for orphans), awarded to girls who have lost one or both parents through death, separation or divorce ('Nice for single mums,' said one fervently). These are non-academic, based on a girl's potential and 'her likelihood to benefit from Godolphin' – and vice versa. There are small variable numbers of academic scholarships (all or part of fees) at 11+ and 12+; Sixth Form

(up to full fees); 13+ boarding award (up to full fees). Also 5 Assisted Places per year.

REMARKS: In good shape – a flourishing and deservedly popular small school for girls that offers an all-round education, runs a full programme, and has good facilities.

Godolphin and Latymer School

Iffley Road, London w6 opg
Tel: 0181 741 1936, Fax: 0181 746 3352
PUPILS: Around 700 girls
ALL DAY
AGES: 11–18
SIZE OF SIXTH FORM: 200
NON-DENOM
FEE-PAYING

HEAD: Since 1986, Miss Margaret Rudland BSc (early fifties), educated at Sweyne School in Essex and Bedford College, London. Read Maths and Physics. Previous post – Deputy Head of Norwich High, and has also taught at St Paul's Girls' School, and at a boys' school in Nigeria. Impressive – very fair, perceptive, warm. An approachable Head and an excellent administrator, she has gained the respect and liking of staff, pupil and parents. President of the Girls Schools Association '96–'97.

ACADEMIC MATTERS: Excellent record of results at both GCSE and A-level, with solid blocks of As and Bs at A-level, and hardly a poor mark in sight. French regularly has a big following and hauls in A grades; History another popular subject, Maths particularly strong (notably Pure with Statistics), also

Chemistry and Biology (which gained 16 A grades out of 25 in '95).

A gentle start as school assimilates large numbers from different educational backgrounds. 22 subjects are taught at A-level, and there is a wide choice of General Studies. Strong Science teaching from the start (a pioneer in the Nuffield Science scheme), but Combined Science only at GCSE. The occasional Bengali, Punjabi, Persian, Portuguese GCSE reflects the cosmopolitan intake of the school.

Pupils are expected to be self-motivated and self-disciplined, and from the start are taught to be academically self-reliant (there is a strong tradition of individual research). Teaching is good, with occasionally mutterings of 'worthy and dull teaching,' but particularly good on individual attention and helping the less able. Classes of 26 for the first three years, far smaller thereafter. Non-competitive, no regular read-out markings. Staff often take courses; intellectual inquisitiveness is a characteristic of the school – as the school mag shows.

Good careers department and discussions, plus really useful programme of work-shadowing.

GAMES, OPTIONS, THE ARTS: Compulsory gym twice a week, own playing fields adjacent and swimming available four evenings a week between 4–6 p.m. at Latymer Upper School. Rowing at Latymer Upper School, coached by 'Rob, Superman of the River'. Extra-curricular activities are busy over lunch time. Out-of-hours and out-of-term travel, field trips, social work, regular exchanges with schools in Hamburg, Paris, Moscow and New York. Good Drama, with weekly classes for all during the first two years, and annual form play competitions and musicals (often written by pupils).

BACKGROUND AND ATMOSPHERE: The 'sister' school to Latymer Upper. Stands in a four-acre site, originally built in 1861 as a boys' boarding school, since when it has evolved through many stages (including LCC aided, voluntary-aided status and during the mid-seventies fought hard not to become comprehensive). It has good facilities for Science, also a good Library. The place is warm, friendly and fairly untidy. Situated in a slightly grotty area of London ('but improving,' says the Head), and lacking in glamour. Liberal progressive tradition. Old 'Dolphins' and parents are dedicated and helpful. Sixth Formers (uniform-free) may lunch out of school. There is a rather ordinary feel to the place, which often appeals to the pressure-cooked potential pupil.

PASTORAL CARE AND DISCIPLINE: Few complaints. Christian values are subtly inculcated. Form teachers have a second colleague to help with pastoral matters. Also new Heads of lower, middle, and Sixth Form, appointed from September 1994. A small group of pupils gather together off the premises to have a quick fag before the school day starts.

PUPILS AND PARENTS: A mixed bunch, but less competitive than St Paul's. A complete social mix from all over London and the outskirts – shopkeepers' daughters, nobs, down-at-heel middle class, lots of working mothers, heaps of first-time buyers, some who have failed to get into St Paul's (but NB it can work the other way). Lots of foreigners (Indians, Middle Easterners and Americans, etc).

ENTRANCE: Consistently large numbers sit for 100 places from 136 schools, half state, half private, and are put through an enormous number of hoops. (NB This school interviews the girls, never the parents as so many do.) Not only interested in high-fliers. According to the school, about 10–15 come in at Sixth Form to fill in for leavers – and even then, there are sometimes spaces. Occasional vacancies in other years.

EXIT: The overwhelming majority to established universities (Bristol, Edinburgh, London and Leeds are all popular at the time of writing), a healthy dozen or so to Oxbridge (more Oxford than Cambridge), one or two to art foundation and teacher training courses.

MONEY MATTERS: Reasonable fees, with few extras. One music scholarship, 25 Assisted Places per year at age 11, plus three to the Sixth Form, some bursaries are available at all levels for special needs. A £500 deposit is required on acceptance of a place.

REMARKS: A solid place, one of the strongest London central girls' day schools, striding confidently forward, but not quite as fashionable as it once was.

Gordonstoun School

Elgin, Moray, Scotland IV30 2RF
Tel: 01343 830445, Fax: 01343 830074

PUPILS: 165 girls, 260 boys (400 boarders, 25 day)
AGES: 13–18
SIZE OF SIXTH FORM: 184
INTER-DENOM
FEE-PAYING

HEAD: Since 1990, Mr Mark Pyper, BA (forties), educated at Winchester, then did one year at Oxford, 'got bored' and finished his degree externally at London University. Married, young family. Previously Deputy Head at Sevenoaks. Always wears a suit. Pragmatic and good with people. Rumour has it that the Governors told him to tighten up discipline – and certainly pupils do seem less wild. He aims to keep Kurt Hahn's philosophy of 'holistic education' in line with the nineties – and would like to see Gordonstoun as the strongest arts school in Scotland. HRH Prince Andrew is a Governor, also HRH the Princess Royal (who is also a parent).

ACADEMIC MATTERS: Not as comprehensive an intake as all that, particularly at Sixth Form where there is considerable competition to get into this fashionable school. One to two forms are streamed at entry and the rest go into mixed ability. Combined History and Geography (Humanities) is now an option and combined Sciences to GCSE, but there seems to be a declining interest in Sciences among both boys and girls. GCSEs are limited to 8 or 9. Modern Languages rather than Classics (but Latin and Greek are available to GCSE), conversational Russian and Japanese, Hungarian and Finnish are on offer. PE is offered at A-level, Drama Studies were recently introduced as A-level.

There are some complaints that the best staff are concentrated on the top set. 'Not enough good staff to go round,' said a pupil. 'Laid back,' said a parent.

The only school in Scotland to follow only the English GCSE and A-level curriculum (i.e. no Highers, etc. NB This means the English league tables are relevant here). The recent results make somewhat depressing reading. French, English, Business Studies, Geography and History are the most popular A-level subjects.

GAMES, OPTIONS, THE ARTS: Extras are the great strength of the school –

both what they offer and what they actually *do*. Mainstream games are getting stronger – and remember the distances for matches against other schools – and there are good sports facilities. Tours go regularly to Europe and further afield, and honours are clocked up at district and national level. In 1995/6 no less than six boys gained places in the Scottish schools rugby squad (Peter Philips being one of them) – 'even beat Merchiston.'

Astroturf, 16 tennis courts under construction; climbing wall, skiing, etc. Outstanding Community Services – fire brigade, mountain rescue, ashore rescue, boat service, helping in mental and old people's homes, nursery schools. 'Service' is an integral part of the weekly programme (and could be one of your reasons for choosing the school) from the Fifth Form upwards. School has its own yacht and charters another and the cruises are the highlights of school life, as are the 'expeds' – outward-bound expeditions. Keen on Music, and Drama is now part of the curriculum (a new theatre building is in the pipeline).

BACKGROUND AND ATMOSPHERE: Founded in 1934 by the German educationalist Kurt Hahn, founder of Salem School in Switzerland, who believed in educating and developing all aspects of children, not just the academic. The grounds and setting are very lovely, half a mile from the Moray Firth, with cliffs and beaches nearby.

Gordonstoun House is a former residence of Gordon-Cumming of card-cheating fame. The beautiful circular stable block (hence the Round Square tag) was converted into a lofted library and boys' house. It can be freezing up here, but Moray Firth has its own microclimate and the weather is better than in a lot of Scotland. Houses are widely spread and pupils have been known to wear out two pairs of shoes per

term. Many exchanges with other Round Square schools – Canada, Germany, Australia, etc: if you have a genius skier he can go to Aiglon in Switzerland for a term. Organises joint international expeditions to India, Hungary, Venezuela, Thailand, Kenya to work on conservation/ecological 'projects' (expensive).

There are minimal exeats – distances are enormous – but pupils often do not want to go home on exeats. 'It is the parents who suffer,' commented a mother missing her children. Food reported to be the 'best school food in Scotland' but even so an FP parent recently supplemented the diet by poaching and barbecuing a local pheasant.

Non-stop social life which swings straight through the holidays – caveat for southerners.

PASTORAL CARE AND DISCIPLINE: Keep them busy seems to be the motto. All Third and Fourth Formers have compulsory Saturday afternoon activity. Every pupil has an academic tutor. There are many talks on 'substance abuse', and drugs are frowned on by pupils. Drinking has been a problem in the past but appears to be less so since the introduction of the Sixth Form bar at weekends. See recent TV programme for handling of bullying. Morning runs are almost a thing of the past.

PUPILS AND PARENTS: 45% Scots, 30% UK and 25% non-British, mainly continental European, some of whom come for the summer school and want to stay. Pupils tend to be cliquey (can be a problem). Parents range from the very grand to the not at all grand, with a parental mix of farmers, landowners, professions, Services and, currently, the Princess Royal (this is a great place for social climbing). FPs include Royals, William Boyd, Eddie Shah, and the composer of *The Flower o' Scotland*, Roy Williamson.

ENTRANCE: CE, with Aberlour the principal prep-school feeder offering guaranteed entry to Gordonstoun from 11+. Also at Sixth Form.

EXIT: 5–10 each year to Oxbridge. 92% go on to further education, very widely spread; art college is a popular option. There is a fair amount of movement of pupils at Sixth Form, in and out – more in than out – with some leaving because they believe they may achieve higher grades elsewhere.

MONEY MATTERS: Assisted Places, many scholarships (the last major appeal went to a scholarship fund), including 10–12 at Sixth Form, and 12–13 at Third Form (13+). There is a hardship fund (financial self-assessment for fee-paying has now been scrapped). Vast sums are accumulated via a flourishing summer school for foreigners.

REMARKS: This is a good choice for those seeking a school with a strong *mens sana* ethos plus a big name, also for parents wanting to get their children away from the over-sophisticated influence of the south of England. But parents should not choose Gordonstoun if they are looking for a high academic performance. Currently one of the fashionable places to go for Scottish prep school children.

Gresham's School

Holt, Norfolk NR25 6EA
Tel: 01263 713271, Fax: 01263 712028

PUPILS: 311 boys, 209 girls (two-thirds board, one-third day)
AGES: 13–18
SIZE OF SIXTH FORM: 220

C OF E
FEE-PAYING

HEAD: Since 1991 Mr John Arkell, MA (fifties), educated at Stowe and Selwyn College, Cambridge, where he read English (and also rowed and acted). Had a spell in the navy (as a submariner) post-school. Formerly Head of Wrekin College, Head of English at Fettes and set up the junior school there. Married with three grown-up children. Teaches English for a third of his timetable. An enthusiast, and fun with it; approachable, and has an informal manner but is decisive. Keeps a boat on the Mediterranean, keen on old cars, rides a motorbike. Tries to encourage pupils to be 'resourceful and energetic'.

ACADEMIC MATTERS: Steady, and does well for the average pupil; has a broad intake, including a handful of high-fliers. Has an outstandingly good Maths department, with the largest following at A-level of any subject (plus some a year early in order to move on to Further Maths); 18 As, 8 Bs in '95. The department is headed by Mr Smithers, who gives potential staff a test ('some walk out'), never uses textbooks, and insists that all six classes work parallel which allows pupils to move up and down sets without affecting other subjects. 'Maths pinches a lot of prep time,' comment other staff. English is another strength. Sciences also do well, Physics especially.

A-level choices are not restricted to picking from columns (this is rare and wonderful) – only about three pupils per year have to forgo one first choice. Theatre Studies are on the menu, also Japanese. 51% As and Bs at A-level in '95. The Head is well aware that Norfolk has been called the graveyard for the ambitious, and he continues to inject new young staff. Pupils now all take 10 GCSEs (and a few may take

Maths/French early). Good careers advice is given (by a master who developed the Oasis careers programme, now widely used in schools).

GAMES, OPTIONS, THE ARTS: Strong and keen sports. Very successful shooting (two Athelings currently), under John Rowley, regular prize winners at Bisley; sailing teams do well (4th in the national dingy finals), and rugby was given a terrific boost recently by the arrival at Sixth Form of an international schoolboy player. Rugger for girls as well. Traditionally strong cricket. Outward-boundish and outdoor pursuits are generally 'easy to sell'. Some swim before breakfast daily. Has a tremendously well-supported D of E scheme – participants must also do CCF (army and RAF): 440 gold medals have been notched up in 20 years. New weights room/Multigyms; rowing machines popular with both boys and girls.

Sophisticated DT; computers are widely used. Music is much encouraged, choral music especially, bumped up in recent years to a good standard. New Theatre Studies and Drama are gathering momentum – an appeal for the new theatre is going well, due to be completed in '97.

A memorable VE day included pupils and staff dressing in Forties' fashion, and eating spam fritters at tables arranged in victory-V formation.

BACKGROUND AND ATMOSPHERE: Set in 170 acres of very beautiful Norfolk landscape, and most definitely out on a limb. Founded in 1555 by Sir Thomas Gresham, and turned into a public school at the turn of the century.

The school has a friendly, happy and fairly homely atmosphere, with good relations between staff and pupils. 'They don't put us under any pressure,' said a pupil. There is a lively social life within the school (a result of geographical isolation?) with a Sixth Form club, Lower and Upper Sixth divided (alcohol for the Upper), and Dave's Diner, the tuck-shop bob-shop for the rest of the school; both are open five nights a week, after prep hot spots.

The Big School is used for lunchtime concerts, performances, assemblies, and has a goldleaf Oxbridge honours boards (including Maclean of spy fame), and one recent addition, misspelt 'Oxen'. Very regular chapel (no complaints). Busy weekend programme (games, outdoor pursuits, including sailing). Boys' houses have maximum 8-bed dormitories, and study bedrooms (shared at first) from 14/15 upwards. Three girls' houses (one with 84) are extremely comfortably furnished. The CFB (Central Feeding Block), known as 'the trough', is drearily functional. The school's Twenties' temporary thatched huts ('scruff shacks') are now listed buildings.

PASTORAL CARE AND DISCIPLINE: One of the first public schools to appoint a counsellor, well-liked, well-used. Sixth Formers have sessions on stress. Gentle tightening up carries on: there have been occasional dismissals for drink in the past. (Local pubs are few and far between and can recognise a Gresh-amite 'a mile off'.) Laziness and non-participation is frowned on (including by pupils).

PUPILS AND PARENTS: Numbers are up, both boys and girls – ratio is now three boys to two girls. Delightful: open and friendly and easy, unpretentious, relatively unsophisticated boys and girls. By and large farmers, solicitors, accountants, etc. Unless they are day, parents are also looking at Oakham, Oundle. Also 25 ex-pats, 12 foreigners. An interesting list of Old Boys includes Sir Stephen Spender, W H Auden,

Benjamin Britten, Sir Christopher Cockerell (inventor of the hovercraft), James Dyson, Lord Reith, Hugh Johnson. Mainly from East Anglia, some from London (especially those with Fishmonger connections), some from the Midlands.

ENTRANCE: From a large number of prep schools, especially Taverham Hall, Beeston, Town Close (Norwich), and fed by its own prep school down the road (225 boys and girls, ages 7–13). Numbers swell at Sixth Form – approximately five leave post-GCSE, and 15 come in (increased interest at this level), via exam.

EXIT: Seven gained Oxbridge places in '95; 95% take degree courses – all over the place, to universities new and old (Newcastle, Edinburgh, Birmingham, Bristol, Bath, Reading), a handful to creative arts. Engineering is popular, also veterinary and medicine, farming.

MONEY MATTERS: There are generous scholarships from the Fishmongers' Company, with whom the school is associated (lots on the governing body), 3 specifically for children entering at 13+ from the maintained sector. Also 3 Art and Music and one for Drama, at both Sixth and Third Forms. An internal scholarship is given to a pupil continuing into Sixth Form and showing most academic improvement. There are also 5 Assisted Places at Sixth Form. Overall numbers (and quality) have been unaffected by the recession, though more have applied for bursaries.

REMARKS: An unusual co-ed school (which started life as a boys' public school) with increased numbers, plenty on offer, a positive outlook and high morale, and currently in good heart.

Guildford High School

London Road, Guildford GU1 1SJ
Tel: 01483 561440, Fax 01483 306516

PUPILS: 495 girls (plus 286 girls in junior school, ages 4–11)
AGES: 11–18
SIZE OF SIXTH FORM: 130
C OF E
FEE-PAYING

HEAD: Since 1991, Mrs Sue Singer, BA (fifties). Sits on GSA Education Committee and Council. An impressive profile – married young (abandoning plans for a medical career), and studied for Open University Maths degree while bringing up three children and running a playgroup. When the youngest was safely ensconced in school, she embarked on a teaching career, with a short period at a comprehensive, followed by St Paul's Girls', where she became Head of Maths. Charming, undaunting, deservedly popular with girls and parents, she teaches a few periods a week as a means of getting to know the girls.

ACADEMIC MATTERS: Formidably strong across the board, one of the top girls' schools in the country. The Head is very keen to develop a European dimension: their lucky 5-year-olds are taught German with their bilingual teacher, and, at the other end, Sixth Formers are strongly encouraged to maintain a language – although not forced to do so (particularly if taking four A-levels). Italian, French, German, Spanish, Russian, as well as Greek and Latin, on offer.
Stupendous numbers of A grades at A-level (54.6% to be precise, in '95, 79.3% A–B; French, Geography and Biology the most popular subjects, in that order). Girls

are very computer literate, although the Head is aware that girls still lag behind boys in state-of-the-art technology; CD-Rom facilities in the library include seven years' (indexed) *Guardian* newspaper plus encyclopaedias: 'really useful' commented one Sixth Former, 'we can research a lot here.' The computer room is full of Apple Macs, with computer courses for first years (open at lunch time for first and second years), and large numbers of Sixth Formers catching up by taking RSA Computer Literacy and IT courses. A highly qualified Careers Adviser is in situ three days a week.

GAMES, OPTIONS, THE ARTS: The school has a heated indoor pool and four acres of games fields two minutes from the school. Very successful lacrosse. There is a very strong music tradition, with a bias towards contemporary music – the late William Mathias composed one of his major works for the centenary in '88. Nine large keyboards link up to computer software (for sequencing and editing) and there are lots of budding composers. Some concerts are arranged jointly with Royal Grammar School; also lots of Drama, with an annual play/musical a co-operative effort with RGS. Debating is taken very seriously.

Girls are very actively involved in running clubs – their Technology Club built an electronic scoreboard for the Games Field. The 'Do-It' club is run by senior girls for first and second years to initiate them into the skills that no good citizen should be without – juggling, sherbert-making, tie-dye, card tricks. Also a very popular science club, Lower Sixth newspaper.

BACKGROUND AND ATMOSPHERE: A modest Victorian main building with pink-decorated walls reflects the general warmth and homeliness of the school. New buildings proliferate, including a light and airy junior school, a fine Sixth Form block, and other building works recently completed, providing assembly and dining halls, music and drama studios.

A very happy atmosphere, with a strong feeling of everyone working at full stretch. The school was founded in 1888, among the seven schools governed by the Church Schools Company providing a 'sound education based on Christian principles'.

PASTORAL CARE AND DISCIPLINE: Works well. First years in groups of six are assigned Sixth Form 'carers' – 'It's easier for them sometimes to talk to us about their problems'.

PUPILS AND PARENTS: Solidly upper-middle/middle class as might be expected in a city (until recently) bursting with prosperity. Guildford, Cobham, Woking and Godalming provide the main catchment area. Middle-class parents fallen on hard times are the ones who most vigorously seek out (and get) Assisted Places. Celia Imrie is an Old Girl.

ENTRANCE: Nearly all junior school pupils progress to senior school. Around one-third of intake at 11+ comes from the maintained sector. A few girls enter the school for the Sixth Form. There is nothing like as much pressure for places as at the top London day schools. Excellent road access and BR Station opposite the school.

EXIT: Almost all to university with between 8–15% to Oxbridge annually.

MONEY MATTERS: There are 5 Assisted Places at 11+. Academic and music scholarships, plus bursaries for the daughters of clergy.

REMARKS: Impressive – a successful, purposeful, well-resourced girls' city day school. Hard to fault, though possibly too 'safe', with its remarkably homogeneous intake and with many girls spending 13–14 years in the school.

Haberdashers' Aske's School

Butterfly Lane, Elstree, Borehamwood, Hertfordshire WD6 3AF

Tel: 0181 207 4323, Fax: 0181 207 4439

PUPILS: 1,100 boys (Plus prep school, with 209 boys, ages 7–11)

ALL DAY

AGES: 11–18

SIZE OF SIXTH FORM: 300

C OF E

FEE-PAYING

HEAD: Since 1996, Mr Jeremy Goulding MA (forties). Previously Head of Prior Park, Bath; went to school in Nottinghamshire, then Magdalen College, Oxford, where he started to read Classics, and switched to Philosophy and Theology. Keen sportsman, rowing and cricket in particular. Taught at Abingdon, Shrewsbury, and comes here from Prior Park, where he was Head. Married to Isobel, who also has a degree in Philosophy and Theology, with four children.

ACADEMIC MATTERS: All bright, but shades within the band. Classes of around 20–25 at the youngest age, then 10–12 for A-level. Remedial help is on hand for mild dyslexia. Particularly strong English, Maths, History, Sciences and Languages. Three separate Sciences at GCSE (Dual Award is not an option). Very computer literate with £150K

worth of Nimbus: there are over 60 networked machines where each boy has his own space and can use machines in his spare time. There is increasing use of IT across the curriculum; CD-Rom machines in the library. A very low turnover of staff; 'terrifically keen teaching', report many parents.

Near the top of league tables year after year – chart-busting again in '95, (32 out of 48 A grades in Eng Lit, 31 out of 54 A grades in Economics, 36 out of 61 A grades in History all at A-level). Hugely successful in a wide range of national Brains Trust-type competitions.

GAMES, OPTIONS, THE ARTS: Beefy on the games field – rugby and hockey are both strong (with regular tours abroad) also some budding athletes and swimming (outstanding water polo – boys play in national teams). Good games pitches, new Astroturf, Sports Hall. Magnificent pottery and Art department. Lively Drama – usually in conjunction with the Haberdashers' Girls', next door. In '95, presented *The Skylark*, a wickedly funny two-hander playlet by two members of staff, concerning Nicholas Serota (Headboy) and Brian Sewell, both Old Boys. Has a distinguished Music tradition, and boys sing regularly at the Westminster Hall or Albert Hall. Many clubs/activities, thriving community service, CCF currently popular.

BACKGROUND AND ATMOSPHERE: Founded in 1690 in Hoxton by the Worshipful Company of Haberdashers, who continue to play a powerful role in the governing body. Moved to the present site in 1961, formerly Lord Aldenham's pretty red-brick home, which houses the admin offices (and accommodation upstairs for young teachers). A distinctly purposeful atmosphere pervades, in a pleasantly green setting.

Haberdashers' Aske's Prep School (Tel: 0181 207 4323, Fax: 0181 207 4439). Head, since 1990, Mrs P A Bryant. A popular choice as a way in to the senior school, heavily oversubscribed, competitive entry exam plus report from previous school, and the (long) short-listed boys and their parents are called in for interview. Bright, airy classrooms, lots of outdoor space. Very rare for boys at 11+ to be directed elsewhere.

PASTORAL CARE AND DISCIPLINE: Tight on disciplinary matters, a school where prefect power counts for something. Staff are beady-eyed over to-ing and fro-ing with the girls' next door. Staff are also watchful of bad language.

PUPILS AND PARENTS: Polyglot (Arabic is part of the core curriculum). Parents are mainly professionals (mothers as well as fathers); the school busily fosters links with 'the home'. Appeals to first-time buyers. Pupils come from an ever-increasing large catchment area: boys and girls are bussed in together (parking permits for the lucky few). OBs include Leon Brittan, Dennis Marks (English National Opera), Michael Green (Carlton TV), racing driver Damon Hill.

ENTRANCE: Tough and oversubscribed. CE at 11+, many from Haberdashers' own prep school; about 25 at 13+. Some at Sixth Form.

EXIT: Very small post-GCSE leakage (mainly to Sixth Form colleges). To university – with rare exceptions – anything between 35 and 45 to Oxbridge annually.

MONEY MATTERS: 35 Assisted Places; some bursaries.

REMARKS: No change: thorough and rock-solid academic day school with high expectations, (except for social climbers), which charges on successfully.

Haberdashers' Aske's School for Girls

Aldenham Road, Elstree, Hertfordshire WD6 3BT

Tel: 0181 953 4261, Fax: 0181 953 5663

PUPILS: 550 girls (plus own junior school, with 300 girls)

ALL DAY

AGES: 11–18

SIZE OF SIXTH FORM: 250

C OF E

FEE-PAYING

HEAD: Since 1991, Mrs Penelope Penney, BA (fifties), educated at Chatelard, Switzerland, and Bristol University. Previously Head at Putney High (five years) and Head of Prendergast School, Catford (seven years). Head of English before that. Married to a 'Management Consultant Cleric', three grown-up children.

President GSA '94. Believes learning should be fun and aims to produce 'confident not cocky girls, who are interesting and interested, with intellectual curiosity. People of integrity, who accept others' points of view.' Important to remember that 'we are educating future Europeans'. Very enthusiastic, 'has never been as happy'. An outstanding Head, who wants girls to have 'a go at things and be able to fail safely'. Has increased the number of staff. 'It's a treat to teach girls like this in surroundings like this.'

ACADEMIC MATTERS: Very strong; always very good. Girls work hard.

Strong Maths and Sciences (three sciences), and Modern Languages and English. Regularly near the top in league tables. No learning support is provided. Set in Maths and French from 12; a large school which makes it easier to adjust the curriculum. Girls are 'encouraged' to take two Modern Languages at GCSE, and can do Japanese and Modern Hebrew in Sixth Form.

The colossal Computer lab has 38 networked Archimedes computers (the second lab is now devoted to the Lower School). CD-Roms are everywhere (two in the library); computers in classrooms, and satellites in language labs.

GAMES, OPTIONS, THE ARTS: Lacrosse team 'strikes terror', loads of county and national players; otherwise netball, tennis, swimming, fencing, badminton, athletics. Lovely Art (hence the new building), and good sculpture; and strong Music (girls can and do play everything, can have a go). The new combined Music and Art building opened May '95. No domestic activities offered – no domestic science, dressmaking or fabric design. D of E award. Masses of debating; regular champions. Some Drama with the boys next door. CDT is good, with girls making serious model cars – for themselves.

BACKGROUND AND ATMOSPHERE: The Haberdashers' Company originally bequeathed money by Robert Aske in 1690; the girls' school was founded in 1901 and moved to its present 50-acre site adjoining Haberdashers' Boys' school in 1974. The two schools, run separately, are joined by 'Passion Gates'; much to-ing and fro-ing at lunch time for joint clubs (for everything). Also share the 58 buses which bring pupils from as far away as Luton, and all over Hertfordshire, North Finchley, Muswell Hill.

A collection of somewhat stark airy red-brick buildings joined by upper and lower walkways – girls say they don't get lost. Specialist classrooms in blocks; a fun drama workshop on the top floor. The Upper Sixth can and do drive to school.

There is a great feeling of peace and purposefulness. Lots of 'girl-inspired' charity involvement. Haberdashers' Company visit in robes on St Catherine's Day – Deputation Day: lots of fun links with the Company.

Haberdashers' Aske's School for Girls, Lower School (Tel: 0181 953 4261). Head: Mrs D Targett (who was previously Deputy Head here). 300 girls, ages 4–11, with fiercely competitive entry, via an hour-long playgroup, followed, for the successful, by an interview later. Attached to the main school building, and shares all the senior school facilities, but have their own Science lab.

PASTORAL CARE AND DISCIPLINE: Form Tutors take a tutorial lesson each week. 'Girls aim to please.' Not much naughtiness: 'two sets of really naughty girls since I arrived,' says the Head. Massive leadership training: prefects are elected by peers, staff, and years above and below; they help with juniors and provide a 'listening ear'.

PUPILS AND PARENTS: Parents are interested and very supportive – currently buying a second Language lab, and have provided seating and an organ in hall etc. There is a strong ethnic mix – Asian, Jewish, (and of those girls who take a 'gap' year, a large percentage of them go to Israel). Also a strong work ethic; parents regard education as a 'family commitment'.

ENTRANCE: 11 and 16. Seriously oversubscribed: five or six applicants to one place. Prospective pupils do a full-day exam in English, Maths and Verbal Reasoning; the successful examinees are called back for interview and some are chosen. No priority for siblings. Everyone is looked at as an individual.

EXIT: A tiny trickle leaves after GCSE (logistic, financial, not many fail to make the grade), 99.9% to university (eventually), with a record-breaking 32 to Oxbridge in '95.

MONEY MATTERS: The Haberdashers' Company provide a generous special fund each year for real emergencies. There are 20 Assisted Places each year (and help is given with extracurricular activities if necessary). Entrance bursaries, and academic and music scholarships. No falling away in numbers because of the recession.

REMARKS: No change: an outstanding, worthy academic girls' day school. An oasis of excellence.

Haberdashers' Monmouth School for Girls

Hereford Road, Monmouth
Tel: 01600 714214, Fax: 01600 772244

PUPILS: Around 545 girls; 130 board (full and weekly), the rest day; plus own junior school, with 95 girls, ages 7–11.
AGES: 11–18
SIZE OF SIXTH FORM: 168
CHRISTIAN FOUNDATION,
  NON-DENOM
FEE-PAYING

HEAD: Since 1992, Mrs D Newman BA Hons in English from University of London, PGCE. Formerly Deputy Head. Unfortunately ill when we visited, and we were shown round by Shelagh Salter, director of PR and marketing. Much re-organisation of offices.

ACADEMIC MATTERS: Offers a good range of subjects. English and Modern Languages are strongest, Science is also popular. A state-of-the-art new Science building opened September 1994 – impressive labs and equipment. Extended Sixth Form provision by offering A-level subjects at either Monmouth School or here. Boys come over for Psychology, Religious Studies, Statistics, Italian and Classical Studies; girls go to boys' school for Russian and History of Art. There are lots of male staff. The excellent careers department has its own Head of Department.

The school has come top of the Welsh league tables in 1993 and 1995 and does consistently well – much to its credit, given the rural position and relatively local catchment area.

GAMES, OPTIONS, THE ARTS: The school has a five star sports hall, also a gym and wonderful pool. Rowing was only recently introduced but already the eights have won the Gold Medal at the National Championships in '94 and '95, joined in '95 by the fours winning the Gold also. Keen lacrosse – West of England Champions in 1995 – though sport shows no signs of dominating the place. Organises jolly events – barbecues, fêtes, etc. School has a drama master in residence – and keen Drama and Theatre Studies A-level. Also has an excellent Needlework department – imaginative and careful work in different areas (well, what would you expect from the Haberdashers?). The super Art department has proper one-to-one teaching. Strong on Outward Bound (with glorious

Welsh hills on the doorstep), D of E. The school holds an Eisteddford.

BACKGROUND AND ATMOSPHERE:
The school has the enormous strength of financial backing from the Haberdashers' Company. Founded in 1892, out of the bequest of a local merchant made good, William Jones, who had provided for the foundation of the boys' school in 1614. The boys' school is slightly eclipsed by the heads-down attitude of the girls, but has strong links – the site is close by in the town, and there are lots of brother/sister links, as well as joining for academic and non-academic activities. The May Ball is the social focal point. Recently redesigned maroon uniform.

Healthy site with a beautiful view over Monmouth, on a hill, with some departments across the road (pedestrian flyover). Lots of walking about to get to different locations and a good sense of space. Rather unexpected large panelled dining room. The boarding house is just behind the main block – modern purpose-built and unremarkable, though in the process of having rooms upgraded. Boarding numbers reduced with national trend/recession, though flexi boarding has been introduced and the number of girls entering at 13 and 16 is increasing. There are lots of weekend and evening activities for boarders. The Sixth Form have their own block with a common room, and wear a different uniform.

PASTORAL CARE AND DISCIPLINE:
School Tutors and Heads of Year; PSE on the curriculum. The senior boarding house has a larky local reputation, but there are no real problems.

PUPILS AND PARENTS:
Children of local business and professionals, one or two from Hong Kong, some from Services. Broad social mix. Friendly. Very supportive parents (but no PTA).

ENTRANCE:
Mainly via the junior school. Also from local primaries and preps. Entry at 11+, 13+ and 16. (Testing in March for entry to junior school in September.)

EXIT:
To an impressive array of universities all over the UK including Oxbridge, London, Bristol, Exeter, Manchester. Some to ex-polys, a few to art school; the breadth of destinations is a credit to the careers department. Girls go on to professions, medicine, Services and the arts – even to Moscow Space School – and become engineers on oil tankers.

MONEY MATTERS:
Owing to the strength of the Jones Foundation, the school is an absolute bargain (fees currently £2,664 per term for boarding) and well worth considering. Academic scholarships of up to 50 per cent of fees at age 11 and into the Sixth Form. One or two Music Scholarships, currently 10 Assisted Places available, and more applied for under the new government scheme. The Haberdashers are very generous to parents in genuine need.

REMARKS:
A good if slightly uninspired performer in the girls' academic schools stakes. Worth a look.

Haileybury

Hertford SG13 7NU
Tel: 01992 463353, Fax: 01992 467603

PUPILS: Around 511 boys, 80 girls in Sixth Form (419 board, 172 day)
AGES: 11–18
SIZE OF SIXTH FORM: Approx 280

C of E
FEE-PAYING

HEAD: From September 1996, Mr Stuart Westley MA, Oxon, (forties). Educated at Lancaster Royal Grammar School, and read Law at Corpus Christi, Oxford; cricket blue, and a serious cricketer. Previously Principal of King William's College, Isle of Man, Deputy Head at Bristol Cathedral School, also taught at Framlingham. Married with one young daughter. Takes over from Mr David Jewell.

ACADEMIC MATTERS: Thorough teaching, on the whole, but one or two weaker departments. Results are good, considering the intake. The school has a whizzo Head of Geography and pretty impressive results. Also impressive results in Mathematics; Chemistry looking strong, and French. Pupils are allowed to take an A-level in a subject even if they are the only one – a rarity this – e.g. Latin, Greek, Spanish, Russian each had a single taker, each clocked up A grade. Photography also on offer. Both Art and Art and Design get consistently good results. Dual Award Science for all at GCSE – excellent results here.

GAMES, OPTIONS, THE ARTS: Famous for producing successful sportsmen (athletics county gold medallists at the time of writing; good rackets; soccer flourishing; ditto cricket). Good fencing and shooting. Indoor sports hall, CCF very popular – girls, too, are going for it. The school's first indoor swimming pool is ready this year, thanks to the generosity of two generations of Old Boys. The old gym has been converted into the Technology Centre.

The Art department under John Higgins continues to produce some stunning results and prizes. Successful public speakers and debaters and the school has come first at The Hague Model United Nations Competition. Other arts, including Drama, are also busy, and there is a small theatre, named after OB Alan Ayckbourn. The school mag looks more like a serious intellectual glossy. A good school for music, with a very wide range of activities, ambitious performances, e.g. Bernstein's *Chichester Psalms*, the St John Passion in German, an annual St Martin-in-the-Fields concert, a tour of Florence and Venice including singing in St Mark's.

BACKGROUND AND ATMOSPHERE: Amalgamated with Imperial Service College, and housed in the defunct East India College, the training ground for generations of boys destined to govern India. Fine William Wilkins architecture, college-style, laid out around a vast quad, with sympathetic additions hidden among trees. Houses are small – 48ish in each – and in 3 out of 13 cases whole houses continue the tradition of sharing one dormitory, which is a popular arrangement, though there are now more smaller dorms and bed-sits, and refurbishing continues. There is a very strong sense of community, partly, say pupils, because the whole school meets together four times a day (morning chapel and at meals in the domed dining hall which has an incredible echo). Cafeteria system – pupils eat at magnificent polished oak tables made by the Yorkshire carpenters who signed their work with a mouse. The school shield is a crossed sword and anchor surmounting three flying hearts.

PASTORAL CARE AND DISCIPLINE: The outgoing Head cared passionately about pastoral care, and was constantly communicating and consulting with parents about everything from the shape of weekends to illegal drugs and cigarette smoking. His letter to *The Times* on discipline was a model of fair-mindedness and common sense, and taken to heart by other schools. At the time of writing, there were few major disciplinary problems. The school operates a policy of testing for drug abuse.

PUPILS AND PARENTS: About one-tenth children of OBs; some from overseas – including some ex-pats; lots of parents in the Services. New boys are still called 'New Guv'nors'. Decent sorts, conventional on the whole, mixed ability. OBs: Clement Attlee, most of the founding fathers of the Royal Air Force, including Sir John Slessor. Also Lord Oaksey, Neville Coghill ×2, Stirling Moss, Rex Whistler, Lord Allenby, John McCarthy. Not to mention 19 VCs and GCs. Girls come from single-sex schools and are sisters with brothers here.

ENTRANCE: Boys numbers were booming at the time of writing, and girl numbers increasing again having declined in '93 (not the only one). Scholarship pupils come from an exotic selection of schools in the area and further afield (e.g. Craiglowan School, Perth, Dodderhill School, Droitwich)

EXIT: Over 95% to further education, with 16–20 going on to Oxbridge. Manchester, Durham, Newcastle, Nottingham, Birmingham, Bath all popular. Traditional careers now the Empire is no longer with us: banking, medicine, accountancy, estate management, the Church.

MONEY MATTERS: Up to 10 academic scholarships and exhibitions of up to half fees (index linked); up to 5 music scholarships and 5 art scholarships. One or two sons of clergy are on reduced fees. The school's wonderful windfall of £3 million (left in his will by OB Russell Dore, who made his money in the City) should help keep recession breezes at bay.

REMARKS: A distinguished, conventional, and rather low-profile traditional public school.

Hampton School

Hanworth Road, Hampton, Middlesex TW12 3HD
Tel: 0181 979 5526, Fax: 0181 941 7368

PUPILS: 947 boys (all day)
AGES: 11–18
SIZE OF SIXTH FORM: 285
C OF E (other faiths welcome)
FEE-PAYING

HEAD: From 1988 until 1997, Mr Graham Able, MA (forties), educated at Worksop College and Trinity College, Cambridge (read Chemistry), who sums up the ethos as 'Giving the boys excellent tuition and ensuring that they develop their abilities.' Dismissive of 'league table games'. Leaving for Dulwich in 1997, and his successor is unknown at the time of writing.

ACADEMIC MATTERS: A strong team of staff (many long-standing), mostly male. A-level strongest in Chemistry, Biology, Sciences and Maths, with large numbers taking these subjects and scores of A grades, but some Ds, Es and below are sprinkled about too. All boys take three Sciences at GCSE. French is taken a year early – followed by Scottish Higher French (the only school in England to do so?) 'because it has some literature in it and is the only course that really acts as a bridge between GCSE and A-level'. Maths is noticeably strong. The numbers of pupils taking Classics both at GCSE and also at A-level are *increasing* – reflecting the impact of a new young head of department? General Studies (examined) for all Sixth Formers. Computing much enlarged. Good (and early) careers advice.

GAMES, OPTIONS, THE ARTS: Exceptionally strong rowing (Boat House at Molesey – a fair way off), three times winners of the Triple since '85, and among the top six rowing schools since early eighties. (Boat news and successes takes up notably more space than any other sporting news in the school's annual report, a dry little booklet.) Rowing all the year round. Rugby and soccer are played in both winter terms, and both do well. Saturday morning sports 'pretty keenly' attended.

A long (one-and-a-half-hour) lunch break accommodates options, e.g. some music, drama, etc, though some longer sessions are held after school for orchestra, CCF. Work experience is taken seriously.

BACKGROUND AND ATMOSPHERE: Old grammar school foundation (1557), went fully independent in 1975. Depressingly unaesthetic functional buildings (1930s onwards) on a main road, plus a new building housing the Sixth Form common rooms, History department, lecture theatre and the cricket pavilion, i.e. multi-purpose. Set on 25–30 acres of playing fields in comfortable suburbs, with Lady Eleanor Holles bang next door (qv). The school has a well-equipped library, and all facilities – sports hall, Technology department, etc – in place. Senior students often use computers/word processors at home for project work, due to pressure on the school's equipment. Purposeful, get-on-with-it atmosphere. Some joint activities (drama, music mainly) with the neighbouring girls. An energetic programme of activities is laid on by staff during the holidays.

PASTORAL CARE AND DISCIPLINE: Beady eyes are kept on boys. Lack of tolerance is considered the worst sin; persistent poor work, etc, merits Saturday morning detentions (on average 5 a week, 'but far more by the end of term').

Smoking: boys caught outside school get instant Saturday detention. Staff are now limited to smoking in a 'fairly unattractive shack'. Four boys have been sacked for drugs during the present Head's reign. Long hair is tolerated in Sixth Form, 'but a skinhead would be sent straight home.'

PUPILS AND PARENTS: Courteous boys, solid and steady citizens from broadly differing social and economic backgrounds. The school's insistence on the boys' involvement in the many aspects of education on offer produces balanced individuals. Pockets of energetically involved parents. Boys bus in (with LEH girls) from as far away as Woking, Windsor, Ascot. OBs: Olympic rowing gold medallists Jonathan and Greg Searle.

ENTRANCE: Selective (top 20% of ability band), and getting harder as more plump for day education. The Head has a firm policy of refusing to take boys at 11 from IAPS prep schools. Between 250 and 300 sit for 100 places at 11+. Approximately 53 at 13. Some (to fill leavers' places) come at Sixth Form. (NB Interesting discovery here – though why, none can tell – that the CE Maths paper is a very good indicator of how well boys will perform at GCSE and A-level in all subjects.)

EXIT: Practically all to university; 2 or 3 to Forces; 2 or 3 to industry. Oxbridge entrants 10–20; Southern/Midland universities preferred; followed by a wide variety of careers.

MONEY MATTERS: Surprisingly well-off foundation (though it certainly doesn't look it). There are 27 Assisted Places at 11+; 4 at 13+; some at 16+. Various scholarships and bursaries at 11 and 13.

REMARKS: A solid place in the grammar school tradition, much appreciated, and doing well, though lacking in pizazz.

Harrogate Ladies' College

Clarence Drive, Harrogate,
North Yorkshire HG1 2QG
Tel: 01423 504543, Fax: 01423 568893

PUPILS: Around 380 girls (250 board, 130 day)
AGES: 10–18
SIZE OF SIXTH FORM: Around 100+
C OF E
FEE-PAYING

HEAD: From September 1996, Dr Margaret Joan Hustler, BSc, PhD (forties), Biochemist (her research degree was industry linked). Taught at Lady Eleanor Holles, Atherley School and comes here from being Head at St Michael's in Surrey. Married, with eight children. Born and bred in Harrogate.

Takes over after an ugly period in the school's history. The previous Head was forced to resign, and so was the Chairman of Governors who supported her, following a parents' meeting which ended in a vote of no confidence in them both. This created bad publicity for the school, which maintained its 'dignified silence' – there is some angst that their side of the story was not given a public airing.

ACADEMIC MATTERS: Good A-level results in '95, especially considering the brouhaha, but still should do better in public exams – Maths good, also English (though only 8 students took this), Chinese results are successful for the usual reasons. GCSEs looking healthy, though Dual Award science came a bit of a cropper in '95. Dual Award or separate sciences on offer at GCSE. Computers are networked throughout the school. Good and stimulating facilities, which have in the past attracted good staff. Girls have a 10-period day.

GAMES, OPTIONS, THE ARTS: Keenly sporty – the girls have been northern lacrosse champions, there is a golf course nearby, lots of tennis courts, a 25-metre pool, riding, six badminton courts – good facilities and much used. Multi-gym, keen D of E (a member of staff is head of Northern scheme). Ballet; strong Music, especially the choir, and no-one misses a class for a music lesson, a masterpiece of ingenious timetabling. The school makes sensible use of local theatre, cinema, concerts and opera (Leeds). Huge Art room (for Art and Design), plus Design Technology department. Amazing radio-transmitting satellite station – the girls have contacts with USA, Japan, etc, run by the infectiously enthusiastic master, Mr Horton. Sub-aqua, windsurfing and ski trips are now on the extra-curricular menu. The school chapel has a – wait for it – two-manual Walker tracker-action classical pipe organ.

BACKGROUND AND ATMOSPHERE: The school was founded elsewhere in 1893. It is one of the 'Allied Schools' (though this does not appear to mean very much today). The present premises are akin to a seaside hotel with mock Tudor beams and gables. Houses are neat but basic, common rooms focused round the telly with easy chairs. Formal, rather old-fashioned feel. All ages mix freely. New boarding house – Oakdale – for 10–14-year-olds. Weekly boarding is available as well as 'day' and full boarding.

PASTORAL CARE AND DISCIPLINE: Manners strictly monitored. At 16+, girls are allowed out one night a week – it is 10 minutes' walk to town centre.

PUPILS AND PARENTS: Many northerners; substantial number of boarders from overseas, including foreign nationals, the majority Hong Kong Chinese. Buddhists, Jews and Muslims in the school. Solidly middle class.

ENTRANCE: Own entrance exam for the 10-year-olds and above, plus previous Head's report and interview.

EXIT: 90% to degree courses; 2–5 to Oxbridge, otherwise widespread including London, ex-polys, universities overseas.

MONEY MATTERS: There are 8 Assisted Places, bursaries at 11 or 12 of up to one-third of fees (which are not unreasonable), plus 2 or 3 into Sixth Form. Discounts for siblings. Also 2 music scholarships of up to one-third of fees. Not a rich school, but run by good housekeeping.

REMARKS: Impossible to comment at the moment as the school is in a period of interregnum as we go to press.

Harrow School

Harrow on the Hill,
Middlesex HA1 3HW
Tel: 0181 422 2196, Fax: 0181 423 3112
PUPILS: 800 boys (all board)

AGES: 13–18
SIZE OF SIXTH FORM: Around 310
C OF E
FEE-PAYING

HEAD: Since 1991, Mr Nicholas Bomford, MA (fifties), educated at Kelly College and Trinity Oxford. Previously Head of Uppingham, before that of Monmouth, and taught at Wellington. Historian, and acknowledged to be a 'brilliant teacher'. Keen on fishing and shooting. His wife plays a full-time Head's wife's role and is one of the team who interviews prospective candidates for Gap; two grown-up daughters. Says he has 'tinkered' rather than made radical changes ('Not a decision-maker, but terribly nice,' from a senior boy). Very much in contrast to his predecessor, the innovative Ian Beer. Some parents wish he had a 'little more get up and go.' Definitely has the staff behind him – 'He's a good listener,' they say, 'and a consolidator.'

ACADEMIC MATTERS: Very healthy exam results (though '95 was slightly down on the previous two years). Strong across the board in A-levels, with brilliant Geography results (yet again) – 25 A grades, 9 Bs, 3Cs, 2 Ds. Chemistry is another strength, with 24 A grades, 12 Bs, 4 Cs, also some Ds and Es in this. French and English also very good. Economics results – as elsewhere – are not so hot, and Harrow has now decided not to continue with the Oxford and Cambridge board in this subject. All boys now take a minimum of 8/9 GCSEs, and all boys must take two Science subjects. The outstanding Geography department has excellent facilities and a splendid young Head of Department, Mr Mel Mrowiec. There is a small take-up of German and Spanish at A-level; Japanese is an option (Arabic is now off the menu), so is Italian.

Latin has a good following. Theatre Studies have recently been introduced.

Steady teaching; the staff are all male except for two, and many have been here for yonks. 10 sets per subject (in general), with larger numbers in the top sets than lower sets; groups of up to 14 for A-levels. Bearing in mind a broadish intake, the results are particularly good.

GAMES, OPTIONS, THE ARTS: Keen on games (including Harrow football), with a great deal of house competition (keenly fostered in the main). Currently a pair of outstanding Eton Fives players in the school. One of the Lord's cricket schools. Has a smart indoor sports complex with magnificent 'ducker' (pool). Each house has its own tennis courts. 'Too much emphasis on sports' from several boys (plus ça change, plus c'est la même chose). Popular CCF, with outstandingly successful marine section, the rifle corps winning the Pringle Competition in 1995.

Extremely lively Drama – given a boost now by the new Ryan Theatre. All manner of productions are constantly on the go, occasionally with girls from North London Collegiate (Rattigan's City of Angels was the most memorable in '95). The Speech Room (Burgess in a restrained mode) is annually transformed into a Globe Theatre replica for the Shakespeare production. There is a good Art department (with an artist in residence). Music has 'transformed' over the last five or six years and is now producing notable music e.g. Purcell's Dido and Aeneas; the piano trio played in the final of the National Schools Chamber Music Competition at St John's Smith Square; and – a recent innovation – the competition for singing self-accompanied on the guitar. Lots of extras in other areas, including the farm, now a dairy farm, but no longer providing milk for the school.

BACKGROUND AND ATMOSPHERE: Founded in 1572 by John Lyon; on a site of more than 300 acres on the hill (the Chapel by Gilbert Scott is very fine; the spire is visible for miles around: an island of dignity and elegance in a sea of hideous suburbia. The oldest buildings date from the 17th century, collegiate buildings are spread along either side of the High Street (a boy met his death crossing over in '93), worlds away from the nearby Betjeman-esque. There is a very fine collection of antiquities in the Museum and fine watercolours (mostly 19th century). The quality of modern buildings is outstanding and should be seen by other schools for the non-carbuncular possibilities. Older teaching blocks were mostly redesigned inside to give spacious and light classrooms. Staff are all accommodated on the Hill – no wonder they like to work here, 'But the trouble is,' said a parent whose sons' schooling spans two decades, 'they tend not to move, so there can be dead wood.'

Splendid uniform, includes straw hats, tail coats on Sundays (and top hats and sticks for monitors). A jolly photograph in the latest Harrow Record shows a dashing clutch of monitors in full fig 'helping' a mini-skirted Liz Hurley to switch on the Regent Street Christmas lights. A pecking order is keenly felt by boys. Some complaints that 'innovative thinking' – e.g. students' union, any mildly left-wing thinking – is 'deeply frowned on by the establishment'. The school is short on exeats. The eleventh and final house has been refurbished (at a cost of £1 million). Most boys share double rooms for the first two years, then have single rooms – no dormitories.

PASTORAL CARE AND DISCIPLINE: Being off the hill without written permission could mean instant dismissal (and usually accounts for the loss of one or two boys per year). 'But most of them don't take advantage of the temptation.' Stiff anti-drugs ruling: drug testing on pupils suspected of taking illegal substances was recently introduced ('96). Housemasters and their tutors are 'pretty beady' about boys' behaviour. One of those schools where housemasters have tremendous power (tenure of housemastering is 12 years). Most boys are law-abiding and respect tradition – they won't survive here if not. Runs an outstandingly good 'way of life' course (run with girls from three local schools) with small groups discussing/reflecting on 'their experience of the environment, society, ourselves and God' – under the guidance of specially trained counsellors. The school also has a consultant psychiatrist on call.

Antagonism between Harrow school boys and local youth hit the headlines in '95, but was largely, says the school, a case of the press making mountains out of molehills.

PUPILS AND PARENTS: Very varied. One of the rare schools that can truthfully claim to be (inter)national; has a long tradition of exotic foreigners, including maharajas and minor royalty. Lots from Scotland and Ireland. Loads of fiercely loyal Old Harrovian families. The school is C of E but currently has 20 Jewish (rabbi comes in), 70+ RCs (priest comes in). Strong links with trade, old landed and aristocratic families, also social climbers and new money. Polite ('though the cad element lingers,' says a distressed mother). OBs: seven Prime Ministers (including Winston Churchill and Baldwin), Byron, Peel, Trollope, Palmerston, Galsworthy, King Hussein of Jordan, the Nizam of Hyderabad. Also the acting Fox brothers.

ENTRANCE: Names down early – at a particular house. 'Housemasters are kings of their castles in this area,' comments the Head. 50% passmark at CE – and no plans to change this. Currently full, and lists healthy.

EXIT: 26 to Oxbridge in '95 (24 is average). A gap year is popular. All over the shop to universities; Bristol, Edinburgh, Newcastle particularly popular, also Durham, Oxford Brookes and Southampton and one or two to American universities. ('95 breakdown of subjects reads: Arts 48, Sciences 36, Engineering/Technology 11, Social Sciences 19). Then to a wide variety of careers. Making money matters less in the nineties than in the previous decade, thinks the Head.

MONEY MATTERS: 20 scholarships per year. 'Everyone thinks we're well endowed, but we're *not* well endowed' emphasises the Head. The school does indeed appear to be rich and definitely comfortable, there is a sense of quality, and it is extremely well kept (freshly painted and no ugly rubbish bins or lurking crisp bags). All is relative. Many parents hard hit by Lloyd's and the recession.

REMARKS: One of the country's most famous public schools, which has never quite regained the top slot following a downslide some years back, but is still very strong (and our impression is, getting stronger), very traditional, very male, muy macho. Marred by the suburban setting, but very splendid and probably worrying about its future less than most schools.

Headington School

Oxford OX3 7TD
Tel: 01865 741968 , Fax: 01865 602608

PUPILS: Around 550 girls in senior school. Plus 200 in junior school (ages 4–11). Mainly day, but board, from age 9, weekly and full 200.

AGES: 11–18

SIZE OF SIXTH FORM: 180

C OF E

FEE-PAYING

HEAD: From September 1996, Mrs Hilary Fender BA (Hons) (forties), educated at the Marist Convent, Devon and Exeter University, where she read History, followed by King's College, London. Married with one son. Previously Head of Godolphin School, Salisbury – and a great catch. Very pro single-sex education, says she 'wants girls to have full lives, to realise they have choices – and to go for it.' Occasionally writes for *The Times*.

ACADEMIC MATTERS: Traditional teaching, and generally the school gets good results all round, though this is variable from year to year, and '95 shows a dip. English, Chemistry, Maths, Biology and Geography are popular at A-level. Newly introduced A-level subjects are Politics, Economics, History of Art, Environmental Science and Theatre Studies GNVQ also starting up in Business Studies. Separate sciences or Dual Award science course at GCSE. IT taken by most girls at GCSE.

GAMES, OPTIONS, THE ARTS: The school is heavy on sporting opportunities, with high standards – county champions regularly in several sports, and girls are often selected for county teams. Keen boat club; new Sports Hall, lovely indoor swimming pool. Hundreds of girls do music – choir, chamber orchestra, chamber choir (tours abroad), groups galore, operatic production biannually (*Carmen* in '95). Not ashamed of doing cookery; takes a traditional approach to

Art. Exceptionally strong D of E (30 gold, 68 silver, 120 bronze enrolments at the time of writing). Young Enterprise county prizewinners.

PASTORAL CARE AND DISCIPLINE: Good at TLC. There is a school counsellor. Form and house staff are 'dedicated to giving personal approach to the girls'.

BACKGROUND AND ATMOSPHERE: Founded in 1915 by a group of Church of England members with faith in the future who 'saw that there was a need in Oxford for a combined day and boarding school where girls could grow up in a Christian atmosphere . . . sense of service . . . fulfil . . .' The school has a generous amount of space, given its position, i.e. bang on (though set back from) the main road, opposite Oxford Brookes. The original Queen Anne-style building is quite mellow; some of the new buildings are very functional, particularly some of the boarding houses, though teddies, posters, etc, are much in evidence.

One particularly glorious boarding house – Davenport (there are four houses in all) – looks on to a mellow garden, and is run by a dedicated staff and matron. Formerly a family home. It has a friendly feel, a loo called Everest, and cosy dormitories with names like Owl, Squirrel, etc, and a real hedgehog hibernating in a cubbyhole in the basement, with brand new kitchens (following Children Act). There is a separate Sixth Form boarding house (the Celia Marsh House) in which girls can (and *do*) do their own thing – particularly in dress – leggings, tights with seams, shirts hanging out. Weekly boarding is available – wistful looks as parents arrive to whisk off the lucky ones. A day school with boarders, rather than vice versa.

Junior School (Tel 01865 61774, Fax: 01865 60268). Head (since 1986), Mrs A A

Boon, Cert Ed. Across the road in a Victorian house set in four acres (with mature trees and a Wendy house). Boarding for the little girls is in the main school boarding houses.

PUPILS AND PARENTS: Bright Oxford daughters of academics and professionals; Hong Kong contingent all the way up, Brunei and Malaysian government scholars, Nigerians (one second-generation), plus 'girls from Europe' in the Sixth Form. Most famous OG is Baroness Young; also the Moderator of the Movement of the Ordination of Women; Olympic long jumper Yinka Idowu.

ENTRANCE: Has a broader ability range than Oxford High, particularly on the boarding front. Entry into senior school at 11+, 12+ and 13+ by Spring CE; entry at 14+ and into Sixth Form by school's own entrance exam.

EXIT: To a surprisingly wide range of practical university and other courses, including Pharmacy, Accountancy, Biotechnology, Business Studies, as well as Law, Philosophy, Veterinary Science, Medicine.

MONEY MATTERS: Has had Assisted Places for the past five years – up to 5 in any one year, of which 3 must come from the state sector. Scholarships at 11+, 12+, 13+, Sixth Form, and also an international scholarship at 14+. No endowment whatsoever. A small proportion of fee income goes to bursaries. Fees are kept 'reasonable' on founders' wishes.

REMARKS: Oxford's second string girls' school with a boarding element, now in the hands of a dynamic new Head.

Heathfield School

Ascot, Berkshire SL5 8BQ
Tel: 01344 882955 Fax: 01344 890689

PUPILS: 215 girls
ALL BOARDERS
AGES: 11–18
SIZE OF SIXTH FORM: 34 in the Upper Sixth in '95 – 'the largest the school has ever known' and 29 in the Lower Sixth. NB This can fluctuate quite considerably, but is showing an upwards trend.
C OF E
FEE-PAYING

HEAD: Since 1992, Mrs Julia Benammar, BA, M es Lettres (early forties). Educated in Manchester and Leeds University, followed by a Masters degree in France, where she met her husband. Both teach – her former post was Housemistress at Wellington (she was headhunted for Heathfield) – her husband is currently head of the British Section of the French Lycée in London. A neat, quiet person, and an outstanding organiser – 'I'm tidy,' she says modestly. Also has what appears to be an outstanding talent for finding good part-time staff. Mrs Benammar teaches the top and bottom forms. May well be head-hunted again.

ACADEMIC MATTERS: No-nonsense all-round place, with excellent academic results both at GCSE and A-level. A creditable number of As at GCSE (including 6 in biology and 3 in physics in 1995), and few below the C mark at A-level. This is particularly impressive, as the school has not had the pick of the academics.

The biggest strength of this school, however, is that although the Sixth Form is relatively small, as Sixth Forms go, it can offer almost any subject you want at A-level in almost any combination – this is extremely unusual, and not surprisingly keeps a member of staff with a permanent worried frown on her face as she tries to sort out the timetable 'It's too complicated for a computer,' she says. Even more impressive – the school does not charge extra for the more unusual choices; the fees cover any three A-levels. The result of this is very small classes (often ones and twos – which some might consider too small) at A-level, getting more or less individual attention, but not being limited in choice. (Last year, for example, they had one girl taking Welsh at GCSE, and one is currently studying Japanese; four did Theatre Studies at A-level.) Staff:pupil ratio is 1:7½.

The school has some enthusiastic, competent and highly dedicated staff who, says Mrs Benammar, have to turn their hand to any number of different things in the school.

Computer lessons are timetabled – Apple Macs for e.g. word processing, Archimedes for scientific applications (with the latter situated handily for the Science labs). All do three separate sciences at GCSE; General Studies are not part of the A-level curriculum.

Years are divided first into two forms – A and alpha (max 20 to a form here), then into three for the main subjects.

The school has a whizzo Head of Languages, not to mention excellent staff, and language students have, among other things, *work* exchanges organised for them, in e.g. *Vogue* offices in Paris.

G AMES, OPTIONS, THE ARTS: This is not traditionally a gamesy school, but in a quiet way is doing rather well at present – six girls are in the county lacrosse under-15s, plus four in the seniors, and one is going for trials to represent the West of England. The games pitches are in constant use, with periods timetabled throughout the day,

which gives a nice feeling of variety. Tennis courts are in constant use, with coaches, and there is a Sports Hall which would be the envy of many bigger schools.

Art is outstanding. Particularly impressive, and again, most unusual, is the Art department's success in fostering totally different styles – from stylised draughtsmanship to embryonic post-modernism. Pottery is also good. The Art room is constantly open – the school feels it is therapeutic to be able to come and potter (or artter) in spare moments (the young must have someone to supervise, but usually there is someone about).

B ACKGROUND AND ATMOSPHERE: Founded by educationalist Miss Eleanor Beatrice Wyatt in London (in what is now Queen's Gate School – note Heathfield House names 'Queen's' and 'Gate') in the last century, and moved in 1899 to this elegant Georgian house in a most pleasant green site surrounded by rhododendrons (the school runs round and through them on what is known as the 'rhodie run'). Behind the rhodies is a busy road, and not far off, Ascot race course. The original house now has any number of additions, but the whole is still pleasant, and the overall impression is one of light, with windows everywhere. Bedrooms are charming – with flower names (Buttercup etc) for the younger pupils, and literary giants for the older girls. It feels very uninstitutional. All this could get ritzier as Nina Campbell is a governor. Younger children are in the Georgian house (above the library, where their leaps from bunk to floor can be heard by passing staff . . .)

The school operates a system of making the Lower Sixth prefects responsible for 'running' the school, so that in the Upper Sixth they shed their community responsibilities along with their uniform and migrate to a modern brick, self-contained Sixth Form house.

The chapel is still very much at the centre of the school, as decreed by Miss Wyatt, and the school motto 'the heart of one is the honour of all' with it, along with a slightly more dubious little motto attached to a particular school prize – 'Power with control' ('they meant self control, of course', says Mrs Benammar).

We think the important thing to realise about this school is that all the girls are boarders (there are no exceptions to this), and the difference in atmosphere between this and a day/boarding mix is very noticeable. The staff room provides desks as well as work and filing space for all members of staff, plus some of the part-timers, though as elsewhere the school does struggle to keep enough staff on the premises at weekends. Exeats are kept to one on each side of half term – from Friday afternoon to Sunday evenings, plus two Saturdays or Sundays out. The distinguishing mark of the Heathfieldian is the huge number of badges for games, etc pinned on their navy sweaters – some end up looking like Chelsea pensioners on Remembrance Sunday.

PASTORAL CARE AND DISCIPLINE: Has its moments of excitement, but behaviour generally is good and responsible. Each pupil has a tutor for both academic and personal matters.

PUPILS AND PARENTS: Well-mannered charming girls, many from London and roundabout, also ex-pats and one or two bilinguals. As ever, a nice place for making friends.

ENTRANCE: The school does its own selective test in November for the following September. Entrance at 11+, 12+ and 13+. Girls come from London preps such as Norland Place and Garden House, also a clutch from Godstowe. Also entry at Sixth Form.

EXIT: Precise paths for '94/'95 not given, but the school magazine lists an interesting collection of 'destinations' over the past 12 years – including many to art colleges, one to Cambridge, four to Oxford, a chunk to Oxford Brookes, London, Newcastle, Manchester, Edinburgh, University of the West of England (Bristol ex-poly), large numbers to the USA (activity unspecified).

MONEY MATTERS: Fees are large for a girls' boarding school – well over £4,000 a term, but for this you get very good value (we cannot see how the Sixth Form can even break even), and the school does amazingly well, given the small numbers. The school operates a flexible scholarship scheme – for academic, for music, and would-be scholars are also invited to bring art portfolios. Around 5% of fee income goes on scholarships, and the school also has the capacity to 'carry' an existing parent in a case of hardship.

REMARKS: This is a super little establishment, offering, particularly at Sixth Form, the staff and flexibility of a crammer, with the pastoral care and sense of community of a school – a place where you get the best of both these worlds. Tomboys and tough academics may still find the place does not offer enough peer group competition.

The Henrietta Barnett School

Hampstead Garden Suburb,
London NW11 7BN
Tel: 0181 458 8999, Fax: 0181 455 8900
PUPILS: 665 girls
ALL DAY

AGES: 11–18
SIZE OF SIXTH FORM: 200
NON-DENOM
VOLUNTARY-AIDED GRAMMAR
SCHOOL
STATE

HEAD: Since 1989, Mrs Jane de Sweit MA (Cantab) (early fifties). Classicist. Formerly taught Classics at City of London School for Girls. Daunting, uncompromising, not a person to suffer fools gladly. An efficient administrator, extremely supportive of her staff. Adamant that this is no middle-class sanctuary. The ideals of the redoubtable Henrietta Barnett, who founded the school as part of her overall vision for Hampstead Garden Suburb, are alive and well.

ACADEMIC MATTERS: Formidable, with better GCSE results than the eight fee-paying schools in the area, and excellent A-levels too. Has very large classes, 31 pupils up to GCSE, cramped into sardine-tin space. The budget is extremely tight due to highly experienced (i.e. higher-income) staff – a Catch-22 situation, leaving the Head without the financial leeway to appoint additional teachers to relieve pressure (the right decision in the light of recent research). Teaching is remarkably strong right across the board.

One of the few state schools to offer Greek at GCSE and A-level, and all pupils study French, German and Latin. Science, now taught as a Dual Award to GCSE, has increased interest in the subject, with lots of girls heading towards medicine. Biology, Economics, French and Latin are particularly strong at A-level.

GAMES, OPTIONS, THE ARTS: Though sporting options have much improved since the appointment of the current Head, sport is still relatively modest (the Head doesn't agree). Karate, canoeing, sailing, squash as well as the usual girls' options. Possibly not enough use is made of the capital's art galleries, theatres, debating forums, etc.

BACKGROUND AND ATMOSPHERE: Safe, and secure; 'pressure from within to do well'. The elegant exterior building is a fine example of Lutyens, with Bigwood House (which has a friendly feel) for the 11–13-year-olds, facing the main school across a pleasant green square. The main school is rather forbidding (but mercifully rescued from terminal gloom by light streaming through beautifully proportioned windows). Redecoration work inside – desperately needed – has taken place, 'at last.'

Overstretched teachers work under extremely difficult conditions – short of space, and books – and still manage to do an outstanding job. 'They are amazing,' said one former pupil, 'better than my university teachers'. A recent injection of £13,000 via the PTA has enabled the library to be updated (cries of hurrah!), and a librarian was appointed (1994). Computers are far more in evidence since we last went to press.

PASTORAL CARE AND DISCIPLINE: Excellent pastoral care is overseen by one of the Deputy Heads. Personal, Social and Health Education for all is now well established.

PUPILS AND PARENTS: The usual multi-cultural city mix. Only a minority of parents could have afforded to pay for a private academic education. 'Most would not have the opportunity of an academic education if they didn't come here,' said a father. Girls are modest, unassuming – and very aware of their good fortune.

ENTRANCE: By exam and interview. Ferociously competitive. Up to 1,500 attend Open Days and applicants for admission are not far short of the 1,000 mark. The school is looking for innate intelligence and potential – 'sparky intelligence shines out' according to the Head. She is emphatic that parents do their children no favours in opting for cramming: 'You can always spot it.'

EXIT: A few girls leave post GCSE – and some return again after discovering that the grass at Sixth Form Colleges is not so green. Virtually all go on to higher education – to top universities, occasionally to ex-polys.

MONEY MATTERS: Voluntary-aided, state grammar. The Department of Education and the Borough of Barnet 'really have no excuse to starve the school – which doubles as an Evening Institute – of funds and overpack the classrooms,' commented a parent. A field centre near Shaftesbury is maintained with parental help.

REMARKS: Undoubtedly one of the top state schools in the country: a tightly organised academic girls school, but with little attention paid to expanding the pupils' social horizons (and sometimes making for difficulties in adjusting to post-school life).

Highgate School

Highgate, London N6 4AY
Tel: 0181 340 1524, Fax: 0181 340 7674

PUPILS: Around 600 boys (in senior school; junior school – see separate entry)
ALL DAY
AGES: 13–18

SIZE OF SIXTH FORM: 200
C OF E
FEE-PAYING

HEAD: Since 1989, Mr Richard Kennedy, MA (forties). Educated at Charterhouse and read Maths and Philosophy at New College, Oxford; taught at Shrewsbury, Westminster and was Deputy Head of Bishop's Stortford. Enthusiastic, ambitious; represented GB at athletics, and a musician (sings with the Academy of St Martin-in-the-Fields). One of the few Heads whose wife (a very high-powered civil engineer, awarded the OBE in 1995) has her separate entry in *Who's Who*. Two young sons both in the junior school. Comments: 'We've got a big job to do here and I'm pleased with the progress we are making.' Governor of Wycombe Abbey.

ACADEMIC MATTERS: Can attract top-quality staff by dint of offering super des. res. accommodation, e.g. 170 people applied for the Deputy Head's post (sensitive subject this, though, as not all get this perk). Academically good all round, and results excellent given the broad intake (59.6% A–B grades, at A-level, and 81.5% A–C grades at A-level – their record – in '95). The school can – and does – cope with the bright who flourish here, 'Though we would really prefer our son to have more competition,' said the ambitious father of one high-flier, the average, the screwballs and the slower learners too. Some remedial help is offered. 'Maximise potential' is one of the Head's favourite phrases. Maths and Science (Physics especially) are traditionally the strongest departments; Economics good. Dual Award Science at GCSE. Good General Studies at Sixth Form. Average class size 25 at lower end of school, dropping to around 8 at A-level. Complaints about lack of careers advice now sorted.

GAMES, OPTIONS, THE ARTS: The school has a strong games reputation – often national champions at Eton fives – 18 fives courts, is this a school record? Keen cricket, with a master class in '95 from Sir Garfield Sobers. Successful athletics; splendid Sports Centre. Also strong Music: Channing girls collaborate sometimes, also on the Drama front, another lively area. Lunch-time activities include a large number of societies (environmental, conjurors, Jewish Circle), also an urban survival course for older boys (how to fill in tax forms, use a launderette), CCF, D of E; Field Centre in Snowdonia. Has an impressive list of visiting speakers, among them recently, Sir Ron Dearing, Jancis Robinson and old boy Jonathan Hill, former political secretary to the Prime Minister. Good track record of raising money for charities.

BACKGROUND AND ATMOSPHERE: Founded 1565. On a fine site between Highgate and Kenwood, buildings are spread over generous acreage and cover many architectural dates and a hotchpotch of styles – with surprising and pleasing patches of greenery and space. The main block is on the main thoroughfare and across the road (via subterranean passage) is another teaching block with an astonishing view over London. In a lovely setting, up above the fumes – one of the school's trump cards. Weekly boarding is now a thing of the past.

PASTORAL CARE AND DISCIPLINE: Quite a caring school. House masters visit boys' homes before they come. The House system is arranged by geography, e.g. Westgate for boys whose families live west of the school. Houses are vertically streamed like boarding schools, and the 'pastoral person' is the Housemaster. There are also Sixth Form tutors who know all there is to be known on getting on to the next stage.

Hit the headlines in 1995 when a group of computer freak boys fraudulently used credit cards, (parents became suspicious when boys turned up with super equipment and expensive clothes), having sussed out how to do this via the Internet.

PUPILS AND PARENTS: Very popular locally (though ambitious parents will still opt for Westminster), and, increasingly, from further afield. Strong on ethnic minorities – cheerful mix of class and culture – everything from sons of city gents to corner shop owners. The distinguished list of Old Boys includes John Tavener, Anthony Crosland, John Rutter, Clive Sinclair, Patrick Procktor, Barry Norman.

ENTRANCE: Via junior school (see separate entry), thereby virtually gaining a guaranteed place, or by entry tests and CE – about 70 from each; the lowest hurdle at 13+ then rising.

EXIT: Most to higher education of some sort. In the last 5 years, 44 to Oxbridge.

MONEY MATTERS: There are 5 Assisted Places at age 11, 1 in Sixth Form.

REMARKS: A London day school with good facilities and plenty of 'buzz', in super surroundings, doing well and giving other North London day schools a run for their money. Good reports continue to reach us.

The High School of Glasgow

637 Crow Road, Glasgow G13 1PL
Tel: 0141 954 9628, Fax: 0141 959 0191

PUPILS: Around 620 (boys and girls
50/50); plus own junior school (qv)
ALL DAY
AGE: 10–18
SIZE OF SIXTH FORM: 172
NON-DENOM
FEE-PAYING

HEAD: Rector, since 1983, Mr Robin Easton OBE, MA (fifties), educated at Kelvinside Academy, Sedbergh and Christ's, Cambridge. A linguist, became Head of Modern Languages at George Watson's. A quietly confident Head, who wants to turn out 'all-rounders' who leave to become 'responsible well-adjusted citizens with a caring attitude to others'. The Rector thinks that the school is 'a happy school, where children feel at home, in a Christian (with not so small a 'c') background where they can learn concern for others'. Although pleased with the academic standards, he does not see the school as a 'hothouse'. Still teaches – 'well, supply teaching in the Modern Languages department'; and has 'no thoughts on changing the size of the school'.

ACADEMIC MATTERS: The school teaches the Scottish system exclusively. For bright children: 100% (in '95) achieved Grades 1–3 at Standard. 18 subjects on offer at Highers, with 'crash' Spanish and Accounting courses available in Sixth Form. Modern studies (Politics, Economics, Modern History and Geography) taken at either Higher or CSYS; Management and Information Studies,

Economics, English, French, German, Latin. Very keen on Sciences (taught separately); the greenhouse attached to the Biology lab had a good selection of geraniums. Limited learning support provided; first few years only and linked with junior school. Scotvec modules available in everything (shortly to be assessed as Highers when several are put together). Keyboarding skills are popular. Has vied with Hutchesons' Grammar School for first place in the West of Scotland league tables in recent years. There are videos and computers everywhere. Max size class 26, with 20 for practical subjects.

GAMES, OPTIONS, THE ARTS: The school is surrounded by 23 acres of games fields and car parks. Masses of county players (Alison Sheppard FP, Olympic swimmer), lots of representatives on West of Scotland rugby but no recent caps. Girls are good at 'no touch' rugby, and shine at hockey – Scottish champions at outdoor and indoor hockey in '94, and indoor champions in '95 too. The four badminton court-sized Games Hall is much used. The PE module is in great demand, also survival cooking.

D of E awards, and excellent debating: winners of the Cambridge Union Society/*Financial Times* Schools debating competition in '95 – and the first ever Scottish school to win this. Fantastic Media Studies. The Art department is flourishing, and the school has a dynamic Director of Music. Choirs tour Holland, and sing at Glasgow Cathedral and Paisley Abbey. The school makes much use of Glasgow cultural activities.

BACKGROUND AND ATMOSPHERE: Founded as The Grammar School of Glasgow in 1124, the school was closely associated with Glasgow Cathedral, but, despite (because of?) its high academic standing, was closed by Glasgow Corporation in 1976. An appeal launched by the High School Former Pupil Club funded the new purpose-built senior school on the sports ground at Anniesland Cross, already owned by the FPs, following a merger with Drewsteignton school in Bearsden three miles away, now the junior school.

Purpose-built between 1977 and over the years, latterly in 1995, with round courtyards, and a buttercup yellow walkway: there is a new Science block and expanded Art room with kiln. The square split-level Assembly Hall doubles as a dining area with pop-up tables and stools.

There is a purposeful air about the school, with wide corridors (full of bags: lockers are too narrow for pupils' clutter) whose walls are covered with noticeboards. Each house has a designated area within the main building.

PASTORAL CARE AND DISCIPLINE: The school has a highly defined house system with colours (but not names) carrying on from junior school: siblings follow siblings and FPs into same house, with house tutors. The 'Transitus' (10-year-old) pupils are lovingly tended with lots of back-up from junior school (particularly with learning support).

The Rector has enormous parental support, and says that he is 'not complacent, but no problems'. Drugs case in '95. Suspensions for bullying, misbehaving at Railway Station. Otherwise punishments range through sanctions, lunch-time detentions, clearing up the school (Black Bags) to school detention after school on Fridays.

PUPILS AND PARENTS: Ambitious, strong work ethos: almost half come from Bearsden and Milngavie and the remainder from different parts of Glasgow and outlying towns and villages within a radius of about 30 miles. Pupils can and do drive to school – there is a large pupil car park. The geographic jump from the centre of Glasgow changed the bias of the school which now has few Asians or Jewish pupils (there is no synagogue in the West End), and raised the school's status amongst the upper middle class. But there is still a large element of first-time buyers.

ENTRANCE: 10 and 11. Automatic (with exceptions as noted before) from junior school (qv), otherwise three times oversubscribed. There are 60 applicants for 20 places at Transitus and 75 applicants for 24 places at first year. One or two vacancies in most year groups. Own exam. Small quantity after Standard grades, but 'not many, not really looking for customers'.

EXIT: A tiny dribble to traditional Scottish public schools, otherwise over 90% to degree courses, with around one-quarter going to Glasgow University, large contingents also to Strathclyde, Edinburgh and St Andrews. The rest are scattered widely, with a regular handful to Oxbridge (five in 1995).

Pupils are occasionally sponsored by some firm and may spend a gap year (if any) working for that firm. Law and medicine are favourite careers, followed by business studies and accountancy.

MONEY MATTERS: 'Always some bad debts', which school makes 'provisions for'; not a major worry, but there are a few chancers. The school is sympathetic to genuine problems. There are 2 academic scholarships a year, and about 40 bursaries awarded on a financial need basis; plus over 50 Assisted Places.

REMARKS: A remarkable success story – a High School truly worthy of its name.

Holland Park School

Airlie Gardens, Campden Hill Road,
London W8 7AF
Tel: 0171 727 5631, Fax: 0171 243 0176

PUPILS: Around 1,500 boys and girls
ALL DAY
AGES: 11–18
SIZE OF SIXTH FORM: Around 300
NON-DENOM
STATE

HEAD: Since 1995, Mrs Mary Marsh MA (fifties), educated Birkenhead High and Nottingham University; diploma in education from Hatfield Poly, MBA at the London Business School. Has wide experience teaching in state and fee-paying schools, day and boarding; most recently Head of Queen's School, Bushey. Also widely experienced on educational committees and think-tanks. Married with four sons. High powered and very respected. Approachable, confident and energetic. She is pumping energy and spark into the place, and is known to be a woman with high expectations.

REMARKS: An extremely bouncy London state school which should be excellent, given its huge budget, support and its geographical location in prime Holland Park – but has not been. The school has had a very high truancy rate in the past . . .
    GCSE and A-level results have dramatically improved (they could hardly have been worse) over the last few years, and are now above the national average. The Head stoutly claims, 'This is a school that is definitely on its way up – and that is certainly one of the reasons why I chose to come here.' She also adds a caveat about private schools playing the league tables: 'If pupils are accepted to do a course here, they can take the exam.'

Howell's School

Denbigh, Clwyd,
North Wales LL16 3EN
Tel: 01745 813631, Fax: 01745 814443

PUPILS: 300 (109 boarding, the rest day)
AGES: 11–18 (also junior school from 3–11, 85)
SIZE OF SIXTH FORM: 64
'BROAD ANGLICAN TRADITION'
FEE-PAYING

HEAD: Since 1991, Mrs Mary Steel, BA (forties). Educated Ogmore County Grammar School and University College, Cardiff – read French and German. Previous post Deputy Head of St Margaret's, Bushey. Loves walking on the Isle of Mull in spare time. Jolly, bouncy and good-humoured.

ACADEMIC MATTERS: The school has a staff:pupil ratio of approximately 1:9. Good wide GCSE curriculum, with very good results. The best A-level results in '95 were in Biology (9 A grades out of 13), English (8 A grades out of 13), Chemistry (7 A grades out of 13). Photography and Art and Design do well every year. There is a small following for Welsh as a second language at GCSE.

GAMES, OPTIONS, THE ARTS: The school has excellent sports facilities including a Sports Hall and much needed all-weather pitch, and excellent sports staff. Games include hockey, lacrosse. Also has a large heated swimming pool. Hill walking, mountaineering, camping and riding at weekends. D of E awards a natural. There is a super choir, as you would expect – it travels to e.g. Notre-Dame, Paris, and tours Italy.

BACKGROUND AND ATMOSPHERE: In 1540 Thomas Howell bequeathed to the Drapers' Company, one of the twelve great Livery Companies of the City of London, the sum of 12,000 golden ducats. The bequest was originally intended to be used for 'marriage portions for Welsh orphan maidens of his lineage', but in 1852 an enlightened parliament passed an Act which enabled the Drapers' Company to set up two girls' boarding schools – this one, and a sister school at Llandaff, for which the maidens of these places have been truly grateful ever after.

The school is tucked away down a side street in Denbigh – once through the school gates you are confronted by a venerable main building, with lots of space, good facilities, a school hall and a general feeling of plenty of money.

Girls wear a cheerful red uniform. There is a busy, head-down atmosphere, and this school is unpretentious. The wonderful feeling that the great outdoors is on the doorstep – canoes, minibuses, ropes, etc – is constantly in evidence. This is a boarding school but 'we welcome day girls'.

PASTORAL CARE AND DISCIPLINE: A pupil is allocated a tutor for two years in the first year – and sees her every morning (briefly) and every afternoon (also briefly) and for more time every Saturday morning to monitor academic progress and iron out problems. No smoking is allowed, no drinking – 'no nothing'.

PUPILS AND PARENTS: Mostly from the surrounding area (the school has a huge catchment, and runs three buses daily – from Colwyn Bay, Mold and the Rhyl), some from overseas, and Forces. Exeat coaches to the Wirral (many pupils

are from this area), plus escorts to London and Manchester. Regarded by locals as being a bit toffee-nosed.

ENTRANCE: Registration and school's own exam (in January) at 11+, 12+, 13+ and 14+. Entrance to Sixth Form, with 5 GCSEs at A–C.

EXIT: Mostly to universities outside Wales, including London, Newcastle, Leeds, 2 to Oxford in '95. Some go on to art courses.

MONEY MATTERS: The school has a rich number of scholarships and bursaries, including Drapers' Company boarding scholarships, Assisted Places (10 a year at 11+; 5 to the Sixth Form), orphan foundationer awards (preferably Welsh), foundation scholarships in Music, Speech and Drama, Sports. Also Sixth Form scholarships.

REMARKS: This is a strong well-funded girls' boarding school doing a good job. It is well worth a long drive to get to.

James Allen's Girls' School (JAGS)

East Dulwich Grove, London SE22 8TE
Tel: 0181 693 1181, Fax: 0181 693 7842
PUPILS: Around 750, plus junior school (JAPS) qv
ALL DAY.
AGES: 11–18
SIZE OF SIXTH FORM: Approx 205
C OF E FOUNDATION but all are welcome
FEE-PAYING

HEAD: Since 1994, Mrs Marion Gibbs BA MLitt (forties). Read Classics at

Bristol University, where she also did her PGCE and part-time research. Previous post – HMI inspector. Previously taught in both private and state schools, including Burgess Hill, and at Haberdashers' Aske's School for Girls, Elstree. Very keen classicist, has been examiner in the subject, author of books and articles (under the name Baldock). Married for second time, no children. Direct, lively lady and good at roping in parents. Very keen on 'shaking off the inaccurate image of JAGS as a hard and uncaring school.'

ACADEMIC MATTERS: Perennially strong, though perhaps not quite as daunting as pressure on places at the bottom of school would lead you to suppose. Very good A-level results, and best ever in '95 – particularly strong English, Maths, Biology, History. Overall 46% A grade at A-level. GCSEs also show impressive results.

All girls do Latin, though not necessarily to exam standard (but NB in '95 out of 32 pupils taking Latin at GCSE, 27 got grade A, 5 grade B). Modern Languages are particularly strong: provision is made for advanced children coming in from hotshot preps (including their own) to steam ahead – they are then encouraged to do German for two years while the rest catch up. Two Modern Languages for all (German, Italian, Russian and Spanish as well as French, also Japanese) and girls must continue to do one in the Sixth Form. Setted for languages, Maths, Science. Dual Award or all three separate sciences at GCSE.

There is a wide programme of General Studies – including an introduction to the wonderful Dulwich Picture Gallery. General Studies programme held in conjunction with Dulwich College at Upper Sixth level. An impressive new careers centre enlists the services of the Cambridge Occupational Analysts, and includes a computer data bank.

GAMES, OPTIONS, THE ARTS: Set in 22 acres, with good playing fields and a sense of space, with a heated indoor swimming pool, and a Sports Hall. Traditional games are compulsory for the first two years, and a range of sports is played in all years. PE is an option at GCSE. Self-defence classes are now compulsory in Year 10. The school has an excellent Art department. Music is under Rupert Bond, founder of the Docklands Sinfonietta, and conductor of London Blackheath Sinfonia (Holst taught and composed here for ages). Drama is intensely keen – the small but inspiring theatre is modelled on the Cottesloe. The school also has a good Design and Technology Department.

Lots of excursions and Outward Bound-ish expeditions, also foreign exchanges. Large number of clubs – chess, computers, debating, etc – which wax and wane depending a bit on the enthusiasm of girls/staff in the school at the time.

BACKGROUND AND ATMOSPHERE: The school was founded in 1741 in 'two hired rooms at the Bricklayer's Arms' – a symbolic beginning. One of the three schools of the Foundation of Alleyn's College of God's Gift at Dulwich, named after James Allen, warden in 1712 of Dulwich College and described as 'Six Feet High, Skilful as a Skaiter; a Jumper; Athletic and Humane' – not a bad role model. The school became girls only and moved to its present 22-acre site in leafy Dulwich in 1886 following an Act of Parliament passed to reorganise the Foundation. It has famous Botany Gardens planted by Lillian Clarke (a pioneer ecologist at the beginning of the century).

Ths school bounces with energy and pride – much stronger than the rather dour façade which greets the visitor on arrival suggests. The new Head has brightened and lightened and generally improved parts of the school, especially the bit you first walk in to, 'to make it more welcoming,' – and is itching to do more.

PASTORAL CARE AND DISCIPLINE: Prefects are elected by the girls. There are regular meetings between the Head and girls to discuss problems/complaints. The most usual punishment is detention (parents are warned in advance). The form teacher is the first port of call, then Heads of section.

PUPILS AND PARENTS: Mostly from south of the river, and as far away as Bromley – all those lucky enough to win a place. There is a wide social mix, articulate, ambitious but unpretentious. Middle classes predominate. OGs are Anita Brookner and Lisa de St Aubyn Terain.

ENTRANCE: About a quarter from their own excellent junior school (on the same site – see separate entry) though all must pass the exam held in January for a place in September. Nearly 50% from state sector. Children come in from three hundred 'feeder' schools. It is constantly oversubscribed and there is hot competition to get in. 'Mental liveliness' is considered an essential ingredient, as well as academic ability. Interview takes place before exam, in an attempt to weed out over-cooked (academically speaking) girls. Also Sixth Form entry.

EXIT: Around a dozen leave post-GCSE – but far larger numbers apply at Sixth Form. 95% to higher education, 12–15 to Oxbridge (a relatively small number for the size and strength of school). Bristol, Nottingham, Edinburgh, and Manchester are popular. Several to art colleges and drama school. Medicine is popular, so is History. Around one third take a 'gap' year.

MONEY MATTERS: Well endowed – has a fixed per capita annual grant from the College Estates (of which most goes towards scholarships, including a bursary element where necessary). There are 20 Assisted Places for 11-year-old entrants; 6 at 13 and 5 for Sixth Form entrants. Up to 20 scholarships per year are offered by the school at 11+, including 1 for music – major scholarships of 50% of fees, minor ones of 30%. In case of need, these scholarships may be increased to 90% and 70%. 1 scholarship is offered for Sixth Form entrants.

REMARKS: A very strong all round girls' day school. Well worth bustling about to get in.

The Judd School

Brook Street, Tonbridge,
Kent TN9 2PN
Tel: 01732 770880, Fax: 01732 771661
PUPILS: 818 boys
ALL DAY
AGES: 11–18
SIZE OF SIXTH FORM: 228 (including a few girls)
C OF E
STATE

HEAD: Since 1986, Mr K A Starling, MA (Cantab) (late forties). A geographer whose teaching experience includes high-profile private and state boarding schools. Considers this to be 'the happiest school I've been in. Boys naturally want to learn.' Relaxed, and at ease with running the establishment, in spite of crowding, bureaucratic overload and a tight-fisted council.

ACADEMIC MATTERS: Good, solid results, with few A-level failures and minuscule Sixth Form fallout. Came high up in state school league tables in '95 (about eleventh nationwide). Slightly stronger in Arts subjects, with 17 out of 20 candidates getting A in English A-level ('95), plus 2 Bs, 1 C. Mathematics are strong, with the top two sets taking the subject at GCSE a year early, and some taking AS-level Maths in Year 11. All pupils sit 10 GCSEs including three Science subjects. Particularly strong results given the class size of 30.

GAMES, OPTIONS, THE ARTS: Sporty and competitive; blessed with three rugby pitches literally on the doorstep (with bi-annual tours of Canada/USA), an open-air pool much used in summer, a cricket pitch plus two all-weather pitches.

Music is strong and vigorous, now inspired by the recently opened Music Centre, with the senior orchestra (one of three) interpreting ambitious works, and the Choral Union performing ambitiously e.g. Brahms' German Requiem. Jazz and Brass groups are active and the bands have groovy names. Several pupils are in regional youth orchestras and bands, and there is usually one in the National Youth Orchestra.

In other areas, there is a fairly traditional mix of options. D of E awards, CCF, voluntary service, debating, drama and plenty of outings and club activities.

BACKGROUND AND ATMOSPHERE: A late-Victorian building in a suburban setting on the edge of Tonbridge, bursting at the seams. Hard to disguise its institutional atmosphere, with cramped, dark classrooms looking much the same as they might have done nearly a hundred years ago, and brown-tiled corridors doing nothing to dispel the gloom, though fresh paint has lightened all this. But outside the main building all is redeemed by a splendid £2-million classroom and Technology block, new Science labs and an airy Art studio: two

fine buildings that have helped greatly to reduce the claustrophobic (we think – this is hotly denied by the school) atmosphere and the pressure on space. Recent decoration also helps.

PASTORAL CARE AND DISCIPLINE: Well in place.

PUPILS AND PARENTS: Well-behaved motivated sons of Tonbridge, Tunbridge Wells and the Kent Weald.

ENTRANCE: Always oversubscribed. Via Kent selection procedure, effectively the 11+. Normally limited to the top 15–20% of the ability range. Catchment area of west Kent includes Tunbridge Wells, Tonbridge, Sevenoaks and the pleasant rural villages of the Weald of Kent. A few 'Governors' places' are reserved for those living outside the catchment area, and a few girls enter at Sixth Form. Not at all affected by the increase in day places at Tonbridge School: pressure, they say, is the other way round.

EXIT: Well over 90% to university, with the Governors awarding one major scholarship and up to four leaving exhibitions. Around 10% a year to Oxbridge.

MONEY MATTERS: In the last century the sensible burghers of Tonbridge, finding the fees for Tonbridge School beyond their reach, requested that the Skinners' Company provide affordable academic schooling for their offspring. The Company obliged, opening The Judd in 1888.

Doubtless the inhabitants of Tonbridge continue to be relieved that their children can enjoy state-funded academic education. They, and Old Juddians, show their gratitude by contributing most generously to the much-needed building funds required as a Voluntary Aided school.

REMARKS: A successful well-run, traditional boys' grammar school which deserves its strong reputation and the high regard in which it is held.

Kilgraston School

Bridge of Earn, Perthshire PH2 9BQ
Tel: 01738 812257, Fax: 01738 813410

PUPILS: Around 173 girls (115 board, including 60 weekly boarders; the rest day). Plus junior school with 47 girls and some boys, ages 5–11 (including 15 boarders).
AGES: 11–18
SIZE OF SIXTH FORM: 63
RC but inter-denom as well
FEE-PAYING

HEAD: Since April 1993, Mrs J L Austin, BA (Hons) (fifties), educated at Downe House and studied English Lang and Lit, Old Icelandic and Medieval Latin at Birmingham University. Taught at Birmingham primary schools, also Downe House and elsewhere. Roman Catholic, married to a trouble-shooting hospital management consultant; one grown-up daughter. Lives in a new house built in the grounds. She is the first Lay Head of Kilgraston. Nuns are enormously supportive of the changeover, and still lend a hand. A shy, thoughtful Head, who has made many changes since her arrival.

ACADEMIC MATTERS: Not the sleepy place it used to be. Run primarily on the Scottish system, SCE standard grade followed by Highers to university the following year, but A-levels are on offer (9 subjects; a small take-up) or Scotvec modules in Upper Sixth. Piloting Scotvec clusters (four modules equals one cluster). English and History, also Maths do well, but pupils are of mixed ability and are set for Maths, French, Latin and (Middle School upwards) for Sciences (three on offer). There are French and German exchanges (pupils and staff) every year (via the Sacred Heart network). EFL is also on offer. Class sizes 8–20. Sixth Year Studies under review. The school has a remedial Unit, with a specialist teacher and special needs catered for. Computers are everywhere, and two computer rooms.

Parents report that pupils taking extra subjects must pay extra money.

GAMES, OPTIONS, THE ARTS: There are 4 PE periods per week, as the school is run on a day-school timetable. The magnificent new Sports Hall is faced in sandstone, and echoes the niches in the stable building (well converted into the junior school with attached nursery) – historic Scotland at its best. There are 9 Astroturf tennis courts; swimming (in Perth) is timetabled and optional before breakfast (6.45 a.m. start), as is the early morning run. A wide choice of other sports is available. Strong Drama, and a magical Art department overlooking the rotunda. An inspired conversion of attics to a Music centre (with keyboards and individual study rooms, guitars and stringed instruments everywhere) means Music is 'on the up', with excellent singing. D of E, debating, leadership courses. Cooking and brilliant needlework.

BACKGROUND AND ATMOSPHERE: Founded in 1920 and one of 200 networked schools and colleges of the Society of the Sacred Heart. Moved to the handsome red sandstone house, after Robert Adam and with masses of additions. Barat wing, light and airy buildings. There is lots of room for expansion, and preparatory work has already been done. New Language labs opened last year.

There are huge wide passages everywhere, a Sixth Form common room, and bed-sits from third year. Dormitories for the youngest are a trifle austere. The uniform is up for change. School stops at 4.10 p.m. on Fridays for day and weekly boarders, but there are masses of alternative activities for those who stay back – there are the usual moans about 'not enough to do', but this appears to be on an individual basis. Computers and sewing machines open throughout. Boyfriends can and do visit at weekends, and there are lots of discos, etc, with Strathallan, Glenalmond, and Queen Victoria's (the military school – better at Scottish Country dancing).

PASTORAL CARE AND DISCIPLINE: The Sacred Heart ethos prevails and staff are enormously caring, but children are not perceived as 'streetwise'. There is a Disciplinary Committee, gatings, and detentions if too many – *NOTES* (Sacred Heart again) for bad marks, then gated and a letter sent home. 'Will ask girl to leave if necessary'. Weekly boarding is championed by local parents. The school can arrange Guardians.

PUPILS AND PARENTS: Day children from all over Fife and Perthshire; a Stage Coach drops and collects from the school front door. Boarders from all over Scotland, and also Old Girls' children. Toffs' daughters. Academically pushy parents may move their children elsewhere, but the school breeds loyalty among those who value 'other things'. Currently there are only 12 foreigners.

ENTRANCE: Exam (not that difficult) – which also serves as a scholarship paper – even from its own junior school,

otherwise 11+ from primary schools, and 12+ from prep schools, or whenever (even at half-term if room is available).

EXIT: 90% to university last year (including one to Oxford in '95). Very occasional departure for Sixth Form in boys' schools; some leave after Highers.

MONEY MATTERS: A rich school though not as rich as all that. There are 50 Assisted Places and waiting lists. Also up to 10 Academic, Art and Music scholarships available at Lower and Upper Fourth, Lower Fifth and both Sixth Form years. Almost one-third receive assistance.

REMARKS: A very small, gentle, caring school, with terrific facilities, enormously popular locally, and seen as a viable alternative to St Leonard's for single-sex education in Scotland. No longer just the Catholic cream of Scottish Society. Happy reports.

King Edward VI High School for Girls

Edgbaston Park Road,
Birmingham B15 2UB
Tel: 0121 472 1834, Fax: 0121 471 3808
PUPILS: Around 545 girls
ALL DAY
AGES: 11–18
SIZE OF SIXTH FORM: 160
NON-DENOM
FEE-PAYING

HEAD: From September 1996, Miss Sarah H Evans, BA, MA, educated at King James' Grammar School, Knaresborough and Sussex, Leicester and Leeds

Universities. Previously Head of the Friends' School, Saffron Walden, and before that taught at Leeds Girls' High School also Fulneck Girls' School. Takes over from Miss Ena Evans.

ACADEMIC MATTERS: Outstanding academically for many years, and undoubtedly one of the country's top academic schools, with some outstanding teaching and an ethos of hard work. Excellent across the board. A staggering number of A grades at A-level. Girls are achievers with high expectations. Wide syllabus. Classes of 'mixed ability' (on a very narrow range, however), maximum class size 26. One-third of pupils take A-level Sciences (and must do English), one-third take Arts (and must do Maths for one year of Sixth Form) and one-third is mixed. General Studies is regularly taken as a fourth (rarely third) A-level. Streams of As across the board – for instance, 31 girls got A grade Biology A-level, the other four candidates got B ('95); all 12 Latin A-level candidates got A grades. Brilliant.

Russian, Italian and Spanish are on offer at Sixth Form. The school has a very strong Classics Department, with Ancient History popular. There are eight Science labs, two computer rooms (free access during day), classrooms double as subject rooms, with old-fashioned desks in the main. Some classes are taken with King Edward's School (qv).

'Outsiders sometimes think teaching here must be a soft option,' commented one member of staff, 'because all the girls are bright – but the fact is that a little doesn't go a long way: they lap it up and want more.' Girls are adept arguers and verbalisers and class discussion is encouraged from earliest forms.

Careers advice and work experience are both on offer.

GAMES, OPTIONS, THE ARTS: There is a formidable hockey team, and lots of county representation; netball is also good, as well as tennis, athletics, fencing and basketball. Strong dance group, aerobics. Girls are picked for county squads in several sports, 'They get madly keen.' Sports Hall. Swimming is outstanding, the school has its own pool; boys have their own next door. Girls in Sixth Form must take some type of exercise but team games are not mandatory; golf, archery on offer. Rifle shooting popular. (NB The previous Head was very sympathetic to the non-sporting, and girls are wondering whether this will prevail?)

The 1983 Centenary Art and Design block is filled with marvellous three-dimensional paper sculptures: textiles and tie-dyeing as well as traditional painting and superb ceramics. On offer is cooking and King Edward boys do it too. For proper CDT (plastics and the like) girls use the boys' facilities.

Masses of fund-raising and community service. Theatre Studies are shared, and popular. Drama is very good, and Music outstanding – combined again. Girls bring out the school newspaper, *High Profile*.

BACKGROUND AND ATMOSPHERE: Part of the King Edward Foundation extension scheme (all bursarial work is carried out jointly), founded in 1883; it followed King Edward's School to its present site in 1940. Shares the same architect and the campus is a pleasing blend of red brick plus usual later additions (not always totally in keeping). A Direct Grant school until 1976. Girls wear uniform to Sixth Form, when free rein is given to fashion.

PASTORAL CARE AND DISCIPLINE: Marked discipline. Staff hold a short weekly meeting to discuss concerns, but have 'been very lucky'. Girls have ongoing Pastoral Care and Personal

Decision-making Programme, and can discuss problems with any member of staff, but normally with Form Tutor, Deputy or Head. There is no prefect system, no Head Girl, no Houses. Masses of parental contact. In principle, parents can contact senior staff, the Head or her Deputies 'certainly within the hour' (other schools please note). There are clear rules on smoking: a 'letter home works wonders'.

PUPILS AND PARENTS: Seriously bright children of professional families, middle to lower-middle class. They share the transport system with boys at King Edward's School; girls come from as far away as Lichfield, Bromsgrove, Wolverhampton, Solihull. 'There's not a school in this league for miles, and precious few anywhere,' say parents. Approx 20% ethnic minorities as you might expect – no problems here. Ecumenical outlook.

ENTRANCE: The school's own very selective test is 'designed to test the children not their teachers' (nice one). The majority come from state primaries. Tough entry post-GCSE.

EXIT: Very few post-GCSE, 10–20 to Oxbridge, and the rest to the top range of universities – Bristol, Leeds, Nottingham, London in droves.

MONEY MATTERS: There are 25 Assisted Places at 11, 5 at 16+. Academic scholarships up to the value of 3 full-fees at 11+ (usually about 50% per pupil) plus the equivalent of 1 full-fee scholarship at 16+. The Parents' Association does the odd bit of fund-raising (though is mostly used as a sounding board and for social activities); there is a second-hand shop in the summer term.

REMARKS: As always, emerging as an incredibly strong school and one of the country's top academic girls' schools, now under a new Head.

King Edward's School

Edgbaston Park Road,
Birmingham B15 2UA
Tel: 0121 472 1672, Fax: 0121 414 1897

PUPILS: Around 870 boys
ALL DAY
AGES: 11–18
SIZE OF SIXTH FORM: 250
C OF E
FEE-PAYING

HEAD: Chief Master since 1991, Mr Hugh Wright, MA (Oxon), (fifties) educated at Kingswood School, Bath, read Greats at The Queen's College, keen sportsman (played rugby and rowed for his college). Formerly Head of Gresham's in Norfolk, before that Head of Stockport Grammar School. Wife, Jillian, is diocesan treasurer for the Mother's Union and much more besides. Three grown-up sons. Chairman of HMC in 1995.

Charming and outgoing, a capable and experienced Head, his motto is 'Expectation breeds confidence' and he expects a King Edward's boy to have 'a certain openness, nicely modest and easy to talk to, used to exchanging views'. The Chief Master holds regular year group meetings at lunch time when the boys put up their own agenda.

ACADEMIC MATTERS: Outstanding academically and gets five-star results. New staff have been appointed to cope with the increase in numbers (the school now has five forms in each year block), including a new Head of Computing, and a full-time Librarian (the library has been updated and extended to include a Resources Room).

All departments are strong. There are 25 to a class, fewer for specialist subjects and A-levels. Streamed for Maths after three years, but not otherwise streamed – difficult across such a narrow ability level. These are bright boys, taking heaps of GCSEs and usually take 4 A-levels each (but this includes General Studies). Streams of As across the board: French, Physics, Chemistry and Maths particularly get immensely impressive results at GCSE and A-level (98 out of 130 A★, 17 A grades in Physics GCSE in '95). Another Chemistry lab was added in '95, because so many pupils do the subject and need the space. Arts subjects have a lesser following at A-level by and large. School 'does not teach to exams, but beyond them'. The school has a proper Classics department (40 A★, 22 As out of 79 Latin GCSE candidates in '95), and Satellite and e-mail are used in Language depts. The school has dedicated staff, and wide and capable Common Room.

G AMES, OPTIONS, THE ARTS: Good games: regular county and even international representation; previous under-15 rugby champions, 'not often beaten in the hockey world'; plus basketball, cricket, table tennis, swimming. 'Embarrassingly good,' says the Chief Master. They hire the hockey Astroturf from the University of Birmingham 'over the road', their own is now in the pipeline.

'Music brilliant,' according to parents; a huge number of pupils play instruments, and combine with King Edward VI High School for Girls on the adjacent site; lots of ensembles, etc. Drama is strong, and there are junior and senior workshops;

boys join with girls to put on plays and concerts post-A-level.

CCF is gaining in popularity, Young Enterprise, D of E and lots of community service. Upper school boys do Technology (Cooking) at High School, and Sixth Formers do the odd bit of 'guinea pigging' and research for the university opposite.

B ACKGROUND AND ATMOSPHERE: The school was founded in 1552 by King Edward VI; and is a flagship for the famous King Edward Foundation, which was expanded in late 19th century to include a further six schools. The Chief Master is Head of the Foundation, though each school is autonomous, but often with shared Governors. The Foundation has a think tank for every subject, and provides serious sums 'on a per capita basis' for matters educational including a children's university run here and in local schools on Saturday mornings; and the Lucas Industrial Fellowship, for careers advice amongst the seven schools.

King Edward's moved to its present 32-acre site, which it shares with King Edward VI High, in 1936. Surrounded by Botanic Gardens, the University of Birmingham, lakes and golf course. It feels like deep country, but is only 10 minutes from Birmingham centre. Very Thirties' red-brick and oak buildings with modern additions for Design and Music. Impressive.

P ASTORAL CARE AND DISCIPLINE: Form Tutors, Housemasters, the Chaplain and Heads of Middle and Lower School take up the slack. The Chief Master instigated a Pastoral Review on arrival, but there are no overt problems, or bullying: 'the school does not suffer from big city syndrome'. Takes a strict line on drugs. Personal and Social Education programme throughout the school.

PUPILS AND PARENTS: A complete social mix, just over 30% from ethnic minorities, but there is 'absolutely no social frisson', plus the usual cosmopolitan mix. The Parents' Association mainly social, but does the odd fund-raising. There are lots of first-time buyers. Boys wear their uniforms with pride (and loads of different ties and hair styles!). Bus companies run a school bus service to the campus during term time.

ENTRANCE: A highly competitive exam at 11+ or 13+, at least four for every place. For Sixth Form entry: school exam plus successful GCSE results – difficult and very selective, but a good number come in at this stage.

EXIT: Rare for a boy not to go on to university. 30–40% to Oxbridge, many getting Firsts. London, Nottingham, Durham, Leeds and all the civic universities are popular, reading everything from Medicine to Classics and even Popular Music and Recording (at Salford, if you're wondering). If you get in to the school, you will probably get on. OBs include J R Tolkien, Bill Oddie and Kenneth Tynan.

MONEY MATTERS: Approximately 40% of all boys are on some form of assistance. There are 40 Assisted Places a year, plus academic scholarships to the value of 5 full fees awarded annually (can be spread), plus 3–4 named scholarships in particular subjects. Funds are available for real hardship; no one need leave in exam years.

REMARKS: Flourishing, and remaining up there as one of the country's top academic boys' day schools with consistently strong results year after year, churning out dozens of well-rounded high-fliers. Fantastic.

King Edward's School

North Road, Bath BA2 6HU
Tel: 01225 464313, Fax: 01225 481363
PUPILS: 628 boys, 44 girls in Sixth Form
AGES: 11–18. Plus junior school, 180 boys ages 7–11
SIZE OF SIXTH FORM: 233, all boys except for 44 girls in the Sixth Form
NON DENOM
FEE-PAYING

HEAD: Since 1993, Mr Peter J Winter, MA (Oxon) (forties), educated at Trinity School, Croydon, and Wadham College, Oxford, where he read French. Taught at Latymer Upper and Magdalen College School (Oxford) before going to Sevenoaks School (Head of Modern Languages, then ran the International Centre, the Sixth Form boarding house for boys from 28 different countries with his Ghanaian-born wife). Two young children. A keen all-round sportsman and Francophile. A live wire.

ENTRANCE: At 11, 13, via exam; also at Sixth Form. There are 18 Assisted Places, mainly at 11+ but also at 12 and 13, and two for 16+.

EXIT: 95% go on to degree courses, 10–15 annually to Oxbridge. Art College is a popular exit line. A small but regular number go on to Service careers.

REMARKS: The school is going fully co-ed (entry points for 7-year-olds, and 11-year-olds, and – as before – at Sixth Form), from September 1997, after much discussion, and as we write, is in the throes of working out the details.

This is a strong day school with an increasingly wide catchment area and a distinguished history. Founded as a grammar school in 1552 (Old Boys include Sir Sidney Smith; Arctic navigator and explorer Sir Edward Parry; the founder of Sandhurst, Major General le Marchant), the school moved from the centre of Bath in 1961 (bringing in funds) to an elegant large house on a hill near the edge of the city (with a splendid view of Bath one way, and cows in the field next door), plus many additions, including a Sixties purpose-built block now converted into a fine new theatre. Theatre Studies has just been introduced as an A-level, and the school has a strong dramatic tradition.

Sciences and Maths are both strong subjects. Modern Languages, especially French, do well. However, 1995 results overall at both A-level and GCSE (despite scores of A*s) have slipped slightly. A long-term plan to increase staff is on the move. Work is taken seriously – but there is also a sense of fun. This is not just a school for medium to high-fliers – art is distinctly good, so are sports ('but it is almost possible to get away without doing anything,' confided one pupil), with particularly successful athletics and rugby. Hockey, cricket and soccer are all 'coming on strongly'. The school runs a hockey festival.

An extraordinary bird-watching club (KEOS) takes pupils of all ages all over the world (Poland, Nepal, South Carolina, Yorkshire, Scotland). Pupils from all walks of life are polite and lively. Fees are kept purposely low. The junior school (behind the main school) is well designed with classrooms centred around the open-plan library), and is a hive of purposeful activity.

King's College

Taunton, Somerset TA1 3DX
Tel: 01823 272708, Fax: 01823 334236

PUPILS: Approx 300 boys and 140 girls (250 boys board, 100 girls board – the rest day)
AGES: 13–18 (also separate junior school)
SIZE OF SIXTH FORM: Approx 200
C OF E
FEE-PAYING

HEAD: Since 1988, Mr Simon Funnell, MA (fifties). Read English at Cambridge. Formerly a Housemaster at Shrewsbury, keen on music. Married, three children, likes golf – seriously.

ACADEMIC MATTERS: Some excellent young and not so young staff, particularly in the History and Languages Departments. Sound in mainstream subjects. A-level results are creditable and steady, given the mixed intake, though there are an uncomfortable amount of Ds, Es, Ns and Us in some subjects. The Head comments that 'it is not our policy to withdraw borderline candidates in order to improve A-level statistics'. Pupils do not take General Studies as exam. The Biology department is working with the United Nations to conserve the giant marine turtle in the Mediterranean. Some parents 'wish there was a bit more pressure put on our children to work really hard'. Does War Studies as a general course (not a lot of places do this).

GAMES, OPTIONS, THE ARTS: Plays rugby and cricket with enthusiasm and success; cricket tour to Australia, one pupil in the MCC Schools England side. The boys were under-14 county hockey champions in '95, and the girls are good too. Games are compulsory until age 15. Won Rosslyn Park Sevens Competition in '94. The school has jolly facilities, including wonderful, big, light, inspiring Art Centre (converted from an old day boys' house), spawning pictures all over the school. There is also a purpose-built

CDT centre and video studio. The school produces zestful Drama – it has produced three large scale musicals in the last three years. Music is also active – the choir sings evensong annually at St Paul's Cathedral and St George's Chapel, Windsor. A notable jazz band plays hither and thither and makes CDs (in '95 they won a competition to spend a day recording in a top West Country recording studio). Keen CCF (marines, army and RAF). Good at good works – granny bashing, etc. The school makes ambitious trips, including to Mount Sinai. It has a busy extra-curricular programme.

BACKGROUND AND ATMOSPHERE: One of the Woodard Foundation schools (muscular Christianity). On a pleasant 100-acre site on the edge of Taunton. A beautiful old Gothic chapel has been converted into an indifferent new library. The present chapel is a more humble white-washed affair and quite jolly (look at the portrait of Bishop Fox in the Lady Chapel). Boarding houses are just across the road from the main buildings – like an advanced housing estate, looking on to Astroturf, hockey fields and tennis courts. More than adequate facilities. The Sixth Form have cosy study bedrooms, done up with tender loving care by some (drapes, etc). Recent upgrading and refurbishing of some boarding houses has brought approving noises from pupils and parents. There are two girls' boarding houses.

PASTORAL CARE AND DISCIPLINE: One or two hairy moments, but on the whole good. Prefects are to be allowed into pubs – a cunning ploy, as 'what do we do when we encounter our illegally drinking non-prefect mates?' asks one. A school in which the word 'community' means something.

PUPILS AND PARENTS: This is an easy option for West Country and Welsh families. The social mix is more to the middle side of middle class, with a strongish army and navy element. There are a number of non-nationals in school – the majority from Germany and the Far East. OBs include Geoffrey Rippon and cricketer Roger Twose.

ENTRANCE: Registration and CE. Also entry at Sixth Form for 'suitably qualified' pupils.

EXIT: In '95, 7 to Oxbridge – about par for the course (usually Oxford). Otherwise to universities old and new all over. 91% to higher education at the latest count.

MONEY MATTERS: A generous percentage of fee income goes on scholarships and bursaries, including those for sons of clergy and school-masters. There are also Art and Music scholarships; one or two scholarships at Sixth Form.

REMARKS: Going forward as a good, solidly performing second-division public school, and doing well.

King's College School (KCS)

Wimbledon Common,
London SW19 4TT
Tel: 0181 255 5353, Fax: 0181 255 5359
PUPILS: 700 boys
ALL DAY
AGES: 13–18
SIZE OF SIXTH FORM: 260
C OF E (BUT OTHER FAITHS WELCOME)
FEE-PAYING

HEAD: Since 1980, Mr Robin Reeve MA (fifties), educated at Hampton, read History at Cambridge. Head of History and Director of Studies at Lancing. Serious and unassuming, a vigorous campaigner for academic standards for high-fliers. Due to retire at the end of '97, i.e. staying here through the centenary celebration year (100 years since the school moved from the Strand to this site).

ACADEMIC MATTERS: Strong, strong, strong – and getting stronger. The Head believes firmly in academic discipline and attainment, though he is well aware that narrow success is the besetting sin of London day schools and to this end constantly tries to enrich the boys' academic diet, encouraging the study of subjects 'because they are intrinsically interesting subjects to study rather than because they're going to lead to X'. Streaming from the first year, then setting. Sciences are examined separately (Dual Award is available for the weaker). Ten GCSEs are the norm (some early), but several take as many as 13.

Maths is an outstanding department, also English, 'But every department is good,' commented a parent. French apart, Modern Languages still appear to have minimum A-level appeal. A grades at A-level alone make up 59.3%, A–B = 83.1% – golly! The school has many distinguished members of staff – some of whom stay decades.

GAMES, OPTIONS, THE ARTS: Everything on offer – 'Boys aren't just eggheads,' said a pupil. Get a copy of the school mag – very glossy, black and white bar the fat section on art – and you will get the gist of the breadth of activities.

Rugby, hockey fields, on site (plus 15 more acres at Motspur Park), cross-country on Wimbledon Common, good rowing from the school's boathouse on the Tideway at Putney.

There has been a renaissance of curricular activities since Saturday was abolished (though up to one-third of the boys come in for sports or rehearsals on Saturdays). The school has extremely good Art, and ceramics must be among the best in any school. Music is also very vigorous and so is Drama with what one mother calls 'Surprisingly sophisticated productions' (an ex-Wembley Stadium stage manager was recently appointed to manage Collyer Hall, the school's excellent theatre). Impressive school newspaper. Societies are busy at lunch time and after school. The great and good are drawn in to talk on all manner of topics – in the last year, for instance, the late Jean Muir, Virginia Bottomley, Lord Archer, Lord Reece Mogg.

BACKGROUND AND ATMOSPHERE: A curious hotchpotch of buildings, including a fine collegiate hall, an elegant eighteenth-century house and sundry modern additions with plenty of elbow room, pleasant grounds, a junior school (qv) on site – all nicely set on the edge of the Common, with a pub opposite. The Sixth Form block has a good common room.

The school was originally founded in 1829 in the Strand, as a junior department of King's College, University of London. It is a sombre and busy seat of learning with bustle and purpose. Lively: boys are involved with all sorts of activities other than excelling at exams.

PASTORAL CARE AND DISCIPLINE: There is a big emphasis on responsibility, and a tutor system is firmly in place. Discipline is not a problem, 'the vast majority of boys are well motivated'; no long hair. The school gives parents advice about weekends. Prefects now sent off on leadership training courses (like many others), and regard themselves as junior managers.

PUPILS AND PARENTS: Middle class, largely from south-west London, Kingston and Surrey, with lots of ethnic minorities. Some Sixth Formers drive in. Professional parents; both parents and pupils are mostly 'life's natural hard workers' joked a parent. 'Boys not born with a silver spoon,' commented another, 'but often well aware that they are the intellectual élite.' OBs include vast numbers of university dons, Dante Gabriel Rossetti, Walter Sickert, Roy Plomley.

ENTRANCE: Two-thirds from the school's own wonderful prep (see separate entry), the rest from a wide variety of schools, pre-tested at 11. CE passmark is 65%, 'but boys need spare capacity as well'.

EXIT: Virtually all to university (conservative in their choices), substantial numbers (25+) to Oxbridge. Engineering, the law, the City and medicine continue to be likely careers. A few leave post-GCSE.

MONEY MATTERS: Up to 15 scholarships at 13+ and one at Sixth Form (all up to a maximum of 50% fees). There are 3 Assisted Places at 13+, 5 at 16+; 2 awards for boys showing 'outstanding promise as classical or modern linguists'.

REMARKS: A remarkable boys' day school, thriving on all fronts, without the hothouse high-pressured atmosphere of some academic establishments, helped in this by being situated in a desirable suburb of London. Occasional comments that the school 'is just a bit pleased with itself'.

King's School Bruton

Somerset BA10 OED
Tel: 01749 813326, Fax: 01749 813426

PUPILS: Around 304 boys, 31 girls in Sixth Form (258 board, 77 day)
AGES: 13–18
SIZE OF SIXTH FORM: Around 156
C OF E
FEE-PAYING

HEAD: Since 1993, Mr Richard Smyth, MA, PGCE (forties), educated at Sedbergh and Emmanuel College, Cambridge, where he read Law and History. Taught at Christ's Hospital, worked in the family business, taught at Gresham's, Housemaster at Wellington College. Keen cricketer (Cambridge blue); Swiss wife and three children.

ENTRANCE: Via CE (not a high hurdle), many through the school's own prep.

Junior School: Hazlegrove (Tel: 01963 440 314, at Sparkford, Yeovil, with around 240 boys and girls, and its own pre-prep, Hillcrest, in a glorious setting, housed in Mildmay's family home, surrounded by parkland. Children mainly go on to King's Bruton, but Sherborne is a popular choice, some to Millfield, Marlborough, Queen's Taunton, and widespread.

EXIT: Small post-GCSE leakage (to Sixth Form Colleges usually). After degree/higher education, careers often in estate management, farming, Services, architecture, the law.

REMARKS: A small, traditional, competent and efficient school – a good place to be a big fish in a small pond, with a broad intake. Thorough teaching (there are many staff of long standing), and very good facilities, with new Physics and Computer departments. Business Studies is now on option for A-level and proving popular. The exceptional Design Centre (for Art, Technology and IT) produces some exciting work, and good art. Pupils are kept busy, though the pace is fairly gentle, with three weekly reports, a record of achievement, regular church services and assemblies, and games three days a week, Saturdays included (there are major sports tours every few years). Serious sports (reports take up a huge chunk of the school magazine), and notably successful at hockey, rugby and tennis.

The school has a caring environment, with a good pastoral set-up and plenty of links with other local schools (Sexey's, Bruton Girls). Numbers have substantially increased (popular with Forces, and girls have doubled) since we last went to press and are healthy, with a record number in the Sixth Form. Results are respectable, steady and rising; the vast majority go on to degree courses (declining numbers opt for a gap year first).

This is certainly a school to consider if you are looking for a small rural school that does everything and has the facilities, set in a charming ancient little town in a lovely part of the country. It is not smart, low profile, but does a good job, giving the average pupil confidence.

Stop Press: The school will be going fully co-ed from September 1997.

The King's School

Canterbury, Kent CT1 2ES
Tel: 01227 595501, Fax: 01227 595595
PUPILS: Around 444 boys, 291 girls
  (605 board, 130 day)
AGES: 13–18
SIZE OF SIXTH FORM: 297

C OF E
FEE-PAYING

HEAD: From 1996, the Rev Keith Wilkinson, BA, MA, FRSA, who comes here from being Head of Berkhamsted, and previously taught at Eton. Went to Hull University; he has worked as a parish priest. Married (his wife is a teacher), with twin teenage daughters.

One-third of governors have or have had their children or close relatives in the school.

ACADEMIC MATTERS: A-level pupils all take at least one subsidiary subject, sometimes at AS-level (44 subjects were taken in '95), anything from Philosophy to Italian, and they must participate in a new modular programme of General Studies. Portuguese and Russian are 'available' at Sixth Form, and there is 'some opportunity to study Japanese and Swahili.' GCSE is almost a fail-free zone (64% of passes at A★ or A grade, plus 27% at B). The brightest can take Maths, Latin and a Modern Language early. Separate Sciences for one third, Double Award for the majority.

The school has a slightly dry talk-and-chalk approach to teaching – the aim is first and foremost to get those exam results, so there is no wandering off into gardens of bright images. Streaming and setting; 'work is taken seriously at King's,' says the prospectus (this is certainly true of mainstream subjects). Supervised evening prep.

Business Studies and IT have been not brilliant, but computing facilities are now receiving major additional investment. The library is housed in Butterfield's first major building. The school owns the personal libraries of both Sir Hugh Walpole and Somerset Maugham.

There were excellent A-level results in 1995, with 48% A grades, and 71% A–B grades. Large numbers of pupils choose

General Studies at A-level. Girls and boys perform 'almost identically' at A-level, but girls do 'marginally' better at GCSE. English, Biology and Chemistry are currently the most popular A-level subjects, with 20 others available. Classics is surviving 'in a healthy condition'.

GAMES, OPTIONS, THE ARTS: We were taken to task for saying only a minority of boys take games seriously – not so, says the dynamic Head of Sport, Roy White (and boys and girls agree with him). The school has a county-standard sports centre, with a pool, six squash courts, blue sports hall, fitness suite, and snack bar, which members of the public can also use (at a price) when the school isn't. Also two Astroturf pitches. This is a rowing school – girls as well as boys. The choice of sports increases as pupils move up the school.

There is a new Director of Music, who 'expects his musicians to perform well.' Several choirs, including one which sings for the school in the Cathedral (though NB this is not the Cathedral choir, which is a separate entity). In '95, the school gained 6 Oxbridge choral awards, and in the same year 15 pupils passed grade VIII (some with distinction).

There are excellent CDT facilities, ditto an Art Centre in the converted 13th-century priory; also a small theatre. The 'climax of artistic endeavour' is the annual King's Week, spoken of lyrically by all as a feast of soul and flow of reason in the last week of summer term.

Our impression, however (and not surprisingly the school disagrees with us), is that extra-curricular subjects are relatively poor relations, and this was volunteered by members of staff: everything is on offer, but there is no room in the busy day to take advantage of it all.

BACKGROUND AND ATMOSPHERE: A romantic setting in the middle of Canterbury in the shadow of the Cathedral (*son et lumière*), and using glorious ancient buildings and a quad owned by the Dean and Chapter, as well as a rich variety of architectural styles for different boarding houses, the Art school and the Music school (this last a monument to Egyptomania). Beautiful at every turn (pretty gardens, flint walls), and, said a housemistress with glee, 'when parents see the place they are instantly won over'.

The atmosphere of ancient customs and traditions is in fact totally at odds with the truth, which is that a small school on the site was turned by Canon Shirley (the Head of King's 1935–62 and one of the great pioneering entrepreneurial Heads) almost overnight into a place with a smart uniform and quaint customs, thanks to a marketing exercise of which any captain of industry would be proud.

Girls now form 40% of pupils and wear a smart uniform, pinstripes and jacket and white shirts with wing collars – like little barristers; pupils are so taken with it that apparently some go on wearing it when they leave school.

PASTORAL CARE AND DISCIPLINE: Some bullying has been reported, both girls and boys, and the school has had a rocky ride to its co-ed status, with logistical problems. The 90 members of staff *DO NOT SMOKE* – how about this for a good example? There are not enough female staff, but the school is 'positively trying to get them'. A personal tutor is assigned to each child, who keeps the same one throughout school. A fortnightly report is made on each pupil. House masters and mistresses are all members of the academic staff.

Discipline is strict – and pupils know what is expected of them. Alcohol is a perennial menace – pubs are right on the doorstep. Pupils learn about safe sex by putting condoms on bananas (could this result in mini-inferiority complexes?) – NB the outgoing Head was unaware of the bananas, and wished we had not mentioned this; and remember this is not the only school to use bananas.

PUPILS AND PARENTS: A rich mix (middle class, upper class, children of Canterbury shopkeepers, and the school has just fielded one minor foreign royal). There are around 60 foreigners (this is a very popular choice for Nigerians). Several Conservative politicians' children are here, also London solicitors, Forces' and diplomats' offspring. Children are outward-looking, confident and conformist.

ENTRANCE: Parents and children choose which house they wish to go into. CE for one and all – and there is considerable pressure on places, both girls and boys. Pupils here come from 70 different prep schools (including King's own junior school in Canterbury). Pupils entering at Sixth Form are expected to have six GCSEs at C or above.

EXIT: A good number to Oxbridge; the rest to 'other universities and colleges', and a clutch to medical schools and to ex-polys (Oxford Brookes still the reigning favourite), the odd one to re-take. OBs include Somerset Maugham (who hated it, and is said to have based *Of Human Bondage* on it), Walpole, Marlowe, Patrick Leigh Fermor (expelled), William Harvey, David Gower, and the first Englishman in space, Michael Foale.

MONEY MATTERS: 'Up to 30' scholarships, including music and art. Bursaries for hardship cases 'when a child is on his/her way to a public examination'. No endowment.

REMARKS: A very popular public school which works well for the reasonably bright, bouncy extrovert in search of straight up-and-down academic education. But this is not the place to send your gentle, shy child (however clever), or what the pupils call 'losers'. Cleverly marketed. A glorious setting.

The King's School

Worcester WR1 2LH
Tel: 01905 23016, Fax: 01905 25511

PUPILS: 790 pupils: 539 boys, 251 girls (95 boarders, the rest day). Plus own junior school with 176 boys and girls
AGES: 11–18
SIZE OF SIXTH FORM: 255
C OF E
FEE-PAYING

HEAD: Since 1983, Mr John M Moore, JP, MA, PhD (fifties). Educated at Rugby and Clare College, Cambridge. Classicist. Previously Head of Classics and director of Sixth Year Studies, before that at Winchester and spent 19 years at Radley. On so many committees, it is hard to name them all.

Author of six books on Classics including *Aristotle and Xenophon on Democracy and Oligarchy*. Friendly and likeable.

ENTRANCE: By registration. Qualifying exam for boarders, competitive exam for day pupils.

EXIT: University for 95%; all over the place, and around 10 per year to Oxbridge (13 in '95).

REMARKS: A steady and solid performer, which has had girls in the Sixth Form for some years and started going fully co-ed in '91. A detailed breakdown of results was not forthcoming (Head comments 'they are so easy to misinterpret'), but '95 was a good year, and results appear especially good in the light of a fairly broad intake.

An ancient foundation (7th century), refounded by Henry VIII after the suppression of the priory. There has been a big expansion and building programme to meet the demands of day co-education, all completed in '95. Set in the precincts of the Cathedral, the school sits compactly between the River Severn and the city. Buildings of many dates (including the 14th-century refectory, now the main hall, and the ancient Edgar Tower, which houses the library) are all grouped around gardens and quadrangles.

The junior school (also co-ed), stands in its own grounds next door (and uses many of the senior school facilities), and provides choristers for the Cathedral choir. Strong muscular Christianity and also a strong Music tradition (organ scholarships to Oxbridge have been chalked up regularly). Very good strong sports, also Drama. There are large numbers of computers and good IT. The prizewinning newspaper, *The King's Herald*, produced by desk-top publishing (high-quality concert/theatre programmes are also produced by pupils). A vigorous careers department, with industrial links. Unusually successful Young Enterprise. The school is very well considered locally. Parents are mainly professionals. Boarders from Wales, also from abroad, ex-pats (Far East, Services).

There is a good extra-curricular programme, especially from the day point of view, said a parent: 'It's a long day, with boarding Value Added available to day pupils.' 'Full of get-up-and-go staff with ideas,' said another. Saturday morning school was recently abandoned, and replaced by extra-curricular activities (school day and year dates have been rearranged to encompass academic life),

giving greater flexibility to boarders, following pressure from the marketplace.

A traditional and flourishing school, producing well-balanced boys and girls – who do not end up thinking the world owes them a living.

The King's School

Wrexham Road, Chester CH4 7QL
Tel: 01244 680026, Fax: 01244 678008

PUPILS: 504 boys (all day)
AGES: 11–18
SIZE OF SIXTH FORM: 136 (Plus own prep school on site, with 160 boys, ages 7–11)
C OF E
FEE-PAYING

HEAD: Since 1981, Mr A R D Wickson, MA (fifties), educated at Whitgift, read History at Cambridge. Previously Head of a Dorset grammar school (since turned comprehensive), before that Housemaster at Ardingly. Infectiously enthusiastic (Gilbert and Sullivan, medieval history), tremendously caring: a good shepherd who observes his boys thoughtfully and watchfully. Exudes positive good humour and has a smiling face. Regards it as 'fundamental' to know all the boys well (teaches top and bottom).

ACADEMIC MATTERS: A strongly and unashamedly academic school, though 1995 results are down slightly on the previous year, and the school now rates 36th on the five-year *FT* rating – quite a sharp fall from when we last went to press, but all is relative, with 42% of A-level results at A grade, 64% at A and B (though NB all take General Studies as an A-level); also one-third of GCSEs starred As. 'We do it because we are selective. The results are what they ought to be,' commented the Head. Maths, Physics, Chemistry, and History show up recently as the strongest departments. There is much emphasis on intellectual challenge, critical thought, and General Studies are taken well beyond the confines of the curriculum. Staff are largely male, many long-standing. The Head sees all boys twice a year with their reports.

GAMES, OPTIONS, THE ARTS: Very strong rowing: the boys are constantly in training for this and winning all kinds of trophies, sometimes beating university teams, and boys have been picked for World Junior Championships. The school has a fine boathouse on the River Dee (in the town centre, two miles away), and excellent coaching. Drama is good (girls corralled), including outdoor Shakespeare and biannual Gilbert and Sullivan, directed by the Head, who also sings (his part is chosen by the boys): sell-out performances. Good on visiting speakers/lecturers, mainly academics. Flourishing and expanding CCF.

BACKGROUND AND ATMOSPHERE: Founded in 1541 and linked to the Cathedral. Moved to its present site (32 flat, bare acres) on the outer edge of Chester in 1960, inconvenient for public transport though double-decker school buses pile up with pupils and parents sweep in and out on school runs. The main block, pleasant brick with dignified proportions, incorporates some items from the original building in the city, but the overall aspect (many later additions) is featureless. However, the atmosphere within hums with activity.

PASTORAL CARE AND DISCIPLINE: Staff chivvy away at loutish behaviour. Poor work, untimely work, untidy appearance, smoking, etc, merit detentions, but serious breaches of conduct are non-existent, says the Head.

A newsletter was recently introduced, to help keep parents in touch, since information sent home by letter often ends up not being delivered.

PUPILS AND PARENTS: Decent, hard-working professional parents (some very rich in this area) send their boys here from miles away. Pupils wear an elegant dark green/blue-striped blazer. Articulate, confident, unpretentious boys with a rich mix of accents.

ENTRANCE: Highly selective at 11+ 'and later by chance'. No automatic entry from the junior school. Entry there at 7 (down from 8) with queues for places and tests.

EXIT: Wide variety of degree courses, Newcastle, Sheffield, Birmingham and Imperial College London in droves; 11 or more to Oxbridge. A huge breadth of careers afterward.

MONEY MATTERS: The Head cheerfully describes the school as 'penniless'. There are 16 Assisted Places at 11; 5 at Sixth Form; bursaries; 1 full-fee academic scholarship for outstanding ability with financial need. Good value (£1,344 per term at time of writing).

REMARKS: A flourishing and impressively academic boys' day school which crams a lot into its day and retains an agreeably personal touch.

The Lady Eleanor Holles School

Hanworth Road, Hampton, Middlesex TW12 3HF
Tel: 0181 979 1601, Fax: 0181 941 8291

PUPILS: 690 girls in the senior school, 190 in the junior school
ALL DAY
AGES: 7–18
SIZE OF SIXTH FORM: 170
C OF E
FEE-PAYING

HEAD: Since 1981 (and staying) Miss Elizabeth Candy BSc (fifties); sees her role as an 'enabler' for both her girls and her staff, for the former to emerge 'confident and assertive' in what she sees as a society 'still rife with sexist prejudice'. Dynamic and perceptive, with a dry sense of humour. Miss Candy is a Chemist, trained at Westfield College London; she commands a lot of respect. 'She's tall and scary and gives evil looks at assembly,' says a Lower School girl, while senior girls find her 'positive, encouraging, involved'. Ex-Putney High second-in-command, she still teaches PSE and General Studies and pitches into school activities.

ACADEMIC MATTERS: Tip-top exam results are achieved without undue pressure. Compulsory Latin for two years (there is a strong but inevitably small Classics department – 7 took Latin A-level, 3 Greek in '95); joint Classics trip with City of London Boys). LEH pioneered Russian in the '50s, and there is still a good department.

Horses for courses: less academic options at A-level include Home Economics, Textile and Design, Theatre Studies (joint with Hampton Boys), Practical Music. Psychology is also on offer. 24 girls in a class (pre A-levels) but under almost exclusively female staff – 'reflecting the well-qualified wives of established professional men in this fairly prosperous area,' comments the Head. Around one-third of A-levels at grade A, and in '95, 80% A–B grades. Girls get an impressive trawl of top grades all at one go

in GCSE. General Studies remains 'an examined course to keep them interested,' although 'league tables are absolutely rubbish,' she adds fiercely.

GAMES, OPTIONS, THE ARTS: This is a top girls' rowing school, listing among its trophies Women's Henley '93 and '94 Schools Head of the River. The squad includes both National and Junior World Championship rowers. The Boat House, five minutes' drive away at Molesey, is shared with Hampton Boys. The school also has an indoor pool (keen scuba diving), 15 tennis courts, badminton courts in an excellent gym, plays lacrosse – 'but you can choose to do whatever you want, or not,' approves an un-gamesy pupil. A recent innovation is the girls' Army and RAF Cadet Corps. Keen Music, good Chess. Popular Art under an 'inspiring' Head of Department. Active fund-raising for charities.

BACKGROUND AND ATMOSPHERE: Founded in the Cripplegate ward of the City of London in 1711; two early 18th-century plaster figures from the original school bear incongruous witness to the transplant to the suburbs in 1936. The school (largely inaccessible by public transport) is a visually tranquil oasis on a suburban avenue. The main building is a cross between a '30s factory and an American high school – light, airy, wide corridors, spacious grounds. There is a new Sixth Form library and classrooms. Girls wear a cherry-red uniform, with ties. For Sixth Form dress, anything goes.

The junior school (Burlington House) is in the grounds: some girls who have been on the same site since the age of seven are keen to 'bolt' post-GCSE.

PASTORAL CARE AND DISCIPLINE: There is small evidence of bucking the system here. 'There's a lot of space to move here and a lot going on to occupy girls physically and mentally,' comments the Head, 'and there's also room to make a noise if you need to.' Two pastoral tutors per class. Sixth Formers can go off the premises at lunch time or invite Hampton boys in: 'They sometimes hang around outside school for the middle years, but we can take them or leave them actually,' disparaged a Sixth Former.

PUPILS AND PARENTS: Daughters of stockbrokers or yuppies (some from ethnic minorities) who bus themselves in via parent-organised buses and coaches over a wide catchment from Weybridge and Windsor to Guildford; lesser numbers commute out from Richmond, Barnes, Kew and Twickenham. Parents are middle-class, comfortably off and involved with the school. Girls are busy, capable, civilised and unpressurised, and get on well with each other.

ENTRANCE: Slightly under half from own junior school, via exam. 'We can afford to be fairly selective in looking for those who really want to be involved in all aspects of school life,' says the Head, who gets 5–6 applicants for each place, about 20% from state schools. A £250 non-returnable deposit is required on acceptance of place. Restless girls leaving at 16+ are likely to go to Westminster, Richmond College, Ardingly, Stowe, Wellington.

EXIT: Most to the longer-established universities: Bristol, Birmingham, Nottingham, Leeds, London, Exeter, only occasionally the new universities. Around 15 annually to Oxbridge.

MONEY MATTERS: A few academic and music scholarships are on offer, plus means-tested Cripplegate Schools Foundation entrance bursaries. There are several Sixth Form scholarships of 40% fees. The number of Assisted Places has been reduced to 13, as too many remained unfilled in the qualifying (well-heeled) area.

REMARKS: An impressive premier league girls' day school, sound and popular, geographically advantaged, and excellent value, steered strongly but calmly by a characterful, unpushy Head. A local favourite for yonks, it has now caught the selector's eye.

Lady Margaret School

Parson's Green, London SW6 4UN
Tel: 0171 736 7138, Fax: 0171 384 2553
PUPILS: 430 girls
ALL DAY
AGES: 11–18
SIZE OF SIXTH FORM: 100
C OF E
VOLUNTARY AIDED
STATE

HEAD: Since 1984, Mrs Joan Olivier BA (fifties). Came from Camden Girls as Deputy in '73. State-educated, read History at London and did her post-graduate work at Cambridge. A splendidly talkative lady, with a totally open-door policy, wedded to the school, though plenty try to poach her. 'I love it here, I say why should I want to move?'

Cheerful, positive, liberal with praise, also sharp in rebuke where necessary. Her husband worked in the City, own son is at a fee-paying school. Constantly in despair over lack of funds, etc, but makes the best of everything. Insists on bright colours on the walls, flowers in the hall – etc. 'People think it's rather odd, but I tell them that if you give children a bright environment, they'll be proud of it and won't wreck the place.'

Enlightened governors.

ACADEMIC MATTERS: Rigorous teaching and expectations; takes a traditional approach. Several staff have both private and state school experience. All are exceptionally committed, and girls do well at all levels. Study skills are keenly taught. Homework at least one hour per night from the start. Class sizes are variable, occasionally up to 33. French and Spanish are options. Good Art. The only state school in the borough to offer Music at both GCSE and A-level. It does quite exceptionally well at GCSEs, rating (in '95) seventh in the country and top of the London comprehensives. A-levels are taken by far smaller numbers (35 girls in '95), and results are less startling but solid. There is a good and well-used library.

Historical note: the success of this school was built on the brave decision to reduce its intake at a time when the rest of inner London was being swamped with huge numbers. However, see Entrance below.

GAMES, OPTIONS, THE ARTS: Imaginative Drama; the Sixth Form put on their own ambitious productions. Netball/tennis courts are on site, and there is an energetic sports matches programme. Good Art, with signs of embryonic fashion designers in evidence. Music another lively department. Loads of outings and trips, sleep-overs in the school, special leavers breakfast (Mrs Olivier is dead keen on ritual).

BACKGROUND AND ATMOSPHERE: An elegant Georgian bow-windowed mansion with Common in front and gardens behind, plus a modern gym, hall, etc. There is a super new Design and Technology building (for which the school energetically raised vast sums). The transformation of the top floor now includes a much needed study room for the Sixth Form. Moral values and a caring aspect breed deep loyalty and a distinctly happy atmosphere, much commented on by parents and staff. It feels like a private school, hardly surprising since it is run along those lines.

School numbers are now set to expand, and new buildings are planned to cope with this. What a pity.

PASTORAL CARE AND DISCIPLINE: High marks for discipline. 'This is a Church school,' says the Head firmly. Truancy is negligible; problems e.g. temper (but this is rare) are sorted out in chapel, where a girl is allowed to sit alone for a bit, 'and cool down'. Girls are neat and tidy (and ticked off if they're not).

PUPILS AND PARENTS: A big mix, including a handful of very keenly involved parents, some of whom are brilliant fund-raisers. Some are refugees from the private sector, and there are more middle-class professionals than many state schools. Girls are polite, articulate and fiercely supportive of each other.

ENTRANCE: Accepts 45 church-going girls (letters from Vicars are needed), 45 others: from 8 boroughs – including Ealing, Barnes, Wandsworth. No preference to siblings. Mainly what was ILEA Band 2, but also Bands 1 and 3. 460 children are tested in December (Maths, English, Verbal Reasoning), all are interviewed. 'I like girls who are going to do something, who have potential, who need a break, who will appreciate the value added here.' NB on numbers: the Sixth Form has now expanded to 100 – a gradual build up, and from September '96, will take in more girls at 11 + – all this due to popular demand.

EXIT: Some always leave post-GCSE, but the majority stay on for A-level, and are joined by pupils from other schools. Increasing numbers go on to further education, (training courses/qualifications/degrees) – and 1 or 2 to Oxbridge annually.

MONEY MATTERS: State-funded. Parents regularly raise money for the school. The Head is keen on boosting coffers by letting the school to Weight Watchers, weddings, etc.

REMARKS: A super school, with a well-deserved reputation for being a nice, small, caring place under an exceptional Head.

Lancing College

Lancing, Sussex BN15 0RW
Tel: 01273 452213, Fax: 01273 464720
PUPILS: Around 460 boys, 76 girls in Sixth Form (mostly boarding; around 48 day – mainly boys)
AGES: 13–18
SIZE OF SIXTH FORM: Around 250
C OF E
FEE-PAYING

HEAD: Since 1993, Mr Christopher Saunders, MA (fifties). Educated at Lancing and Fitzwilliam, Cambridge, where he read Geography. Previously Head of Eastbourne College (and much praised in that role), before that, Housemaster at Bradfield. Soccer and cricket blue. Represents HMC on the Football Association Council. Well liked by fellow heads and described as a 'good man'. Nickname at Eastbourne 'C J' (Head's initials – after *The Fall and Rise of Reginald Perrin*). Married with two children. His study is strategically placed so he can see all who pass.

ACADEMIC MATTERS: Offers a good, wide curriculum – Arts outweigh Sciences at A-level in our opinion, though Head says not so, and separate Sciences offered for all at GCSE (no Dual Award). '94 was a bumper year for Lancing in exam results, '95 also very good, though with slightly fewer As and Bs at A-level. A relatively broad intake of pupils is reflected in results: 'My middling bright son has done better than we hoped,' commented a father, pleased with the commitment and high expectancy of staff here. No streaming, but pupils are setted for English, Maths, Sciences and Languages. The school has a fantastic Electronics department.

Many Modern Languages are offered – and there are exchanges with Russians, Spanish, Italians, Germans. Japanese and Chinese are taken at A-level (though by nationals). Everyone does two languages in the first year – French, Spanish, or German, and can pick up Italian and Russian. Classics is particularly strong with some excellent teaching (three full-time staff) – everyone does either Latin or Classical Civilisation, and about 60% go on to do one or the other at GCSE. Greek is timetabled for anyone to do – it's an 'official' option (not many choose it for A-level, but younger boys are triumphant at inter-school classical reading competitions). Classes in Lower School have no more than 20 pupils; A-level sets are between 6–12, with an upper limit of 15. There are some good, dedicated staff, though parents caution that it is not all singing and dancing. Only ten female staff, and one points out that it's still called the 'Masters' Common Room'; she does not think that will ever change.

GAMES, OPTIONS, THE ARTS: Strong games: this is a good soccer school, with currently terrific tennis too, sailing, etc. A keen mountaineering club goes off to cliffs and to Scotland. A relatively new Head of Art (ex-Marlborough) is empire-building like mad – he already has a huge department in the crypt of the chapel, and is now expanding into a whole new building. Some excellent work is being done. Also a good Pottery department. Strong Music – every corner is alive to the sound of practising. Head of Chapel Music, Welshman Neil Cox, is acknowledged to be a star. The choir tours Europe every year. Strong Debating and Public Speaking – there is a long tradition of success here, and in '95 they made it to the finals of the Cambridge Union Schools Debating competition, and to the semi-finals of the *Observer*'s Mace.

On no account overlook the school's famous farm, in which Brian the Boar, a huge orange-haired brute, takes pride of place. This does wonders for boys and girls interested in veterinary science (there is a steady little flow of these) but also, say staff, they like to go and commune with the animals . . .

BACKGROUND AND ATMOSPHERE: Occupies one of the best school sites in the country, 550 acres on a hill above the A27, looking out to sea. It is dwarfed by a monstrous school chapel of the upturned-pig school of architecture (opinions differ on this, however, and some find it glorious, awe-inspiring, etc). This is a monument to the worldly ambition of the school's founder, Canon Nathaniel Woodard (of Woodard Schools – muscular Christianity – fame), whose tomb takes pride of place within the chapel. Made of sandstone, and slowly sinking towards the sea; inside the acoustics are bad – 'like singing in a sand dune', says the Head of Chapel Music. Beside this edifice (the largest school chapel in the world), the daily round of the school pales into insignificance, though pupils say they get used to it. (Maintenance bills are paid for by Woodard Corporation, by Friends of Lancing Chapel – and by heck, it needs a few – and by English Heritage.)

There are glorious flint-faced cloisters through which the wind whistles – freezing cold as charity (go in spring when blossom is out for best viewing). One of the very few schools where boys' dorms are ritzier than girls'. Girls are in two neat little houses, small and without character. Studies (in girls' case) are aptly called 'pitts'. One is run by Mrs Bentley, an ex-teacher of Kamazu Academy, Malawi (a country with which, coincidentally, the school has traditional links and exchanges). Boys are in rooms worthy of Oxbridge colleges, with much panelling and lots of individual studies; the (inevitable) 'refurbishment' programme has done away with the huge dormitory which vied with Loretto's for being the biggest, most gruesome in the land. (Five hundred matelots were stationed here in the war.)

The atmosphere is friendly – 'they'll knock you down but stop to pick you up again and say sorry', says Registrar Mr Shearwood, who showed us round and knows the school better than anyone. Food: chips with everything, and mountains of tomato ketchup – never seen so much lavished on one meal. Milk shakes are a speciality.

PASTORAL CARE AND DISCIPLINE: Discipline has been considerably tightened up ('It jolly well needed it,' warned a mother). Pupils' appearance has been 'improved' says the Head, 'by substantial changes to the clothing list.' Staff boldly claim they (pupils) now know where they stand and 'have responded very positively to the stricter, but in no way oppressive, regime.' This is, needless to say, not what the pupils say.

The school has an excellent pastoral care system of boys choosing their own tutor after the first year (to give them time to look around). In theory each member of staff is limited to 15 pupils, but popular ones take on more. Each new boy is issued with a copy of *The Pupil's Charter.* Other faiths are welcome, but all must come to chapel.

Achievers – in any field – are liberally praised and encouraged. Staff are ambitious for their pupils rather than for themselves.

PUPILS AND PARENTS: About half of pupils come from the south-east. Popular with ex-pats, and a goodly number of pupils from Hong Kong, Korea, Malaysia, also US exchange. There are around 10 children of clergymen at any one time. Girls come from nearby schools, including one or two from Roedean, and occasionally from Benenden and St Swithun's. OBs include Tim Rice, Tom Sharpe, Trevor Huddleston, Peter Pears (who wowed them in the choir), Evelyn Waugh, and Tom Driberg (who was expelled); also playwrights Christopher Hampton and David Hare. The school has strong links with Korea – the first bishop of Korea was here. Few second-generation.

ENTRANCE: By CE, pass of 55% required. Pupils coming from the state sector are separately assessed. Girls need to register for entry into Sixth Form asap.

EXIT: 10–22 to Oxbridge (12 in '95). Lots to Newcastle, Leeds, Durham, Edinburgh – the fashionable universities, also ex-polys. Some to art college, and e.g. organ scholarships to Oxbridge.

MONEY MATTERS: There are 25 awards a year, including two clergy exhibitions and others for Music and Art (Music and Art scholarships are keenly sought-after and make a real difference to the standard of pupil in the school).

REMARKS: A strong second division public school which has gone a bit quiet recently.

Latymer School

Haselbury Road, Edmonton,
London N9 9TN
Tel: 0181 807 4037, Fax: 0181 807 4125

PUPILS: 1,305 boys and girls (in equal numbers)
ALL DAY
SIZE OF SIXTH FORM: 396
NON-DENOM
STATE

HEAD: Since 1983, Mr Geoffrey Mills BA (fifties), read Modern Languages at Cambridge. Charming, quiet, outspoken, widely respected and considered to be a 'brilliant manager'.

ENTRANCE: Not so easy: heavily oversubscribed, academically selective.

EXIT: Mostly to university, about 12 a year to Oxbridge.

REMARKS: A successful gigantic high-powered co-ed grammar school which gets super academic results with wonderfully devoted staff (they are often in at 7 a.m., and don't leave till after 6 p.m. NB Many have children in the school). 'But it's not the crème de la crème here,' says the Head, 'there's the thin stuff in with the crème.' The school has high expectations and pupils given lots of encouragement, but the Head is mindful of not being complacent (it is regularly way up on the top end of the state league table list), 'I do remind everyone that we have many schools above us in the independent sector,' says the Head, who teaches French to GCSE years. Modern Languages are a particular strength (there are regular exchanges with schools in France and Germany), also Maths and Science – despite labs in desperate need of modernisation. A broad range of subjects is offered at A-level (Photography, Russian, Sociology).

Music is a great strength – the school has three full orchestras, four major choirs, chamber orchestra, madrigal group and wind band, under the eagle eye and ear of David Elliott. Drama is another real strength, and keen sports too – this is a school which takes everything it does seriously and is in the hands of an outstanding Head whose staff work together in close harness – and there are some super staff here. The school is housed in a functional building stretching sideways (with a steamy canteen), and the large Hall which can house the entire school is used daily for assemblies, Drama, Music. The playing fields behind are a pleasing girdle of green in a dreary area of outer London.

If you live in this area, look no further.

Latymer Upper School

King Street, Hammersmith, London W6 9LR
Tel: 0181 741 1851, Fax: 0181 748 5212

PUPILS: 940 boys (Plus own prep school with 136 boys, ages 7–11)
ALL DAY
AGES: 11–18
SIZE OF SIXTH FORM: Around 290 including 25 girls in Sixth Form from 1996 (this number will double next year)
NON-DENOM
FEE-PAYING

HEAD: Since 1991, Mr Colin Diggory BSc (early forties). Married with three school-age children. Educated at Redcar Grammar school, read Mathematics at Durham. Energetic, dynamic, jolly, a total believer in the grammar

school ethos. Started his teaching career at Manchester Grammar School, 'You can only go sideways after that,' moved to St Paul's, then Merchant Taylors' (Head of Maths), came to Latymer as Second Master, took over acting Headship before becoming fully fledged Head. Has had a happy time 'shaking up the curriculum' and is 'consciously raising the academic profile'. Maintains 'We're very good at the top end,' and is keen to 'protect and do very well for those boys capable of three Cs'.

Works with a very strong management team.

ACADEMIC MATTERS: Sound and very thorough, with some very high-powered teaching, and results are sharpening up – rising gently but firmly, reflecting a relatively broad intake. Staff are mainly male, with a sprinkling of young; the Head of English is generally considered 'brilliant and fun', and this is reflected in A-level results. Class sizes have been reduced to around 20, and the number of sets has increased (but staff numbers have remained the same). Sciences are offered as three separate subjects but also Dual Award GCSE. There is a smallish but strong Classics department. Also Strong IT and well-used computers all around the place.

Maths and Physics produce the best A-level results; Biology, Geography, Chemistry, Economics and History all have a big following with grades widespread. Politics does very well.

GAMES, OPTIONS, THE ARTS: Rowing is a special strength – the school has an impressive boat house with an Olympic oarsman as a coach. Saturday morning is a busy time on the river here. One of the few English public schools that rows from home. Under-13s regularly produce winning teams. This is a good place for the sporty types, with lots of matches (864 fixtures of one sort or another calculated during one academic year), 'though you can get away with doing very little,' said a non-sporting pupil. Strong rugby (have been Middlesex champions), also good at cricket.

Art and Drama are both very popular, and there is a strong Music tradition (joint orchestra with Godolphin & Latymer qv).

BACKGROUND AND ATMOSPHERE: The school was founded in 1624; the present buildings (centenary celebrated in '95) are functional red-brick Gothic (now lit up at night), plus many additions – a tight squeeze, and will be more so, presumably, when the girls come in, and every corner is fully used. The school is divided into middle and upper for administration purposes. Bulging, functional and urban: no gracious lawns here. There is a slightly cramped feel in some areas. A sense of busyness pervades; the boys and staff are going places. Unpretentious and stimulating. Visiting parents are hit by their first impression of the school bang on the main road, amid the petrol fumes.

The school has a new Sixth Form common room – and quite a few other changes are afoot, clever tampering with space, adapting to changes (girls and the deliberate policy of an increased size of Sixth Form). Planning permission, etc, is awaited with bated breath for the development of a new Arts Centre, £3 million is ready and waiting for this.

Latymer Preparatory School (Hurrah, it's name has been simplified now) 38 Upper Mall, W6 (Tel: 0181 748 0303, Fax: 0181 741 4916). Head Mrs J Chandler BA, whose family have long ties with the Latymer foundation (she left and came back). Entry via competitive exam, automatic stepping stone to the senior school. Super school, back on form after a wobble, quietly set behind its big brother,

in two elegant 18th-century houses overlooking the Thames. Lively but gentle; Mrs C's four Cs have to be observed - courtesy, consideration, co-operation and concentration.

PASTORAL CARE AND DISCIPLINE: Not a problem. Tolerance really is the keynote of this school. A consultant psychologist has recently been taken on for one afternoon per week. Staff kept on their toes with training sessions on tutoring, pastoral care, etc.

There are complaints from locals of boys loutishly loitering and smoking near the school gates and beyond.

PUPILS AND PARENTS: Many races, many creeds, many colours. Streetwise, polite and (mostly) very hardworking sons of professional men and women. Not the place for social climbers. OBs include Sir James Spicer, George Walden, Mel Smith, legions of MPs, Hugh Grant.

ENTRANCE: At the age of 11 and 13 from a wide variety of state and private schools (an initial exam in January weeds out the non-starters) and boys from Latymer Prep. NB The intake is currently gradually being reduced (from 150 per year to 125 per year, i.e. to six forms of 20 boys each – plus a few) as part of the raising-the-standards plan.

Places at Sixth Form for girls (from September 1996): apply with GCSE B grades, and As in chosen A-level subjects .

EXIT: To a wide variety of universities, old and new: anything between 3 and 20 to Oxbridge per year; Imperial College, Brunel and Manchester show up on the leavers list alongside Wimbledon School of Art, Central Lancaster and John Moores, and an interestingly varied range of subjects – engineering (various), environmental sciences, medicine, business studies. Gap years are in vogue.

MONEY MATTERS: Good value for money, and parents – who are not rich – are conscious of getting their money's worth. There are up to 30 Assisted Places at 11+, up to 5 Assisted Places at Sixth Form (boys and girls), plus scholarships and bursaries (governors are actively keen that gifted boys are not denied places).

REMARKS: A successful and worthy fee-paying grammar school, very thorough on all fronts: no-nonsense, with a slight A-level factory feel, though it is broader than it first appears and boys leave well prepared for the future. Efficiently run under extremely strong leadership. In-coming *girls* being watched with interest.

Leeds Girls' High School

Headingley Lane, Leeds LS6 1BN
Tel: 0113 2744000, Fax: 0113 2752217

PUPILS: Approx 620 girls (Plus own junior school with 330 girls, ages 3–11)
ALL DAY
AGES: 11–18
SIZE OF SIXTH FORM: Approx 150
NON-DENOM
FEE-PAYING

HEAD: Since 1977, Miss Philippa Anne Randall, BA (fifties). Educated at Christ's Hospital and LSE. Subject: History. Tall, handsome and characterful. Member of the Friends of Opera North, skis with the school most years, member of National and Yorkshire Women in Management. The school has a list of aims in a written statement of purpose but basically, says Miss Randall,

'this is a an academic school whose pupils generally get where they want to go.' A very hands-on Head. Declares her aims for girls to leave 'confident, caring and able to play their part in the community.'

ACADEMIC MATTERS: Good results all round: Chemistry, French, Economics, History and Maths do well, Biology is usually a strength. Took a dip in '93 (despite all girls taking General Studies): overall, a big mix of grades (58% A–B grades at A level, with a liberal sprinkling of Ds, Es, Ns and Us). GCSEs super in '94, '95 slightly less good – but still good compared with elsewhere. Setting in Maths, French, and Science but no streaming. Good work in an average class size of around 25. The school has long-standing staff, some cosy figures plus an injection of new and young. Dual, separate and Combined Sciences are all on offer at GCSE. There is a small handful of keen classicists under excellent teacher. The school does not offer exotica. Good careers advice is given, with an outside professional brought in to help girls on choosing a career, interview practice, etc.

GAMES, OPTIONS, THE ARTS: All show flair and imagination, and are pursued diligently. The school has a five-star swimming pool, big Sports Hall, and floodlit tennis courts. There is an excellent Art department under Mrs Fox – 'She's inspiring,' enthuse the girls. Nice sewing work, super Home Economics department. Music is excellent and the school has an impressive Music Centre in an old Methodist Chapel (two organs, and free tuition for two years). Energetic collection of activities, e.g. an exchange programme with the Kamazu Academy in Malawi (the 'Eton of Africa', which seems to have links everywhere), also French and German exchanges.

Some activities e.g. drama productions

and General Studies are joint with the boys at Leeds Grammar (though this school will be moving site and the link may be severed, to general dismay). Very successful Young Enterprise (school won the third prize nationally in '95) – and pupils start at the top of the junior school (Ford House, very nearby), doing YE in their last year.

BACKGROUND AND ATMOSPHERE: Founded in 1876, shares a foundation with the local boys' school; ex-direct grant. Set in pleasant grounds, the buildings vary from original to sixties tat. The Hall has an organ and highly polished floor because pupils sit on it (there are no chairs). Compact and functional – all corners are used, (and pretty battered in places). There are some small teaching rooms for small groups, tutors, etc, some windowless.

There has been much rebuilding in the past two years – four-floored extension, with Language labs, Drama studios, etc. A model of all this is in the entrance hall and is useful to get the hang of the lay-out. The junior school is also having a two-storey extension. (NB Money for all this comes from fees; there are no appeals.) The library is used by Sixth Formers for study, and Sixth have their own computer room and the inevitable common room.

The atmosphere is busy, purposeful and bouncy. The school has a prominently displayed motto – *age quod agis*, which girls all know how to translate.

PASTORAL CARE AND DISCIPLINE: Workmanlike – the school functions competently without making a song and dance about it.

PUPILS AND PARENTS: All sorts of backgrounds. Brothers are at Leeds Grammar. The school has a fairly wide catchment area, and there are hordes of buses to and fro. Friendly and articulate

girls. Many distinguished OGs including Catherine Pestell (Principal of Somerville, Oxford), and Pauline Neville-Jones (Political Director of the Foreign Office), also journalist Jill Parkin.

ENTRANCE: Interview, written exams and report from current school except for those entering at 3+, who have an individual IQ-type test. Entry also at Sixth Form – exam and interview after mock-GCSEs.

EXIT: A small leakage post-GCSE. Around 8–14 to Oxbridge (9 in '95), others widespread to universities mostly old, some new; a few re-takers, a few to art college, a few take a gap year.

MONEY MATTERS: Up to 15 Assisted Places per year for pupils entering at 11+. Also an unspecified number of Music scholarships.

REMARKS: An excellent city academic day school for girls, firmly traditional, even slightly old-fashioned – and none the worse for that.

The Leys School

Trumpington Road,
Cambridge CB2 2AD
Tel: 01223 355327, Fax: 01223 357053

PUPILS: 424; 297 boys, 127 girls. (266 boarders; 158 day).
AGES: 13–18
SIZE OF SIXTH FORM: 182
METHODIST/INTER-DENOM
FEE-PAYING

HEAD: Since 1990, the Rev. John Barrett, (MA), (fifties). Formerly Head of Kent College, Pembury. Educated at Culford School and Durham

University, and Cambridge. Married with two children, and has one of the nicest Headmaster's houses in the business. A Methodist Minister; imposing, and generally thought to be well in control of the situation. 'I was brought in to put the school straight after a shaky period.' Assisted by his excellent Deputy, Mr John Trotman, not to mention his wife. Steering the school into co-education and maintaining boarding numbers steady for the last three years – no mean feat.

Lady Trumpington, appropriately enough, is a governor.

A CADEMIC MATTERS: National curriculum plus. Traditional teaching plus some less formal; strong Sciences (but Dual Award GCSE), traditionally more Science than Arts subjects taken at A-level, but this trend is on the turn, though girls at the junior end of the school are showing scientific interest/prowess in internal competitions. Pupils are set in each and every subject individually. There is a good English department, also Theology. Theatre Studies is popular, also Geography. A-level results were uninspiring overall in '95, which said seven gained Oxbridge places. 97% passed at least 5 GCSEs with grade C and above in '95 but the school has no pretensions about claiming to be other than middle-of-the-road, and it has a very broad intake.

G AMES, OPTIONS, THE ARTS: Keenly gamesy: goes on overseas tours, holds its own against bigger schools. Good shooting; also squash, rowing, judo and hockey, but unboastful about their successes. A super new £2 million sports complex is much in use. The school attracts high-powered visiting speakers (somewhat taken for granted – but then, this is Cambridge). Technology centre is open all the time (except late at night), including weekends (rare), without a member of staff (even rarer) – and much used. A splendid little steam engine knocked up over several years chugs merrily by on high days and holidays ('We can't get hold of Welsh coal, it has to be Cumbrian,' moans the master in charge, Mr George). Lively Drama with nine plays a year. The Head of Chemistry runs the popular 'Challenge' whereby prep schools take part at the Leys ('a good way for us to get them in') in competitive projects. Increasing numbers go for D of E. Good trips for the Art department.

B ACKGROUND AND ATMOSPHERE: Founded in 1875 by prominent Methodists. Set in undistinguished red-brick Gothic plus many additions, it suffers from a lack of cohesion, near the centre of Cambridge, on a 50-acre site (seriously geographically advantaged). There has been a great deal of 'refurbishing' since we last went to press – and reorganising, to allow for co-education. The school went fully co-ed in '94 (a smooth operation), and there are now girls in every year. Brighter looking – and confident with it.

The general atmosphere is relaxed and friendly, and there is a marked sense of community. Inspectors rightly reported on the thread of Divinity teaching throughout (a strong feature) which contributes to the ethos. Less of a split-personality school than some with boarding and day pupils, the latter stay on until after prep. i.e. 9 p.m.-ish. Home boarders have their own house.

P ASTORAL CARE AND DISCIPLINE: Pupils are fairly carefully monitored, though illegal pub visiting has been a menace. A Sixth Form club in the basement of a house is shortly to be opened.

PUPILS AND PARENTS: Popular with non-Brits, particularly for the boarding, including bright Europeans, 5% Methodists. Pupils are mostly local – 'The obvious choice if your child is not The Perse material,' commented a parent don. Very friendly boys and girls, who are mutually supportive. The school prides itself on being able to 'adapt to the eccentricities of individuals,' and, says the Head, prep schools recommend it for odd-balls, 'though we don't want too many!' Old Leysians include James Hilton, author of *Goodbye, Mr Chips*; and Martin Bell, Sir Alistair Burnet.

ENTRANCE: Not very selective. Local prep schools include the Ley's own, St Faith's. Still a popular choice for girls at Sixth Form (fun, relaxed – 'and this is Cambridge').

EXIT: Degrees – 85% have gone to university 'somewhere', and professions of all sorts.

MONEY MATTERS: There are 12 Assisted Places (some at 13, some at 16); an assortment of academic, Art, Music, CDT and all-rounder scholarships; bursaries for the Forces. Home boarders pay £2,900 per term (£3,980 for full boarding), expensive compared with other local day schools – but the elongated day offers more.

REMARKS: A smallish, very friendly school gaining strength by going co-ed.

The London Oratory School

Seagrave Road, London SW6 1RX
Tel: 0171 385 0102, Fax: 0171 381 3836

PUPILS: 1,241 all boys, except for girls in the Sixth Form
AGES: 11–18; plus Junior House with specialist music training, for 80 boys ages 7–11.
ALL DAY
SIZE OF SIXTH FORM: 312, including 50 girls
RC
STATE COMPREHENSIVE GRANT-MAINTAINED

HEAD: Since 1983, Mr John McIntosh, MA.

REMARKS: The first London state school (ninth nationwide) to opt out. It is oversubscribed, and has a selective admissions policy 'but only up to a point' – all ability bands are here, with pupils coming from far and wide (Surrey, Hertfordshire, not to mention Islington). Their most famous Islington pupil is Euan, son of Tony and Cherie Blair. A steady performer in the academic league tables for some years. It has an excellent, popular History department. A tiny handful leave post-GCSE; virtually all pupils go on to university afterwards, with around 12 per year to Oxbridge.

This feels like a public school, with discipline, streaming, and a traditional curriculum including Latin, formal teaching. Motto: *Respice Finem* (Look Towards the End). Connected historically with the Brompton Oratory (half an hour's walk away). Four-fifths go on to university.

Opening in September 1996: a Junior House, for 80 boys ages 7–11, specialising in musical training: the new intake must either be good singers and play an instrument, or be prepared to learn two, and all must be bright too. A large grant has been allocated to this new venture.

Lord Williams's School

Thame, Oxfordshire OX9 2AQ
Tel: 01844 213681, Fax: 01844 261382

PUPILS: Around 2,000 boys and girls
ALL DAY
AGES: 11–18
SIZE OF SIXTH FORM: 410
NON-DENOM
STATE

HEAD: Since 1985, Mr David Kenningham, MA (early sixties). Educated Whitley Bay Grammar School and New College, Oxford, where he read Physics. Started his career in industrial management and research, switched to teaching in the private sector (Marlborough College), then to state, ending up as Head of Cheney School, Oxford, before coming here. A forceful, widely experienced Head with a strong belief in comprehensive education. Full of ideas for improving the school and the energy to carry them out.

ACADEMIC MATTERS: Generally very good, the pupils think very highly of their teachers. It has obtained the best GCSEs of all the Oxfordshire county schools for the last two years (not to be sneezed at). It is a 'proper' comprehensive school, catering for all abilities, including those with special needs, who are integrated into the main school. There is some setting, particularly higher up the school, so that able pupils may be well looked after. All take English Language and Literature, Maths and Dual Award science at GCSE. All take at least one Modern Language (French and German), also Design/Technology. There is a good range of subjects available at A/AS level, and GNVQs (three levels) in the Sixth Form. Business Studies is popular. Biggest A-level uptake on Maths, Geography, Physics and English (overall 37% A-B grades at A level in '95 – but NB not all pupils are doing A-level).

GAMES, OPTIONS, THE ARTS: The Sports and Arts Centre offers some of the best facilities in Oxfordshire. All pupils try out all sports during the first two years, and most continue to take some sports seriously thereafter. Girls were South of England Under-16 netball champions in 1995. Over 300 inter-school fixtures a year, going as far away as London and Stratford to find opponents. Classical Music is extremely strong. There are two orchestras and two choirs, and the school provides many members of the county youth orchestra. Also keen Art and Drama. There are many extra-curricular activities including the Syson Competition, in which every pupil in the school competes at public speaking.

BACKGROUND AND ATMOSPHERE: A large school formed in 1971 by the amalgamation of the ancient Lord Williams's Grammar School and the Wenman Secondary School. Now on two sites in a pleasant setting with lots of space and feeling of room; there is a great mix of buildings. A £3 million project to provide extensive new and remodelled buildings was completed in '95. A former boarding house is used for the Sixth Form library and a new Business Centre was funded by local companies. The school has a super friendly atmosphere – every classroom you go into you are greeted with a smile.

PASTORAL CARE AND DISCIPLINE: The school has a tradition of strong links with parents, and of teachers putting themselves out to help individual pupils. Pupils report that bullying is dealt with immediately and effectively and that there are no other major problems.

PUPILS AND PARENTS: A complete cross-section – no creaming by any other school – from the offspring of Oxford dons (a few) and chief executives to pupils whose families have lived here in rural Thame for generations. Also a large number of refugees from the selective system in Buckinghamshire.

ENTRANCE: Principally via primary schools in Thame, Chinnor and Tetsworth in Oxfordshire, and Brill and Long Crendon in Buckinghamshire. Many pupils join from other schools at Sixth Form.

EXIT: About half stay on to do A-levels, of which 3–5 go to Oxbridge each year, and about 100 to universities and colleges. Some do a gap year. The rest go to Further Education or some sort or employment.

MONEY MATTERS: The school has very good links with local companies, who provide finance for expansion and work experience for pupils.

REMARKS: A huge good broad state comprehensive school, with friendly, articulate pupils and enthusiastic teachers.

Loretto School

Musselburgh, East Lothian, Scotland EH21 7RE
Tel: 0131 665 5003, Fax: 0131 653 2773

PUPILS: Currently 315, including 40 girls in the Sixth Form. All board, except for a handful.
AGES: 13–18 (Plus junior school, The Nippers, with 60 boys, 16 girls, including 52 boarders, ages 8–13)

SIZE OF SIXTH FORM: Around 144
ECUMENICAL
FEE-PAYING

HEAD: Since 1995, Mr Keith Budge MA, Cert Ed (early forties). Educated at Rossall, read English at University College, Oxford, PGCE at Edinburgh. Rugby blue. Previously a Housemaster at Marlborough. Married to Moony, three young children. Early reports are favourable: tough, approachable, respected by the boys. Takes over from the famous Rev Norman Drummond, whose personality dominated the school for many years.

ACADEMIC MATTERS: The school mainly follows the English system – GCSE for everyone, followed by A-levels, though a few pupils take Highers (over two years); some do a combinations of the two. Dual Award at GCSE. Results are OK though not very impressive; there is a general sense of 'could do better'. The school offers only French and German as foreign languages – 'we're a small school,' comments the Admissions Tutor, 'and what we do we aim to do well.' Some splendid new young appointments have been made, including an OL who was President of the Cambridge University Women's Boat Club – and there are a good number of wise experienced staff as well.

GAMES, OPTIONS, THE ARTS: This is a keen rugby school, still competitive, though less aggressively so than ten years ago. It does well at hockey (boys). Also keen cricket; ski boots proliferate in winter; golf also offered and CCF. The school has a good Music Centre and this is a lively department altogether, with much jolly if sometimes off-key singing in the chapel, a focal point of Lorettonian life. Tremendous notes boom out from the new organ in the chapel – the school could almost do with a larger chapel to play it in. Heart-breaking plaques on chapel walls commemorating the many dead in two World Wars. There is also a very keen pipe band (have been school champions). An Art gallery open to the public mounts regular exhibitions.

BACKGROUND AND ATMOSPHERE: Sited in the middle of Musselburgh, which describes itself as an 'honest toun', but obviously not honest enough, as the school has security locks on doors, and panic buttons by girls' beds in case of rape, robbery, arson, etc. A collection of sand-coloured buildings – much brisk walking to and fro, with a tunnel link under the A1. It is charming in summer. There is a civilised girls' house, recently refurbished, and a new five-star one to cater for co-education. The boys' houses are improving dramatically (they were formerly Dickensian, and the atmosphere still has a slight feel of hodden doon generations of schoolboys; School House is the smartest). The famously haunted Pinkie House seems spooky to many, particularly the Gallery with its important painted ceiling – 'some of the messages follow you round,' said a pupil 'and it can be quite frightening'. (It is one of the largest dormitories in the country.) One master claims he heard footsteps – altogether, a groo place, and the Head's house is in part of it.

The school has a new Sixth Form centre. Pupils wear smart bright red jackets; all wear kilts on Sundays, girls wear dark skirts on weekdays with white shirts – pleasing. The school was founded in 1827, and purchased in 1862 by Hely Hutchinson Almond, a distinguished scholar of unconventional convictions – Loretto's answer to Dr Arnold. It went fully co-ed in 1995, with girls coming in at 13 (and Sixth Form). Their numbers are building up from the bottom, eventually (it is hoped) to one-third girls, two-thirds boys, but keeping the total number small (max 340).

Junior School, delightfully named The Nippers (Tel: 0131 665 2628): Head: since 1991, Mr David Clark. Super school, with a family feel, right on site. It is generously staffed (some also teach in the senior school), and has a study centre with six classrooms, science lab and French language listening posts. There are light pretty dorms for the boarders with sag bags. Like the big brother school, it went co-ed in '95. Lots of music.

PASTORAL CARE AND DISCIPLINE: Top-class under the previous Head, and no apparent problems on this score. Fines for smoking. Each pupil ('tutee') has a personal tutor. There is a genuine if sometimes self-conscious sense of goodness throughout the school, with uplifting comments hung around, e.g. 'Where there is love there is peace.' Christianity shows its muscles here from time to time and here, feels refreshing. HM Inspectors' report waxed lyrical about the school's 'warm and supportive community where all pupils were known and treated as individuals by a committed and caring staff'.

PUPILS AND PARENTS: The school feels very Scottish, despite one-third of pupils from south of the border. Some Forces children. Many OL sons and daughters – and grandchildren. Kind and polite, they smile and look you in the eye – much gentle charm. Some rough edges and one or two comments still about boys' 'rudeness to girls'. OLs: Headmasters Mavor and McMurray; MP Nicholas Fairbairn, Denis Forman, Hector Laing.

ENTRANCE: CE, from Scottish and northern preps, and pupils come from the school's own Junior School *en* *masse.* There is a special exam and interview for those coming from state system, etc. Six GCSEs (level unspecified) plus an interview for a place in Sixth Form for girls (boys come in at this stage too – the school is purposely top heavy).

EXIT: Most to degree courses, occasional re-takes and other courses (e.g. HND, HNC). Pupils go on to be Professors of Medicine, industrialists and engineers (currently a popular choice).

MONEY MATTERS: There are 25 Assisted Places at any age, and the school undertakes to underpin each child to the end of his/her school career should the Assisted Places scheme fold. Well-endowed with scholarships throughout the school, and there are wonderful bursaries for those who have 'deserved well of Loretto' to help through university (impoverished parents please note).

REMARKS: A famous Scottish public school which has recently gone co-ed and is in the process of adapting. Perfect for gentle, middling academic souls, in need of nurturing, and a 'proper' school with a designer label.

Lycée Français Charles de Gaulle

35 Cromwell Road, London SW7 2DG
Tel: 0171 584 6322, Fax: 0171 823 7684
PUPILS: 2,770 (including primary and nursery school)
ALL DAY: (but see below)
AGES: 3–18/19
SIZE OF SIXTH FORM: Approx 300
(100 in the English section; 200 in the French last two years)

NO RELIGIOUS AFFILIATION
FEE-PAYING

HEAD: (Principal) Since 1991, M Henri-Laurent Brusa, BA, MA, D Lit, Nice University and Sorbonne. Subject: Literature and Law. Previous post as Principal of the Lycée Naval in Brest.

Head of the English stream: M Rashid Benammar, who was educated in France – at Lille – and taught at Wellington and was a Housemaster there, and whose interest is linguistics. His wife is Headmistress of Heathfield (qv).

ACADEMIC MATTERS: Faites attention, svp, parce que c'est assez compliqué. There are in effect two streams – French and English – and classes run from the sixième year (the first year) to the Terminale (last year). The French pupils follow the French syllabus in preparation for the Baccalaureate (and, by the way, they may have to redoubler – repeat a year – if they are not up to scratch).

The Filière Anglaise follows the French syllabus until the end of the Quatrième year, at which point they choisissent whether to go on and do the Baccalaureate (series ES, L, S offered), or go down the GCSE/A-level route. For the Fr system, pupils choose whether to go down the 'literary' or 'scientific' route, but whichever they choose, have to do around six subjects for the Bac. Class sizes are not above 30, but they could be 32; primary not above 25.

Teaching is very much in the fierce French tradition (pupils are usually far too terrified not to work) and no quarter is given; there is no official remedial help. Staff give hundred and ten per cent passionate energy. Results are consistently excellent (and, examiners please note, the results come in weeks before the English): e.g. 62.5% in '95 'TBs' plus 'Bs'

(Très Bien, and Bien for the uninitiated) with 100% réussite usually. GCSE get 100% pass with 74% A–B, and 60% A–B at A-level. Vraiment, c'est sensas – particularly given the comprehensive intake.

GAMES, OPTIONS, THE ARTS: Not the object of the exercise as far as the French are concerned, and your average London-based Lycée product comes out pretty white and flubby. However, games do form part of the French syllabus, so there is no escape. The Games Master tears his hair at the lack of facilities (so do they all in central London), but volleyball, football, rugby and basketball, ski trips, etc, are all on offer and inter-class competitions, which are 'passionnément suivies par les élèves' (je m'en doute). There is a gym, plus a hall which can be used as a gym. Some evenings and samedi matin there are clubs educatifs such as music, travaux manuels, etc, but the school day is long, and clubs are relatively few.

BACKGROUND AND ATMOSPHERE: The school is now on three sites – the youngest in Wandsworth, a new annexe in Ealing (nursery and primary), and the rest in a huge block on the Cromwell Road, stretching back as far as Harrington Road, and with lovely views over the Natural History museum for some. The interior consists of a huge quad, lots of duck-egg blue corridors and soulless classrooms (few are in the same room for long). Avoid the whole area at delivery and collection times.

The history of the Lycée is intimately linked with that of the Institut Français, and in 1915, what with the influx of Belgian and French refugees, the school opened near Victoria Station with 120 élèves. Then to cut a long histoire courte, a nouveau bâtiment was constructed and inaugurated in 1958 et voilà.

The atmosphere is very, well, French. Institutional even. Et cool. Tinies may be flattened. Do not be put off when they answer the telephone in French, however: if you speak loud enough they will give in in the end and speak English.

NB Sartorial note: the Lycée has an Old School Tie – the only Lycée in the world to have one. Not a lot of people know this (or recognise it).

FOOD: You would expect, would you not, at least a Michelin star in this home from home for the French in London, and indeed the menus are little poems of delight: Couscous Mouton (the chef's speciality, explained the member of staff who very kindly showed us round), Boeuf Bourguignon, Jardinières de Légumes Frais, etc. However, we have to relate that the reality is somewhat different: about three-quarters of pupils were eating hamburgers and frites, and the rest, heaps of grated carrot. Foodie note: marvellous pâtisseries have sprouted up all round the area, to cater for those who could kill for a baguette.

PASTORAL CARE AND DISCIPLINE: The French system decrees that matters spiritual and pastoral are to be mainly the province of the parents and the church (Wednesday afternoons are traditionally for catechism, thus many French schools let the children go home for this). However, the Catholic Church is just round the corner, and Protestants have their own church in Soho.

Where discipline breaks down, there is an elaborate system, ending with a conseil de discipline – rather like a court martial, at which the miscreant can explain himself and be heard by staff and his peers. There are also parent-staff meetings. Some reports of bullying reach us, to which some parents have felt teachers turn a blind eye, but this *could* be the English being wet in the face of French sauve-qui-peut-erie. However, 'There is no drug culture,' reports a parent disillusioned with the English public schools on this score. Pupils register for every lesson. Each pupil has a *carnet de correspondance* – for staff to send messages to parents, and vice versa. Parental involvement is de rigueur (a key to the school's success?).

During the school day, surveillants patrol the building, supervising meals, discipline, etc, leaving the teachers free to teach.

PUPILS AND PARENTS: 60 nationalities, from the French-speaking world, plus mixed marriages, embassy children. Parents come from all walks of life including gardeners, Polish dressmakers, dukes, ex-pats (former French colonies). Three MPs are former pupils, including Olga Maitland. There are 1,600 French children, approx 600 Brits plus approx 400 'others'.

ENTRANCE: Registration, preferably before Easter for the following September, plus interview, plus test. All are welcome, providing they can cope with the exigencies of the French language. For entry at 14 – tests in French, English and Maths; for entry at 16 – test in the A-level subjects chosen. (NB Best not to telephone the school for information during the lunch hours.)

EXIT: To French universities (details not given) and to English ones, particularly in the south-east, (Royal Holloway, UCL, and a handful to Oxford), and reading subjects such as French with Law, International Business Studies, European Law and Languages and other such serious matters. Some do a gap year – though the French tend not to.

MONEY MATTERS: A snip at around £700 a term – subsidised by the French Government. No scholarships or Assisted Places (applied for the latter, but were turned down).

REMARKS: Que voulez-vous? Children are imbued with the French educational ethos – they learn to work and their intellectual curiosity is aroused. This is a vachement brilliant place to get a first-class academic education at a fraction of the cost of anything comparable in the land. It makes one despair of England.

Magdalen College School

Cowley Place, Oxford OX4 1DZ
Tel: 01865 242191, Fax: 01865 240379

PUPILS: 520 boys, (all day)
AGES: 9–18
SIZE OF SIXTH FORM: 147
C OF E
FEE-PAYING

HEAD: The Master, since 1991, Mr Peter Tinniswood, MA, MBA (forties), educated at Charterhouse, read PPE at Magdalen College, Oxford; Housemaster at Marlborough, where he helped introduce Business Studies. Left to do MBA at Insead. Slightly theatrical, funny, with an unusual turn of phrase (which makes the boys laugh), very much a manager. 'I have complete trust in my staff, and they must run their departments the way they think best.' Has a high-powered Swiss-French wife, who works part-time in the fashion business as well as taking her role as Head's wife seriously.

ACADEMIC MATTERS: Strong. More A grades at A-level than ever before in '95, and the highest number of passes on record here; however, also quite a number of Ns and Us, 'but we have a fairly catholic intake'. Sciences are taught as three separate subjects, and all boys do three for GCSEs, a recent introduction – 'And I may fall flat on my face,' says the Head. Good Maths – two-thirds take this for A-level. Setting in Maths and French. The school has very high standards of teaching, many staff are of very long-term standing, but there are few female staff. (Fashion note: bow ties and corduroy jackets, plus one or two sexy looking young '*assistants*'.) Saturday morning school. The school offers good Sixth Form non-examined options, three per term each given two periods per week. Pupils have homework notebooks/diaries all the way up the school; Lower Sixth study periods are supervised. Lovely bright classrooms were recently converted (from choristers' dorms) for the new 9- and 10-year-old intake, with the excellent Mrs Jessop-Burnell. Before that, the youngest were choristers only.

G AMES, OPTIONS, THE ARTS: Keen on games, though not necessarily winners – though the recent season proudly records 'more wins than losses' in rugby. Junior hockey teams do well (the school's own playground version goes back hundreds of years); the main playing fields are adjacent, others 3 miles off; enthusiastic rowing (of course).

The school has a distinguished music tradition (especially organists), and choral societies: madrigals were memorably produced on the river in the hot summer of '95. The choir sings from Magdalen Tower at dawn on May morning, one of the great Oxford traditions. The school is umbilically linked (by governors, etc) to Magdalen College, for whom the school produces choristers.

Good Art (despite cramped facilities), which is taken seriously. CCF; also well-run Community Service – not the usual 'granny bashing' but work in schools, hospitals, Oxfam, etc. The chapel converts to a Drama Hall. Extra-curricular activities (keen politics society, also a new juggling club) and lecture programmes keep students busy (during lunch breaks and after school). Good debating (some with girls from Oxford High), e.g. 'American culture has a negative influence on our society,' provokes high passions.

B ACKGROUND AND ATMOSPHERE: Founded in the 15th century by William of Waynflete, whose original home is in the grounds of the college; Cardinal Wolsey was an early Headmaster. School House (on the roundabout by Magdalen Bridge and the Victorian collegiate building) originally housed boarders and choristers – the Master has wisely moved in and refurbished. Across the road the main school buildings are a mish-mash of flimsy-looking edifices (including the Thirties' pebble-dash block) with many additions; Portakabins have been a necessity. 'Grotty,' said a pupil fondly. Lack of funds is clearly a problem, and facilities certainly don't begin to compare with well-endowed establishments – but it's all here and adequate, and the atmosphere is keen, and unpretentious. There are good relations between staff and pupils. 'They encourage us to make decisions for ourselves,' said a Sixth Former.

P ASTORAL CARE AND DISCIPLINE: Definitely good (the Head's housemaster's instincts and experience are in full play), and problems are spotted early on. The one and only school rule – all boys must at all times behave 'sensibly and well' – actually runs to many subsections. Pupils have daily contact with their tutor; Houses are organised on a geographical basis to help parents. Food is 'much improved', say the boys. Prefects must chide younger boys who arrive late for daily assembly in Chapel. NB 9- and 10-year-olds wear uniform, and the blazer goes up the school 'until you grow out of it,' – the rest in non-uniform sober jackets and trousers plus school tie.

PUPILS AND PARENTS: A big mix of backgrounds (including inevitably dons' sons, and a large contingent of sons of professionals), with 25% on Assisted Places. The catchment area spreads to 20 miles in all directions: there is much gnashing of teeth over Oxford traffic problems. OBs include many academics; also Ivor Novello (a chorister); a batch of 15th- and 16th-century grammarians, including Holt, Thomas More's teacher; and a clutch of 20th-century sportsmen and sports commentators (e.g. Jim Rosenthal of the BBC, John Parsons, the Wimbledon expert), also producers Sam Mendes and John Caird.

ENTRANCE: At 9 and 11 with tests to eliminate the crammed child; CE at 13 (minimum pass of 60%). Also at Sixth Form. (NB until '93, the only 9-year-olds were choristers. Now the doors are open to all, no doubt as a sure way in to the main school, though all boys must take the 11+ entrance examination.)

EXIT: A few leave (for other schools, e.g. Cherwell, Winchester). Virtually all to university (14 in a bad year, 22 in a good year to Oxbridge). Increasingly boys go for a gap year first.

MONEY MATTERS: An inexpensive school. There are 5 scholarships at 13, 1 or more Music scholarships; also Assisted Places.

REMARKS: A good choice for locals wanting a liberal academic school, where boys are treated as individuals, and

not minding the lacklustre appearance and lack of oomph.

Malvern College

Malvern, Worcestershire WR14 3DF
Tel: 01684 892333, Fax: 01684 572398

PUPILS: Around 650 boys and girls.
Around 550 board, 100 day; 180 girls, plus own co-ed prep and pre-prep, Hillston, ages 3–13
AGES: 13–18
SIZE OF SIXTH FORM: Around 300
C OF E BUT ALL FAITHS WELCOME
FEE-PAYING

HEAD: Since 1983, Mr R de C Chapman, MA, from St Andrews (fifties). Read languages. Taught Modern Languages at Glenalmond and Marlborough and was Rector of Glasgow Academy before coming here. Busy committee man, fluent, determined. 1994 HMC chairman. Married with three grown-up children. Retires July 1997.

ACADEMIC MATTERS: Strongish, and, our impression is, getting stronger (girls are not unhelpful here). Mainstream subjects show solid good results – though the breakdown of results only in percentages makes it hard to deduce details. School claims to have a high Value Added factor, particularly with pupils of average ability originally – and parents would agree. Dual Award science at GCSE, about one-third take separate sciences. French, Spanish, German, Italian and Russian are all on offer. Very small numbers do Latin and Greek.

One of the few schools that offers International Baccalaureate – and does so successfully, under the très popular et gentil et sexy M Réné Filho. The school is gaining a good reputation in this, and the numbers of pupils choosing IB versus A-levels increase gradually each year (now around one-sixth) – but quite a hard sell is necessary to parents and pupils, 'Because it is hard work.'

Caveat: the school is now operating a tough policy on 'cutting out the dead wood' – 'grossly idle' pupils are being weeded out pre-exams.

GAMES, OPTIONS, THE ARTS: A keen gamesy school – boys and girls are in various county teams, some in England teams. Football is the main game of the autumn term, with rugby in the spring term. There are enthusiastic team tours abroad. Also rackets, fives, canoeing on local rivers, a climbing wall in the smart Sports Centre, a cottage in Brecon Beacons for adventure training (compulsory for all at some point). The swimming pool has been entirely re-vamped and re-opened in '96. CCF is now an option with Community Service, or D of E award.

A lot is on offer at all times/stages, including exotic Sixth Form summer expeditions, e.g. climbing in the Alps, whitewater canoeing in France or Norway. After GCSE, pupils have a week of Sixth Form experience in which A-level choices are tested. Music (including 90 strong choir and Glen Miller style band) based in converted Victorian monastery with monks' cells as practice rooms. Ritzy Art block. Keen Drama. The school are pioneers of work experience, co-ordinated by a three-man careers team – ranging from architecture to fisheries protection to fashion to Tesco – excellent choice. The new Technology centre (opened in '92) won an architectural award.

BACKGROUND AND ATMOSPHERE: A large Victorian pile on a Malvern hilltop with games fields sweeping out below it. Houses 'One' to 'Nine' plus School Houses are arranged in a horseshoe interspersed with other buildings on the campus. There is some criticism that the school feels like a collection of houses, rather than one school, but attempts to remedy this are in hand at the time of writing. The school recently opened a small Sixth Form House and Sixth Form centre. There are three girls' houses on the campus (with capacity for 180). Occasional reports reach us that this feels like a boys' school with girls attached (the old cry). Has its own prep and pre-prep nearby.

PASTORAL CARE AND DISCIPLINE: An intricate house and tutor system picks up most problems, and there are good reports on pastoral care. In the Lower School pupils are allocated tutor in groups of 12–15 pupils. In Sixth Form pupils select their own personal tutors. Has had drugs in the past.

PUPILS AND PARENTS: Sons and daughters of professionals, mostly within a 2-hour drive; some non-nationals, including some from Europe, also Far East, and lots of Service families (15% discount). Pupils don't suffer from city temptations or over-sophistication, 'It's a blessing it's a bit isolated,' reported parents of a frisky teenager. OBs include Denholm Elliott, Jeremy Paxman, Lord Weatheril, Peter Temple-Morris MP and C S Lewis.

ENTRANCE: Registration and CE or a separate test for state school entrants. And of course via their own prep school (though some opt to go elsewhere). Sixth Form entry by (reasonable) GCSEs, interview and tests.

EXIT: 90% go on to long-established universities (London and Oxbridge are the most popular, followed by Bristol, Leeds, Manchester, Warwick, Exeter, Sheffield, also ex-polys) or other higher education. An average of 15 to Oxbridge each year (in '95 all five History applicants won places). A handful to art college, one or two to work/armed Forces.

MONEY MATTERS: There are Assisted Places, and approx 23 academic scholarships (up to maximum of 50% fees). Also scholarships/exhibitions for Music and Art, and Sixth Form scholarships. Also awards for 'games and all-round abilities'.

REMARKS: A co-ed public school going well and good all round: two trump cards – International Baccalaureate and the introduction of girls throughout – have injected new life into this traditional rural boarding school.

Malvern Girls' College

15 Avenue Road, Malvern, Worcestershire WR14 3BA
Tel: 01684 892288, Fax: 01684 566204

PUPILS: Around 450 girls (390 board, 60 day)
AGES: 11–18
SIZE OF SIXTH FORM: 180
C OF E
FEE-PAYING

HEAD: Since 1994, Dr Anne Lee (forties), BA in Psychology from the Open University – an appointment watched with interest as Dr Lee has no previous teaching experience in schools. Was headhunted out of industry, where she built up a career in Management Development and Manpower Training

and Planning, working for Unilever and Morgan Guaranty before setting up her own company. 'Quite a role model!' approved a pupil. However, one or two parents have commented, 'She doesn't understand how a school works, and is not around enough.' The Deputy Head is very important here. Dr Lee has been on the Executive Council of the London Marriage Guidance Council, is a PCC member, and leads an Adult Study Group.
Stop Press: 'leaving'.

ACADEMIC MATTERS: Comes up with very impressive results indeed. A strong general, all-round academic school, but 'not pressurised', say girls. It gets super exam results (74% A–B grades at A level in '95); Maths, Economics (which has a huge following – London board – with 24 out of 37 A grades, could this be a record?), and Biology are particular strengths; Chemistry, French and History are also very good. Traditional teaching throughout. Computers are everywhere, much used and also in boarding houses. Dyslexia coaching and EFL are available.
General Studies in Sixth Form (exam results are not included in the overall grade totals); also complimentary studies one-year GCSE options of Drama, Italian, and City and Guilds IT. There is a broad variety of A- and AS-levels on offer. One-third of girls go on to study Science-related subjects at university.

GAMES, OPTIONS, THE ARTS: The school is strong on the lacrosse field. A much-used circular sports dome was a controversial 1987 innovation ('How many sports do you actually play in the round?' laughed other schools), and an all-weather pitch has improved the games facilities. Football, rugby, rowing and scuba diving are on offer – beefy stuff – as well as traditional girls' hockey and lacrosse. The indoor pool, with fine old changing cubicles, is a legacy from the Imperial Hotel.

The superb Art department produces really professional work – textile and ceramic – as well as traditional paintings. The school has high standards of Music: 90% of girls study one musical instrument, 50% study two; there are exceptional orchestras and a fine choir. The music standard is generally enhanced by annual music festivals.

This is definitely a Christian school (with a link to a school in the Gambia, which is of course, largely Muslim). There is an emphasis on community service, including a lively Grab-a-Granny scheme. Popular Young Enterprise teams. D of E award; cooking on offer. There has been no more Drama, Music and socialising with Malvern College since it went fully co-ed: sounds of lamentation.

BACKGROUND AND ATMOSPHERE: A huge and forbidding Victorian block, close by the railway, converted from the Imperial Hotel. The school is very institutional, strongly house oriented, with all meals in the house. All houses have now been revamped and refurbished.

Weekend activities have been over-hauled, published weekly for the girls to choose options (riding, aerobics, games coaching). All Middle School houses are locked at all times for security reasons. The Middle School no longer wear ties and may wear slip-on shoes. There is no uniform for the Sixth Form.

The splendid library, with 21,000 vols, was recently equipped with 12 multi-media computers linked to CD-Rom.

The school is busy and purposeful, also tough and worthy, and girls are encouraged to learn from their mistakes. The new prospectus has pictures that could be straight out of ads from a glossy and somehow don't look like a school.

PASTORAL CARE AND DISCIPLINE: The school has a strong caring community via Houseparents, and form tutors. It also has a 'code of conduct' rather than rules. But discipline is strong. The Middle School may only go out in threes (or pairs between College main building and house). There is an impressive Personal and Social Skills Course in the Middle School.

Drugs mean automatic expulsion. Sixth Form girls may drink with House Mistress's permission 'the odd bottle of wine', and smoking in the Sixth Form is reported to Sixth Form Council, 'who may recommend disciplinary action'.

PUPILS AND PARENTS: Fairly traditional: 118 girls from overseas (especially the Far East, where parents know the school to be safe and traditional), plus some British girls whose parents live overseas. There is an interesting cross-section socially, ethnographically and academically. Locals, Gloucestershire, Cotswolds, Wales, the Wirral, London; popular with professionals, farmers and a fair number of first-time buyers. OGs include the late Dame Elizabeth Lane, the first woman High Court judge; Barbara Cartland; Elizabeth Tilberis; and Charlotte Rycroft (former ambassador to Chad).

ENTRANCE: At 11+, 12+, 13+ (progressively more at 13+), between 10 and 15 at Sixth Form. CE and own scholarship exam; for Sixth Form, GCSE results must include Bs in A-level subjects.

EXIT: Around 90% to degree courses, 6–12 to Oxbridge. Careers are taken very seriously. Engineering is now popular, also medicine, the City, Foreign Office.

MONEY MATTERS: Scholarships for Academic, Music, Art and PE and at Sixth Form level. Plus special scholarships for daughters and grand-daughters of Old Girls, plus a selection of bursaries.

REMARKS: A very traditional, strong, somewhat old-fashioned girls' all-round boarding school – suffering a drop in numbers, possibly due to the brother school up the road going co-ed, but doing its own thing anyway.

The Manchester Grammar School

Old Hall Lane, Rusholme,
Manchester M13 0XT
Tel: 0161 224 7201 Fax: 0161 257 2446
PUPILS: Around 1,431 boys
ALL DAY
AGES: 11–18
SIZE OF SIXTH FORM: 410
C OF E LINKS, BUT BASICALLY NON-DENOM
FEE-PAYING

HEAD: High Master since 1994, Dr Martin Stephen, MA, PhD (forties), educated at Uppingham, and Leeds University, followed by PhD at Sheffield (Poetry of the First World War). Read English and History for first degree. Prolific writer on English literature and naval history (15 books at last count; *The Price of Pity* about literature and history in the First World War is the latest). Taught at Uppingham, then Housemaster at Haileybury, Deputy Head of Sedbergh. Last post as Head of The Perse, Cambridge, since 1987, where he detected a change in parents' expectations away from the 'driving, ruthless com-

petition of the academic sweat shop – education from the neck up is no longer enough'. Married (wife is Head of a girls' school), with three sons. Likes drawing and painting as well as writing books. An early achiever, choc-full of the right stuff – direct, immensely likeable, energetic, a fast-talker, who thinks it is 'crucial' for a Head 'to be about'. Also patient. The school has a 'management structure' in place: Mr Peter Laycock, the Second Master, and two 'Surmasters', Mr Ian Thorpe and Mr Niel Sheldon; plus Heads of Junior and Middle Schools, and the takeover was smooth.

ACADEMIC MATTERS: An academic power house, one of the best in the country. It has an outstanding Staff Common Room: some young and enthusiastic, some old and enthusiastic, mostly top-class. An atmosphere of learning, and a love of knowledge pervades the Common Room. Class sizes have now been reduced at the lower end of the school to a maximum 25/26, thinning down to 22/23 boys in Middle School. All must take separate sciences at GCSE, and most take (and pass) nine or 11; As are the norm. Latin now becomes an option after two years. Greek, Spanish, Russian and German are also on offer. Boys are 'banded' for Maths, thereafter classes are set by subject grouping. Modular Maths piloted here, and popular, Modular Science is in the pipeline; also languages. Stunning exam results.

The school offers a huge choice of A-levels, plus a choice of 120 'general studies', ranging from silversmithing (MGS Hall Mark) to Swedish, Arabic, Ukrainian, Welsh and Hungarian – 'going quite well at the moment'. Boys must take 12 'general studies', three in each half-year. NB This is one of the very few top academic schools that does not insist on (some) Sixth Formers taking a fourth A- or AS-level, preferring the breadth of the non-examined general studies programme (it receives massive support for this from parents). The school has gone on record protesting at the unfairness of league tables which take no account of whether General Studies are examined or not.

The staff consider pupils 'often' more intelligent than they are themselves, but here this could be modesty. One member of staff commented, 'Let me put it like this – what we achieve together far exceeds the sum of our individual efforts.' One of the few places you will find staff discussing the tactics of getting in to different Oxbridge colleges.

The school has two busy libraries, with boys helping, a security system and CD-Rom, and also a vast bookshop. The Careers room has everything you ever wanted to know.

'The good learning' as decreed by the founder, starts in the Lower School, under the Head of Lower School, Rodger Alderson, and boys study a broad general curriculum for four years before choosing GCSE subjects.

GAMES, OPTIONS, THE ARTS: Boys are not 'press-ganged' to play in any team, but the school still continues to knock the opposition for six. Rugby, football, and cricket are popular – particularly the latter: Mike Atherton and the Crawley brothers are Old Mancunians. The school has a traditional gym and swimming pool only, but a Sports Hall is next on the appeal agenda. Astonishingly successful water polo teams; national finalists at Under-16 and Under-18 in '95. 'I find it alarming that the boys in the team appear to be able to swim faster than I can run,' comments the Head.

Music is very strong under an enthusiastic Head of Department, with lots of individual instrumental teaching from the BBC Philharmonic or Halle

Orchestra members amongst others; the school gives an annual concert in the Royal Northern College of Music. Drama Course from Second Form and 'Dramsoc' popular. The school has a dedicated Sieff Theatre with wooden benches and seriously sad cushions. Art and Music are still the poor relations in terms of numbers taking these subjects at A-level and results are not exciting.

The imaginative new Parker Art Halls (named after the previous Head) encompass five storeys over the main archway, and CDT is compulsory for the first two years; it is thriving, but again results are not spectacular by Manchester Grammar standards (though they would be quite acceptable anywhere else). CDT – with the emphasis on technology rather than craft – has inspired keyboarding. The school has clubs for everything, particularly chess and bridge, lots of debating, Scouts, masses of foreign trips, treks, camps – the younger boys start with weekends at the Owl's Nest at Disley before graduating to The Grasmere Barn.

The school newspaper *The New Mancunian* has a huge circulation and wins awards.

BACKGROUND AND ATMOSPHERE: Founded in 1515 by Hugh Oldham, Bishop of Exeter, a year before he founded Corpus Christi College, Oxford (with which the school has links), to educate able boys regardless of their parents' means, to go on to university and the professions, and open what the Founder called the 'gate' of knowledge. It is now the biggest private senior school in the country. It moved in 1931 to its present purpose-built site (28 acres) in the des. suburb of Fallowfield, down the road from the university, a huge red-brick-based round central quad with heavy high portals, and green late-Art Nouveau tiles to half-way up the walls.

It has been enormously extended, with rabbit warrens through the lab area, and Senior Biology at the rectory across the road. The Marks & Spencer English Centre is now open (there is already a Marks Lab area) and future funds are earmarked for a Sports Hall and improved CDT facilities. Currently Portakabins house the overflow. The dining room is pretty depressing, functional and noisy. There is a lot of reshuffling going on. New boys are given a map to find their way about (even Mr Sheldon got lost, so take heart). The atmosphere is dynamic and bursting with energy, and happy with it. Slick southerners may find it rough at the edges. Sixth Formers wear mufti, otherwise blue blazers.

There has been some redecoration since we last went to press, and generally the school is a more litter-free zone than previously.

PASTORAL CARE AND DISCIPLINE: The Senior Management team is responsible for both, though initial contact with younger boys is via the Form Master, and Form Tutors in Sixth Form. Easy access for parents. Discipline is 'not too much of a problem'; punishments in the form of a communication slip, to be taken home and signed by parent, followed by detention – less used now. Serious punishments are referred to a senior member of staff, who will talk to boys. Out for drugs, drink 'not a problem', Saturday morning detention for smoking.

PUPILS AND PARENTS: The school has a very wide catchment area, stretching far beyond Greater Manchester. There is regular parental contact, with evenings, meetings and regular discussions at 'crucial points' in boys' career. The cream of the intelligentsia, from a wide variety of ethnic and social backgrounds. No earrings, no ponytails

observed ('though when they were really in vogue, they had to be neat ponytails'). Bright boys, polite as you like at the bottom end, but fairly relaxed about visitors near the top; one chap was demonstrating a particularly fine line in 'Egyptian PT' (i.e. falling asleep), whilst another shoved a half-eaten chocolate biscuit into his pocket in one of the many computer rooms. There are dozens and dozens of distinguished OBs, including 'rows' of FRSs, including Sir Michael Atiyah. Also Ben Kingsley, Mike Atherton, Robert Powell and RSC/ENO director Nicholas Hytner, as well as John Ogden, Thomas de Quincey, plus several members of the Sieff family and Simon Marks.

ENTRANCE: Not easy. Main entry at 11, 550/600 boys vie for 200/210 places. The entry exam is in two parts; the sheep from goats are sussed out via questions like 'Four consecutive odd numbers add up to 96, write down the smallest of these numbers.' Very few leave post-GCSE. Entry at Sixth Form is via chosen A-level subjects with GCSE A grade, plus interview.

EXIT: 98% to degree courses, 50+ annually to Oxbridge. Medicine and Law are very popular, followed by Languages, History and Natural Sciences – 'lads don't look for the soft option'. OMs become civil servants, bankers, scientists, businessmen and teachers.

MONEY MATTERS: There are 40 Assisted Places each year, plus 5 for Sixth Form. There are Bursaries to extend Assisted Places scheme, always means-tested, and much drawn on during the recession. NB For historical reasons only, the Bursar is called 'the Receiver'. Bargain of the century: fees just over £1,300 a term for 1995/6.

REMARKS: A five-star academic day school, one of the strongest in the country.

Marlborough College

Marlborough, Wiltshire SN8 1PA
Tel: 01672 892300, Fax: 01672 892307

PUPILS: Around 812, approximately two-thirds boys, the rest girls. Some day, but the majority board
AGES: 13–18
SIZE OF SIXTH FORM: Around 400
C OF E
FEE-PAYING

HEAD: The Master, since September 1993, Mr E J H Gould, MA (early fifties). Previous post as Head of Felsted, where he earned the nickname of 'Basher' – one which stands him in good stead here; he looks like a professional bouncer. Read Geography at Teddy Hall, Oxford, collected four and a half blues (rugby and swimming), rowed for Great Britain. Before Felsted was Housemaster at Harrow. Comments he is homing in on three main things: 'confidence, morale and attitude – none of which you can pass rules on'.

One or two changes among the governors have allowed new blood in, though there is still a heavy presence of clergymen.

ACADEMIC MATTERS: Picking up again – still some excellent staff and teaching. Dual Award Science only at GCSE. Sciences and Arts are spread pretty evenly as we write. Results are variable – GCSE are good, but there are still too many Ds and Es trailing around in the '95 A-levels though we are still

prepared to give the school the benefit of the doubt here and suggest this reflects the calibre of pupils rather than the teaching, (though, alas, the school no longer gets the outstanding Art results it used to).

Classics, Arabic, Japanese, Mandarin Chinese, plus the usual languages are all possible (though NB exotics like Italian are not offered as a matter of course). The school has a good careers centre – indeed it pioneered this. A-level Theatre Studies is on offer (results *comme ci comme ça* in '95), and GCSE Drama was introduced in '94 (though interestingly enough, no one took it). EFL and help for dyslexics is available and well used. The impressive old library has now been overhauled and is much less dusty.

GAMES, OPTIONS, THE ARTS: The school is traditionally strong on mainstream games, and rugby results have been particularly good recently (one boy even won a rugby scholarship to university). Girls are now also more than holding their own against single-sex schools – they do hockey, netball, lacrosse, athletics. Famously strong on extras. Art facilities are up with the best, a legacy from the previous Head of Department. Every child has to do a 'creative project' in Shell year (first year) as a 'counter-blast' to electronic gadgetry. There are dozens of societies, a beagle pack, and a strong Music department, which tackled the *Dream of Gerontius* recently – no mean feat. The famous brass band, the 'brasser', which, says the Head, 'they just lap up', is still going strong.

BACKGROUND AND ATMOSPHERE: Founded in 1843 for the 'Sons of clergy of the Church of England', though you would not guess so to look at it. Buildings are grouped round a central Queen Anne building at the head of the court, contrasting with the Memorial Hall built after World War I – good for concerts – and earthwork known as 'The Mound'. The school has 'in' Houses and 'out' Houses (i.e. on and off the main campus which is spread about the town). Girls' quarters are cosy and comfortable (there are four girls' houses, plus some girls still in boys' houses but they are 'well segregated now'). NB Choose your house carefully. The school has flogged off land from time to time to finance refurbishment. The atmosphere now feels a little less like a kettle full of hot water on which the lid is being kept with difficulty. Pupils' appearance is much less scruffy than before – but there is no room for relaxing on this or any front. That said, if you visit the school you will – as always – see a couple of characters slouching against columns 'like something out of the OK Corral, looking for trouble,' said a member of staff. The Victorian chapel is imposing and stuffy.

PASTORAL CARE AND DISCIPLINE: Previous inadequacies are now melting into history, and the miraculous tightening up is still showing fruit. The Head comments that his approach is 'we're going to talk this through and get it right'. There have been some expulsions since the new Head's arrival, but real effort has been made at this more positive approach. There is a male and female tutor 'team' in every house. The school tests for drugs. Everything is talked through, with written self-assessments – a new system of continuous assessment for encouragement. The Head is also still reported to be pursuing a more 'hands-on' approach – seeing pupils daily as necessary on a one-to-one basis, and on Saturday mornings – 'there is an academic rogues' queue at 8 a.m'. There have been recent sackings for drugs.

PUPILS AND PARENTS: Middle and upper-middle class boys – sons of accountants, lawyers, dealers, army, one or two clergy; also foreigners. Girls come from a wider background. OBs include William Morris, Anthony Blunt, John Betjeman, James Mason, Peter Medawar, Nicholas Goodison (who is now a governor), Wilfrid Hyde White, James Robertson Justice, Lord Hunt (of Everest fame), Francis Chichester, Louis Mac-Neice, Siegfried Sassoon, Bruce Chatwyn.

ENTRANCE: Registration and CE for boys and girls. Three GCSEs at C and three at B grade is a minimum for entry to Sixth Form.

EXIT: Twelve to Oxbridge in '95 (ie, numbers are up on last year, though still very much down on a five-year average); to art foundation courses; more than half do a gap year; one or two to foreign universities.

MONEY MATTERS: A movable percentage of fee income goes to sons of clergymen – though it is still difficult for them to afford it. Approximately 20% of pupils are subsidised in some way (there are no Assisted Places, however). The school also has large number of scholarships and bursaries, and 'limited' help for parents with children in the school whose income has gone down the tubes: 'We would do our level best to get them on to the next "break point".' Also Music and Art scholarships.

REMARKS: A famous designer-label public school which has been through seriously difficult times, but now at last appears to be steady, and getting a cautious thumbs up.

The McLaren High School

Mollands Road, Callander FK17 8JH
Tel: 01877 330156, Fax: 01877 331601

PUPILS: Approx 700 boys and girls
ALL DAY
AGES: 11–17/18
SIZE OF SIXTH FORM: 180
NON-DENOM
STATE

HEAD: The Rector, since 1985, Mr H A Mathie, MA, MEd (fifties). Read Classics at St Andrews University and has taught in the state system all his life. Married with three children. Quiet but impressive, confident and outspoken. Involved in Church activities, plays golf, played hockey at university.

The school comes officially under Stirling Council from April 1996.

ACADEMIC MATTERS: All mainstream subjects are offered, and the school has a wonderful Classics teacher – second-year Latin is still oversubscribed. Gaelic is also offered – about 10 take it. The school follows only the Scottish exam system. Careful setting, and there are good results – though still a few too many low grades. A points system is in place for good work. The school has excellent computing facilities. There are 58 staff, 18 subject departments.

GAMES, OPTIONS, THE ARTS: Given the time restrictions, the school manages to pack in a lot. Not much emphasis is put on competitive team games – to the relief of some – and the official line is that all must be catered for, 'not just the first eleven'. There are lots of clubs and activities in the lunch hour, and trips, (including skiing) abroad. The school is very keen on Music, with festivals and overseas trip every other year with the school orchestra (and concerts after school). All manner of musical tuition is offered, including the bagpipes. Art and Design are also strong. Annual plays are produced – recently *Joseph* and *South Pacific*. There is an activities week in June for all younger pupils, while seniors are on study leave.

BACKGROUND AND ATMOSPHERE: A stunning setting by the river in Callander (some good fly-tiers among the pupils) in the Trossachs. The Sixties' buildings have received a Civic Trust award – though they sit slightly bleakly among the spectacular scenery, and look pretty institutional, especially inside. The first-class library is served by Central Region Library Service – though there are some limitations of use on it. There is room for wheelchairs through the school, including a staircase, lift, ramps (the school is used for adult classes in evenings). Pupils wear uniform, though this is still not immediately apparent, as they are invariably swaddled up in the latest plush slinky anorak and white socks (shell suits are not allowed). There is a happy-go-lucky atmosphere about the place, and it is tolerant of what a pupil at another school called 'weirdos' (by which they meant 'indivduals')

The Foundation dates back to 1844, endowed by Callander philanthropist Donald McLaren in 1850 with a view to providing a 'salary of sufficient amount to induce men of superior talents and acquirements to become and continue Teachers in the said School . . .' School 'dux' boards go back to 1909 on the walls. Motto: *Ab origine fides.*

PASTORAL CARE AND DISCIPLINE: A brisk and realistic approach. Usually it's punishment 'exercise' and the occasional detention. 'Basically,' says the Head, 'it's a question of contact with parents.' He comments that parental control over children is not what it used to be and even in the comparative calm of Callander 'we feel ripples'. The school is leading an anti-smoking crusade.

PUPILS AND PARENTS: All sorts, from a catchment area of 400 square miles – which obviously makes organising extra-curricular activities difficult.

ENTRANCE: By registration.

EXIT: Farming, university, the arts – a total cross-section. Of those going on to university, virtually all go to Scottish universities, of which Glasgow is the most popular.

MONEY MATTERS A state school with foundation endowment (see above). Well-supported by local industries, and manages to provide subsidies where necessary (e.g. for outings).

REMARKS: A sound, much-admired state school, still going strong as ever.

Merchant Taylors' School

Sandy Lodge, Northwood,
Middlesex HA6 2HT
Tel: 01923 820644, Fax: 01923 835110
PUPILS: Around 740 boys (60 board, 680 day)
AGES: 11–18
SIZE OF SIXTH FORM: 250
C OF E
FEE-PAYING

HEAD: Since September 1991, Mr Jon Gabitass, MA (Oxon) (early fifties),

educated at Plymouth College, followed by St John's, Oxford, where he read English. A rugby blue, he still coaches, and will turn his hand to anything: plays soccer, fives, cricket, is very keen on drama – 'exceptionally high here'. Previously taught at Clifton College, and was Second Master at Abingdon. (No relation of the educational agency – observe the spelling.) His wife teaches at a local primary.

A wandering Head, very approachable, who reckons to know every boy in the school, but doesn't see it expanding much more. He still teaches, and believes that it is important for boys to leave school at 18 'self-sufficient, with good A-levels, good communication skills, languages, IT skills, and a sense of purpose and, above all, confidence in themselves'. Gives pupils lots of responsibility to take the initiative.

ACADEMIC MATTERS: The school has made such spectacular progress over the past few years that you begin to wonder what was wrong before. There is no special provision for learning support, but, says the Head, 'teachers are very willing to help those with problems'. Classes are down to nine or less for A-levels, and NB pupils not up to the academic scratch are chucked out after GCSE, so you need to read the A-level results bearing this in mind. GCSEs are amazing – out of a total of 1,272 exams sat in '95, there were only 21 results below C – not many schools can emulate that. Biology GCSE in '95 got 30 A★s, 20 As – and nothing else; Chemistry 41 A★s, 8 As – and nothing else (all either dual or triple certificated). German and Spanish showed equally good results – but the numbers were far fewer. Most pupils take 9+ subjects, with French and Maths a year early. Languages in general are strong (satellite links with Europe are much used), as are Classics. The outstanding performance in Science is followed through to the Sixth Form.

Japanese, Ethics, etc, are available as modules in Sixth Form. Computers (IBM compatible) which were in the attic, are now in 'satellite areas' around the school (in keeping with progressive thought on the matter) and they are on the Internet. The school now has a five-day week with slightly longer terms.

NB In government statistics you will find Merchant Taylors' listed under Hertfordshire.

GAMES, OPTIONS, THE ARTS: There are superb facilities for everything. Boys take their games seriously: rugby pitches are everywhere, they play every school in sight (and Millfield) – though they do not appear to wipe the floor with anyone.

The parents' society, The Friends of Merchant Taylors', is invited to regular lectures on educational topics, and self-subdivide into groups supporting the Scouts, music, hockey, etc.

BACKGROUND AND ATMOSPHERE: Founded in 1561 by the Worshipful Company of Merchant Taylors'. The original building was destroyed in the Great Fire. It moved from the City of London to deep suburbia in 1933 to a purpose-built school (designed by Sir William Newton), dominated by its great hall. Later additions include a Science and Modern Languages block (opened by Lord Coggan, DMT) which harmonises beautifully with the slightly young Music and the old Science block. Set in 250 acres of trees and playing fields, in sunny suburbia. It was one of the original 'Clarendon Nine' schools which included Eton and Winchester, and once unfairly nicknamed the 'Merchant Failures' (the Head says he has *never* heard this name).

The Manor of the Rose, the boarding house, has its own Head Boy, and a full programme for weekends. There is a general purposeful feel throughout the school.

PASTORAL CARE AND DISCIPLINE: The House system is very strong, with House plays directed by senior boys and starring juniors to get them involved during their first term. Tutors throughout: but 'all staff have a pastoral role'.

Mr Gabitass is 'prepared to sack if necessary'. He has sacked for a physical attack on another boy off campus, and for a boy who sold a bag reputed to be cannabis to another which turned out to be rabbit food! The school is prepared to be 'upfront' about smoking, and believes that 'boys want rules applied consistently'.

Punishment fits the crime: forgotten homework? Do it twice plus a bit. The Head believes that the school's own 'air of tranquillity' produces confident but not brash streetwise children, and certainly the ones we met would bear this out.

PUPILS AND PARENTS: Pupils come from 'up and down' the Metropolitan Line, 20 minutes from Baker Street. The ethnic mix creates no apparent disharmony. Parents are very supportive, joining the Sports Club and using school facilities on Saturday mornings and in the holidays. There is a fair number of first-time buyers.

A regular coach service to Radlett, Beaconsfield and Ealing, etc, combined with St Helen's, is about to be expanded.

ENTRANCE: Very selective. About 40 each year at 11 from local state schools: there is a competitive exam in January. The rest at 13 from local preps: St John's Northwood, Orley Farm, St Martin's, Northwood Prep, York House, Alpha and Quainton Hall. The Head interviews candidates in the Christmas term to suss them out; a suitable candidate will be marked A and assured of a place by

January for the following September, assuming CE is up to the mark. There is a lot of telephoning between the school and Heads of Preps. At 16 after GCSE, stringent tests plus five GCSEs at B or above.

EXIT: After GCSE if pupil fails to get three Bs, or for financial or logistical reasons. The great majority to university or degree courses (no details given), a few to crammers or re-applying for Oxbridge. The school got 19 to Oxbridge in 1993 (not 11 as we stated) and though figures for '94/5 are not given, the school states that 20 is 'about average' – with a strong bias in '93/4 to Oxford.

MONEY MATTERS: The Merchant Taylors' Company will mop up any who suddenly discover financial hardship and it produces countless numbers of bursaries for 'academically suitable candidates who come from families of very limited means'. Otherwise, there are 4 scholarships at 11, 5 major and 5 minor awards at 13, and 1 major and 1 minor at 16+. Scholarships also for music at 11+, 13+ or Lower Sixth, and 4 Internal Exhibitions. Also 10 Assisted Places at 11+, 3 at 13+, and 5 at 16+. Plus travel awards to Sixth Formers, Outward Bound and Sail training as well as leaving scholarships to assist at university. A seriously well-endowed school.

REMARKS: A school which is definitely, if quietly, doing something right. It has re-emerged under the current Head as an excellent public day school with superb facilities, well-endowed and producing charming pupils and impressive results.

Merchiston Castle School
(nickname 'Murkie')

Colinton, Edinburgh EH13 0PU
Tel: 0131 441 1722, Fax: 0131 441 6060

PUPILS: Around 400 boys (290 board, 110 day)
AGES: 10–18
SIZE OF SIXTH FORM: 140
NON-DENOM
FEE-PAYING

HEAD: Since 1981, Mr David Spawforth, MA (fifties), educated at Silcoats and Hertford College, Oxford; former BP Educational Fellow, Keble, Oxford. Has been a Housemaster at both Winchester and Wellington. Linguist. Fruity voice, short, voluble, humorous. Married, with two grown-up children. Constant rumours that he is leaving have so far come to nothing.

ACADEMIC MATTERS: A-levels for the majority, Highers for under one-third (a two-year course, with English a must). The school gets middle-of-the-road, almost plodding results, with one or two notable exceptions (e.g. 5 As at A-level in History in '95 – no mean feat). It has good Science teaching (co-ordinated Science exams have been abandoned, and all boys must do a minimum of two separate Sciences at GCSE). There are 17 A-level subjects on offer; setting in most subjects (classes of around 20). Good Electronics; CDT with Art and Design is successful. Boys do well in national industry and invention competitions. The boys' work and progress is 'well monitored all the way,' commented one parent.

GAMES, OPTIONS, THE ARTS: Beefily sporting, particularly at rugby: almost a religion and the 1st XV are terrifying to look at – massive hunks who tower over the teams from other schools (just a thought: shouldn't rugby teams be weighed like jockeys to make the match fairer?) In '95 the team played an enormous number of matches, losing only to George Watson's and to Colston Collegiate (this last being the reigning rugby champions). Also very strong on cricket and athletics – they shine on the Scottish schools circuit. Has its own golf course, squash, sub-aqua. Acres of playing fields, a Sports Hall, etc. CCF for two years. Skiing and all the Outward Bound activities you can think of (it is very close to the Hillend dry ski slope, too). As the Head puts it, 'Boys are not chained to their desks.' Fine Drama, and lots of it.

BACKGROUND AND ATMOSPHERE: Founded in 1833 by scientist Charles Chalmers, brother of Dr Thomas Chalmers in Merchiston Castle (pronounced murky-ston; it's now ruined). It moved to large, purpose-built, gaunt, Georgian-style buildings in the grounds of nearby Colinton House, fronted by games pitches, across the road from the barracks on the outer edge of Edinburgh and looking out to the Pentland Hills. The school has acres of polished wooden floors, including the Memorial Hall, which doubles up as chapel (services are based on the Church of Scotland) and dance hall: girls are regularly corralled in from St George's for Scottish dancing, with heaps of practices before the 'real thing', and squeals of delight all round (starting with 11-year-olds). Girls (again from St George's) are also much in evidence for Drama – which is both keen and ambitious (Metro Golden Meyer casts-of-thousands style). St George's notwithstanding, St Leonard's and Merchiston started a rather unlikely

official brother-sister relationship in 1994 despite a 1¼-hour geographical separation, joint careers conferences, debating, etc. The school has an unusual house arrangement, whereby boys move with their year group – 'You don't get stuck with one housemaster or tutor,' point out the boys. Music and drama practices are enlivened by getting to know boys of other ages. The refurbishment of dormitories is almost complete, now considerably cosied up, giving individuals more privacy. Pupils have study bedrooms at the top end. The school is very Presbyterian.

PASTORAL CARE AND DISCIPLINE: There is a good rapport between pupils and staff, and carefully drawn lines. The school has good drug education (Phil Cooper visits); 'We have to aim younger and younger'. The horizontal house system means 'bullying is non-existent,' say staff (can this be true?). Prefects have more responsibility than most, with all Lower Sixth pupils given a 'try-out' period before final choices are made. Those chosen become Head of dorms in junior houses, etc. 'They all want to become prefects, so they tend not to step out of line.' Drink is an occasional problem. There are some complaints that there is 'not enough to do' on Saturday nights. The jovial and popular Head of Drama runs Pringle House, for the junior boys.

PUPILS AND PARENTS: Middle class, mainly Scottish, some rough-ish diamonds, but open, friendly and well-mannered. One in six is an ex-pat. There has been a slight shift in pupil profile owing to developments in rival establishments.

ENTRANCE: At 10+ (since 1994, previously at 11, and now in line with many other competitor schools);

also at 11, 12+ and 13+, always via tests/exams. A 55% pass is required at CE. Intake also at Sixth Form.

EXIT: To an interesting collection of institutions in '94, including Business Administration at Napier University, Travel and Tourism at Luton, Aberdeen College of Agriculture, Politics and International Relations at Reading, Glasgow Nautical College, several back whence they came (e.g USA and Japan). Pupils go on to be fully paid-up members of the Edinburgh mafia – law lords, etc.

MONEY MATTERS: Scholarships at 11, 12, 13 and one at Sixth Form. New financial brother/sister reductions for parents who send sons to Merchiston, daughters to St Leonard's. The school took relatively few knocks during the recession.

REMARKS: Now the top boys' public school in Scotland, which extraordinary position has been achieved by defection to co-education by the rest. Tough, well run, middle-of-the-road, preparing boys soundly for their future.

Mill Hill School

The Ridgeway, London NW7 1QS
Tel: 0181 959 1176, Fax: 0181 201 0663

PUPILS: Around 525, (340 day, 185 board) boys except 40 girls in the Sixth Form (new 13+ intake of girls in '97)
AGES: 13–18, plus separate junior and pre-prep
SIZE OF SIXTH FORM: Around 210
NON-DENOM
FEE-PAYING

HEAD: Acting Head since the sudden departure of previous Head, in 1995: Mr William Winfield (forties), educated at William Ellis school in North London and the Royal Academy of Music. Has been in the school for 25 years, and set up the much admired Section Bilingue at Mill Hill in the '70s and '80s. His wife, Margaret, is a professional musician – with the Apollo Consort. A nearby prep school Head comments that since he was made Acting Head 'there has been a new spring to his step' and all the signs are he will be given the Headship on a permanent basis – slightly on a play safe basis. Governors: some changes but there are still some tough eggs.

ACADEMIC MATTERS: There is an extremely enthusiastic Business Studies department – just the place for budding R Bransons. Also keen computing, and good Design Technology – the school is generally stronger at practical subjects, reflecting preferences of pupils. The EFL form has been disbanded, to a certain amount of consternation.

The school has a good network of exchanges with France Institution Join-Lambert in Normandy (the 25th anniversary of these exchanges was in '93), Goslar in Germany and in Salamanca. The library needs an injection of capital. Next to the library is the Murray Scriptorum – James Murray of OED fame was a master and worked on his dictionary here.

League table talk: Detailed results are not given, but they appear to be unspectacular and there is a general feeling that the school could do better.

GAMES, OPTIONS, THE ARTS: This was formerly a famous rugby school with blood matches with Harrow, but this has slightly fallen by the wayside, in spite of a splendid Sports/Social Club which raises around £15k a year for sporting tours. The other main games are hockey and cricket – the school were recently county champions (an ex-county cricketer is coach). Girls play hockey and netball. Minor sports also offered: jolly golf and croquet. The Art school has 'Palace of Fun' written in Japanese above the door of the Junior Department and a no-nonsense approach to basic technique (a boy – clothed in school uniform – was posing on the podium for his fellow pupils to draw when we visited). The school has its own Field Study Centre in the village of Dent in Cumbria for the pupils to observe wildlife, etc.

BACKGROUND AND ATMOSPHERE: Founded as a grammar school in 1807 by Non-conformists (the United Reform Church, though links now are minimal/non-existent) and has vestigial traces of the past in rows of headmasters' portraits plastered (we use the word advisedly) on the dining-room walls, and a much bigger portrait of the School Treasurer. Purpose-built – grandiose main buildings with giant Doric columns, bristling with war memorials and marble, on a gorgeous site in 120 acres with pretty draughty hill-air so clean that lichens grow on the school walls; on a clear day you can see Windsor.

Despite the imposing design (the school dwarfs the pretty surrounding village) the atmosphere is wonderfully informal – reflecting the previous Head's style – with pupils punching each other playfully as we passed, and a quite extraordinary system of queuing for meals then taking empty trays through the aforesaid grand main hall, past the Headmaster's study to stack them on trolleys kitchens are in the basement with lifts, (à la country house). The last Head comments about this that they are stuck with it, and it does mean every pupil has to walk past his study at least once a day, which he considers vital for popping-in

purposes. The atmosphere is tolerant and friendly, bouncy, scruffy. Despite its boarding history, this feels very much like a day school.

Junior School: Belmont, Tel 0181 959 1431, Fax 0181 906 3519. Head Mr J R Hawkins. Ages: 7–13, (plus pre-prep, Tel 0171 959 6884, started in September '94 in a redundant boarding house, suitably tarted up thanks to a donation from an OB). Pupils are tested on entry at 7, and test plus interview at 9, 10 and 11. The great majority go on to the senior school. This is a popular prep which does very well for most of its pupils.

PASTORAL CARE AND DISCIPLINE: Six were suspended for smoking cannabis in '95 and later readmitted. The Acting Head commented (and parents will cheer to hear this) 'If you expel a pupil you don't solve the problem. You simply pass it to the next station along the line . . .' The school has a first-rate chaplain (a recent appointment from Brighton College), and every pupil has a tutor for academic and pastoral matters both. There have been reports of bullying in one of the boarding houses. 'I always thought it a very civilised place to be,' said a gentle old boy.

PUPILS AND PARENTS: Sons of local businessmen – many self-made first-generation parents, also a strong contingent of long-established Millhillian families. Almost equal numbers of Protestants and Jewish boys; of the remaining third, half are Hindu and half Muslim. OBs include Richard Dimbleby, Francis Crick, Nigel Wray, Denis Thatcher, Simon Jenkins and several members of the Wills family – an interesting collection.

ENTRANCE: One of a consortium of North London schools including

Haberdashers' Aske's, Highgate, Merchant Taylors', Aldenham – which co-ordinate their (own) entrance exams, on which places are offered; otherwise CE. Put name down a year in advance. Half the pupils come from the school's own junior school.

EXIT: All over the shop. In '95 5 to Oxbridge.

MONEY MATTERS: Scholarships and bursaries and 'we try and bail them out if possible'. There are 10 Assisted Places per year, plus a provision of 5 a year into the Sixth Form.

REMARKS: A one-time traditional boys' boarding school which has now gone co-ed and, with the abrupt departure of the previous Head, is still in search of an identity as boarding numbers continue to drop.

Millfield Senior School

Street, Somerset BA16 OYD
Tel: 01458 442291, Fax: 01458 841270

PUPILS: Around 1,260 boys and girls (about two-thirds board, the rest day)
AGES: 13–18
SIZE OF SIXTH FORM: Around 500
NON-DENOM
FEE-PAYING

HEAD: Since 1990, Mr Christopher Martin, MA (fifties). Educated Westminster and St Andrews University. One of a group of four governing the Millfield schools. Previous post – was Head of Bristol Cathedral School; was a Housemaster at Westminster. A gentle schoolmaster, and a great enthusiast in a school which has hitherto been run by benevolent dictators. Sometime nickname 'Foxy'.

The school is run by a gang of four, including the junior school Head and Bursar.

ACADEMIC MATTERS: Still getting excellent results, particularly at GCSE, in fact the school is much better than it appears in the league tables, given the school's policy of a mixed ability intake. The school sticks rigidly to the syllabus for GCSE and this can lead to problems for pupils going on to study A-level. Good Science – separate sciences at GCSE if you're up to it, otherwise Dual Award – with an excellent Biology teacher, Dr Price. The Language department is weak, in our opinion. The school is pioneering GNVQs – GNVQ in Business Studies has been on offer from September 1994. There is a good wide range of subjects on offer (including Theatre Studies, Classical Arabic, and Italian) and the school can usually cater for the occasional exotic request. It has a famous and excellent remedial department. The ratio of staff:pupils is approximately 1:8 – allows for very finely tuned setting.

NB This is still a school with a truly comprehensive intake – everything from A-level at the age of 11 for the gifted, to children for whom five GCSE passes is a miracle. As such, a very rare animal in the private sector.

GAMES, OPTIONS, THE ARTS: The school is famous for sporting prowess – generous scholarships entice in talent which is then trained up in 'squads' which win everything and regularly compete at county and national level. Swimming and fencing are strong, also rugby and cricket. 'Their First 15 are giants,' said a pupil from a nearby school, 'five of our team were taken off wounded. They slaughtered us.'

The Lawn Tennis Association recommends the school for would-be tennis stars. Famous for polo (boarding fees for ponies are 'like having to pay for another child'), though the famous Major is no longer in charge. Pupils who are not sports stars are not much encouraged to have a go, but if they persist, they find to their amazement that they are of high standard compared with pupils from other schools.

Music scholars produce results, and overall standards are improving. The Art department is one of the best equipped in the country, with one or two good staff, and permanent wonderful exhibitions of professional painting and sculpture – real feasts for the soul in an area notably short of such. However, one or two parents have queried whether the art teaching is always up to the high standard you would expect of this place.

The school offers lots of extras – but pressure on popular options can be too great for resources.

BACKGROUND AND ATMOSPHERE: Founded in 1935 by 'Boss' Meyer, who, rumour has it, opened a new house every time he came back from the summer holidays, in order to pay off his debts. Meyer's philosophy was to put the individual child's needs before those of the school, and to adopt an aggressive marketing attitude. The rows of Nissen huts which were the hallmark of the school are gradually being replaced with rather uninspired buildings, but the campus as a whole is now pleasing, tucked unobtrusively at the edge of Street, with which the school has links via the big shoe industry (Clark's). The relationship between school and town is uneasy at times.

Highly recommended boys' house: Shapwick – 'there's no bullying there and everyone can get on with what they like,' say pupils. Highly recommended girls' house – still the Grange.

The school is brilliant at marketing itself (and has been so since long before other schools had heard of the word) – and never forgets that it is basically a business. Staff exude excitement even after showing the nth parent for the day around the school. The prospectus is a little masterpiece of fancy promotion – with glossy photographs alternating with text on matt paper, like a photograph album, and lots of mini-interviews with pupils.

PASTORAL CARE AND DISCIPLINE: Excellent in parts at grass-roots level, *but* problems do arise owing to the size of campus and the to-ing and fro-ing in buses between the academic and boarding staff and the resulting responsibility gaps. Perhaps too much latitude is allowed. Non-games players (mostly girls) have lots of scope to get up to mischief, and make full use of it. There are regular sackings for drugs; alcohol is a constant problem. The school was a pioneer of the 'six-inch rule' now copied by other schools. It now has a San (since 1992). According to an admittedly biased parent, the school has a gung-ho attitude to pupils' misdemeanours – sack one and let in another; there is a largish turnover.

The school hit the headlines (not an unknown phenomenon) over the court case of the molesting swimming instructor, who taught the Millfield squad.

PUPILS AND PARENTS: Lots of new money. There is a large local contingent, large numbers of first-time public school patronisers, overseas students, one or two dyslexic Sloanes, and a smattering of film stars' children. Mothers flash large rocks, shoulder pads and stilettos, which sink into the grass on Open Days, and cars (Mercedes, Range

Rovers, Rolls-Royce = boarders; Ford Fiestas = day pupils) have personalised number plates (including the best number plate in the business – FU2). OBs include Duncan Mayhew, Mark Law, Chris Law, Gareth Edwards.

ENTRANCE: Interview and previous Head's report. CE for setting purposes. 96 came in from the school's junior school in '95. There is a large exodus after GCSE, and a large intake (the school has some leeway to pick and choose here – don't assume it's easy-peasy).

EXIT: Widely differing careers reflect widely differing children.

MONEY MATTERS: Generous scholarships for Sports, academic and Music keep the school well up in the performance league. No quarter is shown to parents in financial difficulties: a commercial loan is offered, and 'if they don't pay up we take them to court,' says the Bursar. The school has felt the recession (new money tends to evaporate fast) – but rallied.

Contrary to endless reports in the press, it is not the most expensive school in the country – but more or less on a par with the rest.

REMARKS: A top-class, if difficult school to manage. It has strength and non-academic breadth. This also could be your first choice of school if you have a dyslexic child, providing the child is reasonably robust and determined. It is definitely not a place for wets, nor for social climbers.

Milton Abbey School

Nr Blandford Forum, Dorset DT11 0BZ
Tel: 01258 880484, Fax: 01258 881194

PUPILS: Around 200 boys (a handful of day boys, the rest board)
AGES: 13–18
SIZE OF SIXTH FORM: Around 75
C OF E
FEE-PAYING

HEAD: Since 1995, Mr W J Hughes-D'Aeth (pronounced daith) BA (early forties), educated at Haileybury and Liverpool. Previously a Housemaster at Rugby. Read Geography, and teaches to the juniors. Formerly a 'keen Territorial Army officer' and still occasionally dons uniform to help with the CCF. Married with four young children. Sounds charming. Says of the pupils here that he immediately 'perceived they are gentle men'.

ACADEMIC MATTERS: The school is particularly good at helping boys with a learning difficulty, dyslexics are integrated with the rest (lots of remedial help is given where needed). 20–30% pupils come with an educational psychologist's report (a summary of which stays in the staffroom, and tutors and staff have instant access). In the light of this, most results are a credit to the school – with a sprinkling of A*s at GCSE, and a good wodge of As (Maths, Drama and French being the top earners here). Some of the A-level results perhaps show over-ambition, with too many E–Us for comfort, particularly in Communication Studies, funnily enough, and also, as many other schools, in Economics. Art and Design results are disappointing – few pupils take either subject, and there are no As or Bs. Note: in '95 36 pupils took fewer than 2 A-levels. There were also some 'very bright' boys, including, as we write, one 12-year-old who has done A-level and is studying at the Open University . . .

Most classes are under 12, with individual attention and tutorials often instantly available at any time on any subject. The ratio of staff to pupils is $1:7\frac{1}{2}$. There is a low staff turnover. Academic tutors do Study Skills and monitor progress; teaching staff set aside two periods each week for official tutorials or help with problems.

IT is popular and computers everywhere (most boys have them for private study) as well as Computer Rooms. Business Studies linked to the Economics department. German teaching can be arranged, usually individually taught. Latin is also on offer.

GAMES, OPTIONS, THE ARTS: The school has excellent sports facilities: rugby is the main game and there was a tour to Canada in 1994. Peter Alliss-inspired golf course (his son was a pupil) and a new indoor heated swimming pool – which can be used at weekends. Sailing, good and popular, was particularly successful in '95, winning e.g. both the Southern area and South-West area regattas.

Pupils have compulsory activities on Tuesday and Thursday afternoons, and there is a huge choice: Art, v active theatre (with an actor in residence), boat maintenance, clay-pigeon shooting, fencing, model-making, etc. Natural History is still strong with a moth trap shining through the summer months. Boys do regular head counts of birds. Ferrets. The CDT department has expanded, and CCF is popular; the school has strong links with the Royal Armoured Corps at Bovington, also with the Navy. D of E awards.

BACKGROUND AND ATMOSPHERE: An enormously friendly and truly kind atmosphere here – all are cared for and appreciated, weirdos are not picked on and (almost) without exception boys report that they 'loved it' at the school.

An immensely beautiful, listed Grade 1 building (begun by Sir William Chambers and taken over by James Wyatt), set in a fold of valleys and Dorset hills. The Abbot's Hall and Kings' Room are breathtaking. Magical. The school was founded in mid-'50s. Modern blocks are cleverly hidden, while the stable block has been converted into light classrooms plus Art, Music and CDT, with a stunning theatre. Daily worship in the beautiful Abbey (also occasionally used by local community). Houses are in the main building, each with its own territory. All Housemasters are married, and a family atmosphere pervades; boys know each other well, graduating from dormitory/common rooms (i.e. with working spaces round the beds) to single study bedrooms. The Head has instigated a major programme of refurbishment here to bring the school 'somewhere towards the 20th century', aiming for the 'faded country house look', and commenting that 'buildings and the whole environment is so important . . .' Boys are kept occupied in this isolated school; they wear uniforms of lovat trousers and jerseys (suits on Sunday). Not a girl in sight – boys tend to get slightly restless as they go up the school.

PASTORAL CARE AND DISCIPLINE: Housemasters (who are normally also Academic Tutors) plus Assistant House tutors. The Chaplain's wife is a Counsellor. The school is small enough to pick up any worrying vibes via the bush telegraph. It's out for drugs (but only one expulsion since '91 at the time of writing); 'constructive restrictions' for smoking in building, plus rustications.

There is a good prefectorial system: prefects are called 'pilots', the atmosphere is structured and disciplined, good manners and consideration for others are noticeable. The school is almost OTT in its marketing of the 'caring' image.

PUPILS AND PARENTS: Upmarket. Not so very many first-time buyers, but more than there used to be. Boys are courteous, relaxed and friendly, and responsible, 'have an outstanding sense of belonging' and 'really miss it when they leave'. Geographically widespread. There is a monthly rendezvous for Old Boys at the Duke of Wellington pub, Eaton Terrace.

ENTRANCE: Via CE, flexible. From everywhere, including all the top preps, over 100 feeders, plus the state system. Entry post-GCSE if the chap has the right qualifications and is 'good enough'.

EXIT: Around 70% on to some form of further education, with 50% to degree courses. Ex-polys are particularly patronised – including Oxford Brookes and Manchester Metropolitan, also such colleges of higher education as Cheltenham and Gloucester, plus Harper Adams, etc. Boys tend to opt for careers where 'they have to sell themselves' – very entrepreneurial. Practical subjects such as Rural Land Management, and Hotel and Catering are popular.

MONEY MATTERS: There are up to 8 scholarships, including 3 for music. The school will carry pupils through exam year in cases of financial hardship.

REMARKS: An excellent boys' boarding school ('for gents,' said a parent) which might well be a solution for your less academic son and those with specific learning difficulties needing a boost to get

them through A-level. A great confidence-building place which runs on kindness and encouragement.

More House

22–24 Pont Street, London SW1X 0AA
Tel: 0171 235 2855, Fax: NONE
PUPILS: Around 225 girls
ALL DAY
AGES: 11–18
SIZE OF SIXTH FORM: Around 50
RC
FEE-PAYING

HEAD: Since 1991, Miss Margaret Connell MA (Oxon), unmarried physicist (forties), who was previously Deputy Head of Bromley High and stepped into an uneasy situation following abrupt departure of her predecessor who lasted a brief year in the job. Educated at a direct-grant grammar school in Leeds before Oxford.

REMARKS: A Pont Street Dutch architectural rabbit-warren in a prime location (two minutes to Harrods) where cramped, tough, newly decorated premises make extra-curricular happenings thin on the ground though there is a good choir. Anything goes for clothes (some parents are bothered about the Fast Set); among the pupils are lots of bi- and tri-linguals. The RC status (steady at around half, a draw for diplomats, etc) makes for a less socially cohesive group than nearby Francis Holland, Sloane Square. Results are not startling. Dual Award Science GCSE only (good Biology); competent Maths (with a new computer network); keen History under high-calibre old-hand Mr Hancock; strong Languages (Latin, German, French, Spanish – one to Oxbridge '94).

A solid, supportive, small-scale, set-up with lots of personal attention from caring staff ('who bother about us, take us out for coffee,' approves a Sixth Former), which is important for Miss Connell, in her persuasive crusade to retain girls in the Sixth Form. 'A-levels are tough,' comments the Head, 'girls do need help and encouragement.' The school fills a niche in the pricier end of the not particularly academically selective 'nice girls' day market, though it is still not the draw it was and definitely not for the competitive extrovert. Seriously un-gamesy.

Moreton Hall

Weston Rhyn, Oswestry, Shropshire SY11 3EW
Tel: 01691 773671, Fax: 01691 778552

PUPILS: Around 290 (around 20 day, the rest board)
AGES: 11–18
SIZE OF SIXTH FORM: 85
C OF E
FEE-PAYING

HEAD: Principal, since 1992, Mr Jonathan Forster, BA (early forties), formerly Housemaster in charge of girls and Head of English at Strathallan School. Educated at Shrewsbury and Leeds University. Teaches English to A-level students. Very hands-on, and giving the school a much needed shake-up. Married (his wife is a teacher, English is her subject), with two young daughters (one at the school). Madly keen on 'everyone using all facilities as often as possible'.

ACADEMIC MATTERS: The Head and staff are keen on beefing this aspect up, though this is a school with a broad intake, a place you choose for personality more than anything else, with the emphasis on sound, middle-of-the-road education. Some good solid results (including lots of As) at GCSE in all three Sciences, one or two below the C-line in French and Maths. There are few failures at A-level, though a fair sprinkling of Ds and Es but still, all in all, a fairly steady A-level performer. Theatre Studies and Business Studies are now on offer (Home Economics continues on the menu, though is not well patronised). The school has a good dyslexic unit, and interesting life-skills course for Sixth Formers. The IBM-sponsored IT centre opened in 1995. The Careers department/work experience record is far stronger than many bigger grander schools.

GAMES, OPTIONS, THE ARTS: Gamesy (despite its small size), with a traditionally strong lacrosse record. Keen tennis (the school has an indoor court). Design Technology and Art are both good, and there is keen Drama, 'Lots of it,' enthuse pupils. Music is good (some done with Shrewsbury boys), also social activities, lectures, etc.

The Sixth Form are renowned nationally for Moreton Enterprise and the school travel centre (and now piloting GNVQs as part of this), and took over the local railway station, Gobowen, in '93. Turnover (of the travel business) in 1994–5 was £300,000. 'Excellent, practical, hands-on work experience,' commented a parent. The new enterprise manager is a chartered accountant. Good links are building up (music, drama, careers conference, etc.) with Shrewsbury School (NB the Head is an OB).

BACKGROUND AND ATMOSPHERE: Very friendly and uninstitutional, rather a hotchpotch of buildings in lovely country. The school has flexible exeats; the usual girls' school whinges about weekends, and not enough to do, reach us, though the school is very anxious to point out the extensive range of weekend activities including parachuting and D of E awards (eight girls are currently engaged on this last). NB: a ceiling of 300 in number has now been decided upon following considerable improvements, (cosying up) to dormitories and common rooms.

PASTORAL CARE AND DISCIPLINE: Much changed and much improved from being centrally run (good on paper) to a house system with the house-master/mistresses being given consider-able powers. A tutor system is in place and tutors visit tutees twice weekly – 'General feeling of staff working harder and girls have someone to turn to now,' from a parent. Workshops and widening-horizons weekend programmes are in good shape (compulsory until Sixth).

PUPILS AND PARENTS: A truly mixed bunch, socially and geographically. Some ex-pats; but mostly from Cheshire, Shropshire and Wales (parents might also consider Malvern Girls and Cheltenham Ladies'). Open and chatty girls, jolly. Composer Thea Musgrove is an Old Girl.

ENTRANCE: 11+; 13+ via CE or own entry test and interview at other ages. Also at Sixth Form.

EXIT: 90% leavers go to university; art college is a popular alternative.

MONEY MATTERS: There are 3 scholarships at 11+, 3 scholarships at 13+; 1 tennis scholarship at 13+; also an award at 16+.

REMARKS: An untraditional, unstuffy small school in a rural area that teaches girls to stand firmly on their own feet and does not produce stereotypes.

The school appears to be finding its own feet under its energetic Head. Could be a solution?

The Mount School

Dalton Terrace, York YO2 4DD
Tel: 01904 622275, Fax: 01904 627518
PUPILS: Around 235 girls (120 board –
  25 weekly, 115 day), plus co-ed prep
  and nursery department (see below)
AGES: 11–18
SIZE OF SIXTH FORM: Approx 75
QUAKER
FEE-PAYING

HEAD: Since 1986, Miss Barbara J Windle, MA (Cantab) (fifties), formerly Head of English and Sixth Form and Senior Tutor at Bolton School (Girls' Division). A Quaker, though not proselytisingly so, she rules the school with charm, humour and a core of steel and wants 'to ensure that every child is conscious of being valued and finds something in which she achieves, and that would include extra-curricular as well as curricular activities'.

ACADEMIC MATTERS: Small classes. Maths is strong, Music results are good. Set Maths and French; there is a fabulous and well-used Maths and Science Centre adjoining Arts and Crafts. Computers are everywhere and Technology is taught to A-level. The library is good. Results are solid, though note that General Studies is on the A-level agenda.

GAMES, OPTIONS, THE ARTS: A marvellous, maintained 20-acre oasis in the middle of York, with tennis courts everywhere, an impressive indoor pool and integrated PE block, and the standard collection of all-weather pitches (hockey or tennis).

Two-thirds of all girls learn a musical instrument and there is a steady stream of success in the Speech and Drama field. There are lots of co-productions with the brother school, Bootham. D of E award is very popular, and lots of minor sports: fencing, basketball, riding, etc.

Girls have clubs for everything from bee-keeping to rock climbing or conservation. Ceramics, dressmaking, fabric painting, etc, in Art and Design Centre, open at weekends. College (Sixth Form) girls have joint General Studies at Bootham.

BACKGROUND AND ATMOSPHERE: The school started in 1831, but foundations for 'a good liberal education for the daughters of Friends' were laid in 1785; it moved to its present site in 1857. Approx 10% of the pupils come from a practising Quaker background and ditto staff; this is the only all-girl Quaker school in the country. Quaker values, 'answering that of God in everyone', are fostered: the motto, 'fidelis in parvo', is on the front cover of the prospectus. The morning Meeting is based on silent worship; the school's ethos is purposeful, friendly and caring. The revamped dining room has cafeteria-style choice. Good food, vegetarian option. Girls graduate from cheerful mixed-age dorms in the 'lower' and 'middle' schools to study bedrooms in the separate Sixth Form House – 'College' – with a computer-resourced workroom. New girls are allocated a 'nutcracker' to show them round and help them settle in. The school has an active Friends of the Mount Society (FOMS) which lays on such excellent extras as summer balls and fireworks displays. There are Quaker-inspired exchanges with Quaker schools in Philadelphia.

Junior School: Tregelles. Head: Since 1991, Mrs Lynne Atkinson (forties) Cert

Ed. Tel, etc as above. Ages 3–11, boys and girls. Founded in '91, it is popular and fulfilling a local need. It uses all the senior school facilities, including the dining room. 99% of girls go on to the senior school; boys go on to St Peter's, Bootham, or Pocklington.

PASTORAL CARE AND DISCIPLINE: There are weekly tutorial systems, and the whole Staff and 'College' meet annually as a 'Policy Review Committee to consider general matters of school life'. Each 'College' girl has her own personal tutor to discuss academic and personal issues. A positive self-image is encouraged. Girls are asked to leave for 'extremely serious' offences, otherwise punishment is the withdrawal of privileges ('on report').

PUPILS AND PARENTS: Masses of parental contact; pupils are local or Quaker-related from all over, with over 50 boarders from abroad (including expats). Parents can camp on the school grounds during leave weekends. Pupils wear a tartan skirt and grey/blue sweater, mufti in College.

ENTRANCE: Own entrance exam at 11+, 12+, 13+. Approx 99% of girls from junior school move on to senior school, but they have to take the exam. No previous exam papers are handed out, and the school emphasises that it is 'the potential, not the results we are examining'. Sixth Form entry on GCSE results and interview: 10 or 12 each year.

EXIT: Ten or twelve post-GCSE (to boys' schools and the like). Virtually all girls go to university – a mix of older universities and ex-polys (including Leicester, Sheffield, Sheffield Hallam, Warwick, London), about 3 a year to Oxbridge, otherwise secretarial, nursing, etc.

MONEY MATTERS: There are 5 Assisted Places, 1 full academic scholarship at Sixth Form, and academic awards at 11 and 13 (as long as scholarship remains high). Music, Drama and Art scholarships available, the latter mainly to help with the wherewithal to visit art galleries and buy specialist books, etc. Many bursaries are available for practising Quakers, with preference given to daughters of Old Scholars of The Mount or Bootham, plus bursaries for girls who are not connected with the Society of Friends, and bursaries for girls intending to teach, etc. The school is 'sympathetic' in event of emergency.

REMARKS: A well-resourced, famous Quaker girls' school now establishing itself firmly in the 1990s; academic standards are rising, and the school is well organised and caring.

North Bridge House School

1 Gloucester Avenue,
London NW1 7AB
Tel: 0171 267 2542, Fax: 0171 267 0071

PUPILS: Around 478 boys and girls
ALL DAY
AGES: 7–17, also pre-prep
SIZE OF SIXTH FORM: not applicable
NON-DENOM
FEE-PAYING

PRINCIPAL: Since 1972, Mr Wilcox. Truly amazing seventy-something-year-old owner who keeps a low profile and requested not to be in this guide because, as far as he knew, he had had no parents saying that they had entered their child at the school as a result of reading the guide. (The Founder of the school was Mr Warwick James.) He also owns Akeley Wood School in Buckinghamshire, and the popular nursery Stepping Stone in Hampstead. A wheeler-dealer; he sits like a large spider in his web, watching. Comments he is 'traditional and old-fashioned'. Two of Mr Wilcox's sons are working in the school on the administrative side.

HEAD of Upper School: Mr J Lovelock, BA, MSc, PGCE (whom we have not met).

HEAD of Prep School: Mr R Shaw Cert Ed, one-time publicity officer for Simpsons. Likeable.

HEAD of Lower School: Ms J Battye, Cert Ed (thirties). Dynamic, the secret of the school's success. Works tirelessly and through the holidays. A Head who, according to the Head of a top London senior day school, has 'really got her act together'. NB Boys switch to Upper school at 10+, girls stay in Lower school if leaving at 11+.

ENTRANCE: Put name down at the bottom of the school. All are welcome – there is a wide ability intake. Test at 11+, 12 and 13 for 'outsiders'. A large sum of money is required to keep your place open.

EXIT: Mostly to London day schools – St Paul's (boys and girls), University College School, Highgate, City of London.

REMARKS: Housed in what was the Japanese School (and before that a convent), just over the road from Regent's Park Zoo. Its success is partly due to its catchment area for NW intellectuals – average intelligence is high, and the school understands the needs of bright, easily bored children. Not for wilted flowers.

There is a large Jewish contingent and kosher meals are on offer. A strong cabbagey smell emanates from the school dining room in the basement.

This is the only genuine fee-paying co-ed in central London, though NB no Sixth Form, and GCSE candidates are new (first batch through in '91), and few, and didn't perform too hotly in '95 (15 pupils, 81% A–G passes). Bear in mind, though, that the school has a mixed intake.

The school believes in streaming and setting – 'the children have got to be taught' – and Mr Wilcox has no time for staff who think otherwise. Lots of good, old-fashioned virtues are aspired to, and the school makes no apologies for this. 'Undesirable vicious habits' will result in expulsion, as will even the 'smell' of drink or drugs. The main pastoral role falls to the form teacher, with time set aside at the end of each week for sessions on overall progress.

The school is 50/50 boys and girls in prep department, but this fluctuates higher up, with some classes entirely of boys. Maximum class size is 24, much lower in the Upper School. The school has a small and useful EFL unit so overseas students can be trained up from scratch.

The school plays soccer and rugby, rounders, hockey, netball 'in various places' with permanent buses on tap. It has a teeny weeny playground and pupils are constantly barging into each other in corridors.

The Lower School is outstanding at chess, owing to a member of staff, Russell Fell, who is crackers about it, and excited chess games spill over into corridors after school hours in the 'Juniorate'. Music is keen and sophisticated, with 7-year-olds doing what one termed 'abstracts' from *A Masked Ball*, *Aida*, etc. Some excellent art.

Altogether, a school which is seriously

strong at prep school level, but tails off further up.

North London Collegiate School

Canons, Edgware, Middlesex HA8 7RJ
Tel: 0181 952 0912, Fax: 0181 951 1391

PUPILS: Around 745 girls, plus 254 in the junior and first school
ALL DAY
AGES: 11–18 (plus junior school and first school ages 4–7 and 7–11)
SIZE OF SIXTH FORM: Around 223
C OF E – all faiths welcomed
FEE-PAYING

HEAD: Since 1987, Mrs Joan Clanchy MA (fifties). Educated at St Leonard's, read History at St Hilda's College, Oxford. Previously Head of St George's Edinburgh. Her husband is a lecturer in medieval history; two grown-up children. A delightful, soft-spoken Scot, humorous, self-questioning, sensitive. Widely respected. Aware that the girls in her care 'can be arrogant'. Sees her job increasingly as one of 'finding the right balance' for both pupils, staff and parents: citing, for instance, the balance between academic matters plus pastoral care, the balance between pupils and the staff's responsibility to get good results.

ACADEMIC MATTERS: This is a powerhouse, one of the most academic girls' schools in the country: 81.5% of A–B grades at A-level in '95. There were two E grades in Chemistry (but out of a field of 38, good heavens), and one in Biology and in Spanish, and a sprinkling of Ds in '95, otherwise the most startlingly impressive result was 42 girls taking A-level Maths and all getting

As or Bs (mostly As). Languages appear to be a bit weaker – but all is relative. Some AS-levels taken. 100% A–C passes at GCSE.

It is not a bed of roses to teach here, though. 'The problem,' said the Head, 'is that the staff may feel the success depends increasingly on them.' Girls are also naturally competitive ('with ourselves,' they declare, 'and we are mutually supportive'), and urgently want to do as well as the year above. 'I have had new young teachers coming to me white with shock,' said Mrs Clanchy, 'because of the girls' insolence: they expect and demand a great deal of the staff.'

The Modern Languages staff are still very strong, with 1 Russian, 1 German, 1 Spanish, 2 French native-speaking teachers, plus three native 'assistants'. Nine or ten GCSEs are the norm, though musicians may not take more than eight ('Some staff think we're a music school,' said the Head). Sciences are taught as three separate subjects, and pupils do the co-ordinated Double Award at GCSE (staff keen). Excellent A-level and careers advice is given. League tables put pressure on staff to focus more on exam techniques: they often offer workshops (even occasionally on Sundays) right up to the last moment pre-exams.

Some parents and pupils are beginning to complain of a 'desperate sense of pressure to do well *all* the time.'

GAMES, OPTIONS, THE ARTS: Not a cutting edge on the games field, which said, the school does pretty well at its matches. It has a splendid indoor pool, two gyms (one mainly used for dance), and no lack of space/facilities for sport. There is also a multi-gym exercise hall, 'But we need more instruction about which muscles should be exercised when, etc – we were told, but we've forgotten,' comments a pupil. The school has an outstandingly good Music department,

energetic and ambitious (won the Schools National Chamber Music Competition in '94 *and* '95). There are also two orchestras and two choirs. There is a small Design Technology department (now on offer as an A-level, two took it in '95). Keen on Drama – and the school does some productions with Harrow, though, 'Boys tend to get the best parts, we prefer to do it all on our own.' The main assembly hall doubles as a theatre; the studio theatre won prizes despite the fact that some of the audience can't see, it is now used for Drama workshops. Lively Art.

BACKGROUND AND ATMOSPHERE: A lovely, peaceful, spacious oasis on an ugly outer edge of London. One of the oldest of the well-endowed girls' schools, along with Cheltenham Ladies' College, founded by Frances Mary Buss, a pioneer in the field of women's education. The school moved here in 1929 to the former house of Lord Chandos – and the girls are appreciative, especially Sixth Formers, whose teaching is done in the main house. It is set in fine parkland, 30 acres of it, with cedar trees, two large flower-filled ponds, and girls in dark brown uniforms dotted about everywhere in what appears to be a relaxed and informal atmosphere. The Sixth Form have a common room upstairs in the main house (staff are not allowed in here), with walls well-covered with graffiti, e.g.: 'Question Authority!' and beneath it: 'Why?'

Junior School: Tel: 0181 952 1276, Fax: 0181 951 1293. Head from September '96: Mrs D Francken (who already teaches in the school), who takes over from Mrs Parkinson, who is retiring. Ages: 7+–11, also a new infants' school (now called 'First School') for children aged 4–7. There are tests and an assessment to get into First School, thereafter automatic entry into junior school. Tests for

7+ entry. 99.9 per cent of pupils go on to the senior school. Juniors are in a separate building in the grounds.

PASTORAL CARE AND DISCIPLINE: 'Count the number of offices for interviews,' advises the Head, 'if you want to investigate the pastoral care in a school.' (Lots here.) This is an area the Head works hard on, aware of the difficulties inherent in the situation today. At 14/15 girls revolt against the uniform bit. There is total, silent concentration in the classroom, but girls can be insolent and 'give lip'. The school runs staff training days and always includes two days on pastoral school issues, well aware that some members of the staff (largely female) are champing to get their teeth into curriculum matters. The school has a fierce anti-smoking campaign (with posters everywhere) – not heeded by some.

PUPILS AND PARENTS: Lower-middle to middle class, many coming in from state primary schools. Girls are remarkably articulate, poised, fearless, able to talk to anyone, challenging. 20% of pupils come from ethnic minorities, and there is an even larger Jewish contingency. Catchment area defined by 10 coaches (used by 570 girls from the senior and junior schools), which dip into Radlett, Golders Green. Probably not a suitable place for a shy child (Mrs Clanchy agrees, 'though it pains me to say it'): robustness is needed. OGs include Esther Rantzen, Eleanor Bron, Barbara Amiel, not to mention Susie (*Fat is a Feminist Issue*) Orbach, who was expelled.

ENTRANCE: From the junior school (via exam). Strongly competitive exam at 11+ (children are likely to be choosing between NLCS and Haberdashers' Aske's and South Hampstead

High). Some at Sixth Form: approximately five leave (for boys' schools or Sixth Form College), but 15 come in – and more apply. Candidates sit a one-hour paper for each proposed A-level.

EXIT: All to university, it goes without saying, and around 20% to Oxbridge. Medicine, law and engineering are all popular options.

MONEY MATTERS: Six academic scholarships at 11 (awarded on performance in the 11+ exam), two music scholarships and 12 assisted places a year, all at age 11.

REMARKS: Top outer-London academic school that prepares girls well for ambitious careers, with consistently brilliant exam results. Some pupils and parents describe the place as 'over-pressurised' and it is our impression that this is getting worse. Greatly helped by a wise Head and the elegant green acres.

Norwich High School for Girls

95 Newmarket Road,
Norwich NR2 2HU
Tel: 01603 453265, Fax: 01603 259891

PUPILS: Around 650 girls, plus 250 in the junior school
AGES: 11–18, junior school 4+–11
SIZE OF SIXTH FORM: Around 158
C OF E (JUNIOR SCHOOL IS NON-DENOM)
FEE-PAYING

HEAD: Since 1985, Mrs Valerie Bidwell, BA (forties), brisk, businesslike and hot on discipline.

ACADEMIC MATTERS: The one and only serious girls' academic day school in Norfolk – there is a huge catchment area and pressure on places means girls are from a fairly narrow ability band and standards remain consistent. It provides traditional grammar school teaching, with regularly strong results in Sciences (Biology especially, and in '95 this was the most popular A-level) and Maths, while language teaching is boosted by satellite TV. A-level Spanish and GCSE Italian are on offer from 1996. All Sixth Formers do General Studies for an A-level (and almost all get A–C in it, thus bumping up the league table results nicely), plus a minority subject, e.g. Sociology or Theatre Arts or Geology as a GCSE; French or German AS-level. There are few young staff; three Old Girls are on the staff, and many have connections (husbands/wives) with the University of East Anglia. There is a fine well-stocked library. Four classes of approximately 25 girls per year group, no streaming.

GAMES, OPTIONS, THE ARTS: Keen swimmers (good indoor pool); successful lacrosse; tennis popular ('I wish we had more courts'); rowing and fencing are also available. Games space is on the tight side; the grounds contain listed trees. The school has good Music (performances in the glorious Norwich Cathedral) and high expectations in musicianship, with large numbers of girls taking part in choirs and orchestras (main practice times are after school). Good D of E and Young Enterprise take-up rate. Girls have a long lunch hour for extracurricular and some musical activities; the school tries hard to produce visiting speakers for senior girls. There is some wonderful poetry in the school magazine – inspired.

BACKGROUND AND ATMOSPHERE: The school was founded in 1875 (the first GPDST outside London). The main building is an attractive Regency house (the fine conservatory used as the staffroom is 'very cold in winter'), with many later additions. The Sixth Form centre was previously a private Victorian house (as was the Music house); it has large common rooms and girls prefer to eat here. Girls fit a lot into a busy day, with some long journeys either end (parents organise buses and spend hours ferrying about girls who have friends at opposite ends of the county). The atmosphere throughout suggests a worthy grammar-school ethos, and the school feels much smaller than it actually is.

Junior School. Head of Junior Department: Mrs J A Streatfield, but apply to the main school for information on entry. This is the power house of Norwich High – lively, jolly, buzzing with excitement. In a separate house in the grounds. Maximum class size is 20–25, depending on age. Entrance is via tests and interview, virtually everyone goes on to the senior school.

PUPILS AND PARENTS: A hardworking sprinkling of daughters of landed gentry and gentlemen farmers, as well as middle class, and a few clever working class. Ethnic minorities are a rarity – as indeed they are in East Anglia in general: white faces everywhere. There are substantial numbers of parents connected with UEA, also several second and even third generation. Girls are cheerful, pleasant, unsophisticated and unspoilt in their unflattering sage green and beige uniforms (Burberrys are an option instead of the utilitarian brown mac for Fifth Formers).

ENTRANCE: At 11+ by exam (oversubscribed) and some at Sixth Form.

EXIT: Most to university (an enormous spread up and down the country of both old and some ex-polys), a few to other further education colleges. On average 8 per year to Oxbridge; a gap year for a small minority.

MONEY MATTERS: There are 30 assisted places for 11-year-olds, 5 more at Sixth Form. Also occasional bursaries. Scholarships are given at 11+ and at Sixth Form level.

REMARKS: In the last edition we suggested that the school was stodgy. The Head comments: 'no we are not'. Whatever: a strong local reputation, the obvious choice for parents seeking really solid traditional day school education which may differ but little from their own schooling. NB In September '94 Norwich Boys opened its doors to girls in the Sixth Form, potentially good news for the girls – and boys – but not, obviously, for Norwich High. The junior school, however, continues as strong as ever.

REMARKS: An extremely popular (heavily oversubscribed) and successful GPDST day school. It is strong on the academic side (early pupils were among the first women in the country to get degrees) and there are plenty of subject-related activities to back up – foreign exchange trips, lectures, conferences, etc. Girls go on to university nowadays – between 8–13 to Oxbridge. Large numbers go on into medicine. Art, Drama and Music are all up and running strongly.

Clubs/activities are better attended than at many other day schools. The girls are self-confident and motivated, their parents often unusually involved with the school. There is a broad social and cultural mix – many Eastern Europeans as well as Asians and some Afro-Caribbean descendants etc. Assisted places are available. It has a super junior department. This is a popular choice for bright locals who lack the extra oomph and cash required for St Paul's. Good reports.

Notting Hill & Ealing High School

2 Cleveland Road, London W13 8AX
Tel: 0181 997 5744, Fax: 0181 810 6891

PUPILS: Around 560 girls
ALL DAY
AGES: 11–18, plus own junior school with 270 girls, ages 5–11
SIZE OF SIXTH FORM: Around 150
NON-DENOM
FEE-PAYING

HEAD: Since 1991, Mrs S M Whitfield BSc (forties). Read Science at Cambridge. Previously taught Biology at St Paul's Girls' School. Married with five children.

Oakham School

Chapel Close, Oakham,
Rutland LE15 6DT
Tel: 01572 722487, Fax: 01572 755786

PUPILS: Approx 510 boys, 510 girls. Approx 520 board, 500 day
AGES: 10–18
SIZE OF SIXTH FORM: Approx 300 (50:50 boys to girls)
C OF E
FEE-PAYING

HEAD: From September 1996, Mr Tony Little, ARM MA (forties), who takes over from Mr Graham Smallbone who is retiring. Mr Little was educated at Eton and Corpus, taught at Tonbridge, Brentwood and was Head of

Chigwell School before coming here. Married, and has a daughter joining the school. Has two golden retrievers, is an accomplished musician and produces plays.

ACADEMIC MATTERS: Good, particularly given its ability intake and huge numbers and the school's policy of not weeding out weaker candidates. There was a bias towards Sciences and Maths in '95 A-level results (71 taking maths). One or two taking exotic languages at A-level (Japanese, Italian – could these be nationals of the countries in question?) and in general a good wide spread of subjects is on offer, including such items as Theatre Studies and French for professional use. 99% pass in A-levels. Computers are everywhere and much used. The school has a special separate Oxbridge swot house started by Christopher Dixon, so potential candidates get suitably hotted up; the Oxbridge House is a ghetto-blaster-free area. There are occasional comments from parents that social life has greater priority than work.

The school is known for its dyslexia unit, which is, to quote a parent 'very very good' – helps up to six a year; two dedicated teachers. EFL is also available.

GAMES, OPTIONS, THE ARTS: Keen on music, with regular players in the National Youth Orchestra. NB The school gives free music lessons if you pass Grade VI with merit. Arts and crafts are strongly supported.

Strong on games (as one might expect from a school this size) of all kinds. Good shooting (with a new range) and squash (regularly wins Squash National School Championships); didn't do so well at soccer in '94/5. There is a new Astroturf pitch. Lots of D of E Gold Awards. An enormous range of extras are on offer, so much so that pupils commented that the school did not always have the proper coaching back-up and the danger was you got overwhelmed, flying off in too many directions at once. (NB The school queries this, pointing out they have a number of distinguished county and national games coaches.)

The amazingly glossy, A3-size school magazine – the *Oakhamian* – looks very much like a PR production.

BACKGROUND AND ATMOSPHERE: Founded in 1584, by Robert Johnson, Archdeacon of Leicester. A small local boys' school until 1970s, when it changed from direct grant to full-blown co-ed almost overnight with loads of money given by a grateful old boy (the Jerwood Foundation). A high-tech £2 million Library, Resource and Study Centre (complete with CD-Rom and computerised library) opened in 1994. Cosy stone buildings. Boarders are mainly housed in comfy twin bedrooms. The atmosphere is very difficult to pin down as the school is large and widely spread. Co-ed activities: 'we encourage them, after all we are co-ed'.

PASTORAL CARE AND DISCIPLINE: There is a competitive house system. Expulsions for 'serious anti-social behaviour', persistent bullying, drugs and sex. A £10 fine to Cancer Research for smoking. Pupils who are not self-disciplined have been known to go off the rails.

PUPILS AND PARENTS: 30% parents are local, 25% from overseas (ex-pats and foreign). The rest are scattered, pupils come from 'up and down the A1'; from a hotchpotch of backgrounds, a fair number from London, and a contingent from Scotland. It is less spotty than many co-eds but some are on the wild side. Girls wear smart checked kilts up to 'Seventh' Form (i.e. Upper Sixth – Oakham has a rudimentary language of its own). OBs include Thomas Merton the Trappist monk, Matthew Manning the Faith Healer, plus the current Heads of Pembroke and Jesus College, Oxford.

ENTRANCE: 10, 11+, 12+, 13+ and Sixth Form. The school sets its own exam for pupils from state sector, CE for the others – the school quotes a 50% pass mark, but 'other factors are always taken into account'. Sixth Form entrants have their own exam – and are expected to have seven respectable GCSEs.

EXIT: A few leave after GCSE, otherwise 95% to higher education; 10 to Oxbridge in '95.

MONEY MATTERS: £600K of hand-outs annually: 6 Assisted Places per year plus 10 academic for Sixth Form, 10 academic at 13+, and 'about a dozen' assorted other scholarships (Music, Drama, Chess!!, Art and Design) are awarded each year. 'Some internal, some upgrades, and some external.' Plus bursaries. Automatic help is given for those in exam years who fall on hard times.

REMARKS: A large and lively co-ed boarding school for independently minded, average children. Difficult to get the hang of, particularly as it goes through a change of Head. But it is not a cosy environment, and: 'I wouldn't contemplate sending a child here,' said a prep school Head, 'who was not very highly motivated.'

Oban High School

Soroba Road, Argyll PA34 4JB
Tel: 01631 564231, Fax: 01631 565916

PUPILS: Around 1,100 boys and girls.
  Mainly day, but boarding is available

AGES: 11–18
SIZE OF SIXTH FORM: Around 100
NON-DENOM
STATE

HEAD: Rector since 1990, Mr B R Mitchell, BSc (Edinburgh) (forties). Formerly Deputy and Assistant Rector in this school.

REMARKS: A state school with a very large catchment area and pupils coming from 26 associated primary schools covering North Argyll and the Islands. Pupils (approx 55) from large distances board in the school hostel, which has four staff on evening duty and academic staff on hand to help with studies (next door to each other, with communal feeding and much else besides – according to pupils). There is a seven-class intake, and staff of about 80 – making a good staff:pupil ratio. The staff are a 'good blend of youth and experience'.

  The Art department is still good, as is Music, and there is a new English, secretarial and Maths building; 1950s Home Economics (for both sexes) has been revamped. Gaelic studies are available (and taken up), also excellent computing and secretarial courses, as well as the mainstream subjects. The school does Highers. Extra-curricular activities take place in the lunch hour – difficult otherwise because of large distances and buses. Pastoral care is provided by special 'guidance' teachers who support pupils with problems. Some reports of wild behaviour. The school celebrated its centenary in 1993, and is currently in the middle of a £9 million rebuilding and refurbishment programme, working towards new modern accommodation for several subjects.

Old Palace School (of John Whitgift)

Old Palace Road, Croydon,
Surrey CRO IAX
Tel: 0181 688 2027, Fax: 0181 680 5877

PUPILS: Around 598 girls in the senior school, 191 in the preparatory department, including 40+ in the infants' department
ALL DAY
AGES: 4–18
SIZE OF SIXTH FORM: Around 150
C OF E
FEE-PAYING

HEAD: Since 1974, Miss Kathleen L Hilton, BA (late fifties). Educated Queen Mary, Lytham and Royal Holloway College, London, where she read History. Previously Head of History at Manchester High, following a period at Malvern Girls'. Formerly a member of the Schools Council, and a Chairman of Advanced Level subjects (JMB as was). Presiding over a period of great expansion and outstanding success. Lively, energetic, forward-looking; her enthusiasm for the school and its community are underpinned by Christian beliefs.

The school has some super kind and friendly staff.

ACADEMIC MATTERS: Detailed results are not given, but the school is strong right across the board and comes high in any GCSE league table you care to look at. All take (and nearly all pass) 9+ subjects at GCSE. There is a wide choice of languages – French (their prep pupils start at seven), Italian, Spanish, Greek, German, Russian as well as Latin (33 pupils got A or A★ at GCSE in '94 in Latin). All hone French skills in the Sixth Form. A handful of students take exams in their mother tongue – ranging from Polish and Afrikaans to Gujerati and Hindu. The Head teaches A-level History – results are impressive. Maths is very popular, from prep school upwards. Science is still strong (separate Sciences or Dual Award at GCSE – and there were 31 A grades in Physics out of 34 taking separate sciences), which leaves staff wondering how to provide for the large numbers now choosing Chemistry A-level (a lab with bright yellow tables, and a lecture/demonstration area with raised seating provides a most attractive environment).

The school prides itself on 'choice' – letting Sixth Formers opt for any combination of subjects – 'a nightmare to organise', but an indication of the staff's energy and willingness to tailor the timetable to individual needs. The school has an outstanding Design Technology Department, headed by a former Goldsmith College lecturer on the teaching of technology. The 11- to 13-year-olds produce stunningly designed moulded plastic clocks, design and build their own radios, devise travelling games, etc. Computers are used as a tool right across the curriculum – their Nimbus network is one of the most up-to-date in the country. NB All pupils take General Studies as an A-level exam (and lots get A in it).

GAMES, OPTIONS, THE ARTS: There is no room on this medieval site for sport, therefore pupils are bussed to Whitgift for netball, Trinity for hockey (just introduced), and use the nearby YMCA for swimming and weight training. Only one page in the school magazine is devoted to sport – is this a record?

Young Enterprise is strong – as you might expect in this thriving commercial centre; the school produced winners of the Croydon Young Achiever of the Year in '93 and '94/5. Also high-profile Drama, and Theatre workshops, with the emphasis on speech in drama lessons, and GCSE Drama an 'out of school' option. Dance is also popular. Debating is vigorous, via the English Speaking Union, Rotary Club, United Nations Association. Music is thriving, with two orchestras and choirs which have performed at e.g. St John's, Smith Square.

BACKGROUND AND ATMOSPHERE: The former residence of the Arch-bishops of Canterbury, full of atmosphere and architectural interest. Thoughtfully designed new buildings next to Grade 1 14th- and 15th-century buildings. The latter include a Great Hall where Henry VIII and Catherine of Aragon were entertained, an outstandingly beautiful Chapel, a Guard Room where the young James I of Scotland was held prisoner (now the library), Queen Elizabeth's Room (she visited a number of times), Laud's bedroom (part of the staffroom), and small courtyards joined by low arched passages. Can't call that nothing, though the downside of the wonderful buildings is that space is severely limited (and upkeep expensive).

This is not a school in which God is forgotten.

PASTORAL CARE AND DISCIPLINE: Welcoming 'open door' policy, particularly at the infant end – where parents can talk to staff from 7.45 a.m., before the start of the school day, or after school. There is genuine feel of a 'family' school built on the Christian ethos of the founding Sisters of the Church, with a notable emphasis on parental participa-tion. Strict monitoring of homework diaries can reveal 'a surprising amount; we can often tell if there are difficulties'. Pupils raise large amounts for charity.

PUPILS AND PARENTS: The school has a lively social mix with offspring of professional high-fliers and those from inner-city estates. At the infant end it is Asian and Afro-Caribbean parents who seem most willing to commit themselves to financial sacrifice so their children can be taught in small classes.

ENTRANCE: At 4+ (16 children) into a newly opened and already oversub-scribed infant department, or at 7, 8, 9 via exam to the preparatory department (virtually all go on to senior school) and via 11+ entrance (oversubscribed by 3:1). All applicants are interviewed with parents.

EXIT: To strong universities such as Exeter, Imperial College, Man-chester, St Andrews, and some to do exciting courses at ex-polys, such as Marketing and Business Law at North London University, Mechanical Engineering at Kingston. Well-known OGs reflect a wide range of career choice – from BBC weather girl Helen Young, to the first BA woman pilot, Wendy Barnes, and harpist Rachel Harris.

MONEY MATTERS: The school became part of the Whitgift Foundation in September '93 – a foundation formerly for the two local boys' schools, Whitgift and Trinity, but finally the feeling that 'something must be done for the girls' has won through to action. This means more money for bursaries, and altogether more financial muscle. There have been 35 Assisted Places at time of writing and more have been granted by the government's latest handout, plus generous bursaries. Basic fees are kept at the lower end of the scale: 'We've always been good housekeepers.'

REMARKS: An outstandingly success-ful school with a lively, open and friendly atmosphere. All parents we have talked to appear well satisfied with the school – definitely still voted best in the area.

The Oratory School

Woodcote, Nr Reading,
Berkshire RG8 0PJ
Tel: 01491 680207, Fax: 01491 680020

PUPILS: Around 411 boys; 275 board,
136 day
AGES: 11–18
SIZE OF SIXTH FORM: 136
JUNIOR HOUSE: 30
RC
FEE-PAYING

HEAD: Since 1992, Mr Simon Barrow, BA (fifties). Educated at Stonyhurst and the University of Reading (History – 'does a bit of teaching'), he has been at the Oratory for 23 years. Has a low profile and diffident manner – 'deceptively so, it hides an immensely kind man who really bothers about the individual,' comments a parent. No PR man, indeed somewhat grey – 'but his thoughtful speech to parents genuinely impressed us,' says another. Supportive wife, two children.

ACADEMIC MATTERS: The flexible curriculum means almost any subjects can be linked. Boys have their own individual prep times peppered thoughout the day – 'an impetus for boys to be self-organising,' says a parent. French, Spanish, German, Italian, Portuguese, Latin and Greek available at A-level; the school has language links with Caversham Park BBC external monitoring service. Nearly all boys do three separate sciences, and IT is compulsory until GCSE – about eight of these are the norm. There is a good staff:boy ratio, though 'some

teachers are not high enough calibre' according to a high-flier's mother. Boys are given fortnightly progress and effort ratings. A detailed breakdown of '95 results was not given, but overall percentages appear very respectable at both GCSE and A-level.

GAMES, OPTIONS, THE ARTS: The school has good facilities, though weekly boarding takes the edge off commitment. There is a superb cricket pitch giving a view right across Berkshire, 14 tennis courts, a good indoor swimming pool and squash courts. Shooting, rowing and sailing at nearby Goring and Theale. The sports complex has the first real tennis court to be built in the UK for 80 years. The former gym/theatre has now been refurbished exclusively for Drama. An annual trawl of ex-chorister music scholars from Westminster Cathedral Choir School makes for a lively Music department: more than half the boys learn an instrument; the orchestra and choir perform for National Trust Music Days. Art is strong and entrance scholarships are on offer. CCF is popular, especially the navy, where boys can spend a night in a warship.

BACKGROUND AND ATMOSPHERE: The school was founded in 1859 by Cardinal Newman at the time of the Oxford Movement, to provide an intentionally lay Catholic public-school education for the sons of a growing number of upper-crust converts. 'Married housemasters, lay staff with mortgages, and our own chaplain give it the feeling of a parish,' says the Head. The imposing Georgian stone-faced house on a remote spur of the Chilterns with a cluster of new buildings – still being added to – is politely described as functional.

PASTORAL CARE AND DISCIPLINE: Regular retreat and daily Mass (led by an ex-RAF padre) for those who want it, without proselytising. 'Religion is not too obvious but it is taken seriously,' says a parent. The school has a fairly relaxed ethos. Boys have 'chores' and are expected to wash their own clothes (i.e. Mummy does them). Pastoral care is provided by live-in married House-masters – choose your house with care. There is a detention system for slackers.

PUPILS AND PARENTS: Mostly from the Thames Valley and London, around 10% from overseas, including some from Ireland. By and large from the Catholic middle class, 85% of total pupils are RC. Popular with parents of mixed marriages, the school is less suspicious in the lay environment of 'monkey business', to quote one. OBs include Hilaire Belloc, Lennox Berkeley, Michael Berkeley. Gerald Manley Hopkins taught here.

ENTRANCE: Presents no particular problem. Regular intake from own prep school.

EXIT: Around two-thirds to univer-sities old and new; also to US colleges, Business Studies, art school. There is some post-GCSE leakage to Sixth Form Colleges (e.g. Peter Symonds in Winchester).

MONEY MATTERS: 'As many scholarships on offer as good candidates' – including the Sixth Form Newman bursary – given generous provision for academics, artists, musi-cians. The Old Boys' Foundation and '200 Club' make financial provision for hard times.

REMARKS: A smallish, worthy, caring, advantageously located establishment, taking trouble over a broad ability range. It produces solid, respon-sible middle-class citizens, but lacks the social cachet of its senior northern monastic rival. Possibly a bit dull.

Oundle School

Oundle, Peterborough PE8 4EN
Tel: 01832 273536, Fax: 01832 273564

PUPILS: Approx 620 boys, 200 girls (more coming). All board. Also Laxton School (see below) 180 boys and girls, all day.
AGES: 11–18
SIZE OF SIXTH FORM: Approx 360
C OF E
FEE-PAYING

HEAD: Since 1984, Mr D B McMurray, MA (Cantab) (fifties). Formerly Head of Loretto (and he was a pupil there too), and previously taught at Fettes. Tall, with a rather jolly Australian wife and very popular with parents. He is a keen governor of other schools, and a keen visitor of schools as well ('he's often away,' comments a parent). Comments that if Oundle produces a 'type', then he will have failed. On the school's move to co-education, he says that 'to try to inculcate sensible attitudes and expec-tations of the opposite sex, while keeping those sexes separate, is like teaching people to swim without allowing them to get wet'. (Parental comment: 'Lots of to-ing and fro-ing, but they'd have to do a lot of work to sleep together'). Nickname 'Big Mac'. Contracted until the year 2000.

ACADEMIC MATTERS: The school has seriously strong Science and Tech-nology departments. Good in several subjects. The History department is dynamic. Even scientists do languages right through. The Latin master is 'a kick'. Three out of eight sets take French GCSE early 'and they don't get Bs'. The latest addition is the Anglian Water Board Building which has been turned into the Modern Language block – hi-tech lab style (push buttons everywhere); also housed here is the Music school, and the terrifically impressive IT labs.

The school pioneered CDT and the idea of learning through doing at the turn of the century – but in our opinion other schools have now outstripped it. The 13-year-olds spend an afternoon each week in the school's magnificent workshops to design and construct something – the atmosphere here is more like industry than a school – with a foundry, lasers, wind tunnels, microelectronics and lots of computers. Some staff are impressive. A breakdown of results is not given.

GAMES, OPTIONS, THE ARTS: The school has a 50-yard swimming pool, three climbing walls, a new Sports Centre, a running track, two rifle ranges (with regular successes), and grounds stretching as far as the eye can see. Strong rowing – the club was founded in 1886. The superb rugger coach, Terry Cobner, leads lots of trips abroad (Canada, South Africa) and produces national squad players. Good hockey for girls. The average Oundelian is considered 'a pretty competitive animal' – including the girls. Pupils 'can't escape Oundle without some music' as it is compulsory for the first year.

The school's orchestra tours Europe most years and there are regularly members of the National Youth Orchestra. The Stahl Theatre in a converted church in Oundle High Street puts on both professional and pupil productions, which are good and popular and give pupils a feel for 'the real thing'. There are artists in residence and a huge variety of arts on offer. There is a massive Frobenius organ in the school chapel and a marvellous John Piper window. CCF,

Community Service and Adventure training. Organises a regular exchange programme with American school.

BACKGROUND AND ATMOSPHERE: Beautiful mellow buildings – see Pevsner – are scattered throughout the pretty medieval town of Oundle, with pupils scurrying to and fro like university students. The furthest boarding house is a good ten minutes' hike to the central quad (the Head says six minutes – but he has very long legs). The official tour of the school for potential parents takes a record one and three-quarter hours – wear comfortable shoe for this one. (Look out for the Oundle walk, by which OOs recognise each other in later life.)

Wonderful avenue of trees, games fields, etc. The boarding houses are massively built; the most recently revamped have smaller dorms and lots of bed-sits. Recommended house: St Antony's with a five-star Housemaster, Mr Vic Northwood. Girls' houses look more like an American Hilton ('nuts', said one American parent, 'girls' houses look more lived-in now'). Lots of chaps in striped shirts, looking keen and purposeful (girls have a red or blue option). Massive 18,000-volume library in converted gym plus a Muniments Room, which includes the 1626 School Register. Many Oundle traditions continue after school, with strong clubs, including a Masonic Lodge.

The Merchant Master of the Worshipful Company of Grocers and Lord Mayor of London, Sir William Laxton, left provision in his will for the re-endowment of the grammar school he attended, which dated back to 1485. In 1876 the schools divided into Laxton Grammar School, for inhabitants of the town who did not want Classical Studies, and Oundle, for sons of gents who did. Today the two schools co-exist with separate Heads (Head of Laxton, Mr Bob

Briggs), separate buildings and (some) activities, but they do academic studies and sport together. Laxton is a day school with approx 180 pupils plus a junior school (136 pupils). NB: You may need a damp towel round your head to work this out.

PUPILS AND PARENTS: There is a large percentage of Old Boys' children, many Oundle families, with fathers, uncles, cousins all here. 'Fair number from overseas' (approx. 10%), with Hong Kong Chinese and sophisticated Malays predominant. There is much parental involvement and good staff/parent contact. Steady middle class. OBs include Arthur Marshall, Peter Scott, Cecil Lewis the aviator, A Alvarez, Anthony Holden, Archie Coulson.

PASTORAL CARE AND DISCIPLINE: Pastoral care is very much on the house tutorial system, and each pupil has his/her own tutor throughout his/her time at school. 'Pupils need to have clear-cut boundaries,' says the Head, 'but push those boundaries out as far as they dare.' 'Instant out' for drugs. Drink: 'a can of beer is different from being blotto'; for alcoholic offenders it's the 'one, two, three out system'; i.e. 1) gated, 2) rusticated, 3) expelled. The school has a few lively offenders. The Head stands firm on exeats – they are few and far between. Newcomers from cosy-ish preps find the going 'tough'.

ENTRANCE: Own exam at 11+ or CE at 13. There is an assessment day for borderline cases – the Head comments he would like to see 140 pupils sit for 140 places and not have pupils sitting who will not get in. IQs show wide fluctuations, but a 'switched on' IQ of 110 would probably get in, depending on demand. Five GCSE passes for Sixth Form entry

(even within the school). The school has been known to reject a pupil and change its mind later.

EXIT: A large percentage to degree courses, a steady stream to Oxbridge. Pupils thereafter go on to be captains of industry, entrepreneurs and engineers.

MONEY MATTERS: Not as well-endowed as it is perceived to be and there are no Assisted Places. It claims to be the sixth most expensive school in the country. However, there are many scholarships, including Music and Art. There are only 2 scholarships for 11-year-olds, plus Continuation Scholarships for 8 pupils to 'remain at their Preparatory School with an Award of 15% of Oundle's Junior House fees per annum' before joining Oundle at 13, when the scholarship is worth 20%. Also 2 scholarships for incoming Sixth Form pupils. Recently sold some of the (more cramped) buildings they were using in town to make the new IT centre, etc (see above).

REMARKS: Firing on all cylinders and well spoken of, riding high and definitely popular though parents wonder if it hasn't reached a plateau. It is not an easy option – pupils from cosy preps can be quite shell-shocked.

Oxford High School for Girls

Belbroughton Road, Oxford OX2 6XA
Tel: 01865 59888, Fax: 01865 52343

PUPILS: 550 girls. Also 100 girls in Lower School, ages 9–11.
ALL DAY
AGES: 11–18

SIZE OF SIXTH FORM: 150
NON-DENOM
FEE-PAYING

HEAD: Since 1981, Mrs Joan Townsend, MA (Oxon), MSc in Maths (fifties), educated at Wigan High and Hawarden Grammar School. Previously Head of Maths at St Helen's in Abingdon, Mrs T claims to have 'chalk in the blood'. Her husband is a professor at Cranfield University. A challenging Head, exuberant, charming, fun, who has mellowed in the last few years. Intellectually stimulating, sympathetic – particularly when ME and parental discord upset academic activities. Has made things 'better for the less clever. Not the hothouse the myth has it'. Hopes that girls will 'have something to offer' and 'that they shall go out with confidence and own individual strengths developed'. Works with Heads of Lower, Middle, and Upper schools. Decentralises. Teaches Current Affairs to Sixth Form only, but does an in-depth interview at Lower Sixth.

ACADEMIC MATTERS: Strongly academic – thanks to the Oxford environment. 'The brains are hanging off the wall,' said a visiting parent. The school has some outstanding staff – and there is no problem recruiting here. Streaming in Maths, Languages (French, German, Russian, Spanish, Latin, Greek, Italian). It is compulsory to take English, a language, Maths, Dual Award Science at GCSE. Girls take GCSE 'in their stride', 100% A–C in five subjects or more, and we notice a growing number of As over the past five years. Computers are everywhere and in subject rooms. Some pupils do Textiles at A-level. Parents complain that there is not enough choice in A-level combinations. The Head says she 'Honestly didn't see the league tables', adding that they are not important.

GAMES, OPTIONS, THE ARTS: Games up to Upper Fifth. The school has a Sports Hall, a swimming pool, and offers traditional games, as well as rowing, weight training, trampolining. Parents can use facilities in the holidays. The first netball team were runners up in the Oxfordshire Schools Championships, ditto the first hockey team. Music magical, the Head of Music is particularly keen on choirs; also very strong Drama; lively Art (there are murals everywhere – even on the ceiling).

BACKGROUND AND ATMOSPHERE: Started in 1875 by the Girls' Public Day School Trust in St Giles', with a view to educating dons' daughters. The school expanded at a great rate, and a series of moves brought it to its present site (mostly pretty grizzly boxes surrounded by a garden, filled with herbs and games pitches) but the new junior department has an attractive pitched roof. It has ecumenical and sparky assemblies (there was a Jewish-Arab combined service the day the peace accord was signed). Stimulating, and intellectually vibrant, combined with laid-back underlying discipline, and a good sense of humour throughout. Girls are required to do a regular self-assessment. The school uniform includes navy cord trousers and jolly sunflower sweatshirts.

PASTORAL CARE AND DISCIPLINE: The school depends on a tutorial system, and House Mistresses; there have been no sackings (drugs would be automatically out). Even the smallest has her say. Problems are picked up early; there are good parental vibes, and regular class parent meetings so that parents can suss out exactly what their little darlings are up to 'when everyone will be there'.

PUPILS AND PARENTS: 50% come from Oxford, including many dons' daughters; local schools pride themselves on the number of girls who get places here. But pupils are bussed from as far away as Swindon. The school has the occasional problem 'with over-articulate donnish parents' who like arguing for arguing's sake, though on the whole parents are very supportive.

ENTRANCE: Queues of keen local applicants; apply one year before the September term of entry. There is a serious multi-assessment day at 11+ – written English, Maths, Science, VR, and numerical and perceptual reasoning. Children are encouraged to bring in hobbies or examples of art. Doubly oversubscribed. Sixth Form entry on good GCSE results plus previous Head's report (20 annually).

NB Stop Press: Oxford High is linking up with two popular local prep schools – Greycotes and Squirrels – to provide what is planned eventually to be Oxford High's prep and pre-prep (keeping their own sites however).

EXIT: After GCSE, 8–16 may leave; St Edward's is the obvious choice. Otherwise about a quarter to Oxbridge and most of the rest to other degree courses, in particular the big city universities e.g. Manchester, Newcastle, Leeds, and popular ex-polys ('girls are becoming increasingly picky about which courses and universities to go to'). A handful go on to art foundation courses. OGs include Miriam Margoyles, Josephine Barnes, Maggie Smith and Sian Edwards, plus dons, lecturers and other high-powered academics.

MONEY MATTERS: Good value. There are 20 Assisted Places at 11+ and 5 for girls in the Sixth Form. Bursaries for brains, Music and Art. The Head will 'hunt around for extra bursaries for those with genuine hardship'.

REMARKS: A challenging, demanding and exciting school which produces many distinguished pupils, and which long ago outgrew its GPDST label. The Number One academic choice for Oxford and round about, though Dragon girls sometimes find the bottom classes rather undemanding, and not all parents are 100% happy.

Pimlico School

Lupus Street, London SW1V 3AT
Tel: 0171 828 0881, Fax: 0171 931 0549

PUPILS: Around 1,350
ALL DAY
AGES: 11–18
SIZE OF SIXTH FORM: Around 160
NON-DENOM
STATE

HEAD: Since 1991, Miss Kathleen O Wood BA, MIMgt, FRSA (forties). Chairman of governors is Jack Straw, who has two children here.

ENTRANCE: Complicated – don't apply to the school direct but e.g. through your primary school, or – depending where you live – your local education authority. If in doubt, telephone the Westminster Council School Admissions and Benefits Section (Tel 0171 828 8070) and ask for a Westminster Application Form.

REMARKS: A popular oversubscribed inner-London state day school, which appears to be getting its act together again. Pupils find it jolly, but residents comment that pupils are unruly. Pupils stay together for nearly all lessons in the first three years and meet with their tutor at the beginning of every morning and afternoon (unauthorised absence 3.7%

in '95). The school has a good Art department (with good exam results).

Music is also very lively and outstandingly good (jazz in particular – won a distinguished Jazz competition in '95) and the school has the Pimlico Special Music Course for people admitted to the school by audition. NB Twenty-nine pupils took Music A-level in '95 and 18 got A*-Bs. It is housed in an award-winning 1970 building which feels like a super tanker – huge glass windows set at an angle – light, with staircases running up the middle of the school.

The Head points out that the school has a 'below average ability profile' for students at 11+ – and results should be read in the light of this (NB 'average' comes out pretty low), not forgetting that, unlike many London private schools, Pimlico's exam policy is to enter every pupil who completes the course, with no weeding out of the weaker candidates. A-level results have come on by leaps and bounds in '95 – 72.3% A–C passes (compared with an average of 51.7% and 56.1% for Pimlico last year). GCSE results did not look so statistically impressive however. Vocational qualifications are also offered, including BTecs, City & Guilds and GNVQs (including performing arts) and some pupils sit these.

The Perse School

Hills Road, Cambridge CB2 2QF
Tel: 01223 568300, Fax: 01223 568293

PUPILS: 500 boys all day, around 15–20 girls in the Sixth Form (the Boarding House was abolished in 1993), plus junior school ages 7–11
AGES: 11–18
SIZE OF SIXTH FORM: 140
NON-DENOM
FEE-PAYING

HEAD: Since September 1994, Mr Nigel Richardson (forties), educated at Highgate School and Trinity College, Cambridge. Previous post as Deputy Head of King's School, Macclesfield ('92–94), and before that he had a difficult couple of years as Head of the Dragon (prep) School in Oxford ('89–92, where he was described as 'survivor of the year' by a visiting headmaster ...) An enthusiast, the author of six history books for children, he does freelance writing for the TES, etc. Wife Joy is high powered, confident and also an author – with nearly 50 information books for children under her belt plus children's guides to museums. She is also an Ofsted inspector. Two sons.

ACADEMIC MATTERS: Provides rigorous and traditional teaching in classes of around 20–24 (this is a drop on average class size since our last edition) with mostly male teachers though there are around ten women (including cheery youthful science mistresses). The school shows a distinct bias to sciences (NB no Combined Science Award at GCSE) and Maths and Physics results in '95 and '94 were outstanding. Also strong History and Classics; Russian is a GCSE option in the Sixth Form, the numbers taking German doubled from '94 to '95. Keen pot-hunters for National Physics Challenge and the school has also won British Maths Olympiad gold medals and were National Worldwise Geography Quiz finalists and Classical Association Competition Prize winners.

The school has an interesting tradition of teaching younger boys English through acting and mime (the 'Play Way') in the 'Mummery', a small theatre equipped with lights, music, costumes where boys cast and direct their own productions from traditional ballads to Shakespeare, with minimal intervention from the calmly presiding master.

Saturday morning school has now been abolished, following the abolition of boarding, though inter-school matches and some Music still take place then.

GAMES, OPTIONS, THE ARTS: There are 28 acres of prime Cambridge greenbelt for compulsory rugby (twelve rugby teams, the 1st XV went to Prague), though the *Pelican* magazine reported 'one of the worst seasons on record' for the '94 1st XV, and the hockey didn't look too good, though a talented young team is coming along nicely. Thriving chess and bridge. CCF or community service (good works include boys helping at neighbouring Addenbrooke's Hospital), D of E awards and Scouts. The Head of Music has done much to raise standards (a 'colours' music tie sports a treble clef) and introduced a Music Technology course: 100 now learn an instrument. Keen Art and ceramics in a new, brick, studio block (GCSE Art is taken a year early), all do a GCSE architectural project, with much to inspire them a few minutes walk from the doorstep. There is an annual art show and sale of boys' and local artists' works in the school's Pelican Art Gallery (the school emblem, recalling Sir Francis Drake's eponymous ship circumnavigating the globe) and Friends of the Pelican Gallery was recently launched. Stunning ceramics. There is also busy Drama in a newish theatre and Form drama evenings at ages 13 and 14 to encourage self-confidence in public speaking – a good idea. Perseans are three-time winners of the Young Businessman of the Year award.

BACKGROUND AND ATMOSPHERE: The school has a 400-year historic background – it was founded in 1615 by Stephen Perse, a Fellow of Gonville and Caius, though the endowment has sadly long since been embezzled. The school feels somewhat lost in Sixties, purpose-built, ecclesiastical-cum-chalet style, red-brick premises in the Cambridge margins. It is uncomfortably close to the school's greatest threat – the Hills Road Sixth Form College. Direct grant until '76, it retains a non-exclusive small friendly ethos with scions of the middle classes (including ethnic minorities) in grey herring-bone tweed jackets and purple ties; the school has only a 'dress code' for the Sixth Form with fairly staid results. In the airy high-ceilinged dining hall, staff pull up a corner Formica table to eat corned beef unnoticed among the mêlée. Immaculate corridors and manicured grounds (NB no crisp packets) give a slightly soulless feeling of underused space.

Junior School: Head (The Master): Mr P C S Izzett. Tel: 01223 355377, Fax: 01223 568273. On a separate site in Trumpington Road, about 1½ miles from the senior school. Entrance by exam – this is the sure way into the senior school.

PASTORAL CARE AND DISCIPLINE: The school has a strongly pastoral tutorial system and a safety-net innovation of a prefect appointed as 'minder' to individual younger classes as a method of detecting bullying. Lots of staff time is spent boosting the weaker academic end (with results apparent). There is a fierce anti-drugs policy.

PUPILS AND PARENTS: Across the economic and social divide, and until recently provided the last bastion of all-boy secondary education in Cambridge. 20–25% sons of Cambridge-associated professionals, otherwise teachers, farmers, employees of the Science Park and 'parents who ten years ago would have boarded their sons'. The catchment area of around 35 miles' radius reflects a migration of families from housing-starved Cambridge. The school produces well-adjusted, articulate, unstuffy boys from the upper intelligence band. Girls are in the Sixth Form only, so there is no home grown product to judge. OBs include two (scientific) Nobel Prize winners, F R Leavis, Sir Peter Hall, Marius Goring, Mel Calman.

ENTRANCE: 60 boys at age 11 (two-thirds from the associated prep, the rest from local primaries); 2–3 applicants for each place are judged on IQ, Maths, English and an interview; 20–40 at 13 (and an extra form at 13+ was added in 1995). Those applying at Sixth Form need a minimum of six GCSEs at grade B.

EXIT: Virtually all to universities; approximately one-quarter of Upper Sixth to Oxbridge. Regularly wins Forces university scholarships; to the occasional arts foundation, but Science rules.

MONEY MATTERS: Across-the-board low fees are kept to around £4,500 p.a. (i.e. cheaper than most Cambridge preps). Scholarships are therefore understandably not an item here, though there are 'some' of 10 per cent; also 55 Assisted Places on offer.

REMARKS: This school has just carried out possibly the most blatant piece of backstabbing in the history of private schooling – by the introduction of girls in the Sixth Form when it has a good sister school on the doorstep (see The Perse School for Girls below). However, it still provides good academic grounding for the able sons of the Cambridge middle class. It is too early to say how the new regime will develop.

The Perse School for Girls

Union Road, Cambridge CB2 1HF
Tel: 01223 359589, Fax: 01223 467420

PUPILS: Around 520 girls. Plus a
  separate junior school ages 7–11
ALL DAY
AGES: 11–18
SIZE OF SIXTH FORM: 110
C OF E
FEE-PAYING

HEAD: Since 1989, Miss H S Smith, MA (Oxon) (forties), educated at King Edward's Birmingham and St Hilda's, Oxford, where she read Mathematics. Previously Head of Maths at The Perse, and before that taught at Cheltenham Ladies', also at the International School in Brussels.

ACADEMIC MATTERS: Very strong Modern Languages, with all girls doing two at GCSE (French plus either German, Italian, Russian or Spanish). The school is hot on exchanges and visits abroad. In '95, 9 girls out of 14 got A grade at French A-level and 13 out of 16 girls got grade A in Maths A-level – Maths and English are both strong departments. GCSE results are a sea of A*s and there were a mere six Ds and Es out of 890 exams sat. All girls take all three Sciences at GCSE. Setting by ability in Maths and Languages. Classes are largish (up to 27), 'but this isn't a problem here, the girls apply themselves'. The school offers a new and very popular modular course in creative subjects for girls in their third year. The much prized, wonderful and enthusiastic Head of Computer Studies, Mrs Handcock, is still going strong. There are good facilities for IT and also terrific Electronics. Staff here are of extremely high calibre, as you might expect in Cambridge.

GAMES, OPTIONS, THE ARTS: The main playing fields are 10 minutes away and the new Leys Sports Hall is used for 8 hours a week. There are several girls in county squads for both hockey and netball, but this is not really a gamesy school, though there is an element of compulsion. Girls swim in the Leys pool, and elsewhere. Drama is popular (lots of Speech and Drama exams passed with distinction); also high standards in Music. Some charming poetry can be found in *The Persean* – worth a look. There is a fairly busy lunch time programme for extra-curricular activities – debating, chess, bridge, music, etc, though by comparison with some other schools, these are relatively thin on the ground, and the Head makes no bones about the fact that 'We are an academic school', (though she points out 'we also value recreational activities').

BACKGROUND AND ATMOSPHERE: Cosy, squashed, rather sedate institution with carpets, polish, wallpaper and good pictures on the walls. Some parts are reminiscent of the worst of St Trinian's, said to have been modelled on The Perse, with new buildings helping to diminish the sense of cramp. The school, founded in 1881, looks like students' digs, overlooked by the university Chemistry lab. The latest addition is a Sixth Form Centre (converted from a parish institute) near the school's back gate, with an Art studio, quiet study rooms, common room, teaching rooms, etc. Much use is also made of the basement.

Junior School Head: Mrs D N Clements. Tel: 01223 357322, Fax: 01223 467420. Ages: 7–11. Around 170 girls, in class sizes 15–24. Entrance is by tests at the beginning of the year.

PASTORAL CARE AND DISCIPLINE: Potential problems are likely to get spotted at an early stage via Form teachers plus the Head of Year.

PUPILS AND PARENTS: Dons' daughters and distinguished academic names litter the school list, but there is a fairly broad social mix. The self-confident and hard-working girls know where they're going. OGs include Jean Rhys; Philippa Pearce; and Lady Wootton, considered a particularly good example: 'High-powered, sceptical, detached, non-conformist.'

ENTRANCE: Examinations (The Perse's own) and an interview all on the same day; registration by December of the year prior to entry. Also via the junior school.

EXIT: To all manner of universities, including, in '95, a fair number to ex-polys including Sheffield Hallam, Leeds Met, Greenwich, and one or two to arts foundation courses, even one to an acting school. Also a good number to Oxbridge. A gap year is popular.

MONEY MATTERS: One of many schools very dependent on government money in the form of 15 assisted places at 11+, 5 at 16+. Some bursaries are also available, and Sixth Form scholarships.

REMARKS: A strong and highly sought-after city day school with a distinguished academic rating.

The Portsmouth Grammar School

High Street, Portsmouth PO1 2IN
Tel: 01705 819125, Fax: 01705 870184

PUPILS: Around 612 boys, 215 girls. Also pre-prep school of 150 boys and girls aged 4–8, and lower school of 210 boys and girls, ages 8–11
ALL DAY
AGES: 11–18
SIZE OF SIXTH FORM: Around 210
NON-DENOM
FEE-PAYING

HEAD: Since 1983, Mr Tony Evans, MA (Hons), M Phil (early fifties). Educated at De la Salle School, London, followed by the French Lycée in Kensington, then Paris University and Oxford, where he read Modern Languages, and University College, London. His mother was Jersey French and he has a French wife and two children. Previously taught at Dulwich before ultimately becoming Master in College at Winchester. Chairman of HMC in 1996, he made a very thoughtful inaugural speech on the problems of children today and the need not to sweep them under the carpet.

The buck stops with Mr Evans for all three schools, but he is totally responsible for the senior school. He teaches French plus RS and will substitute teach – he enjoys it, and speaks French at home all day. An outgoing, chatty Head. Maintains he produces 'no typical child, they come from such mixed backgrounds, academically pretty good and confident, but difficult to guarantee social ease'.

ACADEMIC MATTERS: The school is 'quite strong' in Maths and regularly takes part in the Olympiad. Science is strong and all take three separate sciences at GCSE; Biology, Geography and Chemistry are popular A-levels. Languages are also strong (particularly French – the position of the school is a help for jumping on ferries and whizzing over to France; also, the Head of Modern Languages, Mr Perry, is well-known

outside the school for running excellent pre-A level courses in France at Thonon-les-Bains). Also German, Spanish and Japanese. Latin and Classical Civilisation are also around but, after a struggle, Greek has apparently dropped off the curriculum. Latin and IT for the first two years only: IT is not an option. Most pupils do 10 subjects at GCSE, including two or three options and 'AO things'. Classes are now only set for Maths (one term in) and thereafter sets are decided by option choice. Results have gone up since de-banding.

Mild dyslexia is catered for via the Winchester and Portsmouth Institute, primarily outside school hours.

GAMES, OPTIONS, THE ARTS: Pupils are bussed to games fields at Hilsea, with swimming either in the pool at the junior school or in Victoria Baths. Cross-country is very strong (regular finalists), also successful athletics – 'a whole range of international athletes here'. Sea-rowing (clinker rowing), also sailing, as you might expect, plus rugby and hockey. Pupils may choose their sports after GCSE. Girls play netball, with aerobics, modern dance and fencing. Girls are also more enthusiastic at CCF, and there is a whole girls' team competing in the Ten Tors Long Endurance race. Art and Music are very much part of the curriculum, and the whole of the lower school must play some instrument. Pottery and ceramics are exciting. There is a new-ish Sports Hall on the site of the Headmaster's house, plus a Music Hall – with a marvellous upside-down falling angel made out of Frosties packets – from the proceeds of an '88 appeal.

BACKGROUND AND ATMOSPHERE: The school was founded in 1732, formerly direct grant, becoming 'independent' in '76 at which point girls were first admitted to the Sixth Form.

The school went co-ed from the bottom in '89 and became fully co-ed in '95.

The main School House is in a conservation area (so nothing can be done to buildings, not even the verandahs removed); the campus is in the centre of Portsmouth. The Head is still hoping to buy an about-to-be-redundant naval building on an adjacent site (they already have half of it). Space is at an enormously high premium.

PASTORAL CARE AND DISCIPLINE: The Head is deeply concerned on matters pastoral: Portsmouth has the highest record of homeless after Glasgow, and many have suffered some form of 'distress'. There is a very strong pastoral structure, now house-based rather than form-based, with the same tutor over four to five years. The school has two trained counsellors plus Chaplain, and a part-time Chaplain as well, not to mention five staff acting as counsellors to help the 'growing number of pupils with problems'. 'Pupils here have sampled the lot,' says Mr Evans, who loathes to expel – he prefers to use suspensions (particularly for theft, plus counselling), or to get pupils to 'do something useful'. About bullying he says there is 'not a lot of it'. A programme is on hand to 'educate parents'. The number of children coming to school without breakfast is so high that the Head has introduced breakfast.

PUPILS AND PARENTS: See above. Pupils come from as far afield as Havant, Lancing, Winchester and the Isle of Wight. Not the middle-class dream. There is a percentage of 'public school drop-outs', either for recession or logistical reasons. Not many come from ethnic minorities.

ENTRANCE: Competitive exam at 11, approx 50% come from lower school – 'virtually all do, but three or four might not make it'. A trickle come from traditional preps at 13 – Prebendal, Great Ballard, Oakwood, West Hill Park, Twyford (all local). An interview and GCSE results for entry at Sixth Form (seven needed, but As and Bs not necessarily required).

EXIT: Two or three go to local schools. 'All but one or two a year' go to university – London, Leeds, Birmingham, 17 to Oxbridge in '94.

MONEY MATTERS: The locality (Navy, IBM, Marconi, etc) is one of the worst hit by the recession. The school will 'see through as far as it can' at any intermediate (i.e. exam) stage. It is quite a poor school, the fees are low. Scholarships are available 'from time to time' for 13-year-olds. The school is very dependent on Assisted Place money from the government – there are 30 Assisted Places at 11, 6 at 13 and in the Sixth Form, plus an equivalent number of bursaries.

REMARKS: A seriously strong grammar school offering the best possible academic facilities under the leadership of an outstandingly sympathetic Headmaster. Changes to all this may be in the offing as the school goes co-ed throughout.

Portsmouth High School

Kent Road, Southsea,
Hampshire PO5 3EQ
Tel: 01705 826714, Fax: 01705 814814
PUPILS: Around 540, all girls
AGES: 11–18
SIZE OF SIXTH FORM: 120
NON-DENOM
FEE-PAYING

HEAD: Since 1984, Mrs J M Dawtrey (who says she doesn't refuse any age attributed to her – we wouldn't dare hazard a guess), BA from Westfield College, London, in French. Formerly Head of Modern Languages department and academic assistant to Head of Rickmansworth Masonic School. Widow, with two adult children. Came to the interview with us as though going to the dentist, and suffered a very painful extraction. However, she did divulge that she likes reading, gardening and theatre, and that her purpose in the school's life is to 'prepare the girls for the future . . . for life'. Laconic. Plays her cards close to her chest.

ACADEMIC MATTERS: The school shot to national fame by coming top of the A-level league tables the first time they were published, beating all comers. Mrs Dawtrey commented that it was an 'exceptional year', and she had to spend much time encouraging the year below not to get disheartened if they did not do as well. However, results are very steady, and a former pupil comments that the school has 'always been like that'.

The school achieves absolutely solid results in the subjects covered – which includes all major academic subjects but not much breadth (a small clutch was doing Government and Political Studies, however). Pupils wanting to do something exotic are steered towards the mainstream A-levels which will get them into the (exotic) course of their choice. (It is often a strength, as Mrs Dawtrey points out, not to have done the exotic subjects at A-level.) The proximity of cross-Channel ferries is useful for the Modern Languages department – accents well brushed up. Individual sciences are offered at GCSE; outstanding English Literature results at GCSE, which is unusual, and good at A-level as well. A handful are doing Scottish Highers as

options, which is also unusual. An interesting observation on the academic staff: almost all come from anywhere but Oxbridge – could this be a key to teaching success? The ratio of staff to pupils in the senior school is the 'standard GPDST', i.e. 1:13.

GAMES, OPTIONS, THE ARTS: There is little in the way of games facilities – the school rents Southsea Common from the council – 'freezing,' say pupils. Games are mostly thankfully abandoned at Sixth Form, though some exercise (aerobics is very popular) required. The school had an enthusiastic cricket team; however, the enthusiast in charge has now retired, and now it's a football club instead – for those who wish to make a statement.

The school has an outstanding Music department, housed in a rather seedy-looking converted Victorian building. The Director of Music, Mrs Dearsley, is tireless – 'never stops,' comments the Head. Mrs Dearsley is also in charge of string training for the Hampshire County Youth Orchestra. The numbers taking music exams at high levels exceed that of many of the traditional music schools. It offers all manner of different instruments, too – oboe, flute, viola, treble recorder, singing, trumpet. It also appears to wipe the floor with other schools in the Portsmouth annual music festival.

The Art department looks like a giant greenhouse but, reports the school, is no longer as hot as hell in summer owing to a solar film which cuts down the heat.

BACKGROUND AND ATMOSPHERE: One of the Girls' Public Day School Trust Schools (see introduction). Founded in 1882 on a dreary site though efforts have been made to brighten up the outside areas. Housed in a red-brick building (shiny brass plate) tucked behind the seafront at Southsea (bracing).

Behind the red brick, which looks as though it was designed to accommodate about a hundred girls, the school now has any number of bolt-on extras, and has just finished a major rebuilding to eke out yet more space in the existing site (the Head points out that the school's site has in fact doubled in the past ten years). There is a slightly institutional smell – but this could be because of overcrowding owing to building works. The school has a small not very inspiring library (though Deputy Head points out that there is a panelled well-stocked Sixth Form library and the main school library is computerised). There are no fields and minimal grass/garden – very urban feel, despite the sea.

The Sixth Form are treated very much as young adults with privileges, responsibilities. There are new Sixth Form facilities including a garden. The school did away with Sixth Form uniform in the '70s.

PASTORAL CARE AND DISCIPLINE: Pastoral care is in charge of the individual form mistresses (or masters). The Head seems stumped to think what the main disciplinary problem might be – 'there's the normal teenage high spirits,' she says doubtfully. The question of smoking, drinking, etc, is tackled in 'Personal and Social Education' lessons.

PUPILS AND PARENTS: Bouncy: pupils look you straight in the eye and smile. Parents work in IBM, some Service families, professionals. On the middle side of middle, with some humble backgrounds coming in on bursaries, etc. OGs include Managing Director of Framlington Unit Management, Anne McMeehan; Mrs Justice Ebsworth.

ENTRANCE: Put name down in autumn for the school's own exam the following February for entry in September for 10–11-year-olds. There is

a very modest registration fee. There is no advantage to putting down name early – the school is academically selective only. Separate Sixth Form prospectus.

EXIT: Remarkably few to Oxbridge (about four a year, if that), given their performance in A-levels – this could be a reflection on the teaching, or on pupils' aspirations, probably both. Otherwise – to nearby universities (Bristol and Southampton are popular), ex-polys, a gap year, one or two to Higher Education colleges and to Project 2000 (nursing).

A number leave after GCSE to go to local Sixth Form Colleges, and to the newly co-ed Portsmouth Grammar.

MONEY MATTERS: There are 24 Assisted Places at 11 (part of the school's secret league table weapon), plus 5 at Sixth Form. The Head has a small bursary fund, plus support from a central trust, and access to an emergency fund run by the Friends of the GPDST. By girls' school standards – jolly good.

REMARKS: A successful girls' day school which beavers away to consistently outstanding exam results. It deserves a better site. It appears to be holding its own in the face of potential poaching by the grammar school.

Putney High School

35 Putney Hill, London SW15 6BH
Tel: 0181 788 4886, Fax: 0181 789 8068
PUPILS: Around 600 girls
ALL DAY
AGES: 11–18 (also junior department)
SIZE OF SIXTH FORM: 130
NON-DENOM
FEE-PAYING

HEAD: Since 1991, Mrs Eileen Merchant BSc (fifties), educated at a Convent School in East London and studied Chemistry at Sheffield. Previously Deputy Head of Latymer School. Teaches Maths, visits classrooms regularly and sees girls when they 'sign the excellence book'. Keen Games supporter.

Described by parents as 'impressive, cool and detached; very clever and terribly honest'. Strict: 'the girls know where they are with her.'

ACADEMIC MATTERS: Fluctuating results. More all round than many GPDST schools, and also less formal. There are 22 subjects offered at A-level, including History of Art (strong), Economics and Italian (also at GCSE). Nine basic subjects are available at GCSE plus Classical Civilisation (Classics is also good and popular), Greek, German and Computer Studies. Modern Languages are outstanding (HMI Centre of Excellence), but Maths is good, also Biology and Chemistry (Dual Award at GCSE).

GAMES, OPTIONS, THE ARTS: Gym is either in the main hall or the traditional gym, plus Barn Elms and Putney Leisure Centres and Bank of England Sports Grounds. Tennis and netball teams are successful, but much emphasis is put on individual exercise: aerobics (very popular), fencing, abseiling. Rowing from the Thames Rowing Club; girls are surprisingly successful at Regattas.

CDT is popular, and Home Economics – Textiles taught to A-level, but there is possibly a slight lack of imagination. Ditto Art, competent rather than inspired. Music is good, with many external orchestras, and players in The National Youth Orchestra and Stoneleigh. School choirs were in the finals of Music For Youth at Royal Festival Hall.

BACKGROUND AND ATMOSPHERE: A leafy suburban site half-way up Putney Hill, three large Victorian villas (one for the junior school) plus sundry modern revamped and about to be upgraded purpose-built additions. There is a new octagonal hall for Music and Drama. Girls wear purple (no uniform for Sixth Form) with rather jolly sweat shirts, and any combination of purple and white for summer dresses.

Junior School: Head Miss C J Attfield. Teaching cert. Approx 275 girls ages 5–11, all day. Entrance by assessment and interview. Name down by mid-November for following September. Very popular.

PASTORAL CARE AND DISCIPLINE: Via Form tutors, and have strong links with parents, but Mrs Merchant is perceived as very strict: cross the line and you're out. The school has an excellent anti-bullying policy and a recent clampdown on bullying was successful, not strident. Only the Sixth Form is allowed in the street during the day. 'Girls are very co-operative and keen to do well,' says Mrs Merchant.

PUPILS AND PARENTS: Predominantly Putney locals and those from the surrounding areas of Richmond, Twickenham, Fulham and Barnes. Parents come from the professions including a fair amount from the media. OGs include Amanda Waring and Virginia Bottomley (the latter was Head Girl).

ENTRANCE: 50% via junior school, a fair number from state schools. At 11+, interview plus very stiff CE – 320 girls sit for 84 places. There are vacancies in other years, however. Sixth Form entry needs six GCSE passes with A or B for A-level subjects, plus interviews (about 12 a

year). Competitive. No sibling concessions.

EXIT: After GCSE, 10–12 leave either
to Westminster and the like or to
Sixth Form Colleges (more than previous
years?). Otherwise, most leavers to
university, including Oxbridge. 'Fair
number do gap year before taking up
university place.'

MONEY MATTERS: There are 20
Assisted Places annually plus 5 in
the Sixth Form. Assisted Places can be
topped up to 100% by the school.
Academic, and Music scholarships
available, plus GPDST bursaries. Short-
term assistance is on hand for need.

REMARKS: No longer the power
house it once was, but nevertheless,
a popular local school. Happy reports
from (most) parents and pupils – with two
or three dissenters. 'Slightly tunnel-
visioned but good as far as it goes'.

Queen Anne's
School

Caversham, Reading, Berkshire
RG4 0DX
Tel: 01734 471582, Fax: 01734 461498
PUPILS: Around 325 girls. 200 board
(including the odd weekly boarder),
120 day
AGES: 11–18
SIZE OF SIXTH FORM: 111
C OF E
FEE-PAYING

HEAD: Since 1993, Mrs D Forbes,
MA (Oxon) (forties), educated at
Bath High School, and read English at
Somerville. For the past ten years taught

English at Cheltenham, ending as Head of
English. Married to a writer; two grown-
up children.

Taking over after an interregnum, she
is quietly rebuilding confidence in the
school with a minimum of fuss and a
maximum of humour and consultation –
'with everyone'. 'It is difficult to know
what traditions are sacred and what they
are longing for you to change.' But
'doesn't want to tamper with the ethos of
the school, the changes are more
superficial'. Instituted a School Council
to consider changes.

Looks to produce 'good all-rounders
with good academic education and plenty
of other things besides'. She is very
committed to boarding and not so keen
on weekly boarding.

ACADEMIC MATTERS: Standard
English, Maths, French, German
and Spanish: The Language lab is popular.
Latin, plus Greek is available on demand
(no one taking it in '95 though). The
school gains respectable A-level results,
with the usual disappointments in
Economics.

Very keen Science, and some girls
become medics. Both single certificate
and separate sciences are offered at
GCSE. There is no sign of computers yet
linking to CDT, or Geography – still in
the pipeline. The school has no specialist
dyslexia unit or teacher, but mild dyslexia
is not a bar. Four libraries, including one
super new octagonal double-decker
showpiece; the old library is now a lecture
hall. Good careers advice is given.

GAMES, OPTIONS, THE ARTS:
Lacrosse is still strong, with a USA
tour in '95, though they are no longer the
under-15 county champions. Serious
tennis coaching throughout the winter
(with a ball thrower); all-weather tennis
courts are much in demand. There are
lots of external activities, particularly at

weekends – skating, dry-skiing, sailing. Girls are also good at rowing. The swimming pool with underwater lighting and music is equally popular. Masses of Music; Drama is good.

The school also has a strong Art department, and super 3D textiles, with girls making their own clothes including ball gowns: sewing machines are available at weekends, but the computer rooms are not open. Keyboard skills and RSA qualifications. Young Enterprise and D of E Award.

BACKGROUND AND ATMOSPHERE: The history of the school reaches back to 1698 and the opening of the Grey Coat Hospital in Westminster. In 1706 Queen Anne granted a charter to Grey Coats, and in due course part of the endowment was used to found a boarding school in the country. Grey Coat Hospital is now in the state sector and links with its 'country arm' are somewhat tenuous, though relationships were strengthened for QA's centenary in 1994. The school has magical new(ish) combined Performing Arts Centre and 250-seater theatre.

Purpose-built in 1894, the charming red-brick complex sprawls round two sides of the 40-acre grounds less than five minutes from the centre of Reading. There are massive games fields. Girls flow happily in long red cloaks throughout the campus, and are based in one of four boarding or two day houses.

Sixth Formers have their own houses and wear mufti (not jeans for lessons), give dinner parties and stay out later than the rest of school. Boys are welcome for tea in the house and most girls have their own rooms (Head Girls have either a private shower or bath).

Visits to Reading are allowed on the basis of responsibility via 'The List' (which gives one term's advantage over the others). The school does an enormous amount of girl-inspired charity work.

PASTORAL CARE AND DISCIPLINE: Pastoral care under chain of command via 'pastoral deputy head', House Mistress and Tutor to Head; There is a strong Christian ethos. School Counsellor. The school has sensible rules: sacking for drugs ('not in Head's time'); smoking means a letter home, suspension for repeated offences; booze, not without permission, but OK at school parties – in moderation.

PUPILS AND PARENTS: From within a 50-mile radius: Home Counties. Delightful, not particularly streetwise, mainly 'the unmentionable middle class, good solid citizens whose values are straight' (still). There are 40–50 non-Brits (who sit a stiff English exam), and a similar number of ex-pats, plus a fair number of first-time buyers and OGs' daughters. OGs include: cartoonist Posy Simmonds, Jenny Seagrove. NB a Parents' Association has just been started.

ENTRANCE: Mainly 11+, rest at 12+, or 13+. CE and interview. Pupils come from local schools, and prep schools such as Godstowe, Maltman's Green, Rupert House, St Mary's Henley. Places are 'usually' available at Sixth Form level: five GCSE passes A-C, and interview.

EXIT: Some leakage post-GCSE, 95%+ go to university particularly the popular ones – Nottingham, Edinburgh, Exeter, Manchester; 4–5 to Oxbridge annually.

MONEY MATTERS: Well funded (by girls' schools standards). All funding comes from the Foundation Office in London, which also deals with bad payers. Help is always available for genuine hardship, particularly in exam years. Otherwise there are 2 open scholarships for the Sixth Form, and 4 internal ones based on GCSE results. Also 6 scholarships at 11, 12 or 13. There is a major bursary for day girls.

REMARKS: A nice low-key girls' boarding school which delivers the goods – both sporting and academic – in a quiet sort of way. Worth a look.

Queen Elizabeth's Grammar School

Blackburn, Lancashire BB2 6DF
Tel: 01254 59911, Fax: 01254 692314

PUPILS: Around 1,100 pupils, all boys
   except for 50 girls in Sixth Form
ALL DAY
AGES: 7–19
SIZE OF SIXTH FORM: Around 300
INTER-DENOM ON C OF E
   FOUNDATION
FEE-PAYING

HEAD: Since September 1995, Dr Hempsall, MA PhD (late forties). Read History at Cambridge. Previously Head of Scarborough College. Took over following an interregnum following the departure of the long-serving and excellent Head, Mr Johnston.

ACADEMIC MATTERS: The school has a very strong Science bias (there are lots of serious engineering businesses around – ICI, Volvo, British Aerospace, etc) with streams of As in Biology, Chemistry and Mathematics at A-level. Also many As in General Studies at A-level. Maximum class size 30, fewer for GCSE and A-levels. There are language labs (French, Spanish and German on offer, with a Russian option in Sixth

Form if there are enough takers). Latin and Greek are also possible to A-level. The school is divided into blocks of subject-taught areas – IT and CDT, and some Business Studies. There are computers around, but not as many as one might expect from a school this size. A good hard-working ethos prevails. Eight or nine GCSEs are the norm. The staff are high-powered; no remedial help is given.

GAMES, OPTIONS, THE ARTS: This is a soccer school (note to fans: Blackburn Rovers wear school colours, train on school grounds) and there is a lot of county representation in cricket, netball, cross-country and athletics. Not much rugby. All England Croquet Club Schoolboy Champions, and the school has two Olympic swimmers, with a superb swimming pool (which locals use in the evenings).

Music is taught in a converted Christian Science church – 'v short on facilities' – but orchestras, bands and ensembles abound. Sent four organ scholars to Oxbridge recently and there are regular major productions in Cathedral. Drama is strong, and there is an annual mega production on its own stage, but the auditorium is too small to hold the whole school; Gilbert and Sullivan popular.

The school makes regular trips abroad, soccer to US, cricket to Holland, Classics scholars to Italy, Politics to Russia, Linguists to France and Germany, and lots of foreign exchanges. Scouting is popular, with trips to Switzerland, Young Enterprise, and D of E Awards. Masses of extra-curricular involvement.

BACKGROUND AND ATMOSPHERE: The school was founded in 1509 by the second Earl of Derby (the current Earl is the school Visitor) and incorporated by Royal Charter from Queen Elizabeth I in

1567. Went Direct Grant in 1944 and returned to the private sector in 1979. It moved to its present site in 1882, and much of this building remains, with elegant stained glass and serious 'boy-proof banisters' (with knobs on). Portraits of previous Heads and school silver are proudly displayed. Recent extensions and the acqustion of neighbouring buildings make the campus somewhat crowded. Games fields and the Sports Hall are 15 minutes' walk away; pupils are bussed. Grounds are immaculate, with the junior school (Horncliffe), sharing premises and facilities. The next project is to convert two Victorian villas into a Sixth Form Centre and study area. A light airy library at the top of Queen's Wing gives a good feeling of quiet purposeful study.

PASTORAL CARE AND DISCIPLINE: Problems are relayed via Form Masters (Tutors in Sixth Form), Heads of Year to Vice Head and Head. Two ex-Headmasters and the Chaplain run an informal counselling service, and staff get in-service training. Punishments range from Saturday morning detentions, to temporary or permanent removal from school (the latter mainly for drugs). The school has a hot policy on bullying and verbal abuse, seminars on drugs.

PUPILS AND PARENTS: 'Genuinely sociologically much more comprehensive than many in Lancashire', lots from ethnic background, one-sixth Asian, with 'lots of parents seriously disadvantaged'. Open to anyone, and pupils wear the school uniform with pride. Parents are expected to turn up for PTA meetings, and Sixth Formers accompany them to Sixth Form meetings. The PTA is hot on fund-raising, 'make money hand over fist to subsidise Assisted Place pupils to go on trips'. Catchment area all over NE Lancs, from Preston to Bolton to Brierfield: the school

bus service covers 13 routes. OBs include Russell Harty; the former bishops of Woolwich and Chester; Sir Kenneth Durham (former chairman of Unilever).

ENTRANCE: At 11, a school test in English, Maths and verbal reasoning, with a strict academic cut-off, but preference is given to siblings, OBs' children, and those 'with the X factor'. There is no automatic entry from Horncliffe. At Sixth Form, via interview and good GCSE results.

EXIT: Most to universities, 16–24 to Oxbridge, often sponsored by local industries (Shell, BP, National Coal Board).

MONEY MATTERS: Tough on those who 'refuse to pay when we know they could', but the school will carry any child in exam year, tries to keep fees down, arranges delayed payments, etc. Can support 'in proven need and academic worthiness'; otherwise there are 30 Assisted Places at 11, 5 at 12–13, plus 5 at Sixth Form and limited bursaries available. (NB This means 275 Assisted Places at any one time – in our view the school is over-dependent on this government funding.)

REMARKS: A tough, thrusting, successful school, achieving the academic ambitions and aspirations as set out by its original Foundation, despite hot competition from the local state sector. It is too early to comment on the new regime.

Queen Elizabeth Grammar School Wakefield

Northgate, Wakefield,
West Yorkshire WF1 3QX
Tel: 01924 373 943, Fax: 01924 378 871

PUPILS: Around 749 boys, plus junior
school of around 235 boys
ALL DAY
AGES: 11–18, plus junior school 7–11
SIZE OF SIXTH FORM: Around 190
INTER-DENOM
FEE-PAYING

HEAD: Since 1985, Mr R P Mardling, MA (Oxon), FIL, FRSA (fifties), and educated at Nottingham High School, read languages (German and French) at St Edmund Hall and teaches German Business Studies in the Sixth Form. Previously Deputy Head of Arnold School in Blackpool and before that at Nottingham High. A keen teacher manqué, he 'fits in'. Sits in on exam Boards and does 'a lot of work with the joint girls' school' – Wakefield Girls' High School.

Aims to produce 'self-confident, caring, modest, open-minded children who will have a go at things' and encourages 'good organisational skills and respect for others'.

ACADEMIC MATTERS: The school shows a bias towards Science and Maths (the school is bursting with mathematicians, a fair number of them not too hot, to judge by the '95 results). Physics has a pretty steady collection of D–U grades as well, in fact results across the board seem to indicate a more mixed intake than is normal with a grammar school. Some languages are studied with the Girls' High; boys can opt for an extra language in Sixth Form, Russian, Italian or Business French or German. The Head of English has 'added impetus' to the department – very pleasing A-level results in English Literature (though not in Language).

All the Sixth Form do General Studies at A-level (40 As in '95), which bumps up the school's position in the league tables nicely. Remedial help is on hand for mild dyslexia, children are screened, and additional help can be organised, usually at lunch time. Lap-tops are allowed.

GAMES, OPTIONS, THE ARTS: Rugby (keen), hockey, cross-country, cricket, tennis and athletics, plus ancillary badminton, basketball – the rugby team toured to Australia and NZ, and the cricket team to Holland recently. The school 'has use of' over 27 acres of playing fields, the senior boys play 'up the road' (which is also used by the nearby Police Academy as a helicopter landing pad – great excitement).

Art has blossomed and is a good and popular A-level subject; the department is very energetic; screenprinting and photography are popular (has its own dark room). The school has an enthusiastic Head of Music, with over 200 individual players, and swing bands, junior swing bands are hired out for weddings and things – money earned goes to funding trips abroad. Concerts are often held in Wakefield Cathedral, for which the school is the choir school. Drama is popular, with regular blockbusters, *My Fair Lady*, *Amadeus*, *Macbeth*, etc. The theatre has a superb stage and doubles as assembly hall.

Marvellous CDT development, with super new labs and IT moving into its own slot, out of DT; computer lab and in departments. The library has expanded with a false floor (the brilliant Victorian roof is still visible through the mezzanine) and CD-Rom.

BACKGROUND AND ATMOSPHERE: The school was founded by Royal Charter in 1591, and moved to its present site in 1854. From 1944 to 1976 it was a Direct Grant School, and reverted to fee-paying in 1976. The marvellous Victorian Gothic façade hides a multitude of extensions and make-overs; some are very imaginative, some less so. The junior school is also on site, the small learning pool is used by juniors and those learning to swim, including the junior girls' school. There is no real swimming pool or Sports Hall.

PASTORAL CARE AND DISCIPLINE: All boys carry a record book at all times which can be inspected by staff at any time, and must be signed by parents at preordained intervals. If a boy misbehaves in public, the line is to remove the record book and send it back to the school, which will then reprimand the owner. Brilliant: it works well, other schools could do well to copy. The school will tail boys if they complain about being bullied; there is no problem with drugs (as yet) but the school speaks to the Drugs Squad – the Head says drink is the biggest problem of the middle classes. Tuesday p.m. 'staff detention' for minor sin, Saturday morning detentions for serious infringements – two lessons in two of the pupil's weakest subjects (as determined by him and confirmed by a master). Suspensions and exclusions (the Head expelled four recently); vandalism, bullying and aggressive behaviour are stamped on hard. *And it works.*

PUPILS AND PARENTS: There is a fair number of first-time buyers (at least 50%); the school is regarded as a local option for boarding or for those disaffected with the state system. The strong middle-class ethic about getting value for money is evident everywhere: boys work hard. The school has a fair ethnic mix. 50% have a Wakefield postcode, the rest come from as far away as Doncaster, Sheffield and Wetherby. Parents organise school buses.

ENTRANCE: 11+, 13+ CE paper (boys use girls' CE paper *pro tem*). 12+ own exam, plus Head's report plus Head's judgement. About 50/55% of boys come from own junior school, but there is no automatic entry, and from local preps – Westbourne, Sheffield, plus state primaries. Sixth Form entry: good GCSEs – B or over required for A-level subjects. Boys can and do move into the school at all other times, subject to academic ability and space available.

EXIT: Some post-GCSE; of the rest, one or two drop out, one or two to Art Foundation courses, one or two to employment, a handful to Oxbridge, some to re-takes or improved offers but the majority to degree courses all over Britain (Sheffield, Durham and Newcastle were popular in '95).

MONEY MATTERS: Numbers are steady – the recession was less harmful than the miners' strike. 'Special arrangements in place' for some, but there is lots of parental commitment and a very efficient Clerk to the Governors. Recently, 27 hadn't paid one month into term; four or five were being kept through their exam year. Lots of encouragement to opt for Direct Debit. There are 23 Assisted Places throughout the school and all are taken up, plus bursaries. 25% of pupils are on some sort of fees assistance, and the fees are reasonable. There are 12 Sixth Form scholarships, and Music scholarships (deserving case), plus bursaries in junior school for choristers, one-third paid by Cathedral and one-third by school.

REMARKS: The best boys' city day school in this area.

Queen Margaret's School

Escrick Park, York YO4 6EU
Tel: 01904 728261, Fax 01904 728150

PUPILS: Around 367 girls, all board except for 25
AGES: 11–18
SIZE OF SIXTH FORM: Around 100
C OF E
FEE-PAYING

HEAD: Since January 1993, Dr Geoffrey Chapman, MA (fifties), educated at St Bartholomew's Grammar School, Newbury; read Classics at Trinity College, Oxford. Teaches A-level Greek (to one or two). Previously Head of Classics at Christ's Hospital, Horsham, and before that was Professor of Classics at the University of Natal. Known for serious research on Aristophanes, keen on golf. Wife (a popular lady) teaches Drama, two children at university.

Keen on breadth and choice. 'No one can excel at everything, but everybody can excel at something.' A listener.

ACADEMIC MATTERS: The school has made a big push on the Sciences, which have been 'the Cinderella subject', comments the Head. Sciences every which way at GCSE. English and French are still especially popular, otherwise everything is on offer – Politics, Economics, one or two doing Music, History of Art, Religious Studies, Classical Civilisation, Business Studies – these less mainstream subjects dominate the A-levels. There are three streams.

This is one of the few schools to run a one-year Sixth Form course for non-A-levellers (Business Studies, Modern History, typing, etc).

GAMES, OPTIONS, THE ARTS: Lots of healthy outdoor life – games are keenly played; the school has a 9-hole golf course, also lacrosse, hockey, squash, tennis; and masses of girls ride (there is a Riding School next door, some box their ponies over for the term). Very good Art, keen on DT. Cooking lessons for all. Strong Choral Music, and enthusiastic Drama (the Drama Hall transforms into chapel). Mass is held for the Catholics in the adorable tiny Lady Chapel.

BACKGROUND AND ATMOSPHERE: Founded in Scarborough in 1901, the school moved to this fine Palladian house (by John Carr) in 1949. It was originally part of the Woodard Foundation, but was taken over by parents in a 1986 drama. In a lovely setting in 65 acres of parkland, with Victorian additions, clever conversions and recent additions. The school is extremely uninstitutional (chintz and carpets and flowers), and the Head is working hard at making the dorms parent-friendly (cutting down in size). There is a splendid library (panelling, wood, open fire, huge windows looking out on to lawns). Some weeding out of Housemistresses. The circular dining hall (once an indoor lunging school) has dreadful acoustics.

Girls live in year groups (which 'prevents them growing up too fast,' observes a pleased parent), though Dr Chapman is keen to encourage more vertical interaction between elders and youngers. Girls are kept 'pretty busy', weekends not excepted. There is a calmness felt throughout the school (not always true in the past). It may be benefiting from likely rivals falling from favour for various reasons.

PASTORAL CARE AND DISCIPLINE: Girls are in the slow lane – this is a rural boarding school, protective of its inmates. 'There are no silly rules,' say parents and girls. Sixth Formers are given a fair amount of freedom (e.g. they can go into York during free time on Wednesdays and Saturdays), which they are mostly keen not to abuse, and also a fair amount of responsibility.

PUPILS AND PARENTS: Girls are friendly and supportive of each other, and inwardly contented. Mainly upper and upper-middle class; landowners, farmers, one or two from abroad (keenly encouraged), lots from Scotland, Cumbria, Northumberland, the Peterborough area and, of course, Yorkshire. Criticised by some as 'the smart school', by those who consider the girls 'precious' and 'think the world owes them a living'. Brothers might be at Ampleforth.

ENTRANCE: By CE at 11+, 12+ and 13+ (a far tougher hurdle at 13 than 11), and at Sixth Form. The school has a broad ability intake.

EXIT: Virtually everyone goes on to further education (everything from Oxbridge – 1–8 annually – to minor erstwhile polys; some medics). Some leave at Sixth Form to go to Repton, Uppingham etc.

MONEY MATTERS: Scholarships at 11, 12, 13 and Sixth Form; Music scholarships at 11; some bursaries. School is a charitable trust in its own right – no longer part of the Woodard Foundation.

REMARKS: A lively, small, rural boarding school which offers a good deal, and is well worth consideration, especially by southerners seeking an escape route from the fast lane.

Queen Mary's School

Baldersby Park, Topcliffe, nr Thirsk, North Yorkshire YO7 3BZ
Tel: 01845 577425, Fax: 01845 577368

PUPILS: Around 225, 90 day, the rest board
AGES: 7–16
SIZE OF SIXTH FORM: not applicable
C OF E (Woodard school)
FEE-PAYING

HEAD: Since 1978, Mr Peter Belward (fifties), educated Coleshill Grammar; and Mrs Belward, Cert Ed, educated at St Elphin's, Derbyshire. Mr Belward teaches Maths, Mrs Belward teaches Art and primary classes. The Belwards comment that they do not recognise the place from our description.

REMARKS: Traditionally looks after the children of local gents who are not overly worried about how their daughters fare at school, though one parent has written to us to say that this is no longer the case, and pupils are now all sorts from all walks of life. Some leave at 11 to go on to Tudor Hall, etc. Otherwise on to Oundle, Uppingham, Gordonstoun, etc. Has a *very* mixed-ability intake: the school says the pupils' IQs range from '140 down to the seventies' – though how it manages to cope with this huge range, given the small size of school, is a mystery.

Streaming and setting. The school has a dyslexia unit for 10 children.

Baldersby Park is a grand Palladian mansion – a good selling point – and girls live in converted flats, with posh bathrooms and good-sized dormitories; there are also good conversions of the farm buildings and outhouses. This is a happy place, though there are some reports of boarding pupils feeling 'isolated'. Day numbers are reported to be increasing, which is causing slight ruffles in the cosy boarding atmosphere.

Queen's College

43–49 Harley Street, London WIN 2BT
Tel: 0171 580 1533, Fax: 0171 436 7607

PUPILS: Around 367 day girls
AGES: 11–18
SIZE OF SIXTH FORM: Around 86
C OF E
FEE-PAYING

HEAD: Since 1991, The Hon Lady Goodhart MA Oxon (fifties). Educated at St Michael's Limpsfield and St Hilda's, Oxford, where she read History. An Honorary Fellow of St Hilda's.

Daughter of missionary Lord Hemingford, married to QC Sir William Goodhart. Lady Goodhart is beady but kind. Brought up three children (one patronised Queen's College), taught part-time both here and at Westminster Tutors before returning to full-time work outside the home. On all manner of committees, including President of the London Marriage Guidance Council, Vice President of Youth Clubs UK. She makes a good role model for pupils. Passionately believes in girls getting qualifications as well as university degrees and says it is vital to see university as a stepping stone not the be-all and end-all. And passionately doesn't believe in forcing girls to suffer on the hockey field – shudder.

ACADEMIC MATTERS: The school still has on the whole an excellent Common Room, though the school has recently lost a real star, plus an excellent teacher. The teaching is good – enthusiastic, competent and able to instil some breadth as well as getting the troops through exams (100% pass rate in '95 A-level – very good). Classes below third form are on the large size (25-ish). The school has a Language laboratory, and a very strong Language department with lots of different languages on offer, including (ancient) Greek, Latin, French, Spanish, Italian, German, Russian – and results are usually good. All children do Latin and French; and at thirteen have to choose a third language.

The school has stopped taking separate sciences at GCSE (Dual Award now) but Science labs are modern, and, says *The Other Prospectus* (a very jolly tract written by the Sixth Form), if you do Biology A-level you get your own vacuum-packed rat to dissect. Geography has been excellent.

The charming and dedicated Senior Tutor, Mr Hutchinson, teaches computing – all pupils have hands-on experience and can do Computer Studies at GCSE and A-level (good GCSE computing results). The school is currently pushing AS-levels. There is a nice atmosphere in the library (the Kynaston Library) which has a good budget for periodicals and new books; warm, elegant and conducive to learning.

The school has a helpful careers department and lots of good advice is given: 'sometimes painful', say the girls. Good networking.

Caveat: the school operates a policy of bumping pupils off particular exam courses half-way through if they are failing in tests 'in order that they can concentrate on fewer subjects'. Pupils are given heavy amounts of homework, (e.g. 11 topics/essays to do for one GCSE subject over the Christmas holidays). This also makes for an effective weeding out or constructive dismissal of less keen pupils.

GAMES, OPTIONS, THE ARTS: Not exactly famous as a games school, but surprisingly good, and regularly trounces neighbouring schools at hockey; recently it also came second in British Schools Fencing Championships. Everyone up to 16 goes to Regent's Park to do games. The school has a lively Art department. There are five Music rooms, a choir, orchestra, and children learning a wide variety of instruments. Clubs are after school – keen debating, fencing. The school has its own printing department.

BACKGROUND AND ATMOSPHERE: The school is housed in good big buildings in Harley Street wedged between seas of doctors and marked out by smart white columns. It was founded in 1848 by F D Maurice, Professor of History at King's College London as 'the first institution to provide a sound academic education and proper qualifications for women' (hurray for him), and all the best governesses studied here, accompanied by their chaperones.

There are elegant staircases, lots of parquet, and a microscopic playground on site ('good atmosphere, stairs – which do wonders for your thighs – pretty building until the third floor' says *The Other Prospectus*). It has a good School Hall by Inner London standards, with wooden chairs engraved with the names of Old Girls. There is a new Sixth Form 'suite' with common room, kitchen, etc.

The Head and Second Head wear their gowns, which adds a touch of style to an otherwise depressingly scruffy image – indeed, they have now overtaken Bedales as possibly the scruffiest school in the business – not just pupils, but also some members of staff, not to mention parents. There is no uniform – jeans and tee shirts are quite in order, and not necessarily clean or untorn ones at that: 'we took the line,' says Mr Hutchinson, 'that there are more important things to worry about ...'

There is a voucher system for lunch (planned by pupils), popular and lots of choice, all taking place in the basement – lots of room by London standards.

PASTORAL CARE AND DISCIPLINE: The school is quite prepared to expel where necessary. The recurring problem is children wandering round London after school (with all its temptations) – parents are too busy working. The school takes endless trouble to liaise with home.

PUPILS AND PARENTS: There is a slightly floating population of children en route to or from country boarding schools. Some media and government. Also a Jewish contingent (and Jewish prayers said for them). Parents come from all shades of the financial and social spectrum; there are a large number of families in which both parents work full time. Popular with foreigners. Pupils appear slightly tough and street smart compared, for example, with Francis Holland down the road. OGs include Gertrude Bell, Katherine Mansfield, Emma Freud, Jennifer Ehle, not to mention Miss Buss and Miss Beale.

ENTRANCE: Interview, reference from previous school, and school's own exam. There is a £500 registration fee at the time of writing.

EXIT: A fair exodus after GCSE. Most to higher education of one sort or another – London university is the favourite choice. An interesting range of jobs thereafter.

MONEY MATTERS: Nearly 25% of pupils are on some sort of scholarship or bursary. There are Assisted Places at entry and Sixth Form. The school is generously funded by girls' school standards. It is sympathetic to parents who have fallen on hard times.

REMARKS: A serious and lively central London school with some very good staff. In need of a touch of glamour/publicity. It deserves to be better known.

Queen's Gate School

133 Queen's Gate, London SW7 5LE
Tel: 0171 589 3587, Fax: 0171 584 7691

PUPILS: 222 girls
ALL DAY
AGES: 11–18
SIZE OF SIXTH FORM: Around 30
NON-DENOM
FEE-PAYING

HEAD: (Principal) since 1987, Mrs Angela Holyoak Cert Ed. Elegant, efficient, enthusiastic. Generous with praise, enormously positive and humorous. Runs the whole school with panache and terrific attention to details. Cares passionately about the individual, 'Which is why we never put pressure on parents or children at any stage to stay here if they think their talents might be better suited elsewhere.' Well aware of the difficulties of shedding the image of the past. Pupils admire and like her.

Headmistress: Miss Skone-Roberts, BSc, PGCE, previously Head of Physics at Heathfield, Queen's Gate's sister school.

ACADEMIC MATTERS: A breakdown of results was not given, but the school tells us that one star pupil got nine A*s at GCSE in '95. Not a place you would choose for a potential Oxbridge girl who needs continual challenge, but this school does extremely well for the average ('those with an IQ below 105 really won't fit in') and has enough competition for the above average. X and Y streams (flexible). The school has an outstandingly good French department (A grades galore, both at GCSE and A-level, under Miss Singh) – and has had this forte for years. It also has very good History of Art (under Miss de Leeuw), who lives on the premises, and is also a careers adviser, cleverly bouncing the ball in straight at the girls: 'If they want to read English at university, I tell them to do the research on courses and come back to present it to the whole class.'

The Science labs (in the basement, along with a new Sixth Form sitting room and bar) have recently been renewed and refurbished, duly strengthening the department. 'An even newer computer room' has been kitted out on the fourth floor since we last went to press, with new Apple Macs, even laser printers; there are also computers in the (small but well-equipped) DT department for graphic design. All pupils learn word-processing.

The school has a very small Sixth Form (size variable; 31 in 1993, 13 in 1995), with often 50% leaving to do A-levels elsewhere (some have been here since the age of 4). But there are interesting and not unusual cases of girls returning, having tried somewhere else for a short spell. Having said that, the Sixth Form, alas, appears to be dwindling away – 'not good for morale' comments a bystander.

GAMES, OPTIONS, THE ARTS: To Battersea Park for sports. Good Art in a large new Art room on the new fifth floor with inspiring views over London. (NB Nearby Museum resources are constantly drawn upon.) Keen Music and Drama (enhanced by a hall built across two of the houses, thanks to much fund-raising). Good on trips and outings. 'They're always doing things and going away,' said a parent.

BACKGROUND AND ATMOSPHERE: Three large mansions in South Kensington house the school. 'We've more space than you first imagine,' points out the Head, and broom cupboards in erstwhile mansions of this size provide useful dark rooms/tutorial rooms. It is well kept; walls are full of notice-boards, photographs, work. Children are amazingly quiet during classes ('Some visiting parents ask if all the children are out'), the silence broken excitedly at break times. The school has a very friendly atmosphere; a big family where the littles know the big ones – and aren't scared. There are particularly good teacher/pupil relationships. The black glossy dining room for seniors is used by staff at break. Good food (children may bring packed lunches). No uniform.

PASTORAL CARE AND DISCIPLINE: Something Mrs Holyoak cares passionately about. There are lots of links with parents, and a Tutor system throughout the school. Sixth Formers are allowed out at lunch time: 'I'm not terribly keen on them hanging around South Ken, but they are 17 or 18.'

PUPILS AND PARENTS: Pretty upper class. Streetwise in a sophisticated way, articulate and poised girls. The school has several foreigners, encouraged by the Principal, as long as their English is up to it, 'This is London and we're a cosmopolitan city.' And, observes Mrs Holyoak, it also sets up a useful worldwide network. The school breeds fierce loyalty. OGs include the Redgraves, Sieffs, Guinnesses, Amanda de Souza, Camilla Parker-Bowles.

ENTRANCE: From its own junior school qv (three-quarters of junior girls come on to the senior school), and a huge variety of other schools.

EXIT: Girls are keen on a gap year, and all nowadays keen on degrees; art college is popular. 'Our girls are ambitious and getting more ambitious all the time,' says the Head, 'but we don't talk about it so loudly as some schools.'

MONEY MATTERS: There are 2 internal scholarships for Upper Sixth.

REMARKS: A cosy, friendly, lively, small, unpressurised school – an unusual phenomenon in the centre of London.

The Queen's School

City Walls Road, Chester CH1 2NN
Tel: 01244 312078, Fax: 01244 321507

PUPILS: 420 girls
ALL DAY
AGES: 11–18
SIZE OF SIXTH FORM: Around 121
C OF E
FEE-PAYING

HEAD: Since 1989, Miss Diana Skilbeck, BA (fifties). Splendidly forthright, down-to-earth, doesn't stand upon ceremony, modest and humorous. Warmly appreciated by children (who are not afraid of her), also by staff and parents. Has worked in both state and private schools (previously Head of Sheffield High). Read Geography at London University.

Determined to 'educate the whole person and help every pupil live up to their potential – I know it's what everyone says, but it really IS what matters'.

ACADEMIC MATTERS: The school is traditionally a powerhouse, but '95 results are not going to knock them in the aisles. A fair number of A-levels were taken with 'Studies' in the title – Business Studies, Classical Studies, Religious Studies, not to mention General Studies (NB this last produced the best results). Fairly competitive with the boys at King's (the schools are unrelated, though there are many brothers/sisters at both). It provides traditional teaching (some Old Girls are on the staff), with classes of 24 (no streaming, no orders). There is a broad-based General Studies programme for all Sixth Formers.

Good careers/university advice is given under Mrs Falcon. (NB This is a real department; she visits universities regularly, and her time is not reduced by teaching.) Staff are incredibly hard-working: girls lie in wait for them outside the staff room.

GAMES, OPTIONS, THE ARTS: The girls share the swimming pool with Nedham House, Queen's Junior School, five minutes away by car ('Slightly annoying having different sites to fetch and carry on different days,' commented a mother). Wedge-shaped playing fields over the road produce some good lacrosse (some girls have been chosen to play for Cheshire), 'we even beat some of the boarding schools'. Good, sometimes powerful Art. Keen on charity fundraising, successful YE, D of E popular. There are several music groups, including the operatic society with King's. Cooking and Textiles/Dressmaking are available, with good standards in both.

BACKGROUND AND ATMOSPHERE: The original Victorian building is red-brick Gothic (many sepia photographs of Queen Victoria are dotted about the school), on the edge of the city, backing out to the cathedral, looking out over the city walls and river; a pleasant site, donated by the first Duke of Westminster. Heaps of additions have been tacked on for new essentials (IT, Science labs, Language block the newest), with the playground area endlessly encroached on. 'Every time you dig foundations to build here,' explains the Head, a keen archaeologist, 'you come across Roman remains.' Unpressurised, friendly atmosphere. Girls wear cheery, red sweaters. The school magazine – called *Have mynde* – has a quote from its 1897 issue: 'in these days of much reading, much hearing, much doing, and much talking, there is some danger lest the noble industry of thought should be neglected. HAVE MYNDE my dear girls . . .'

PASTORAL CARE AND DISCIPLINE: The school places a firm emphasis on consideration for others.

PUPILS AND PARENTS: Solidly middle class, mainly from professional and business backgrounds, also farming; traditionally the popular choice for Welsh parents (easy by train). Enthusiastic and hard-working girls. The school has a huge catchment area: long journeys for some (train plus bus).

ENTRANCE: By own entrance at 11 – and highly selective, though the numbers trying dropped with the recession, 'but we still have plenty of choice'. Pre-prep and prep entry by assessment.

EXIT: One or two to higher education colleges, but almost all to universities, with, in '95 a fair number to ex-polys, three to Oxbridge. Both the (nearby) Sheffield and Leeds Universities are popular. A good wide variety of subjects chosen, though the bias is still towards sciences. The school has produced a huge number of doctors. OGs include Anne Clwyd MP.

MONEY MATTERS: Fees are extremely reasonable (£1,440 per term at time of writing).

REMARKS: The automatic choice for parents with academic daughters in the area. It hit the headlines when the league tables started, by coming in at the top, but it hasn't kept this up. General Studies are keeping the results looking very good, however. Small, caring and good value.

Queenswood

Shepherd's Way, Brookmans Park, Hatfield, Hertfordshire AL9 6NS
Tel: 01707 652262, Fax: 01707 649267

PUPILS: Around 410 girls. Mainly board, but a 'small quota' of day girls (since '91)
AGES: 11–18
SIZE OF SIXTH FORM: Around 110
C OF E
FEE-PAYING

HEAD: From September 1996, Ms Clarissa Farr MA (thirties). Read English at Exeter and has taught in a Sixth Form College, a High School, a Grammar School, and abroad before coming to Queenswood as Deputy Head (academic) in '92. Married to the sports news correspondent of *The Times* – they have a baby daughter. Hobbies include marathon running. Takes over from the great Mrs Audrey Butler, who was Head here from 1981.

ACADEMIC MATTERS: The '95 results are quite impressive (and considerably stronger than '94) – excellent Language results (Spanish, French and German); five took Art A-level and all got As; History of Art is also good and popular. Theatre Studies is on offer. Setting in Maths, French, English and Science (Dual Award at GCSE) but there is no one fast stream, 'What counts is confidence in the classroom.' Nonetheless, academically a competitive school where high expectations are fostered. Staff are very lively, and the previous Head took much trouble to find people who can 'turn the key – though they're like gold dust'. (NB Not many Heads are realistic enough to admit this.)

The school offers amazingly good Computing/IT and is fun with it – the outgoing Head says 'whatever we can do to prepare our students for life in the fast-changing world, we must do'. Sixth Formers all have to study a Modern Language and modular six-week General Studies courses of their choosing alongside their A- and AS-levels. There are weekly visiting lecturers on anything from space travel to funding for the arts (followed by dinner with Head and speaker, girls by rota). Enormous library with CD-Rom.

GAMES, OPTIONS, THE ARTS: Sports are 'high on the agenda'. The school is a national LTA clay court centre (it now has twelve courts) and has a staggering thirteen all-weather courts, two indoor courts – not surprisingly, the school hosts the National Schools Championships each year, and the Lawn Tennis Association suggests it for would-be tennis stars. It also has a new all-weather Astroturf hockey pitch, indoor swimming pool, and a huge Sports Hall.

Keen on Music, with impressively high standards – particularly Choral Music – involving tours of the Continent, and a lively choice of works are performed. Weekends are full of rehearsals and inter-house competitions. Good Drama and Art; regular Art History trips to the Continent. D of E Awards scheme; the keen exploration society – Queenswood

Raven Exploration Society – has regular canoeing and caving expeditions; thriving Engineering Club. Also a Model United Nations Association. Girls raise between £5,000 and £7,000 for charity each year. The 1995 (centenary) school magazine runs an interview with Gillian Shephard tucked away in the middle, not to mention quotations from Lord Archer, Michael Portillo and other political luminaries.

BACKGROUND AND ATMOSPHERE: Only just out of suburbia, set in 150 acres of woodland and sports fields. Founded in Clapham in 1884, the school moved to these purpose-built neo-Tudor beamed blocks in 1925. Parts are warren-like, parts are first class, e.g. the academic facilities, and the lecture theatre in the Audrey Butler Centre. The Sixth Form common room has the anonymity of an airport lounge. The school is functional throughout, unprepossessing. Sleeping quarters up in the eaves are the most popular (for Lower Sixth), nicknamed by girls the 'West End'. Girls wear a purple and grey uniform. The school has a purposeful, get-on-with-it atmosphere, disciplined and institutional. Daily chapel.

PASTORAL CARE AND DISCIPLINE: Each house of 40–60 girls is run by teaching housemistresses with assistants and a team of academic tutors. The Deputy Head (pastoral) monitors boarding matters and arranges in-service training. There are resident SRNs on site. The Sixth Form choose their own individual personal tutors.

PUPILS AND PARENTS: Solidly middle class, with 30% from abroad, including 17% non-Brits (from across the globe). Popular with the Forces. Very friendly, very career-minded. Some impressively bright and articulate pupils.

ENTRANCE: Via CE at 11, 12 and 13, and a few at Sixth Form: selective. Pupils outside the CE organisation are assessed separately by the school.

EXIT: The school is losing largish numbers (around 16 a year at the moment) post-GCSE – to go on to boys' schools. 95% go to universities, some to Oxbridge. Noticeably increasing numbers go into business and commerce, fewer into the professions. Large numbers take a gap year.

MONEY MATTERS: There are 2 Sixth Form scholarships, 3 academic scholarships (for 11-, 12- and 13-year-olds); 2 Music scholarships; 2 Tennis scholarships please note. Bursaries and grants are available.

REMARKS: Not to be sneezed at. A quietly impressive girls' boarding school, highly structured, active, busy producing good and bouncy citizens for tomorrow's world. Academic results are good (particularly given the brain drain to boys' schools at Sixth Form), and extra-curricular activities excellent.

Radley College

Abingdon, Oxfordshire OX14 2HR
Tel: 01235 543000, Fax: 01235 543000

PUPILS: Around 600 boys. All board
AGES: 13–18
SIZE OF SIXTH FORM: Around 240
C OF E
FEE-PAYING

HEAD: Warden since 1991, Mr Richard Morgan, JP, MA. Educated at Sherborne and read Law at Gonville and Caius, Cambridge. Previously Head of Cheltenham College and before that – secret weapon this – was Housemaster here. Married with three daughters. Took a sabbatical year before taking up the post here. Famously outspoken, which upsets some parents. Comments that the 'way forward is not games but employment' – and that changes he proposes for Radley will reflect this top priority. Plans to give the school a 'turbo charge'; comes from the Rhondda, and aware of need for 'grit'.

ACADEMIC MATTERS: Results are very, very good given the intake (see Entrance). Maths A-level results are outstanding, Physics very good. Economics is popular, though results, as elsewhere, are disappointing. GCSE is a walkover for pupils in all subjects – not a weak link. The Head is keen on Europe and has shaken the whole Language department from head to toe (46 pupils did A-level French in '95). He has gathered round him a dynamic, excellent young staff to build up a top-class common room, as he did at Cheltenham.

All pupils are now 'expected' to leave the school with one (spoken) language under their belt, though those headed for four As at A-level are exempt. Well-subscribed History, English and Maths, otherwise pupils spread their interest over a traditional range of studies, sitting mostly Oxford and Cambridge Board A-levels. The top three sets do single sciences at GCSE.

GAMES, OPTIONS, THE ARTS: This is a very keen games school, both traditionally and currently. Its ambition is to beat Eton on the river – rowing is hot stuff with cups everywhere. Rugby in Michaelmas term – Wellington are the oldest rivals. Hockey in spring term for 'dry-bobs' and in summer, the school is strong in cricket and tennis. Has its own beagle pack. Also a stunning swimming pool with probably the best diving

facilities in the private sector in the country. (The school in general has a slight aura of a country club at times with tip-top facilities all round.)

The school is twinned with seven schools in Europe, and has links with European Youth Parliament. For four years, all boys have to give two weeks each year in the school holidays to community service (a recent introduction) e.g. running a camp in Romania for 250 Romanian students. There is a strong Arts department – the Sewell Centre. CCF is compulsory at 14½ until a proficiency test is taken.

BACKGROUND AND ATMOSPHERE: In a green and pleasant site – even Turner was moved to paint it in his youth – lots of mellow red brick (1720) and Victorian Gothic, overlooking the school's golf course, lake, games fields and pavilion: 800 acres of prime Oxfordshire, totally self-contained and away from the rest of the world. The school was founded in 1847 on the Oxford college model – with cloisters, quads, 'dons' (masters), shortish black gowns. The idea of the founders (the Revs William Sewell, don at Exeter College, and Robert Corbet Singleton) was to give boys an aesthetic education (some may laugh hollowly) and the school is blessed with a wonderful collection of furniture, and the Lenthall picture collection on loan. The Warden's house is listed (NB the Warden and Common Room are both tucked away from the coal face). There is an old-fashioned dining hall though the school has succumbed to self-catering (institutional fare). The library is still in need of overhauling and buildings much in need of decoration (there are some truly gruesome colour schemes as we write). The clock tower is a meeting point. Sixth Formers have much pride in the 'JCR' in the basement – a cosy black hole. There is a brilliant tuck-shop at which all boys have what is aptly called a 'jam account' – bacon butties are available at all hours. Jolly red theme to school and uniform, though pupils are allowed to wear any sensible dark jacket and shirt – the status of a pupil is marked by the type of tie. The school still feels slightly inward-looking and its strength and current status are a source of amazement to some other schools, not to mention some OBs.

PASTORAL CARE AND DISCIPLINE: There is a complicated hierarchy of 'stigs' (new boys) – each with a 'nanny' – to 'pups' (prefects). Housemasters ('tutors') preside over 'Socials' – Houses, e.g. Social A, Social B (traditionally the gamesy houses); Social E is currently popular. Staff lean on 'pups', who have intricate privileges in exchange for their responsibilities. The school has compulsory evensong four nights a week. 95% of staff are on campus in school accommodation – brilliant for packing in the talent. Staff, young, new and old, have the occasional 'MOT', one-to-one meetings with Head at which they can air grievances/produce ideas, etc. Recent Drugs expulsions.

PUPILS AND PARENTS: Pupils are a very homogenised British middle-class lot – not much room for anyone else, given the previous Head's intake policy and success. Despite hands-across-the-sea-policy on foreign language speaking, there are still no foreign pupils here. OBs include Mark Carlisle, Christopher Hibbert, Ted Dexter, world rackets champion James Male.

ENTRANCE: Still largely on a first-come, first-served principle, which explains why lists have been consistently full for years ahead. So – name down asap. However, the Head has introduced a 'Warden's list' here of up to 10 places which he can dole out to deserving late arrivals. Note the weedy little pictureless prospectus – the new status symbol.

EXIT: On to the usual universities. OBs then go on to be Headmasters, servicemen, one or two barristers, one or two art dealers, 'general management'.

MONEY MATTERS: One new 'Silk' bursary (named after the previous Warden) on money raised. There are 5 instrumental Music scholarships and several exhibitions, also bursaries for the needy. 2 Art scholarships, up to 12 academic scholarships and exhibitions, and 3 Thompson scholarships for all-rounders.

REMARKS: Good and popular traditional public school – one of the very few left with boys only. Designer label. Satisfied reports from parents.

Rannoch School

Rannoch, Perthshire PH17 2QQ
Tel: 01882 632332, Fax 01882 632443

PUPILS: Around 190 boys, 60 girls
AGES: 13–18. Plus junior school, with 45 boys and girls, ages 10–13
SIZE OF SIXTH FORM: Around 80
NON-DENOM
FEE-PAYING

HEAD: Since 1982, Mr Michael Barratt, MA (fifties). Educated at Merchiston and Oxford (read English). Previously a Housemaster at Strathallan, and taught at Epsom. Froebel-trained wife is very active in school affairs (this is true of most staff wives/husbands here), liaising with parents. Head's fervent wish is for a 'happy school which provides an all-round education'.

ACADEMIC MATTERS: The school has very small classes, and occasionally reaps spectacular results with even the most unpromising of its pupils. The school has a reputation for employing gifted if unorthodox teachers, most of whom have some outdoor skills.

Highly professional learning support is given (send for information on this) with extra staff for English and Maths, and scribes and dictating machines for exams. Also a small EFL 'facility'. The majority of pupils follow the Scottish exam system. Half- or whole-term exchanges can be arranged to France, Germany, Australia and Canada.

GAMES, OPTIONS, THE ARTS: Very muscular and gamesy – the kit list includes a rucksack as well as a winter-weight sleeping bag. The school has a fine Sports Hall. Mainstream games on offer, also skiing and a 6-hole golf course. The Duke of Edinburgh Award scheme plays a prominent part in school activities, and 500 pupils have achieved gold awards to date – is this a record? Duke of Edinburgh award winners are listed on a smart honours board in the dining room.

The Rannoch Marathon is run each year. True to Kurt Hahn's principles, community service plays an integral part of school life: fire-fighting, mountain rescue, ambulance service, loch patrol. There is also a building service. Pupils helped renovate the very beautiful chapel and the Art/Music complex was converted from out-buildings. Service projects (expensive) to promote ecotourism in Venezuela, the earthquake zone in India, sailing tours in the Med. Enthusiastic Music, with almost half the pupils learning an instrument. The choir toured to Malta in '94 and has appeared on television.

BACKGROUND AND ATMOSPHERE: Founded in 1959 by A J S Greig and two teaching colleagues from Gordonstoun. In a wonderful Highland setting, but very remote: there are stories of hand-to-hand chains to get bread to school in bad snow conditions. The school recently received a grant from the Scottish Historic Buildings for external renovation, and the exterior (Victorian Scottish baronial) is stunning. Considerable sums of money have been spent tidying up the inside and there is now a refurbished dining hall, boys' house, new careers department, new classrooms, mixed Junior Common Room and Staffroom, etc. (If you go into the staff room it looks like an Outward Bound hostel, with plaid shirts and hiking boots.) A member of the Round Square group of schools (20 worldwide) which follow Kurt Hahn's principle of educating the whole child. Rannoch hosted the organisation's International Services Conference in '93, at which an impressive group of young from all over the world spoke of their community service projects. The estate (120 acres) is on the south side of Loch Rannoch, 25 miles from the nearest town. The midges in the summer are huge. Healthy-looking pupils have ruddy complexions.

PASTORAL CARE AND DISCIPLINE: All staff act as shepherds; plus tutors as academic watchdogs. Cigarettes and alcohol are the main problem areas (two or three expelled for booze misdemeanours over three years). PD (punishment drill) includes good works in the grounds, alternatively physical exercise; and 'wearing uniform not home clothes at the weekend is very effective,' notes the Head.

PUPILS AND PARENTS: Mainly from Scotland, but an increasing number from Europe; one or two from Africa, one or two refugees from the snobbery of the public school system. Around 80% first-time buyers in private education; popular with hoteliers, farmers and business people. Happy and self-confident children, relaxed, robust, energetic.

ENTRANCE: To Junior School by interview and report from primary schools. At 13, via CE. Very, very low IQ children are not admitted.

EXIT: Typically, 31 out of 41 leavers in '95 went on to further education, including one to Oxbridge (the whole school had a holiday to celebrate). Some go straight into business, farming or re-take exams elsewhere.

MONEY MATTERS: Several academic awards of 50% worth of fees, and 5 Assisted Places at 13 (which are over-subscribed).

REMARKS: A Scottish public school which is an excellent choice, particularly for the non-academic and those requiring learning support. It is good at bringing out the best and providing all-round education (go easy on entering your wilting urban flower here). Very popular with parents and children. No longer the place for daft Scots.

Repton School

The Hall, Repton, Derbyshire ED6 6FH
Tel: 01283 702375, Fax: 01283 701468

PUPILS: Around 560: 425 boys, 135 girls. 400 board, 160 day
AGES: 13–18
SIZE OF SIXTH FORM: 252
C OF E (other faiths welcome)
FEE-PAYING

HEAD: Since 1987, Mr Graham Jones, MA (early fifties), educated at Birkenhead, read Economics at Fitzwilliam, Cambridge. One-third of timetable is taken up by teaching (more than most) – 'that's what it's all about'. A good manager, enthusiastic, humorous. Married, no children.

ACADEMIC MATTERS: A broad intake, with five sets for most subjects. The school has a strong English department; Chemistry is popular, also Economics. There are too many D–U grades in most subjects in A-level (e.g. 3 Ns and Us in French, 4 Ns and 4 Us in Economics). Several good results in Chinese at A-level. Study the statistics carefully. Classics has had a bit of a 'renaissance' led by bright young staff. The school provides traditional teaching; computers are mainly kept in the IT room. There is a very fine library in the old priory building, though the most ancient and valuable tomes are kept locked away. Modern Languages (nothing fancy on offer) are taught almost entirely in the native tongue.

Sciences are examined singly or Combined or Dual Award at GCSE. Practically all Sixth Formers do General Studies as a fourth, occasionally fifth or third A-level ('the northern universities like it') – and this bumps up their league table results no end. A fairly broad programme of options is available to Sixth Form; the courses on relationships and study skills are the only ones which are compulsory.

GAMES, OPTIONS, THE ARTS: An outstanding tennis school (recommended to tennis-mad parents by the LTA). Tennis is played all the year round, outdoors and indoors (on two courts); there was a recent successful summer coaching trip to Roger Taylor's tennis school in Portugal (pupils loved watching themselves on video). Regularly wins inter-school tennis championships. Also has a fine cricket record (has produced astonishing numbers of test cricketers), strong football and hockey; girls' sports are 'picking up', said one. Daily games. There is a huge indoor Sports Hall, and a new Astroturf pitch (now 3 in all). The vast indoor swimming pool was completed (summer '94). CCF is compulsory for all for a time; big D of E take-up. Unusual and good Art (with currently 3 artists in residence). The school has a good music tradition – ambitious chorally and orchestrally, always one or two outstanding players in the school, generous with scholarships. House Drama is enthusiastic and ambitious.

BACKGROUND AND ATMOSPHERE: Very much a part of the village and proud of it, with houses, the Art department, etc., spread hither and thither. 'We feel part of life,' commented a boy; 'Less of an ivory tower atmosphere,' said a master. A Bloody Mary Foundation, with a long and interesting history dating back to the medieval monastery, still at the heart of the buildings. Attractive rugged pinkish stone, and mellow; the Hall is finely proportioned and still one of the largest boarding houses of any public school (numbers are being decreased as a matter of policy; there were over 100, now 80).

Repton went fully co-ed in '91 (though girls are relatively thin on the ground still); but 'of course,' said the Head, 'there have been girls in the Sixth Form since the late '70s: we ran training days for staff, but they didn't really need it' – a view not necessarily shared. The school wants to improve boy:girl ratios to 2:1. 'But we're happy to settle where the market demands it,' says the Head realistically.

The girls' boarding house is extremely well designed (has won prizes), centred around a courtyard, with a walk through the common room (which prevents cliques and is good for the shy). Girls' bedrooms 'where they can make nests', as suggested by Miss Lancaster, ex-Head of Wycombe and an ex-governor of the school.

Boys' houses have mixed-aged studies (a fairly unusual arrangement) – Sixth Form down to 13-year-olds, no peer groups. 'It's good,' confirmed a boy, 'you don't muck about so much, olders can help youngers with work and you get to know people outside your own age.' Study-beds are available for some Sixth Formers, though they don't necessarily choose to have one. A very house-orientated school: and one of the few where pupils eat in their houses. (Good food in the Brook.) Bedders (= dorms) go by peer groups.

PASTORAL CARE AND DISCIPLINE: Strong lines are laid down, and are (by and large) adhered to. Gating for two weeks for smoking (on second/third offence). Instant out and no quarter is shown for drugs (recent case). The school has good staff–pupil also staff–parent links. 'We're treated as human beings,' commented a boy. The limited exeats (half-term plus one, occasionally two) – breed no discontent. Many local pupils go home regularly on Sundays.

PUPILS AND PARENTS: Largely middle-of-the-road, middle class (lots of muck and brass, according to a member of staff), from the big industrial conurbations of Sheffield, Leeds, Bradford and Doncaster. Day pupils stay till 9 p.m. Unspoilt, conservative and pleasant pupils, relatively unsophisticated. Many overseas pupils (including some foreigners); a sprinkling of landed gentry.

ENTRANCE: 40% from own prep, Foremarke Hall (nearby, co-ed, and

NB pupils go on to a diversity of schools). The rest from a large number of prep schools. There has been quite a selective entry for girls at Sixth Form, but now they will come up through the school and, following the national trend, selection possibilities have narrowed down as fewer girls apply for places at Sixth.

EXIT: Judging by the 'Valete' section in the school magazine for '95, large numbers go on to popular ex-polys e.g. Sheffield Hallam, Leeds Met, Nottingham Trent; pupils also go on to art foundation, one or two to crammers. Conservative choices of subjects and ultimately professions.

MONEY MATTERS: Up to 9 academic scholarships, worth between 50% and 20% of the fees, up to 9 Exhibitions worth 10% of the fees. A few Music awards, worth up to 50% fees. Also 4 Assisted Places at 11+, 5 at 16+.

REMARKS: A pleasant low-profile school which has ridden the recession well and is actually expanding as co-education moves up and through the school remarkably smoothly – though it currently feels like a boys' school with some girls; free from the ivory-tower syndrome.

Roedean School

Brighton, East Sussex BN2 5RQ
Tel: 01273 603181, Fax: 01273 676722

PUPILS: Around 450 girls. Most board, but there are now a number of day girl places
AGES: 11–18
SIZE OF SIXTH FORM: Around 160
C OF E, but other faiths also
FEE-PAYING

HEAD: Since 1984, Mrs Ann Longley, MA (fifties), educated at Walthamstow Hall School and Edinburgh University (Modern Linguist). Taught in Australia and was Head of a school in California, USA. Widowed with three grown-up children. Charming, an impressive speaker, immensely efficient (she has streamlined school management American-style). Convinced that flexibility is essential in boarding nowadays, 'We're trying it out.' A fierce defender of single-sex education (and has publicly defended girls' schools' emphasis on keeping them at A-level in the teeth of boys' schools 'poaching').

ACADEMIC MATTERS: Pupils report a fair mount of old-fashioned chalk and talk in the teaching. The school has a long tradition of fine Sciences (with half the pupils taking three separate GCSEs, the others Dual Award). Girls are encouraged to make electronic cars, satellite dishes, laser photography. Dr Bailin, Head of Sixth Form Studies, ensures that girls choose the most appropriate mix of A- and AS-level subjects to maximise their university options. One-third of the pupils study Sciences at A-levels, one-third Arts subjects, one-third mix Sciences with Arts (often a language).

A breakdown of exam results was not given for '94–'95 but parents report 'strings of As and very happy with them'. For the first three years, girls are taught in house groups of 18–20 (unusual); setting in Maths and French. Latin for everyone for the first two years. Interestingly, the School Inspectors recommended 'challenging the ablest girls even further through greater use of differentiation', whatever that may mean.

GAMES, OPTIONS, THE ARTS: Participation is the key note. Sport is very successful and keen; this is one of the few girls' cricketing schools (they play against local prep schools, boys' schools and the House of Commons team). Also beefy hockey, lacrosse, squash. There are excellent facilities, including, of course, a Sports Hall, indoor pool, 15 tennis courts. Very active D of E participants, also Young Enterprise. Strong Drama, Dance (especially keen on this) and Music (good choirs).

BACKGROUND AND ATMOSPHERE: Bracing sea air blows up treeless cliffs to the forbidding pebble-dashed buildings, set in 40 acres, just east of Brighton. Founded in 1885 by the Misses Lawrence, the school is modelled on a boys' public school – functional, structured, traditional (female staff, i.e. the majority, called 'Madam').

Roedean enjoyed the reputation for many years of being one of the two most famous girls' boarding schools in the country, and it is still the one foreigners have heard of – as well as inspiration of many a popular ditty, e.g. 'We are good girls, good girls are we. We take a pride in our virginity . . .'

There are good facilities for everything, with a recently completed development plan which includes, amongst other things, a new Humanities department, library ('this was my first priority,' declares the Head) and Resources Centre, and an impressive Performing Arts complex (brilliant theatre) opened in 1994 by HRH the Prince of Wales. Sixth Formers are heavily involved on school committees; Mrs Longley is hot on girls learning 'leadership and committee skills'. Most houses (which are highly competitive) are undergoing renovation ('not before time,' mutter parents). The junior house is cosy. The Sixth Formers' house (single rooms for all) has the usual semi-detached air of domesticity with clothes drying, etc. The Head is strongly aware of the 17- and 18-year-olds' needs for increased indepen-

dence, freedom and decision-making, while also being firm about keeping the structure of the school very much in place. There is a purposeful and busy no-nonsense atmosphere; also a strongly international flavour throughout the school, which is – and always has been – multiracial, multinational. Freezing (not indoors, though).

PASTORAL CARE AND DISCIPLINE: Pupils are well catered for with a good individual care system; particularly cosy at the bottom of the school. 'Everyone knows the rules and the behaviour boundaries,' commented a pupil. Smoking is on the wane ('they're health and environmentally conscious'). Staff are watchful and concerned over fashions, dieting, etc. The school has flexible weekend arrangements now, under careful surveillance and apparently popular, with families often scooping up children on Saturday afternoons (post-match) and coming back some time on Sunday. However, there is no mass exodus and the weekend programme runs hard, with riding, shopping, cinema trips.

PUPILS AND PARENTS: One-third live overseas (FO, Services, business), 20% are non-nationals (increasingly from Europe; also Canada, USA, Africa, Middle East, Malaysia, Hong Kong, Japan and elsewhere). That said, this still feels very much an English boarding school – hence its popularity with foreigners – with most parents professionals living in London and the south-east. Pupils are mutually supportive. 'The global environment breeds tolerance,' commented a parent.' It also means they are not tunnel-visioned,' added another. Girls are confident, outward-looking, sometimes unsophisticated and often very articulate. OGs include Baroness Chalker, Sally Oppenheimer MP, Verity Lambert, Dame Cecily Saunders, the founder of the Hospice movement.

ENTRANCE: At 11+, 12+ and 13+ CE or the school's own exam. Likes girls with a wide range of interests. Often from co-ed prep schools. NB The school observes more girls coming in at 13+ ('Mothers don't want to part with them at eleven'). Far more come in at 16+ than leave.

EXIT: 10+ a year go to Oxbridge. And to all the top universities; medical schools; a few to Art and Design or Drama School. After that, high-powered careers. Loses one or two to Lancing and elsewhere at Sixth Form.

MONEY MATTERS: About 4% of fee income goes towards scholarships; about 35% scholars/exhibitioners in the school at one time, including Music scholars. Also bursaries and the school is good at lending a helping hand in hard times.

REMARKS: A strong girls' public school with clout which does not waver much from its traditional stance, though it has become slightly softer at the edges and notably more flexible, demanding robustness from pupils – this is no place for shrinking violets/sensitive souls (though NB the Director of Admissions says this is no longer the case). What it lacks in charm it makes up for in achievement, and keeps its reputation high. Now taking day girls.

The Royal Grammar School

High Street, Guildford GUI 3BB
Tel: 01483 502424, Fax: 01483 306127

PUPILS: 840 boys. All day
AGES: 11–18

SIZE OF SIXTH FORM: 240
NON-DENOM
FEE-PAYING

HEAD: Since 1992, Mr TMS Young, MA (forties). Educated at Eton, read History at Cambridge. Previously a Housemaster at Eton; has taught in California and New Zealand. Charming. High-powered wife (consultant radiologist), one child.

ACADEMIC MATTERS: Outstanding, as you would expect from the high calibre of pupil. The school has rigorous standards, many staff of long standing, and high expectations all round, with boys buckling down to hard work – the grammar school ethos in action. Maths and Sciences are traditionally the strongest subjects, and substantially more boys take Science rather than Arts at A-level.

GAMES, OPTIONS AND EXTRAS: Sports are also taken seriously (the playing fields are two miles away), and this is Bob Willis's old school. The sailing club is still very successful, and shooting is currently even better.

There is a nice drama studio. The school does well in public speaking competitions. Car maintenance is on offer, not to mention ballroom dancing (with local girls' school) and bachelor cooking. Helen Sharman, Britain's first astronaut, was a recent and popular visitor to the school's radio ground station.

BACKGROUND AND ATMOSPHERE: The school was founded in 1509 in the centre of Guildford, which is a London dormitory town, and also popular with retired people (NB housing is expensive here). The main teaching block is bang on the main road, a faceless and dreary '60s hulk, to which the Science and Technology block, among other things, have been added. Across the road, however, is the delightful tall white ancient original building now used by the Sixth Form.

Prep Department: Lanesborough School, Tel : 01483 502060, Fax: 01483 306127. Head: Mr S Deller. Around 300 boys, all day. Ages: 4–13. No automatic entry to the senior school. In an Edwardian house plus many extensions set on the green north-east edge of Guildford. Lively and traditional; also acts as the Choir School for the Cathedral – the choir is very good, and Music is excellent.

PASTORAL CARE AND DISCIPLINE: The boys' development is well taken care of. The Head gives parents guidelines (not so easy in the G + T area, and Guildford is not un-druggy), and is keen on good citizenship. On the whole, boys make 'active and purposeful use of their time'.

PUPILS AND PARENTS: The brightest and best, academically speaking, in the area. Parents include lots of middle-classes; stockbroker belt-ish. Ambitious.

ENTRANCE: CE, with 65% pass required. Hot competition. Many come in from the prep department, and from the state sector.

EXIT: Now *averages* 30 a year to Oxbridge – and this is a genuine figure.

REMARKS: A powerfully strong grammar school, which happily creams the brightest 10% from its juicy catchment area and, on the whole, does them proud. Its appearance is somewhat at odds with its performance.

The Royal Grammar School

Eskadale Terrace, Newcastle upon Tyne NE2 4DX
Tel: 0191 281 5711, Fax: 0191 212 0392

PUPILS: 930 boys. Plus junior school, 150 boys, ages 8–10
ALL DAY
AGES: 11–18
SIZE OF SIXTH FORM: 290
NON-DENOM
FEE-PAYING

HEAD: From September 1994, Mr J F X Miller, MA (forties), previously Head of Framlingham, and before that a Housemaster at Winchester. Economist. Positive and friendly.

ACADEMIC MATTERS: With a distinguished academic record, the school rates highly on the national league tables. All boys take 10 GCSEs, 40+% of A-level results at A grade is the norm, but there are sprinklings of 'Fs'. The '95 GCSE results show 40 Fs and 175 Cs, but a staggering 327 As and results in both public exams show a consistent trend over the past few years to better results (or easier exams). The school has a strong Maths and Science tradition (47 A grades at A-level Maths in '95), and a good History department (though '95 results were a bit disappointing).

On average, about half the Sixth Form do at least one AS, which is increasingly unusual. Class sizes vary throughout the school, but at present some first and second years have as many as 30, there are 28 in the third year, with GCSE sets becoming 'significantly smaller'; 15 would be the maximum in the Sixth Form (usually fewer). Follows a rigorous programme, with traditional teaching (one or two very long-serving staff).

GAMES, OPTIONS, THE ARTS: Strong on sporting matters (the school has produced runners for Britain) with an enormous number of sports on offer and keen followers in many of them. The First Fifteen played in the *Daily Mail* under-18 final at Twickenham in '94 (lost to Mount St Mary's Sheffield) – and they won 25 out of 27 matches (though '95 was not nearly as successful). Cricket also had a very successful year in '94. A new sports centre opened in '96.

Successful chess, and the school were HMC North East champions in '94 and '95. Some Drama with the girls from Central Newcastle High. Art is OK. The school has well-developed and well-used computing. CCF thrives.

BACKGROUND AND ATMOSPHERE: *The* Tyneside grammar school, which celebrated its 450th anniversary in '95. Handsome buildings, plus functional additions, with playing fields at the back (the Music Room was built when a slice of land was removed for the building of the motorway). There is a fine old school hall with pews, organ and honour boards. Lively noticeboards everywhere. Also a good indoor pool and a lecture room. There is a slightly sauve-qui-peut atmosphere about the place: parents are warned from the start that boys need to be self-motivated. 'True,' said a father. 'There is not much of a helping hand for boys bumping along the bottom or those who just do the bare minimum.'

Down the road is what used to be a synagogue, which now serves as a coffee shop used by Sixth Formers of both RGS and the girls of Central Newcastle High – a super place, very nice atmosphere.

PASTORAL CARE AND DISCIPLINE: The latter has been somewhat 'iffy',

with well-founded complaints beyond the school gates of the loutish adolescent behaviour of a minority. Head says that pastoral care is one of his main priorities – 'good,' said a parent.

PUPILS AND PARENTS: All sorts, and the social mix is getting richer as the traditional boarding market turns day-ward. Lots of first-time buyers. Boys on the whole are decent, but occasionally accused of arrogance by other schools. Some travel in from a long way – there is good local transport.

ENTRANCE: The 'standard route' is through the school's own entrance exam at 11 and 13: highly selective and highly competitive. Some boys come in via CE. Some come from the on-site junior school. Entry also at Sixth Form.

EXIT: To a wide spread of universities, around 25 per year to Oxbridge (more bridge than Ox); Imperial College, King's and UCL all popular, though by and large top northern and Midland universities are preferred (e.g. Manchester). Law, Social Sciences and Sciences, also engineering degrees in large numbers, but even more, says the Head, to medicine and in '94 'we supplied just under 1% of the year's male medical students' (can he mean that?).

MONEY MATTERS: There are about 220 Assisted Places at the moment, mainly at 11 and 13, and 5 at Sixth Form. However, no scholarships. Features almost at the top of the *Financial Times'* admittedly rather tortuous 'value for money' figures.

REMARKS: Charges on and up, in the traditional strong grammar school mode. Unrivalled in the area.

The Royal High School

Lansdown Road, Bath, Avon BA1 5SZ
Tel: 01225 313877, Fax: 01225 420338

PUPILS: see below
DAY AND BOARDING, GIRLS ONLY
SIZE OF SIXTH FORM: see below
C OF E
FEE-PAYING

HEAD: In due course: Mrs Emma McKendrick, BA (early thirties). Deputy Head to her predecessor for four years (and taught German), previously Senior Housemistress, also Head of Sixth Form. Husband in the banking world. Modern linguist (she read German and Dutch 'just to be difficult') at Liverpool. Both shy and friendly, and charming. Comments that 'school is very much about preparing girls for the next stage and not an end'.

REMARKS: Amalgamation in process over two years of the Royal School, Bath, and Bath High to become a different (GPDST) animal by September 1998. Impossible to comment at the moment as major reorganisation is in train, with the junior school being (re)located in the old Bath High premises, and the seniors in the old Royal School.

Rugby School

Rugby, Warwickshire CV22 5EH
Tel: 01788 543465, Fax: 01788 553914

PUPILS: Around 730 in all: 400 boys boarding, 100 day; 170 girls boarding; 60 day
AGES: 11–18 (day pupils only at 11 and 12)

SIZE OF SIXTH FORM: Around 360
C OF E
FEE-PAYING

HEAD: Since September 1990, Mr M B Mavor, CVO, MA (late forties). Educated at Loretto and Cambridge. Previously Head of Gordonstoun (got his gong for supervising the schooling of HRH The Duke of York and HRH Prince Edward – no mean task). Keen fisherman. Wife brought up in Peru, graduate of London University, two teenage children, dog. Particularly good at public relations.

ACADEMIC MATTERS: There were good Maths results in '95. Three separate sciences at GCSE for the top three sets, Dual Award for the rest. GCSE Drama and A-level Theatre Studies are offered – the curriculum now has a good number of 'new' subjects. Every subject is setted. Huge Design and Technology centre, and pupils can get real, solid, hands-on experience of a practical subject. The school's fantastic Language lab, with computer programmes in different languages, wouldn't disgrace a university. Mandarin Chinese and Italian are offered as non-examined 'options'. Economics and English are still popular. The Common Room now has new young energetic staff (the average age has fallen considerably), including 20 female ones – 16 more than when we last went to press. There is a super careers department.

GAMES, OPTIONS, THE ARTS: The school has a smart Sports Centre, also used by the town. Keen but voluntary CCF. Strong Drama, with at least three school plays a year, plus house plays and visiting professional productions in school's own theatre, and good enthusiastic staff. There is a professional-standard photographic studio (which is indeed used by professionals as well as by pupils). Design and Art is now all go (23 As at A-level in '95). A fantastic media studio has all the gear for pupils to practise making tapes, videos.

BACKGROUND AND ATMOSPHERE: Founded in 1567 but metamorphosed as a Victorian 'railway' school in the 19th century. Home of the famous Dr Arnold of *Tom Brown's Schooldays*. The Head still uses the study at one end of which is a door leading to a staircase built by Dr Arnold through which the boys could slide in without having to run the gauntlet of the school secretary.

There are imposing buildings very much in the middle of and dotted about the town – with heavy traffic on one side of the campus. It feels rather like north Oxford. The Sixth Form 'Social Centre' has a bar in it. House prefects are allowed out into Rugby on a Saturday night.

The school went fully co-ed in 1993. There is one Day House for girls and one for boys. All pupils now eat in their own boarding houses. 'Social' eating is allowed in each others' houses by invitation. Girls houses, as usual, are very civilised, particularly the Sixth Form one, Stanley (and the food is good here too). Boys' houses have been less ritzy (to put it mildly), but since our last edition money has been thrown into upgrading them, particularly School House, right in the middle of the school, which was Dickensian, and is now beautifully thought-out, state-of-the-art, but retaining the old panelling and structure.

PASTORAL CARE AND DISCIPLINE: The geographical layout and position of temptingly near pubs, etc, in town make this a difficult school for staff to police. The Head has centralised disciplinary matters (boarding houses used to

be run very largely by boys on traditional lines, with some horrendous results). Responsibility is now being 'handed back' to the pupils, but 'in a controlled manner'. On drugs, the Head comments: 'the school is in the process of reviewing its drugs policy to include increased education, counselling, urine testing which in most circumstances would not result in expulsion . . . Pupils may also be tested if their work or general performance falls behind'.

PUPILS AND PARENTS: Mainly from the Midlands, a sprinkling from overseas, still some from Scotland, the North of England, and an increasing number from London. OBs include Rupert Brooke (a girls' house is named after him), Hugh Montefiore, Ian Lang, Robert Hardy, Tom King, Tom Brown. 12% of pupils are sons and daughters of OBs – who usually regard the place with nostalgia.

ENTRANCE: Interview first, 'then weed' and entrance exam. Not stiff, but stiffening. School comments that an IQ below 110 would be struggling. The choice of house may be deferred until nearer time of entry. Fed by Midland and East Anglian preps, such as Bilton Grange and Beeston Hall, and by a wide mix of schools from Arnold Lodge to Llandaff Cathedral School and Yarlet Hall.

EXIT: 100% to university (Edinburgh and London are particularly popular at time of writing), 10% to Oxbridge.

MONEY MATTERS: There are around 15 scholarships at 13; 10 at 16; 4 music scholarships at 13, 2 music scholarships at 16 – all up to 50% of fees, but can be augmented by a bursary in case of need. There are 6 all-round bursaries, 2 major 'foundation' scholarships and 4 minor ones to entice bright day pupils (major scholarships are 100% of fees and pupils must live within 10 miles of the school). The Head points out that the original foundation was for 'local boys' to be educated. Also help for the needy and for sons of Old Rugbeians. The overall percentage of income devoted to scholarships is now 11%. The school owns a London estate in Great Ormond Street.

REMARKS: A famous public school which has undergone huge changes in the last five years and is now one of the most popular choices among the 'Midland' schools. Friendly, hard-working and, say pupils, (particularly the girls) 'fun'.

PS We failed to include the girls in our head count for the last edition and concluded, erroneously, that numbers were down. Overall numbers are in fact up.

St Alban's High School

Townsend Avenue, St Albans, Hertfordshire AL1 3SJ
Tel: 01727 853800, Fax: 01727 845011

PUPILS: 680 girls
ALL DAY
AGES: 11–18
SIZE OF SIXTH FORM: 120
C OF E
FEE-PAYING

HEAD: Since September 1994, Mrs Carol Daly, BSc, graduate of Chemistry and Geology from Nottingham University. Previously Head of Forest Girls' School in Snaresbrook E1. She took over from Miss Elizabeth Diggory, who in her eleven years here put

the school in a strong league-table position.

REMARKS: A strong traditional girls' day school serving local needs and also popular with families in the furthest reaches of Hertfordshire and, increasingly, north-west London. Ten school buses ferry girls to and fro daily (up to one hour away). Morale is high, partly due to the school's league-table results, 'And the parents do take notice.'

The school was founded in 1889 (as a boarding school) by the Church Schools Company (it retains strong links with the Abbey), and moved here later to this purpose-built Queen Anne-style block with many later brick additions, not far from the centre of St Albans. The setting, once rural, is now suburban. There is a large tarmac playground; outdoor swimming pool; big, much-used Sports Hall; one grass half-size pitch; games fields five minutes' walk away.

The school provides thorough teaching on all fronts in functional classrooms (walls are on the bare side). Latin for all for two years; a choice of German (most popular) or Spanish, plus French (sensible exchanges). Girls are worked hard 'but we're not pressurized'. Science GCSE Dual Award exam. The timetable follows a circus rota for Music, Home Economics and Art; Sports, IT, Design Technology are all fitted in to a tightly packed day.

A breakdown of results was not given, but English Literature and Biology A-levels have done particularly well in the recent past. Most girls go on to degrees (2–5 to Oxbridge).

Class sizes (sometimes up to 28) are balanced by a small-school feel. 'You can't get lost here,' said a pupil. Sixth Formers are all encouraged to share responsibilities: they run the houses, organise fund-raising. Girls are polite and enthusiastic.

Barry Rose recently arrived to take

over as Head of Music, amid great excitement.

Many girls come in – via 11+ – from the school's own super lively junior school over the road (and a pre-prep is under consideration here); the rest from a large number of private and primary schools. The numbers of post-GCSE leavers (to Haileybury or local Sixth Form college) have dropped and a few extra come in too. Though the school is very firmly Christian, there is a strong Jewish contingent, and a few Muslims. 'On the whole our girls emerge happy from the tunnel of adolescence,' says the Head.

St Antony's-Leweston School

Sherborne, Dorset DT9 6EN
Tel: 01963 210691, Fax: 01963 210786

PUPILS: 270 girls; two-thirds board, one-third day. (Plus pre-prep and prep, with 80 boys – tinies only – and girls, ages 3–11)
AGES: 11–18.
RC (but 50% are not)
FEE-PAYING

HEAD: Since January 1993, Miss C Denley Lloyd, BA (Hons), Dip Ed (fifties), previously Deputy Head here. Tremendously characterful and competent, a firm lady of the old school, realistic, with clear-cut aims for the school and girls.

ENTRANCE: Not a problem. CE at 11+, some later. Also at Sixth Form.

EXIT: Lots to practical degrees and Further Education courses (hotel management, business, nursing, etc), often after a year out.

REMARKS: Originally a boarding school for nice Catholic girls run by a Belgian order of nuns, St Antony's now caters for girls of widely varying abilities, of varying religions and varying degrees of day-boarding (it is very flexible on exeats as well). Housed in a fine park and house with many additions and extras, not least the Science block. Has excellent arts and crafts in a very well-equipped block (which NB is open on Sunday afternoons). The Biology department is popular. Interesting collection of A-levels (including Japanese, Ancient History). There is a joint orchestra with nearby Sherborne boys' and girls' schools.

The school has a very good remedial department, also EFL for foreign girls.

St Bees School

St Bees, Cumbria CA27 0DU
Tel: 01946 822263, Fax: 01946 823657

PUPILS: Around 154 boys, 137 girls. 114 board (50% weekly), the rest day
AGES: 11–18
SIZE OF SIXTH FORM: 90
C OF E
FEE-PAYING

HEAD: Since 1988, Mr Paul Chamberlain, BSc (forties), educated at a 'now defunct state school in Cheshire', followed by Zoology at Durham. Previously taught at Haileybury – 'something else kept coming up so I stayed' – and ended up as Housemaster. Teaches juniors 'a very little' and RE to seniors. Aims to turn out 'quietly self-confident pupils with clear aims'. Son and daughter in school, wife is a local JP.

Charming, thoughtful, deeply into the organisation, with a sparkling sense of humour. Knocks on all classroom doors before entering. Pupils obviously like him.

354

ACADEMIC MATTERS: The school is traditionally not for high-fliers, though some recent GCSE and some A-level results are excellent. The usual compound of subjects is offered with peer group emphasis on Science (three sciences at GCSE); the school has a vast science block. Computing and IT are popular, and French and German are taught with the aid of satellite televisions. Pupils use the mega-successful Management and Language Training centre on Campus for Computer Studies and languages. The school gets excellent Art results. The timetable follows a 5-day week.

GAMES, OPTIONS, THE ARTS: An outdoor school – there are lots of hill climbs, and the school makes great use of local facilities, the Lake District's natural resources, and the sea half a mile away. The St Bees' Award is taken by the Sixth Form in four terms and is 'very much tougher' than the D of E award, which they also do. The Housemaster of a senior boys' house has sea canoes and a camper van parked outside his house; there are more canoes in the swimming pool.
CCF and Voluntary Service in the community. Games fields are everywhere. Sellafield (nuclear power station) is just up the road.

BACKGROUND AND ATMOSPHERE: Founded as a grammar school in 1583, set in 150 acres of rural splendour close to the coast and Lake District: the original school building is now the dining hall. Masses of red sandstone everywhere. Girls were admitted in 1976; girls' houses are a jolly collection of upgraded terrace houses on the other side of the railway line (footbridge) across the games fields.
The St Bees Management Centre, a professional conference centre built without cost to the school in 1992 by local industry, is used by the school and adds a whole dimension to the place. Popular and successful (it even smells successful) and with its own catering.

PASTORAL CARE AND DISCIPLINE: Housemaster and spouse in houses, plus matrons; also small tutorial groups (under review). Sackings for sex (the school follows the six-inch rule), also drugs; will sack for booze, or repeated smoking; otherwise internal punishments, fines for Cancer Research for smoking, gating. 4 were sacked for cannabis in '95.

PUPILS AND PARENTS: Mostly local lads and lasses, including the children of farmers and local industrialists. Day and weekly boarding parents are very supportive. About 20% of full boarders are from abroad; several Hong Kong Chinese, the rest ex-pats with Cumbrian connections.

ENTRANCE: At 11, mainly from state schools, and occasional entry at Sixth Form 'to pull up their exam results'.

EXIT: All to Higher Education this year, some to Oxbridge, otherwise Aberdeen to Exeter – no 'northern bias'. No bias on courses. Lots of engineers (girls too). One or two leave after GCSE.

MONEY MATTERS: Bursaries for 'proven need' – can be anything. 50% Academic, Music and Art scholarships. There are 11 Assisted Places and several are available at 16.

REMARKS: A good local school fulfilling Cumbrian needs with boarding. Links with industry (Sellafield, etc.) are amazing and working well.

St Benedict's School

54 Eaton Rise, Ealing, London W5 2ES
Tel: 0181 862 2010, Fax: 0181 862 2199

PUPILS: Around 549 boys, plus 40 girls in the Sixth Form. (Plus own junior school, 240 boys ages 4–11)
ALL DAY
AGES: 11–18
SIZE OF SIXTH FORM: Around 175
RC
FEE-PAYING

HEAD: Since 1987, Dr A J Dachs MA, plus PhD from Cambridge (early fifties). Historian. First lay head of a Benedictine secondary school. Married with four children. An effective leader.

ENTRANCE: Middle school entrance exam for entry at 11. CE or special exam set by the school for entry at 13. Reference from previous school. Fed by RC day preps and state primaries, e.g. St Philip's. Also Sixth Form entry.

EXIT: Almost all to university, one or two to Art Colleges.

REMARKS: A Benedictine foundation (surprise, surprise), attached to Ealing Abbey, and useful to know about as being the only RC private day school for senior boys in Greater London, and not difficult to get into. Also useful for girls coming from local schools without Sixth Forms. Facilities have greatly improved in recent years and discipline has gradually tightened up. The school provides good pastoral care, and results are creditable, given the intake. History and Science GCSE '95 have too many D–F grades.

NB The junior school only takes RCs (has its own Head, Father Martin) and does not prepare for CE (i.e., you may need to switch at 11).

St Christopher School

Letchworth, Hertfordshire SG6 3JZ
Tel: 01462 679301, Fax: 01462 481578

PUPILS: Around 325 boys and girls (189 boys, 136 girls); 181 board, 144 day pupils. Plus own on-site junior school (ages 5+–11) with 64 boys, 43 girls (all day except for 9 boarders). Plus pre-prep with 35 children, ages 2–5.
AGES: 11–19
SIZE OF SIXTH FORM: 93
NON-DENOM
FEE-PAYING

HEAD: Since 1981, Mr Colin Reid, MA (fifties), educated at Brentwood School, read History at Cambridge. Came here from Atlantic College, and before that taught at Tonbridge. His wife, Betsy, teaches Geography and Humanities at this school. A charming, confident, unassuming and capable Head – incidentally, only the third in the school's history.

ENTRANCE: By interview at 11 (lots come up from the junior school), 13 and 16. Always a contingent from abroad (parents working overseas, diplomats, British Council); sons/daughters of Old Boys/Girls. Has extremely broad social and ability intake. Help is given for (mild) learning difficulties, and a few 'special needs' places are available.

EXIT: Most stay till Sixth Form. Then increasingly to Further Education, (anything from Oxbridge to fairly lowly ex-polys) also Art, Music and Drama Colleges in substantial numbers.

REMARKS: A successful alternative school, founded (with Theosophical links) as a co-educational progressive school in the Twenties, and is true to its original aims, i.e. that of developing the whole child – heart, body, spirit and head. Quaker aspects are alive, with moments of silence (before meals, at some meetings/assemblies).

A breakdown of results is not given, but they appear weak, given that pupils (though of very varied abilities) are all required to be 'average plus', and that there are occasional scholar refugees from highly pressured establishments.

The school has keen and good Drama, well above average Art, and puts an emphasis on Craft. It is very Third World conscious – notice boards are alive with posters, talks, fund-raising events for Save the Children, etc.

There is a strong emphasis on challenge, adventure and outdoor pursuits – all the usual games, some on the premises, others – squash, riding, golf – are within easy reach. Also rock-climbing, canoeing, orienteering, and famously busy end-of-summer-term expeditions for all years.

Pupils are extremely supportive, friendly, and tolerant. The school has an informal atmopshere, no uniform, all staff are called by their Christian names, and pupils play a vital role in running the school, 'We are teaching freedom and that means responsibility,' said a member of staff. 'And we are all – pupils, parents, staff – involved in the same way of life here.' (The school claims the oldest Parent Teacher Association in the country).

Parents on the whole are caring types, and looking for something different. Reports still continue to reach us from

parents who are 'very happy' with their children's development here – though some suffer niggling worries that 'the caring aspect may need stronger academic underpinnings' given the current climate. The school comments that it has responded to this with an 'increased use of setting'. 'Idealism and wanting to save the world are all very well,' commented a committed parent, 'but our children must survive in the world of the hard-nosed business nineties.'

Now housed in Edwardian mansions (one was Laurence Olivier's childhood home). NB Letchworth was the first of the garden cities. The school has many additional and varied buildings with plenty of space and grass; the overall effect is of a well-worn patchwork. Some of the original Arts and Crafts aspects (settles, big bow window seats, plain wooden floors, etc.) are intact in boarding houses, (all are mixed age, mixed sex), underpinning the pleasantly homely atmosphere.

NB Vegetarian food only; excellent and varied – the school is extremely health- and diet-conscious. There are cookery lessons for all in the 'well-equipped vegetarian centre' (very popular).

St Columba's School

Duchal Road, Kilmacolm, Renfrewshire PA13 4AU
Tel: 01505 872238, Fax: 01505 873995

PUPILS: senior school 146 boys, 193 girls
ALL DAY
AGES: 11–18
SIZE OF SIXTH FORM: 85
NON-DENOM/EPISCOPALIAN
FEE-PAYING

HEAD: Rector, since 1987, Mr Andrew Livingstone, BSc (Hons) (Aberdeen), Dip Ed (Glasgow) (forties), educated at Campbeltown Grammar School. Previously Deputy Rector of Paisley Grammar School. An educationalist (he served on the Scottish Exam Board), he is the first Rector of this previously traditional girls' school which went co-ed in 1978. Teaches Maths and occasionally Computing.

ACADEMIC MATTERS: Fluctuates – only four failures in 363 Standard Grades, and fourteen failures out of 180 Highers candidates. Pupils take Scottish Standard Grades, with Highers the following year and then Sixth Year Studies. Accountancy and Finance are on offer, as well as the usual subjects. The school's reputation has been enhanced by new Economics, Accountancy and Secretarial departments.

Learning support is given to registered dyslexics – either by part-time staff with the children being extracted from lessons, or by tutors after school.

GAMES, OPTIONS, THE ARTS: The centenary project for 1997 is to improve the Art, Science and Technical department in the main school.

Tennis courts are a couple of hundred yards away, and the main games field is near the junior school, along with a recently completed massive Games Hall (costing £500,000).

The orchestra is popular, and there is a lot of choral work; also good Drama, Art and Pottery.

BACKGROUND AND ATMOSPHERE: The original school was founded in 1897. Red brick, in very tidy and rather cramped surroundings. The imaginative Sixth Year Common Room has a microwave. Learning is structured, with masses of parental encouragement and a strong work ethos. Parents do catering for matches and clubs.

Junior School: Tel: 01505 872768. Head Mr Alan Maclean. Just over 200 boys and girls, ages 4–11, plus nursery school. Entrance by assessment and interview at primary 1 stage 'or at any time throughout primary'. Automatic transfer to senior school.

PASTORAL CARE AND DISCIPLINE: There are four houses, and inter-house everything. Discipline is done through the house system; order marks for 'not covering books [in brown paper] or non-attendance at hockey club'. 'We don't really have problems,' says the Head. Theft or drugs would be out automatically.

PUPILS AND PARENTS: Local professional families, bussed in from all over Renfrewshire and North Ayrshire (to the detriment of traditional Glasgow schools, which are still losing boys like mad). Approx 2–3% of pupils are from ethnic minorities. Massive parental support. Very middle-class with traditional values, including first-time buyers who like the same.

ENTRANCE: Automatic from junior school; waiting lists at 10, 11, 12. Own test and interview. Priority to siblings, FPs' children.

EXIT: Very occasionally to traditional public schools. The occasional leaver after Standard Grade, otherwise 80+% to university, with one or two to Oxbridge.

MONEY MATTERS: Scholarships and bursaries are provided for 'hard times rather than academic'. There are 38 Assisted Places, not all filled.

REMARKS: A good flourishing local school.

St David's College

Gloddaeth Hall, Llandudno, Gwynedd,
North Wales LL30 1RD
Tel: 01492 875974, Fax: 01492 870383

PUPILS: Around 240 boys, 175 board, 65
day
AGES: 11–18
SIZE OF SIXTH FORM: 60
NON-DENOM
FEE-PAYING

HEAD: Since 1991, Mr William
Seymour, MA (forties). Educated at
Aldenham School and Christ's College,
Cambridge. Wife, Shirley, helps in the
school. Two children (one educated at St
David's).

REMARKS: Founded in 1965, initially
with 37 boys, on a pretty site on the
end of Snowdonia. The school is a
mishmash of architectural styles, including beautiful old hall and Portakabin
classrooms stacked one on top of the
other. There are also minuscule departments in an old cottage. Boys come from
all parts of the UK; the school places
much emphasis on building up self-
confidence and self-reliance, initiative
and individualism, and it has a deservedly
high reputation for helping boys with
difficulties – including dyslexia, late
developers, etc.

Boys are shown lots of care and
understanding. This is a good place to
gain maturity through Outward-Bound
activities: the challenge of hill walking,
and tough outdoor pursuits, e.g. sailing
3,000 miles to the Azores, a mountaineering trip to Iceland. Falconry is on offer,
with two buzzards now fully trained, and
two Harris hawks. A travel scholarship is
awarded for a 'holiday which involves a
purpose'.

The school breeds athletic champions,
not to mention mountain-bikers and

board sailors who have represented
Wales. Also reached the rugby seven-a-
side quarter-finals at Rosslyn Park '93.
Produces keen Art; strong Technology
and Computing.

Boys are in small groups (18–20 is large)
for academic work. Separate sciences are
offered at GCSE; A-levels include
Business Studies, Philosophy and Theatre
Studies. GCSE results are good, considering the intake.

The dyslexic unit is much in demand
and very good; early registration is
important. Each year a handful of boys go
on to university, the majority to ex-polys
and technical colleges. Muscular Christianity. Good reports.

St Denis and Cranley School

Ettrick Road, Edinburgh EH10 5BJ
Tel: 0131 229 1500, Fax: 0131 229 5753

PUPILS: Around 140 girls; 60 board, the
rest day. Plus small lower junior
school with about 25 day girls age 5–
8; nursery of 12 boys and girls, ages
3–5, not to mention day care for
babes from 3 months, which service
is 'thriving' at £2 an hour
AGES: 9–13,
SIZE OF SIXTH FORM: Approx 38
INTER-DENOM
FEE-PAYING

HEAD: From 1996, Mrs Sally M
Duncanson, MA, who was previously Assistant Head at The Mary
Erskine. Takes over from Mrs Munro,
who is retiring.

ACADEMIC MATTERS: A confidence-
builder. Lots of learning support is
given where needed. Of those pupils who

do stay for Sixth Form, some 60% do either SYS (mainly the Arts) or A-levels (predominantly Science, at which the school is strong). The exciting Science and Technology building encompasses CDT, Geography, Computing (Business Studies is on offer) with Home Economics – currently under-used, it could cope with expansion. The school is keen on work experience, and practising interviewing techniques.

GAMES, OPTIONS, THE ARTS: Music and Drama is strong. The school was in the throes of a Drama Festival when we visited, and everyone was playing or singing something. The school has a Games Hall and tennis courts, and much use is made of local facilities, e.g. the swimming pool at Merchiston Castle.

BACKGROUND AND ATMOSPHERE: St Denis School, founded in 1855, has traditional links with La Maison d'Education de la Legion d'Honneur outside Paris, and merged with 'Cranny' School in 1979. Links with St Denis continue. The school is cosily encompassed in Morningside's splendour, with eight acres of gardens, five Victorian villas, tennis courts, etc. Two of the boarding houses are run by couples, the third by the school nurse. A vegetarian option is available at all meals.

PASTORAL CARE AND DISCIPLINE: No aggressive disciplining; there is the odd spot of anti-social behaviour – but rare and the school will suspend if there is a serious problem. The emphasis is on self-discipline.

PUPILS AND PARENTS: Mainly professional middle classes, many from echnic minorities (including Asians allowed to wear traditional costume – in school green). 50% of boarders from abroad, mostly ex-pats, but a few Hong Kong Chinese. OGs include Hannah Gordon, Catriona Smith (of Scottish Opera).

ENTRANCE: At 10/11, boarders from 8. Either from own tiny junior school or from local pre-preps. Tests in Maths and English (no tests from junior school) at 10 or 11, thereafter by interview. Girls may join the school at any time, in any term.

EXIT: There is a slight leakage post-Standard Grade, otherwise a strong preponderance of Science-based university entrants.

MONEY MATTERS: The school has written off the occasional bad debt, because 'the child is the important one'. Discounts for the Forces and clergy, also for siblings (50% for a third daughter), plus Assisted Places (as available) and 6 scholarships, including 2 post-Standard Grade.

REMARKS: A kind and friendly small local girls' school, with some boarders. Has a useful nursery, but the upper school is struggling a bit with numbers.

St Edward's School

Woodstock Road, Oxford OX2 7NN
Tel: 01865 319323, Fax: 01865 319242
PUPILS: Around 507 boys, 66 girls (all in Sixth Form). 435 board, 138 day
AGES: 13–18
SIZE OF SIXTH FORM: 270
C OF E
FEE-PAYING

HEAD: Warden, since 1988, Mr David Christie, BSc Econ (London), BA (Strathclyde) (fifties), educated at

Dollar Academy. Came via George Watson's College, Edinburgh, and Moray House, where he taught Economics while researching the 'economics of education'.

A kindly Scot ('I like that'), who enjoys a debate, sees the world as a meritocracy, and is keen to broaden the entry base of the school, also keen on promoting three-way communication despite the boarding environment: pupils/school/parents. No thoughts of moving 'it suits me fine, and is now coming on course'.

Married, three children (youngest at Oxford High, others grown up). An active member of the HMC hierarchy, publishes books, articles on literature, and – his overruling passion – plays golf.

ACADEMIC MATTERS: The traditional belief is that Teddy's is more brawny than brainy. Recent results suggest the school is on a par with other middle-ranking boarding schools. Given its position in north Oxford it perhaps ought to be doing better than this, particularly given the intake of girls at Sixth Form, but NB we have not been given detailed results by the school. It does not offer every A-level under the sun, but separate sciences at GCSE, Latin for all, and Greek, German and Spanish as options; Economics is still popular. A General Studies course is taught throughout Sixth Form, plus one period a week on religious/moral issues. Pupils are streamed (after first term) and setted for Maths, etc. Some help is given for mild dyslexia for the first two years.

GAMES, OPTIONS, THE ARTS: In line with the brawny/brainy upheaval, it has now taken to losing matches, but cricket is still hot stuff, and sports are nonetheless extremely well served: there are 90 acres of pitches (hockey and rugby official games), and a classy Sports Centre (though the indoor pool could be improved) popular with non-school locals. Water sports, especially rowing, are a speciality, and the Boathouse is much in demand by local schools. Activities on offer range from archaeology, archery and (extra) art via science and engineering society to woodwork. Masses of Drama and ditto Music. The school has a new Art and Design centre, and Art is flourishing on the back of it. Week's management course and debating, CCF is compulsory until proficient (naval side popular), active D of E scheme.

BACKGROUND AND ATMOSPHERE: The school was founded in 1863, and moved to its present site in 1873. Imposing red-brick round busy quad, with masses of unobtrusive additions, a mile from the dreaming spires, tucked into the homelier Summertown district of north Oxford. Playing fields run down from the school to the canal on the other side of the busy Woodstock Road (connected by an underpass). There is a marvellous library. Boarding houses: some comfy old, some sparkling new. Daily life features large amounts of (popular) sliced white bread delivered for toasting in mini kitchens (everywhere). Not a school known for especial smartness and style, social or otherwise, of pupils. Girls have their own boarding house and boys are not allowed in, full stop. But day girls, boarders and day boys work (etc.) in boys' study dorms. Day pupils stay until 9 p.m. (two hours' homework given nightly, an hour and a half on Saturdays). A major rebuild of kitchens and dining hall has just been carried out – and not before time, say some.

PASTORAL CARE AND DISCIPLINE: Pastoral and parental links via a network of Housemasters and Tutors, 'but lots of people on hand to talk to,' plus two trained counsellors on tap. Bullying is picked up early by the prefecting system (Sixth Formers) – the Head is 'constantly staggered by how good they are'. Staff do duty patrols round Summertown and pubs to pick up any possible problems. Very tough on under-age drinking – police brought in – but the bar (with parents' permission) offers senior pupils beer and cider. Bouncers go round pubs and root out boys. Pupils are put out for drugs and sex, and the school 'wages ceaseless war' against cigarettes.

PUPILS AND PARENTS: Mainly from the professional middle classes. Tranches of day boys whose fathers are at Oxford (teaching and poor), plus a slight touch of the north Oxfords. This is a popular Sixth Form choice for girls (e.g. from Oxford High and Headington, also from London). OBs include Sir Douglas Bader (who was largely excused his fees), Lord Olivier, Kenneth Grahame, Judge Stephen Tumim (the liberal education coming out) and George Fenton (*Shadowlands* musack).

ENTRANCE: Down-payment of £300 at 11 guarantees a place on the successful passing of CE; last-minute places are often available. Test and assessment for state school entrants. Streams of Dragons (first and second choice), Winchester House, Caldicott – prep school Heads are not ashamed to mention that their pupils are patronising St Edward's. Sixth Form entry: five GCSE's at B or above, plus the school's own test and interview. This is a popular place for girls at Sixth Form and entrance requirements are far more demanding than results would suggest.

EXIT: Some leakage after GCSE, otherwise 90% of the Sixth to Higher Education (70–75% to trad universities). The remainder, drop-outs apart, to

Armed Forces, family and other businesses.

MONEY MATTERS: There are no Assisted Places, but fairly plentiful help is given. Up to 13 scholarships and exhibitions, 2 Service exhibitions, 30% bursaries for sons of clergy, Music and Art scholarships (the numbers vary from year to year), 4 continuation scholarships offered with a group of prep schools, plus a Dragon/St Edward's School scholarship for a 9-year-old at State School. Also the Arkwright Design scholarship for a 16-year-old, plus new Rotherfield and Bader Awards for 'bright all-rounders'.

REMARKS: A worthy middle-ranking school which has had some puzzlingly disappointing results recently, but coming up in the fashion stakes. It has good facilities and is seen to be trying hard.

St Elphin's School

Darley Dale, Matlock,
Derbyshire DE4 2HA
Tel: 01629 732687, Fax: 01629 733956

PUPILS: Approx 230 girls; 75 board, 155 day
AGES: 3–18 (boys aged 3–7)
SIZE OF SIXTH FORM: Approx 40
C OF E
FEE-PAYING

HEAD: Since 1994, Mrs V E Fisher BA (forties), who read Theology at Manchester. Previously Head of The Assumption School in Richmond, Yorkshire. A positive soul. Married, with one son. Takes over from Mr Peter Pollard.

REMARKS: The school was founded in Warrington in 1844 and named after a little-known saint who perished in battle in the 7th century. It moved to Derbyshire countryside in 1904 (now on A6) and has a huge chimney stack in the background. (NB The Head says this is an unfair description as the chimney does not dominate, and the school is a very fine Victorian building with newly built classrooms, etc.) There are small classes, and a wide range of ability. No streaming in first year, but thereafter streamed and setted according to ability in Maths and French. All girls take French, and Latin and German are on offer. Seven girls did Chinese GCSE in '95 and all got A*s – is this a record? One did Hindi (another A* here). The majority of girls did General Studies at A-level in '95. A very small Sixth Form makes the results difficult to report on, but they look healthy. All girls are reported to go on to university. OG Richmal Crompton, creator of *Just William*.

The new junior school block is very popular. Swimming for all is at the nearby Matlock Lido, and there is a good range of playing games fields, including an all-weather games pitch. Girls are keen charity workers and fund-raisers. The school is represented at the annual Buxton Festival of Speech, Drama and Music. Also produces some excellent and lively Art. Girls wear smart kilts. Friendly, with good pastoral care. Fees are reasonable and there are some scholarships on offer, including 2 of half fees.

The school fulfils a need in an area not noted for private schools.

St Felix School

Southwold, Suffolk IP18 6SD
Tel: 01502 722175, Fax: 01502 722641

PUPILS: Around 270 girls, 180 board, 90 day
AGES: 11–18

SIZE OF SIXTH FORM: 65
NON-DENOM
FEE-PAYING

HEAD: Since 1991 Mrs Susan Campion, MA (forties), previously Head of a girls' grammar school: this is her first post in the private sector and boarding. 'I'm a total convert.' Married to an inventor, with two sons. Energetic, humorous, ambitious for the school (but not unduly so), extremely able, likes to be closely in touch with each department. Describes herself as a pragmatist and an opportunist. Knows the girls well, and is much respected. Comments that some 'girls are over-ambitious and have to be dissuaded, others need to be revved up'.

ACADEMIC MATTERS: Results are average, reflecting the intake (IQs 110 plus), with some girls not necessarily going for the easy options. Arts subjects rather than Sciences (currently examined as three subjects at GCSE, and staff are determined to keep it this way; excellent laboratories); Classics is alive and all do Latin for three years minimum; also a good French department. There are regular exchanges with Spanish and German schools. Some help is given for dyslexia. All girls do 9 GCSEs and 3 A-levels. Drama Studies is offered as an A-level choice and included on the curriculum from the start, a hugely popular innovation. The school provides early and definitely good degree and careers advice (the Head is present in the school during the whole of August).

GAMES, OPTIONS, THE ARTS: Strong on sports of all kinds, especially all water sports, also tennis. There is a huge choice of activities which are compulsory for girls lower down the school, between lessons and prep: this could include sport (including football), riding (NB there is quite a strong pony contingent and some may be kept at livery down the road), woodwork, current events, friendship-bracelet-making. Girls produce good Art, some wonderful pottery, also Photography and DT. Music is keen (always one or two for A-level), with Copeman Hart in the chapel, good singing, and now at last the school has an orchestra. There are plenty of other groups, and the school does quite a bit with the local community. Parachute training, wine appreciation, etc, are available at Sixth Form. YE does well, and the Head has initiated a multinational YE scheme. Tough survival courses (includes skinning a rabbit) are on offer for 12–13-year-olds.

BACKGROUND AND ATMOSPHERE: A lovely secluded site not far from the North Sea, surrounded by 75 finely kept acres of own land. Unlike many girls' boarding schools, this one is well endowed, its fine facilities all in good nick. Victorian red-brick buildings plus additions, well designed, with pleasant sense of space and light. The Lower Sixth are given most of the leadership duties – they are charming with the younger girls and mutually supportive within their own house. The Upper Sixth House (where girls breakfast) is a little way off, a good school to university stepping-stone. There are good libraries and studies and common rooms for working – with an agreeable atmosphere. The school has a good weekend programme, and a sensible exeat time-buying system so girls must be committed when they are in school.

PASTORAL CARE AND DISCIPLINE: Non-teaching house staff; and Tutors: fierce on anti-smoking. Discipline is not a problem – this is a caring school.

PUPILS AND PARENTS: Mainly from Suffolk and Norfolk and the London

A12 corridor. A few from Hong Kong, and Germany (for a term or year). Natural and unspoilt girls, moderately ambitious. OGs include Lady Waley-Cohen, Olga Detterding, Lady Prior, Helen Lowenthal (Founder Vice President of NADFAS).

ENTRANCE: Via exam at 11+, though some come later.

EXIT: To an interesting variety of degree courses, including Music at Cambridge, Nursing at Surrey, Production Engineering at UMIST, plus one or two to Norwich Art School, a couple a year to Oxbridge (Cambridge particularly). Some do a gap year.

MONEY MATTERS: There are varying numbers of scholarships (minimum value 33% of current fees) and exhibitions (minimum value 20% of current fees) at 11, 12 and 13; also some at Sixth Form. A few Assisted Places at 11+.

REMARKS: An attractive gentle school with an agreeable atmosphere and fine facilities in a super area (though it takes a bit of getting to), which deserves to do well.

St George's School

Ascot, Berkshire SL5 7DZ
Tel: 01344 20273, Fax: 01344 874213

PUPILS: Around 287 girls; 173 board, 114 day
AGES: 11–18
SIZE OF SIXTH FORM: 77
C OF E
FEE-PAYING

HEAD: Since January 1989, Mrs Anthea Griggs, BA (fifties); educated North Foreland Lodge, and

Edinburgh University, where she read Religious Studies as a mature student.

Previously Deputy Head of Oxenfoord, and Upper Sixth Housemistress and careers adviser at Harrogate Ladies' College. Teaches ethics to Sixth Formers, 'reads to the little ones on Sunday evenings' and is much involved with pastoral life. Has a pleasantly firm, slightly confiding manner interspersed with giggles. An approachable Head, she sees St George's as producing 'competent, confident and compassionate girls' who are 'steady all-round performers'.

ACADEMIC MATTERS: GCSE results are surprisingly good for the mixed-ability intake (a deliberate policy here), with 53% of a (small) total of A-level candidates getting As and Bs. But the school is just as proud of the girl who gets two Es. Classes are set after first three years, with a maximum size of 24. No EFL on offer but the school can cope with mild dyslexia, and has a visiting tutor (a special needs unit is being set up). The previous bias towards English and the Arts is now levelling up with more scientists (nine doing A-level Maths, Chemistry and Physics in '95–'97). Classical Civilisation is still popular, and there were good French A-level results in '95. Altogether, hardly an E or less in sight.

GAMES, OPTIONS, THE ARTS: Girls have a choice of many games in a new four-badminton-court-size Sports Hall and the surrounding 30-acre campus. The Sports Hall has enviable weight training and ballet/aerobics, fencing, an exercise area on the top floor, but the swimming pool is outside (heated) across St George's Lane. Games are important here, with players in the national and county squad for lacrosse and tennis (all the year round). There was a lacrosse tour to America in '95. Timetabled self-defence in third year.

Inspired Design Technology (incorporating textiles and art rather than wood and plastics) and good Art and Ceramics. The Craft club (with sewing machines, etc) is open for making ball gowns at weekends. Computers are everywhere, and girls can do keyboarding and RSA exams.

Impressive Music, with computerised (music) keyboarding. Drama and Public Speaking are popular, with regular awards for the former (large numbers gaining distinctions in LAMDA exams). Photography is strong and the school's own dark room is very much used; also taught at GCSE. D of E (pottery features highly), Young Enterprise and lots of charity work.

BACKGROUND AND ATMOSPHERE: Founded in 1877 as a boys' prep school and converted to a girls' school at the turn of the century. Tucked down St George's Lane on the edge of Ascot High Street, with recently purpose-built dorms and interlocking classrooms (and incredibly narrow staircases everywhere). The new buildings were funded by the sale of Queen's Hill.

There are no timetabled lessons on Saturdays, day girls are called 'day boarders' and there are 'one or two flexible boarding arrangements' (i.e. weekly). Boarders move from small six- or eight-bed dorms to study bedrooms, with common rooms and kitchens for each year group. Sixth Formers can take driving lessons and entertain boys in the Common Room. Girls 'graduate' via a set of increasing privileges – half-blues, blues, etc, and a great feeling of being in the social whirl still pervades. There is no uniform in the Sixth Form; girls are ambivalent about marvellous Red Riding Hood cloaks.

PASTORAL CARE AND DISCIPLINE: There are good pastoral links via the house and prefectoral system; Housemistress and Form Tutors work in tandem (day girls are assigned to boarding houses). The school is 'run on trust, with open communication' and lots of open discussions, particularly discussion and a current awareness of anorexia. Automatic expulsion for drugs, but otherwise each incident is 'treated on its merits'; smoking very much a 'no-no'.

PUPILS AND PARENTS: Most from the South rather than London, with tranches of social parents from further afield, some first-time buyers. Popular with Service families (though less of these) and ex-pats, as well as a small number of foreigners.

ENTRANCE: CE at 11+, 12+ and 13+ (progressively more at 13); mixed ability intake, essentially girls who have something to offer, assessed via time spent at the school a year before entry. The Head comments: 'No problem if they get 60% in practice papers.' Foreigners on interview and internal comprehension exam, ditto for Sixth Form entrants plus the previous Head's report and six GCSEs at A, B or C.

EXIT: Some leakage post-GCSE, but most will stay on to do three A-levels, and 90% go on to 'tertiary education'. Otherwise 27 to further education in '95, plus three deferred entries; History of Art the most popular subject.

MONEY MATTERS: Lost a few because of the recession; the school 'will cover in crisis in exam years', and extended payments are popular. There are no Assisted Places but 2 annual scholarships for academic and Music promise. Also Sixth Form scholarships, and bursaries. Junior *boarding* scholarships are sometimes available.

REMARKS: A pine and rhodie girls' boarding school with increasing numbers of 'day boarders', doing well by the less academic.

St George's School for Girls

Garscube Terrace,
Edinburgh EH12 6BG
Tel: 0131 332 4575, Fax: 0131 315 2035
PUPILS: 897 girls; 822 day, 75 board, and nursery 27
AGES: 5–18
SIZE OF SIXTH FORM: 160
NON-DENOM
FEE-PAYING

HEAD: Since 1994, Dr Judith McClure, MA, DPhil (Oxon) FSA Scot (forties), educated Newlands Grammar School, Middlesbrough (was briefly a nun), studied Law, later took a first in History at Oxford. Lectured at Liverpool and Oxford Universities, and was previously at St Helen and St Catherine's, and Head of Abingdon, Kingswood School and Royal School Bath since 1987. A super, enthusiastic Head, larger than life, though some would say OTT, and 'not to everyone's taste' says a parent.

Dr McClure believes that girls do better in a single-sex environment, and looks forward to 'building characters, and running a happy school with capable, confident and committed teachers'. She puts pupils, parents and staff in that order of importance. Refreshingly honest. An educationalist, but recognises that there is no time for a Head to teach in a large school. Married to 'portable' historian husband, Dr Roger Collins, who specializes in 7th–9th-century Spain. No children.

ACADEMIC MATTERS: Very much a grammar school feel to the place – straight academic performance with not many frills. Three distinct departments: Primary, Lower School and Upper School. Girls take Highers in one year and A-levels (if they wish) the following year – or do the complete A-level course. Seriously strong Science. Also marvellous French with interesting computer courses (Château and Courier) designed and taught by Mrs Williams, who is extending her expertise to German and Spanish. IT provision has recently expanded. A good General Studies course is followed and careers advice is also good. Support learning is on offer throughout, both for those with learning difficulties and for the gifted child. NB League tables are meaningless in this school, given that two systems are followed.

GAMES, OPTIONS, THE ARTS: The school has a fabulous Centenary Sports Hall with a good viewing area over the hall and squash courts, marvellous lacrosse, including a flood-lit 'synthetic' pitch (believe it or not, the Lockerbie disaster fund was dedicated to boosting the game, for obscure reasons). The Robertson Music Centre is the home of three orchestras, with choirs, wind groups, and chamber music – over 600 musicians. Art is popular (in a new Art and Design Department), as is Drama. D of E Award. Great use is made of computer graphics to enliven letters, exam results, etc – really jolly.

BACKGROUND AND ATMOSPHERE: A cluttered collection of modern extensions round the purpose-built 1912 complex in Murrayfield (including boarding houses), surrounded by sports grounds and an excellent selection of wilderness areas. Pupils have a purposeful air. There is no uniform for the Sixth Form. Does things (play and dance) with

Merchiston, though traditionally it is linked umbilically with Edinburgh Academy.

PASTORAL CARE AND DISCIPLINE: Problems are dealt with on an 'individual basis' with much parental involvement, under the aegis of a 'head of guidance'. Occasional sackings.

PUPILS AND PARENTS: Unashamedly élitist and hard-working. A mixture of Charlotte Rangers, incomers and first-time independents. Parent Teacher Forum and The Friends of St George's for social events.

ENTRANCE: Serious test from 4½. Selective. Parents have been known to cram their tinies for entrance to the junior school (and to weep copious tears when their darlings are refused entry), otherwise by exam. Some come in at Sixth Form.

EXIT: Post-GCSE, 10% leave after GCSE. The rest go on to degrees and Higher Education of all sorts – Scottish Law is popular, as are the Sciences. Around 60% of university entrants go to Scottish universities – Aberdeen and Edinburgh have been particularly popular.

MONEY MATTERS: Assisted Places, selection of scholarships, discounts for siblings, including those at Edinburgh Academy.

REMARKS: A straight-up-and-down academic girls' day school, now back on track as the number one Edinburgh girls' day school. Still regarded as a bit 'narrow' by some Edinburgh parents.

St Leonards School

St Andrews, Fife KY16 9QU
Tel: 01334 472126, Fax: 01334 476152

PUPILS: Around 350 girls (including junior school). 252 board, 98 day

AGES: 12–18, plus junior school ages 7–12 of around 64 girls, both day and boarding

SIZE OF SIXTH FORM: 97

NON-DENOM

FEE-PAYING

HEAD: Since April 1988, Mrs Mary James, BA (Hons) York, (forties). Previously at Queen Ethelburga's, where she had been Headmistress for four years after teaching at Sedbergh and Casterton. First-class History Honours at York, followed by postgraduate research at Oxford; and married to fellow Historian author Lawrence James, two sons. Cheerful socialiser. Prepared to wait for good staff and not afraid to appoint a younger Head of Department over his/her peers.

Encourages independent thought, and believes St Leonards is still one of the best schools in the country and one of the very few girls' schools able to 'look the major boys' public schools straight in the eye where facilities, horizons and aspirations are concerned'. Not a highly selective school, but one where the 'ethos is such that girls will find sparkle and ability in the right environment and learn to work under pressure'. Aims at producing 'whole women'. *Very keen* on single-sex education.

ACADEMIC MATTERS: Conflicting reports – some say the school is strong, others that it should do better. Difficult to assess given that the school follows both English and Scottish exam systems and has not given us details of exam results. Scottish Standards are not offered, and most pupils do A-levels (though a few do A-levels and Highers). However, many staff have links with the University of St Andrews, and the school uses some of their facilities. Computers are much improved, old Science labs now computer-aided; the Design and Technology department is linked with Science (and has ties with Textiles and Colour Chemistry). Science results have been weak; there is strong resistance to 'heavy metal'. Careers advice is on offer from 13. General Studies produce 'independent thought'. There are one or two complaints from parents on the lack of flexibility on subjects on offer, e.g. German and Spanish are alternated.

GAMES, OPTIONS, THE ARTS: Very strong games for Scotland, but now more fun. A Lockerbie disaster-funded Lacrosse Museum is in the offing; also judo, trampoline, badminton, all-year tennis, swimming. Adrian Watson-West (ex-Queen Ethelburga's) is Head of the brilliant Art department. Music is much improved (Bob Steedman, husband of the previous Head, designed the centre). D of E Award. There is a feeling of lots going on all the time.

BACKGROUND AND ATMOSPHERE: Founded in 1877, known as 'Smellie Lennies', the 'mother' school of Wycombe Abbey (qv), purpose-built (and slightly awesome) with many additions, very near the sea – the air is bracing (track suits are popular for games) – in a bustling university town. Golf, riding and going to the beach as well as making trips up town and forays to the surrounding countryside. The school has recently established links, e.g. careers conferences, with Merchiston Castle School (one and a half hours' drive, and a rather odd choice). There is a mega library and a selection of Maryana in Queen Mary's House.

Houses are civilised – NB girls do their own laundry and ironing – and pupils wear Chris Clyne-designed uniforms (skirts are not cheap, but second-hand stuff now available), including Barbours and cloaks. There is a marvellous (Bob Steedman-designed) popular Sixth Form house with study bedrooms and glitzy bathrooms.

Junior School: St Katharine's (St Kays), The Pends, St Andrews, Fife KY16 9RB. Tel: as above. Joint Heads: Mr Trevor Bayley and Mrs Gail Robson-Bayley - a good team. Entrance is via interview and the previous Head's report. Most girls go on to the senior school. The junior school uses senior school facilities. Pleasant atmosphere in boarding house. There are lots of satisfied reports from parents, who don't always continue sounding quite so enthusiastic when their children transfer to the senior school.

PASTORAL CARE AND DISCIPLINE: School rules feature punctuality, security and civilised behaviour: sackings for OTT (for drugs involvement off school), 6–8 since 1988. Also two sackings for untruthfulness – claiming to be going to friend for weekend and turning up at an all-night party in Edinburgh. Mrs James makes an issue of every suspension (drinking and smoking) and brings in police where theft is involved. Phil Cooper (a reformed street druggy) gives annual anti-drug talks.

PUPILS AND PARENTS: Strong Scots contingent, though the switch to co-education in Scottish public schools siphoned off some of 'Smellie Lennies' traditional fodder. Around 13% of pupils come from England, with fewer foreigners and ex-pats. Lots of daughters of 'Seniors' (famous Seniors Betty Harvey Anderson, Dame Kathleen Ollerenshaw).

ENTRANCE: CE at 11, 12, or 12. Own exam for state school entrants (the junior school take 12+ CE).

EXIT: A slight leakage post-GCSE. Otherwise 95% to university, a small fluctuating number to Oxbridge. Newcastle, Bristol, Exeter, Durham and Scottish universities are popular – particularly Edinburgh and Aberdeen.

MONEY MATTERS: Well-endowed for a girls' school, rich in scholarships, for Music, Seniors' daughters, older pupils, etc. Also sibling discounts with Merchiston Castle. There are 33 Assisted Places.

REMARKS: A famous traditional girls' boarding school with far less nervy sophistication than at many southern academic establishments. There are some complaints, both pastoral and on the academic front.

St Leonards– Mayfield School

The Old Palace, Mayfield,
East Sussex TN20 6PH
Tel: 01435 873652, Fax: 01435 872627
PUPILS: Around 525 girls, 320 board, 205 day
AGES: 11–18
SIZE OF SIXTH FORM: 160
RC
FEE-PAYING

HEAD: Since 1980, Sister Jean Sinclair, BSc (early sixties), whom we could not meet. The 1986/7 President of the Girls' School Association. Shy, humorous, gentle and popular. Educated at Wycombe Abbey, a mathematician and former athlete, she is a convert to Roman Catholicism – strongly against personal publicity. 'There is no truth in the rumour that she is Sir Clive Sinclair's sister, nor that she is about to retire – though as a religious, she may be moved at any time,' says a spokesperson. There are three full-time nuns still in the school – though not now teaching.

ACADEMIC MATTERS: Strong on English, Sciences (Dual Award science at GCSE, streamed at 15). Also streamed for Maths, English, French. Maximum class size 20, for first two years, then 16–18. The school can supply-teach any language – French, Spanish, Italian, Russian, German, Chinese and Portuguese are currently on offer. Hot on Religious Studies – as one might expect. Has links with the Neighbourhood Engineers scheme, and five girls a year regularly go into engineering; also medics, biochemists, etc. Mild dyslexia is 'no problem', and the school can deal with a certain amount of physical and visual handicap (though wheelchairs are a bit tricky). EFL is in demand. Less than 10% of staff male.

GAMES, OPTIONS, THE ARTS: Strong games, and the games pitches are stunningly situated. Sixth Formers can opt out of team games and plump for fencing, judo. The school has a marvellous covered swimming pool designed by a nun-architect, and is used by local villagers, also there is an inter-schools cross-country riding course. Young Enterprise and D of E Awards. Superb ceramics (with GCSE results to match), good Art. Home Economics is also offered, and pupils are prepared for the City & Guilds Cooks professional exams.

The Music Director is Kenneth Pont, founder of the Gibbons Consort, director of Mayfield Festival, and adviser to Oxford University Press. The school has five choirs now, which perform regularly with local Glyndebourne soloists and London orchestras, but some parents voice disappointment that more is not done in the way of educational trips, etc.

BACKGROUND AND ATMOSPHERE: Mayfield School was founded by Sister Cornelia Connelly in 1872 in the grounds of The Old Palace of the Archbishops of Canterbury (the magnificent 13th-century Chapel was restored by Pugin and is used for worship by the whole school daily). Sister Cornelia Connelly founded the Society of the Holy Child Jesus in 1863, and the school amalgamated with an earlier foundation at St Leonards-on-Sea in 1954. Boarders must be RC, but day girls are mixed.

On a marvellous site, with sympathetic developments (though girls complain they feel 'isolated'). Dormitories and classrooms are scattered throughout, with the two junior years in separate Aylwins House, above the Art Centre; otherwise, houses are in clusters, with communal lunching in the dining hall and own individual refectories for supper. Second-year Guardians are assigned to new girls. Sixth Formers have study bedrooms. The revamped library has CD-Rom and anti-theft devices and computer-tagged books. Blue uniform for all but the Upper Sixth, girls carry their worldly possessions around in blue school bags.

PASTORAL CARE AND DISCIPLINE: A strong religious background, with regular prayer groups and retreats plus lots of advice on where to go if worried. Discipline – 'not many problems'. Some parents comment that the girls are allowed 'too much freedom'. Someone from the Navy comes during the pupils' fifth year and delivers the drug lecture given to the ratings – terrifying. There is a £10 fine for Cancer Research and a letter to parents if caught smoking.

PUPILS AND PARENTS: Mainly from south-east England, and a collection of diplomatic and army families. Also around forty foreigners, including Hong Kong Chinese, Nigerians and Europeans (particularly Spanish). Europeans often come for one year only. Charming and articulate; local parents are very supportive.

ENTRANCE: 11+, 12+, 13+, occasionally 14+ and Sixth Form entry. By CE from local preps, more now at 13+ than 11+; 14+ by interview and previous school report, and Sixth Form ditto. CE results are no bar from A-level attempts, but five Bs at GCSE is the norm.

EXIT: Some leakage after GCSE, but most stay: some may try boys' schools and return to base! 74 to university last year, with three Oxbridge.

MONEY MATTERS: Will carry exam-year crisis, otherwise ISBA form and means-tested scholarships and bursaries awarded to Roman Catholic girls at 11+ or 13+ for academic ability, Art, and Music.

REMARKS: A wide-ability Catholic girls' boarding school where pupils are expected to be self-motivated, 'but we lean on them pretty hard'. A large social and ethnic mix, which works well. Offers a good strong range of non-academic subjects as well as the usual.

St Margaret's School Edinburgh

East Suffolk Road,
Edinburgh EH16 5PJ
Tel: 0131 668 1986, Fax: 0131 662 0957

PUPILS: Around 660 girls; 50 board, 610 day
AGES: Girls 3–18. 8–10 boys, age 3–8
SIZE OF SIXTH FORM: 150
NON-DENOM
FEE-PAYING

HEAD: Since May 1994, Miss Anne Mitchell, MA (Hons) English (forties). Previously Deputy Head of Dunbar Grammar School. Educated at Lossiemouth High, Elgin Academy and Aberdeen University. Miss Mitchell's aim on taking over the school following the sudden departure of her predecessor, was to provide a 'period of stability and consolidation' in the school.

ACADEMIC MATTERS: Results are not given. EFL and remedial help are on offer throughout, with pupils being withdrawn or given support in class.

Pupils sit A-levels only 'if Heads of Departments prefer the courses', otherwise Highers and SYS. Difficult to judge results because of the Scottish system of appeals, whereby prelims and previous year's work can be taken into consideration and exam results improved. French, Spanish, Latin and German are available, but Greek is extra-curricular.

The school has a super, enthusiastic computer expert who has set up clubs everywhere, and an expanded Business Studies department which includes external adults – very successful. Careers advice is given from age 13. There are over 70 staff, with many part-timers.

GAMES, OPTIONS, THE ARTS: Games are at the University of Edinburgh's Sports Grounds. The gym is above the Music Studios in a converted church. Music is improving, and there is an excellent choir. Also brilliant Ceramics; Home Economics is on the increase.

BACKGROUND AND ATMOSPHERE: 'Awfully cosy', comments a parent. A cluster of Victorian villas in bedsit land of South Newington, including a dead cushy boarding house (ex-Oratava Hotel) with private bathrooms everywhere, (excellent letting prospect). A £2.8 million property portfolio. Some, but not all, buildings show signs of the previous Head's recent programme of revamping (coral and pale turquoise preferred).

PASTORAL CARE AND DISCIPLINE: No recent expulsions. 'Seeing the Head is enough'.

PUPILS AND PARENTS: Eclectic – gentrified children departing for their country estates on the one hand, and solid Edinbourgeoisie, plus children whose parents work at the local supermarket on the other. Surprisingly only 'half a dozen or so' came as a result of the demise of Oxenfoord – though places were offered to all. Also 30 or 40 from abroad.

ENTRANCE: Throughout the school, but primarily, at 5, 11 and 16. Boys only up to 8. Interview and assessment, entrance test.

EXIT: One or two leave after Standard Grades, but the majority aim for degree courses.

MONEY MATTERS: Few debts or bad payers but the school is 'always happy to help with financial problems'. 6–7% of pupils are on Assisted Places; 'keen on market forces, but not to the detriment of education'. The school is 'absolutely not financially stretched'. Currently places an emphasis on high-fliers to the extent that discretionary 'bursaries are available' throughout.

REMARKS: A cosy Edinburgh girls' day school which is now ticking over (though numbers are down since our last edition) without making waves.

St Mary's School

Ascot, Berkshire SL5 9JF
Tel: 01344 23721, Fax: 01344 873281
PUPILS: Around 340 girls; 330 board, 10 day
AGES: 11–18
SIZE OF SIXTH FORM: 89
RC
FEE-PAYING

HEAD: Since 1982, Sister Frances Orchard (formerly known as Sister Mark – she has reverted to her baptismal name), IBVM, BA, PGCE (fifties), educated at St Mary's Ascot and London University. A firm, tireless Head who leaves much of day-to-day running to her Deputy. A shrewd businesswoman, though parents comment (slightly, it seems, to their surprise), that 'she has a human face'. Likes skiing, dog-walking, doing tapestries, reading and Scrabble. Parents comment that you can feel the difference almost immediately when she is not in residence – 'the school sags a bit'.

ACADEMIC MATTERS: The school has a strong bias to the Arts, with History of Art, Classical Civilisation and Religious Studies featuring strongly in the A-level results, though '95 shows a slight increase in pupils doing Sciences. All pupils take Religious Studies at GCSE and, at the time of writing, do very well in them. Languages are the school's biggest academic strength – note for example the dear little poems in four different languages in the school magazine. Dual Award Science for all at GCSE.

GAMES, OPTIONS, THE ARTS: Tennis is the top game, and the keen coach is at the nets morning, noon and night. Also fencing. Good Art, Drama (including house plays), community service and D of E Award, not to mention dressmaking and computers. Music is very popular – the majority of girls learn one instrument, several learn two 'or more'. The size of the Music School increased by 100% in '94 (not as difficult as it sounds), owing to a new Director of Music (from Bluecoat's in Reading).

BACKGROUND AND ATMOSPHERE: Set in commuter-belt rhododendron country – impeccably kept. The Head's house is bang in the middle of the school grounds, though, she says, compared with where she was before, it is the height of privacy. Purpose-built in 1885, it has since been extended in similar red brick. The Head and Deputy in charge of boarding are members of the Institute of the Blessed Virgin Mary, founded in the 17th century by Mary Ward, one of the great English educationalists.

There are civilised bedrooms for older girls, and even dorms are more like rooms, with much privacy. Houses are given the responsibility of running the school in rota, and this system helps break school age barriers vertically. There is no uniform for the Sixth Form, who live apart in a new Sixth Form block. Sheltered. The soothing chapel has a slightly cloistered feel – a wonderful sanctuary from the shrill world outside.

PASTORAL CARE AND DISCIPLINE: No alcohol – the place for a smoke and drink is down in the woods. Regular larks with Eton boys get into the national press, and do the school's image no harm at all. There is a strong tradition of pastoral care and, says the Head, there is 'virtually no homesickness as juniors have 24-hour access to the Deputy Head in charge of boarding' – a brave claim. The school could be a bit short of weekend activities.

PUPILS AND PARENTS: Top Catholics. Conventional. A few smart foreigners, diplomats' daughters, OGs' daughters, and 20% from overseas, mainly ex-pats. OGs include Caroline of Monaco, the Spanish infantas, Sarah Hogg, Marina Warner.

ENTRANCE: By registration – lists close 18 months ahead of entry at the time of writing.

EXIT: A few leave after GCSE, otherwise the majority to universities. A handful to Oxbridge in '95/'96. Psychology appears to be enjoying a small vogue. Careers in the City, law, medicine and teaching. Secretarial and cookery skills are often acquired in the gap year.

MONEY MATTERS: OG scholarship for Sixth Form entry. Also a Sixth Form Science scholarship, Music scholarship and discretionary bursaries for pupils currently in the school. Fees are 'as high as the market place will allow'.

REMARKS: A still excellent establishment with a quiet sense of community and purpose, and contented reports from parents. An oasis of tranquillity which has changed remarkably little over the decades, despite all. OGs still complain that the school does not prepare pupils for the hurly burly of 'life' today.

St Mary's School

Calne, Wiltshire SN11 10DF
Tel: 01249 815899, Fax: 01249 822432

PUPILS: Around 306 girls; the majority board, about 35 day
AGES: 10–18
SIZE OF SIXTH FORM: Around 73

C OF E
FEE-PAYING

HEAD: From 1985 to Easter 1996, Miss Delscey Burns, BA, MSc (Oxon). New Head: Mrs Carolyn Shaw BA Hons (English). Married, two children. Previously at Cheltenham Ladies. Miss Burns will be a hard act to follow.

ACADEMIC MATTERS: Results are not given, but reports suggest that Maths, Economics and Physics are the weaker subjects in exam terms, and Science as a whole is not popular. No-frills mainstream subjects are on offer, including Latin, compulsory up to 14; the school is 'too small for esoteric subjects,' as a parent put it, though GCSE Drama is a recent sop to demand. 9–10 GCSE subjects are the aim, all on the toughest boards, 'because the universities like it', and with minimum coursework. There is keen peer pressure to work – and they do, in a chalk-and-talk regime.

Sciences are taught for Combined Award only – 'overtaught but still not the ideal base for A-level', was a comment. The strong team of teachers includes a fair sprinkling of men (e.g. for Physics, Art, Drama, PE). The first fortnight in July, post-GCSE, is set aside for 'taster' induction A-level courses. Eng Lit is predictably the most popular A-level plus keen Geography, History of Art and Bible-based Divinity. A new addition is Theatre Studies. Italian is offered in the Sixth Form, also the Cambridge Computer Course leading to diploma.

GAMES, OPTIONS, THE ARTS: Take second place to academia, though several girls currently represent Wiltshire for lacrosse. The school has a fairly old-fashioned gym and no indoor pool, but keen tennis – 'the best time to grab a court is during *Neighbours*,' confides a player. Keen riding, says one eventer who chose Calne 'so I can stable my pony and keep in with one-day eventing'. Very well-subscribed D of E.

There is a new theatre for recent rousing successes and alternate-year Form Shakespeare competitions. Also weekends trip to Bath for plays. The Upper Sixth fashion show produces glossy pics of budding socialites heading for *Tatler* pages. Girls are keen and good bridge players ('because of the lack of facilities', explained a parent).

RSA typing classes in Calne are offered to the Sixth Form; also driving lessons. The school has a somewhat fusty prospectus (but a new one is imminent), and a livelier school mag, with good varied photographs of impressive art projects, bungee jumping, glacier skiing, etc. Effective fund-raising, e.g. Romania, and a staggering £128,000 for the John Radcliffe Hospital teenage cancer ward following a pupil's leukaemia.

BACKGROUND AND ATMOSPHERE: Not a school you would choose for its facilities. A functional, practical, purpose-built building, founded in 1873 by Canon Duncan (Vicar of St Mary's Church, Calne) in 25 Alsatian-patrolled acres of central Calne, an unglamorous little Wiltshire town best known as the home of the now defunct Harris' sausage factory. Houses are divided horizontally; pupils move each year while remaining throughout in 'companies', accumulating 'red points' for good deeds, and each house has an annual black-tie dinner. There is a Junior House for new girls, who move on and up via cosy self-catering cottages to a newly extended Upper Sixth Form House. The school has a fairly rigid boarding system with fixed exeats.

PASTORAL CARE AND DISCIPLINE: Non-teaching Housemistresses and a quietly supportive tutorial system keep a careful watch – 'We are well aware of social pressures,' say staff, and those have reputedly resulted in a 'mini-outbreak of anorexia' despite a clocking-in system for lunch. Gating for smoking and (occasional) suspensions for alcohol ('No, they are not plaster saints'), and straight out for drugs (no recent expulsions). Each new girl gets met at the door by a 'school mother' from the year above.

PUPILS AND PARENTS: 90% establishment intelligentsia, no nouveaux, in a strongly C of E ethos (though other faiths are accepted, including RCs, Jews, Muslims). Some Forces children, otherwise London and the local smart, with Yorkshire and Scottish additions. Bright-eyed, unhearty, upper-crust girls whose parents tend to know each other. 'Confident, friendly all-rounders,' said a satisfied parent, 'full of initiative and well poised to partake in normal life' while remaining 'feminine and full of fun'.

ENTRANCE: Mainly by word of mouth from the dinner-party circuit, many pupils from the cream of London preps. No one takes the exam, or even registers, till parents and child are vetted at around the age of 9 by Head (or vice versa?). 'We are looking for signs of ability and creativity; we can always get the mechanics right later,' says the Deputy Head. Stiff CE requirements – 'we do not have a pass mark, it is a qualifying examination' – at 11 and 12. Younger sisters are encouraged.

EXIT: Some post-GCSE leakage. But the majority to English universities including a handful to Oxbridge in a typical year; also a handful to US and Canadian colleges, otherwise teacher training, art foundation.

MONEY MATTERS: There is 1 academic scholarship at 11+, 1 at 12+; 1 at 11+ or 12+ for an Old Girl's daughter. Also 2 Sixth Form academic, 1 Art, 1 Music scholarships.

REMARKS: The school has been suffering from having its brightest and best Sixth Formers pinched by boys' public schools going co-ed, and the departure of the dynamic Miss Burns will not help matters. Still seen, however, as a fashionable choice (although no longer *the* fashionable choice) for smarter daughters with well-bred brains who will safely mix with their own kind in the resultant somewhat socially limiting atmosphere.

St Mary's School

Shaftesbury, Dorset SP7 9LP
Tel: 01747 854005, Fax 01747 851557
PUPILS: 300 girls: 220 board, 80 day
AGES: 9–18
SIZE OF SIXTH FORM: Around 70
RC
FEE-PAYING

HEAD: Since 1985, Sister M Campion Livesey, MA (Cantab) (early forties), educated at Lady Eleanor Holles and Cambridge – a historian. Her sister is Head of Drama at Wycombe Abbey. Clever, energetic, informal, inspiring, and closely involved – sees younger girls to bed at night. Says, 'Your relationships with God and other people are what count.' 'She's switched on and keeps her finger on the pulse while really bothering to understand the girls,' approves a parent. 'You can have a giggle with her,' says another (NB she wears no habit and joins in with the barn dances), adding 'but she's a holy lady and commands a lot of respect.'

ACADEMIC MATTERS: Teaching is a 'bit of a curate's egg,' comments a high-flier, but English is singled out as the exception. Choosier than it used to be while looking for all-rounders who can pull off 9+ GCSEs. Setting for Maths, French, English and Science – this last is taught as Dual Award only. Flexible A-level combinations, and options such as Desk-Top Publishing and Theatre Workshop are available outside the curriculum. Drama at GCSE and Theatre Studies at A-level are now on offer. Trouble is taken over the B stream, though some parents feel that the younger end could be pushed harder and earlier and teaching could be 'livelier'. Computerised print-outs give twice-termly grades for achievement and effort. Results are steady. All do Religious Studies at GCSE.

GAMES, OPTIONS, THE ARTS: Good games teaching produces county champions at netball for Under-13, Under-14, Under-15 with Under-14s representing the South-West of England at the nationals. Strong hockey with players at county level. Good PE in a newish Sports Hall (opened '92 following a parents' appeal). Also Yoga and riding. Weekend trips (e.g. to Bath) include day girls (to the mild irritation of some boarders). Most take the D of E to silver. Drama GCSE; YE. The school has the usual bands and orchestra and a 'lovely' choir has toured Italy and Budapest. Also imaginative community service.

BACKGROUND AND ATMOSPHERE: A large château-style Edwardian house converted some 40 years ago – a shrine to Mammon. Lots of space, well-used, well-kept (freshly decorated dormitories), with stunning rolling Dorset/Wiltshire views. Previously a convent and many mourn the nuns' lost era. The school is now a charitable company, with a separate legal existence from the religious community to whom it belongs. Sister Campion and one nun Housemistress are the last relics of the IBVM order, and the school now admits non-RC boarders in an atmosphere that is easy and broad-minded, though all must attend Sunday Mass (optional during the week). The IBVM chaplain is shared with the sister foundation at Ascot, and the school also has a full-time priest chaplain.

Bread and cheese 'fasting' lunch once a week. Some Housemistresses are described as 'on the fuddy-duddy side' – and possibly not always in tune with their charges, or their parents. The truly grim chocolate-coloured uniform has now been replaced by kilts, bottle green sweaters, wax jackets.

PASTORAL CARE AND DISCIPLINE: 'Freedom is yours till you blow it,' says Sister Campion disarmingly. Only one has paid the price in recent years – for cannabis. Girls are allowed a generous measure of rope, especially at the top of the school – e.g. Sixth Form trips to the local pub; three 'late passes' a term; plus permission to drive your own car back to school. Conforming ethos. There is a lack of counselling 'in time of real need', according to several parents.

PUPILS AND PARENTS: Less flash/London-orientated than its linked foundation, Ascot. Some commuter townies (NB the school coach picks up at Fleet and Woking), otherwise local middle class plus farmers' children and 30% from the Forces, including ex-pats; also a regular contingent of Spanish. OGs include the clever Waugh progeny.

ENTRANCE: At 9, 10 and 11 via the school's own exam (English, Maths, IQ) and at 12+ and 13+ via 50–60% CE pass mark. Many from country preps, e.g. All Hallows, Port Regis.

EXIT: 95% to degree courses; the University of West England at

Bristol is popular and Oxford Brookes; also one or two to Cambridge and Oxford. Otherwise Business Courses, Nursing, Art Foundation.

MONEY MATTERS: There are 2 Sixth Form scholarships; 1 Art and 1 major Music scholarship; 2 minor Music scholarships. New 'all round' award from '96. Relatively reasonable fees.

REMARKS: An unstuffy, liberal, small country RC girls' school through which winds of change have blown refreshingly since the *ancien régime*, which was geared to turning out good wives.

St Paul's School

Lonsdale Road, London SW13 9JT
Tel: 0181 748 9162, Fax: 0181 748 9557

PUPILS: Around 750 boys
MAJORITY DAY: Two boarding houses (around 75)
AGES: 13–18
SIZE OF SIXTH FORM: 300
C OF E
FEE-PAYING

HEAD: Since 1992, Mr Stephen Baldock MA (early fifties). Educated St Paul's (where he captained the cricket) then read Classics (Part One) and Theology (Part Two) at King's College, Cambridge. Came back to St Paul's to teach Classics, headed the boarding house, was Surmaster (Deputy Head in St Paul's speak) for eight years before being appointed to the present job. Married to a GP, lives just across the road, has four children; likes sports and plays in staff teams. Knows the school inside out, obviously, and this should be a great help to him. More 'hands on' than his predecessor, and spends more time in the school. Thoughtful, easy to talk to, and – that much overused word – approachable.

ACADEMIC MATTERS: Unquestionably outstanding. Just to give you an idea: of 1,616 subjects taken at GCSE in '95, only five were below C; Chemistry got 57 A*s, 10 As – and nothing else; Maths, Physics and Biology show similar patterns. If there is a poor relation it is Economics, but we suspect that this may be more to do with the examination board than the standard as it afflicts practically the whole country. Teaching staff are on top of the job. Lively debating style of teaching.

The curriculum was recently revised, so that all boys have to take an option in a practical subject from the second year. Most boys take GCSE French and Maths at the end of the second year, and carry on with the modular A-level French syllabus, which gives them extra strength in this.

Outstanding Modern Languages, with French, Italian and German *assistants*. Japanese is taught for the Cambridge Certificate at Sixth Form. Very strong Science (separate Sciences and Nuffield Co-ordinated Sciences – Dual Award). Also some outstanding English and History teaching.

Generally very strong Common Room (sabbaticals and exchanges are encouraged to gee up flagging enthusiasms). Maximum of 24 per class; A-level classes average nine or ten. Impressively long detailed reports each term can reduce the non-brilliant to despair.

Three A-levels is 'the norm', but almost all do AS as well, interestingly enough, plus non-examinable General Studies.

GAMES, OPTIONS, THE ARTS: The school has a two-hour lunch break daily during which boys are involved in a non-academic activity – e.g. rowing (impressive), Music, swimming. Saturday mornings are also taken up with games, rehearsals, extras (though not compulsory).

Games are traditionally and actually strong, though 'it's OK', said a pupil, 'if you're no good at them.' Cricket and rugby are particularly lively – results are variable from good to so-so. The school is recommended by the Lawn Tennis Association for keen would-be tennis players. There is a good indoor pool, and the fencing salle is said to be the best in Western Europe; fives is a major game here. Rowing school.

Music news: there is a new Director of Music in '96 – Mr Mark Tatlow, whose previous post was Chorus Master at the Swedish Court Opera, no less. A new Music building is 'in the pipeline'. There are some outstanding musicians in the school, and one or two top-class staff. Some concerts are given with St Paul's Girls'.

A stunning, recently built palatial Art department has space for exhibitions, and every resource and facility known to man – probably the best school Art Centre in the country. Head of Art is David Wakefield. CDT flourishes – there are super modern facilities. Drama, too, is keen.

The school has the cleverest student newspaper in the business, *Black and White* – heavy topics written in bright dynamic style, interspersed with witty bits, e.g. 'Will Carling? Or more pertinently, Did Carling?'

BACKGROUND AND ATMOSPHERE: On a super site, with 45 grassy acres (formerly reservoirs) sweeping straight down to the River Thames, the view of which has been much spoilt by ghastly boarding-house buildings and other purpose-built grimbo monstrosities –

aesthetic considerations are very low on the St Paul's agenda. The entrance hall/atrium in the main block is the central gathering place – like Grand Central Station – where messages are relayed out and boys are to be seen congregating at all hours.

The school was founded in 1509 by Dean Colet, friend of Erasmus and Thomas More, whose humanitarian principles still stand firm. The Trustees of the Foundation are the Worshipful Company of Mercers, who provide much (too much?) of the governing body. The school moved to its present site in 1968. New boys coming from London preps may find Pauline life a bit unstructured. To participate in 'Apposition' is every boy's aim (four outstanding pupils speak/make music, etc., to assembled distinguished visitors, governors and parents).

Boys are bussed in from all corners of the metropolis – it can be difficult when clubs and societies demand their presence after bus leaving hours. Boarding houses are very useful for short-term stays, either through the demands of school, or when parents are away.

The school has a very down-to-earth, scruffy, grammar school feel, with academic work the overriding priority. A very male atmosphere, without being macho.

PASTORAL CARE AND DISCIPLINE: A Tutor system, which the Head is keen to use as 'a springboard' to promote a feeling of the school as a community and to 'teach them that people matter' (i.e., not just academic priorities). The Head sees the 1993 school photo (the first time the whole school was photographed together since 1959) as a 'big moment'. Parents are asked to invite the Tutor (plus wife, if he has one) home for a meal in the early days: communication is intended to be frequent and open. PSE courses (relationships with girls, drugs, etc.) have been newly instigated, and a pre-university course on life with a capital F.

The Head agrees, somewhat uncertainly, that any boy 'in possession of illegal substances should expect to be expelled', but adds the rider that 'you can't do a belt and braces on school rules'. The school has regular visits from a psychiatrist/counsellor. This is a lively place, and not easy to keep the lid on – many a slip between school and home, and endless excuses for being anywhere but in the right place.

PUPILS AND PARENTS: Drawn from all around London and from as far away as Guildford and Windsor. Some from state schools. All sorts, no types, though qualities which come up over and over again in OBs are doggedness, head-down approach to life, street smart. Very articulate – always winning public speaking competitions. OBs include John Milton, Edmund Halley, Jonathan Miller, Peter Shaffer, Montgomery of Alamein, G K Chesterton.

ENTRANCE: Tough: all but the brightest and best are weeded out at 10/11; intake is 150–160 per year – 75 from Colet Court (see separate entry), the rest from prep schools all round London – Newland House, Milbourne Lodge, Durston House, Hill House (lots from here), Rokeby, The Hall, The Mall, Tower House, North Bridge House. At 10 or 11, all prospective pupils and parents come to the school: the Head interviews parents, the Surmaster sees the boys and afterwards they compare notes. Main lists close then and CE follows on as qualifying exam. Boys must perform well in every subject.

EXIT: To Oxbridge (40–50 a year), with still more bridge than Ox. Also

4–5 a year to art college. Otherwise, the older, popular universities. Pupils go on to be lawyers, doctors, civil servants, one or two to the Church.

MONEY MATTERS: No Art scholarships on entry, but at Sixth Form (assuming the two other subjects are up to scratch as well). There are 153 scholars (as many as the miraculous draft of fishes – scholars wear a silver fish badge): scholarships are mainly awarded on entrance, some develop in the 'Eighth', i.e. Sixth Form. Scholars are integrated with the rest of the school. Cases of genuine need are catered for – the school is very well endowed. Assisted Places. The basic term fee at time of writing is just under £2,700 for day boys, plus £1,425 for boarding.

REMARKS: Still reigns as one of the two top London academic boys' day schools, if not the top one. More of a grammar school-y atmosphere than the other one (Westminster), and maybe rather more prepossessing pupils.

St Paul's Girls' School

Brook Green, London w6 7bs
Tel: 0171 603 2288, Fax: 0171 602 9932

PUPILS: Around 620 girls
ALL DAY
AGES: 11–18
SIZE OF SIXTH FORM: (known as Seventh and Eighth Forms) around 214
ANGLICAN FOUNDATION
FEE-PAYING

HEAD: (High Mistress): Since 1993, Miss Janet Gough, MA, PGCE (fifties). Read History and English at Cambridge. Was interregnum Head for a year before her appointment as Head was confirmed, stepping into the breach created by the departure of the previous Head. Before that Deputy Head. Gets the seal of approval from girls: 'Really cool,' said one. A strong, calm presence. Knows the school inside out – has been here for 30 years (much of it teaching English) and at 8.15 a.m. every morning you will see her standing 'on the marble' (in the entrance hall) being approachable, and at noon, she says, the door is also open. Comments on her academic pupils, 'we are a dying breed'. Five-star Head. Her brother (retired now) was Headmaster of Forest School.

ACADEMIC MATTERS: Outstandingly strong and consistently so. History – 'if you take History you can't fail,' said a pupil, 'it's so good'. English also very strong indeed. Science relatively less so, though not to be sneezed at. Languages – Russian, French, Spanish, Italian and German all offered and taken up. Girls take up to nine GCSEs, but often less – the idea being to leave time to pursue a broader curriculum than the rather constrained demands of the GCSE syllabus. This causes no problems, says the Head – universities know St Paul's is strong. Now setting in Maths after the first term. No setting in languages. Non-examinable General Studies (from the Middle School up). Dual Award science at GCSE. There is a newish building for IT.

There is a very strong Common Room (some housing for staff is available). Always comes at or near top of the A-level league tables, which is no surprise, but still, all credit for sustained effort.

GAMES, OPTIONS, THE ARTS: Very strong Music. The new-ish Music Director, Dr Derek Bourgeois, MA, MusD is the ex-Director of National Youth Orchestra, a composer, and he did a stint at Bristol University. The school is lucky to have him, though given the tradition of musical stars at St Paul's (Gustav Holst was Director of Music here, and wrote wonderful things for 'SPGS'), filling this post is never a problem. The senior Music teacher, Carl Jackson, is also seriously good. Eight out of 8 GCSE Music candidates got A in '95.

Art, on the other hand, is the poor relation, certainly in terms of time given, according to the Head of a good Foundation Course (there are outside assessors for Music and Art) – though all 7 pupils taking Art at A-level got As in '95.

There is an Olympic-sized swimming pool, two lacrosse pitches, a gym, tennis courts, etc. but not a school that worships team games. Much keener on intellectual matters such as debating, language exchanges, exchanges with the US, etc. There is work experience for all after GCSE, and job shadowing.

BACKGROUND AND ATMOSPHERE: The school opened in 1904 with money hived off from John Colet's Foundation, run by the Mercers' Company (Mercers abound on the governing body). A large, red-brick, purpose-built but mellow building nestling in Brook Green, surrounded by houses occupied by parents of would-be Paulinas. There is a calm but dynamic atmosphere: the school does not stand still, but neither does it strive to change. Good big imposing hall, plus Music Hall, new Science classrooms. There is no uniform but 'we like to be formal sometimes,' says the Head.

PASTORAL CARE AND DISCIPLINE: Has a slightly I'm-All-Right-Jack approach to discipline and care, both within and outside the school, but the school does produce a helpful leaflet full of telephone numbers for e.g. the Eating Disorder Association, and British Pregnancy Advisory Service, etc. Anna Ford's glamorous brother is (still) chaplain here and is one of the people who interviews candidates.

PUPILS AND PARENTS: Solid professional classes, with a sprinkling of barristers, cabinet ministers. A large Jewish contingent is a feature of the school. Pupils are incredibly articulate, with views on everything (no easy ride for parents) and a teeny tendency to intellectual arrogance. Pupils are mentally very tough indeed. Robustness on all fronts is essential for survival. 'Fine if your face fits,' said a pupil who was unhappy here.

An impressive array of OPs including Rosalind Franklin, Evelyn Sharp, Harriet Harman, Brigid Brophy, Joan Robinson, Shirley Summerskill, Shirley Conran, not to mention Carol Thatcher.

ENTRANCE: Regarded by most prep school Heads as the equivalent of finding the Holy Grail. Potential Paulinas are treated like Derby winners by their prep schools. The school sets its own exam papers in February for the following September, with a fine disregard for would-be pupils sitting other London girls' schools exams. It chooses pupils for their potential as much as their performance. A number from Bute House (formerly called St Paul's Girls' Preparatory School), otherwise one here and one there from London preps all over, including Hill House and Norland Place. It draws a good number from state primaries (and is always on the look-out for intellectual fodder).

EXIT: Look at the school honours board in the entrance hall – packed with Oxbridge entrants. Medicine is still very popular.

MONEY MATTERS: Foundation awards for Music and Art, a bursary named in honour of ex-High Mistress Baroness Brigstocke, but the real strength (or weakness, depending how you look at it) is up to 15 Assisted Places each year, including 5 in the Sixth Form.

REMARKS: St Paul's continues to reign confidently as the utterly wonderful, top girls' academic day school in London if not in the country. Much sought-after, and deservedly so.

St Swithun's School

Winchester, Hampshire SO21 1HA
Tel: 01962 861316, Fax: 01962 841874

PUPILS: Around 457 girls, 225 board, 232 day. Plus junior school, ages 3–11, including boys up to the age of 8.
AGES: 11–18
SIZE OF SIXTH FORM: 115
C OF E
FEE-PAYING

HEAD: Since 1995, Dr Helen Harvey BSc, PhD Bedford College, London (forties), was at school at Lordswood School, Birmingham, did her PhD in cancer research at the Royal Marsden in Surrey. Previously Head of Upper Chine School on the Isle of Wight. Dr Harvey is married to a medic, has two children, one in the school. Keen on sailing (crews for a boat moored at Cowes) and on music. Has an easy authority, is competent, and we feel the school is in safe hands. She says (fighting talk) that she has 'no plans for going co-ed'. The school has a nice Deputy Head.

Governing note: the visitor is the Bishop of Winchester, the Vice Chairman of the council is the Rev J A Cranmer, council members include the

Dean of Winchester, the mayor of Winchester, not to mention the Head of Winchester College. A Winchester production, in fact.

ACADEMIC MATTERS: 'Girls go in here,' said an observer, slightly bemused, 'and with no particular song and dance seem to come out with incredible A-level results'. This is one of the very few schools which will actually give exam statistics both with and without General Studies (all pupils do General Studies at A-level).

Very good, very steady results right across the mainstream subject board, e.g. Physics gets 79.2% A★/A grades at GCSE ('95) out of 45 pupils taking it. Also strong is General Studies – not simply the A-level paper, but the whole field of general education: 'we feel there are many things – to do with politics and philosophy, for example – which no girl should leave without knowing'.

Streaming for Maths and Modern Languages. All take nine GCSEs – there are no timetabling blocks, you can choose what (within reason) you wish. Three separate sciences for the majority. Some very pleasant classrooms, particularly in the English department – most conducive to study. NB Most teachers are women.

GAMES, OPTIONS, THE ARTS: The school has a modern Sports Hall opened by Princess Anne; and a swimming pool opened in '95 (built with the aid of an appeal) in which girls have buried a time-capsule. Also netball, riding, karate, cross-country, tennis, archery, D of E Award scheme – you name it.

There is an impressive technology centre under the five-star male Head, Mr Vaughan Clarke, where goggled girls operate industrial robots, and develop the most amazing ideas including, for example, a shuttlecock which makes a hum as it whizzes through the air – for partially sighted people, and a wonderful Heath Robinson device to separate clean hay from dirty in a rabbit hutch. St Swithun's girls won the Hampshire Technology Competition three years running and yet again in '95, and were regional winners of the Young Engineer of Britain.

Home Economics is compulsory in the first and third years – all part of the quest for a useful education – in gleaming kitchens.

Music is reputed to be good – as we write they are doing the wonderful but quite taxing Chichester Psalms. There are many orchestral groups, etc., and 'you can have a bash at anything, including the harp,' says a pupil. Art appears to be the poor relation – in an unloved small building with no sign of life, still or otherwise (though Art exam results are good).

There is a popular 16+ pre-driving course in Winchester.

BACKGROUND AND ATMOSPHERE: Founded by the Dean of Winchester in 1884 for the Christian education of the daughters of Winchester dons and clergy. Now housed in a huge '30s red-brick Queen Anne-style purpose-built building, which looks like an elegant army barracks, with lots of space, set a bit bleakly between motorway escarpment and main road in a green belt 20 minutes' walk into Winchester, with several additions and extensions plus the adjacent brick junior school. There are wonderful flower arrangements inside though, plus lots of polish, lots of light – big windows – and a statue meant to be St Swithun . . .

The separate day and boarding houses are cosy and warm. Lots of weekly boarders (very successful). The half-and-half breakdown of day/boarding 'makes for split in friendships', comments a pupil – except in the Upper Sixth when girls have their own mixed day and boarding house. There is also the familiar baleful feeling of girls stuck in boarding houses while the day pupils – as they perceive it – are larking about in Winchester.

There is no Saturday school but the new Head volunteers that there is a 'degree of compulsion' about weekend activities (what joy to a mother's ears) – otherwise it is so easy for them to loll in front of the television all day. Compulsory chapel. Rather uninviting libraries.

The atmosphere is generally one of 'good work ethic' and purposefulness plus sensible discipline. Occasional activities with 'or against' Winchester College, including dances, but despite St Swithunites putting up notices in town 'for God's sake communicate!' Wykehamists are largely unaroused and understandably viewed by some girls as 'off this planet'.

The uniform has a 'violently disliked' (by some) daisy on the front, the legacy of the school's wonderful ample-bosomed Victorian benefactress, Charlotte M. Yonge, authoress of *The Daisy Chain*.

Junior School: Tel 01962 852634, Fax: 01962 841874. Head: Mrs V A Lewis MA MSc, Dip Ed. Nursery, pre-prep and prep (boys go on at 8 to local prep schools, e.g. the Pilgrim's School, Farleigh). In the grounds of the main school, but autonomous. A fair number go on to the senior school, but also to girls' boarding schools, Downe House, St Mary's Calne, etc. There is no automatic entry to senior school.

PASTORAL CARE AND DISCIPLINE: Housemistresses are said to be 'caring and bothering' and individual teachers are largely well thought of – parents' rumblings, however, of 'failures of communication' and 'lack of supportive help' in the minefield of university applications (though Dr Harvey comments that pupils' hands are held every inch of the way and she cannot see what more could be done). 'It's out for drugs,' approves a parent living in Winchester, which manages to combine a safe middle-class environment with being the drugs capital of Wessex (NB there has been only one school drugs incident in recent years). The school is pretty strict on permission to go out or have visitors; fines for smoking and drinking of 'around £15'.

PUPILS AND PARENTS: 'Middle of the road grammar school' – pupils with IQs of 115+ – to quote the previous Head. Mostly from within a 50–100-mile radius. Children of middle-class professionals and business people, sisters of Wykehamists, a fairly large contingent of ex-pats, including Forces children, as well as a few foreigners, otherwise Londoners, many with weekend cottages off the M3. OGs: Baroness Warnock, Professor Joscelyn Toynbee.

ENTRANCE: Oversubscribed for CE at 11, 12, 13. Between a fifth and a quarter come up from the junior school. A handful of girls join at Sixth Form – no hard and fast qualifications for entry here: each pupil is judged on her particular merits.

EXIT: A fair number leave after GCSE – to Peter Symonds Sixth Form College in Winchester, and to boys' Sixth Forms. Otherwise, almost all to universities, including a good number to Oxbridge (e.g. a quarter of the Upper Sixth has been offered Oxbridge places as we write).

MONEY MATTERS: An unspecified number of scholarships are available (exams late January). Music scholarships give free music tuition. Also scholarships and some Assisted Places (not always taken up) for new intake at Sixth Form. The school has some hardship back-up money.

REMARKS: *The* academic girls' school in the Winchester area, in a strategic position just off the M3, less than an hour-and-a-half to London. Suffers slightly from the 'split-personality' of a school with day and boarding in almost equal make-up.

Sedbergh School

(Pronounced 'Sedber')

Sedbergh, Cumbria LA10 5HG

Tel: 01539 620535, Fax: 01539 621301

PUPILS: Around 350 boys. 340 board, 10 day

AGES: 11–18

SIZE OF SIXTH FORM: 140

C OF E

FEE-PAYING

HEAD: Since 1995, Mr Christopher Hirst MA (forties), educated at Merchant Taylors' and Trinity Cambridge. Previously Senior Housemaster at Radley under Dennis Silk, before that was Head of Kelly College. Historian and cricket blue. Currently chairman of HMC Sports Committee. Describes himself as a 'genuine enthusiast for boys' full boarding'.

The governing body shows a pretty solid and strategic body of academics.

ACADEMIC MATTERS: There is more pressure at the top to aim higher and work harder, and results are steady, rising gently: 'There's a sense of "getting boys through",' commented a parent. The school has a fairly broad spectrum of IQs, and good support groups for the less able. Maths and Sciences are the strongest

departments, Modern Languages has a new Head of department.

A detailed breakdown of results is not given, though a smart bound leaflet lists lots of statistics, e.g. 9 boys passed five A-levels in '95, 76 per cent of them at A grade, two boys passed one A-level etc – which is of limited use but we would add that the '95 A-level league tables list the school as averaging 6.4 points per subject, and that General Studies is an examinable subject.

The school gives unusually good careers advice and interview experience (with Old Boys and parents).

GAMES, OPTIONS, THE ARTS: Famed for its rugger and the Wilson Run – a 10-mile fell race open to ages 16+. Also a good cricket school. Takes regular trips abroad with games. There is a sports hall, and a 25-metre indoor pool. CCF (medals for shooting), strong naval links. D of E.

Good CDT and workshops, interesting Art and pottery. There is a magnificent Music School and good Drama. 'Not bad,' (said a father) on visiting speakers, and most societies are well supported. The CCF military band is much recommended.

BACKGROUND AND ATMOSPHERE: Founded in 1525 by Roger Lupton, a Provost of Eton, the original seven houses have been joined by a 'baby' house, Cressbrook, for state school entries at 11–13. Traditional dorms (large) have now been converted and updated. The limestone houses are throughout the tiny town: Music is in the former Bursar's House, Guldrey, on Main Street. The school made an impressive conversion of a Georgian building on the site of Lupton's original school into the Churchill Library (roof now mended, we are relieved to hear). The innovation of a Sixth Form House was vetoed by boys fiercely loyal to houses. A recent, jolly radio programme about life in a boarding school might be helping recruitment of pupils.

PASTORAL CARE AND DISCIPLINE: Some reports of bullying and booze reach us. The school has a well-thought-out punishment system, with points/endorsements, driving-licence style, pink cards for minor offences (a boy is 'pinked'), green for major. Also a good house system, with some 'super house-masters', according to pupils, parents and prep schools. Staff are caring: there is a positive atmosphere, with older boys and staff on a good footing. The programme is kept fairly busy at all times – possibly to lessen the sense of isolation: the school is miles from anywhere* in wonderful fell country, wild and wet.

*The Head points out that the school is in fact 5 minutes from the M6, 15 mins from a main line station and 70 mins from an international airport.

PUPILS AND PARENTS: Mainly local, some from Scotland. Professional and country parents. Boarding numbers are way down (there is room for many more) and the school has been busy recruiting. A healthy social mix, 20 ex-pats and 20 foreigners. OBs include Brendan Bracken, Will Carling, Sir Christopher Bland, Robert Swan, James Wilby.

ENTRANCE: CE, or to the Junior House via 11+ and interview.

EXIT: 2% post-GCSE; 80% to degree courses – reading subjects right across the board.

MONEY MATTERS: There are 5 Assisted Places for the Junior House, also scholarships, Assisted Places at Sixth Form, bursaries and music scholarships.

REMARKS: A traditional, all-male and well-structured games-orientated boarding school in an isolated area. Good at producing well-balanced, normal, unaffected boys with a strong sense of comradeship. The possibility of going co-educational has been rejected – at least for the time being.

Sevenoaks School

Sevenoaks, Kent TN13 1HU
Tel: 01732 455133, Fax: 01732 456143

PUPILS: Around 510 boys, 430 girls; 160 boys board, 350 day boys; 160 girls board, 270 day girls
AGES: 11–18
SIZE OF SIXTH FORM: 400
NON-DENOM
FEE-PAYING

HEAD: From 1996, Mr T R (Tommy) Cookson MA (early fifties), previously Head of King Edward VI Southampton where he made waves (metaphorically speaking). Takes over from Mr Richard Barker, who was here from '81 and built the school up from a fairly second-division place to a very popular, much-sought after one.

ACADEMIC MATTERS: The school has a determinedly up-to-date approach to teaching. One of the few public schools which offers (and has offered for some time) the International Bacca-laureate as an alternative to A-level – a course which is proving increasingly popular and hard to get in to do. (NB For the IB, three main and three subsidiary subjects are studied, including a Science, Maths, a Language and a national literature. The French may consider this the soft alternative, but for Brits only the academically OK will be allowed to take it.) In 1995, 150 Sixth Formers were reading the full IB diploma. (Astronomy is on offer and the school has its own observatory.)

Does particularly well at GCSE; also a good performer at A-level, though more Ds (and down) are noted here. A-level and IB results are lumped together (which is misleading). English, Maths and History are by far the most popular subjects here at the moment. Science has relatively weak results at A-level.

The school's great strength is Modern Languages – the IB course attracts keen linguists, who are well provided for, with unusual languages, e.g. Dutch, Norwegian and – newcomer – Japanese – on offer. There is a system of exchange visits during term to/from France, Germany, Spain, the Eastern bloc – pupils are 'expected' to go on 'one, two or three exchanges' (or four or five if double linguists) during their time at the school – including one or two before GCSE (this will bump up their results no end).

Results are also bumped up by the weeding out of weak pupils at Sixth Form and the injection of fresh academically able blood. This means that the school is far stronger academically at the top than at the bottom (see Entrance below).

GAMES, OPTIONS, THE ARTS: The school has several claims to fame on the games field: soccer has been 'exceptional' (even beat the Corinthian Casuals 6–1); girls' teams have represented the South-East in netball and squash. Sailing, shooting and tennis are all strong – victories include the Glanvill and Youll cups. The school has – among other things – three covered tennis courts, and is recommended by the LTA for budding tennis players. CCF is voluntary and popular and includes many girls.

Strong all round. There is plenty of scope for budding musicians. Also a thriving Drama department (with its own

theatre), and a public festival every year with 30 major productions, including an annual performance of a play in a foreign language. Most children do a creative subject (specialist craftsmen are employed for this). The school also has a studio for budding TV reporters. National pioneers for the Voluntary Service Unit: boys and girls are much encouraged to be community-minded.

BACKGROUND AND ATMOSPHERE: The school was founded in 1432 (it is now thought) by William Sennocke, Mayor of London and a friend of Henry V, as a thank-you for his share in the victory at Agincourt. A purposeful air of efficiency pervades. It is right in the main town of Sevenoaks, and its position and cramped buildings (new and old) give an almost claustrophobic feel to the place, but the school actually has 100 acres and opens up onto the gracious acres of Knole Park behind.

Two-and-a-half new boarding houses have been built recently – numbers of boarders have actually risen, also the number of girls, so that the school is now more balanced. However, it is still predominantly day, and the nightly exodus can be disruptive, causing some pretty heavy resentment on the part of boarders who see themselves locked up while their day pupil peers lark about in town.

NB The school feels like two different animals – a powerful and international Sixth Form (mainly boarding) on the one hand, and an ordinary town day school running up to GCSE on the other. The two co-exist a bit uneasily.

PASTORAL CARE AND DISCIPLINE: Considered good and firm. The school is giving more emphasis to the 'planned development of personal and social skills'. A school counsellor has been appointed to work alongside the house staff. Strong house system. The out-going Head regularly and tirelessly sends letters to day parents, giving guidance on social life, parties, etc. The school tests pupils for drug abuse.

PUPILS AND PARENTS: Largely local, favoured by professional and media parents, some diplomatic. Many bilingual hybrids and budding linguists, attracted by the school's reputation for languages. 20% of pupils are foreigners, many of them European, from 42 different countries. 'And it's so fashionable to be foreign,' said an English parent. 'Your child comes back speaking with ze foreign accent.' Don't expect them to want to settle down in this country afterwards.

Old boys and girls include Professor Simon Donaldson, Oliver Taplin, Lord Prout, Jeremy Harris, Paul Adams, Emma Johnson (Young Musician of the Year), Chris Tavare, Paul Downton, Emma Hope (shoe designer).

ENTRANCE: At 11 and 13 via the school's own exam or CE for entry from 11–16. No automatic entry at Sixth Form, however, and parents of 11–13-year-olds would do well to bear this in mind when applying. A £1,000 deposit is required on the offer of a place. Eighty pupils come in at Sixth Form – strong candidates and the school is over-subscribed; parents wanting the IB have been known to consider bribing the school in their keenness to get in.

EXIT: Fluctuating numbers to Oxbridge. The University of London is popular, otherwise to a wide variety of universities (including overseas). Expolys are popular for Business Courses. Medicine and engineering are favoured careers. Some do a gap year.

MONEY MATTERS: Offers 55 academic scholarships a year and 5 Assisted Places.

REMARKS: A popular day and boarding co-ed school (formerly boys' only) which has built up its strength on the back of its International Bac programme, taking in able students at Sixth Form for this.

Sheffield High School

10 Rutland Park, Sheffield s10 2PE
Tel: 01142 660324, Fax: 01142 678520
PUPILS: Approx 797 pupils, including 252 in junior department
ALL DAY
AGES: 4–18
SIZE OF SIXTH FORM: Around 115
NON-DENOM
FEE-PAYING

HEAD: Since 1989, Mrs Margaret Houston, BA (early fifties). Educated at St Hilda's, Whitby, and read English at Leeds University. Has been teaching all her life in grammars and comprehensives. Previous post as Deputy Head of Harrogate Grammar School. Married with two children. Husband teaches in a Sixth Form college.

ENTRANCE: Automatic entry from the junior school; tests in English, Maths, verbal reasoning for entry to senior school from elsewhere.

EXIT: Some post-GCSE (the expansion of neighbouring Birkdale hasn't helped); the majority to go on to Higher Education (Sheffield and Sheffield Hallam, Newcastle, Birmingham and Bristol are favoured), 6 to Oxbridge in '95.

REMARKS: This useful GPDST girls' day school should be a star in Sheffield but for many reasons, not least the resistance in the area to private education, it is not. It is solid and worthy rather than inspiring, and perhaps a bit lacking in energy in some areas. Latin is taught to all, however, and separate sciences. German, Russian, Spanish and Greek are offered.

A flyer in the prospectus announces that '95 saw 'our best results ever' and government data show average A-level points per subject as 7.2 though NB all girls do General Studies at A-level which bumps up the school's league table position considerably.

The buildings are in a quiet backwater tucked away in the smarter area of Sheffield. The Victorian main building has bits and bobs added on: no frills and not much space – but adequate. The school has two newish Information Technology labs with Nimbus Network and computerised careers and library areas (pleasant library). Also a Sixth Form Centre. Has in the recent past joined with Birkdale School (qv) for some Sixth Form studies, but this arrangement has been terminated. This is a pity for the High School, and it is now losing pupils to the newly co-ed Birkdale on the doorstep. There are 16 Assisted Places in each year group, some bursaries for the needy.

The recently opened junior school on the same site has helped stabilise numbers.

Sherborne School

Sherborne, Dorset DT9 3AP
Tel: 01935 812249, Fax: 01935 817511

PUPILS: Around 620 boys, all board except for 30

AGES: 13–18

SIZE OF SIXTH FORM: 260

C OF E

FEE-PAYING

HEAD: Since 1988, Mr Peter Lapping, MA (fifties), educated at St John's College, Johannesburg, University of Natal (read History) and Lincoln College, Oxford (PPE). Contracted until retirement (next century). Previously Head of Shiplake College. Solid presence, a good manager. His apparently gentle manner belies an inner steel. Keen on producing boys 'who have their feet on the ground, are equipped to face life and don't think the world owes them a living'. Has made strenuous efforts over the last few years to ensure more personal contact between staff (himself included) and boys.

ACADEMIC MATTERS: Results are steady, with a handful of lively staff among many traditional practitioners. Best results are in Maths and Modern Languages (small numbers doing exotic languages e.g. Japanese invariably get As at A-level). Science results are reasonable. There are eight sets of varying ability. The Classics department is still waving the flag – two did Greek at A-level in '95 (both got As), eleven took Latin. Changes to the curriculum mean all boys now take 10 GCSEs. French is no longer compulsory, but one Modern Language (in a well-designed teaching block) is essential. Since '93, all boys must take three separate science exams, 'though we are prepared to review this in special circumstances'. Prep ('Hall') on Sunday evenings.

The school has a well-stocked, well-used careers department under Mr Craig Bryson, assisted by the great and good Mr Rob Lloyd.

GAMES, OPTIONS, THE ARTS: The games record is still extremely strong and playing fields cover 50 acres. Games are compulsory till 16, and many boys continue thereafter. Very strong CCF (marines an option).

The school has a successful Art department under the enthusiastic, flamboyant Trevor Boyd, and runs excellent inexpensive trips to Paris and Amsterdam. Very good Drama, and plenty of it, at various levels (the Powell Hall theatre is used by visiting theatre groups). There is a lively and thought-provoking programme of talks by visitors (and sometimes boys) often given in masters' drawing rooms. Some 'study options' at Sixth Form are undertaken with Sherborne Girls (qv).

The school has a new structured minority studies programme to ensure breadth and continuation of more non-examinable subjects, including an excellent Modern Languages course pioneered here by the Head of department. Lots of discussion and debate – boys do well in public speaking. Good Music – ambitious programmes, two orchestras (with girls), jazz groups; over half the boys learn an instrument.

BACKGROUND AND ATMOSPHERE: A glorious setting, with rich honey-coloured ancient buildings around a huge gravelled courtyard, in the shadow of the Abbey. There are many later additions. Founded by Edward VI as a grammar school in 1550 (though its origins go back to 8th-century Benedictine Abbey links), the school has a splendid library with a famous hammerbeam roof. (The loveliness of the setting and the collegiate atmosphere bring in a nice little income from visiting film companies.)

The school has nine houses (choose with care), some scattered around the town; boys in dark blue guernseys with files/books scurry everywhere (the townspeople speak well of boys on the whole). Most boarding houses have been refurbished and more study bedrooms introduced (bedsits, usually shared, from second/third year onwards). The Abbey House outsize dorm (32 beds) has been kept and now carpeted – by popular request (the boys love it), despite the Inspectorate's recommendations. A lack of privacy in study areas has worried some

parents/boys in the past. A strong sense of tradition and moral fibre pervades.

Lively social life with both Sherborne and Leweston girls (aka 'bimbos on the hill' by the former). 'The Stick' (a pretty grizzly Sixth Form common room) is open to Sherborne boys and girls on Saturday nights. Food is plentiful; parents have complained in the past that it is a bit 'heavy on chips' but the school points out it has recently won the Heartbeat Award by Dorset County Council for 'healthy eating options'. Supper at 6 p.m. – boys' pantries are in full swing after prep at 9.15 p.m.

PASTORAL CARE AND DISCIPLINE: The Head is not afraid to sack for drugs (about one a year) and occasional OTT behaviour (ditto). There is a resident Tutor (sometimes two) in every house, plus Housemaster (and family); now two chaplains. Firm rules; slacking is frowned on. The school has a well-thought-out programme of personal development, health education, etc., for Fourth Formers; parents are called in *en masse* to co-opt for potential difficult times. The school operates a policy of testing for drug abuse. Physical exercise (runs, etc.) as a punishment have been 'adjusted' as a result of the Children Act inspectors. The emphasis is on responsibility (care and concern) not power/ privilege of authority: there is a clever initiation course for new prefects – a mini managerial teach-in with an Outward Bound-ish session with staff on Exmoor, when boys must run everything, including budgeting, role playing, etc., to give them confidence with their peer group.

PUPILS AND PARENTS: Sensible, self-confident, civilised, relatively unsophisticated – applies to pupils and parents alike. Appeals to parents in the professions and Services (lots and lots of the latter). OBs include David Shepherd, Nigel Dempster, Jeremy Irons, John le Carré (also, appropriately enough, the Head of MI6), A N Whitehead, Christopher Chataway, Richard Eyre, Michael Hopkinson the architect, the King of Swaziland.

ENTRANCE: At 13 via CE.

EXIT: To a broad spread of universities (93%), between 15–20 to Oxbridge each year, Scottish unis, Newcastle, Southampton, Bristol, Reading for agriculture; medicine, law and other conservative careers are popular.

MONEY MATTERS: The recession took a swipe, and numbers were down – but not by much and, on paper, they appear strong for the future. Unusual fiscal move: all departments in the school are now responsible for their own budgets. The Bursar shows them the annual figures. The school also owns the Study Centre, a school for foreign boys, mainly from the Far East, teaching English and preparing them for other schools/public examinations; this tidy little earner will soon provide a scholarship fund for Sherborne Boys'.

There are 3 academic scholarships at half fees, 2 at quarter fees. Also 8 exhibitions worth one-fifth fees (especially for those with proficiency in Science); one full-fees' worth of Music awards each year, plus up to 2 full-fee Sixth Form scholarships – well worth knowing about as it is now unusual to have scholarships of more than 50%. Various bursaries and other awards are available.

REMARKS: A traditional and strong public school charging on, doing a thorough job producing young men who are healthy in body, mind and soul, if perhaps sometimes a little over-sheltered?

Sherborne School for Girls

Sherborne, Dorset DT9 3QN
Tel: 01935 812245, Fax: 01935 814973

PUPILS: Around 420 girls; boarding except for about 18
AGES: 11–18
SIZE OF SIXTH FORM: 155
C OF E
FEE-PAYING

HEAD: Since 1985, Miss June Taylor, BSc (fifties). Home-grown: educated at Sherborne School for Girls (Head Girl) and Sussex University (Mathematics). Taught at Sherborne, and was a Housemistress here for fifteen years before becoming Head. Imposing, and extremely perceptive about 'her girls' – though pupils have little chance to get to know her during their years in the school and (wrongly) suspect that she does not know them. Fiercely wants the best for them and urgently desires girls to make the most of their talents. Accused by her critics of 'not listening'. Invited to spend a sabbatical term teaching Maths at St Hugh's College, Oxford.

ACADEMIC MATTERS: The school provides thorough and solid teaching all round, and facilities are exceptionally good. However, there is some dead wood among the staff – girls (particularly at Sixth Form) find a lack of inspiration in some areas and some parents feel their daughters deserve better. There are occasional beefs from parents and pupils about not being able to mix subjects at A-level despite claims of flexibility. As one parent commented, 'It seems strange in a big strong school.' Careers and university advice could be improved. Class sizes vary from 20+ to far fewer; girls are streamed early on into four bands (and can be shifted). NB Girls in the lower stream may finally gain better results than those in the top. Strong English, Sciences and Maths; also Russian is outstandingly successful under the wonderful Dr Daphne West. The school provides good Modern Language teaching in general (satellite reception for foreign broadcasts is well used). Sixth Form options and the General Studies programme are under review – the Head is dead keen on breadth, 'also on getting girls to discuss issues', and a good new Cultural Studies slot does just this.

GAMES, OPTIONS, THE ARTS: This is a strong games school (with large numbers of Sixth Formers in teams), hockey and lacrosse, good tennis teams, squash. There is a splendid new Sports Hall. The school has a fine Music department, especially on the choral side (including a notable madrigal group – Emma Kirkby is an OG), all run by the ever-dynamic Miss Augusta Miller. Some orchestral playing with Sherborne Boys. The school has a splendid Art block, with jewellery making, Design Technology. Home Economics, Textiles, dressmaking, Drama are all available, though the girls 'yearn' for more drama and better facilities for it. There is some criticism that the school could/should coerce the girls to participate more in extra-curricular activities.

BACKGROUND AND ATMOSPHERE: Founded in 1899, the school is a large, architecturally dreary purpose-built conglomeration on a 40-acre site on the edge of the town, looking out over open country, with many later additions (particularly depressing compared to the boys' school). It has close links with the (glorious) Abbey. There are daily prayers at school assembly. Food is good and all meals are eaten in houses (with accompanying emphasis on table talk and

table manners). Recommended House: Aylmar. The new Upper Sixth House (Mulliner) known as the Sherborne Hilton (where the food gets far lower marks), opened in '93 and is spacious, with a lift, though bare white walls have also earned it the nickname of the Lunatic Asylum.

Girls are kept busy and occupied most of the time, and a purposeful atmosphere pervades, though the usual girls' school complaints of not enough happening at weekends persist, and visitors comment on kilted girls 'wandering aimlessly about the town at weekends'. Social life with Sherborne Boys is available (and occasionally distracting), sometimes officially (dinner parties, discos, etc.). There is an underlying ethos of working hard and playing hard.

PASTORAL CARE AND DISCIPLINE: There are eight houses (competitive), mixed ages: choose carefully. House staff vary in fierceness or otherwise, many have dogs (useful for night walking/ checking). A Tutor system exists more in principle than in practice. Which said, girls are well cared for. The school has a sensible outlook on discipline, though some parents are critical of the amount of television watched. The number of exeats has slightly increased (and exceptions can be made).

PUPILS AND PARENTS: Homogenised. Sizeable numbers of daughters of Old Girls; also popular with army families (80 girls at last count), diplomats, Londoners with south-west connections. Girls are friendly, supportive, high-spirited. There is the occasional public school tendency of the privileged to think the world owes them a living. Among the OGs are Maria Aitken, Dame Diana Reader-Harris, and the first woman to make the board of M & S – Clara Freeman.

ENTRANCE: Two-thirds come in at 12+, one-third at 13+. From 1996, there is also 11+ entry and the school sent letters to likely prep schools announcing this. Very definitely selective. Also at Sixth Form.

EXIT: Practically all go on to university (a good number to Oxbridge). The fashionable choices – Edinburgh, Manchester, St Andrews, Nottingham, Durham, Bristol – are all popular. Substantial numbers do medicine and languages. Also to Art and Music colleges. A gap year is favoured.

MONEY MATTERS: There are 5 major academic scholarships, 2 exhibitions; 3 Music scholarships; 1 Sixth Form scholarship.

REMARKS: Just holding its ground as a strong traditional all-round girls' boarding school, with a slight sense that it needs to shake up its act in order to maintain this. Very much a girls' only school despite loads of social life and some joint undertakings with Sherborne Boys'.

Shiplake College

Henley-on-Thames,
Oxfordshire RG9 4BW
Tel: 01734 40255, Fax: 01734 402455

PUPILS: Approx 310 boys. 235 board, 75 day
AGES: 13–18
SIZE OF SIXTH FORM: 116
C OF E
FEE-PAYING

HEAD: Since 1988, Mr Nicholas Bevan, MA (Oxon) (fifties), educated Shrewsbury and Balliol College, Oxford. Soldiered for five years before deciding to become a teacher (trained at St John's College, Cambridge). Taught at Westminster, then Shrewsbury, where parents latterly considered him one of the best Housemasters. Charming, approachable, dead honest (not all are). Married with four children. Teaches 'a very little' Geography, knows the boys, and is to be found 'everywhere' – he will cover for most emergencies. Very proud of Shiplake (he insisted on showing us the view himself, despite the boy-guide standing in the background) and is almost boyish in his enthusiasm. Very go-ahead, and very good at Public Relations. Recently advertised a school Open Day on Classic FM; keen on local involvement.

ACADEMIC MATTERS: Copes well with less able boys and has an excellent unit for those with dyslexia and specific learning difficulties (one of the first in the country; 16–24 boys are admitted each year, remedial English is timetabled instead of French, but there is no overall use of lap-tops). Remedial English is offered throughout. The school is well spoken of by many preps, who use it as a standby for those who fail to make their first choice of mainstream academic school. The less able shine here and numbers are viable, despite contingency plans having been made for a fall-off in numbers.

Small classes, maximum 16. Career planning starts early, timetabled from Fifth Year, and sensible advice is given on appropriate GCSE and A-level options. Boys are not academically submerged, the policy being 'to obtain the maximum results with the minimum of fuss' in the words of the late Head. The 'best chap' in '95 got four As at A-level, 'and you can't do much better than that', comments the Head. 17 A-levels are offered. Pik 'n' Mix A-level boards – depending which suits best.

No shame is attached to retakes. Maths and Physics are still the main strengths, but Classical History is popular, as are Media Studies and Geography. French and Spanish are on the up. A new academic Tutor system has been introduced, as well as a supervised study period. Computers are everywhere.

GAMES, OPTIONS, THE ARTS: Games are thriving – particularly rugby, hockey (beat Pangbourne – deadly rivals), squash, tennis and cricket. Astroturf. There is a huge and much used Sports Hall; rowing is seriously popular with regular tours abroad: Amsterdam, the Ukraine and the States. The school has a tradition of producing Olympic rowers. Compulsory CCF, adventure training (trips to Kenya and South Wales) and Young Enterprise; as well as work experience.

CDT is very strong, with good workshop and draughting facilities. The school has a brilliant ceramics teacher and very strong Art (a new Head has just come from King Edward's Birmingham). Enthusiastic public speaking. Music and Drama are particularly inspired – with regular plays in the tithe barn and fabulous spectaculars round the main house in the summer term organised by Malcolm Woodcock.

BACKGROUND AND ATMOSPHERE: Established 1959, in a stunning setting overlooking the River Thames. There is a Great Hall in the main school used for assembly and a dining room (all beautifully newly lit). The school has a big building programme – the newest thing is a pavilion/day boy house complex which includes a Conference Centre, flats for staff as well as a ritzy room for day boys. There are strong house bonds, very traditional with an emphasis on developing self-discipline. Boys graduate from largish dorms to study bedrooms.

Houses have Common Rooms (the upholstery is being revamped, the Head assures us) with a kitchen, and senior boys run the 'Junior Common Room' with bar.

PASTORAL CARE AND DISCIPLINE: Boys are fiercely caring of each other; this is a small school, so 'no real problems'. A good House Master/Tutorial system is run on old-fashioned lines. Very good handling of bullying (not much anyway); smoking equals a fine; drink is no problem (own bar); drugs mean automatic expulsion. The Head will sack and has: three cases in five years – mainly bullying. Perceived as a 'tough' school.

PUPILS AND PARENTS: From all over, traditional parents and lots of first-time buyers (close to London – lots of Londoners). Boys are a polite and gentlemanly breed of chaps. About 35 'from abroad', with 12 'real' foreigners. There are regular parent/staff consultations.

ENTRANCE: Mostly from prep schools: CE at 13+, plus the school's own English paper. School's own English, Maths and IQ paper from state schools. And the Head's report in both cases. Boys with difficulties in English need to book early: they are assessed by the Remedial Department nine months before entry and 25% are turned away at interview. 60+ boys from over 50 prep schools. Sixth Form entrants come on the basis of five GCSEs and the Head's report. In all cases, the Head's report rules supreme.

EXIT: Some leakage after GCSE (often financially based), otherwise around 24 to universities (one to Oxbridge), plus 13 to Diploma Courses, and in '95 an excellent 8 to Art Foundation courses.

MONEY MATTERS: A few bad payers. Will 'try to help with financial crisis during exam years'. The occasional music scholarship (usually awarded internally), plus 1 bursary a year for Services, plus discounts for sons of prep school masters and the occasional discretionary bursary for outstanding boys, plus a 10% reduction in Sixth Form for the best GCSE results.

REMARKS: A super, confidence-building establishment in the public school mould. Academically now more challenging, much sought-after for the Remedial Department. Under-achievers elsewhere can come up trumps, and boys of quite mediocre ability achieve degree courses previously considered unthinkable.

Shrewsbury High School

32 Town Walls, Shrewsbury, Shropshire SY1 1TN
Tel: 01743 362872, Fax: 01743 364942

PUPILS: Around 600 girls in total: 405 in the senior school; plus junior school, with 175 girls ages 4–11.
ALL DAY
AGES: 11–18
SIZE OF SIXTH FORM: Around 80
FEE-PAYING

HEAD: Since 1990, Miss Susan Gardner, MA (forties). Born and bred in the Home Counties, grammar-school educated, read History at University College, London. Previously Head at a co-ed voluntary-aided school in Essex. This is her first time at a single-sex school. Most charming, open, a listener, girlish; her style is in tremendous contrast to her predecessor, and is appreciated by

staff ('we're all on Christian name terms') and parents ('we can talk to her and she listens'). Spends a good deal of time with the girls, 'as an ex-classroom practitioner'.

ACADEMIC MATTERS: The one and only academic girls' private day school for miles around: it has a huge catchment area. Solid results. 20 did General Studies at A-level in '95. Only 32 pupils actually sitting A-levels in the Upper Sixth – i.e. not a large Sixth Form. A second Modern Language (German) is introduced at the age of 12, along with Latin. Greek is no longer automatically on offer. DT is well established and extremely well taught (by a colourful ex-lecturer in 20th-century design at Lancaster University). The school gives good university advice, involving parents and daughters (urged to start looking/ thinking in the pre-Sixth Form summer).

GAMES, OPTIONS, THE ARTS: Some county athletes, hockey, netball and tennis players; tennis is probably their strongest sport (though they produced a national hockey player in '95). The school has the use of six local tennis courts and a swimming pool, to supplement its own games pitches: sport is relatively low profile (the lot of many day schools, especially those which cater for pupils travelling long distances). Rowing is available at Sixth Form, thanks to Shrewsbury School, and some girls go on to row for their universities.

Keen on Drama ('But I wish we could do more,' from a pupil) and Music. Also nice Art. Some careers talks, Drama, etc., with Shrewsbury (lots of girls have brothers over the river).

BACKGROUND AND ATMOSPHERE: The school was founded in 1885 (GPDST), in a lovely setting (away from the town centre), south-facing, with grounds sloping down to the River

Severn, directly opposite Shrewsbury School (whence boys were seen jogging in the snow on the day of our visit). Buildings are a mixture of old and new, including a separate Sixth Form House and a Music block. A lively and stimulating ambience.

The thriving junior school nearby has all its own facilities (including Technology) on site (entry at 4, 7 and 9).

PASTORAL CARE AND DISCIPLINE: The school is small enough to allow staff to know individuals well; Miss Gardner is 'dead keen' on working closely with parents.

PUPILS AND PARENTS: A very broad social mix of backgrounds, including lawyers, doctors, farmers and landowners. From Staffordshire, Wales, Cheshire as well as locally. Bright and bushy-tailed girls, with pleasant manners; not afraid to state their own views, and relatively unsophisticated compared with metropolitan pupils, but polished Sixth Formers.

ENTRANCE: Many from the junior school; 11+ selective exams. Entry possible in other years. Some leave pre-Sixth Form; places are quickly filled.

EXIT: A gap year for some, the bulk straight on to a big cross-section of old and new universities – 5–6 to Oxbridge in a good year, some to Welsh unis – to read anything from Marine Biology to Fashion with Technology, from American Studies to Medicine; a surprisingly large number went on to read Business Management or Administration in '95.

MONEY MATTERS: There are 14 Assisted Places at 11+, 2 at 16+; 3 scholarships at 11+ and 4 at Sixth Form. Some bursaries. Fees are very reasonable.

REMARKS: A girls' school with a deservedly good local reputation that prepares pupils well for the next step.

Shrewsbury School

The Schools, Shrewsbury,
Shropshire SY3 7BA
Tel: 01743 344537, Fax: 01743 340048
PUPILS: Around 690 boys, 550 board,
140 day
AGES: 13–18
SIZE OF SIXTH FORM: 271
C OF E
FEE-PAYING

HEAD: Since 1988, Mr Edward Maidment, MA (fifties) ('Ted'), educated at Pocklington School, Scholar and Choral Scholar at Jesus College, Cambridge. Read History. Previously Headmaster of Ellesmere College. A bachelor and a keen singer; jovial, larger-than-life, refreshing (though some find his tongue a wee bit sharp). Definitely good at selling the school, and witty. Widely considered one of the best Heads in the business. Knows the boys remarkably well, and is convinced that 'the heart of a good and successful education is not quantifiable'.

Fosters strong links with prep schools – 'important at a time when curriculum developments do not favour the 13+ entry'. Most interesting and articulate on the subject of boarding, adding to familiar arguments 'the deep and detailed knowledge of the individual' by Housemasters, Tutors and academic staff, plus strong resources which mean far more is possible in terms of achievement for the individual. Enjoys quoting Cecil Day-Lewis, 'Selfhood begins with a walking away/And love is proved in the letting go.'

ACADEMIC MATTERS: Does very well indeed for boys of all levels (a fair number of scholars, the majority are average, some below average). The school has some excellent staff (the Head believes in waiting till he gets the right person and is encouraged by governors to cast far afield: two new members – including the Second Master – were previously in the Green Jackets, two more have come in direct from industry). Sciences are still very popular (though Chemistry A-level results were a bit disappointing for '95). The Biology department, under Ian Lacey, is particularly noteworthy. It has an electronic microscope, and an amazing collection of pickled organs. A new Chemistry and IT building open in '96. Maths is also strong; and languages are on the up – Japanese and Russian have been added to the menu.

The wonderful ancient library is one of the most important scholarly public-school libraries. In '95, 17 took General Studies at A-level (helping the league table position look healthy), Business Studies and Religious Studies were also very popular. Nine pupils took AS-levels (French and Maths). There were six full-time, eight part-time women on the staff at the last count (compared with none in 1987).

The school has a strong careers department and solid industrial links. School workshops are flourishing.

GAMES, OPTIONS, THE ARTS: Famous for rowing, and strong on most games, aware 'of our superior fitness', as one Salopian commented. Music is very vigorous, 'talent brought out and developed' according to parents. (A new Music block is in the pipeline; current facilities are not up to the talent). Art is taken seriously (pottery notable) and Drama is highly thought of by locals as well as the school. Art and History

departments combine for trips (Italy – Rome and Urbino; France – Paris and Versailles) – hugely successful, adding extra dimensions for all.

The school has a reputation for Outward Bound-ish activities (basic camping, fell walking – tough leadership skills and all that), and serious community work (the Head is dead keen). Also attracts many visiting speakers ('No, we don't feel isolated'). Boys are definitely encouraged to be outward-looking, especially towards Europe. The highly successful annual conference on European Affairs (requiring considerable stamina from the Lower Sixth) brought officials from their London embassies for debates following pupils' strenuous efforts to recruit their help.

BACKGROUND AND ATMOSPHERE: Founded in 1552 (at one time reckoned to be the largest school in England), revived by Samuel Butler at the end of the 18th century and moved from the town to its present splendid position, fortress-like, across the river. A lovely campus: buildings on 'the site' are spread out, boys seen scudding about everywhere. The grounds are superbly kept. A terrific refurbishment programme to all houses is still in progress (cost: £4 million). Day boys have their own houses. All houses eat at their own table in the communal dining hall (good food). NB Breakfast and supper are cafeteria-style, lunch is formal, with set tables, grace, lower boys serving from trolleys and prefects giving out notices. ('Some formality helps the table manners no end,' observed a father.) Chapel is three times a week; Moreton Hall girls and Shrewsbury High girls combine with boys for some Music, Drama, etc., not to mention socializing.

PASTORAL CARE AND DISCIPLINE: 'Know your boys' is still the Head's motto on discipline. Houses are now for 55, with a well-used/structured tutor system. Boys choose their own Tutors. Housemasters are very much encouraged to contact boys' parents. All staff are trained up to be watchful shepherds: the Head is forever watching the boys, 'but caringly, not critically,' said one.

PUPILS AND PARENTS: Steady civilized chaps with an ease of manner. The catchment area is vast – Norfolk, Scotland, the North of England. Having said this, many are local. Lots of sons of Old Boys (loyalty is a strong point). The fascinating list of Old Salopians includes Sir Philip Sydney, Monsignor Ronald Knox, Charles Darwin, Edmund Hillary, Michael Heseltine, Michael Palin, Richard Ingrams, Willie Rushton, Paul Foot, Michael Abrahams, John Peel (the DJ, that is).

ENTRANCE: By CE, but early registration is recommended. Droves of boys via all the top prep schools for miles around, Abberley and Prestfield especially, also Malsis. There are also some places at Sixth Form.

EXIT: A good number to Oxbridge, and it is rare for the rest not to take a degree. Many take a year off 'which is a state of mind', the Head tells them. 'You can go to just as distant places within yourselves working among the handicapped at home as travelling exotically.'

MONEY MATTERS: There are 17 academic, 4 music scholarships at age 13, 2 at Sixth Form. Two hundred boys are supported by the school (thanks to a Foundation recently set up along American lines to provide extra funds).

REMARKS: Still one of the strongest public schools in the country,

despite being geographically disadvantaged. One of the very select few left with boys only. Has a good blend of tradition and forward-looking attitudes, and produces self-confident boys. There are one or two comments from educationalists that the school could be in danger of becoming complacent, but this could be competitive gripes. A connoisseur's choice.

South Hampstead High School

3 Maresfield Gardens, London NW3 5SS
Tel: 0171 435 2899, Fax: 0171 431 8022

PUPILS: 630 girls, plus junior school of about 250 girls, ages 4–11
ALL DAY
AGES: 11–18
SIZE OF SIXTH FORM: Around 150
NON-DENOMINATIONAL
FEE-PAYING

HEAD: Since 1993, Mrs Jean Scott BSc (forties), educated at Wellington School, Ayr, and Glasgow University; read Zoology, teaches Biology. Previously Head of St George's School, Edinburgh, and before that Deputy Head of Ipswich High ('So I understand how GPDSTs work and think'). Widowed, with two grown-up children. Precise, spruce, straightforward, sensible. Keen on music, jazz included. 'I had imagined that I might find the girls very much more sophisticated here – but they're very like Edinburgh girls ... they have the same pressures on them to achieve.'

The dust is beginning to settle after a particularly difficult start to Mrs Scott's reign.

ACADEMIC MATTERS: Very strong, and Science is no longer the poor relation – Maths and Chemistry are among the most popular A-level subjects (also French, History, English). Interestingly, although Chemistry attracted 21 candidates for A-level in '95, almost half of them only got Ds or Es. However, expectations, as we said before, are extremely high here, and teaching is of a high calibre and challenging: staff are desperately committed.

To avoid competition, there is no grading internally, 'And they've got to be bright to be here anyway – but they all know precisely who is best.' Girls are kept on their toes in all subjects, with the emphasis on breadth (the Head is very keen on this), and there is a wide programme of non-examinable General Studies in the Lower Sixth.

Teaching is rigorous; sloppy thinking is not allowed. An AS-level is increasingly popular as a fourth examined subject. IT is well established; Art is very good indeed.

GAMES, OPTIONS, THE ARTS: Not a gamesy school though girls always do very well in netball (girls play for Middlesex at various ages); there is also a strong tennis team and currently one or two notably talented gymnasts and judo practitioners. Girls walk to Swiss Cottage for swimming and the Sports Centre, and to Hampstead Cricket Club for athletics and hockey.

Lots going on: 'a real buzz'. Girls organise speakers regularly. The Music department continues to be strong under Dr Parmley (appointed '93), especially in singing, with 40 visiting teachers (not nothing), a new Music Studio made out of two classrooms, a new wind band, and e.g. a tour of the USA in '94.

The school has a programme of exchanges with France, Germany and Spain, culminating in work experience placements for Sixth Form students in 'their' countries. Some drama with University College School (qv) boys. A sprouting of computers, both in the senior and junior schools.

BACKGROUND AND ATMOSPHERE: Unprepossessing red-brick North London buildings tucked conveniently behind Swiss Cottage. The school was founded in 1876 – the ninth of the GPDST schools – and moved to its present site in 1882, and has been added to and adapted ever since. The dining area has circular tables (much friendlier than traditional school refectory tables) and there is a swipe-card system for paying for school lunches.

Intake has been increased to four classes per year and the size cut from 26/8 to 24 – this overall increase has been made possible by the acquisition of Oakwood Hall next door, which is now a Sixth Form centre, plus crèche for staff babies in the basement ('very trendy,' comments the Head). Some areas of the school are still down at heel, and there are some austere and traditional old-fashioned classrooms, though the Head has been addressing this, adding carpets, etc. There is no prefect system, but all Sixth Formers submit a CV and have an interview for the post of Head Girl and her (three) Deputies. The sensible uniform allows trousers or skirt.

Junior School: South Hampstead High Junior Department, numbers 5 and 12 Netherhall Gardens NW3 5TG. Tel: 0171 794 7198, Fax 0171 431 2750. Head: Miss K M Stayt BEd, London. Entrance at 4+ (kindergarten entry started in '94) and 7+ via telling testettes (no longer at 5+). NB If you flunk first time you can now resit at 7+. Register 2 years before date of entry. All go on to the senior school. Very pressured indeed. Bright and very active. In a cul-de-sac, with plenty of space –

good selling point for London, and it's got the kindergarten attached.

PASTORAL CARE AND DISCIPLINE: Hard working, though not pressure-cooked. 'This place breeds survivors,' comments a parent. There is a structured Personal, Social and Health Education syllabus for the senior school.

PUPILS AND PARENTS: Large numbers from bright Jewish and Asian families ('very strongly family-minded they are too,' comments the Head, who thinks this may be what restrains over-sophistication). A wide social mix from far corners of North and North-West London as well as many locals. Among parents are Hampstead media, actors, psychotherapists. 'Pretty pushy' commented a recent parent. Girls are (despite the school's ethos) competitive, ambitious, hard-working, self-confident, notably articulate and totally unfazed about putting forward their own opinions with adults, however distinguished. They are also friendly and relaxed. OGs include Rabbi Julia Neuberger, Helena Bonham-Carter, Dilys Powell, Fay Weldon.

ENTRANCE: Highly selective and oversubscribed. Searching entry tests and interviews. Increasingly via the school's own (enlarged) junior school. Many from state schools. About 10 places at Sixth Form – to fill leavers' places and new places available to clever girls (entrance exams in proposed A-level subjects, plus you need three As at GCSE in the subjects).

EXIT: Practically all to university, reading all manner of subjects; sometimes a gap year. 18 to Oxbridge in '95, 19 in '93. Tough careers follow naturally.

MONEY MATTERS: There are 1 (or 2) scholarships of half fees for girls who top the entrance exams. Also 1 (or 2) Sixth Form scholarships (available internally and externally). 10 assisted places at 11+, 2 at 16+. Like all GPDST schools, good value and relatively inexpensive, though very dependent on the government for (assisted place) funding. A Music scholarship is available at 11+.

REMARKS: An excellent no-nonsense academic day school for girls bright enough to cope with the pressure. Has gone a bit quiet recently.

Stonar School

Cottles Park, Atworth, Melksham, Wiltshire SN12 8NT
Tel: 01225 702309, Fax: 01225 790830

PUPILS: Approx 500 girls; approx 290 board, 210 day
AGES: 4–18
SIZE OF SIXTH FORM: Around 102
C OF E
FEE-PAYING

HEAD: Since September 1985, Mrs Susan Hopkinson, BA (fifties). Educated at Howell's School, Llandaff, and St Hugh's, Oxford (History). A very enthusiastic and bubbly business lady (some would say her application of business principles has gone too far). She says, 'The experience of being at school should prepare you realistically for a career; I don't want to produce little misfits who can't get a job.' Aims to help girls develop an awareness of the possible conflicts that they may encounter over working and bringing up a family. She herself is a mother of two. Husband used to teach in the school, is now retired.

ACADEMIC MATTERS: Results are not given, but government tables for '95 list an average of 4.9 points per A-level subject taken, with 38 girls taking two or more subjects – ie, not brilliant, though NB intake is non-selective. There are good, modern Science facilities. The school follows the National Curriculum; three separate Sciences at GCSE are available for a 'minority of girls each year'. Some subjects get one-to-one tuition at the top of the school. The staff:pupil ratio is 1:10 – including ten 'full-time males'. Tailor-made Sixth Form courses can include e.g. Photography, Theatre Studies. One of very few private schools forward-looking (or could it be brave?) enough to be pioneering GNVQs in Business Studies.

GAMES, OPTIONS, THE ARTS: The school has stabling for over 60 horses, and a covered and open-air riding school with a mini-Badminton cross-country course. Guinea pigs and other pets are also welcome. The school is mostly famous for holding the British Inter-Schools One Day Event annually (for riding, not guinea pigs), which attracts around 500 competitors from schools all over the country. Has its own covered swimming pool, plus a new centenary Sports Hall. Strong in cross-country; has had several county hockey players; has an All-England netball coach.
There is a purpose-built Music School.

BACKGROUND AND ATMOSPHERE: A charming neo-Gothic building, behind which lies a slightly scrubby collection of outer buildings, and a Bath stone-fronted junior school and purpose-built Sixth Form complex on a collegiate model, all set in 80 acres of beautiful Wiltshire countryside.
The school has a gentle, uninstitutional atmosphere, generally happy, homely and relaxed.

PASTORAL CARE AND DISCIPLINE: Has a small-school feel – staff keep a close eye on everyone.

PUPILS AND PARENTS: The school suggests we describe pupils as 'a cheerful cross-section of late twentieth-century young womanhood'. Boarders are mainly from the southern counties and London, also weekly boarders (started 1986). There is a strong overseas contingent: 40 or so ex-pats, a small proportion from Japan and Hong Kong, and a number from Service families.

ENTRANCE: Easy peasy. At 9+, the school's entrance exam (though the school is listed as non-selective); at 14+ interview plus report and recommendation from previous school.

EXIT: Details are not listed, but to an interesting variety of courses including Equine Studies; 2 or 3 to Art College.

MONEY MATTERS: A discretionary bursary for the lower school for a particular talent. Also 4 Sixth Form scholarships – 2 for those already in the school (which helps stop the leakage to boys' schools). Half-fees scholarships available at 11+; Music, Riding and Athletics bursaries.

REMARKS: A boarding school for ponies. A successful and efficient girls' school – its success is based on clever marketing and giving the punters what they want (e.g. ponies).

Stonyhurst College

Stonyhurst, Clitheroe,
Lancashire BB7 9PZ
Tel: 01254 826345, Fax: 01254 826732
PUPILS: Approx 380 boys, 319 board, 61 day

AGES: 13–18
SIZE OF SIXTH FORM: 161 boys, 9 girls
RC
FEE-PAYING

HEAD: Since 1985, Dr Giles Mercer, MA, DPhil (forties), educated at Austin Friars, Cambridge and Oxford. Head of History at Charterhouse, then worked for the Ministry of Defence. The first married lay Head of any Jesuit College in the English-speaking world. Delightful and boyish.

ACADEMIC MATTERS: The thorough teaching is continually commented on by parents. There are small groups, setting for languages and Maths, questioning and probing so that Sixth Formers learn to think for themselves.

Results do not shine in league-table terms, reflecting the very wide ability intake, 'in which we take pride'. A significant number are taking Chinese, who invariably do well, which helps bump up league tables.

The school follows a broad curriculum (including, for instance, astronomy – it has its own observatory for this and a newly acquired remarkable telescope), strong languages (plus EFL for boys whose mother tongue is not English). Recent strengthening of international Jesuit links aims to broaden everyone's outlook. Study habits are acquired via a daily 8.15 p.m. prep period, plus prep on Saturdays and Sundays (very rare).

GAMES, OPTIONS, THE ARTS: The school has a strong Outdoor Pursuits tradition, with fell walking, canoeing, sailing, fishing on the Hodder for trout and salmon, successful shooting teams, and strong sport all round (rugby is the main sport), with good facilities and lots on offer. There is a fairly strong take-up of D of E, and an emphasis on community service (more meaningful than at many schools, with an annual trip to Lourdes). Boys have access to a new theatre at St Mary's Hall, the on-campus junior school. Good Music (free instrumental lessons). The school's most vigorous society *Past*, has regular visiting academics to speak, and trips to places of historical/artistic interest.

BACKGROUND AND ATMOSPHERE: An imposing (and vast) building (previously the property of the Weld family) – reputedly the largest boarding school under one roof, set in fine parkland. Somewhat isolated, definitely dignified if daunting. The school was founded in France in 1593 (for RCs forced to be educated out of England). It is full of treasures (paintings, ethnographica, largely donated by OBs), with a sense of history at every turn. Religion is taken very seriously (with boys very much encouraged to think for themselves).

The school is centrally run, with everyone sleeping under one roof. Boarding accommodation has been cosied up recently, with large study bedrooms for Sixth Formers. Boys are divided into year groups (Playrooms). The sleeping-out exeats policy is softening up (i.e. negotiable on an ad hoc basis), but basically half-terms only.

The ritzy prospectus in a wallet looks like a company report, and the very fat school magazine is perfectly bound.

PASTORAL CARE AND DISCIPLINE: This is a caring school – all the staff are shepherds. Consciences are carefully developed. Prefects have far more clout than at many schools (though staff most certainly run the place). Alcohol and smoking occasionally pop up, but the Head reassures us that these are not now 'troublesome'. There is a bar for Upper Sixth.

PUPILS AND PARENTS: A broad social and geographical mix, but mainly from middle-class professional backgrounds; 10% not RC. 25% come from abroad (including Ireland, Canada, France, Hungary, the Spanish-speaking world, and Hong Kong, often via Jesuit Colleges; boys must speak good English): the international dimension 'goes back a long way and is something we nurture and cherish'. Pleasant, articulate and mature boys. OBs include 12 martyrs (including 3 canonized saints), seven VCs, also Arthur Conan Doyle, Charles Laughton, General Walters, Paul Johnson, Lord Devlin.

ENTRANCE: Via the school's own prep – St Mary's Hall (on site), and St John's Beaumont, Windsor (this latter, incidentally, has been well recommended to us), also from a wide variety of other prep schools. Entry at Sixth Form as well.

EXIT: Far fewer to Oxbridge in '94 and '95 than reported in our last edition (about four in each year, not 10%). London is the most popular university choice. Business/Management/Politics/Economics and related subjects are currently in vogue here.

MONEY MATTERS: Not short of a bob or two: endowment money is entirely for bursaries, but, of course, this frees up money for other things. There are up to 9 academic scholarships (depending on the quality of applicants), several Music scholarships, also for Art and Design, plus bursaries. Also 35 Assisted Places at 11+, 13+ and also 16+.

REMARKS: A distinguished and interesting traditional Jesuit establishment with a clear vision of its educational role. Suffering as elsewhere from a drop in the boarding roll.

Stowe School

Stowe, Buckinghamshire MK18 5EH
Tel: 01280 813164, Fax: 01280 822769

PUPILS: Around 432 boys, plus 100 girls in the Sixth Form only; around 30 day pupils, the rest boarding
AGES: 13–18
SIZE OF SIXTH FORM: Around 307
C OF E
FEE-PAYING

HEAD: Since 1989, Mr Jeremy Nichols, MA (fifties). Educated at Lancing (captain of everything) and Cambridge, where he read English. Previous post as Eton Housemaster. A good teacher and good at bowling over potential parents with his charm. Married with four children – three girls, one boy (only two children on the cover of the prospectus, however). Keen on Dickens and has a springer spaniel called Mr Boffin. Mr Nichols is quoted on the front cover of the new prospectus as saying: 'A Stowe education teaches young people to *think* deeply, to *think* for themselves and to *think* about others'. So there you have it.

ACADEMIC MATTERS: Note that over half the school is Sixth Form and that it is large. Separate Sciences for all at GCSE. Pupils are streamed, and there is some setting. Also timetabled computing – keen. History of Art is on offer. Maximum class size 20 – less higher up the school. There were some rather nice A-level results in '95 in a good wide variety of subjects including Urdu, Religious Studies, Theatre Studies, Dutch (two candidates), Japanese, Music, Photography. The general standard of results is still climbing up, though Economics results are disappointing (as everywhere else) and wild fluctuations are not entirely ironed out – French, in particular, looks too awful: out of 33 A-level candidates in '95 *nineteen* got D–U. However, the school comes out well in ALIS Value Added ratings. The Head has worked hard to get fresh blood in the Common Room – but it's a big task.

GAMES, OPTIONS, THE ARTS: The school has its own beagle pack, (which the school sounds a bit shifty about), fishing (with its own hatchery) CCF, D of E and all that.

Excellent art results (13 A grades at A-level in '95, out of an entry of 19, and this is a typical sort of year). Lots of singing, and the school is famous for its Drama and Opera. Contrary to our report that girls do community service while boys play rugby, the school points out that *both* boys and girls do community service.

BACKGROUND AND ATMOSPHERE: Architecturally outstanding – a Grade I former ducal palace in a stunning setting, with gardens once tended by Capability Brown. The garden follies alone are worth a detour and now, luckily for the school, their upkeep is in the hands of the National Trust (whose kiosk is sitting in the grounds), with injections of cash from English Heritage. The National Trust now owns all the 700-acre park, including the games fields. This has made a vast difference to the look of the place – now, once more, gracious; it utterly wows potential parents.

Acres of roof still belong to the school, however; recently overhauled, but it's a never-ending task and school has a constant slightly down-at-heel look. This is not helped by the truly awful modern classrooms run up in the grounds which provide a constant eyesore. Some of the boys' houses are also pretty gruesome ('spartan' would be a more accurate description, says the school's Marketing Director), heavy with old wooden honours boards and the smell of suffering (long past, of course).

The school was founded in 1923 by, among others, Montauban (cf the school library, which is good and mellow), under the famous first Head – J F Roxburgh.

Worth a browse is *The Stoic*, which has been revamped and turned into a coffee table number, full of nostalgia trips, reports on the doggy Birtathon, the riding school, etc and aimed at the deepest pockets of Old Stoics. See also the arty farty prospectus. Pupils have their own racier newspaper, *The Voice*, full of exciting little snippets, e.g. grouses about why the tuck-shop isn't open on Wednesday, and 'overheard' quotes, e.g. 'A good journalist never relieves his sources.'

The original aim of the school was to break away from traditional public-school tradition, and, my goodness, it has succeeded.

Commercial Notes: The school, with its National Trust connection, is in the forefront of the trend to turn an honest penny in the school holidays, etc. The latest wheeze is to rent out the place for civil marriage ceremonies and this, we are told, is going like hot cakes. Gardens are open – a family ticket £9 at the time of writing, and 'refreshments and light lunches' are available, also 'powered wheelchairs'. Allow two hours, or you can rent a temple (via the Landmark Trust), and should this pall, there is always the Silverstone circuit just down the road – throaty roars on summer days.

PR note: The school featured in *Hello!* magazine in Feb '96 . . .

PASTORAL CARE AND DISCIPLINE: Fewer high jinks have come to our notice since the last edition. Current parents report that they are confident and the school comments that 'enterprising antics with the "unacceptable" are swiftly dealt with!'. There is a tutorial system in the lower and middle part of the school – not before time. The school suffers a tiny bit from the over-reaction of the media to pupils' peccadilloes (the word 'Stowe' helps make a small, smart headline). A very popular young chaplain is still packing the punters into the school chapel, and he is one of the school's real strengths.

PUPILS AND PARENTS: All sorts, socially, geographically, racially and academically. Lots of Londoners; a loyal Scottish contingent. Some parents are bemused by the school's grandeur. OBs are an individual lot, though there is a good deal of entrepreneurial talent, including Richard Branson, Nigel Broakes, Nicholas Henderson, Leonard Cheshire, David Shepherd, Lord Ampthill, Christopher Wates, Peregrine Worsthorne, Billy Butlin's offspring, George Melly (who has written lyrically about who seduced whom in his day), Lord Sainsbury, David Niven, Gavin Maxwell (the GM literary prize was once won by R Branson).

ENTRANCE: Common Entrance. Not difficult. From prep schools all over. Once more an acceptable choice if you aren't Eton material.

EXIT: 90% to 'university courses'; lots to a gap year. Look in the school's Sixth Form Courses guide for detailed destinations of recent leavers.

MONEY MATTERS: A Bursar's nightmare – the most expensive school buildings to keep up in the country, with the endowment not nearly up to the constant drain on resources (not to mention energy). Has help from English Heritage, however, not to mention the

Getty Foundation. There is an 'Enhanced range of Scholarships and bursaries, art, music and academic'. The school has a 'Marketing/Commercial Director'. There is also a 'finance director'. At Sixth Form, 6 Assisted Places.

REMARKS: A famous and fondly regarded public school beginning to see the light at the end of a difficult tunnel. Good for 'middle- (and end-) of-the-road' pupils looking for a designer label.

Strathallan School

Forgandenny, Perthshire PH2 9EG
Tel: 01738 812546, Fax: 01738 813269
PUPILS: About 345 boys, 160 girls
ALL BOARD: Except for 25 (half of them are staff's children)
AGES: 10–18
SIZE OF SIXTH FORM: 175
NON-DENOM
FEE-PAYING

HEAD: Since 1993, Mr Angus McPhail, MA (Oxon), (late thirties), educated at Abingdon School, read PPE at University College, Oxford. Came from Sedbergh, where he was a Housemaster. Started his career as a banker, switched to teaching ('far more satisfying') and first taught at Glenalmond. A delightful man with ease of manner, many talents and interests (a keen cricketer, all-round sportsman, very musical, sings, plays the violin and guitar). Wife and three young children. Fond of children: 'You can't be a good teacher unless you like children – and I've met lots of people in the profession who don't like them.' Cites resilience and adaptability as being key qualities the young need when they leave here.

ACADEMIC MATTERS: The school gets steady and OK results across the board, both in Highers and in A-levels (though bear in mind the different standards of the two exam systems). Around 60% take A-levels, the rest do Highers (over two years). English and History are the most popular subjects at A-level in '95. There has been a U-turn on the move to Dual Award Science at GCSE which we reported in the last edition – all pupils must opt for at least one science and most do all three. CDT continues to be outstanding, with brilliant electronics teaching (the Head of Department has devised a build-up method of Montessori simplicity); sophisticated computer design equipment, and pupils can work here in their spare time. Also two separate computer rooms, with a variety of computers. There is a smallish, effective learning-support room.

GAMES, OPTIONS, THE ARTS: Sport is taken seriously, especially rugby and cricket. The school also has its own golf course, skiing, CCF (boys and girls, voluntary), flying, sailing, fishing in own loch, plus 12 permits on the River Earn. Girls and boys both cook. The indoor pool is prehistoric (does not deter some from swimming daily at 7 a.m.).

Good Music (the school has a Copeman Hart manual organ), including a keen traditional Scottish music group. Lots of Drama, with a small theatre, a clever conversion from what was a boys' boarding house, its insides scooped out. The Head has introduced an 'expressive arts' programme to the curriculum (emphasis on Mime, Drama). New Head of Art in '94.

BACKGROUND AND ATMOSPHERE: The school was founded in 1912, the nucleus in a 19th-century country house, with masses of additions, set in 150 acres. It has a nice chapel, a hideous dining room (like a huge aeroplane hangar), main classroom blocks 300 yards away. Co-education is working well, with girls doing everything boys do, and everyone kept extremely busy. Strong on trips to Edinburgh and Glasgow for theatre, exhibitions, etc. The school has a refurbishing programme (accommodation is particularly important to first-time buyers, notes the Head) – spanking new(ish) boys' (T-shape) houses, like a university hall of residence with study bedrooms, lock-up cupboards, even for all 14–15-year-olds, pantries everywhere. Junior House Riley is currently being extended (to take in new 10-year-old entry) and enlarge space. The Sports Hall has also been tarted up – not before time.

PASTORAL CARE AND DISCIPLINE: Good, despite large houses (75), with two staff on duty every night. The Head is clamping down on smoking (HM report – means bookwork near his study in all free periods); there is a punishment system for misdemeanours of 'fatigues', jobs around the buildings and grounds ('no shortage of jobs'). Drinking means rustication or gating (and pupils might be kept back for a week of the holidays). There has been one drug expulsion within the last three years. The Head banned Doc Martens for smart occasions – antagonising parents who had to buy new shoes.

PUPILS AND PARENTS: 20% come from abroad (though only three or four foreigners), many oil-related parents. Popular with Scots; it is an hour from central Edinburgh and ditto Glasgow. An increasing contingent from the south – about 50 living in England at the time of writing. Mainly solid middle class. A popular choice for first-time buyers. Pupils are chatty and enthusiastic. FP – Dominic Diamond (computer games whizzo).

ENTRANCE: At 10 or 11 for the Junior House (interview and test), then automatic or by CE (children may have more than one attempt). Not a high hurdle, but popular. Later entry points if spaces.

EXIT: A few leave post-GCSEs for Sixth Form college. 90% to universities, mainly Scotland (Aberdeen popular). Some exit to creative arts.

MONEY MATTERS: Variable scholarships both for junior and senior school. Music awards (when merited); discounts for siblings, sympathetic bursaries. 7 Assisted Places per year. Fees are being kept down as a matter of principle, and are cheaper than comparable English public schools (£3,685 a term at the time of writing).

REMARKS: A successful and vibrant co-ed school, with an awful lot on offer, which came up fast under the previous Head and is still doing well, though no longer as fashionable as it was when we last went to press.

Streatham Hill and Clapham High School

Abbotswood Road, London SW16 1AW
Tel: 0181 677 8400, Fax: 0181 674 0175

PUPILS: 420 girls. (Plus junior school at Wavertree Road, London SW2 3SR)
Tel: 0181 674 6912, with 147 girls, ages 4–11)
ALL DAY
AGES: 11–18
SIZE OF SIXTH FORM: 88

NON-DENOM
FEE-PAYING

HEAD: Since 1979 (and on an open-ended contract) Miss G M Ellis BSc, (early fifties), unmarried. 'The school is her life,' comments an approving parent – ex-Senior Mistress of Croydon High, read Chemistry at Glasgow University. Forceful, direct, friendly, energetic, 'not afraid to come down hard if she needs to'; has turned what was something of a sinking ship into a sought-after, achieving establishment. 'Education isn't for life, it is life,' she says, and she knows every girl.

ACADEMIC MATTERS: 'I sit in on a lesson taught by shortlisted staff candidates – qualifications don't tell me all I need', says the Head. The ratio of 7:3 female:male staff teach a traditional academic curriculum with compulsory three separate Sciences to start off with; a proportion switches to GCSE Combined Science ('and that's a better option than dropping two'), with a slight bias towards Sciences at A-level. Strong French from the first year, Latin added in the second, plus options of German, Spanish and recently introduced Italian. Pupils may be bumped off courses at the last minute, if their performance looks dodgy (protecting those league table results?).

Economics is an option at Sixth Form and Classical Civilisation is popular. There has been a steady rise in A grades at GCSE. A-level percentages were not as good in '95 as they have been in recent years – but then they were outstanding. The Head comments: 'There are girls here for whom a grade C at A-level represents a tremendous achievement.'

GAMES, OPTIONS, THE ARTS: Improved facilities at the Tooting site have eased pressure on space, though 'it's not what you have but how you use it' comments the Head. New tennis and netball courts in '95 (to replace weedy ones). The school has a dance studio for gymnastic dance, a large gym hosting Surrey acrobatics championships; also basketball, volleyball, swimming in local pool.

Strong Art is much in evidence; pencil drawings in the school magazine point to good teaching in draughtmanship (a rare virtue). Also Home Economics; keen D of E. The Hall/Theatre is used for regular school plays with girls playing male roles – 'Yes, it is a drawback that we have no links with local boys' schools,' sighs a pupil. Busy fund-raising activities.

The Sixth Form speakers' club includes among visiting speakers card-carrying women of influence – Mary Archer, Jane Asher, Dame Cicely Saunders.

BACKGROUND AND ATMOSPHERE: A functional if rather uninviting brick building (rebuilt after a 1944 direct hit by a flying bomb) in South London suburban wastes near Streatham bus garage is now home to the junior school only while the senior school has moved to new premises in Cynthia Payne country. No frills, suburban environment, purposeful and hard-working.

The slightly startling and deeply unflattering lettuce-green uniform (which can't help with the acknowledged aggro from the local comprehensive) is topped by the occasional black Islamic shawl (there is a white tight rule to 'smarten us up') and gives way to own clothes in the Sixth Form – with a notable absence of front-line sophisticate dressers.

PASTORAL CARE AND DISCIPLINE: Evident warmth and protection from day one include a personal tutor for every GCSE girl, who acts as a trouble-shooter. There are some reports of sex, drugs and rock 'n' roll, but no more than elsewhere.

The Head has a fierce anti-bullying policy: 'I cannot tolerate any injustice that hinders a child's chance in life.' There is a hands-in-pockets rule in the pre-lunch queue – 'to prevent thieving,' explain girls.

PUPILS AND PARENTS: A social and racial melting pot from a sizeable chunk of South London, taking in Brixton, Dulwich, Streatham and, in increasing numbers, Clapham. Most from the state sector and lots of first-time buyers. Daughters of teachers, solicitors, redundant architects, the medical world. OGs include Angela Carter, and – from the days of the occasional boy pupil – Norman Hartnell.

ENTRANCE: Via exam at 11. The Head interviews every applicant herself. 'National Curriculum reports at 10 plus tell me nothing.'

EXIT: 70–90% to universities for medicine, law, humanities; a couple a year to Oxbridge; also to business, computing, teacher training, Art School, nursing.

MONEY MATTERS: Strict screening for up to 24 Assisted Places ('Yes, we have had the odd fiddle'), of which scheme the Head is a staunch supporter and has been on Channel 4 to say so. Girls' Public Day School Trust Scholarships at Sixth Form, and a hardship fund for those genuinely fallen on hard times, contributed to through active social fundraising by the Friends' Association. Low fees from centrally administered GPDST give good value – parents tend to know it and pay up.

REMARKS: An unflash, achieving smallish girls' day school which still presents a serious alternative to its smarter South London cousins JAGS and

Alleyn's, though several parents have commented to us that the school is 'not as good as we make it out to be' and has gone off the boil.

Taunton School

Taunton, Somerset TA2 6AD
Tel: 01823 348200, Fax: 01823 349201

PUPILS: Around 513 boys, 419 girls; 267 board, 665 day
AGES: 3–18
SIZE OF SIXTH FORM: 204
INTER-DENOM
FEE-PAYING

HEAD: Since 1987, Mr B B Sutton, MA (Cantab), JP (fifties), educated at Eltham College – which was evacuated to Taunton School in the war – then read History at Peterhouse. Previously Head of Hereford Cathedral School, he teaches History; his wife teaches Maths.

REMARKS: A useful local school in which you can put your child at age 3 and leave it there for the next fifteen years. To all intents and purposes it is a day school. Traditionally stronger on Science, but it still offers both Latin and Greek. A breakdown of results is not given but the average number of points per A-level entry according to government statistics is 6.1.

The school is lucky enough to have Trevor Hill, a whizz on Radio Astronomy. There is an excellent and enthusiastic Design department, very on the ball, and Maths, Physics and Design make a popular option.

The popular EFL Centre provides English tuition at no extra charge, which has changed the school profile from Middle Eastern and Eastern pupils to European (though the Head comments

that the school tries to keep the number of children with foreign passports to around 12%).

Music is popular, as is Drama and Art. Flourishing D of E Award, and keen CCF. All games fields are within walking distance; the railway runs at the bottom of the cricket pitch in front of the main school. Traditionally strong at rugby, but there are proper facilities for girls to play games and they are expected to do two main sessions a week.

The school was founded in 1847 as a school for children of dissenters – Baptists and Congregationalists – of which there were many in the South-West (Queen's, Taunton, was for Methodists). It has been co-ed from 13 since 1971.

After GCSE, 10–15% leave; otherwise a steady stream to university. The school has generous scholarships and bursaries and some Assisted Places at 11+ and Sixth Form. Also scholarships up to 50% fees for children of ministers of all recognised denominations, plus 5% bursaries to Service children. Boringly middle class (but Head comments that the school 'draws from a wide cross-section socially').

Successful summer school in the holidays.

Tiffin School

Queen Elizabeth Road, Kingston-upon-Thames, Surrey KT2 6RL
Tel: 0181 546 4638, Fax: 0181 546 6365

PUPILS: 952 boys
ALL DAY
SIZE OF SIXTH FORM: 300
NON-DENOM
STATE (opted out in '93)

HEAD: Since 1988, Dr A M (Tony) Dempsey, BSc, PhD (fifties).

Educated at Tiffin and Bristol University where he read Chemistry. Previously Deputy Head of Feltham Community School (has also taught in the private sector). Married, with one son; a keen walker and industrial archaeologist.

Dr Dempsey 'covers' lessons, but says it is 'unrealistic to expect a Head to teach and know all the boys' (apart from which, his time costs three times more than most staff), but he expects to know the 'goodies and the baddies' and those who naturally come to the fore. Parents can (and do) have free access to him.

ACADEMIC MATTERS: An academic school. Boys take 10 GCSEs and do very well in them – around a third get A/A★ in any subject, with Maths and Science strongest at this level, though NB at A-level the Sciences and Maths tail right off and results in '95 show perhaps too many Ds and Es for a school of this nature. All take three A-levels, however. Classics (particularly Latin) are popular and strong at GCSE, with Dual Award science on tap for those taking Classics or German and French. A certain amount of dead staff wood at the top still needs pruning, but most departments are fine: English and Geography are particularly strong. Nationals are expected to cover their own language at GCSE, hence the Polish, Modern Greek and Arabic results.

GAMES, OPTIONS, THE ARTS: There is a games pitch on the slightly cramped 1½-acre site, with extra rugby and cricket facilities at Grists by Hampton Court, and a boathouse on the Thames. Also a mega ritzy new Sports Centre (Sports Studies is on offer at A-level). The fabulous new Chester Centre houses dramatic Art (including pottery) and really good IT, computer-linked. Masses of Music and Drama, with serious representation at many of the London venues – Festival Hall, the Royal Opera House, Albert Hall and Covent Garden – as well as regular school performances in-house.

BACKGROUND AND ATMOSPHERE: The school was founded in 1638 and moved to its present site in the middle of leafy desirable Kingston-upon-Thames in 1929, incorporating Elmfield House (circa 1770 – much watched by English Heritage, but fairly scruffy inside). A hotchpotch of handsome red brick (with later additions) and the current Head's brilliant extensions; the school is amazingly tidy considering the sheer numbers operating in the space.

There are 30 computers on line and more in the pipe line. There is a slightly scruffy Sixth Form centre in Elmfield House and a very nooky library. The uniform is fairly strictly adhered to, but Sixth Form wear mufti, and occasionally feel the urge to express their personalities via hair. A purposeful atmosphere. NB Local transport is excellent.

PASTORAL CARE AND DISCIPLINE: Form Tutors, plus subject Tutors as the child progresses through the school. There is a strong house system, and everyone has someone with whom they can talk. Good PHSE programme, with drugs lectures from Customs and Excise. The sight of addicts gravitating towards the Kaleidoscope Centre next door for their daily methadone fixes is a grim warning.

PUPILS AND PARENTS: Kingston is essentially middle class, so lots of those, with about 25% ethnic minorities. 95% of pupils come from within eight miles – including Richmond, Merton, – plus a 'sprinkling' from further afield. Very supportive, with lots of parental input, not to mention car boot sales and associations.

ENTRANCE: Very, very selective. By verbal and non-verbal reasoning tests for entry into year 7 (marks are 'age-weighted'). Apply before October (the exam is taken in November) for the following September. Seriously over-subscribed – this is Mecca for the impoverished and left-wing intelligentsia of the area: 140 pupils are accepted out of a staggering 1,250 applying, though here, as elsewhere, the figures are misleading as parents 'play the system' and some potential Tiffinians will be offered places by St Paul's and Westminster. Indeed, the private sector has been known to troll almost at the gates of the school, enticing bright pupils away with lures of scholarships. Extra pupils are accepted at 11+, and around 10% of new intake goes to the Sixth Form (you need at least 5 GCSE A or B grades, including Maths and English and proposed A-level subjects).

EXIT: 90% to Higher Education, traditional universities more popular than modern add-ons; about 15 a year to Oxbridge. Engineering and medicine are still the most popular subjects.

MONEY MATTERS: State-funded. There is a lot of parental input. Only 19 pupils currently receive free lunches, and these are helped (discreetly) to do essential field trips.

REMARKS: A beacon in the state system and indeed in the area – a strong traditional academic school in the old grammar school tradition.

Tiffin Girls' School

Richmond Road,
Kingston-upon-Thames,
Surrey KT2 5PL
Tel: 0181 546 0773, Fax: 0181 547 0191
PUPILS: 880 girls
ALL DAY

AGES: 11–18
SIZE OF SIXTH FORM: 245
NON-DENOM
STATE (NOT OPTED OUT)

HEAD: Since 1994, Mrs Pauline Cox BA (forties). School at High Storrs Girls' Grammar School in Sheffield, read Geography at Birmingham and did an MA at the London Institute of Education. Previous post as Deputy Head of Cranford Community School, Hounslow. Started her career in the British Embassy in Poland, spent three years in Accra teaching, and has taught in various places in the plusher parts of South London. Married with two teenage children. Keen on sport including skiing ('avid but hopeless'). We have not met her yet but early showing suggests a winner.

ACADEMIC MATTERS: A top South London state academic girls' school which nevertheless reflects an ethos of the best of comprehensives rather than of the more competitive fee-paying schools with their loads of extras. This is no academic forcing house and has not got an Oxbridge obsession. Classes are large – 30 – though smaller for practical subjects. GCSE choices include IT, Design Technology, Latin and either Dual Award or three separate Science subjects. One or two AS-levels are also taken. The '95 GCSE results look very healthy (considerably more so than '94), with a slight blip in Design and Technology. A-level results are also excellent – with a good range of subjects, not just the mainstream ones but Theatre Studies, Psychology, Computing. Judging by '94 and '95 results, Geography is a weak link at the moment.

For what it's worth: the school was second in the *Sunday Times* state league tables for '95, after Reading School and before Dr Challoner's High.

GAMES, OPTIONS, THE ARTS: Courts and playing fields are on site, also two large gyms – dance and aerobics are on offer as well as the more traditional sports. The school places a big emphasis on sport; netball is particularly strong with the Under-16 team National Netball Champions in '90. Raising money for charity is also important – £2,000 was raised in a single day – and the Sixth Form (which has its own building) has formed an Amnesty International group. The School has a Drama Studio. Once a week Sixth Form group discussions with Tiffin Boys' are 'more beneficial for the boys than for us,' commented a girl.

BACKGROUND AND ATMOSPHERE: The school moved to its present building, formerly housing a secondary modern, in 1987. The faceless two-storey extension, set in a flat suburban landscape, is deceptive – inside all is calm, spacious, light and very friendly. It is also refreshingly unstuffy. There are excellent facilities, with Design Technology, computer rooms and libraries particularly impressive. The atmosphere is one of co-operation not competition.

The school has an extremely complicated history, starting with Thomas Tiffin and his brother John who in 1638 and '39 left £150 in trust for the education of 'some honest poor men's sons'; moving on to Elizabeth Brown, who left dwelling houses in St Bride's to her son to be conveyed to the town of Kingston and a small yearly income to be paid to 'some honest industrious poor woman . . .'; moving on to Edward Belitha who had needlework for 'honest respectable women' in his sights; and so to the foundation of the Tiffin Schools in 1880. That's enough history.

PASTORAL CARE AND DISCIPLINE: This is a caring school, with supportive pupils and staff. The policy of appointing older pupils as form 'associates' for first years seems to work particularly well: 'They really take time to notice you and spend time caring about you.'

PUPILS AND PARENTS: Open and unpretentious, with girls generous in their praise for both Head and school. Words tumble out: 'atmosphere really good', 'It's such a cliché but we really are one happy family', 'It is a second home – if someone has a problem with a topic everyone wants to help.'

ENTRANCE: Getting tougher as the Greenwich Judgement (a recent court ruling) means that the Borough of Kingston boundaries are no longer sacrosanct and the school can and does take able children from the neighbouring boroughs of Twickenham, Richmond, Wandsworth. This is inevitably narrowing the ability band of the local intake (from the top 15% of ability range to the top 8% is estimated), which *should* mean gains for neighbouring comprehensives.

There are very few opportunities for Sixth Form entry – only 10% of applicants are accepted. Around 100 apply from the private sector alone. All Sixth Form applicants sit entrance tests in their A-level subjects in the spring of their final GCSE year.

EXIT: Almost all to Higher Education. The '95 'entry' includes 10 to medical colleges and 14 to Oxbridge. One or two go straight into employment.

MONEY MATTERS: State-funded. Grateful parents raise £30,000 a year (which NB is £10K more than they were raising when we last looked) – most recently for their computer rooms and Drama Centre.

REMARKS: A super duper state girls' grammar school with an outstanding record but delightfully unassuming and lacking in intellectual arrogance.

Tonbridge Grammar School for Girls

Deakin Leas, Tonbridge, Kent TN9 2JR
Tel: 01732 365125, Fax: 01732 359417

PUPILS: Around 955 girls
ALL DAY
AGES: 11–19
SIZE OF SIXTH FORM: Around 250
NON-DENOM
STATE

HEAD: Since 1990, Mrs Wendy Carey, BA (Hons) in English (late forties), from the University of London. Previously Deputy Head of one of the King Edward foundation schools in Birmingham. Born in Australia, grew up in Africa, moving between South Africa and Zimbabwe (where she took an external London BA in English) – came to England when civil war broke out, bringing her four young children with her. Articulate, dynamic and perceptive. Her experience includes fee-paying, state, co-ed and single-sex schools. Is a firm believer in the advantages of single-sex education for girls: 'They don't have to hold back, can take risks, question things, push themselves, be innovative,' she argues. Finds the school's grant-maintained status 'hugely enabling'.

ACADEMIC MATTERS: Results are not given, but usually they are excellent. A wide-ranging choice of subjects includes Latin (compulsory in the first year), Greek, Textiles and Fashion, Government and Politics: strengths

extend right across the curriculum. The school is also at the cutting edge of technological development. It is unusual in a girls' school to encounter such serious commitment to planning and resourcing of technical options: the school's dynamic policy deservedly generates much enthusiasm. The school has made a large investment, too, in AppleMacs. The most recent inspection ('92) gave a glowing report. (Ofsted is due to inspect in '96)

GAMES, OPTIONS, THE ARTS: All the normal options are available on their spacious and airy site with the popular open-air pool recently refurbished and equipped with changing rooms. The local Sports Centre is also put to good use and a nearby artificial ski slope enables pupils to hone their skills for the national Ski Championships.

There are plenty of opportunities for Drama and Music, with the Head commenting that many choose the school for its commitment to music. Also some joint debating, drama and music with The Judd School, and some joint activities with Tonbridge School, including a Model United Nations day.

BACKGROUND AND ATMOSPHERE: The main school is bright and cheerful, though with signs of wear and tear. Countless temporary classrooms are dotted around a fine 19-acre hillside site overlooking the Weald of Kent. Facilities will be vastly improved by a £1.25 million Science and Technology teaching block – due for completion in '96. Although Sixth Form provision is neither ideal nor generous, there is remarkably little post-GCSE drop-out – a testament to the school's ethos, teaching and the breadth of subject and extra-curricular options.

PASTORAL CARE AND DISCIPLINE: The '92 inspection praised the 'exceptional high quality of pastoral care reflected in excellent relations between pupils and teachers and among pupils'.

PUPILS AND PARENTS: The majority are middle-class offspring of fairly well-to-do Weald of Kent parents, with brothers at the Judd, some at Tonbridge School. Large numbers come from Sevenoaks (the town). Girls are friendly, unassuming. The uniform is particularly nice; Sixth Form – very casual, no uniform. There are strong links with OGs. OG of the moment: Rebecca Stephens, first British woman to climb Everest.

ENTRANCE: 140 places via Kent selection procedure: 11 + exam; it is essential to pass the exam, but not necessary to live in Kent. The school is oversubscribed. Its main criteria, after sibling preference, is placing in the exam. Up to 15 normally enter at Sixth Form level; at the height of the recession that number rose to 25.

EXIT: Almost all to university. Pupils display a dazzling diversity of choice, ranging from Fashion, Marketing, Aeronautical Engineering and Business Information Technology, to the more traditional career areas, including Veterinary Science, Medicine and Law. Some to Oxbridge.

MONEY MATTERS: State-funded.

REMARKS: One of the country's top state grammar schools.

Tonbridge School

Tonbridge, Kent TN9 1JP
Tel: 01732 365555, Fax: 01732 363424

PUPILS: Around 678 boys; 424 board, 254 day
AGES: 13–18
SIZE OF SIXTH FORM: 276
C OF E
FEE-PAYING

HEAD: Since 1990, Mr (J M) Martin Hammond, MA (early fifties), educated at Winchester and Balliol College, Oxford, a scholar at both. Previously Headmaster of City of London School, and before that taught at St Paul's, Harrow, also Eton, where he was Head of Classics, then Master in College. A keen classicist, he has published a translation of the *Iliad*, and is now at work on the *Odyssey*. Married (his wife has her own teaching career) with two children. A five-star Head.

Described by former colleagues as a man of 'iron determination' and 'creative ruthlessness'. Positive, affable and, to some, daunting. Still declares he is 'most interested in the ordinary guy and what he gets out of it all'. Hugely busy on the massive building projects – and loving it.

Management note: this is a very efficiently run school.

ACADEMIC MATTERS: The school is formidably strong in a wide range of subjects. Streaming from the start, and some setting (Maths and Languages). Maths, French and Latin GCSE are taken one year early by a substantial number of boys (most pupils take ten in all). Separate sciences at GCSE: all must take two and most take three. The school has very thorough and rigorous teaching throughout: 'Boys are really taught how to work, and have to work hard,' commented a parent. 'There's no let-up.' Teaching groups have about 17 boys, down to 8 at A-level. A firm emphasis on the critical and analytical approach to study – how to think, reason and argue – starts well before the Sixth Form.

The school has excellent facilities (constantly being improved) with each department housed in its own area, with offices and (usually) its own library. Geography, History and Economics were recently ('92) rehoused, the English department much expanded. There is an impressive main library. Computers are everywhere. Also an impressive seminar lectures programme.

Invariably coming very high in the league tables, it was in '93 the first and only HMC school to achieve a 100% overall pass rate at A-level. All three Sciences are strong. Mathematics continues to be outstanding (and currently the most popular A-level subject); English, Modern Languages, Physics are also very strong and popular, not to mention Economics: Tonbridge is one of the very, very few schools to teach Economics successfully.

The enormously committed staff who put in many over-and-above hours. There are A-level reading and revision groups in the holidays in Cornwall, and at Lindisfarne for Oxbridge students: 'brilliant,' said a boy. A generous and useful early retirement scheme for staff has 'proved beneficial' (Head). Ten new Heads of Department have been appointed in the last three years (this must be a record).

GAMES, OPTIONS, THE ARTS: This is a very sporty school: games are still compulsory even for Sixth Form, and there are huge numbers of squads and teams at all levels. The school are proud of their sporting reputation: powerful cricket, hockey and rugger sides, with 100 acres of pitches. Sports on offer (20+) include rackets, fives, sailing, golf and rowing (results in matches more mixed than their academic equivalent but still good). There is a marvellous all-weather athletics track with pole vaulting, shot putting, high and long jumps; also two all-weather pitches.

The dynamic Head of Music, who looks like a teenage stick insect and is an outstanding teacher, Mr Hilary Davan Wetton, comes from St Paul's Girls' (chief conductor of the Wren Orchestra, the City of London Choir). Under him Music is booming; the fine Chapel Choir has new chorister scholarships for trebles from local prep schools. The new organ in the restored chapel (see below) is generating much inspiration: 'the difference made to the whole feel of the school is almost tangible', says the Head. NB The school regularly produces organ and choral scholars for Oxbridge.

Drama is also strong (girls from local grammar schools take part) and gets increased emphasis with two or three plays each term (some small-scale), with a new theatre complex under way. D of E Awards, CCF compulsory for one year. The school has good language exchanges, and foreign expeditions are 'particularly well thought out and organised,' commented a parent.

BACKGROUND AND ATMOSPHERE: The school was founded in 1553 and rebuilt in the 19th century (Gothic style) in the centre of the town. The chapel was destroyed by fire in 1988, but restoration completed in late '95 – an incredible feat – at a cost of £7 million, including £800,000 for a new organ built by Marcussen of Denmark, with four manuals, and 66 stops, which stops people in their tracks. The school is undergoing a massive £20m development programme (started in '92), by far the largest of any public school in recent years, including an integrated Arts, Technology and Theatre complex generating huge excitement (and envy). All this involves cunning decanting.

Houses (eleven; the school is very house-orientated) are scattered around the town (though all are near the main campus): boys still eat in their houses.

Day boys and boarders keep to separate houses; a new day house recently acquired in tandem with the school's expansion schemes. There is a slight element of 'we/they' split personality. 'Marvellous for day pupils,' commented a parent. 'They get all the advantages of a big, strong, round-the-clock boarding school.'

The planned expansion to a total of 680 by '95/6 has been achieved. This is a highly structured environment, and boys admit the pace is 'fairly pressurised' ('They mean very pressurised indeed,' translated one mother.) Sixth Form have a bar and there is a new social centre with a café. Occasional social life (house by house) with Benenden.

PASTORAL CARE AND DISCIPLINE: The school traditionally (but not, we are assured, deliberately) projects an image of a tough rugger-playing place – but this image is now slightly at odds with reality: TLC is on hand and pastoral care is taken seriously. The Tutors' brief is 'get to know the boys' and they do their best; in the first two years groups of three or four visit the tutor at home; there are small group pupil/tutor meetings for Sixth Formers to discuss/explore intellectual matters. The Head is fiercely anti-smoking (jacked up the first-time fine to £10; detention, letter home, rustication): 'But you never entirely get rid of it.' Alcohol is reported to be 'under control' and (appropriately aged) Upper Sixth boys are allowed to local pubs on Saturday evenings. The Head comments that, 'Boys nowadays appear to be law-abiding, docile and well behaved.'

PUPILS AND PARENTS: A fairly broad cross-section, especially in view of the generous scholarships. Mostly local, also Londoners, and not socially upper crust. Many sons of the solid and worthy middle class, not flashy. Few are non-

English. Boys are open, well informed, and look you in the eye. There are occasional mutterings of complacency. OBs include Colin Cowdrey, E M Forster, Sidney Keyes, Sir Patrick Mayhew, Vikram Seth.

ENTRANCE: Tough, but not as tough as it has been. Draws from over 50 prep schools round about; not from state schools and it is very much at the sharp end of competition with extremely good grammar schools on the doorstep. Two-thirds come via CE at 13+, one-third through the scholarship exam (but not all with awards). The Head notes (as others do) that parents are leaving the choice until later.

EXIT: All to university, including Oxbridge. Medicine, law, engineering continue to be popular.

MONEY MATTERS: A rich school, whose endowment is administered by the Skinners' Company. Up to 25% of boys receive an award of some kind. 21 academic awards each year between full and one-quarter fees, as well as 9 Music and 5 Art or Technology scholarships. There are extensive resources for the unexpectedly needy.

REMARKS: A tip top and now first division traditional public school with outstanding facilities, going from more strength to more strength under a widely admired Head. Uncompromisingly all boys, and now expanding the day element.

Truro School

Trennick Lane, Truro,
Cornwall TR1 1TH
Tel: 01872 72763, Fax: 01872 223431

PUPILS: Around 599 boys, 236 girls. 658 day, 177 board. Plus separate prep and pre-prep ages 3–11 of 200+ boys and girls (see below)
AGES: 10/11–18.
SIZE OF SIXTH FORM: Around 245
METHODIST FOUNDATION
FEE-PAYING

HEAD: Since September 1993, Mr Guy Dodd, MA (fifties). Read History at Cambridge; taught in New Zealand, then (16 years) at Cheltenham College and Lord Wandsworth College, where he was Head for eleven years.

ACADEMIC MATTERS: Good results on the whole – one or two weak links in '95 A-levels (in particular, Biology and French). Maths is strong and very popular, Physics also popular. The school has 16 Science labs; excellent Technology and IT. History is well taught. AS-levels are also taken. A large entry at Sixth Form helps beef up things here.

GAMES, OPTIONS, THE ARTS: Dynamic and original projects and extras. This is *the* school for chess and it won *The Times* inter-schools competition in '93. A keen take-up of D of E Awards, bronze, silver and gold. Still firmly into Young Enterprise (the first school to create a real aeroplane, which was flown across the Channel). Good Art. Does well with swimming, sailing, also rugby. There is a huge list of extra-curricular activities on offer; good on expeditions, keen on the great outdoors.

BACKGROUND AND ATMOSPHERE: The school was founded in 1880, a move described by the prospectus as a 'step of faith' taken by Cornish Methodists.
Glorious site 'on the ridge' overlooking the River Truro and the Cathedral – a position which brings tears to the eyes of property developers. ('High on the hill, with the City below' sings the school song.)
Grounds run down from the ridge, and playing fields stretch out at the back. Rather lumpen school buildings, as befits what was formerly the grammar school, with higgledy-piggledy annexes and extra Science labs. Boarding houses are dotted around the town (NB boarding numbers dwindled significantly during the recession), including one house in an elegant mansion house with most beautiful grounds.
NB: Went fully co-ed in 1990; before that, absorbed many actual and potential pupils from the closure of Truro Cathedral School.

Junior School: Treliske Prep School, Highertown, Truro, Cornwall TR1 3QN. Tel: 01872 72616, Fax: 01872 223431. Head: Mr Russell Hollins BA etc. Entry is by registration at pre-prep, assessment and report at 7+ plus interview and a day spent in the school. Almost all go on to the senior school, but the school has recently won scholarships to other schools e.g. Bristol Cathedral and Bath High. Pleasant light building, a super, enthusiastic place, good pastoral care. Boarding and day (draws from a wide area); one of the very few prep schools in the area. Two miles away from the senior school, it has 10 acres of its own plus good facilities. Scholarships and bursaries are available. Remedial help is also available.

PASTORAL CARE AND DISCIPLINE: Firmly in place; Christian and spiritual values are positively instilled, with an emphasis on the individual.

PUPILS AND PARENTS: The pupils come from all over Cornwall, from Scilly to Saltash. Straightforward and unpretentious; sundry parents in farming and the Services, a few from abroad (Far East). OBs include Robert Shaw, Bryan Pearce, David Penhaligon, Ben Luxon, Alan Opie.

ENTRANCE: Via the school's own exam at 11+ (i.e. neatly timed in with state system); grammar school ability is required (though this is pretty mixed). Lots come in via the school's own prep. Between 30 and 40 pupils join at Sixth Form (largely from state schools).

EXIT: Some to green welly universities, one or two to Falmouth Art College, to banking, Scottish universities, 10 to Oxbridge in '95 (about par for the course recently) and a contingent to the new universities for Business Studies, Hotel Management.

MONEY MATTERS: Good value, this is one of the least expensive private boarding schools in the country (apart from the genuine charity schools). Boarding fees, at the time of writing, are £2,860 per term in the main school, but there are few scholarships (the school is not endowed, and they come out of fee income).

REMARKS: Cornwall's only HMC school, traditional but liberal, which scores well. It feels more like a day school than a boarding one.

Tudor Hall School

Wykham Park, Banbury,
Oxfordshire OX16 9UR
Tel: 01295 263434, Fax: 01295 262777
PUPILS: Around 263 girls, 231 boarding, 32 day
AGES: 11–18
SIZE OF SIXTH FORM: Around 78

C OF E
FEE-PAYING

HEAD: Since 1983, Miss Nanette Godfrey, BA (early fifties), educated at Northampton School for Girls and London University (read English). Taught at the Royal Ballet School, Abbots Bromley, and Ancaster House (Deputy Head). Magistrate; keen traveller (recently asked to lecture to teachers in Kiev), and keen theatregoer. Professional and highly respected, purposeful and shrewd beneath an apparently timid manner. Girls comment, 'We can talk to her.' Teaches all ages: 'If you're going to discuss pupils with your staff, you must know them.' Enormously positive about the benefits of a small school. Took a sabbatical term in '95 immersing herself in the works of Edward Lear.

Deputy Head: Harriet Granville.

ACADEMIC MATTERS: '95 GCSE results had 100% success with grades A–C, with an average of 9.2 subjects per girl and 'what really delighted me,' says the Head, 'was that every girl had English, Maths, Science and a Modern Language'. Now that really tells you something. Average points score per subject at A-level was 6.9, however – which doesn't look quite so impressive.

Rising Sixth Form numbers (but NB still small) mean a wider choice of courses are now available. A-level Theatre Studies has been added under the live-in Drama teacher, – 'Brilliant' say the girls. History of Art still one of the most popular A-level subjects, with good results. The school provides good language teaching, with Russian, Greek, and Italian crash courses available. It also now offers an exchanged scheme with Le Caousou near Toulouse and those who go on it are 'plunged effectively into French life and education'.

About one-third of pupils take two or three separate Sciences at GCSE, Dual Award for the rest. Setting in Maths, Science and Language. There are some complaints of 'patchy teaching', though the Head acts swiftly and decisively when necessary. Girls are given loads of encouragement by staff.

GAMES, OPTIONS, THE ARTS: This is a fairly gamesy school, with lacrosse and hockey, tennis courts in the old walled garden, and a new covered tennis court for year round playing, plus a resident tennis coach. Also two new squash courts, a large Sports Hall, an outdoor swimming pool. Riding is available (quite a lot do). Has competed in a cross-country run with Radley, and had a joint debate with them.

Good Art, with a lively Art department and energetic Art club. Also good needlework and a big Home Economics department (not offered for examination), and all Sixth Formers do a hostess cookery course. There is also a Sixth Form community-service scheme for all girls. Girls learn to type, as well as use word processors. There is a good CDT block.

The school has a strong debating and public speaking ('they'll need it') tradition. Visiting speakers are drawn from Oxford and Stratford. 'Good feeding ground,' observes a parent contentedly. Geographically conveniently placed for cultural outings, which are given a high priority. The school is planning a trek to Borneo in '96 – all carefully thought out and mapped out already ('95) in the school magazine, with fascinating account of the previous year's expedition (Venezuela). YE companies are flourishing and work experience is compulsory for every pupil.

BACKGROUND AND ATMOSPHERE: Large charming country house, much extended, in pretty grounds produces a very uninstitutional atmosphere. The school was founded in 1850 elsewhere. Additions and conversions of old stables provide very good academic facilities, blends well architecturally (NB the Head has a keen architectural eye). Quite a lot of weekend activities are on offer. Good food. Girls live in very well-furbished houses/rooms (very cosy newly renovated 11+ house), and live by age (vertical houses exist for competitive purposes). Sixth Form accommodation is five-star with loads of space and light. The Japanese garden has been restored.

PASTORAL CARE AND DISCIPLINE: Good on both fronts, with positive pupil/staff relations. There are firm rules and no major problems. 'Biddable girls,' commented a parent. The Head resolutely refuses to take in any girls who have been 'asked to leave' other establishments. She writes astute letters to parents (e.g. following on from a drinking incident), encourages parents to get together to discuss their stand on booze, boys, etc. Most recently gave parents guidelines on detecting early signs of anorexia.

PUPILS AND PARENTS: Pretty and pleasant girls with good manners, unspoilt, friendly, conventional, capable and practical – like their parents, many of whom are county or City Sloanes, from far and near. A very cohesive lot. The school motto is *Habeo ut dem*.

ENTRANCE: Getting in is not difficult as such, but the school continues to be high on popularity stakes, so register early. Entry at 11+, 12+ and 13+, a few at Sixth Form to fill in when girls leave for wider horizons.

EXIT: Three-quarters to university (the green welly and fashionable variety is favoured – Edinburgh or Newcastle if possible). Art, Design and Fashion training are also popular, as is the gap year.

R EMARKS: Formerly a boarding school for thick toffs' daughters, now a happy, strong, small girls' boarding school with good facilities, plenty going on and with an academic achievement which is not to be sneezed at. Rave notices from delighted parents.

University College School (UCS)

Frognal, London NW3 6XH
Tel: 0171 435 2215, Fax: 0171 431 4385

PUPILS: Around 690 boys. Plus separate junior school ages 7–11
ALL DAY
AGES: 11–18
SIZE OF SIXTH FORM: 200
NON-DENOM
FEE-PAYING

H EAD: From September 1996, Mr Kenneth Durham, BA from Oxford in PPE. Comes from a post as Director of Studies at King's College Wimbledon (before Wimbledon he was at St Alban's). Has written some natty books on economics, including resource packs for primary, GCSE and A-level studies. Keen on acting, film, books, music. Takes over from Mr G D Slaughter who retired in August '96.
    Chairman of the appeals committee is Sir Colin Marshall.

A CADEMIC MATTERS: The school provides good sound teaching, and very professional assessments, but is sometimes lacking in imagination, say parents. Traditionally renowned for

excellence in Classics, Maths and Sciences – some feel to the detriment of other subjects, e.g. Modern Languages (surprisingly, in so cosmopolitan an environment, only French and German were on offer until very recently, though Spanish has now been grafted on). Maths was much the most popular A-level subject taken in '95 – excellent results as usual here. Next in popularity, Chemistry – and good results here too. There are good Economics staff. Theatre Studies is now offered. A-level results show a few fluctuations in individual subjects from year to year, but are usually very good. The average number of GCSE subjects taken is nine. The Technology department is excellent.

G AMES, OPTIONS, THE ARTS: The school has good games facilities, especially given that this is expensive, built-up Hampstead; tennis and fives courts, Sports Hall and an indoor pool are all on the premises; its own playing field and all-weather pitch are nearby. Had a very strong first fifteen in '94/95.
    The excellent well-equipped school theatre is regularly borrowed by professional theatre companies. Jazz is still very strong – David Lund, the well-known jazz buff, retired as Head of English here in '95, but still runs the jazz concerts. The choral society is very popular, but parents comment that Music appears to be put on hold at various times of the term, e.g. when exams are coming up. Visiting speakers – particularly from the media (David Frost, Michael Grade) – are a regular feature. Art is 'surprisingly good', according to a visiting parent.

B ACKGROUND AND ATMOSPHERE: Founded in Gower Street in 1830 (as part of University College London) for non-Christians at a time when Oxford and Cambridge required membership of C of E as condition of entry. An arson attack in 1978 gutted the great hall – splendidly restored and rebuilt – and twenty-two classrooms. Religion is still not taught and a liberal outlook is still true of the school's educational policy. The emphasis is on self-discipline; boys are given a good measure of responsibility for running activities outside the classroom. There are no bells. A masculine atmosphere.

The school has just completed phases one and two of a giant squillion pound development plan, including the new Sports Hall, a new library, a 'medical suite' – facilities, says the outgoing Head, are now 'second to none'.

Junior School: 11 Holly Hill, London NW3 6QN. Tel: 0171 435 3068, Fax: 0171 435 7332. Head: Mr J F Hubbard, previously Head of Science and Housemaster at the senior school. Ages: 7–11, which means NB that pupils cannot easily work towards senior schools starting at 13. Competitive entry at 7 and 8 – around 160 children sitting for 40 places. All children are interviewed before taking the exam. Automatic entry to senior school. A further 20 places are available at 8. A good and thorough grounding is provided which teaches independent thought at an early age. There are good facilities, plus use of some of the senior school's.

PASTORAL CARE AND DISCIPLINE: A non-authoritarian regime. No complaints at the time of writing.

PUPILS AND PARENTS: Solidly middle class, often rich (though mothers are more intellectual and less designer-dressed than other Hampstead schools). There is a strong Jewish element, who do their own thing on the Sabbath and indeed, say one or two parents, do their own thing altogether, to the possible detriment of the social life of the school

(though NB there are some who would disagree with this comment). OB Professor Sir Roger Penrose.

There are a fair number of media brats – parents in journalism, publishing, show business. Pupils are accused of being 'cynical, self-assured and worldly wise'. The outgoing Head disagrees – the boys are independent and confident, but certainly not cynical, he says.

ENTRANCE: Two-thirds at age 11+ come from UCS's own excellent prep in Holly Hill (see above). The others from preps and primaries all over north London.

EXIT: The majority of leavers go on to Higher Education. A great many lawyers, doctors and accountants and civil servants result. Also successful businessmen (often third and fourth generation at the school).

MONEY MATTERS: There are Assisted Places and bursaries at 11+. Exhibitions, bursaries at 13+, but these are (largely) honorary. Also Assisted Places at 16+. The school is very quick to respond to parental financial crisis where appropriate.

REMARKS: A top second (plus) division London day school, very strong, and left in good shape by the outgoing Head. It could do with some new energy.

Uppingham School

Rutland LE15 9QE
Tel: 01572 822216, Fax: 01572 822332

PUPILS: Approx 620 pupils, 130 girls (all in Sixth Form). Mainly boarding, but some day pupils, and a new day facility for 11-year-old boys opened in 1994

AGES: 11–18
SIZE OF SIXTH FORM: Around 320
C OF E
FEE-PAYING

HEAD: Since 1991, Dr S C Winkley, MA, (forties), educated at St Edward's College, and read Greats at Brasenose; his Doctorate is in Medieval Greek Poetry. Previously Second Master at Winchester, and in charge of scholars there. Married with young children. Well spoken of. He is proud that parents 'choose the school on the feel of the place – it's friendly without being cosy'. He is fiercely against pupils 'wasting time'. The Second Master, Mr David Gaine, is popular and very jokey.

ACADEMIC MATTERS: Gets the best out of its pupils – weak, strong and average. There is an even balance between Arts and Sciences, and the school avoids the problem of 'Maths and Science' being for the boys. A-level results reflect the mixed ability intake. A wide collection of A-levels is taken (including Photography, Political Studies, Theatre Studies, Ancient History, and Geology as well as the usual mainstream subjects). The school gets remarkable Oxbridge results, and is 'really good at giving help to Oxbridge students,' said a parent, using contacts, building confidence. The strongest A-level results are in English, Geography and Maths, though there are plenty of Ds and Es in many subjects. Economics was the most popular A-level in '95, followed by Maths. The Head comments: 'pupils have to work far harder these days'. A fair number of AS subjects are taken.
Dyslexic pupils are accepted, but there is no separate teaching unit.

GAMES, OPTIONS, THE ARTS: The school claims the largest playing field in England (over a mile round): the

Middle. Main games are rugby, hockey, cricket and athletics for boys and hockey (National Hockey Finalists in last two years), netball and tennis for girls.
Arts are a particular strength of the school. It has an outstanding Music department, one of the strongest in the country, with 60 ex-cathedral choir and collegiate music scholars in the school. Also a full symphony orchestra and a celebrated choir. Neil Page is Director of Music, a position which has a distinguished tradition here – Douglas Guest was director from 1945 to 1950. Music is taught by a resident department of seven with thirty peripatetics, including musicians teaching regularly on a 'consultancy' basis, pioneered by the school. Ambitious works are performed regularly and the orchestra, concert choir and chapel choir perform a full professional repertoire to a very high standard.
Also excellent Art, Design and Applied Technology – now housed in a magnificent and inspiring new building designed by Piers Gough, an Old Boy of the school. The Head of ADT, Andrew Wilson, is well spoken of. Artists-in-residence augment the regular teaching.
The Computer Centre is on a par with most universities – the result of the school's arrangements with British Aerospace and Akhter Computers. A centre of excellence for Windows.
Popular and enthusiastic Drama, with several major productions a year in the school's own theatre and an additional workshop humming with extras (filmmaking, scenery-making), and experimental drama.
Also has an excellent shooting record – a regular winner at Bisley (won in '95). Strong D of E tradition.

BACKGROUND AND ATMOSPHERE: Founded in 1584, the school completely dominates the tiny and charming market town of Uppingham, 'a sleepy place' according to one or two pupils, a safe place according to the Head.

The school is distinguished in the present day by having small boarding houses and keeping to a system of house-feeding. The Head fought hard to keep this – which makes an enormous difference: pupils are friendlier, manners better, and there is a much stronger feeling of community, and less likelihood of boys and girls falling by the wayside because they have been overlooked.

There are two main clusters of buildings, and 13 boarding houses around them, some a brisk 7 minutes' walk from classrooms. A third girls' house opened in September 1994. 'Nearly all' pupils have their own studies, and most Sixth Formers have their own bedsits.

There have been girls in the Sixth since 1975, so the school is well used to them. The tuck and coffee-shop is for all; a bar for seniors (one hour, three times a week). The uniform is a bit sombre, but due for change. House and Games Colours ties have already been introduced. There is an informal and friendly feel about the place, relatively unsophisticated.

PASTORAL CARE AND DISCIPLINE: Good pastoral care is provided via small houses and a tutor system. The little book of school rules makes no reference to sex, but plenty of guidance is given.

Discipline is 'firm but relaxed' with an absolute line on drugs (sacking last year) and progressive fines for smoking. No complaints from parents about discipline have come our way recently. There are no exeats but 'parents are welcome for weekends' (and sometimes friends come to stay).

PUPILS AND PARENTS: Straight-up-and-down middle class, nothing flashy. The main catchment area the northern Home Counties – Essex,

Cambridgeshire, Herts, East Midlands, East Anglia and South Yorkshire, within two-and-a-half hours' drive, though some from Scotland. A very British place.

Very polite and at ease, with no neurotics. Approx 15% are second-to-fourth generation Uppinghamians. There is a strong system of overseas placements for gap-year activities, thanks in part to a good Old Boy network. OBs include Stephen Fry and the author of *Raffles*.

ENTRANCE: Not too difficult for boys. CE at 13+, plus school report and interview. Also 11+ entry (own tests) for day boys. About 25 prep schools regularly send boys in quantity. Girls, however, have a selective entry by interview – no competitive entrance exam, but they must have at least five GCSE passes and register at least two years in advance. NB: a thoughtful touch in the prospectus is a list of recent parents who are prepared to be grilled by prospective parents of pupils about what the school is like.

EXIT: Details are not given, but the Head points out that 33% of the school's '91 'girl intake' is now at Oxbridge.

MONEY MATTERS: There are no Assisted Places, but 12 academic, and 20 Music scholarships awarded annually plus an Art, Design and Technology all-round scholarship or a combination of all four.

REMARKS: Could be just what you are looking for and haven't thought of – a gentle rural boarding school, with large co-ed Sixth Form, which can turn out As if your child is reasonably bright. Friendly, and we have constant reports that pupils 'really love it here'.

Wellington College

Crowthorne, Berkshire RG11 7PU
Tel: 01344 771588, Fax: 01344 771725

PUPILS: Approx 750 boys, 54 girls (girls all in Sixth Form). Approx 130 day boys, the rest board; virtually all the girls board (4 day)
AGES: 13+–18 boys; 16–18 girls
SIZE OF SIXTH FORM: Approx 350
C OF E
FEE-PAYING

HEAD: (The Master) Since 1989, Mr C J Driver (nickname 'Jonty'), BA, BEd (both at University of Cape Town – contemporary of the *Daily Telegraph* education correspondent), M Phil Oxon (Trinity), FRSA (fifties). At school at St Andrew's, Grahamstown, South Africa, sometime *persona non grata* of this country and imprisoned for activities as head of the National Union of Students. Before current appointment was Head of Berkhamsted, Principal of Island School, Hong Kong. Also taught at Sevenoaks and was Director of Studies at Matthew Humberstone Comprehensive School. Governor of Benenden.

'Fanatical' about long-distance running. Also has alter ego as poet and novelist – four novels so far. Has an imposing presence somewhat at odds with a complicated character. Unusually honest and outspoken (for a Headmaster). Rushes into print without any encouragement, and is editor of the Headmasters' official magazine, *Conference & Common room* (NB we apologise profusely for calling it a 'comic' in the last edition). Is slightly detached from the school and the everyday life of pupils. Not a fan of the *Good Schools Guide*.

Wife, Ann, is an occupational therapist by training and works on the Hospital Advisory Committee for Broadmoor. Three children.

There are a sprinkling of Army and Navy chaps among the governors. HM The Queen is the official 'visitor' and any alteration to the Statutes have to be approved by Buckingham Palace.

ACADEMIC MATTERS: The school is traditionally stronger on the Science side, but in '95 the two most popular A-level subjects were History and English, and the best results were in Classics – all five entries got As in Greek and half the 18 taking Latin got A (and all six taking Greek got As in '93). Economics and Politics were among the weakest A-level results in '95, and at GCSE, Religious Studies had only a 76.9% pass rate.

Separate sciences are offered at GCSE, and all must do English, Maths, French, Physics and Chemistry. The school has 20 laboratories. Maximum class size at this level is 24 (large, by public school standards). All pupils must take three A-levels. Girls' results are 'outstanding', says the Head – one of few to admit this and 'results look quite good in boarding terms' (over-modest, this).

GAMES, OPTIONS, THE ARTS: Compulsory CCF, as you would expect of an army school, but only for 'about a year' (and the RSM at time of writing is a girl . . .). Girls play hockey and lacrosse: 'girls pile in, have to join in'. All must do games – even the weakest would be expected to don rugger boots and turn out for the house if needed. The school is seriously keen on games (80 acres of playing fields, a giant Sports Hall), and particularly strong are rugby, cricket, hockey – it is almost taken for granted that the school will be among the winners. No games scholarships, however, and the Head has put pen to his (anti) feelings on this.

There are excellent CDT facilities – though could be made more use of. Keen Drama, and Art is strong (planning permission for a new Art School was recently granted).

The Head is keen on the school's 'leadership programme', which has been run now for five years – Housemasters and others get trained up, then they train up the pupils. After GCSE boys go on a 'team building' course run by Outward Bound – 'the idea is to make kids work better with each other'.

BACKGROUND AND ATMOSPHERE: A conglomerate of John Shaw red-and-white-brick buildings designed in 1854, plus lots of well-blended additions and a glorious avenue of oaks, Wellingtonians and Andean pines. The college was founded in 1853 in memory of the Iron Duke. The main quad has porters in peaked caps at the entrance dispensing tuck. Shades of the Empire – heavily bewhiskered portraits, bleak cloisters, though the school yearbook records that school slang (bims, tishes, ushers, etc.) is fast disappearing, and fagging is now vestigial.

The atmosphere is still a bit male, military and tough – though an official spokesman for the school disagrees with this. Unusually, girls appear to have had little impact on the place. Definitely not cosy.

The majority of boys' houses are in the main buildings, some out in the grounds. All dorms now refurbished (boys live in 'tishes' – derived from Partitions). The girls' house, Apsley, is jolly and popular. The previous Master had a wonderful crypt chapel for quiet thought constructed below the main, very handsome chapel by Sir Giles Scott.

PASTORAL CARE AND DISCIPLINE: The Head comments there were 'a lot of drugs in the school when I arrived and I had two miserable years'. Recent drugs scandal. The Head feels one of his main contributions to the school's welfare

has been the overhauling of the prefect system so that there is a proper chain of command. He comments that every house now has a 'decent, traditional housekeeper/matron'. A parent picked up by the school in a time of distress says 'cannot speak too highly of the place'.

All pupils have a 'quiet time' on a Saturday evening between 6.45 and 8 p.m. – a clever way of blunting the edge of Saturday night rave-ups. Girls are reported to be 'very happy'; still, slightly less lyrical reports from boys lower down the school. Occasional reports of bullying still reach us. Mutinous rumpus over Head Boy's misdemeanour in '95.

PUPILS AND PARENTS: A large number of Service children – but their numbers are dwindling. Army families, and OWs heavy with decorations (including 15 VCs). OBs include Harold Nicolson, Robert Morley, Rory Bremner, Sir Horace Rumbold, James Hunt (who apparently hated it). Approx 25% of parents are OWs.

ENTRANCE: At 13+, 155 boys a year from 60–70 different preps, plus 10 to 15% from Wellington's own prep, Eagle House. CE for boys; an interview and test for girls (mostly from nearby boarding schools, and some because it's Daddy's Old School). Sixth Form entry for boys also. The five-star prospectus has super black-and-white photographs by Jane Bown in it (but no address or telephone number . . .).

Prep school Heads do not appear to be wildly enthusiastic about Wellington at the time of writing.

EXIT: One or two post-GCSE to Sixth Form colleges, etc. GAP was founded here, and is still popular. Otherwise on and up to Birmingham, Bristol, Southampton, Bath universities, etc. Several to Oxbridge. Some on to the army – including army scholarships. Medics.

MONEY MATTERS: Reckons to 'get child on to next stage' when parents have fallen on hard times, though this is not always possible. There are 19 scholarships, plus bursaries, plus 5 Assisted Places at 16 and 3 at 13. A brilliantly run endowment fund, according to Master, was set up by Frank Fisher in the '70s. Has also set up a Heritage Fund, to plough in land sales (400 acres in all belong to the school). The College's charter allows for children of deceased Army officers (and, latterly, other Services) to be educated here on a means-tested basis – currently seven of these, though numbers fluctuate (went up after the Falklands).

REMARKS: A traditional boys' boarding school with girls grafted on at Sixth Form. Best for the 'all-round enthusiast,' says the Head. Not a place to send your little weed to be made a man.

Wells Cathedral School

Wells, Somerset BA5 2ST
Tel: 01749 672117, Fax: 01749 670724

PUPILS: 617; 314 boys, 303 girls. 277 boarders, 340 day. Plus junior school ages 4–11
AGES: 11–18
SIZE OF SIXTH FORM: 184
C OF E
FEE-PAYING

HEAD: Since 1986, Mr John Baxter, BA (fifties). Not a musician, but keen and knowledgeable. Married with two sons (one a teacher). Direct, open,

much admired and respected by staff. Previously Head of History at Westminster (and has taught in New Zealand), and sees a likeness between the excellence of academic life at Westminster and the excellence of Music at Wells, but loves 'the peace and quiet here after the neurosis of central London'.

ACADEMIC MATTERS: Results *comme ci comme ça*. Music and Art A-levels are excellent, as you would expect; Maths also is good. A worrying number of D–U grades in the sciences, however. Very hard-working, devoted staff – for whom the school is a way of life. Musicians are timetabled separately, and take far fewer exams (typically 7 GCSEs, 2 As).

GAMES, OPTIONS, THE ARTS: Music is, of course, outstanding: 85 specialists – the Music School (patron HRH the Prince of Wales) is highly selective in its choice of pupils, looking for talent, motivation and potential. Huge amounts of time (from 8.15 a.m.) are devoted to music-making each day, though pupils mingle with the rest in houses. Plus 50–60 'special provision' music pupils, all able musicians who follow the full academic programme and spend more time than mainstream mortals on music – though some of these, as in any school, also play instruments. There are about 10–12 full-time music teachers, 50 visiting teachers.

This is not a particularly sporty school, but the First Fifteen are strong at the time of writing, and it's all happening, without much pressure to take part. Plus all the usual extra-curricular public-school activities, including enthusiastic Drama.

BACKGROUND AND ATMOSPHERE: This is an ancient foundation – note the list of headmasters going back to 1188. In beautiful medieval and 18th-century buildings, as well as grotty new additions, spread about the glorious small city (John Betjeman called it 'the most beautiful square mile of Britain') and in the shadow of the cathedral (pupils are in and out constantly). Vicars' Close is often recalled by students in later years as one of the delights; 'It gets through by osmosis,' say staff. One or two hideous teaching huts and Portakabins still sprout incongruously and untidily in a warren-like complex behind the main school buildings (but a new building programme is in the pipeline). There are some distinctly scruffy classrooms and dorms. Music is a permanent presence that pervades absolutely everywhere. There is a split between boarders and day pupils. The middle years – 12 and 13 – are the low ones: it is not uncommon for parents to be casting about elsewhere at this period (especially if children are very bright), but many come back to roost. The smart prospectus has cutouts, like an advent calendar.

Junior School: Head (since 1995) Mr Nicholas Wilson, BA, formerly Head of Berkhamsted Prep. Tel: 01749 672291 (Fax same as above). Ages: 4–11. Some boarders, but mostly day. No tests into the pre-prep, but 'friendly' tests into prep for all. The majority of pupils go on to the Wells' middle school, and thence to the senior school. This is a very lively school, particularly at the pre-prep stage, and indeed there are many who think the junior school is Wells' greatest strength. It has taken girl choristers since September '94 and issues a very nice pamphlet saying 'Could *your* daughter be a chorister at Wells?' (though NB no scholarships for them as yet).

PASTORAL CARE AND DISCIPLINE: Has been *laissez-faire* in the past, considerably tightened up by this Head, who comments he feels he has been 'working closely with parents'. Pupils

have a fair amount of freedom: no sense of rigorous discipline, tight rules. 'More discipline wouldn't come amiss,' comments a parent. Town locals observe pupils are slightly 'woolly about the edges'. There was a drugs problem in '93. The school has good pupil/staff relations.

PUPILS AND PARENTS: All sorts – including, e.g., a child from Soweto and several whose parents moved to Wells to send them here – for the music; more Service children proportionately than many other HMC school (children can stay put during exeats). Otherwise, locals. Friendly, happy and laid-back: 'an attitude some of us,' said a parent, 'see as a criticism'.

ENTRANCE: Many from its own junior school. Some at Sixth Form. Not a high hurdle academically, but all manner of auditions for musicians.

EXIT: Musicians to Music Colleges, and Conservatoires, and a distinguished record of Music scholarships to Oxbridge. Of the rest, some go straight into employment, a regular few retake A-levels, others to read a wide variety of subjects at universities and ex-polys.

MONEY MATTERS: This is not a rich school; it has no endowments. The beady Bursar and an astute Financial Director discuss finances regularly. There are generous Music scholarships: 50 'specialists' are funded by the Department of Education. Also Assisted Places.

REMARKS: An orderly, steady co-ed school, ordinary on the academic front, but flavoured throughout by the extraordinary music dimension, in a stunning setting. The only one of four music schools (Chetham's, Purcell, Menuhin) that operates in the context of a 'normal' school: hard for the aesthetics not to rub off on a pupil.

Westminster School

17 Dean's Yard, London SW1P 3PB
Tel: 0171 963 1000, Fax: 0171 963 1006

PUPILS: 597 boys, 77 girls (all in Sixth Form). 444 day boys, 153 weekly boarders; 47 day girls, 30 weekly boarders

AGES: 13–18

SIZE OF SIXTH FORM: 290

C OF E

FEE-PAYING

HEAD: Since 1986, Mr David Summerscale MA (fifties), previously the Master of Haileybury, educated at Sherborne and Trinity Hall, Cambridge (played squash, tennis, cricket for university teams). French wife, two children. Started his teaching career in India, where he maintains strong links. Unassuming, gentle and quiet.

Complaints that 'he doesn't know the boys' could now be out of date, and it has been pointed out to us, by one who should know, that in fact his knowledge of the pupils is 'encyclopaedic'. Some yearn for a firmer hand on the tiller, but the Head also earns 'he's doing a very good job here' praise from many.

The recent Ofsted report describes the school as having 'effective and thoughtful leadership', but 'some limitation in the ability, where necessary, to establish and monitor corporate practice' (whatever that may be).

ACADEMIC MATTERS: The school is powerful beyond question – with subjects strong right across the board. Politics teaching is particularly good. The calibre of the Common Room on the whole is outstanding, with lots of wacky intellects who can play equally (or more) brilliant boys (droves of such) on a line. 'When I go to a parent/staff meeting at Westminster,' comments a parent, 'I know what I am paying all this money for.'

There is a huge amount of academic pressure, with no apparent consideration given to how boys cope. 'There is no mercy,' said a parent. Pressure escalates as A-level heaves into sight, with the trend to take four or more subjects. There is Saturday morning school, with weekly boarders bent over their books on the train home. The fabulous Science laboratories are still being visited by other schools. Girls coming here from girls' schools (i.e. most of them) are consistently 'amazed' by the high-powered teaching, by the demands, 'and we have to learn to debate and argue and make ourselves heard'. Exam results are as you would expect of possibly the most selective school in the country – lists groan with A grades (74% GCSEs, 62% A-level in '95).

The school sends troupes of boys with masters (parents pay) on pre-A-level booster trips e.g. classicists to Greece on a boat ('impossible to escape,' noted a parent).

(NB Ofsted commented on the pressure put on boys doing 4 A-levels; the school commented that there was a 'culture clash' between the school and the inspectors . . .)

GAMES, OPTIONS, THE ARTS: The sad-looking gym under the cloisters has a vintage smell of sock. Water sports and fencing are both successful at national and international levels. Also some keen cricket (this and tennis are played in Vincent Square). Had a good football season in '94/95.

Good Art (under a delightful Head of department); Music can be threadbare and under-rehearsed. Both Art and Music tend to be slightly overlooked in the face of such strong academic demands. Also good Drama. Debating, chess and other intellectual sports are popular.

There is a strong expedition society, compulsory for all lower school and part of the Head's broadening ethos – everything from white-water canoeing to chamber music weekends for aesthetes. As you would expect, there are impressive lists of distinguished lecturers and speakers, 'who are often', said a member of staff, 'given a good run for their money by questioners afterwards.'

BACKGROUND AND ATMOSPHERE: Historic buildings; umbilically tied to Westminster Abbey, in which school services are held thrice weekly, and Latin prayers once a week on Wednesdays. Founded in 1560 by Queen Elizabeth I, following her father's provision for 40 King's Scholars at the Abbey (whose privileges include queue-jumping Commons debates). Under the patronage of the Abbey, the Dean is the chairman of the governors, and the school is very much in the glare of the world. Beyond the calm of Dean's Yard lies a warren of buildings, some very ancient, often anything but calm – noisy, scruffy and seething with pupils and staff coming and going, not to mention sudden seething masses of tourists. The place hums with activity, argument and discussion.

Complaints about the food persist (though – unlike pupils' manners – it's better than it was), eaten in the erstwhile Abbot's State Dining-room. Also, the state of the sagging beds in dormitories cheek by jowl in some of the boys' houses brings a shudder of horror to many a mother.

The school has a liberal tradition and not much structure beyond the classroom for boarders. It was recently described by a French father as 'a université for ze children' – which about hits the nail on the head.

PASTORAL CARE AND DISCIPLINE: Very conflicting reports. Some parents claim there is little evidence of pastoral care (lip service apart), particularly for day pupils. 'They don't seem to care what happens once a pupil is outside the school gates,' comments a parent. However, other parents (especially of boarders) wax lyrical about perceptive understanding and the good care taken of their offspring. Some boys who fall between the exceptional and the inevitable 'muckers' at the bottom become 'driven' and during the growing years have leanings to 'any life beyond work and more work' snuffed out. There 'seems to be a lack of care for sensitive boys, manners, and property,' comments a parent. Vandalism has been a problem, so have drugs. Some reports of bullying reach us.

The recent Ofsted report singled out the providing and monitoring of pastoral care as a key issue for action.

PUPILS AND PARENTS: Street-smart. Highly articulate, often nervously brilliant, with a reputation for being difficult to teach, they can be mocking and irreverent; they can also be true charmers, though the veneer of sophistication is often thin. Up to 50% have one or more parents from abroad; bilinguals in profusion; rich Middle-Easterners; heavy middle-class intelligentsia; and the offspring of ambitious parents, broken homes, also two-income, suburban, not to mention computer and chess geniuses. What day boys need (but don't all have) is a supportive family to pick up the pieces. Robustness is an absolutely essential ingredient to survive here, and this applies to girls as well as boys.

OWs include six prime ministers, the original William Hickey, Warren Hastings, Sir John Gielgud, Peter Brook,

Angus Wilson, Tony Wedgwood Benn, Ben Johnson, John Locke to pick a few famous names at random.

ENTRANCE: Continues to be one of the most sought- and fought-after schools in London.

Put the boy's name down at 10: interview and CE (highly competitive, minimum pass of 65%). Large numbers of bright boys are encouraged to sit for scholarship (the Challenge), even if they don't have a real chance, thereby giving the school a more finely tuned exam to test able boys. 25% come in from the Westminster Under School (qv) but not automatically.

EXIT: All to university, with around 30 going to Oxford and the same again to Cambridge at the last count. The other two overwhelming popular choices are London and Edinburgh. Some take a gap year (much encouraged by James Cogan, an English master, previously John Rae's (the previous Head's) Deputy, and the founder of Schools Partnership Worldwide, SPW).

NB: Owing to the high-powered, university Common Room atmosphere of the school, Westminster boys often find university a bit of a disappointment.

MONEY MATTERS: There are 10 scholarships per year (including 2 for Music): scholars must board (worth half the current boarding fees). Assisted Places (38 of them in all at time of writing) are carried through from Westminster Under School. The school has the A A Milne royalties.

REMARKS: Outstanding in academic and allied matters. A school for the tough and the clever, it vies with St Paul's as the top London academic public school, full of cut-and-thrust. It's also the only public school in central London with a significant number of boarders, and with Sixth Form girls. Regardless of this school's very high reputation, do not choose it for your son if he is in any way likely to be an underdog.

Westonbirt School

Tetbury, Gloucestershire GS8 8QG
Tel: 01666 880333, Fax: 01666 880364
PUPILS: 250 girls. 221 board, 29 day
SIZE OF SIXTH FORM: 60
AGES: 11–18
C OF E
FEE-PAYING

HEAD: Since 1986, Mrs Gillian Hylson-Smith, BA (Hons) (fifties), educated at Wycombe Abbey and Leicester University, plus a postgraduate diploma (which she took aged 40) at Hatfield, 'because I thought my Classics were looking ropey'. Previously taught at Haberdashers' Aske's London, and has taught in boys' schools. Grown-up children. Describes her husband, bursar of an Oxford College, as 'a weekly boarder'. Clear-headed. One or two parents have commented that Mrs Hylson-Smith 'spends too much time out of the school, drumming up business'.

REMARKS: A small girls' boarding school which has gained a reputation of helping middlebrows to shine and gain confidence. 'I want girls to feel good about themselves.'

GCSE results are respectable (the third best in Gloucestershire), but A-levels still 'need gingering up', though '95 has seen a bit of ginger, we're happy to report – e.g. 19 A–C grades in English at A-level, and a terrific 17 A*s at GCSE. Sciences are almost non-existent at A-level – though five sparkling labs and a lecture theatre in the new Science block may improve this state of affairs. English and Drama are both prominent, History of Art still very popular (the most popular A-level subject in '95, along with Business Studies, funnily enough). There are small teaching groups throughout the school. Given the league tables, prep is now compulsory after supper – and evenings are not as free for friends and clubs. Reports from parents that staff 'do not always inform parents when a girl is slacking'. The school has a good Music tradition, and strong Art.

All the usual sports are on offer, plus riding locally and golf. Successful Young Enterprise; D of E also gets a good take-up. 'There's plenty on offer for girls to get their teeth into,' commented a parent.

In a stupendous large neo-Renaissance pile (built for the Holford family), listed Grade I, with wonderful grounds and gardens ('only four gardeners'), and a glorious arboretum now in the hands of the Forestry Commission. 'Doesn't feel like a school at all,' said a visiting educationalist. There is a beautiful library, and some dorms in splendid bedrooms with old painted furniture. Committedly Christian (Low Church). Girls come in at 11+, 12+ and 13+, and are a rich mix socially, including Sloanes, first-time buyers, Londoners, Forces' daughters. Girls are good mixers, happy and articulate. Most girls go on to a degree, (mainly to ex-polys e.g. de Montfort), one or two to Art Foundation courses, to secretarial.

William Ellis School

Highgate Road, London NW5 1RN
Tel: 0171 267 9346, Fax: 0171 284 1274

PUPILS: Around 855 boys; 629 boys 11–16, Sixth Form 226
ALL DAY
AGES: 11–18
SIZE OF (JOINT) SIXTH FORM: 470, increasing to 1,000 in a consortium of four schools, 'La Swap'
STATE

HEAD: Since 1988, Mr Michael Wheale (forties), MA in Politics and Government from King's College, London. Enthusiastic, open-minded and friendly. Relishes the liberating effects of running his own budget and organises it with flair. Travels in daily from north Oxford – but is usually in the school shortly after 7 a.m., as are the majority of the staff. Plays down the effects of the maelstrom that has hit schools for the best part of a decade, but nevertheless does not underestimate the effects on staff.

ACADEMIC MATTERS: The school provides a stimulating environment, with dedicated and energetic teachers. Over the past few years efforts have been focused on the comprehensive nature of the intake, with a less narrow academic approach accepted. Consequently GCSE results are only fair, with around 30–35% achieving 5+ GCSEs, and too many down among the low marks, particularly (in '95) in Mathematics and Design and Technology. This is improving as the current intake moves up the school, and '95 A-level results look promising. A wide range of A-level subjects is taken including Bengali, Portuguese, Philosophy, Sociology, Theatre Studies and Economics, as well as the mainstream subjects. One of the few local schools offering 3 separate sciences at GCSE; also Music and German as a second language are now on offer. GNVQS are available – a wide range at all levels and 'very popular'. AS-levels also on offer, but not so popular. There is a huge ability range and classes currently run at 30+, with IQs ranging from 160+ down to 85+.

Intelligent, long-sighted options include offering Geography GCSE in Spanish (studying the Madrid ring road system, rather than the socio-geographic considerations of the local leisure centre). Computer and technical programmes are also well thought out, encouraging questioning, challenging minds, and a practical attitude to problem-solving.

The giant combined Sixth Form 'consortium' – called La Swap – draws pupils from William Ellis, Acland Burghley, La Sainte Union and Parliament Hill, to provide the numbers/funding for a huge range of subjects (all four schools to be used for classes).

GAMES, OPTIONS, THE ARTS: Rugby, soccer, basketball, cross-country running, tennis and athletics mainly take place on the school's playing fields at Edgware. There is also a cricket enclosure next to the school. More sporty than the normal inner-city comprehensive, although sport is not an obsession for most.

The school owns a very pleasant semi-rural residential centre – a converted water mill – which is much used by the first year, who spend a week under canvas, and for Biology and Geography Field Studies; for adventure activities; and for Sixth Form revision.

Music is considered to be a strength of the school; debating is robust; and there is a fully equipped television studio, with all third-year students taking Television and Media Studies.

BACKGROUND AND ATMOSPHERE: The school is full to breaking point and spilling over into every square millimetre of space. It is waiting for DfE funding for an extension to allow for smaller classes, but land on the edge of Hampstead Heath is obviously at a premium. There is a tremendous feeling of a community at full stretch: some decoration is carried out by OBs, and teachers have rewired and decorated the staffroom. Computers are interspersed with potted plants to humanise the most impressively resourced computer rooms (50 Apple Macs – with more to come: not surprisingly there is a queue to join lunch-time computer clubs).

A third of staff are women, including the Deputy Head and Head of Science. On a rainy day, the degree of co-operation and comradeship between the boys was noticeable – no sign of bored teenagers slouching around the immediate vicinity of the school.

PASTORAL CARE AND DISCIPLINE: This is a non-judgmental, purposeful, happy and confident community, with reward rather than punishment a central part of the school's ethos.

PUPILS AND PARENTS: A multi-racial intake, mainly from families of neighbouring manual workers, with a liberal smattering of Hampstead liberal middle classes. Lively, open, friendly and street-wise. Motto: '*Rather Use than Fame*'. OBs become diplomats, lawyers, scientists (Toby Young an exception here).

ENTRANCE: Around 120 a year from local primary schools – mainly Hampstead, Camden Town and Kentish Town. Also 12 musical children, some from further afield.

EXIT: Around 35% to university.

MONEY MATTERS: State-funded, and in need of more money.

REMARKS: A super North London state school with tremendously hard-working, innovative staff, providing a real sense of community. The school is still failing to provide a slice of middle-ability pupils with adequate qualifications, but there are one or two little green shoots to suggest things may be improving.

Wimbledon High School

Mansel Road, London SW19 4AB
Tel: 0181 946 1756, Fax: 0181 944 1989

PUPILS: 569 girls (plus own junior school with 257 girls, ages 4–10)
ALL DAY
AGES: 11–18
SIZE OF SIXTH FORM: 146
NON-DENOM
FEE-PAYING

HEAD: Since 1995, Dr J L Clough BA London, PhD Hull. Educated at Colston's Girls' School, Bristol and Queen Mary College, London, read English. Previous post as Head of the Royal Naval School for Girls in Haslemere. Dr Clough is a FRSA and a member of the Admiralty Interview Board, and has three daughters.

ACADEMIC MATTERS: A rigorous and largely traditional 'blend of old and new' teaching styles with largish teaching groups (25–28). 'It works because they're all high ability: they stimulate each other.' Long-serving mostly female staff ('only because fewer men apply').

The school follows the National Curriculum plus, with an initial choice of French, German or Spanish. Latin in the second year; virtually the entire group get As at GCSE, and all As in Greek. Three separate Sciences at GCSE (the Combined award has been phased out) in a modern airy block teeming with busy goggle-wearing girls in lettuce-green overalls. Gujerati, Bengali and Japanese are all on offer at GCSE. A-level options include Geology, Economics, Business Studies, with Maths the most popular in '95 (16 As, 6 D–Es): 'We are not particularly vocationally orientated here but more into pure study,' comments the outgoing Head. A-level results are strong – 69.8% As and Bs at A-level in '95 for example. One or two AS-levels are taken. GCSE results are Division One – only ten papers below C in '95 – Physics the chief offender. Conscientious careers advice is given.

GAMES, OPTIONS, THE ARTS: Netball, tennis, and an athletics track are within walking distance at the school's own Nursery Road playing field. Also golf and self-defence. The school has a new 25-metre swimming-pool, and a Sports Hall opened in September '94. Plays, debates, Music and Liberal Studies are all in collaboration with nearby boys' King's Wimbledon. Jazz is popular (with keen saxophonists) plus numerous instrumental groups, madrigals and a choir. D of E Awards; lots of keen community service, e.g. handicapped playgroup helpers, visitors for the lonely, old. Exchange Art trip, and also Classics trip (to Sorrento and Pompeii).

Committed work experience: hospitals, vets, business.

BACKGROUND AND ATMOSPHERE: Functional Victorian gabled red-brick buildings front a tree-lined suburban street in the heart of prosperous SW19 (near tube and BR). Fairly cramped for space; steep staircases open off a galleried main hall ('too small for all of us') in cream and brown. A new block houses an enlarged library and Art Studio. Adjacent is a fairly faceless addition for

Science and a Sixth Form 'villa-style' house for very much the inner-city teenage girl with regulation uncombed tresses, hooded tops, jeans, DMs, ethnic knapsacks, clearly relieved to cast off the rather austere navy pinafore and sweater of her juniors. Multi-cultural, multi-ethnic girls create an easy blend – a recent Hindu-style assembly featured Hindu readings, music and prayers and Indian religious dance.

Junior School: Tel, etc as above. Head: Mrs Jacqueline Compton-Howlett (formerly Deputy Head here). Entrance via playgroup and interview at 4, tests at 7; register names one term early – the school is selective and oversubscribed. On the same site as the senior school and uses some of their facilities. Does a 'carousel' of languages in years 5 and 6. Popular and flourishing.

PASTORAL CARE AND DISCIPLINE: The school has a strong pastoral and tutorial system. Counselling for 'social problems, divorce, abuse' can be arranged outside the school. The occasional girl 'who is not right for the school' is asked to leave. PSE classes cover health, sex, 'personal presentation' and how to write a business letter.

PUPILS AND PARENTS: A wide catchment area south of the river and from as far as Surrey brings in all backgrounds 'from daughters of office-cleaners to publishing magnates'. 'They're kind, caring girls and good listeners,' comments a parent, 'I particularly like the tradition of older girls involved in teaching and helping the younger ones – they both benefit.'

ENTRANCE: There are five applicants for every place at 11: girls come from the junior school (not all of them make it), almost equal numbers from other

schools, with tests involving English, Maths, Verbal Reasoning. 'We're looking for academic calibre and interests.' The 16+ intake hinges on minimum grade Cs in six subjects, with A or B in prospective A-levels.

EXIT: Most to Higher Education, with a predominance of scientists, engineers and medics. London medical schools, and Manchester university are popular; 9 to Oxbridge in '94. Also the Liberal Arts, teaching training, Arts Foundation, even one to do Equine Studies at Writtle.

MONEY MATTERS: There are up to 10 assisted places a year; plus GPDST bursaries for hard times.

REMARKS: A strong and strategically placed local school with the cutting edge to produce impressive academic results in the usual bargain-no-frills GPDST tradition, producing bright, unpampered city girls with a trace of sophistication as well as kindness.

Winchester College

Winchester, Hampshire SO23 9NA
Tel: 01962 854328, Fax: 01962 842972

PUPILS: 675 boys, 1 girl: 652 board, 24 day
AGES: 13–18
SIZE OF SIXTH FORM: 264
C OF E
FEE-PAYING

HEAD: Since 1985, Mr James Sabben-Clare, MA (fifties). Educated at Bramcote, Winchester College (got top scholarship) and New College, Oxford, then did a spell at Marlborough before bolting back to the old alma mater, where he was Head of Classics and Second

Master before his current appointment. Wife was a barrister, now teaches law as a non-examinable subject in the school – has 60 pupils at the time of writing. Two children, one at Cambridge, the other a qualified barrister. They also have a Jack Russell.

Comes from a theatrical family. Unassuming, disarming, and clearly and understandably regards Winchester as paradise. One of the few Heads who really does go quietly about his business, acknowledged by staff and by boys with affection as one of the team. A new maintenance man didn't even recognise him. 'Pomp', he says, with classic understatement, 'is not my style.'

Mr Sabben-Clare sees his task as 'providing the best for bright boys', and believes it is of great importance that they should be happy. Since his appointment, he has set himself the task of 'changing the ethos a bit', and changing the image projected by the school. Not easy tasks, either of them.

ACADEMIC MATTERS: The school provides outstanding academic education, with 150 options to choose from. It is impossible to do more than scratch the surface in the space available here. GCSE is taken on the wing at different moments – endless shadow of exams might daunt lesser mortals. The Classics department reports the largest number taking up Greek for years. The Head has started a school for Oriental Studies, teaching Mandarin and Japanese, plus Oriental culture and civilisation. Enormous numbers take Maths at A-level, often in strange combinations. Physics and Chemistry are well patronised – the school's Arts-orientated image is no longer accurate. A handful take Classics (and always do brilliantly). Modern Languages, the school tells us, are no longer the poor relation, and to prove the point they cite 125 taking French at

GCSE with 48 A*s in '95. A handful still carry on the tradition of studying Russian at GCSE.

A little general learning is imparted by 'div' – unexamined General Studies (the school doesn't do General Studies at A-level). Each boy has one period a day at this with the same master ('don'), covering aspects of European history in whichever way the don sees fit, e.g. he might look at Zola's novels in the context of social upheaval in France. More general knowledge is also sucked in in the 'transition period' created by taking GCSE early. The library has a budget of £20,000 a year – excellent collections, both old and new. The main library is housed in an old brewery and still smells faintly of this.

League table talk: the school comes consistently at or near the top of league tables, which, given that boarding schools – even Winchester – are necessarily less selective than day schools, is outstanding.

GAMES, OPTIONS, THE ARTS: The perfect place for a boy who is shaping up to be bolshie about team games. Individuals are allowed to do their own thing here, and there are a huge number of things on offer. The 'main' games, soccer, (the school's own variety of football) and cricket, are not compulsory after the first year: joy for some. The school has glorious grounds with one of the most beautiful cricket pitches in the country, stretching down to the River Itchen, where the school's famous fishing club (founder member: Lord Grey of Falloden) still flourishes under the eye of keeper Mr McCarthy and his black Labrador.

The water polo team – bolstered by the school's Hong Kong contingent, for whom swimming is the Number-One sport – is virtually unbeaten. Basketball is also good – 'not many schools do it,' says the Head modestly. And the school is, as we write, one of the strongest in the south at cross-country.

The school is very lucky to have one of the earliest Sports Centres, built large and well enough by the vision of the former Head, Sir Desmond Lee – it is still in use a punishing 85 hours a week, not only by boys but also by outsiders. There is no big all-weather surface – city planners won't allow it. The Head also says they could do with more tennis courts (rich OBs please note).

There is a keen CDT centre, currently expanding and lobbying for a bigger budget. The Carpentry room is much patronised not only by boys but also by staff. The large light Art department has a fabulous collection of watercolours – Cotmans, Rowlandsons – all on the walls to inspire undeserving pupils.

Music is outstanding and it has been pointed out with justification that we have not made enough of this in previous editions. The school has maintained the 14th-century tradition of having 16 quiristers selected from all over the country and trained up by the Director of Chapel Music to sing in chapel. On the non-classical front, it won the '93 Schools Jazz Competition. There is a magnificent 1960's concert hall, decorated with panelling by a pupil of Grinling Gibbons (taken from elsewhere in the school). Two-thirds of pupils learn an instrument. Seven did Music at A-level in '95: four A grades.

Drama is also considered strong – keen, with a good theatre to work in. It is impossible to list everything – but NB, the idea is that pupils make a choice and stick with it: commitment is expected. CCF is compulsory for one year.

Some granny bashing, but in no way does the school feel part of the local community.

BACKGROUND AND ATMOSPHERE: The centre of the school is still the 14th-century quad built by William of Wykeham, Bishop of Winchester and chancellor to Richard II. Other buildings have been bolted on at regular intervals, giving a glorious but slightly rabbit-warreny feel to the place, where every other stone has a history. The chapel has the christening robe of Henry VII's son Arthur, embroidered with red and white roses symbolically linked, and some original stained glass. The grounds are outstanding – on one side the town, on the other the cathedral close, and long acres of playing fields stretching lushly down to water meadows. Architectural gems are dotted all over the place, including a 17th-century Sick House beside which a 17th-century-style herb garden has been planted. Everywhere, a feast for the eyes and soul.

Boarding houses are dotted around the town, cosy, in narrow ancient lanes and backstreets (it is difficult to park). Meals are still eaten in the house – one of the very last schools to retain this civilised custom (NB there are some complaints by boys that supper can leave you hungry). Sign seen in one dining room: 'No Mandarin to be spoken at mealtimes'.

Scholars live in a separate 14th-century house 'College', where, they report, they are worked like stink. Several buildings are still used for the purpose for which they were originally built – a strong sense of continuity and purpose.

PASTORAL CARE AND DISCIPLINE: Housemasters reign here, but there are no unhappy reports of any particular house at the time of writing. A central laundry system is now installed, so there are no more comforting sounds of spin driers on summer eves.

There is a system of young and old pupils working side by side in 'toys' for the first 2 years (study cubicles – NB Winchester has a well-developed language, as befits its old age). Generally a

Good Thing, as new boys are kept in sight, and pupils of different ages mix; more like a family than many schools. Also, there are weekly meetings in groups with House Tutors – boys of all ages. Pupils seem for the most part happy and well cared for. The school does not go in for fleets of counsellors: 'If there is a problem,' says the Head, 'we expect to deal with it.' Parents confirm that this is so, and that the Head in particular is brilliant at it.

Alcohol is generally regarded as the menace – there are lots of pubs within a stone's throw and reports by locals of noisy carousing by Wykehamists on Saturday nights. Ten boys were 'sent home' in summer '94 for being caught smoking cannabis (the city of Winchester reeks with the stuff).

Given the strong collegiate system, there is still a slight sense of several entities beavering away in separate corners rather than working as a community, and the Head is still talking of 'drawing more threads into the middle'.

The school has a brilliant second-hand shop.

PUPILS AND PARENTS: Bright to brilliant. Largely from intellectual (upper) middle class, also a contingent of bright Hong Kong Chinese. Overwhelmingly, reports are of charming pupils, with good manners. Slightly inward-looking, but nothing like as inward-looking as Eton. Pupils from more down-to-earth backgrounds comment still that Wykehamists are a 'touch out of touch with the real world'.

OBs include Willie Whitelaw, Hugh Gaitskell, Richard Crossman, Geoffrey Howe, the great Prof Dyson, and Montague John Druitt (possibly Jack the Ripper). Also Sir Jeremy Morse (warden of the College), George Younger, Tim Brooke-Taylor, the Nawab of Pataudi, Richard Noble.

ENTRANCE: Rumoured to be full to bursting, with boys being farmed out in dons' houses. Register after the child's eighth birthday. Interview at 11, with IQ test for selection to take the school's own entrance exam at 13+. Pupils are drawn from 170 different prep schools. Traditional 'feeds' are the Pilgrims' School (qv) on the doorstep, Horris Hill (qv) and Twyford (qv).

EXIT: Oxbridge as always – 40–50 a year. Other universities. Pupils go on to be lawyers, bankers, doctors, accountants and backroom experts.

MONEY MATTERS: Underpinning parents through the recession has been stretching the currently considerable resources to the limit. One or two pupils even so have fallen by the financial wayside. Each hardship case is considered on merits. The Bursar has been heard to comment that the school is 'full of pupils who can't afford to be here'.

There are 70 scholars, around 6 exhibitioners a year, plus up to 6 bursaries for boys from Hampshire state schools, plus up to 6 Music exhibitions. Also 5 Assisted Places per year. Five-star value.

REMARKS: Traditionally and currently still one of the best and brightest public schools in the country. Outstanding all round. Enormous muscle, both mental and financial. Our only criticism is a continuing tendency towards ivory-towerishness, despite the school's protestations that this is not so.

Withington Girls' School

Wellington Road, Fallowfield, Manchester M14 6BL
Tel: 0161 224 1077, Fax: 0161 248 5377

PUPILS: Around 590 girls
ALL DAY
AGES: 7–18
SIZE OF SIXTH FORM: 120+
NON-DENOM
FEE-PAYING

HEAD: Since 1986, Mrs Margaret Kenyon, MA (Oxon) (fifties). Educated at Merchant Taylors', Liverpool, and read Modern Languages at Somerville. Previously at Cheadle Hulme in Manchester, she also doubles as the school's Bursar (historically the two jobs go together), which has allowed her to give rein to a rolling improvement scheme. 'Can't imagine being free to teach.' Mrs Kenyon was President of the GSA 1993–4.

Positive, quick-talking, she has clearly defined priorities: she wants girls to feel they have 'every right to approach the next stage of their life with confidence. Girls are expanding within themselves, and going for more things . . . the world is their oyster.'

ACADEMIC MATTERS: The school provides seriously good teaching throughout, with computers dotted around, and a good careers department with strong links to industry, and girls are encouraged to arrange their own work-shadowing – embryo doctors do this very early. The school invites lots of speakers, often parents, or senior hospital figures. There is a state-of-the-art language lab (two languages at the same time and touch-screen operations), and a new IT Centre.

Exam results are outstanding. GCSE got only one grade below C (D) in '94 and none in '95 and more A*s than anything else (357). A-levels show a sprinkling of Ds and Es but are still impressive – with more than twice as many As as anything else. Science is still very popular; one-third do A-level Sciences (with large

numbers of As), followed by Maths, English, History and French. All girls do either three separate Sciences or Dual Award to GCSE, and modular Maths and Science coming on stream. The school regularly features in the Science Olympiads. Girls do original research for the Royal Society at school level, and publish results.

Very little streaming, Maths and French only; maximum class size 25.

League table note: almost all girls do General Studies as an A-level (most getting As) and this bumps up the school's position.

GAMES, OPTIONS, THE ARTS: Tennis is outstanding still (usually Lancashire finalists), and lacrosse. The school has no pool, but a super Sports Hall, with trampolines and a viewing gallery. Sailing is currently on offer.

Music is super, getting better and better, with two orchestras, a wind band, jazz group, and very inspirational staff (who have strong links with the BBC Philharmonic). Drama is strong (clubs) in a fabulous new hall in the round, with lots going on: much is done with Manchester Grammar (qv) plus house play competitions and visits to local theatres. The whole school hums with Mancunian cultural contacts.

Good Art, and Ceramics – the Art Rooms were revamped as part of the Centenary Appeal. Also good Fabric Design and Textiles, and Home Economics (also revamped, and full of cooking and green-room activities when we visited). The school has good charity links (Barnardo's is tops). Girls have a choice of clubs and masses of extra-curricular activities and trips hither and yon.

BACKGROUND AND ATMOSPHERE: The school was founded in 1890 by a group of prominent Mancunians, whose original aims still hold good: to provide 'efficient and liberal education for girls: to make work interesting and stimulating in itself, eliminating prizes; to remain small; to stress the importance of Natural Science'. The school is set in an oasis of green (building on this is forbidden by Founders' orders – but a Sports Hall was OK), and the Centenary Appeal has resulted in a massive rebuild – with the school still in residence.

There are superb new(ish) labs, with more being revamped, and new class-rooms all in the space previously occupied by the old hall. Also good new Geography and Art Rooms; dining room and kitchens are next in line for an upgrade, with extra library space, and revamping of the junior school.

PASTORAL CARE AND DISCIPLINE: A chain of support via Form Teachers, Tutors in Sixth Form, formalised PSE programme (timetabled), working up to a girl's Personal Statement and Record of Achievement. Plus lots of speakers, including the Police.

The school has no written rules, other than 'Respecting other people and Respecting self'. No detention: ad hoc punishments, like sorting lost property. 'Has never sacked', 'no whisper of drugs, drink not a big issue'. One or two anorexia problems, but the school 'keeps an eye' ('-wide', adds the Head).

PUPILS AND PARENTS: An ethnic mix, including Chinese. Girls come from a wide catchment area. Lots of university and medics amongst parents: good role models. Good parental contact. OGs include the first female director of Price Waterhouse in Manchester, C A Lejeune (Mrs Louisa Lejeune was one of the school's Founders); Judith Chalmers; Catherine Stott.

ENTRANCE: Own exam at 7, 8, 9 or 11; about 28 come in from own prep

school, plus 50 from outside. Over-subscribed by 3:1. There are some places at Sixth Form (good GCSEs needed, and interview).

EXIT: Some leave after GCSE (the Upper Sixth year is currently about ten girls fewer than the GCSE year). All Sixth Formers go on to degree courses, with the emphasis on Medicine and Law (seven of each in '95); 13 to Oxbridge, the rest scattered, mainly to old civic universities – Birmingham figures largely in the '95 exodus.

MONEY MATTERS: 'Very reasonable fees', 'best value around, all our developments are based on northern thrift'. Fees at the time of writing are £1,250 a term, with lunches and individual music extra.

There are 15 Assisted Places annually, plus 3 in the Sixth Form 'invariably, not all taken up'. Bursaries at discretion, flexible and sympathetic, but means-tested.

REMARKS: A very strong, stable girls' day school which thrives on the back of Manchester's cultural and educational resources. Highly sought-after (and deservedly so).

Woldingham School

Marden Park, Woldingham, Surrey CR3 7YA
Tel: 01883 349431, Fax: 01883 348653
PUPILS: Around 540 girls, 430 board, 110 day
AGES: 11–18
SIZE OF SIXTH FORM: Around 135
RC
FEE-PAYING

HEAD: Since 1985 Dr 'Phil' (Philomena) Dineen (fifties, retires at sixty, and according to our records has been in her fifties since 1985). Educated at a small convent in Wales before an English degree at the University of Cardiff and a PhD at the University of London. Ex-Head of a Sussex church state school; half her teaching background ('this is my sixth school') has been in state co-education. Strongly respected, vital, an ex-nun. Says firmly, 'As far as I'm concerned a girl needs a better education than a boy'; talks of 'inner reserves, confidence and self-respect as foundations for decisions with peace'. A late marriage to now retired economist Peter Dineen provides, as she says, 'a grandfather figure on the campus'.

Workaholic Dr Dineen (puts in 12 hours a day seven days a week) delegates briskly from her chintz and repro office (a portfolio project for her Arts Foundation hopefuls) following early-morning lengths at the pool and an RE lesson with juniors. Admits herself to be 'demanding of unrealistic commitment' from staff, who counter cheerfully, 'Yes, it is rather like working for Margaret Thatcher.' A highly successful Head. Retiring, alas, in Summer 1997.

ACADEMIC MATTERS: The school doesn't pretend to be a hothouse, nevertheless encompasses some high-fliers, a bulk of middle-of-the-roaders, and a few stragglers – 'all gifts are equal; we are here to identify talent,' comments the Head. Most staff are Dineen-appointed (about a third are male, including the Deputy Head). Hot on languages and all must take two modern ones (mostly French, Spanish, German) in addition to Latin or Classical Civilisation. (NB a rather paltry three candidates at GCSE in '93/94 but these have been bumped up to 15 for '95). One-third of pupils do separate sciences,

the rest Dual Award sciences in a modern science block; very strong computer technology. 9 or 10 GCSEs are the norm; all must take RE; keenly successful Geography. English Lit is the most popular A-level, followed by History of Art. Choices include Business Studies, Theatre Studies, Theology, Sociology. NB A breakdown of results is not given, but government data lists the school's average A-level points score per entry as 6.3.

Exceptional careers advice is given by Mrs Bagley.

GAMES, OPTIONS, THE ARTS: Strong tennis; also hockey and netball; an athletics track and a popular fitness studio. A new Sports Hall opened in '95, financed by a 6% fees surcharge over three years ('fairer than an appeal where less well-off parents tend to give proportionately more,' says the Head). Lots of training in 'responsibility', e.g. leadership courses. Good debating, community service, D of E Awards. Busy Drama; strong Art includes life class, plus art trips to Florence and Amsterdam; Photography. Young Electronic Designer Award winner. Flourishing Music (BBC Young Musician of the Year entrants).

BACKGROUND AND ATMOSPHERE: In a glorious rural setting (with an extra 700 acres of rolling farmland recently acquired), though suburbia is only a few miles off. The leafy grounds are immaculate, with manicured topiary, etc. 'I never tell girls to hurry to class in such surroundings,' says the Head. Formerly a convent of the Sacred Heart (the order founded in 1800 by a French nun following the turmoil of the French Revolution – four elderly nuns hang on in school bungalows), the school has been lay-based since '85. It transferred here in 1946 to a spreading mellow late 17th-century (fire-damaged and partially re-built) château-style house (mentioned in

John Evelyn's Diary) with sympathetic additions including a luxury-motel-style Upper Sixth house.

Senior girls eat with the juniors housed in a nearby more functional barracks-style addition (younger girls house their own pets in Hamster Hall and Guinea Pig Gallery). Good food, with lots of choice. The school has an open, friendly, no-clique atmosphere. 'Ribbons' (prefects) are elected by pupils (a coveted honour); senior girls can earn weekend and evening money manning the reception, school bank and shop. There are discos, etc., with Worth, Wellington, Charterhouse, Cranleigh; Upper Sixth can ask boys for dinner and cook it in their own kitchen-diner. 'Flexible boarding' – weekly boarding is particularly popular.

Unstuffy spirituality with alternating C of E and RC confirmation years – 'this is no Ascot,' comments a relieved mixed-marriage parent – under a female chaplain from the RC Oxford Team Chaplaincy and visiting religious from nearby Wonersh seminary; leaving girls attend Mass with a highly charged Ceremony of Commission.

PASTORAL CARE AND DISCIPLINE: 'I'm rarely let down,' boasts the Head, while admitting, 'some fire fighting when I came'. Reputedly 'not a whiff of drugs' in this steadily middle-class suburban community: 'We operate on trust, like a good home,' says the Head. There is no going to pubs, strict screening on videos. Health Education is taught, and there are visiting tellers of cautionary tales, e.g. a reformed drug addict, a HIV-positive man, and an Old Woldingham high-flier single mother. The Head concedes the need for inspection 'so bad schools have to do something', while deploring Children Act inspectors' 'loo counting'. Head visits most ex-pat parent families and invites every visiting family in for a meal.

PUPILS AND PARENTS: More than half are Catholics; 19% from families living overseas; also very handy for Londoners. The ratio of day to boarding pupils is 1:4. The school breeds great loyalty among Old Girls; droves return to be married (at least 12 wedding bookings are listed at any time, for which the choir returns to sing), plus some to be buried alongside the nuns in the school's own cemetery. A wide social mix encompasses lots of first-time buyers. OGs include Caroline Charles, Caroline Waldegrave.

ENTRANCE: Currently popular. A pre-selection day at 10–11 before CE. Only half a dozen fall at a fairly soft-edged CE and all siblings are automatically accepted. There is a new parents' dinner and treasure-hunt plus ploughman's lunch for all on Parents' Day, 'so they can compare problems and solve them,' suggests the Head cannily. Sixth Form entry also possible.

EXIT: To medical school, business management, art courses, secretarial, teaching. Also a gap year. Post-GCSE, 6–8 leave to Sixth Form colleges, etc.

MONEY MATTERS: Not short of a bob or two, in fact, coffers are bulging (see land purchase above). There are 9 scholarships (some academic, others for Music and Art) plus internal scholarships for Sixth Form.

REMARKS: A strongly steered, good-value family boarding school in the liberal ecumenical RC tradition, best for the average pupil. Super.

Worth School

Paddockhurst Road, Turners Hill, Crawley, West Sussex RH10 4SD
Tel: 01342 715207, Fax: 01342 718298

PUPILS: Around 363 boys; almost all board
AGES: 8–18 (includes junior school from 8–11)
SIZE OF SIXTH FORM: Around 97
RC
FEE-PAYING

HEAD: Since 1994, Father Christopher Jamison, OSB, MA (Oxon) (forties). Educated at Downside and Oxford, where he read Modern Languages. Recently wrote a book on developments in the Catholic church since Vatican 11. Parents comment, 'He's good news, a doer.' Father Christopher comments, 'Pupils in RC schools learn as much about how to be human as how to be RC.' (Oh, good.) Also comments that he sees himself 'leading a community of learners into a changing world ... a unique animal with deep monastic roots and modern technological wings'.

ACADEMIC MATTERS: This place is not an academic ball of fire (average A-level points per entry in '95: 6.4) and there were rather a depressing number of D–U grades in '95, being let down in particular as so often by Economics which, unfortunately, is currently the school's most popular A-level subject. The staff of 40+ teachers include six monks, plus partnership with the Dyslexia Institute. The school has a good old-fashioned teaching system.

Combined or separate sciences are available at GCSE. Languages – Spanish, with German and Italian as 'extras'. All take Religious Studies at GCSE. One or two take AS-levels. Business, Media, Theatre Studies are on offer as well as the mainstream subjects. Father Christopher comments: 'We aim to make silk purses out of sows' ears.'

GAMES, OPTIONS, THE ARTS: This is a fairly games-orientated school with a strong rugby tradition (acres of mud-strewn pitches) – an ex-Head Boy was capped for England Schoolboys. There is a Sports Hall, also a seven-hole golf course. No CCF, but active D of E.

There has been a revival of Music under a Director who favours early(ish) Music; the choir toured to Paris in '95 and sang at Notre Dame, but boys pursue their own music-making from heavy metal to modern. Boys can play in the Worth Community Orchestra.

The school has recently been given money to expand its IT provision, and is doing this with a will – there are two network rooms and work stations dotted about the school – but more importantly, every member of staff is being made to learn about it, so that different skills can be imparted in different subjects (e.g. word processing in English).

The school is heavily into granny bashing – playing guitars at a school for the handicapped, manning a soup kitchen in Brighton.

BACKGROUND AND ATMOSPHERE: The original building was Lord Cowdray's late 19th-century house in 500 acres of rolling Sussex parkland, with many additions, plus a painful-looking circular '60s weathered concrete Abbey Church. Founded in 1933 as a prep school for Downside, it became a senior school in 1959. Thirty monks are currently in the Community, of whom two are Housemasters of the five autonomous houses.

Younger boys can fag if they want to – £10–20 a term, fetching newspapers, vacuuming prefects' rooms, etc. All boys are expected to clean their own rooms. A Benedictine ethos permeates; the school makes trips to the Holy Land and Lourdes. Boys comment on the 'fantastic unmonkliness of the monks – they teach us to be Christian and we try to explain to them the rules of American football' (a quotation from the prospectus, this).

The school empties at weekends ('but not till Saturday night and there are activities for those still here', comments the Head). Non-stop social life – e.g. dances with other schools. The uniform is grey suits and house ties; cheerful colour-coded collared sweaters denoting year are worn in the Junior House; conventional navy jackets in Sixth Form.

A major development plan is in the pipe line – for 'Worth in the year 2000' – starting with the computers and going on to a new Arts Centre, etc.

PASTORAL CARE AND DISCIPLINE: Careful monitoring and strictish rules on going out so 'boys know where they stand'. Gatings for having boys in rooms after 11 p.m. and 'for playing canasta in prep'; also a £20 fine for smoking. Flexible exeats. Two recent drugs cases were swiftly dealt with – parents written to within 24 hours.

PUPILS AND PARENTS: Approximately a quarter of boys have parents in the Services or diplomatic corps. 'Popular with island dwellers' says the head, 'from Jersey to St Lucia'. The rest live within an hour's drive of the school. Happy, friendly boys. OB Harry Enfield apparently loathed it.

ENTRANCE: Mainly at 8, 11 and 13. Interview for Junior House. Otherwise, 'nominal' pass rate for CE plus recommendation from prep school. No line is drawn between the weak and strong: the school pledges to accept 'any pupil who would flourish here'. 'Resolutely' single-sex and developing a partnership with Woldingham (qv) – e.g. same term dates, socials, joint staff training – a brilliant idea, and it is amazing how unusual this is.

EXIT: Almost all to universities old and new (overwhelmingly in Arts and Theology); 9 to Oxbridge in '94. Also Building, Agriculture, Business, Arts Foundation courses, the Forces.

MONEY MATTERS: Some new scholarships (and assisted places) are available at 11+. There are 7 or 8 academic scholarships at age 13 up to half fees plus a special 25% award for excellence in Science or Maths, Latin or Greek. Also Sixth Form scholarships up to 50% of fees. The 5 major music scholarships, plus 4 minor ones, offer free music tuition. Also choral and instrumental awards for Junior House.

REMARKS: A small RC boarding school taking increasing numbers of non-Catholics. Boys coming from/going elsewhere comment that the school feels 'very nice, very friendly . . . but limited' to quote one.

Wycombe Abbey School

High Wycombe,
Buckinghamshire HP11 1PE
Tel: 01494 520381, Fax: 01494 473836

PUPILS: 500 girls, all board except for 20
AGES: 11–18
SIZE OF SIXTH FORM: 164
C OF E
FEE-PAYING

HEAD: Since 1989, Mrs Judith Goodland, BA (fifties), educated at Howells, Denbigh, and Bristol University, where she read French and Spanish. Previously Head of St George's Ascot. Divorced, with grown-up son and daughters. Business-like, with a faintly diffident and defensive manner, but above all hugely proud of the girls and the school. Very capable. Well aware of the dangers of laurel-resting: 'We are not complacent.' Due to retire in 1998.

ACADEMIC MATTERS: A high-powered Common Room – particularly unusual in a girls' school – provides some excellent stimulating and challenging teaching, with good attention to detail. There are many long-standing staff, and the staff are mainly female (one or two Old Girls); the emphasis is on girls thinking for themselves. Senior Mistress Mrs Best is 'absolutely super' according to a parent.

The school get outstandingly good A-level results (78% A–B grades in '95). Strong in all subjects taken (though not a notably wide range of subjects being taken). AS-levels are also well patronised. Girls have a choice of German, Russian, Spanish and Italian to add to French; three pupils did Japanese A-level in '95 (all three got As). There are no set prep periods: 'We like girls to work out how to use their time', except in the first year; after that, they must fit it in during the day (using libraries, studies, classrooms, not overseen). Girls are worked like stink and report themselves 'exhausted' (ditto staff). Sciences – both combined and single at GCSE. Also English (both lang and lit) and Modern Languages – there are regular exchanges with schools in France, Germany, Spain.

Hot on IT – girls were involved on an RAF project at the time of our visit, working out how to get aid parcels to remote areas of Third World countries. High expectancy rate: Head notes that parents occasionally put 'too much pressure on girls – we don't', and observes that Wycombe girls are 'ambitious: they want to do things'.

GAMES, OPTIONS, THE ARTS: A very sporting school: lacrosse is played keenly (the Under-15s 'won everything last year'); also tennis (coaching round the year), with 25 tennis courts. D of E is well supported.

It is not just an academic hothouse here – everyone does sewing, everyone does cooking (non-examinable, of course). There is also terrific Drama, with a first-rate theatre in the Arts Centre (local artists put on exhibitions here, and the theatre is used by the outside world as well), a triumph of modern architecture rising above the lake. Good Photographic department. Inspired Music – many girls play instruments (several to Grade VIII), and there are chamber groups, orchestras, and good singing.

The school has a rich variety of societies – with notices up all around the school concerning these, far more sophisticated than at most schools.

BACKGROUND AND ATMOSPHERE: Castellated grey stone Gothic (James Wyatt), decorated in pretty soft colours, set on the edge of High Wycombe, girdled one side by the wall so that most of the boarding houses back on to an extremely busy road. Houses are fiercely competitive; the Lower Sixth are in charge of younger girls; girls sleep in mixed-age dorms (actually rooms), but 11-year-olds live together in the Junior House further up in hill. Another Sixth Form house, new(ish), is coolly elegant, happily partially hiding the other Sixth Form house, the hideous hot red-brick Clarence – an excellent school-to-university stepping stone, with girls living in groups of ten (study bedrooms), and cooking their own breakfast and supper (provisions are laid on, plus a weekly allowance for some fresh foods). Houses are interconnected, with one main sitting room.

NB Television is not much watched: Wednesdays and weekends, with *Neighbours* and *Home and Away* videoed for bumper sessions. There are regular visits to theatres, exhibitions, lectures (London, Oxford, Stratford). And at the top end, increasing activities with boys' schools – Drama, Music, debating, shared lectures, with Eton, Radley, Harrow and Winchester. 'Just enough,' sighed one girl wistfully.

The school was founded in 1896 by Dame Frances Dove from St Leonards, Scotland, and faint links are retained. Daily chapel. The atmosphere is definitely busy, though not driven, with pupils going to and from classes calmly carrying heavy book bags.

PASTORAL CARE AND DISCIPLINE: This is a 'grown up' place – children are treated as adults and even 11-year-olds are allowed into Marlow on the bus (with a chum). Self-discipline is the key. The Head is very fierce about smoking and drink ('I suspend at once'). An independent counsellor runs a surgery on Sunday afternoon (fairly well attended).

Revolutionaries are few and far between in this tight pastoral system, backed up all down the line. Exeats either side of half-term mean the whole school shuts down: pupils and staff need the breather. The Head is currently resisting pressure to offer weekly boarding.

PUPILS AND PARENTS: From nationwide – one of the few schools to claim this nowadays (and it is especially rare among girls' schools). 'A good cross-section,' said a parent 'with brains as the common demoninator'. Parents are the well-heeled upper classes, professional intelligentsia, civil servants, solicitors, city folk. Girls are poised, stylish, remarkably articulate, and often more mature than their peer groups elsewhere. Also very energetic: 'You won't survive here,' said a 16-year-old, 'unless you do lots of things. You can't just work.' OGs include Elizabeth Butler-Sloss, Elspeth Howe, the late Judith Chaplin.

ENTRANCE: At 11, 12 and 13, with a 55% pass at CE (the bottom line in a girl's weakest subject): 'They must be academically able, and most important, they must be able to cope – and still have energy and enthusiasm for all the rest,' stresses the Head. From a wide variety of schools. It is increasingly popular to come at 12, 13 or even (if space) at 14. Also entry at Sixth Form. Now offers 20 places to day girls (hitherto limited, for historical reasons, to daughters of the clergy), an expensive choice, given that there are some very good day schools locally.

EXIT: Around 15 to Oxbridge in '95 at the time of writing; the others to top universities, Edinburgh popular, to read a variety of subjects – medicine and anthropology are currently popular – and then to high-powered careers. Gap years are popular 'and well planned', say parents. NB A surprising number leave after GCSE – to co-eds.

MONEY MATTERS: There are several scholarships, including three at two-thirds fees, plus various other scholarships and bursaries (including some for seniors' daughters/granddaughters); 2 open Sixth Form full-fees scholarships, and 1 at half fees.

REMARKS: Once again one of the top academic girls' boarding school in the country; in very good shape, strongly traditional but making a conscious effort to mingle more with the world outside.

Wymondham College

(NB pronounced wind'em)

Norfolk NR18 9SZ

Tel: 01953 605566, Fax: 01953 603313

PUPILS: 940 boys and girls; about 550 board (both sexes), 390 day
AGES: 11–18
SIZE OF SIXTH FORM: Approx 300
NON-DENOM
STATE (opted out); parents pay boarding fees

HEAD: Since 1992, Mr John Haden, MA, BPhil (early fifties), Oxford Chemist; taught in King's School, Worcester, in Uganda, also state schools. Previously Head of King Edward VI School, Louth. Comes from a family of teachers (his father was a Head). Well liked. Married with two sons. Chairman of the Boarding Schools' Association 1991–3.

ACADEMIC MATTERS: Pupils are set by ability in major subjects (25 per class). They get notably good GCSE results considering the raw intake (the school does well among the Norfolk league tables – indeed, the best GCSE results of any state school in Norfolk or Suffolk for '94 and '95, not that that is overpoweringly difficult). A-level results show some worrying pockets of failure, though the school points out that its UCAS point score average has increased every year since '93. However, there were encouraging Physics results in '95; also in Design, Art, Geography, Sociology and – unusually – Economics. Science is still the school's biggest, most popular department at A-level, though results here are adequate but not impressive (Dual Award science at GCSE). General Studies A-level was taken by 23 students in '95. The school is developing strength in Design and Technology with a new Technology department (opened '94).

The school has an extremely good library, with over 14,000 useful tomes, a large budget and excellent staff, and a large collection of careers material which has been identified by the County as a Centre of Excellence, and deservedly so. 'Individuals are expected to do well,' says the Head.

GAMES, OPTIONS, THE ARTS: The school has plenty of playing fields, and good facilities (Sports Hall, indoor pool). Keen games, with matches against state and private schools throughout East Anglia. Two England caps in '94/95 (badminton and athletics). CCF continues to be strong – this is very unusual for a state school, possibly reflecting Services parents; and the school was a USAAF hospital base during the war. It is now developing a link with the Royal Anglian Regiment in Colchester. The school is said to have produced more RAF pilots than any other school in the UK. Good Art department; enthusiastic Drama. The extra-curricular programme includes car maintenance. There are good computer, video, animation facilities.

BACKGROUND AND ATMOSPHERE: Founded in 1951 by Norfolk County Council Chief Education Officer Sir Lincoln Ralphs, who apparently designed the boarding houses with two separate staircases so that boys and girls could reside under one roof as though in a family. Cosy and clean. Genuine co-education. Heavy TV-watching school. Tangible commitment ('We chose to come here,' commented boarders). The atmosphere, as we said before, is fairly steamy.

In humble surroundings in wind-swept Norfolk. Nissen huts (desperately bleak without, actually quite spacious inside) which are used for teaching are now disappearing in a seven-year development plan, 'but we will keep clusters as part of our heritage'. Since opting out, the school has changed to being brisk and purposeful with cheerful, dedicated, excellent staff, now dressed less in Crimplene more in little Chanel-type numbers. Copies of *RAF News* and the *Norfolk Young Farmers* handbook are littered about in visitors' waiting room.

There has been a reorganisation of the boarding in response to growing numbers. New boys and girls now spend their first year in Peel House, which is specifically for them, and provides a safe base form which to get to grips with this large institution. The 17-year-olds in the Lower Sixth play a 'key leadership role' in the 12–17 houses. There is a separate Sixth Form house for final year students.

PASTORAL CARE AND DISCIPLINE: Staff are amazingly committed. Norwich, 12 miles away ('Not a Babylon,' commented a parent), is a magnet for some boarders. Day pupils can arrive early in the morning and stay until 9 p.m. The school has more than its fair share of children from troubled backgrounds (single parents, etc.) and deals with problems kindly and wisely. Flexible, it judges each case on its merits. Being on the wrong staircase means instant expulsion.

PUPILS AND PARENTS: A social ragbag; claims to be classless. A growing number of students from the EU, in particular from France, Germany and Spain (International House was set up in 1993) but most children are from Norfolk. Also children from all ranks of the RAF and Army, Colonels to airmen/women (35% of boarders). A slight tendency to roughish manners. There is an increasing number of ex-private school pupils (at all ages, including Sixth Form).

ENTRANCE: No tests, but previous school report and interview. A small number of grant-aided places are available for Norfolk children, but the great majority are 'choice' boarders. Boarding numbers are growing.

EXIT: Approximately 77% went on to take degree courses in '94 as well as a similar number of '95 leavers – ex-polys are popular. Norwich City College is also a popular destination. Handfuls take gap years, retake A-levels, nursing training, etc. Some leave post-GCSE. Some go straight to employment.

MONEY MATTERS: Now grant-maintained – and in control of the situation. The school opted out in 1991, and now operates on a £6.2 million annual budget. One of the relatively few state boarding schools in the country, with a fee-paying element to make the boarding pay for itself – approximately one-third the cost of its private sector equivalent (i.e. at the time of writing, around £4,293 per *year*). Norfolk County Council has a bursary scheme for some very low-income families and 'disadvantaged children'.

REMARKS: A friendly, lively school which claims to be by far the largest state boarding school in Europe. Since opting out, has had lift-off. Well worth consideration by the impoverished, wanting boarding and traditional ethos but not too concerned about social polish.

MAPS

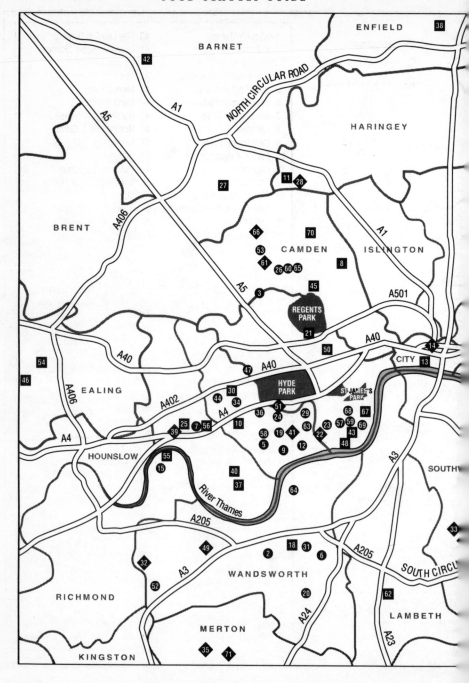

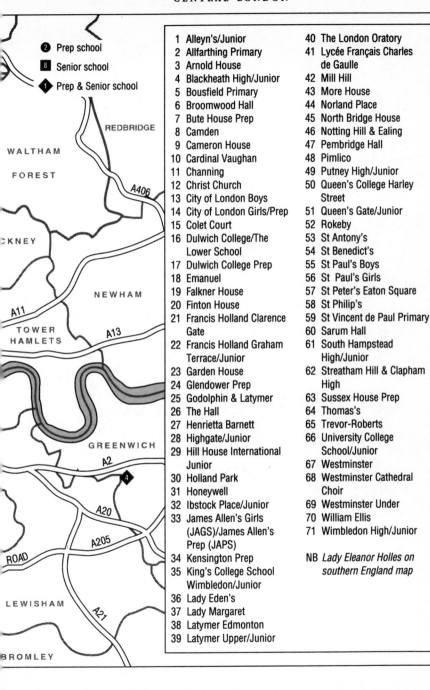

Prep school
Senior school
Prep & Senior school

REDBRIDGE

WALTHAM
FOREST

A406

CKNEY

NEWHAM

A11

TOWER
HAMLETS

A13

GREENWICH

A2

A20

A205

ROAD

LEWISHAM

A21

BROMLEY

1 Alleyn's/Junior
2 Allfarthing Primary
3 Arnold House
4 Blackheath High/Junior
5 Bousfield Primary
6 Broomwood Hall
7 Bute House Prep
8 Camden
9 Cameron House
10 Cardinal Vaughan
11 Channing
12 Christ Church
13 City of London Boys
14 City of London Girls/Prep
15 Colet Court
16 Dulwich College/The Lower School
17 Dulwich College Prep
18 Emanuel
19 Falkner House
20 Finton House
21 Francis Holland Clarence Gate
22 Francis Holland Graham Terrace/Junior
23 Garden House
24 Glendower Prep
25 Godolphin & Latymer
26 The Hall
27 Henrietta Barnett
28 Highgate/Junior
29 Hill House International Junior
30 Holland Park
31 Honeywell
32 Ibstock Place/Junior
33 James Allen's Girls (JAGS)/James Allen's Prep (JAPS)
34 Kensington Prep
35 King's College School Wimbledon/Junior
36 Lady Eden's
37 Lady Margaret
38 Latymer Edmonton
39 Latymer Upper/Junior

40 The London Oratory
41 Lycée Français Charles de Gaulle
42 Mill Hill
43 More House
44 Norland Place
45 North Bridge House
46 Notting Hill & Ealing
47 Pembridge Hall
48 Pimlico
49 Putney High/Junior
50 Queen's College Harley Street
51 Queen's Gate/Junior
52 Rokeby
53 St Antony's
54 St Benedict's
55 St Paul's Boys
56 St Paul's Girls
57 St Peter's Eaton Square
58 St Philip's
59 St Vincent de Paul Primary
60 Sarum Hall
61 South Hampstead High/Junior
62 Streatham Hill & Clapham High
63 Sussex House Prep
64 Thomas's
65 Trevor-Roberts
66 University College School/Junior
67 Westminster
68 Westminster Cathedral Choir
69 Westminster Under
70 William Ellis
71 Wimbledon High/Junior

NB *Lady Eleanor Holles on southern England map*

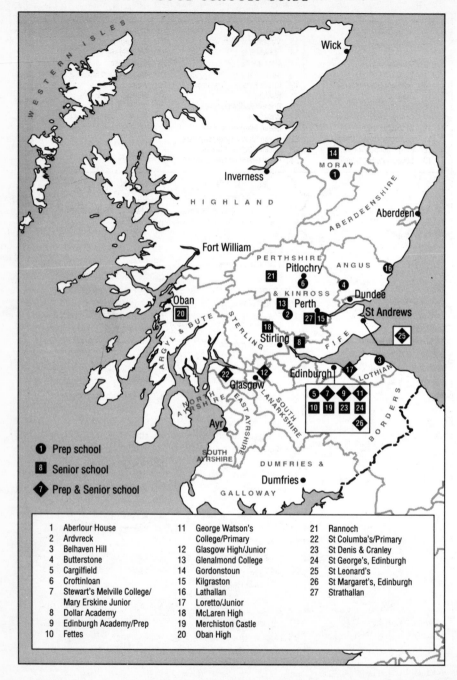

1 Prep school

8 Senior school

7 Prep & Senior school

1	Aberlour House	11	George Watson's	21	Rannoch
2	Ardvreck		College/Primary	22	St Columba's/Primary
3	Belhaven Hill	12	Glasgow High/Junior	23	St Denis & Cranley
4	Butterstone	13	Glenalmond College	24	St George's, Edinburgh
5	Cargilfield	14	Gordonstoun	25	St Leonard's
6	Croftinloan	15	Kilgraston	26	St Margaret's, Edinburgh
7	Stewart's Melville College/	16	Lathallan	27	Strathallan
	Mary Erskine Junior	17	Loretto/Junior		
8	Dollar Academy	18	McLaren High		
9	Edinburgh Academy/Prep	19	Merchiston Castle		
10	Fettes	20	Oban High		

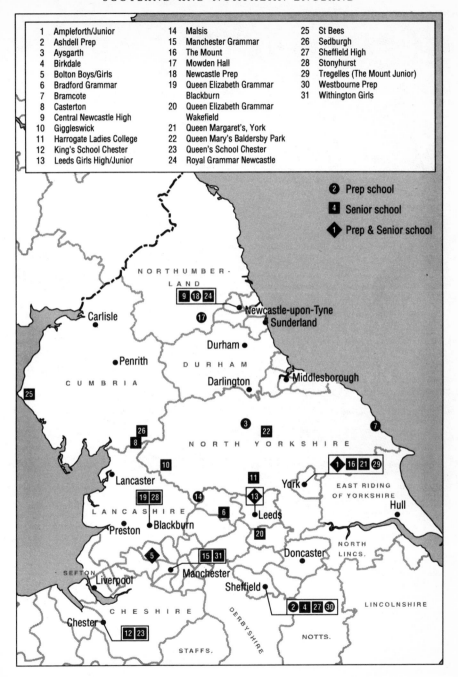

1	Ampleforth/Junior	14	Malsis	25	St Bees
2	Ashdell Prep	15	Manchester Grammar	26	Sedburgh
3	Aysgarth	16	The Mount	27	Sheffield High
4	Birkdale	17	Mowden Hall	28	Stonyhurst
5	Bolton Boys/Girls	18	Newcastle Prep	29	Tregelles (The Mount Junior)
6	Bradford Grammar	19	Queen Elizabeth Grammar	30	Westbourne Prep
7	Bramcote		Blackburn	31	Withington Girls
8	Casterton	20	Queen Elizabeth Grammar		
9	Central Newcastle High		Wakefield		
10	Giggleswick	21	Queen Margaret's, York		
11	Harrogate Ladies College	22	Queen Mary's Baldersby Park		
12	King's School Chester	23	Queen's School Chester		
13	Leeds Girls High/Junior	24	Royal Grammar Newcastle		

Prep school

Senior school

Prep & Senior school

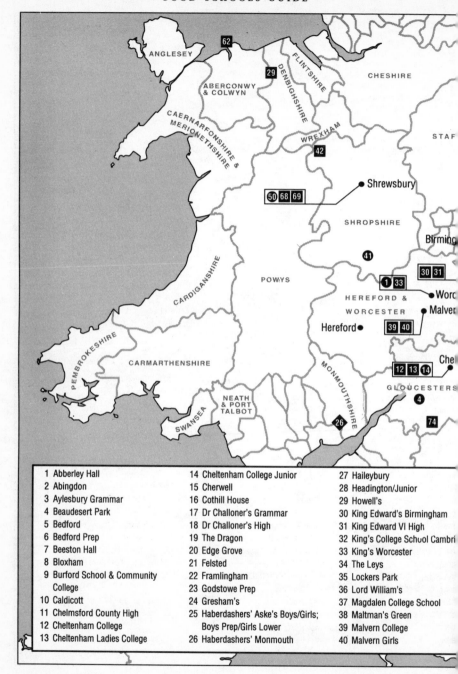

1 Abberley Hall
2 Abingdon
3 Aylesbury Grammar
4 Beaudesert Park
5 Bedford
6 Bedford Prep
7 Beeston Hall
8 Bloxham
9 Burford School & Community
   College
10 Caldicott
11 Chelmsford County High
12 Cheltenham College
13 Cheltenham Ladies College

14 Cheltenham College Junior
15 Cherwell
16 Cothill House
17 Dr Challoner's Grammar
18 Dr Challoner's High
19 The Dragon
20 Edge Grove
21 Felsted
22 Framlingham
23 Godstowe Prep
24 Gresham's
25 Haberdashers' Aske's Boys/Girls;
   Boys Prep/Girls Lower
26 Haberdashers' Monmouth

27 Haileybury
28 Headington/Junior
29 Howell's
30 King Edward's Birmingham
31 King Edward VI High
32 King's College School Cambri
33 King's Worcester
34 The Leys
35 Lockers Park
36 Lord William's
37 Magdalen College School
38 Maltman's Green
39 Malvern College
40 Malvern Girls

Legend:
- ❶ Prep school
- ■2 Senior school
- ◆25 Prep & Senior school

55 Repton
56 Riddlesworth Hall
57 Royal Grammar, High Wycombe
58 Rugby
59 St Alban's High
60 St Anselm's
61 St Christopher's, Letchworth
62 St David's College
63 St Edward's, Oxford
64 St Elphin's
65 St Felix
66 St John's School
67 St Mary's Wantage
68 Shrewsbury

69 Shrewsbury High
70 Stowe
71 Summer Fields
72 Tudor Hall
73 Uppingham
74 Westonbirt
75 Winchester House
76 Wycombe Abbey
77 Wymondham College

Moor Park
Moreton Hall
New College School
North London Collegiate School
Norwich Girls High/Junior SP
Oakham
Orwell Park
Oundle
Oxford High
Packwood Haugh
The Perse Boys
The Perse Girls
Queenswood
Radley

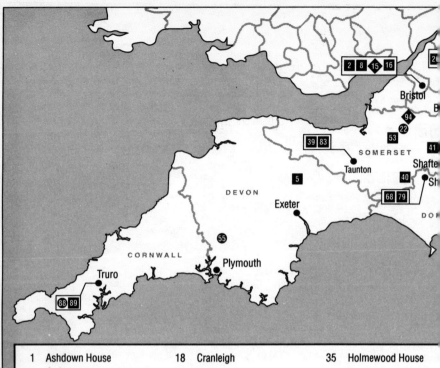

1	Ashdown House	18	Cranleigh	35	Holmewood House
2	Badminton	19	Downe House	36	Horris Hill
3	Bedales	20	Downside	37	The Judd
4	Benenden	21	Dunhurst	38	King Edward's, Bath
5	Blundells	22	Edgarley Hall	39	King's College, Taunto
6	Bradfield College	23	Elstree	40	King's Hazlegrove
7	Brambletye	24	Epsom	41	King's School, Bruton
8	Bristol Grammar	25	Eton	42	The King's School, Can
9	Bryanston	26	Farleigh	43	Knighton House
10	Canford	27	Frensham Heights	44	The Lady Eleanor Holle
11	Chafyn Grove	28	Godolphin	45	Lambrook
12	Charterhouse	29	Guildford High	46	Lancing College
13	Cheam Hawtreys	30	Hampton	47	Lanesborough
14	Christ's Hospital	31	Hanford	48	Ludgrove
15	Clifton College/Prep	32	Harrow	49	The Mall
16	Clifton High	33	Heathfield	50	Marlborough College
17	Cottesmore	34	Highfield	51	Merchant Taylor's

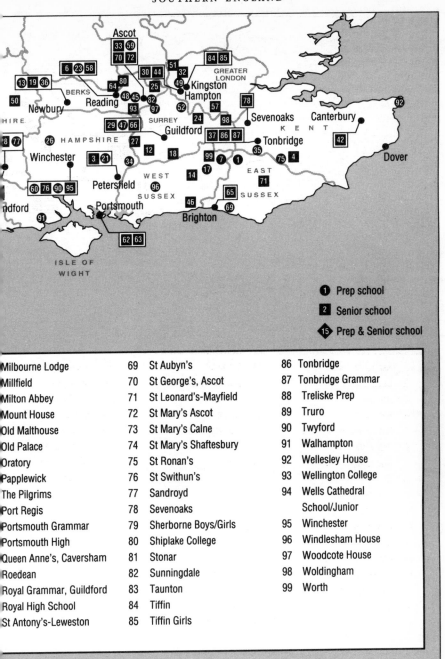

Prep school
Senior school
Prep & Senior school

Milbourne Lodge	69	St Aubyn's	86	Tonbridge
Millfield	70	St George's, Ascot	87	Tonbridge Grammar
Milton Abbey	71	St Leonard's-Mayfield	88	Treliske Prep
Mount House	72	St Mary's Ascot	89	Truro
Old Malthouse	73	St Mary's Calne	90	Twyford
Old Palace	74	St Mary's Shaftesbury	91	Walhampton
Oratory	75	St Ronan's	92	Wellesley House
Papplewick	76	St Swithun's	93	Wellington College
The Pilgrims	77	Sandroyd	94	Wells Cathedral
Port Regis	78	Sevenoaks		School/Junior
Portsmouth Grammar	79	Sherborne Boys/Girls	95	Winchester
Portsmouth High	80	Shiplake College	96	Windlesham House
Queen Anne's, Caversham	81	Stonar	97	Woodcote House
Roedean	82	Sunningdale	98	Woldingham
Royal Grammar, Guildford	83	Taunton	99	Worth
Royal High School	84	Tiffin		
St Antony's-Leweston	85	Tiffin Girls		

Index